G. D. H. COLE

The Post-War
Condition
of Britain

77341

HD6664
.C68

London
Routledge & Kegan Paul

First published 1956
by Routledge & Kegan Paul Ltd.
Broadway House, Carter Lane, E.C.4
Printed in Great Britain
by Butler & Tanner Ltd.,
Frome and London

Second Impression 1957

CONTENTS

CONTENTS

* The Reader's attention is specially drawn to this Appendix.
See the Preface.

LIST OF TABLES

I POPULATION

II FAMILIES AND HOUSEHOLDS

III CLASS STRUCTURE

IV MAN-POWER AND EMPLOYMENT

V PRODUCTION

PREFACE

A NY book that attempts to deal with current statistics is bound to be out of date in many respects before it appears. Both official and unofficial statistics are published at various times throughout the year; and there is no one date at which all the statistics for a particular year are available and none of them have been superseded, or rendered of only historical interest, by later figures. In finishing this book, I did my best to pick a time of year—late October 1955—at which most of the figures for the previous year, 1954, were available; but I am now correcting the paged proof sheets in June 1956, and already a good many, though not nearly all, of the data for 1955 have come to hand. It is quite out of the question, for reasons of cost, to insert these later figures in the text, as this would mean re-setting many of the tables; and accordingly the account of post-war Britain rendered in the main text ends, for the most part, with 1954, though I have inserted a number of references to conditions during the first half of 1955. In addition, I have provided an Appendix giving the more important figures that have become available since my book went to the printers. This of course means that, as far as the main text goes, the record is closed before the beginning of the 'credit squeeze' and the return to high interest rates which have considerably altered the economic situation in 1956; and there are quite a number of points at which I should need to express myself differently if I were writing now. Similarly, my chapter on Monopolies and Restrictive Practices was written before the Government produced its Bill, now before Parliament, dealing with these matters; and the widespread discussion of 'automation' and the 'redundancy' crisis in the motor-car industry have flared up since my book was sent to the printers. Such time-lags are unavoidable, and I do not need to apologize for them. Nor is it my fault that books take nowadays a long time to produce, or that this particular book was unfortunate in being in the printers' hands at a time when production was being seriously interfered with by a trade dispute. The reader who is particularly concerned with the most recent developments must be left to search out the latest figures for himself with the aid of the fairly full list of sources given in the bibliography.

A work of this sort is necessarily based to a very great extent on official statistics; and I have to thank the Director of the Stationery Office for allowing me to make full use of these sources. I have not thought it necessary to indicate for each table or set of figures the precise source on which I have drawn, mainly because many of the tables are composite and include figures from a number of sources. I think the bibliography will provide guidance enough for anyone who wishes to refer back to the original sources—there to find, of course, a great many additional data which I have had to omit for reasons of space.

Among the many sources used the most important naturally include the *Annual Abstract of Statistics* (latest issue No. 92, 1955) and the *Monthly Abstract*, and also the annual Blue Book on *National Income and Expenditure* (latest issue 1955) and the annual *Economic Survey* (now available for 1956). To these should be added the *Statistical Year Book of the United Nations* and the U.N. *Monthly Bulletin of Statistics*. All these cover a wide field. Unfortunately the invaluable report, *National Income Statistics—Sources and Methods*, prepared by the Central Statistical Office in order to explain how its annual estimates are arrived at, has only just been published as I write these words, and I have not been able to make use of it in the present volume. For the rest, I must refer readers to the bibliography.

G. D. H. C.

All Souls College,
Oxford.
June, 1956.

INTRODUCTION

IT was in 1937 that *The Condition of Britain* was first published. The book now offered to the public is not a revised version of its predecessor, but an entirely new work. Even if it were possible—and in many cases it is not—to take the facts and figures of twenty years ago and supplement or replace them with more recent facts and figures, the purpose underlying the present volume would not be served. The situation has so changed in many respects that to a considerable extent the questions to which answers are needed in order to evaluate the condition of Britain to-day are different from those which had to be asked before the second world war. No doubt, many of the old questions still stand good; but even so, the entire balance needs to be different. Problems that were acute twenty years ago have receded into the background, or even disappeared; and new problems have taken their place, or displaced them from the centre of attention. Some questions that were unanswerable with any approach to accuracy have become much more answerable; for there has been an unquestionable advance both in the collection of statistical data and in the methods used in handling such data. But, as against this, a good many of the new questions are very difficult to answer accurately—not so much because the required statistics are not available as because their very nature rules out the possibility of directly statistical answers. Twenty years ago, with unemployment rife and a considerable section of the people manifestly going short of the basic requirements of healthy living, it was obviously correct to focus attention on unemployment and poverty as unquestionable sources of widespread unhappiness and ill-fare. To-day, on the other hand, unemployment, though it continues to exist, is for the time being not a major problem, except in the sense that the fear of it is still powerfully present in many people's minds. The extent of unemployment can be measured: the fear of it cannot be, or at any rate has not been. In respect of unemployment, the statistics no longer tell the most important part of the story.

As for poverty, in a more general sense, it is easy enough to show that, in its physical effects, it presses less hard to-day than it did in the 1930s on a large proportion of the worse-to-do; but it is not so easy to translate this improvement into terms of greater well-being. It is indeed clearly a great gain that fewer people, young or old, have to face continual near-starvation on account of sheer poverty; but well-being depends on many factors, and we cannot pronounce upon it without considering them all. Nor can we even, outside the medical and nutritional factors, hope to arrive at an undisputed definition of what well-being is—for its meaning has subjective as well as objective elements. We can, however, safely affirm that the medical evidence conclusively demonstrates a large and significant improvement in the state of the public health, and that in this respect poverty is now a less destructive force than it was less than a generation ago.

This makes it possible to set out on a contemporary survey of the condition of Britain in a happier mood than was objectively justifiable twenty years ago. Then, even apart from the evident danger of war, the clouds on the British horizon were indubitably menacing. Although the world depression had passed its worst, and the British economy had shared in the recovery from the acute crisis of the earlier 'thirties, the persistence of unemployment and the unfavourable state of the balance of payments showed plainly enough that the days of Britain's world economic leadership were over and that there was likely to be increasing difficulty in selling enough British exports in the world market to procure the imports needed for feeding the people and keeping them steadily at work. This crowded island—crowded as a consequence of its high economic capacity—seemed to be getting too populous to continue supporting its people at the rising standards of living to which they had been used. No doubt, the birth-rate was low, and falling; and the statisticians were forecasting a sharp fall in population in the near future. But this was cold comfort, because it foreshadowed an ageing population likely to prove economically less efficient than a population with a higher proportion of young workers and also held out the prospect of more elderly people to be supported out of the product of those able to work. No doubt, there would also be, if the existing trends continued, fewer unproductive children to be supported, and for some time the proportion of employables to non-employables in the whole population would not be much affected; but even so the prospective decline in population seemed likely to worsen Great Britain's competitive capacity and to raise costs in terms of human labour. Moreover, to the extent that unemployment led to emigration, the emigrants were likely to be drawn mostly from the more productive sectors of the people, so that their departure would worsen instead of improving the outlook. Even if there were, as the pessimists contended, too many people in the country, the prospective reduction in their numbers was calculated to make matters not better but worse.

This pessimism was widespread in the 1930s, and there appeared to be good warrant for it, even without taking account of the danger of war. This danger was, however, clearly very great, and held out even then very alarming prospects. War, it was clear, would be very destructive, especially to a densely inhabited and highly urbanized country such as Britain. While it lasted, it would cut British industry off from a large part of its world market and would also make it much more difficult to obtain the imports needed to keep the people alive. No country could be so easily starved out by successful submarine warfare; and at the worst, if immediate starvation were averted by surrender to the enemy, as some pessimists deemed possible after the early disasters of 1940, it would still be no easy matter, with impaired productive capacity and under subjection to the Nazi yoke, to recover lost markets or make good wartime devastation. Even victory in war would leave productive capacity impaired and would thus aggravate the unfavourable economic factors.

The Condition of Britain, then, was written in a prevailing atmosphere of national pessimism, which the course of events was making deeper from year to year. It is remarkable that to-day, ten years after the end of the greatest war in history, and with the threat of a third, infinitely more devastating, world war still hanging over us, we are able to record, not only in many respects, a great and unmistakable improvement over pre-war conditions, but also, despite Great Britain's serious difficulties over the balance of payments, a more favourable economic outlook than that of the 1930s, and therewith, I believe, a much more optimistic temper among the people despite the appalling possibilities of destruction involved in war waged with atomic weapons. This situation is possible partly because the second world war was in certain ways much less destructive than had been expected—notably in terms of human life; partly because under the stimulus of war there has been a great and largely unanticipated advance in productive power; and also partly because, from one cause or another, our productive capacity is being more fully used and, for the present, is not being stultified by inability to sell our products to other countries in exchange for what we need to keep ourselves alive and to maintain our standards of living unimpaired.

I am not suggesting that to-day everything in the British garden is lovely—or would be but for the danger of war. Obviously, a great deal is still amiss and there are serious dangers ahead. But this book is concerned mainly not with the future but with the present in comparison with the recent past; and the results of such a comparison are undoubtedly in many respects highly favourable. Whether there is more happiness to-day in Great Britain than there was twenty years ago may be a moot point; for happiness is not a measurable condition. But that there is less of many things that clearly make for unhappiness is evident enough. There is less sheer physical privation due to poverty; there is less disease and, on the whole, improved health; and there is less immediate worry about the material means of living because there is greater economic security. On the other side of the account there is the new uneasiness engendered by the fear of atomic warfare—a fear which still greatly outweighs the hopes raised by the prospect of advantage from the peaceful use of atomic power. But this cause of mental unhappiness cannot be weighed in any balance against the actual advances in material welfare.

Between June 1939 and June 1954 the population of the United Kingdom rose by 3,024,000, or 6½ per cent. Between 1938 and 1954 the gross national product rose from £5,132 million to £15,130 million, or nearly threefold; but of course the major part of this increase was accounted for by the general rise in prices. There is no general price index that can be used to eliminate the effect of price-changes. Wholesale prices of commodities (1938 = 100) stood at 325 on the average of 1954 and retail prices at 232. Weekly wage-rates stood at 238 and weekly earnings in April 1955 at 342. It is not possible, for lack of the relevant data, to make any exact estimate of the total increase in real output since 1938. The rise in industrial output can however be put approximately at 44 per cent between 1938 and 1954. Total consumers' expenditure at current prices increased from £4,534 million in 1939 to £11,702 million in 1954. Measured at constant prices (those of 1948) it rose from £8,317 million in 1939 to £9,298 million in 1954—an increase of 12 per cent, or nearly twice that of population. This, to be sure, means only a modest increase of about 6 per cent in consumption per head over the fourteen or fifteen years; but, as we shall see, fairer distribution has made an important contribution to the welfare of the poorer sections of the people.

There will no doubt be some who will accuse me of overestimating the economic advances that have been made since the 'thirties. Such critics will point out how small the aggregate increase in consumption has been, especially in the case of food. They will stress the fact that food consumption per head is still a good deal less in large than in small families, and that at any rate up to 1953 the average calorie value of family diets was no better than before the war. They will argue that in the 'thirties the British people were getting the advantage of favourable 'terms of trade', especially in the form of imported foodstuffs exchanged on very favourable terms with the primary producers, and that these conditions greatly mitigated the effects of the world depression on British standards of living. These contentions are correct; but the fact remains that, even if the standards of workers in steady employment were reasonably well maintained, there were many depressed areas, including the colliery districts and the shipyards, in which very great privations were suffered: so that general averages gave a very misleading impression. As for the smallness of the rise in total consumption, especially of food, what is most remarkable is the narrowing of the gap between the wealthier consumers and the main body of the working classes, and also the undoubted improvement in the position of the less-skilled workers. There are, of course, still immense differences in consumption between the rich and the poor; and despite high direct taxation there are still considerable groups able in one way or another to live lives of conspicuous luxury at the expense of the common people. These groups are, however, a good deal less numerous than they used to be; and—what is much more important—there is much less sheer privation at the bottom end of the social structure. There has been a real and, in this respect, effective re-distribution of purchasing power, dependent partly on the improvement of the social services but even more on the continuance of full employment over the whole post-war decade.

A large part of this re-distribution of spendable incomes occurred during the war, as a result of more steeply progressive taxation on big incomes, of steady—and indeed excessive—employment and greater employment of women, and of the payment of separation allowances and other special grants to those in need. Rationing of scarce supplies and subsidies to keep down the prices of essential foods also helped to bring about a better distribution of what was available. To a large extent the measures taken after 1945 to develop the social services had the effect not so much of further improving the distribution of consuming power as of preventing the wartime gains from being lost. Both during the war and for some time after it the United Kingdom was spending above its current income and was able to do this partly by the sale of British-owned assets overseas and partly by borrowing. It took time to recover from the wartime diversion of productive capacity to war purposes and to get production for post-war needs fully re-established; and without loans from abroad there would have been an unavoidably sharp fall in current standards of living. This phase, however, did not last long; and when it was over it became possible to maintain standards out of British production, though not without serious difficulties due to the shortage of dollars for buying necessary goods that could not be acquired on other terms. As we shall see, the British current balance of payments was restored to parity by 1948, though the dollar balance continued to be adverse. Thereafter, it was a question of not allowing the distribution of British-produced income to slip back, so as to reproduce the privations of the 1930s; and in general the improved distribution was maintained, though certain groups—notably the pensioners—got less than a square deal, and children's allowances became inadequate to meet the needs of the larger families.

The chapters which follow this brief introduction embody an attempt to show as clearly as possible what has happened in each particular field. Beginning with population, we shall see what have been the outstanding changes since 1938 and how far they have been the consequences of deliberate social policies and how far of other causes, such as improvements in productive techniques, or medical knowledge, or of changes in the situation of the United Kingdom in relation to other countries My main purpose, however is to describe rather than to assign causes: it is not at all to make prophecies about the future.

CHAPTER ONE

POPULATION

IN the years before 1939 there was much discussion of the consequences to be expected from a falling population. The British population seemed to be almost on the point of entering into a decline
which, if the existing trends continued, would become very sharp well
before the end of the present century. According to one much-quoted
estimate, based on a continuance of the trends of the rates of births
and deaths as they were in 1933, total population in England and
Wales would have fallen from well over 40 millions to under 36 millions
by 1965; and thereafter the fall would have become much more rapid.
Even if the rates of 1933 remained unchanged, population would be
down by 1965 to about 38,500,000, and the proportion of the total aged
over 60 would have risen from 12·5 per cent in 1935 to 16·8 per cent
thirty years later, while the proportion of children under 15 would
have fallen from 23·2 to 19·0.

Effects of Falling Population. These estimates were not wrong, unless
they were taken as prophecies of what was bound to occur: they were
quite correct *on the assumptions on which they were based.* Nor was
Great Britain exceptional in being faced with this prospective decline,
which was common in varying degrees to most of the advanced Western
countries. In the light of these expectations there was much argument
about the probable effects. Would an ageing population prove more
or less productive per head? Would a smaller population forfeit the
economic advantages of providing for a large market, and thus occasion
a fall in living standards? On the whole the economists were pessimistic
about the effects, even though, for a considerable time to come, the fall
in the proportion of children would roughly cancel out the increase in
that of the aged, leaving the population of working age in much the
same proportion to the dependent population that would have to be
maintained by its labour.

The Post-war 'Bulge'. In practice, the anticipated decline has not come
about. There has been a 'bulge' in the birth-rate, especially during the
years immediately after 1945, whereas the death-rate has fallen more
sharply than was expected: so that the pre-war forecasts of population
have already been falsified. At present the number of female children
born and likely to survive and become mothers is more than enough

to reproduce the existing population in the future, unless a substantial part of it is wiped out prematurely by atomic warfare.[1] It can, of course, be argued that present appearances are misleading, on the ground that many of the marriages of 1945 and the subsequent years were hurried forward by the return of peace, so that the rise in the number of births during these years really represents births that came sooner than they would have come normally and should be deducted from the anticipated births of years still to come. This, however, is a questionable, though not necessarily an unfounded assertion. At all events, the British population, despite war casualties, has risen since 1939 by a good many more births than the forecasters of that date expected; and although the number of old people has also risen more than was anticipated, on account of a sharp fall in the death-rate, the age-balance of the population has changed less than it seemed likely to change.

In these changed circumstances, there is now much less discussion of the population problem than there was twenty years ago, and much less alarm about future possibilities. This is partly because we have passed in the interval from a situation of severe unemployment to one of labour scarcity. It was not at any time very plausible to argue that fewer persons in the country would mean less unemployment; for the decline would have affected the size of the market as well as the power to produce. Nevertheless, when a state of full employment exists, both the man in the street and the experts are likely to pay less attention to the problem of population, except that part of it which concerns the proportion of old people who need to be supported by the efforts of those at work. The problem becomes one of the burden likely to be involved, in a 'Welfare State', in providing for the maintenance of the retired and of the proportion of this burden falling on taxes or compulsory insurance payments. It no longer presents itself as a problem of prospective 'national decline'.

Population Problems in Underdeveloped Countries. Indeed the boot is now on the other foot. The countries which are to-day most disturbed about their population problem are among those whose population is rising very fast, where fears are entertained that the increase may bring with it a fall in the standard of living. These fears are not felt in the Soviet Union or in the satellite States of Eastern Europe; for the rulers of these countries are confident of their ability to increase production fast enough to provide for the needs of their additional citizens. It is in India and in other crowded peasant countries that the real difficulty arises. The area under cultivation in these countries can be increased only by means of costly capital works for which it is difficult to find the

[1] The net reproduction rate in 1953 was 1·033 for England and Wales and 1·121 for Scotland.

money; and though there is scope for great improvements in the quality of cultivation and livestock, it takes a long time to raise agricultural standards, even when the peasants can afford to apply them. Accordingly there is danger that for a time population may run ahead of agricultural production and these countries may be unable to pay for imports of needed foodstuffs on the scale required. In the long run the problem will almost certainly disappear, both because production will rise and because the increase in population will be slowed down when the fall in infant mortality has achieved its main effects. For the time being, however, the difficulty is great; for these countries, in order to raise their production as fast as possible, need much more capital than they can save out of their low national incomes, but find great obstacles in the way of borrowing from wealthier countries on a big enough scale. Nor have gifts from the wealthier countries gone beyond the provision of technical aid designed to help in increasing production in the poorer parts of the world.

The British Population Problem To-day. Great Britain's population problem, on the other hand, would become pressing only if the world demand for British exports were to fall short of what is needed to pay for enough imports of foodstuffs and materials to feed and employ the people, or if the relative prices of imports and exports were to change seriously to Britain's detriment. These are no doubt real dangers; but they are not pressing enough to cause deep disquietude about population at the present time. The more immediate of them, the danger of an adverse movement of the 'terms of trade', will be discussed in a subsequent section. It takes the form of a threat to the standard of living which would be little affected by any probable change of population for a long time to come.

The present concern of British demographers is much less with the absolute numbers of the British people than with its age-distribution and its productive quality. Age-distribution affects the proportion of total population that is available for productive work, as against the proportion that has to be maintained out of the product of their labour. Quality, affected both by physical health and by intelligence and training, affects productivity and is a vital factor in determining standards of living. It is particularly important for a country which has to depend largely on imports for feeding its people and processing the raw materials on which they work; for it obviously affects the ability to produce goods for export at prices competitive with those demanded by other manufacturing countries. Great Britain's prospects of prosperity depend on the maintenance of a high and rising level of technical and scientific efficiency as the necessary condition of procuring the requisite imports on favourable terms of exchange.

With this preamble, we can proceed to a study of the plain facts and of the trends which they reveal. Comparisons will be made, wherever possible, with the conditions that prevailed in the 1930s, and in some cases over longer periods.

Total Population. In June 1954 the population of the United Kingdom was 51,066,000, made up of 24,689,000 males and 26,377,000 females. These figures include members of the British forces serving abroad, but not members of Commonwealth or American forces serving in the United Kingdom. The *de facto* population, excluding the former but including the latter, was rather smaller—50,784,000, made up of 24,411,000 males and 26,373,000 females. As compared with June 1939 *de facto* population had risen by just over 3 millions—1,449,000 males and 1,574,000 females. At the Census of 1951 *de facto* population was 50,212,000—24,127,000 males and 26,085,000 females.

Here are the separate figures for England and Wales, Scotland and Northern Ireland in June 1954:

TABLE 1

Population of United Kingdom by Countries, 1954
(*thousands*)

	Total		Per cent		Per cent of
	Males	Females	Males	Females	Total (M. and F.)
England and Wales *	21,288	22,986	48·1	51·9	87·2
Scotland	2,447	2,676	47·8	52·2	10·1
Northern Ireland	676	711	48·7	51·3	2·7

* Wales alone, approximately 2,600 = 5·1 per cent of total.

Age-distribution. The total population in June 1954, including home forces abroad but excluding other forces temporarily in the United Kingdom, was divided into the following age-groups:

TABLE 2

Population of United Kingdom by Age-groups, 1954
(*thousands*)

		Total	Males	Females	Excess of Males
Under Working Age:	0–4	3,894	1,994	1,900	94
	5–9	4,258	2,179	2,079	100
	10–14	3,464	1,767	1,697	70
Working Ages:	15–19	3,323	1,681	1,642	39
	20–24	3,351	1,692	1,659	33
	25–29	3,517	1,762	1,755	7
					Females
	30–34	3,978	1,977	2,001	24
	35–39	3,268	1,609	1,659	50
	40–44	3,794	1,869	1,925	56
	45–49	3,726	1,832	1,894	62

	Total	Males	Females	Excess of Females
Working Ages: 50–54	3,411	1,642	1,769	127
55–59	2,879	1,299	1,580	281
60–64		1,085		
Over Working Age:	2,487			
60–64			1,402	317
65–69	2,102	887	1,215	328
70–74	1,657	676	981	305
75–79	1,125	442	683	241
80–84	568	212	356	144
85 & over	264	84	180	96

Thus, the entire population can be divided into the following age-groups:

	000's		Per cent
Under 15	11,616	= Under Working Age	22·7
15–44	21,231		
45–64 (M.) or 60 (F.)	11,101	= Of Working Age	63·3
Over 65 (M.) and 60 (F.)	7,118	= Over Working Age	13·9
	51,066		

Population of Working Age and Occupied Population. This definition of 'working age', though usual, is of course arbitrary. Many women in these age-groups are not 'gainfully occupied'; many young persons remain in schools and colleges after 15; and a number of men over 65 and of women over 60 continue to be 'gainfully occupied'. The 'occupied population' is substantially smaller than the population of 'working age'. In June 1954 the actual working population, including all sorts of 'gainfully occupied' persons, but excluding housewives, was estimated at 23,816,000—made up of 16,049,000 males and 7,767,000 females. For their distribution among occupations and industries see pages 47 ff.

These estimates leave the following differences between population of 'working age' and 'occupied' population:

TABLE 3
Working Population and Population of Working Age, 1954 (*thousands*)

	Males	Females	Excess of Males
Population of Working Age	16,448	15,884	564
Working Population	16,049	7,767	8,282
Difference	399	8,177	

These differences are accounted for by able-bodied men and women not 'gainfully' employed, and by disabled persons, and are partly offset by persons over retiring age who are still at work. The figures of working population exclude all children under 15, but include part-time as well as full-time workers. Less than half the female population of working age is actually 'occupied' for gain, whereas the number of males of working age not so occupied is small, and is mainly accounted for by young persons still receiving full-time education after 15 and by disabled persons. For the numbers still receiving education after 15 see page 37.

Of the males of 'working age', approximately 64·5 per cent were under, and 35·5 per cent over 45 years of age. Of the females, about 67·3 per cent were under 45 and about 32·7 per cent over 45. This difference is due mainly to reckoning the retiring age for females at 60 and for males at 65. If 65 is taken for women as well as men, the percentages become 61·8 under and 38·2 over 45, as the proportion of females is greater in the higher age-groups. In the age-groups 15–64 females outnumbered males by 845,000; but in the population of 'working age' (15–64 for males; 15–59 for females) males outnumbered females by 549,000. The male preponderance in the actual 'working population' was, as we saw, much greater, being 8,282,000.

Births, Marriages and Deaths. The total population is continually increased by births and decreased by deaths, and is also affected by migration. Here are the figures of births, deaths and marriages in recent years.

TABLE 4

Births, Marriages and Deaths, 1935–54

(*thousands*)

	Live Births	Deaths	Excess of Births	Marriages
1935–8 (average)	722·7	574·9	147·8	403·3
1939–44 „	764·3	600·9	163·4	
1945–9 „	907·2	575·5	331·7	445·8
1950	813·1	590·1	223·0	408·0
1951	798·8	632·8	166·0	411·4
1952	792·5	573·8	218·7	399·8
1953	801·9	577·2	224·8	395·3
1954	794·3	578·4	215·9	392·9

Thus, the number of births reached a peak during the post-war years 1945–9, and has not varied a great deal since 1950, but remains substantially higher than in 1935–8 and higher than during the war. Moreover, there has been a sharp decline in infant deaths under one year of age. The numbers of such deaths, excluding still births, averaged 43,200 in 1935–8, but was only 24,800 in 1951, 22,900 in 1952, 22,200 in 1953, and 20,900 in 1954. How far this fall has been due to medical causes and how far to better nutrition and other environmental factors must be left over for consideration later (see pp. 373 ff.).

In 1951, of the total population of Great Britain (excluding Northern Ireland, for which particulars are not available) 24,357,000, or 50·3 per cent, were married, 3,204,000, or 6·6 per cent, widowed or divorced, and 20,880,000, or 43·1 per cent, of all ages single. These figures are available only for Census years.

Urban and Rural Population. In June 1954, out of a population of 50,784,000 in the United Kingdom, 39,979,000 were living in urban and 10,806,000 in rural areas—approximately 79 and 21 per cent respectively. The particulars for the main countries were as follows:

TABLE 5
Urban and Rural Population, 1953

	Numbers	(*thousands*)	Per cent	
	Urban	Rural	Urban	Rural
England and Wales	35,640	8,634	80·5	19·5
Scotland (cities and burghs)	3,602	1,522	70·3	29·7
Northern Ireland	737	650	53·1	46·9

These figures follow administrative areas: rural areas are, of course, not purely agricultural.

At the same date, 18,661,000 persons were living in the seven major conurbations, as follows:[1]

TABLE 6
Large Cities and Conurbations in the United Kingdom, 1953
(*thousands*)

Greater London	8,319	including	London County	3,343
West Midlands	2,256	„	Birmingham	1,118
West Yorkshire	1,681	„	Leeds	507
		„	Bradford	287
S.E. Lancashire	2,411	„	Manchester	699
Merseyside	1,389	„	Liverpool	786
Tyneside	838	„	Newcastle-on-Tyne	287
Central Clydeside	1,755	„	Glasgow	1,083

The most populous cities, apart from London, were:

Birmingham	1,118	Bristol	445
Glasgow	1,083	Nottingham	312
Liverpool	786	Kingston-upon-Hull	300
Manchester	699	Bradford	287
Leeds	507	Newcastle-on-Tyne	287
Sheffield	503	Leicester	287
Edinburgh	469	Stoke-on-Trent	274
Belfast	449	Coventry	265

The largest city in Wales, Cardiff, had 246,000.

[1] For 1951 figures see p. 392.

Population by Regions.   England and Wales are officially divided into 10 standard Regions. Here are the populations of these Regions in 1939 and 1954:

TABLE 7

Regional Populations, 1939 and 1954 (*thousands*)

	1939	1954	Change
Northern	3,003	3,151	+ 148
East and West Ridings	3,976	4,098	+ 122
North Western	6,237	6,441	+ 204
North Midland	3,065	3,437	+ 372
Midland	3,987	4,490	+ 503
Eastern	2,691	3,258	+ 567
London and S.E.	11,046	10,960	− 86
Southern	2,317	2,773	+ 456
South Western	2,673	3,065	+ 392
Wales	2,465	2,601	+ 136

Thus, all Regions except London and S.E. have increased since 1939; but the increase has been most rapid in the Eastern (21·0 per cent), Southern (19·7 per cent), South-Western (14·8 per cent), Midland (12·6 per cent), and North Midland (12·2 per cent) Regions. The increase has been 5·6 per cent in Wales, 4·7 per cent in the Northern Region, 3·3 per cent in the North-West, and 3·0 per cent in the East and West Ridings. In London and the South-East there has been a fall of nearly 1·0 per cent. The cities showing the largest increases are Coventry (45,000), Nottingham (33,000), Bristol (26,000) and Leicester (24,000).

Over the same period mid-1939 to mid-1954, the rise in population for the United Kingdom and its constituent countries was as follows:

TABLE 8

Population Changes: United Kingdom, 1939–54 (*thousands*)

	1939	1954	Increase per cent
England	38,995	41,673	6·8
Wales	2,465	2,601	5·5
Scotland	5,007	5,123	2·3
Northern Ireland	1,295	1,387	7·2
United Kingdom	47,762	50,784	6·4

Birth Rates and Fertility: Size of Families.   Of the 795,000 live births registered in the United Kingdom in 1954, about 37,000, or 4·65 per cent, were illegitimate. The percentage was lowest in Northern Ireland (2·8 per cent), and highest in England and Wales (4·75 per cent). It was 4·55 per cent in Scotland, and 3·5 per cent in Wales alone. Still births numbered 18,400 for Great Britain as a whole. The birth-rate per 1,000 was 15·6 for the United Kingdom, 15·2 per cent for England and Wales

(15·5 for Wales only), 18·0 per cent for Scotland, and 20·8 per cent for Northern Ireland.

The 795,000 live births were made up of 409,000 males and 386,000 females. In 1953 the net (or effective) reproduction rate was 1·033 for England and Wales and 1·121 for Scotland. For both areas it has been above 1·0 in every year since 1946, whereas in 1938, it was only 0·805 for England and Wales and 0·933 for Scotland. This change has substantially modified population forecasts. Long-run forecasts are now made with a good deal more caution than they used to be before 1945.

The Royal Commission on Population, reporting in 1949, made some attempt to estimate the extent of differences in size of family between parents belonging to different social classes or different occupational or income groups. On the basis of figures collected for the Family Census of 1946 the Commission concluded that, in respect of marriages entered into between 1900 and 1929, manual workers had families from 41 to 44 per cent larger than non-manual workers, with little variation over the whole period. They also concluded that among both manual and non-manual workers, parents either or both of whose education had gone beyond the elementary stage had on the average substantially smaller families than parents who had both ceased their education at this stage. The average family sizes for the two categories of parents were found to be among manual workers 2·80 and 2·23 and among non-manual workers 2·29 and 1·75 respectively. These differences are of long standing, and are not mainly attributable to the development of modern methods of family limitation. There has been a steady falling trend in the average size of families, irrespective of class differences, from an average of 3·37 live births from marriages entered into during the years 1900–09 to an estimated 2·19 for those entered into from 1925 to 1929. The latter figure includes an allowance of 0·09 for births still to come in 1946 from the later marriages.

The Birth-rate. From 1934 to 1939 the United Kingdom birth-rate was almost constant at between 15·2 and 15·5 per 1,000 of population and between 63·0 and 63·6 per 1,000 women aged 15–44. From 1942 it began to rise, and for the eleven years up to 1954 the two rates were as shown in Table 9 (overleaf).

Reproduction rates are the rates at which female population of child-bearing age is being replaced by births. 'Net' rates take account of deaths before the end of the child-bearing period, at the current rate of mortality. 'Effective' rates further take account of current trends of mortality rates. There are no statistics for Northern Ireland.

The 'bulge' in the birth-rate in 1946 and the following year has now subsided; but the rate in 1954 was still appreciably higher than in the 1930s. It has resulted in a corresponding bulge in the school population

TABLE 9
Birth-rates, United Kingdom, 1944–54

	U.K. per 1,000 population	U.K. per 1,000 women aged 15–44	Reproduction Rates— E. and W. Effective	Scotland Net
1944	17·9	76·7	1·021	1·041
1945	16·2	69·9	0·936	0·978
1946	19·4	84·3	1·138	1·192
1947	20·7	91·5	1·244	1·346
1948	19·1	81·4	1·107	1·208
1949	17·0	77·5	1·056	1·168
1950	16·2	74·6	1·017	1·150
1951	15·8	73·0	1·001	1·098
1952	15·7	73·3	1·003	1·118
1953	15·9	74·9	1·033	1·121
1954	15·6	74·7		

at the primary level, and this bulge will soon be transferred to the secondary schools (see p. 338).

Death-rates and Infant Mortality. Crude death-rates rose during the war years for males, but not for females. From 1934 to 1938 the male death-rate was between 13·7 per 1,000 population in 1937 and 12·6 in 1938. It rose to 16·2 in 1940 and then fell gradually to 15·2 in 1944 and 14·9 in 1945. From 1934 to 1937 the female rate fluctuated between 11·9 in 1937 and 11·0 in 1938. It rose to 13·0 in 1940, but was down to 11·0 in both 1944 and 1945. Here are the figures for the years since 1946.

TABLE 10
Death-rates per thousand, United Kingdom, 1946–54

	1946	1947	1948	1949	1950	1951	1952	1953	1954
Males	13·4	13·6	11·9	12·6	12·4	13·4	12·2	12·2	12·3
Females	11·1	11·4	10·3	11·2	11·1	11·8	10·6	10·6	10·6

Thus, there has been an all-round improvement since the 1930s, though not a very great one. For the five years ending in 1938 the average male death-rate was 12·9; for the five years ending in 1954 it was 12·5. For females the corresponding rates were 11·4 and 10·9.

The improvement in infant mortality rates (under one year) has been much more substantial. Between 1934 and 1938 the rate for the United Kingdom per 1,000 live births fell from 61 to 53. After a rise to 60 in 1940 and 63 in 1941 it fell to 53 in 1942 and thereafter fell almost continuously to 26·4 in 1954, when it was 29·6 for males and 22·8 for females. The improvement, from a higher rate, has been especially marked in Scotland, where the rate in the years 1934–8 fluctuated between 82 in 1936 and 70 in 1938. It then rose to 83 in 1941, but fell to 69 the following year and thereafter improved almost continually to 31 in 1954 (35 for males and 27 for females). There has been less improvement in Northern Ireland, where in 1954 the rate, though tending to fall, was still as high as 33 (males 37, females 29).

For male children aged 0·4 years the death-rate during the years 1934 to 1938 lay between 20·4 in 1934 and 18·0 in 1938. It reached 19·4 in 1941, but thereafter fell almost continuously to 7·0 in 1954. For females the range in 1934–8 was from 16·4 in 1934 to 14·3 in 1938. There was a rise to 15·5 in 1941 and then a similar fall to 5·7 in 1952, 5·8 in 1953 and 5·3 in 1954.

One of the most remarkable improvements in recent years has been the fall in maternal mortality. In 1938 the number of deaths in the United Kingdom due to various causes arising out of maternity was 2,665. By 1946 the number had fallen to 1,511, and by 1954 to 571.

The causes of the fall in death-rates remain somewhat obscure. Improvements in medicine and in nutrition have undoubtedly played an important part; but the fall appears to be of much the same order for all social classes and occupational groups: the relative mortality among the poorer does not seem to have become less—a somewhat surprising fact in view of fuller employment and the growth of social services. The evidence on this point is however still inconclusive, though. It is well established that death-rates are higher in the lower and lower in the higher income groups.

Causes of Death. Out of 578,400 deaths in the United Kingdom in 1954 natural causes accounted for 554,370 and 'violence' for 24,030. Of the latter suicides numbered 5,393 and homicides, including war operations, 324. Transport accidents accounted for 6,364 (motor vehicles 5,280) and other accidents for the rest. The causes of natural deaths, which accounted for the largest numbers, were as follows:

TABLE 11

Causes of Death, 1953

Arteriosclerotic and Degenerative Heart Diseases	133,362
Malignant Neoplasm*	100,276
Vascular Lesions affecting Central Nervous System	83,790
Bronchitis	27,847
Pneumonia	20,378
Tuberculosis	9,276

* Including Intestines and Rectum (17,818), Stomach (16,185), Trachea, Lung, etc. (18,406).

Long-term Population Changes. The population of the United Kingdom (present area, excluding Southern Ireland throughout) at successive Censuses from 1821 has been as follows:

TABLE 12

Long-term Population Changes, United Kingdom, 1821–1951

(*thousands*)

	England	Wales	Scotland	N. Ireland	Total	Increase Number	Increase Per cent
1821	11,206	794	2,092	1,380	15,472		
1831	12,993	904	2,364	1,574	17,835	2,363	15.2
1841	14,868	1,046	2,620	1,649	20,183	2,348	13·2
1851	16,765	1,163	2,889	1,443	22,259	2,076	11·0
1861	18,780	1,286	3,062	1,396	24,525	2,266	11·0
1871	21,299	1,413	3,360	1,359	27,431	2,906	11·2
1881	24,402	1,572	3,736	1,305	31,015	3,584	11·3
1891	27,232	1,771	4,026	1,236	34,264	3,249	11·1
1901	30,515	2,013	4,472	1,237	38,237	3,973	11·2
1911	33,649	2,421	4,761	1,251	42,082	3,845	11·0
1921	35,231	2,656	4,882	1,258	44,027	1,945	10·5
1931	37,359	2,593	4,843	1,243	46,038	2,011	10·5
1951	41,148	2,597	5,096	1,371	50,212	4,174	10·9

Thus in every decade from 1831–41 up to 1921–31 total population increased by not less than 10·5 and not more than 11·3 per cent. But over the twenty years from 1931 to 1951 the rate of increase was almost halved, being less than 11 per cent for the whole period. Of course, the figures would look considerably different if Southern Ireland were included up to 1921; for the population of Ireland fell sharply from 8,196,000 in 1841 to 4,390,000 in 1911, because of heavy emigration, especially in the earlier decades.

Changes in Age-distribution. The age-distribution for the United Kingdom, excluding Southern Ireland, has been as follows:

TABLE 13

Changes in Age-distribution, Great Britain, 1871–1951

(*thousands*)

	1871	Per cent	1901	Per cent	1931	Per cent	1951	Per cent
Under 15	9,909	36·1	12,422	32·5	11,175	24·2	11,388	22·6
15–24	5,071	18·5	7,501	19·6	8,013	17·4	6,542	13·0
25–34	4,004	14·6	6,141	16·1	7,325	15·9	7,271	14·5
35–44	3,078	11·2	4,659	12·2	6,223	13·5	7,622	15·1
45–54	2,396	8·75	3,403	8·9	5,614	12·2	6,818	13·6
55–64	1,640	6·0	2,301	6·0	4,262	9·3	5,195	10·3
65–74	944	3·4	1,277	3·3	2,460	5·3	3,686	7·3
Over 75	390	1·4	531	1·4	957	2·1	1,765	3·5

Thus, the proportion of children under 15 has fallen from 36·1 in 1871 to 24·2 in 1931 and 22·6 in 1951; whereas the proportion over 65 has risen from 4·8 in 1871 to 7·4 in 1931 and 10·8 in 1951. These changes have left the proportion of population of working age, here taken as 15 to 64 for both sexes, relatively stable, but increasing steadily, at 59·1 in 1871, 62·8 in 1901, 68·4 in 1931, and 66·6 in 1951. If women over 60 are excluded, these proportions are reduced to 57·6 for 1871, 61·3 for 1901, 66·2 for 1931, and 63·9 for 1951. The increase in the proportion over working age has been more than offset by the decline in the proportion of children. But the proportion of the working population in the older age-groups has been rising. In 1871 44·3 per cent of the total population were between 15 and 44 years of age; by 1951 this proportion had fallen to 42·6, whereas the proportion between 45 and 64 had risen from 14·75 to 23·9. The number of males aged 15–44 rose from 5,807,000 in 1871 to 10,517,000 in 1951, whereas that of males aged 45–64 rose from 1,923,000 to 5,588,000. Of course at the earlier dates a substantial proportion of children under 15 were at work: so that, despite earlier retirements, the change in the age-composition of the working population was rather greater than these figures indicate. The important fact is that the proportion of working to total population has increased, and this has made it easier for society to carry the economic burden of a higher proportion of retired persons. For Great Britain only the number of persons recorded as 'retired' in the Census of 1951 was 1,846,000—1,543,000 males and 303,000 females.

The Effects of Migration. Population is of course affected by migration as well as by births and deaths. Up to 1931 there was each decade a net outflow of emigrants, varying considerably from decade to decade. Thereafter the conditions changed; and between 1931 and 1951 there was a substantial net inward movement. Here are the figures for the successive decades:

TABLE 14

Net Migration, 1871–1951

(*thousands*)

	Net Outflow		Net Inflow
1871–81	415	1931–51	423
1881–91	959		
1891–1901	190		
1901–11	820		
1911–21	919		
1921–31	672		

It should, however, be noted that between 1931 and 1951 both Scotland and Northern Ireland continued to show a net outflow. For

England and Wales the net inflow was 745,000, partly offset by Scotland's net outflow of about 220,000 and Northern Ireland's of 73,000.

Aliens in Great Britain. Many persons have an exaggerated idea both of the number of aliens residing in the United Kingdom and of the numbers who are granted certificates of naturalization. At the end of 1954 the total number of registered aliens was under 357,000—211,000 males and 146,000 females. The great majority of them—nearly 319,000 —came from Europe: the entire American continent contributed only 22,400, Asia 7,800, and Africa 1,200. The largest European contingents came from the following countries: Poland (119,000), Germany (37,000), Italy (35,000), Russia (19,000), France (14,000), Switzerland (10,000), Austria (9,500), Yugoslavia (8,500), and Holland (8,500). 21,000 came from the United States. The largest Asiatic contingents came from Iraq (2,000) and Japan (1,000), and the largest African group from Egypt (950). Of course, these figures do not include settlers from territories within the British Commonwealth, as they are not aliens. But this inflow is not large: even the Jamaicans, about whom there has been so much comment, have been arriving this year past at an annual rate of only about 10,000. The total coloured population of Great Britain in 1955 was certainly not above 80,000.

Nor are certificates of naturalization granted to aliens in at all large numbers. The total number granted from 1946 to 1954 was 70,470, of whom 63,260 were Europeans, 1,743 Asians, 389 from the United States, 149 Africans, and 122 from other American countries. But the majority of these certificates were granted in the years 1947 to 1949, which together account for 42,443. The totals for more recent years have been as follows: 1950, 7,033; 1951, 4,332; 1952, 3,529; 1953, 4,122; and 1954, 5,381. Poland is the only country from which there has been a substantial continuous inflow, averaging about 2,000 a year.

Town and Country. We have seen that in 1954 approximately 79 per cent of the population of the United Kingdom were living in urban and only 21 per cent in rural areas, and that in England and Wales the urban population was over 80 per cent. These urban areas are of very different sizes, from large conurbations to quite small places which have acquired the administrative status of Urban Districts. Much the greatest concentration is in Greater London, with a population of 8,319,000 in 1954. Only 3,343,000 of these were living in the area covered by the London County Council—an area whose boundaries were fixed by the Metropolis Management Act of 1855, so that the growth of London over the past century has taken place largely outside its administrative frontiers. The total population of London can indeed be defined in a number of different ways. The boundaries are differently drawn for different purposes: the Metropolitan Police, the Metropolitan Water Board, the Metropolitan Postal District, and the Greater London

Planning Area are all differently defined, and the Standard Region—London and South-Eastern—which is the unit for decentralization of the various departments of the Central Government, differs from all these. The total population of Greater London can be put at any figure between 8,334,000 and 10 millions, according to the area chosen.

No other conurbation—which can be defined as a growing together of towns and urban areas into a combined mass of built-up districts—approaches London in size. The six next largest (see p. 7) had together in 1954 10,530,000 inhabitants, apart from London's 8,319,000, making 18,949,000 in the seven main urban concentrations, or about 37 per cent of the total population of the United Kingdom.

The further eleven centres mentioned on p. 7 had in 1934 a combined population, excluding suburbs outside their municipal boundaries, of 3,851,000—another 7·6 per cent out of the total. Thus, 44·5 per cent of the people of the United Kingdom in 1953 were concentrated in these 18 major centres.

There were in all 72 cities and urban districts in the United Kingdom with populations of more than 100,000, including those within conurbations. Of these, 63 were in England, 4 in Wales, 4 in Scotland, and 1 in Northern Ireland. Of those in England 19 were in Greater London and 4 more, including Oxford, in the Home Counties. 11 were in Lancashire and Cheshire, 7 in Yorkshire, 6 in the West Midlands and 3 in the East Midlands, 4 in the North-East, 4 in the Southern Counties, 2 in the Eastern Counties, and 2 in the South-West.

In England and Wales 81 towns had in 1954 the status of County Boroughs, exclusive of London. 49 of these had populations of more than 100,000, and another 29 exceeded 50,000. There were only 3 with fewer than 50,000. All these areas are governed by their own local authorities, and are outside the jurisdiction of the administrative County Councils. In other areas local government is divided between the County Councils and the municipal non-county boroughs; but there were 3 urban districts with populations of more than 100,000 and another 14 with more than 50,000. Two of those over 100,000 and 11 of the others are in the neighbourhood of London.

The extent to which administrative boundaries coincide with the real limits of urban areas differs greatly from place to place, according to the extent to which towns have been allowed to annex the areas over which their populations have spread. The County Councils usually oppose the extension of County Boroughs, as well as the grant of County Borough status to growing towns, for fear of losing valuable rateable areas. In the major conurbations, some towns are surrounded on all sides by others and have no room to expand. Many towns have suburbs which extend considerably beyond their municipal frontiers.

Regional Specialization. The most heavily urbanized regions are closely associated with particular industries—South-East Lancashire with cotton and engineering, the West Midlands with the motor industry and light engineering and other metal trades, the North-East with coal-mining, iron and steel, shipbuilding and engineering, Clydeside with the same groups of industry, Merseyside with shipping, engineering, and a wide range of miscellaneous trades, the West Riding with the woollen industry, coal and engineering, and London with shipping and engineering and with many consumer trades. We shall consider the regional distribution of industry more fully in the chapter dealing with Occupations (see pp. 52 ff.).

Urban Birth- and Death-rates. In 1953 birth- and death-rates per 1,000 inhabitants for the most populous cities were as follows:

TABLE 15
Urban Birth- and Death-rates, 1953
(per thousand)

	Birth-rate	Death-rate		Birth-rate	Death-rate
London	15·2	11·6	Bristol	15·6	11·6
Birmingham	18·7	11·8	Nottingham	16·8	10·6
Glasgow	16·6	10·6	Hull	19·1	10·9
Liverpool	20·3	10·7	Bradford	16·0	13·8
Manchester	17·4	12·3	Newcastle-on-Tyne	17·1	10·9
Sheffield	13·9	11·9	Leicester	16·0	11·2
Leeds	15·1	11·4	Stoke-on-Trent	16·4	10·9
Edinburgh	15·4	12·3	Coventry	15·2	10·7
Belfast	18·9	10·3	Cardiff	17·9	11·3

The highest birth-rate was in Liverpool, and the lowest in Sheffield. The highest death-rate was in Bradford, and the lowest in Belfast. Of other large towns, the following had birth-rates of more than 20 per 1,000—Bootle, Hartlepool, Jarrow, Middlesbrough, Wallsend, Clydebank, Greenock; and the following birth-rates of under 10—Chelmsford and Dudley. The following had death-rates of over 15—Brighton, Colne, Halifax, Hove, Huddersfield, Leyton, Nelson, Oldham, Warrington, Llanelly; and the following death-rates of under 8—Dagenham, Malvern, Thurrock, Welwyn Garden City. Both sets of rates are largely affected by the average age of the population. Thus, many resorts where there are many retired persons have high death-rates and relatively low birth-rates, whereas new settlements, such as Dagenham, have low death-rates.

Of *all* boroughs and of all urban districts with more than 20,000 inhabitants in Great Britain 50 had in 1953 birth-rates of 20 or more per 1,000, and 11 birth-rates of less than 10. More than half of the former are in Scotland. 8 had death-rates of more than 20, and 57 others of more than 15. 14 had death-rates of less than 8 per 1,000. Birth-rates were on the whole higher in Northern Ireland than in Great Britain, and in Northern Ireland no death-rate was either above 15 or below 8·8.

CHAPTER TWO

FAMILIES AND HOUSEHOLDS

THE predominant type of social unit in Great Britain is the family, consisting of husband, wife and children. These commonly constitute or form the nucleus of a household, which may also include other relatives, such as grandparents or other elderly persons or brothers or sisters of the husband or wife. The children, as they grow up and marry, or sometimes before they marry, commonly leave the households and set up house for themselves, and thus cease to be members of the family household, though not of the family itself. There are also many households that are not based on a family group—mainly single persons living alone; and of course many households include persons who are not members of the family, such as lodgers and domestic servants. There are also many persons living in institutions of various kinds—hospitals, 'homes', barracks, hotels and boarding-houses, schools and colleges and, of course, prisons. Some of these persons live permanently outside family life: others are but temporarily alienated from it.

The Family Household. The family household remains the norm for the great majority of the population; but on the whole an increasing proportion of time is spent outside the home. Greater distances travelled to and from work reduce the proportion of employed persons and schoolchildren who go home for the midday meal. There is more attendance at outside entertainments, especially for young people, more journeying from villages to near-by towns for shopping and amusement, and, last but not least, much greater liberty for children and young persons to go out on their own. As against this, the rapid development of television during the past few years has led to some increase in home-keeping and has had some effect on cinemas and other outside attendances; but it is still difficult to know whether this represents a long-term trend. Married women have certainly more freedom to 'gad about' than they used to have, largely as a consequence of rising standards of living. Old people too, if they are able-bodied, can mostly get about more than used to be possible for them.

It is often suggested that the family is gradually breaking up; but there is no real evidence to support this view, as far as it refers to the family household. It is doubtless true that increased geographical mobility has to some extent loosened the bonds between relatives. When members of a single family, or group of related families, become scattered over a wide area and lose the possibility of more than rare personal meetings, there is a natural tendency for more of them to lose touch with one another altogether or to reduce their contacts to a minimum. This applies especially to men: women tend to maintain closer contacts with their mothers than men with their fathers: whether this is also the case with sisters as compared with brothers is less certain. With both sexes, contact is more easily lost in big towns than in villages; but even in villages there is more migration than there used to be and the enlarged family groups characteristic of village and small-town life are less prevalent than they were. There is, however, still much turning to relatives for help and comfort in times of adversity; and the family bond, though often contracted within a narrower circle, remains strong within these limits. The development of Old Age Pensions has actually strengthened it in certain respects, by making the presence of aged relatives in the household much less a burden than it used to be.

The size of the average family has fallen as a result of the fall in the birth-rate; but this trend has been arrested since 1945. The size of the family household is, however, affected by housing conditions. When houses are scarce, some persons who would prefer to set up households of their own remain in the parental homes for a period. This factor of house shortage affected the number of households shown in the Census both in 1931 and in 1951. Even to-day much remains to be done to bring the number of dwellings into balance with the numbers of families wishing for separate accommodation.

Households on New Estates. Family life has undergone large changes as a result of improved housing standards. Many households have been transferred from crowded housing tenements to houses on new estates, and have had to adapt their ways of living to their changed environment. The result, up to the present time, has been a decline in 'neighbourliness' as well as in inter domestic quarrelling; for in the main the households on the new estates 'keep themselves to themselves' a good deal more than those in the older working-class areas. It is not easy to measure the social gain and loss resulting from these changes: the loss is clearly at its greatest where the new settlements have been built with little or no provision for the community aspects of living.

In general, there has certainly been a notable improvement in the care of children, who are markedly better fed and clothed and provided with toys and opportunities for games than they used to be, as well as better looked after at school and in matters of health. Pride in children has grown more ostentatious, and the proportion of neglected children has fallen, despite the immediate adverse effects of war.

Children's Allowances. Children's allowances constitute, however, a much smaller proportion of family incomes in Great Britain than in some other countries—notably France, where as much as half the total family income may be derived from this source when the chief bread-winner's earnings are low and the children numerous. Children's allowances have, indeed, failed to keep up in recent years with rising costs of living; and in Great Britain they are in any case not payable for the first dependent child in a family, except by way of supplements to insurance benefits or national assistance in cases of unemployment or incapacity for work.

In 1947 children's allowances in Great Britain cost £58 million, and in 1954 £109 million. In the latter year the total bill for wages, salaries and forces pay was £9,432 million, and the total of all personal incomes was £14,544 million: so that these allowances amounted to much less than 1 per cent of all personal incomes and to not much more than 1 per cent of total wages and salaries. Of course, there were in addition allowances paid in respect of children under national insurance and assistance and also allowances to income-tax payers in respect of dependent children; but even when account has been taken of these the provision made remains much smaller than in France.

Nor is as much attention paid in Great Britain as in many continental countries to the family as a social unit. Such bodies as the Family Welfare Association and the Family Service Units are chiefly concerned with families in special need of assistance or advice in connection with the social services, public and voluntary, and have few contacts with normal families which do not ask for such help; whereas in France, for example, the family is not only the subject of continual and extensive sociological studies but also the point of focus for a great deal of voluntary effort designed to improve the quality of family life.

Composition of Households. The majority of persons in Great Britain live in private households, which are commonly composed of members of a single primary family. These households range in size from single persons living alone up to large groups usually based on the primary family. At the Census of 1951 there were in Great Britain (excluding Northern Ireland) about 14,481,500 private households, of which 1,556,100 consisted each of one person only. These are the numbers of households consisting of 2 or more persons:

TABLE 16

Households by Sizes, Great Britain, 1951

2 persons	3,998,500	5 persons	1,393,500	8 persons	129,300
3 „	3,592,800	6 „	645,200	9 „	61,400
4 „	2,760,500	7 „	288,500	10 „	55,700

These figures include all persons living in the households, whether members of the family or not.

Households and Incomes: Number of Children. Of the heads of households consisting of 2 or more persons, 1,781,400 were married, 600,000 were single, widowed or divorced males, and 1,544,100 were single, widowed or divorced females. 3,666,500 of these heads of households were aged under 40, and 3,381,800 over 60. In 2,032,000 households, including 924,800 one-person households, there was no earner of income; in 6,784,500, including 631,700 one-person households, there was only one earner; in 3,807,700 there were 2 earners; and in 1,857,300 there were 3 or more earners. Of those with 2 earners 996,100 consisted of 2 persons only, and of those with 3 earners 259,700 of 3 persons only. Thus more than 1,887,500 households had no non-earning members. In 8,228,100 households, including 1,555,200 one-person and 3,873,600 two-person households, there were no children under 16. In another 3,079,900 households there was only one child under 16; in 1,997,000 there were 2 children; in 1,010,000 there were 3 or 4; and in 165·7 there were 5 or more. These figures must not, of course, be taken as measuring the proportion of families of different sizes, as distinct from actual households. They include, on the one hand, families still incomplete and on the other households where some or all of the children have left the parental home. For the total size of families it is necessary to turn to the Census Tables dealing with fertility. These relate only to legitimate live births. They cover, for Great Britain in 1951, a total of 7,867,000 married women aged 16–49,[1] who had produced altogether 13,544,700 legitimate children. Here are the numbers in each group, according to the number of children produced:

TABLE 17

Married Women (aged 16–49), by Number of Legitimate Live Births,
Great Britain, 1951

No child	1,687,800	6 children	100,300
1 „	2,374,600	7 „	55,400
2 children	2,034,300	8 „	36,000
3 „	945,800	9 „	19,800
4 „	408,900	10 „	10,300
5 „	180,400	More than 10	13,500

Births and Duration of Marriages. Of those who had produced no legitimate children, 38,400 were under 20 in April 1951, 349,400 between 20 and 25, and 347,000 between 25 and 29, 221,700 between 30 and 34, 211,000 between 35 and 39, and 522,100 between 40 and 49. Here are the figures showing the duration of married life for the whole group of 7,867,200 women.

[1] Out of a total of 12,244,900 married and 2,577,100 widowed women of all ages.

TABLE 18

Duration of Marriages and Number of Live Births
(Women aged 16–49), Great Britain, 1951
(*thousands*)

	Women	Number of Live Births	Legitimate Live Births per Mother
Under 1 year	363·5	55·3	0.15
1 year	355·8	183·4	0·51
2 years	345·7	271·0	0·78
3 „	375·0	371·9	0·99
4 „	357·1	420·1	1·18
5 „	345·9	463·0	1·34
6 „	265·0	388·8	1·47
7 „	267·2	416·8	1·56
8 „	305·2	494·1	1·62
9 „	364·3	608·7	1·67
10–14 years	1,830·9	3,426·3	1·87
15–19 „	1,321·0	2,807·8	2·12
20–24 „	963·3	2,394·1	2·48
Over 25 years	407·3	1,243·5	3·05
All durations	7,867·2	13,544·7	1·72

The number of live births varies not only with the duration of marriage but also with the age at marriage—that is, at the first marriage. The averages were as follows, according to age at marriage:

TABLE 19

Age at First Marriage and Number of Legitimate Live Births,
Great Britain, 1951

Age of Marriage	Number (000's)	Average number Live Births	Age of Marriage	Number (000's)	Average number Live Births
Under 20	1,221·5	2·35	30–44	492·9	1·13
20–24	4,145·1	1·78	35–39	161·6	0·72
25–29	1,786·7	1·45	Over 40	59·4	0·39

Fertility by Social Class. Fertility differs also in accordance with class. Here (see Table 20) are the averages for the five Social Classes recognized in the Census of 1951 (for Social Classes see pp. 25 ff.).

Relation of Households to Families. Of the total of 14,481,500 private households in Great Britain in 1951, about 12,501,200, or nearly 86½ per cent, consisted entirely of members of a single primary family. These primary households covered 37,025,000 persons, of whom 1,637,000 were persons living alone—11·3 per cent of the households and 4·4 per cent of the persons living in primary households. A further 1,980,300 households, containing 8,503,300 persons, were 'composite'—i.e. including persons other than members of the primary family group. These households contained 60,100 ancestors and 93,900 other near

TABLE 20

*Fertility by Social Classes (Women Married Once only),
Great Britain, 1951

Social Class	No. of Married Women (000's)	No. with no Legitimate Live Births (000's)	No. of Live Births (000's)	Percentage with no Live Births	Live Births per Woman
I	242·6	61·6	343·2	25·4	1·41
II	1,142·2	270·2	1,707·2	23·7	1·49
III	3,851·0	839·1	6,342·1	21·8	1·65
IV	1,100·9	202·6	2,153·5	18·4	1·96
V	712·0	136·6	1,542·9	19·2	2·17
Total	7,048·7	1,510·1	12,088·9	21·4	1·72

* Enumerated with husbands in Census.

relatives. They also contained 3,860,600 other persons, some of whom constituted distinct private families. These 'family nuclei' numbered 914,200, of which 810,000 were closely related to the head of the primary family household with which they lived. These family nuclei numbered 2,757,900. Of persons outside these nuclei and also outside the primary families, 368,800 were relatives of the head of the family household, and 733,900 were unrelated lodgers.

The Fall in Domestic Service. In 1951 only 1·2 per cent of all private households in Great Britain included one or more domestic servants, and only 0·1 per cent more than one. This is a sharp fall since the previous Census in 1931, when, in England and Wales only, 4·8 per cent of private households included one or more domestic servants, and 1·1 per cent two or more. Scottish figures are not available for 1931, but the Scottish percentages for 1951 are practically the same as those for England and Wales. Even in 1931 the resident domestic servant was confined to a quite small class of households; but the fall in the percentage by more than three-quarters between 1931 and 1951 is the sign of a highly significant social change. The fall continued after 1951; but there was a small increase in spending on domestic service in 1954 (see p. 88).

Size of Households. The average private household in 1951 consisted of 3·1 persons, or, if one-person households are excluded, of 3·5 persons. The average household consisting wholly of a single primary family, again excluding single-person households, consisted of 3·25 persons. Of such families, 3,551,800 had no children, 3,467,200 had one child, 2,295,200 two children, 919,400 three children, 499,300 four or five children, 117,600 six to eight children, and 13,700 nine or more.

Persons Living in Institutions. There were in 1951 in Great Britain,

2,404,300 persons who were living, not in private households, but in institutions of one sort or another. The following is the broad distribution between institutions of different kinds:

TABLE 21

Population in Non-private Households, Great Britain, 1951
(*thousands*)

Hotels, Boarding Houses, etc.	835·9	Places of Detention, Prisons,	
Educational Establishments		Borstals, etc.	26·5
and Children's Homes	122·0	Defence Establishments	501·2
Civilian Hospitals and		Civilian Ships, Barges, etc.	47·2
Nursing Homes	377·1	Other Establishments	201·5
Mental Hospitals, etc.	221·9	Others (Vagrants, Campers,	
Homes for the Disabled or		etc.)	4·0
Aged	67·0		

Total = 2,404·3

Of these, the hospitals undoubtedly include a number of old people who would be more suitably provided for in special homes for the aged. The miscellaneous group includes hostels restricted to particular kinds of persons. The defence group excludes members of the armed forces stationed abroad. The educational group includes only a small fraction of the total numbers receiving full-time education, which stood at 7,289,000.

CHAPTER THREE

CLASS STRUCTURE

VISITORS, especially from the United States, sometimes describe Great Britain as a 'class-ridden' country. When one asks what they mean, they sometimes answer that they are disturbed by the respect paid to royalty and to hereditary titles; but oftener they speak of the social distinction between 'gentle folk' and 'others', which appears to them to have little relation to present-day realities. When one answers them back, by asking whether they prefer the worship of the 'almighty dollar', they are apt to say that there are, at all events, no *class* distinctions in the United States. If one then enquires whether there is not in effect a class distinction between whites and negroes and even between such families as the Lowells and the Roosevelts and the immigrants from South-Eastern Europe, most of them answer that such distinctions, even if they are drawn in some quarters, are unimportant and do not dominate American society as our class distinctions seem to dominate ours. At this point, it does not appear to be worthwhile to carry the conversation any further, unless one is prepared to embark upon what promises to be an interminable argument about the meaning of the word 'class'.

What is 'Class'? 'Class' is indeed a term of singularly elusive meaning. When it is used in ordinary conversation, one has usually a fairly clear notion of what is meant. But it remains very difficult to offer any precise definition. Although there can be no doubt about the existence and the continued importance of class distinctions in British society, this does not mean that persons, or families, are arranged in a simple hierarchy of superior and inferior classes, either objectively or in the agreed opinion of the British people. Many different factors go to the making of 'class'; and those which are singled out for attention differ from one group or section to another. Villagers in mainly agricultural areas have not the same notions of class as dwellers in big towns: different notions are apt to prevail in the North and the South of England, in Clydeside and in the Highlands of Scotland, and in South and in North and Central Wales. Bath and Cheltenham do not view the question in quite the same light as Birmingham or Manchester, or a Working Men's Club as the Oxford and Cambridge Club or the bodies responsible for Henley Regatta. Each group sees classes in the light of its own experience and environment; and most people have but a hazy notion of the class structure of those parts of society of which they have no personal knowledge.

Common Distinctions. Yet class distinctions, though they are often said to be breaking down, preserve a considerable vitality in most people's minds. The classes most spoken of in everyday speech are the 'working' and the 'middle' classes—the latter very often divided into 'upper' and 'lower'. In a different connection, the words 'gentleman' and 'lady' are often used by way of contrast to 'common' people. 'Aristocracy' and 'upper class' have still their uses, though they are much less frequent in our speech than they used to be. For most purposes, the 'upper class' has become merged in the 'upper middle class'; but the term still keeps a restricted meaning with reference to what is called 'society' in an exclusive sense. It has, however, changed its denotation: by no means all titled persons, or even peers of the realm, can now be thought of as belonging to it in these days of Labour and Co-operative peers and of countless business men, civil servants, and persons of distinction in almost any walk of life who are entitled to be addressed as 'Sir' or 'Dame' or 'Lady'.

'Upper' and 'Middle' Class. Capitalism and the advance of political democracy have in effect gone far to destroy the political and economic importance of the 'upper class', which now maintains, except in the countryside, only a vestigial significance in terms of 'social' prestige. In public opinion polls, when people are asked to state to what class they deem themselves to belong, only a few claim to be of the 'upper class'; whereas a great and increasing number describe themselves as 'middle class'—though nothing like so high a proportion here as in the United States. 'Middle' and 'working' are the two main class categories of present-day Britain, both when people are assigning themselves to a class and when they are speaking generally of class distinctions.

'Working' Class. 'Working class' is a term which has evidently in the main an occupational reference. The 'working class' has as its core those who are regularly engaged in manual work for wages, together with their wives and families, except where the latter have some personal claim to be regarded as belonging to another class—for example, as school-teachers or sons or daughters of manual workers who have found their way to a University. The 'working class', however, is no longer restricted—if indeed it ever was—to manual workers. Almost everyone would agree to-day that shop assistants belong to it, except perhaps a few who serve in very exclusive shops; and many extend its meaning to cover large groups of other blackcoated workers, such as clerks, typists, postal and telegraph workers, hospital nurses, draughtsmen, and other minor professional workers. At this point, however, precision is no longer possible. Professional workers, as such, are

ordinarily thought of as belonging to the 'middle classes', in the plural rather than the singular. It then becomes a question of deciding what is to be regarded as a 'profession'; and each man makes his own, often rather indefinite, judgment on this point. The Trade Union is often thought of as a characteristically 'working-class' institution; but nowadays many professional workers are organized in Trade Unions, or in associations that are very like Trade Unions, and quite a number of these bodies are even affiliated to the Trades Union Congress, though others stand aloof—for example, the Teachers, the National and Local Government Officers, and some of the Civil Servants.

Grades of Workers. The words 'working class' indeed denote to-day not so much a clearly delimited body of persons as a wide section of society grouped round a central nucleus consisting of the manual workers and their households, rather than their families in a larger sense. This central nucleus is often broken up into sub-groups— 'skilled', 'semi-skilled' and 'unskilled' workers; but the lines of division between these sub-groups are very imprecise except where the old institution of apprenticeship to a skilled trade persists. Mass-production methods have immensely increased the proportion of manual workers who cannot properly be characterized as either 'skilled' or 'unskilled'; and the allocation of those who can be regarded as belonging to the intermediate 'semi-skilled' group is bound to be largely arbitrary. Anyone who attempts to use the Census figures assigning persons to Social Classes III, IV and V, which are supposed to rest on this distinction, will soon find reasons for distrusting some of the assignments, but will be puzzled to find a better alternative.

Supervisory Workers. There is also a considerable difficulty over the class assignment of supervisory workers, such as factory foremen, colliery deputies, and supervisors of non-manual work. The Census puts most of them into the 'working class', to which, undoubtedly, most of them belonged in the early stages of their working lives. Their functions, however, differentiate them from the main body of wage-workers, and they are in reality on the border-line between the 'working' and the 'lower middle' class.

The 'Middle Classes'. Despite these uncertainties 'working class' is a much simpler term than 'middle class', which has, occupationally, a much greater diversity. The 'middle classes'—note the plural—clearly include the members of all the 'higher' professions—doctors, lawyers, upper civil servants, authors, artists, the higher ranges of actors and musicians, as well as business men (owners or managers of industrial or service concerns), highly qualified scientists and technicians, and most persons living on incomes from property (excluding those few who may be assigned to the 'upper class'). They include many journalists; but there is a doubt about reporters, as well as about rank-and-file musicians and actors. They include chefs, but not cooks as such; military and naval and air-force officers; upper civil servants and upper local government employees. But do they include insurance agents, clerks (or perhaps only certain of them, such as law clerks, cashiers and salaried accounting clerks, and the like)? Do they include or exclude qualified draughtsmen, qualified nurses, school-teachers (or only some of them), minor technicians, rank-and-file civil servants and local government employees, and a host of other persons engaged in specialized forms of non-manual work and in many cases holding some sort of diploma or certificate of competence? Finally, what about farmers and shopkeepers—two big groups which are not at all easy to fit in or to regard as belonging all to the same social stratum?

'Upper Middle' Class. These questions are unanswerable without recourse to the sub-division of the 'middle classes'. But even if we subdivide them into 'upper' and 'lower', or even into 'upper', 'middle' and 'lower', considerable difficulties remain. What, for example, is the 'upper middle class'? It clearly includes the members of the 'higher', but not of the 'lesser' professions, and also the responsible owners and managers of considerable business concerns. It is marked off in part by the size of its members' incomes; but neither income nor occupation provides a sufficient clue to it. Indeed, most people's notion of the 'upper middle' class rests in part on a distinction in terms of education and manners rather than of wealth or calling. To a great extent, in most people's minds, 'upper middle class' is as 'upper middle class' *behaves.* The 'upper middle class' family is recognized by its social habits—by the meals it takes and when it takes them, by the sort of house it lives in and by the house's location, by the service in the house and by the furnishings, by the subjects of conversation and the books and periodicals that are read, and so on; but not by any one of these things taken alone so much as by a number of them together. Clothes used also to be a distinguishing sign, but are much less so to-day; and the same may be said of voice and accent, though these still count for more than everyday clothing. 'Upper middle class' is a mixed notion of superior occupation, or none; of well-to-doness; and of social behaviour. It does not involve a standardized accent; but only certain local variants are admitted—Scottish more readily than Welsh, Yorkshire more readily than Lancashire, and either than 'Cockney'.

The 'upper middle' class is still, in the main, a servant-employing class, though many more of its members than formerly begin their married lives without resident domestic staff. It is of course in these days a motoring class; but the motoring habit extends well below it, and the chauffeur-driven car is only for a small section of it. On holiday, it betakes itself to hotels, rather than to boarding-houses or lodgings. It used to have, with the 'upper' class, a near monopoly of foreign travel for pleasure; but that has now been lost. It does, however, enjoy a near monopoly of air transport, except on business. It has its own social clubs and in some cases its own sports clubs as well. It plays golf, but so do other classes, especially in Scotland; and it ranks Rugby above Association football. It attends the cinema, like other classes, but is less addicted to television than the 'lower middle' and 'upper working' classes. It used to entertain largely, but has almost given up its dinner-parties and formal private dances. It includes the main body of what is known as the intelligentsia, but is by no means confined to intellectuals.

'Lower Middle' Class. The 'lower middle' class is even less socially homogeneous. Its four largest sections consist of the very small employers and the lesser business managers and officials; the members of the lesser professions; the main body of shopkeepers; and a large section of the farmers. With these are ranged at any rate some of the routine non-manual workers in business and in the public services; a fair number of the lesser technicians, and, doubtfully, the supervisory grades in industry, commerce, and a variety of service occupations. These heterogeneous elements have more in common negatively than positively: they neither are manual workers for wages nor feel for the most part solidarity with the manual workers. They differ greatly among themselves in accent, vocabulary, dress, feeding and other domestic habits, and attitudes to life. Their inclusion in a single class is based on a mixture of occupational and income characteristics, and also in some degree on educational standards. Many of them earn no more than many skilled manual workers or than routine blackcoats who are close to the manual workers; but they are marked off either by being their own masters or by possessing some sort of superiority in occupational prestige. The salary-earners among them have something in common with the manual workers and belong in many cases to bargaining bodies closely analogous to the Trade Unions of the manual workers and the rank-and-file blackcoats. But a high proportion of them work not for salaries but for profit; and these groups have much in common with the 'upper middle' class: indeed, no clear line can be drawn between the two.

Farmers and Shopkeepers. Classification is particularly difficult in the case of two of the main 'lower middle class' categories—farmers and shopkeepers. A 'shop' may be anything from a vast department store down to a minute 'selling point' conducted by the wife or widow of a husband with an occupation of his own: or it may be a branch of a multiple or Co-operative concern. The more important shopkeepers and shop managers in a town commonly gather together, with some sense of solidarity, in a Chamber of Trade or Rotary Club. But these bodies do not extend their membership to the lower ranges of retail trading; and the excluded groups can be regarded only by courtesy as belonging to the 'middle class'. They stand, in effect, outside the main class structure—certainly not above the higher sectors of the 'working class'. Farmers are rather similarly placed, though as a group they have gone up recently in the social scale. The big farmer, who employs a substantial labour force, clearly does not belong to the same class as the smallholder who uses only family labour; but there is no valid way of telling where exactly the line between 'middle-class' and other farmers is to be drawn. Moreover, countrymen and townsmen would on the whole probably classify farmers differently: indeed, townsmen might not feel able to classify them at all. The country hierarchy, though partly assimilated to the dominant culture of the towns, is still different from the urban hierarchy, especially in the deep countryside. If one puts the big and middle farmers into the 'lower middle' class, where is one to put the smallholders? It is a strain of ordinary usage to assign them to the 'working' class, hard though they in fact work. In truth, they do not fit into a classification conceived mainly in urban terms. The Census puts them all into Social Class II, with the main body of the 'lower middle' class; but it has a second classification, into Socio-economic Groups, in which it sets agriculture apart from other occupations in a group of its own. It also uses a third classification, by 'status', according to which it divides the farmers into 'employers' and 'self-employed' categories.

Class Nuclei.   The fact that a line is difficult to draw in practice does not mean that the categories it is sought to distinguish are unreal. It means rather that there are central nuclei of the various classes, but that between these there are doubtful groups which can be plausibly put on either side of the dividing line. Some sociologists have aimed at greater precision by dividing the 'middle' classes into three sub-classes instead of two—with a 'middle middle' in between the 'upper' and the 'lower'. This will not work, for purposes of practical measurement; for it involves cutting right through the middle of a great many occupations, and occupation is for the most part the only basis on which any attempt at class assignment can be begun. There is no doubt, in a sense, a 'middle middle' class; but it defies even the most approximate attempt at enumeration.

The 'Census' Classes.   We can now turn from these generalizations to such quantitative estimates of class structure as are available. This means primarily, for our purpose, the Census returns for 1951. The Census authorities, as we saw, recognize five 'Social Classes', delimited exclusively on an occupational basis and for the most part restricted to occupied males because of the difficulty of assigning occupied women to a class. This difficulty arises because so many women who go out to work do so only until they get married, and their occupations while they are working may bear no relation to their class after marriage.

Married women can indeed be classified according to the class assigned to their husbands; and this is done in the Census.

The five Social Classes recognized in the Census are nowhere exactly defined; but they consist broadly of the following groups: Class I. Employers, Upper Professional and Higher Managerial Workers; Class II. Lower Professional and Managerial and Upper Clerical Workers; some Self-employed Workers, and very small Employers; Class III. Skilled Manual Workers and Routine Non-manual Workers; Class IV. Semi-skilled Workers; Class V. Unskilled Workers. In each case all the persons enumerated as following the same occupation are assigned to the same class; but occupations are broken up and entered separately to a greater extent in some cases than in others, so that in practice there is some element of class distinction within an occupation.

The summary results of the Census classification, for occupied males and their wives only, are as follows:

TABLE 22

Occupied Males and Married Women by Social Class, Great Britain, 1951
(*thousands*)

	Occupied Males	Per cent of Total	Married Women	Per cent of Total
Class I	567·8	3·3	385·7	3·4
Class II	2,542·2	14·8	1,923·3	17·2
Class III	9,035·2	52·5	5,799·8	51·8
Class IV	2,826·0	16·4	1,777·4	15·9
Class V	2,234·3	13·0	1,317·1	11·7
	17,205·5	100	11,203·3	100

= 28,409 (excluding unmarried women and unoccupied of both sexes)

It will be observed that this classification assigns four-fifths of the whole occupied male population to the 'working class'—that is, to Social Classes III, IV and V—and upwards of half the whole to Class III —that of the routine blackcoats and skilled manual workers, together with the supervisory, as distinct from the managerial, grades. A companion analysis, limited to heads of households, gives much the same result, with 49·5 of the total in Class III and another 28·9 per cent in Classes IV and V. For some purposes it is useful to break up Class III into its main constituent elements. On the basis of this second analysis, we find that nearly 39 per cent of all heads of households are classified either as skilled manual workers or as engaged in personal services— roughly the manual group, whereas rather more than 12 per cent belong to non-manual or supervisory occupations, including that of shop assistant. The figures are shown in Table 23 (overleaf).

If the shop assistants are grouped with manual, rather than with non-manual, workers, we get 41·8 per cent of all heads of households in the

TABLE 23

Occupied Heads of Households in Social Class III as a percentage of
all Occupied Heads of Households, Great Britain, 1951

Clerical Workers	5·1	Skilled Manual Workers	34·6
Shop Assistants	3·1	Workers in Personal Service	4·1
Supervisory Workers	4·0		
	12·2		38·7

'upper' working class, and another 9·1 per cent in the routine clerical
and supervisory groups, which are on the border-line between the
'working' and the 'lower middle' class.

Classes I and II.   Classes I and II, ranging from the highest groups of
employers, administrators and professionals to shopkeepers, small employers, farmers and the lesser professions (including teachers), together
make up 22·1 per cent of all occupied heads of households. Class I
cannot usefully be broken up into its constituent elements: Class II can
be. Here are the particulars:

TABLE 24

Occupied Heads of Households in Social Classes I and II as a percentage
of all Occupied Heads of Households, Great Britain, 1951

Social Class I		Social Class II	
Higher Administrative, Mana- gerial and Professional Workers and Large Employers	3·3	Lesser Administrative, Mana- gerial and Professional Workers	11·2
		Shopkeepers and Small Employers	4·9
		Farmers	2·7
	3·3		18·8

Social Class I here corresponds roughly to our conception of the
'upper middle' class. Class II contains the greater part of the 'lower
middle' class, which also includes a part of the 8·2 per cent consisting of blackcoats and supervisory workers assigned in the Census to
Class III. The 'middle classes', ignoring the small factor of the employed 'upper' class, thus form something between 22 per cent and
30 per cent of all occupied heads of households. The 'working' classes
—Social Classes III, IV and V, less such of the 8 per cent as we choose
to assign to the 'lower middle' class—form from 69 per cent to 78 per
cent.

I have used 'heads of households' in preference to all 'occupied persons' in making these estimates in the knowledge that the effect is to
swell the relative size of the higher groups because a high proportion of

occupied persons who are not heads of households would be in the lower grades. As we saw, the use of the figures for all occupied males and their wives gives over 80 per cent in the three bottom Social Classes.

The Social Pyramid. The pyramid of British society in 1951 thus had as its apex an 'upper' *plus* 'upper middle' class embracing roughly 3·3 per cent of the whole; and beneath this was a second stratum including about 19 per cent, or up to 27 per cent if we include the doubtful 8 per cent from Social Class III. Then come the 42 per cent comprising the skilled workers, or 51 per cent if we include the doubtful groups of blackcoats and supervisors; and below these again were the 27 per cent of semi-skilled and unskilled workers. Say, one quarter above and one quarter below the central group forming half the total. This is, I think, a reasonable general impression of the contemporary class structure in Great Britain.

Class and Political Opinion. It is a picture of the class structure, but evidently not of political opinion. If the 'working-class' groups voted solidly, even without the support of a single blackcoat or supervisor, they would always be sure of returning to office any Government they wanted. They could indeed do without all the workers engaged in personal service, and still poll over 60 per cent of the votes. In practice, however, nothing like this occurs. Even when the Labour Party wins an election it does not receive anything like the whole of the undoubtedly working-class vote. Mr. John Bonham, in his recent book on *The Middle Class Vote*, has set out to give an impression of the voting tendencies of the different classes. Mr. Bonham makes use of a very wide definition of the term 'middle class', which gives it nearly a third (30·4 per cent) of the total voting power. He divides the 'middle class' in four groups, which he arranges as follows:

TABLE 25

The Middle Classes

		Per cent
Proprietorial and Managerial	4,300,000	12·6
Higher Professional	900,000	2·6
Lower Professional	1,500,000	4·4
White Collar	3,700,000	10·8
	10,400,000	30·4

Mr. Bonham then attempts to analyse the ways in which the members of these groups actually voted in the General Elections of 1945, 1950 and 1951. He divides them into three sections—those who voted Conservative, those who voted Labour, and those who either voted for other parties or did not vote at all. Here are his results:

P.-W.C.B.—D

TABLE 26

Middle-class and Manual Working-class Voting, 1945–51 (Bonham)

Group	Conservative per cent			Labour per cent			Rest, Inc. Abstentions		
	1945	1950	1951	1945	1950	1951	1945	1950	1951
Business a	66	70–73	80	10	9–10	8	24	21–23	12
b	63	70–72	73	12	8–10	10	25	22	17
c	37	53–56	64	27	17–19	15	36	28–25	21
d	47	56–58	65	23	18–21	19	30	26–23	16
Professional:									
Higher	58	68–68	78	15	7–12	6	27	25–20	16
Lower	41	45–45	52	23	24–26	24	36	31–29	24
White Collar:									
Higher	49	60–60	63	20	14–16	13	31	26–24	24
Lower	33	43–43	48	30	28–29	29	37	29–28	23
Intermediate	24	33–34	41	32	38–43	39	44	29–23	20
Manual Working Class	20	26	28	42	48	51	37	26	20
Total	29	36	40	35	39	41	36	25	19

According to these calculations, the Labour Party received in 1950 48 per cent and in 1951 51 per cent of the total manual working-class vote. In 1945 it got only 42 per cent, but the number of abstentions was much greater and there were many more Liberal candidates in the field. The Conservatives got 26 per cent in 1950, 28 per cent in 1951, and 20 per cent in 1945. Abstentions, or voters for other parties, were 26 per cent of the manual workers in 1950, 20 per cent in 1951, and 37 per cent in 1945.

The 'Business' and the 'Professional' Vote. At the other end of the social scale, where abstentions were fewer, the Conservatives got in 1945 66 per cent of the top-level business vote and 58 per cent of the higher professional vote, as against the Labour Party's 10 and 15 per cent. In 1950 they did better, with from 70 to 73 per cent of the top business vote and 68 per cent of the higher professional vote, Labour getting 9–10 per cent of the former and 7–12 per cent of the latter. In 1951 the Conservative advantage increased further, with 80 per cent and 78 per cent. In the next highest business group, the voting was not much less favourable to the Conservatives, who got 63 per cent in 1945, 70–72 per cent in 1950, and 73 per cent in 1951, as compared with Labour's 12, 8–10 and 10 per cent. In the third business group, the Conservatives did relatively ill in 1945 with only 37 per cent against

Labour's 27 per cent. But the case was altered in 1950 and 1951, with the Conservatives getting 53–56 per cent and 64 per cent and Labour 17–19 and 15 per cent. Finally, in the lowest business group the Conservatives got 47, 56–58 and 65 per cent, and Labour 23, 18–21 and 19 per cent.

In the lower professional group too the advantage was all with the Conservatives—41, 45 and 52 per cent as against Labour's 23, 24–26 and 24 per cent. This leaves Mr. Bonham's 'white-collar' groups.

The 'White-collar' Group. We come last to Mr. Bonham's 'white-collar' groups, higher and lower, and to the group which he calls 'intermediate'—that is, nearest of all to the manual workers. Among the higher 'white-collar' workers, the Conservatives were nearly as strong as in the higher professions. They had the support of 49 per cent in 1945, of 60 per cent in 1950, and of 63 per cent in 1951. But in the lower 'white-collar' group the position was different. In 1945 Labour polled 30 per cent to the Conservatives' 33 per cent. In 1950, however, the Conservatives were well ahead, with 43 per cent to 28–29 per cent; and in 1951 they did better still, with 48 per cent to 29 per cent. Only among the 'intermediate' did Labour draw ahead, even in 1945, when it polled 32 per cent to the Conservatives' 24 per cent. In 1950, Labour still just led, with 38–43 per cent as against the Conservatives' 33–34 per cent. In 1951 this scanty lead had been lost: the Conservatives had 41 per cent and Labour 39 per cent, the abstentions and 'third-party' voters having dropped from 44 per cent to 20 per cent.

These figures, rough though they may be, suffice to show that class has more than a little to do with political attitude, and indeed that the correlation has been getting closer. The Labour Party actually polled a higher proportion of the manual workers' votes in 1951, when it lost the election, than in 1945, when it won a handsome majority of seats. Between these dates, its share in the votes of the higher professional workers dropped from 15 to 6 per cent, whereas it held its own among the lesser professionals. In the top 'white-collar' group it dropped from 20 to 13 per cent, whereas in the lower it dropped only from 30 to 29. In the higher business groups there was not much change, but in the lower the Labour vote fell from 27 to 15 and from 23 to 19 per cent. Evidently votes were being cast more in accordance with what were deemed to be economic interests. The shake-up of the war years was losing its effect: class politics were increasing their hold. The Conservatives were indeed polling more manual working-class votes; but these were drawn from Liberals and abstentionists, not from Labour, which also added to its proportion. In 1951 Labour, though it lost the election, still polled more votes than the Conservatives, thanks mainly to getting more working-class electors to the poll.

The Higher Professions. Who are the professionals? According to the

Census figures of 1951 the 'higher professions'—those in Social Class I —numbered 404,000, made up as follows:

TABLE 27

The Higher Professions, Great Britain, 1951

Clergy	48,100		
Lawyers (including solicitors)	26,100		
Doctors	44,100		
Dentists	13,600		
High Civil Servants	12,100	Total	144,000
Engineers:			
Mechanical and Metallurgical	31,900		
Civil	27,700		
Electrical	20,600		
Mining	4,000		
Marine	2,100		
Architects, etc.	19,100		
Surveyors	37,600		
Chemists	24,700		
Other Scientists	17,300	Total	185,000
Authors and Journalists	28,800		
Armed Forces Officers	46,200	Total	75,000
		Grand Total	404,000
Other Groups in Class I			93,100
		Total of Class I	497,100

The Lesser Professions. The lesser professions are harder to classify. Here are the main groups, excluding technical, managerial and administrative staffs in industry and commerce.

TABLE 28

The Lesser Professions, Great Britain, 1951

Teachers	356,700	Navigating Officers and	
Librarians	15,200	Pilots	12,500
Social and Religious Workers	31,600	Producers and Stage	
Physiotherapists	10,300	Managers	4,600
Radiographers	5,100	Auctioneers and Valuers	23,500
Pharmacists	13,800	Land Agents and Estate	
Opticians	8,800	Managers	2,400
Trained Nurses and Midwives	171,900	Executive Civil Servants*	68,900
Other Medical Auxiliaries	27,800	Local Government Officials	29,000
Draughtsmen	126,800	Other Public Officials	6,000
Industrial Designers	6,200		
		Total	925,700

* Excluding 12,100 'higher' Civil Servants assigned to Social Class I.

This enumeration is to some extent arbitrary; but it includes all the professional categories that can be identified in the lists given in the Census as assignable to Social Class II. Of course, some of those included really belong with the 'higher' professionals—e.g. some teachers; but it is not possible to say how many should be transferred. The broad impression given by the figures is undoubtedly correct. They indicate the growing importance of the lesser professions in the class structure as a result of technological development and the increasing range of recognized professional qualifications.

Class and Education.   Another approach to the study of class structure is by way of education rather than occupation. Here the most significant measurable characteristics are the duration of school life and the numbers in Universities and other institutions of higher or specialized study. Here are the figures showing the proportion of juveniles in England and Wales who continue to attend school or college—full-time or part-time—after the minimum leaving age of fifteen:

TABLE 29

Full-time and Part-time Education (over 15), England and Wales, 1953
(*thousands*)

Age	Attending Full-time	Not Attending Full-time	Part-time	Full-time Ratio
15 plus	212	425	10	1 in 3
16 ,,	113	507	21	1 in 6
17 ,,	62	544	30	1 in 10
18 ,,	34	572	25	1 in 18
19 ,,	30	554	21	1 in 20
20 ,,	26	611	17·5	1 in 25
21 ,,	21	629	13	1 in 31
22 ,,	17	636	9	
23 ,,	15	644	10	
24 ,,	8	670	8	
25 and over	30	31,495	57	

Between fifteen and sixteen roughly one child in every three is still at school full-time. But the figure is not of much significance, as it includes those who stay on only a little while after they are fifteen. The next age-group is much more significant: it marks off those who stay for at least a full year beyond the minimum leaving age, and this indicates the relative size of the group which enters on earning a living with more than the minimum of full-time schooling. The passing of another year reduces the group from one-sixth to one-tenth of the total; and one more year brings it down to one in every 18. The difference between one in 6 and one in 18 shows the relative sizes of the groups that begin their earning lives at 16 and at 18, thus stopping short for the most part of the university or college level. The recruits to earning at graduate or professional diploma level—i.e. at 20 or more years of age—number one in every 25—a mere 4 per cent. But even this—and indeed all the figures—represents a large advance on the position as it was in the 1930s or earlier. The full-time university population has risen from about 50,000 in 1938-9 to well over 80,000 in 1955, and was as high as 83,500 while the Further Education and Training Scheme for those with war service was in force. For further details of educational advance see pages 329 ff.

The Changing Class-structure. The class-structure of Great Britain, then, is still a very real thing, though it has changed its shape in recent years. It is less hereditary than it used to be: there is more mobility from class to class over the generations. But this mobility is very difficult to estimate with any accuracy—above all, because of the difficulty in finding a suitable basis of classification. As we have seen, the Census assigns the skilled manual workers and the bulk of the blackcoats to the same Social Class; and, though it is possible to separate them, it is not correct to place either group as a whole above the other in the social hierarchy. Now, a great deal of mobility exists between these two groups; but it cannot be counted as class mobility if they are both put in the same class. Consequently, a great deal of the actual mobility is left out of account, even when there is in reality a movement up or down—say, from the less prestigeful kinds of skilled manual work to the more prestigeful blackcoated occupations.

Class Mobility. Professor Glass and his associates, in their recent book on *Social Mobility*, have attempted to measure the extent to which sons rise above or fall below their fathers' social class. They have used for this purpose not the Census structure of five Social Classes but an amended seven-class structure; but the change affects only the higher classes—I and II of the Census—and still leaves the skilled manual workers and the routine blackcoats together in Class 5, which corresponds to the Census's Social Class III. Here are the figures given by Professor Glass on the basis of a number of field studies.

TABLE 30

Class Mobility in Great Britain—Estimated Percentage

Level of Father	Same	Level of Son Higher	Lower
1. Professional and High Administrative	38·8	—	61·2
2. Managerial and Executive	26·7	10·7	62·6
3. Higher Inspectoral and Supervisory	18·8	13·6	67·6
4. Lower Inspectoral and Supervisory	21·2	17·2	61·6
5. Routine Non-Manual and Skilled Manual	47·3	23·1	29·6
6. Semi-skilled Manual	31·2	33·3	15·5
7. Unskilled Manual	27·4	72·6	—

Upward and Downward Movements. According to this estimate, downward class mobility far exceeds upward mobility in every Class down to Class 4, and appreciably exceeds it even in the biggest Class—Class 5, which is broadly equivalent to the Census's Class III. How can these figures be reconciled with the almost general assumption that more persons move upwards than downwards in the social scale, or with the known increase in the proportion of professional and other higher jobs? A part of the explanation no doubt is that many of the sons have not finished moving and will rise to a higher class before they retire. But this does not appear to be a sufficient reason for so large a discrepancy. A further reason is that much of the upward movement takes place within Class 5 and thus goes unrecorded; but it is to be observed that even in this Class less than half the sons are in the same Class as their fathers.

I confess that I entertain some doubt about the accuracy of these estimates, which do not rest on a large enough foundation of factual ascertainment to be beyond dispute. They are, however, the only figures available, and it seems better to give them for what they are worth than to provide nothing at all.

Age and Class. Age is, of course, a factor in class. Many persons rise to higher jobs as they get older; and many fall back to lesser ones in old age, or retire on pensions which lower their standards of living and therewith their social prestige. These fallings away are for the most part not recorded in the figures, which do not attempt to classify retired persons; but the age-consideration affects the figures of class mobility from father to son. The following table attempts to show the effects of age on social class: it is derived from the Census Tables for 1951.

TABLE 31

Social Class Distribution in Great Britain, 1951

(Occupied or Retired Males only)

(*thousands*)

	Under 25	25–45	45–60	Over 60	Total	Per cent of Total
Class 1	61·3	252·0	144·7	109·8	567·8	3·3
Class 2	157·9	1,039·4	782·1	562·8	2,542·2	14·8
Class 3	1,771·2	3,888·4	2,060·6	1,315·0	9,035·2	52·5
Class 4	464·5	1,105·5	730·3	525·7	2,826·0	16·4
Class 5	310·2	774·9	623·7	525·5	2,234·3	13·0
	2,765·1	7,060·2	4,341·4	3,038·8	17,205·5	100

Percentages of each Age-group in each Social Class

Class 1	2·2	3·5	3·3	3·6
Class 2	5·7	14·7	18·0	18·5
Class 3	64·1	55·1	47·5	43·3
Class 4	16·8	15·7	16·8	17·3
Class 5	11·2	11·0	14·4	17·3
	100	100	100	100

TABLE 31 (*continued*)

Percentages of each Social Class in each Age-group

Class 1	10·8	44·4	25·5	19·3	100
Class 2	6·2	40·9	30·6	22·2	100
Class 3	19·6	43·1	22·8	14·5	100
Class 4	16·5	39·1	25·8	15·6	100
Class 5	13·9	34·7	27·9	23·5	100

It will be seen that the percentage of older is substantially higher than that of younger men in Social Class I and very much greater in Social Class II, which offers most opportunities for promotion. Social Classes I and II both contain much greater proportions of older than of younger men, whereas in Social Class III the position is reversed. In Social Classes IV and V the position of Classes I and II is reproduced, especially in the lowest Class, which includes a large preponderance of elderly persons. These figures seem to contradict the apparent implications of the Social Mobility Table.

Sex and Class. It remains to say a few words about the sex aspect of

TABLE 32

Status Aggregates by Sex, Great Britain, 1951
(Total occupied and retired population aged 15 and over)
(*thousands*)

	Males	Per cent	Females	Per cent	Total	Per cent
Employers	405·9	2·6	54·0	0·8	459·9	2·1
Managers:						
General and Directors	167·0	1·1	18·4	0·3	185·4	0·8
Branch or Primary Departments	368·9	2·4	81·3	1·2	450·2	2·1
Office or Subsidiary Departments	101·2	0·6	11·4	0·2	112·6	0·5
Operatives:						
Class I and II	1,299·7	8·5	761·5	11·2	2,061·2	9·3
Others	12,106·0	79·0	5,633·4	82·9	17,739·4	80·0
Working on own account	887·4	5·8	237·2	3·5	1,124·6	5·1
Total Working	15,336·1	100	6,797·2	100	22,133·3	100
Out of Work	326·1		119·1		445·2	
Retired	1,543·3		302·5		1,845·8	
Total	17,205·5		7,218·8		24,421·3	

class. As we have seen, the Census returns make no attempt to analyse the Social Class of unmarried women; and it is necessary to fall back on the figures of what the Census calls 'Industrial Status', which embodies a classification according to the 'status' of the groups studied as employers, managers, workers on own account, and operatives—these last alone being divided into two groups according to Social Class. The figures relate of course only to occupied persons; but they cover all such persons, females as well as males.

It will be seen from this table that, in relation to the numbers occupied, male employers and managers in all the groups far outnumber female employers and managers. This is true also, though not quite to the same extent, of workers 'on own account'. Conversely, a higher proportion of women are to be found in the 'operative' grades. It should, however, be noted that this applies to the higher as well as to the lower grades of operatives, because of the considerable number of women engaged in non-manual occupations, including professional services. This type of employment tends to mitigate the social inferiority of occupied women regarded as a single group. This inferiority is nevertheless marked enough. 94 per cent of all occupied women are 'operatives', as against 87·5 per cent in the case of men. The lower marriage age of occupied females is of course a factor, as it narrows the opportunities for promotion.

Such, then, is the class structure of British society, as far as it can be measured statistically from the occupational data. I have not in this section considered the alternative way of measuring, in terms of income. That is considered in another section (see pp. 221 ff.).

Changes over Sixty Years. To one who can look back over more than sixty years, it is remarkable how conditions in Great Britain have changed. The class structure remains, not unaltered, but in its essentials the same: yet its consequences in respect of the conditions of living are immensely different. At the very bottom of the social structure there is still deep poverty; but sheer starvation has almost disappeared, and the size of the submerged 'tenth' has been very greatly reduced. When I was young, both adults and children dressed in sheer rags were a common sight, not only if one sought them in the slums but nearly everywhere outside a limited number of 'superior' areas. Squalor obtruded itself on the vision of the ordinary citizen; and there were many who, like me, were made ashamed of it and were impelled by our sense of shame to set about the tasks of reform. Above this bottom level stood the main body of unskilled workers, still separated by a very wide gulf from the skilled workers, and manifestly ill-clad and underfed. Even the skilled manual workers, or most of them, were widely separated from the middle classes by differences of manners, speech, clothing, and behaviour. There was, of course, even then a 'superior' working class to which these distinctions applied much less than to the majority; and these were the men and women who manned both the chapels of working-class Nonconformity and the centres of Trade Union and Labour activity. But between them and the mass they were attempting to influence there were barriers not easily surmounted.

Assimilation. Nowadays, on the other hand, it is often impossible to tell by looking at a man—or woman—and by hearing them talk, to what class they belong. There has been a remarkable assimilation, above all in clothing, but also in speech and in everyday behaviour. It is still, no doubt, possible to pick out some persons, at sight, as members of the upper middle class or as manual workers from their dress and ways of holding themselves and moving their limbs; but there are many more who carry no such evident signs about them. One can try to 'place' the people one encounters in trains or buses or in the streets; but one is quite often wrong.

It may be argued that these changes are only superficial and do not affect the real differences of class. But they do affect them, because they affect the relations between men and women who belong to different classes. Many of the old obstacles to mutual understanding and intercourse have vanished, or at any rate have become much less formidable. This is not only because the physical gulf has been narrowed, though that counts for a good deal. It is also because the entire way of life has become more democratic, and because the 'lower' classes no longer feel the same sense of exclusion from power and from equal intercourse as they used to feel. They have become citizens, with a share both in political power and, up to a point, in the means of decent living.

Class Changes since 1939. When I look back, not to my youth but only to the 1930s, when I was in my forties, I find the contrast much less striking. The 'thirties were a period of depression, during which there was a great deal of dreadful suffering among the old people and the unemployed. But they were not, for all that, a period of *general* working-class misery. The suffering was sectional and limited in its effects. It hit terribly hard the ship-building centres, many of the coalfields, and all those places which felt the full impact of the depression; but because of low prices and of wage-rates not ill-maintained, its effect on the majority of the workers was greatly mitigated. A substantial part of the gains won during and after the first world war were left intact. That was why social discontent, acute in the depressed areas, did not become more intense over the country as a whole.

Nevertheless, the advance between the 'thirties and now has been considerable, and has significantly altered the effects of the class system, if not the system itself. To take an example from my own environment, when I was an Oxford undergraduate in the first decade of this century undergraduates of manual working-class parentage were known, but were unfamiliar and exceptional, and very conscious of being so. In the 'thirties that was no longer the case; but there were still barriers between them and the common run of students that do not exist to-day. Nowadays, their presence is taken for granted; and there is often nothing to mark them off as different from students who come from middle-class families—unless indeed they choose to stress their origin.

Class Struggles.   In these circumstances the struggle between classes, though it does not cease to exist, necessarily changes its human character. It becomes more and more a contest, not between unlikes, but of like with like, carried on with more mutual knowledge and understanding. Moreover, the respective attitudes of the parties are to some extent reversed. To-day, few even of the more class-conscious workers *hate* the capitalists as human beings, or respond to the propaganda of hate. There is more hate among the 'superior' classes for those whom they still regard as their inferiors. Let anyone who doubts this pay a few visits to superior watering-places, such as Brighton or Bournemouth, whose hotels are full of snobbish persons bitterly resentful of high taxation and of the 'pampering' of the poor through the social services. It is in such places, and not in Labour or Trade Union meetings, that the modern 'hymns of hate' are sung. No doubt, the singers are unrepresentative of the whole class to which they belong. They are largely retired 'ladies' and 'gentlemen' who are trying to keep up their superiority on incomes that are less ample than they used to be; and at the back of their hatred lies fear—fear that their days are numbered. They are indeed a decaying section of the classes that live on unearned incomes, rather than a fair sample of those classes in general. Nevertheless, there they are, lamenting in a social vacuum, and only less hostile to Mr. Butler than to Mr. Attlee, or even to Mr. Aneurin Bevan, whose memories of a depressed area in his young days sometimes lead him to use the old language in speaking of the 'superior' classes.

Having visited these haunts of decay, my supposed enquirer should next betake himself to a few really expensive restaurants and bars, where he will find crowds of prosperous-looking persons eating and drinking at a great rate, apparently regardless of the cost. He will not find these persons nearly so much addicted to 'hymns of hate' against the workers. Probably they will not be discussing politics at all. If he were to ask them how they manage, in face of high taxes, to have so much money to spend, and could get them to answer truly, he would find that a great many of them are not really paying for what they consume. They are entertaining themselves, or are being entertained, out of 'expense allowances' which benevolent Chancellors of the Exchequer permit them to charge up to the companies that they serve, or preside over: so that their real incomes greatly exceed the incomes on which they pay tax. These blessings are showered very unevenly: they accrue mainly to business men—to the busy rather than to the idle rich; but they are to-day among the main supports of luxury spending and are a great help in making 'exorbitant' taxation tolerable to the business section of the higher middle class. Luckily for them, the working classes do not visit such places, and are but vaguely aware of this aspect of the working of the Welfare State.

Such 'goings-on' are, indeed, only a minor nuisance. They do not make it the less true that, as matters stand now, the lot of the common people has substantially improved and the gulf between the classes been appreciably narrowed, even since 1939.

CHAPTER FOUR

MAN-POWER AND EMPLOYMENT

WE have already seen (on p. 5) that the 'occupied' population, including therein those for the time being unemployed, differs from the population of working age, both in including persons over the normal retiring age who are still at work and in excluding persons who are not gainfully occupied, even if they in fact work hard as housewives or in some form of voluntary service. The 'working' population, as officially defined, includes all those who normally work for payment, whether they are at the moment working or not. It excludes those who remain in full-time education after the minimum school-leaving age; those who are physically or mentally incapable of earning a living; those who have in fact retired; those who do not work for gain because they are wealthy enough to live on unearned incomes; women and girls, chiefly housewives, who work at home without receiving payment; and, of course, infants and children who have not yet reached working age.

The Working Population. This working population has to provide by its labours for the maintenance of those who do not work, and the proportion it bears to total population is therefore a matter of considerable economic importance. When a population is rising fast, because of a high birth-rate or a low infant death-rate or both, the large number of children in the population reduces the proportion of workers to persons of all ages, and thus tends to reduce income per head, especially if it goes hand in hand with an improvement in the expectation of life among elderly persons. Historically, countries have tended during the two past centuries to experience first a sharp fall in infant mortality, accompanied by a smaller fall in death-rates at later ages. In the absence of social changes increasing the range of persons going out to work this phase involved both rapid increases in total population and a decrease in the proportion of 'workers' to 'non-workers'. This decrease is accentuated if over the same period more children are taken from work to attend school, or if fewer elderly persons continue to work. Following on this period of rapidly rising total population there has come, in one country after another, a period of falling birth-rates, usually accompanied by a further fall in both infant mortality and adult death-rates. These factors work in opposite directions in their effects both on total population and on working population. If the birth-rate falls

faster than infant mortality, the proportion of children in the population declines. But falling adult death-rates increase the proportion of
old people, so that the combined effect on the proportion of working
to total population may be small. As we saw on page 12 recent changes
in birth- and death-rates in Great Britain have not significantly affected
the proportion of total population that is of working age.

The definition of 'working' population is, of course, to some extent
arbitrary. It is a convention and not a law of nature that married
women are not paid for their work in the home and are not counted
as members of the working population unless they are also gainfully
employed. The proportion of women so employed increased sharply
during the war, but fell back thereafter, though the industrial employment of women remained high. The countervailing factor was chiefly
a sharp decline in the number of domestic servants, partly offset by an
increase in institutional employment in hotels, restaurants, hospitals
and other service occupations. The raising of the minimum school-
leaving age to fifteen, without any exemptions, appreciably decreased
the size of the working force at the younger end.

The Fall in Unemployment. The volume of work done, as distinct
from the size of the working force, has of course been substantially increased by the very great fall in long-term unemployment, which has
been reduced to nearly negligible proportions since the war. Short-term
unemployment too has been much reduced. Against this has to be set
some reduction in the length of the normal working week, especially
for young persons; but the increase in overtime working has counterbalanced this reduction, except in the case of juveniles. The average
industrial worker does not in fact work fewer hours in a year than he
did in the 1930s—indeed, the adult male works on the average a full
hour a week longer than he did in 1938—and of course the productivity
of each hour worked is on the average substantially larger than it was
before 1939. It is mainly among women and juveniles and in certain
non-manual occupations, where overtime payment is unusual, that the
actual number of hours worked has been reduced. Hotel and other
institutional services provide an obvious example.

The supply of man-power, then, bears in general much the same relation to total population as it did in the 1930s: the main change has been
in its utilization. Any attempt to consider its comparative efficiency, in
terms of productiveness, is left for consideration later (see pp. 58 ff.).

At the end of 1954 the working population of Great Britain, exclusive
of Northern Ireland, numbered 23,816,000, including part-time workers
—16,049,000 males and 7,767,000 females. Of these, 280,000 were registered as unemployed or temporarily stopped—less than 1·2 per cent.
This high level of employment stands in marked contrast with the situation that existed when the previous version of *The Condition of Britain*
was published in 1937. In July 1936, registered unemployment in the

United Kingdom stood at 1,717,000, or 12·7 per cent, and had re-mained at a high level for many years on end. Continuously from July 1930 to June 1935 the monthly totals of registered unemployment had exceeded 2,000,000; and from January 1931 to May 1933 the percentage had always exceeded 20. Even during the period of re-armament before the outbreak of war in 1939 unemployment seldom fell below one million, or below 10 per cent of the insured population.

Shortage of Man-power. As against this, during and since the war there has been in general a continuous shortage of man-power. There have been periods at which employment in particular trades has fallen off; but there has been, up to 1955, no recession serious enough to lead to a return of unemployment, over the country as a whole, on any significant scale. There was substantial recession in the textile and clothing industries in 1952, with local pockets of unemployment; but there has been since 1940 no unemployment problem even remotely resembling that of the years between the two world wars. In general there have been at least as many jobs as workers looking for them—and most often more; and this change has had an enormous effect both on the economic security of the working population and on its attitude—above all in those areas in which unemployment was previously most severe.

Distribution of Man-power. In June 1939 the occupied population of Great Britain numbered 19,750,000—part-time workers being then counted as one-half and workers in private domestic service and also men over 65 and women over 60 who were still at work being omitted altogether. The pre-war and post-war figures are thus not strictly comparable: revision of the figures in 1948 resulted in increasing the

TABLE 33

Distribution of Man-power, Great Britain, 1948 and 1954 (*thousands*)

	June 1948	December 1954	Change	Change per cent
Agriculture, Forestry and Fishing	1,178	1,022	− 156	− 13·3
Mining and Quarrying	876	865	− 11	− 1·2
Manufacturing Industries	8,137	9,171	+ 1,034	12·8
Building and Contracting	1,450	1,438	− 12	− 0·8
Gas, Electricity and Water	321	376	+ 55	17·1
Transport and Communication	1,787	1,692	− 95	− 5·3
Distributive Trades	2,484	2,802	+ 318	13·0
Professional, Financial and Miscellaneous Services	3,954	4,037	+ 83	2·1
National Government Service	682	583	− 99	− 14·5
Local Government Service	700	728	+ 28	4·0
Unemployed	282	280	− 2	− 0·7
Armed Forces and Women's Services	846	830	− 16	− 1·8

estimate of total man-power for June of that year from 20,274,000 to 22,904,000, from which it rose to 23,816,000 in June 1954.

Of this last total, 830,000 were serving in the armed forces (including 21,000 in the women's services). This left 22,984,000, of whom 22,714,000 were in some form of civil employment, including employers and self-employed as well as employed persons. The broad distribution is shown in Table 33, with comparative figures for June 1948.

Thus, the manufacturing industries have increased their man-power since 1948 by over a million—nearly 13 per cent—and the distributive trades by 318,000—just 13 per cent—whereas there have been substantial decreases in agriculture (13·3 per cent), transport (5·3 per cent), and national government services (14·5 per cent). There have also been increases of some size in gas, electricity and water services (17·1 per cent), and in the professional and financial group (2·1 per cent).

Employment in Manufacturing Industries. The large total for the manufacturing industries evidently needs to be broken up. This can be done only for employed persons, not for employers or self-employed. For employees only, the main groups are as follows:

TABLE 34

Numbers Employed in Manufacturing Industries,
Great Britain, 1948 and 1954 (*thousands*)

	June 1948	December 1954	Change	Change per cent
Treatment of Non-metalliferous Mining Products (other than coal)	312	341	+ 29	9·3
Chemical and Allied Trades	439	507	+ 68	14·8
Metal Manufacture	530	564	+ 34	6·4
Engineering, Shipbuilding and Electrical Goods	1,776	2,020	+ 244	13·8
Vehicles	934	1,176	+ 242	25·9
Other Metal Goods	501	511	+ 10	2·0
Precision Instruments, Jewellery, etc.	127	142	+ 15	11·8
Textiles	922	986	+ 64	7·0
Leather, Leather Goods and Fur	78	72	− 6	− 7·6
Clothing, including Footwear	597	637	+ 40	6·8
Food, Drink and Tobacco	726	881	+ 155	21·4
Manufacture of Wood and Cork	283	307	+ 24	8·5
Paper and Printing	463	542	+ 79	17·0
Other Manufacturing Industries	242	285	+ 43	17·8

Thus, every group, except the small leather group, has increased its man-power since 1948; but of the total increase of 1,041,000 more than half— 530,000—has been in the metal, engineering and vehicle groups, and the only other group to add more than 100,000 is Food, Drink and Tobacco.

The Metal-workers. The huge metal and engineering groups need further breaking up in order to show what has been happening. Here are the figures for some of the more important branches.

TABLE 35

Employment in Metal, Engineering, Shipbuilding, Vehicle, etc., Industries, Great Britain, 1948 and 1954

(thousands)

	June 1948	December 1954	Change	Change per cent
Blast Furnaces, Smelting, Rolling, etc. (Iron and Steel)	229	244	+ 15	6·6
Iron Foundries	122	127	+ 5	4·2
Sheets and Tinplates	37	34	− 3	− 8·2
Non-ferrous Metal Smelting, Rolling, etc.	100	144	+ 14	14·0
Shipbuilding and Repairing	227	205	− 22	− 9·7
Marine Engineering	78	80	+ 2	2·6
Agricultural Machinery	39	40	+ 1	2·5
Machine Tools, etc.	84	108	+ 24	28·6
Textile Machinery	74	66	− 8	10·8
Constructional Engineering	74	83	+ 9	12·2
Boilers, etc., and Stationary Engines	45	58	+ 13	29·0
Other Non-electrical Engineering, etc.	632	711	+ 79	12·5
Electrical Machinery	166	182	+ 16	9·8
Electrical Wires and Cables	58	61	+ 3	5·2
Wireless Apparatus, Gramophones, Valves and Lamps	102	182	+ 80	78·4
Telephone and Telegraph Apparatus, etc.	196	244	+ 48	24·5
Tools and Cutlery	54	48	− 6	− 11·1
Bolts, Nuts, Nails, etc.	41	42	+ 1	2·4
Iron and Steel Forgings	38	39	+ 1	2·7
Wire	38	38	—	—
Hollow-ware	53	61	+ 8	15·1
Brass Manufactures	52	50	− 2	− 3·8
Scientific, Surgical and Photographic Instruments	76	88	+ 12	15·8
Clocks, Watches, Jewellery, etc.	43	45	+ 2	4·7
Motor Vehicle and Cycle Manufacture	279	324	+ 45	16·2
Aircraft Manufacture and Repair	144	239	+ 95	66·0
Manufacture of Motor Vehicle and Aircraft Parts	92	165	+ 73	79·4
Locomotives, Carriage and Tram Manufacture and Repair	177	165	− 12	− 6·8
	3,250	3,843	+ 593	18·3

Here note the very big increase in the Wireless and Gramophone Industries, in Motor Vehicle Parts and Accessories, and in Aircraft Manufacture, as against the decrease in Shipbuilding, Textile Machinery, Tinplate, Tools and Brass.

Here are some figures for the textile and clothing industries:

TABLE 36

Employment in Textile and Clothing Industries, Great Britain, 1948 and 1954
(*thousands*)

	June 1948	December 1954	Change	Change per cent
Cotton Spinning, Doubling, etc.	169	168	− 1	− 0·5
Cotton Weaving, etc.	122	122	—	—
Woollen and Worsted	207	212	+ 5	2·4
Rayon, Nylon and Silk	83	91	+ 8	9·7
Hosiery and other Knitted Goods	102	126	+ 24	23·5
Textile Finishing	84	93	+ 9	10·8
All other Textiles	150	174	+ 24	16·0
Tailoring	246	271	+ 24	10·1
Dressmaking	100	92	− 8	− 8·0
Underwear, Shirts, Overalls, etc.	59	72	+ 13	22·1
Boots and Shoes	138	140	+ 2	1·4
Leather Trades	68	63	− 5	− 7·4

Here the changes are relatively small, except in Hosiery and Underwear. And for Food, Drink and Tobacco:

TABLE 37

Employment in Food, Drink, and Tobacco Industries, Great Britain, 1948 and 1954 (*thousands*)

	June 1948	December 1954	Change	Change per cent
Grain Milling	39	40	+ 1	2·6
Bread and Flour Confectionery	181	185	+ 4	2·1
Biscuits	33	63	+ 30	91·0
Milk Products	50	60	+ 10	20·0
Cocoa, Chocolate and Sugar Confectionery	59	114	+ 55	93·3
Other Food Industries	164	215	+ 51	31·2
Drink Industries	152	162	+ 10	6·6
Tobacco	48	42	− 6	− 12·4

Observe here the very sharp rise in Biscuits and Sugar Confectionery, and the fall in Tobacco.

For other branches of manufacture:

TABLE 38

Employment in Other Manufacturing Industries, Great Britain, 1948 and 1954
(*thousands*)

	June 1948	December 1954	Change	Change per cent
Paper and Board	78	95	+ 17	21·8
Printing and Publishing	311	347	+ 36	11·0
Cardboard Boxes, Cartons, etc.	37	52	+ 15	40·6
Other Paper Manufacture	38	48	+ 10	26·4
Timber, Sawmilling, etc.	94	97	+ 3	3·2
Furniture and Upholstery	121	142	+ 21	17·4
Rubber	97	120	+ 23	23·8
Toys, Games and Sports Goods	26	31	+ 5	19·3
Gas, Electricity and Water	321	376	+ 55	17·1

Here the outstanding changes are the sharp increases in Containers and
Paper, Rubber, Toys and Games, and in Gas, Water and Electricity
supply.

And for selected non-producing services:

TABLE 39

Employment in Service Occupations, Great Britain, 1948 and 1954
(*thousands*)

	June 1948	December 1954	Change	Change per cent
Railways	649 (Dec.)	594 (1953)	55	− 8·5
Shipping	—	—	—	—
Docks (Live Register)	76 (Dec.)	77 (1952)	+ 1	1·3
Road Transport—Passenger	308	275	− 33	− 10·7
Road Transport—Goods	183	169	− 14	− 7·6
Dealing in Industrial Materials and Machinery	219	252	+ 33	15·1
Wholesale Distribution	393	452	+ 59	15·0
Retail Distribution	1,387	1,524	+ 137	9·9
Catering, Hotels, etc.	684	654	− 30	− 4·4
Laundries, Dry Cleaning, etc.	194	173	− 21	− 10·6

Note the rise in Distribution and the falls in most branches of Transport.

Finally, for some other important groups:

TABLE 40

Employment in Other Occupations, Great Britain, 1948 and 1954 (*thousands*)

	June 1948	December 1954	Change	Change per cent
Agriculture	849	755*	− 94	− 11·0
Civil Service: Non-industrial	715	633	− 82	− 11·5
Coal Mines	724	708	− 16	− 2·2

* June.

Outstanding Changes in Employment. For the British economy as a whole the outstanding changes are the much larger numbers employed in the metal-working industries, above all in the motor industries and in aircraft manufacture, in the machine tool trades, and also in the wireless and gramophone group; the considerable increases in the food processing trades, in paper and printing, in hosiery and underwear, and in chemicals and rubber and toys and sports goods; the increase in gas, electricity and water services; and the recovery of man-power by the distributive trades. On the other side are the large falls in the numbers employed in agriculture and transport and shipbuilding, and in the Civil Service. The man-power changes in mining and building have been small, and also those in the size of the armed forces and the general run of professional and financial services.

These changes have been accompanied by some shift in the relative numbers of employed workers in different parts of the country. The following table shows the figures for each of the Regions of the Ministry of Labour in mid-1948 and in mid-1954.

TABLE 41

Numbers of Employed Workers by Regions, Great Britain, 1948 and 1954
(*thousands*)

	1948	1954	Change per cent
London and South-Eastern	5,092	5,385	+ 5·8
Eastern	1,058	1,125	+ 6·3
Southern	952	988	+ 3·9
South-Western	1,083	1,096	+ 1·2
Midland	1,972	2,064	+ 4·7
North Midland	1,386	1,434	+ 3·5
East and West Ridings	1,775	1,808	+ 2·0
North-Western	2,906	2,971	+ 2·2
Northern	1,228	1,256	+ 2·4
Scotland	2,120	2,138	+ 1·0
Wales	928	925	− 0·2
All Regions	20,500	21,190	+ 3·4

The London and South-Eastern and Eastern Regions show substantial increases, and the Southern and the two Midland Regions are
also above the average. The rest are below the average, but only Wales
shows a very small absolute decrease.

Unemployment.   At no time since 1939 has unemployment in Great
Britain reached at all serious dimensions. In 1938 the average number
of persons registered as out of work, including temporary suspensions,
exceeded 1¾ millions. In no year since 1945 has it averaged as much as
half a million. The nearest approach was in 1947, when the average was
480,000. In that year the figure for February actually reached 1,874,000,
but fell two months later to 443,000, the very high totals for February
and March being due entirely to the fuel and power crisis of those
months, which caused very large numbers of workers to be temporarily
stood off. In no other month since 1945 has the total reached half a
million, and only in a few months has it exceeded 400,000, out of a
labour force always above 20 millions. The following table gives the
totals for Great Britain for each year from 1939.

TABLE 42

Numbers Unemployed in Great Britain, 1939–55

(*thousands*)

	Wholly Unemployed		Temporarily Stopped		Total
	M.	F.	M.	F.	M. F.
1939	982·9	315·0	137·2	78·5	1,513·6
1940	507·7	295·2	100·6	59·2	962·7
1941	153·2	139·2	29·3	28·1	349·8
1942	74·0	43·2	3·2	2·8	123·2
1943	53·1	26·9	0·8	0·8	81·6
1944	50·7	22·9	0·4	0·5	74·5
1945	83·7	52·1	0·6	0·7	137·1
1946	257·5	113·5	2·1	1·2	374·3
1947	239·0	86·5	102·7	52·0	480·2
1948	227·5	75·0	4·3	3·2	310·0
1949	223·2	76·9	4·8	3·1	308·0
1950	215·0	90·6	5·1	3·5	314·2
1951	153·4	83·6	8·1	7·8	252·9
1952	196·1	132·6	31·8	53·8	414·3
1953	204·3	115·6	13·9	8·2	342·0
1954	176·5	95·1	7·9	5·3	284·8
1955 (Jan.–Aug.)	141·5	77·4	12·6	10·7	241·0

Over the whole period 1946 to August 1955 unemployment in Great
Britain averaged 332,000, including those temporarily stopped. The
yearly average was highest in 1947 and next highest in 1952, and lowest
in 1955 (up to August) and in 1951. In January 1955, when the total

was just under 298,000, the percentage out of work was 1·4—the same for males and for females. This is a very small figure as compared with even good years in times of peace before the war. The total, moreover, is made up largely of short spells of unemployment between jobs. Out of the 298,000, temporary stoppages accounted for 17,000, and another 98,000 had been out of work for not more than two weeks. Nearly 73,000 had been out for between two and eight weeks, and nearly 110,000 for more than eight weeks. These last were the 'hard core', including a high proportion of elderly and partially disabled workers. 184,000 were men over 18, and 92,000 women over 18: the juveniles numbered nearly 22,000. By industries and occupations the largest groups were in building and contracting (38,800, of whom building alone accounted for 27,300), the distributive trades (29,800), the catering trades (25,500), and transport (21,300). The entire engineering, shipbuilding and electrical group, numbering more than 2 millions, had under 17,000 out of work, and even the textile industries only 10,700, of whom the cotton industry accounted for only 3,000. The high figure for building and contracting was of course accounted for mainly by the discontinuous nature of most of its employment, as well as by the fact that January is a very bad month for much of its work.

Unemployment by Regions. There have been considerable differences in the degree of unemployment in different areas. In August 1955 the percentages out of work ranged from 0·5 in London and the South-East and in the two Midland Regions of the Ministry of Labour to 2·0 in Scotland and 1·6 in Wales (in Northern Ireland the percentage was 6·1). Table 43 shows the regional figures in thousands for July 1939 and for the years 1947–1954.

In only one Region, and there in only one year—1952—has the annual average of those unemployed been above 100,000. This was during the recession of that year, which hit the cotton industry particularly hard. Both Scotland and Wales have shown as a rule unemployment percentages well above the average; but even there the post-war rates have been low, as can be seen by comparing the numbers out of work with the numbers insured in the various Regions.

Full or 'Overfull' Employment? This decline in unemployment has meant a vitally significant social change. In the 'thirties there was continuously a 'submerged tenth' of the working population suffering from unemployment; and the sufferers included a large body of long-term unemployed consisting mainly not of disabled or elderly persons but of fully able-bodied persons attached to the depressed industries—many of them in places where total employment had fallen to a terribly low level. These black spots have been, if not entirely eliminated, at least reduced to a very few. Indeed, over the country as a whole, when allowance is made for very short-term unemployment arising out of

TABLE 43

Numbers Out of Work by Regions, Great Britain, 1939 and 1947–55
(*thousands*)

	London & S.E.	Eastern	Southern	S. Western	Midland
1939 (July)	193·9	37·5	20·7	32·5	82·2
1947 (average)	71·4	18·7	11·0	12·6	48·1
1948 ,,	51·9	10·9	11·3	13·9	12·2
1949 ,,	54·2	11·6	12·8	14·9	12·2
1950 ,,	55·7	12·8	13·7	15·7	9·9
1951 ,,	45·7	10·1	10·8	12·6	8·5
1952 ,,	66·8	14·5	13·5	16·5	18·0
1953 ,,	63·4	13·7	13·3	17·6	21·3
1954 ,,	51·7	13·2	11·2	15·8	12·3
1955 (Jan.–Aug.)	40·2	10·9	8·7	12·7	10·1
Numbers Insured Mid-1954:					
Males	3,382	751	663	741	1,345
Females	2,003	374	325	355	719
Total	5,385	1,125	988	1,096	2,064

	N. Midland	Yorks E. & W.R.	N. Western	Northern	Scotland	Wales
1939 (July)	70·7	131·0	272·0	129·3	190·3	106·3
1947 (average)	23·2	32·0	99·1	43·5	68·5	52·1
1948 ,,	7·7	15·7	54·9	32·5	57·9	41·1
1949 ,,	7·4	15·2	48·9	32·3	62·1	36·4
1950 ,,	8·5	16·6	47·3	34·9	64·7	34·4
1951 ,,	7·3	16·2	35·8	27·5	53·4	25·0
1952 ,,	14·7	34·4	107·3	32·6	69·3	26·6
1953 ,,	9·1	21·7	60·6	29·4	64·1	27·8
1954 ,,	8·6	17·1	44·2	28·3	59·5	22·9
1955 (Jan.–Aug.)	8·0	13·8	41·8	23·9	53·0	17·9
Numbers Insured Mid-1954:						
Males	967	1,186	1,849	897	1,395	669
Females	467	622	1,122	364	743	256
Total	1,434	1,808	2,971	1,256	2,138	925

change of work, the number of unfilled vacancies at the Employment Exchange has been greater than that of persons looking for jobs. Here are the figures showing the number of such vacancies recorded in June and December each year from 1946. (See Table 44.)

Thus in June 1955 the number of unfilled vacancies was higher than at any time since 1951, and was more than twice as large as the number of workers unemployed. This comparison, which includes only vacancies actually notified to the Employment Exchanges, shows a real condition of full employment, though hardly such a condition of 'overfull'

TABLE 44

Unfilled Employment Vacancies in Great Britain, 1946–55
(*thousands*)

	June	December		June	December
1946	635	547	1951	487	313
1947	605	517	1952	305	230
1948	490	367	1953	296	270
1949	427	346	1954	381	338
1950	384	347	1955	460	—

employment as some writers suggest. It is probably a sound state of affairs to have a small excess of jobs looking for workers over workers looking for jobs, and a difference of half a million out of a total working population of nearly 24 millions does not seem to be too high. Certainly it helps to sustain the power of the Trade Unions and to make employers keen to keep their working force and to do what they can to diminish the rate of labour turnover.

CHAPTER FIVE

PRODUCTION

IT is a simple matter, in a country where the required statistics are kept and collected, to say that in any particular year so many tons of coal have been mined, so many motor-cars manufactured, or so many letters sent through the post. We can therefore also say without much difficulty at what rates the output of these things changes in quantity from year to year. But it is another matter to add them together and so arrive, with the addition of a large number of similar data, at an estimate of total production or of the rate at which total production is rising—or possibly falling. Obviously, one cannot add tons of coal or steel to numbers of motor-cars or letters—even apart from the fact that one kind of motor-car may take much more work to manufacture than another, and indeed one ton of coal much more labour than another to get.

Methods of Measuring Production. There are, in practice, only two possible methods of measuring production in general, so as to arrive at an estimate of total production in a particular period, or of the rise or fall in total production from one period to another. One method is to reckon, for each kind of output, the time taken in producing it, including an estimate of the time taken in producing the materials of which it is made and the time represented by the wear and tear of the capital goods used in making it, and also the time taken in 'overhead' services required for getting it to market. This could yield an estimate of the total man-hours applied in each kind of production; and this total could then be compared with the total for some other period— say the previous year—so as to yield an estimate of the change, not exactly in production, but in productive effort expended. There would be, however, two serious flaws in such an estimate. In the first place, as it would measure productive effort rather than production, it would fail to take any account of changes in productivity per man-hour, and might thus conceal the existence of large actual changes in output. Secondly, it would involve either treating all kinds of labour as of equal man-hour value or making estimates of the relative values of different sorts of labour and then treating an hour of one kind as equivalent to more than an hour of another kind. This would be very difficult, and indeed arbitrary; and this method of measuring total production therefore breaks down.

There remains only the alternative of adding up the outputs of different kinds of productive effort in terms of the selling value of what is produced. If the average selling value of a ton of coal, or of a particular type of coal, is x shillings and the corresponding value of a particular kind of motor-car £x, we can not only estimate the money value of all the coal and all the motor-cars produced but also add these values together and, by adding similar totals for all other products, arrive at an estimate of the money value of total production. This is the actual method used in measuring total production. It is not without serious difficulties; for some products are made not for sale but for direct use without charge to the users—for example, roads and hospitals—and their value has to be estimated from the money costs of producing them and keeping them in working order.

The Effect of Price Changes.   Moreover, when goods are measured in terms of their money value, we are faced with the problem that prices are not fixed but changing: so that so many tons of coal may be worth more or less money at different times. If prices are rising, the money value of total production will rise without any change in the quantity of things produced. It may be legitimate to ignore price changes occurring within the period for which the estimate is being made, though this sometimes leads to anomalous results. But we cannot ignore price changes in comparing one period with another; and therefore, if we are to measure changes in total production from, say, year to year, we must make the comparison in terms of constant prices, taking as the standard either the average prices of a particular period, say a year, or the average of a number of past years.

By this method it is possible to arrive at a sort of estimate of the real change in total production from one year to another. But the results are very rough, and it sometimes makes a good deal of difference what year or years we take as the standard, because the relative prices of different goods vary and those which are most highly priced in the base period are therefore given a greater weight in the total. There is no practicable way of overcoming this difficulty; and for this and other reasons estimates of changes in total production can never be very accurate. They have, however, a limited value, and have to be used for what they are worth—for example, in estimating by how much incomes can be increased without inflationary consequences.

Total Production.   The total production of a country is the outcome of a number of factors—of the number of man-hours worked and the composition of the labour force as between skilled and less skilled workers; of the amount of machinery and other capital goods employed to aid the workers in their tasks; and of the productivity of both workers and machines as affected by technological advances and, in the case of workers, by the trained expertness and energy they put into their tasks. There are very great difficulties in isolating the effects of these factors. Productivity may increase either because the workers work harder or with more skill or because they are provided with better machinery and conditions of work, or for both reasons combined; and it is seldom possible to say how much is due to one factor rather than to another.

Production and Productivity. The greatest difficulties of all arise when attempts are made to compare productivity, as distinct from actual production, in different countries. No two countries have exactly the same way of estimating their total production; and differences in economic structure make valid comparisons very difficult to arrive at. We should greatly like to know how much more productive an average unit of labour is in the United States than in Great Britain, or in Great Britain than in the Soviet Union or in India. But, though such estimates are made, the wise man receives them with a good deal of scepticism. They can show only, at best, the relative selling value of an average unit of labour-time in the countries compared; and this, on account of price differences, is not the same thing as relative productivity. It is of course obvious that productivity per head is much higher in the United States than in India—or indeed than in Great Britain; but *how much* higher it is not really possible to say.

Yet the level of productivity is obviously a most important matter; for on it the standard of living in each country is bound largely to depend. It is true that, if the world demand for a particular commodity —say, uranium—rises sharply, the value of the product of a country which is well endowed with it will rise quite apart from any change in the quantity produced; whereas if the demand for a product falls off, the opposite result will follow. A country's purchasing power over the products of other countries can therefore increase or decrease without any change in physical productivity; and the standard of life can be affected by such changes. But higher physical productivity is in most cases the foundation for a rising standard of living; and it makes a great difference whether productivity rises at the same or different rates in countries which are competitors in the world market. For, if costs of production rise or fall faster in one country than in another, the country with the higher costs may lose its export trade and therewith its power to buy needed imports; and this may lead to unemployment and to a further rise in costs as the scale of output has to be reduced.

The countries which depend on imports for the means of life and work have therefore to maintain or improve their productivity as fast as their competitors, if they are not to be faced with serious economic difficulties. Their relative productivity—relative to that of other countries—as well as their absolute productivity affects the standards of living they are able to sustain. Knowing this, their economists and their Governments want to find some way of making international comparisons of productivity—but despite the attention that has been given to this question since 1945, not much progress has yet been made. Countless 'Productivity Teams' have visited the United States and have reported on their return that production per head is higher in America than in British factories. How much higher they have not often ventured to say; and still less have they been able to provide the basis for an all-in comparison of American with British productivity. Such attempts at this as have been made are already a long time out of date,[1] and even for the period to which they apply they fall a great way short of precision.

Production and Consumption. With these warnings in mind, we can now proceed to assemble such information as does exist about British production and productivity and the rates at which they have been advancing in recent years. As we have seen, total production of goods and services in a country can be estimated only in money value or by means of index numbers based on money values, as there is no other way of adding together tons of coal, yards of cloth, transport facilities, and the countless other things that form part of the national product. This means that estimates of total production will be affected by changes in prices as well as in quantity of output, unless the goods and services are valued at fixed prices—say, at those prevailing at a particular time. There are, broadly speaking, two main ways of arriving at estimates of total production. One way is to estimate the money value of the production of each industry and service at the prices prevailing in a particular year or other period, and to add these totals together. The other is to estimate the total amounts spent by the various kinds of buyers of goods and services, at home and abroad, to deduct the sums spent on imports of goods and services, and to add or deduct the value of any estimated increase in physical stocks of materials and unfinished work in progress. It has to be borne in mind that both the value of production and the amount of expenditure upon it are affected by taxation; and in order to make the two methods yield comparable results it is necessary to eliminate this influence and to estimate both value of production and expenditure at what is called 'factor cost'— that is to say, in terms of the cost of the factors used in producing the goods and services in question. This involves deducting taxes levied on production or on sales, but adding any subsidies provided by the State so as to reduce the cost of producing certain goods and services. Ideally, the totals arrived at by the two methods should tally; but they

---

[1] For example, L. Rostas, *Comparative Productivity in British and American Industry*, published in 1948, but dealing chiefly with the 1930s.

are unlikely to do so exactly in practice because of difficulties in the way of making complete and accurate estimates by either method.

Gross National Product. For 1954 the gross national product of the United Kingdom, *measured at factor cost*, was officially estimated at

TABLE 45

Gross National Product at Factor Cost, by Origin, United Kingdom, 1948–54

£million	1948	1949	1950	1951	1952	1953	1954
Agriculture, Forestry and Fishing	642	687	675	722	772	784	760
Mining and Quarrying	383	406	412	446	501	536	549
Manufacturing	3,722	3,938	4,366	4,952	4,922	5,360	5,902
Building and Contracting	656	705	711	766	817	894	950
Gas, Electricity and Water	209	225	251	273	307	338	363
Transport and Communication	828	871	923	1,086	1,135	1,111	1,170
Distributive Trades	1,393	1,480	1,602	1,744	1,673	1,751	1,944
Insurance, Banking and Finance	282	300	333	376	381	410	471
Other Services	927	978	1,025	1,134	1,180	1,242	1,304
Total Production and Trade	9,042	9,590	10,298	11,499	11,688	12,426	13,413
Public Administration and Defence	705	723	747	849	921	955	990
Public Health and Education	257	309	346	387	429	456	480
Ownership of Dwellings	348	370	404	423	457	490	544
Domestic Service to Households	113	105	103	100	99	98	100
Services to Non-Profit-making Bodies	72	58	61	64	65	66	67
Deduct Stock Appreciation	− 325	− 200	− 650	− 750	50	75	− 75
Residual Error	− 20	− 18	20	− 4	38	27	− 5
Gross Domestic Product at Factor Cost	10,192	10,937	11,329	12,568	13,747	14,593	15,514
Net Income from Abroad	187	162	337	217	114	212	204
Gross National Product at Factor Cost	10,379	11,099	11,666	12,785	13,861	14,805	15,718

TABLE 45 (*continued*)

Production measured in Fixed Prices

(These figures, with estimates for 1946 and 1947, can be re-expressed so as to
eliminate the effects of changing prices by measuring output at the factor cost
of a selected year—in this case 1948:—)

Indices of Gross Domestic Product at 1948 *Factor Cost*
(1948 = 100)

	1946	1947	1949	1950	1951	1952	1953	1954
Agriculture, Forestry and Fishing	97	93	105	106	110	114	116	115
Mining and Quarrying	92	95	103	104	108	109	109	110
Manufacturing	86	92	107	116	121	115	123	133
Building and Contracting	88	92	105	105	101	103	110	111
Gas, Electricity and Water	91	94	107	116	124	127	132	142
Transport and Communication	89	93	106	109	113	117	121	124
Distributive Trades	89	97	105	109	106	103	110	116
Insurance, Banking and Finance	94	99	101	104	108	108	109	115
Professional Services	92	95	105	108	109	110	112	114
Other Services	97	98	97	95	95	95	98	101
Public Administration and Defence	157	115	97	95	101	102	103	102
Total	94·6	95·5	104·4	108·6	111·4	110·0	115·1	120·4

£15,514 million, to which must be added, in order to arrive at the total
sum available for spending, a net sum of £204 million representing
income from abroad, i.e. the excess of payments due to persons or
bodies in the United Kingdom from persons or bodies abroad over the
payments due the other way. This sum of £204 million formed no part
of the product of the United Kingdom; but it was available for spending in the United Kingdom equally with income derived from home
sources.

The origin of this total domestic product of £15,514 million, and of
the corresponding totals for previous years, was estimated to be as
shown in Table 45.

From the other angle of approach—that of expenditure—we get the
following:

TABLE 46

Gross National Product, at Factor Cost, by Categories of Expenditure, United Kingdom, 1946–54

£million	1946	1947	1948	1949	1950	1951	1952	1953	1954
Consumers' Expenditure	6,111	6,743	7,197	7,595	8,004	8,564	8,961	9,448	10,116
Public Authorities' Current Expenditure on Goods and Services	2,247	1,702	1,717	1,932	2,011	2,364	2,805	2,980	2,983
Gross Domestic Capital Formation	818	1,429	1,524	1,557	1,401	2,321	1,990	2,321	2,563
Exports of Goods and Services	1,231	1,427	1,951	2,263	2,722	3,385	3,526	3,285	3,454
Deduct Imports of Goods and Services	− 1,668	− 2,051	− 2,197	− 2,410	− 2,809	− 4,066	− 3,535	− 3,441	− 3,602
Gross Expenditure on Domestic Product	8,739	9,250	10,192	10,937	11,329	12,568	13,747	14,593	15,514
Net Income from Abroad	44	114	187	162	337	217	114	212	204
Gross National Expenditure at Factor Cost	8,783	9,364	10,379	11,099	11,666	12,785	13,861	14,805	15,718

Production and Prices. All the above figures, except the index numbers on the preceding page, which are in terms of fixed prices, are affected by price changes. These there is no ready way of eliminating; for there is no comprehensive index covering all kinds of prices that can be applied.

Price Movements. It would be misleading to correct the figures by applying either the wholesale or the retail price index, as these both cover only a limited range. They do, however, serve at least to indicate the broad trend of prices over the period; and for that reason they are cited here. They will be further discussed later on (see pp. 210. ff).

TABLE 47

Movement of Wholesale and Retail Prices, 1946–54

	1946	1947	1948	1949	1950	1951	1952	1953	1954
Wholesale (1938 = 100)	173	189	216	237	259	315	323	323	325
Retail (June 1947 = 100)	(100)	100	108	111	114	125	138	141	142
Agricultural (E. and W.) (1936–8 = 100)	207	241	249	260	270	296	306	312	301

Industrial Production. The only available means of measuring production in general—or rather industrial production exclusive of agriculture and services—that eliminates price movements and attempts to measure quantities only is the index of Industrial Production. This shows the following movements since 1946; but it should be borne in mind that in 1946 and 1947 output was affected by the change-over from war to peace production.

TABLE 48

Index of Industrial Production, 1946–54
(1948 = 100)

	1946	1947	1948	1949	1950	1951	1952	1953	1954
Index	87	92	100	106	114	117	114	121	129
Rise per cent		6	9	6	7	$2\frac{1}{2}$	$-2\frac{1}{2}$	6	$6\frac{1}{2}$

The above figures embody a weighted summary of movements in a number of different branches of production. Here are the figures for the main branches:

TABLE 49

Index of Production for Various Branches of Industry, 1946–54
(1948 = 100)

	1946	1947	1948	1949	1950	1951	1952	1953	1954
Mining and Quarrying	92	95	100	103	104	108	109	109	110
Manufacturing	86	92	100	107	116	121	115	123	133
Chemicals	90	92	100	109	124	134	132	151	166
Metal, Engineering and Vehicles (all groups)	84	92	100	106	114	122	122	125	137
Metal Manufacture (Ferrous)	83	87	100	104	109	113	117	118	125
Metal Manufacture (Non-ferrous)	89	102	100	94	102	116	116	99	117
Engineering, Shipbuilding and Electrical Goods	81	92	100	106	116	127	127	129	140
Vehicles	87	91	100	111	121	124	124	138	155
Textiles and Clothing	83	89	100	109	117	116	99	114	116
Food, Drink and Tobacco	96	96	100	104	107	105	108	114	116
Paper and Printing	90	96	100	115	133	140	118	133	155
Building and Contracting	88	92	100	105	105	101	103	110	111
Gas, Water, Electricity	91	94	100	107	116	124	127	132	142

Volume of Production. A few of the less important branches of production have been left out. In only a limited number of cases is it possible to measure directly the total output of a particular kind of product, without introducing any question of money value. Here are some of the more important: in each case the year of highest production is given in italic type.

TABLE 50

Production of Certain Commodities (Quantities), 1946–54

	1946	1947	1948	1949	1950	1951	1952	1953	1954
Coal (million tons)	190	197	209	215	216	223	*226*	224	224
Gas (million thermo)	2,239	2,300	2,413	2,490	2,616	2,706	2,754	2,721	*2,816*
Electricity (million units)	42,742	43,984	48,036	50,624	56,540	61,519	63,897	67,362	*74,706*
Refined Petrol, etc. (million tons)	2·5	2·6	4·4	6·1	9·3	16·2	22·0	24·5	*26·0*
Pig Iron (million tons)	7·8	7·8	9·3	9·5	9·6	9·7	10·7	11·2	*11·9*
Steel Ingots and Castings (million tons)	12·7	12·7	14·9	15·6	16·3	15·6	16·4	17·6	*18·5*
Cotton and Rayon Cloth (million linear yards)	1,974	2,012	2,441	2,593	2,810	*2,961*	2,292	2,633	2,775
Woollen Cloth (million square yards)	346	359	415	439	*450*	418	378	412	414

TABLE 50 (*continued*)

	1946	1947	1948	1949	1950	1951	1952	1953	1954
Paper, Newsprint (thousand tons)	295	258	298	472	544	527	537	603	*612*
Paper and Board, Other (thousand tons)	1,441	1,477	1,596	1,823	2,070	2,193	1,803	2,084	*2,467*
Bricks (millions)	3,450	4,535	4,600	5,227	5,921	6,080	6,622	7,195	*7,247*
Ships (thousand gross tons)	987	949	1,221	1,361	1,376	1,343	1,271	1,223	*1,493*
Tractors (thousands)	47	86	151	116	150	*178*	154	137	167
Rail Locomotives, Steam (number)	790	678	779	*826*	808	719	559	500	583
Rail Locomotives, Diesel (number)					515	519	651	603	*687*
Motor Cars, Private Passenger (thousands)	219	287	335	412	523	476	448	595	*769*
Motor Cars, Public Service (thousands)	146	155	173	216	261	258	242	239	*269*
Motor Cars, Goods (thousands)	137	142	160	202	250	247	233	232	*261*
Motor Cycles	93	112	133	153	171	172	158	154	*180*
Radio Sets (thousands)	1,380	1,984	1,630	1,345	1,809	*2,089*	1,234	1,183	1,965
Television Sets (thousands)	6	28	91	212	541	711	812	1,147	*1,205*
Footwear, Non-rubber (million pairs)	115	123	137	*142*	139	130	120	140	137
Footwear, Rubber (million pairs)	11	18	22	29	31	31	30	31	*32*
Gloves (million pairs)	30	35	37	39	42	47	44	47	*51*
Fountain Pens (million)	7	10	18	*28*	25	22	22	27	*28*
Matches (million boxes)	1,788	1,706	1,828	1,742	1,748	1,812	*1,940*	1,770	1,744
Beer (million barrels)	*31*	30	28	26	25	25	25	25	24
Spirits (million proof gallons)	12	17	26	31	32	29	30	29	*36*
Meat, Home-killed (thousand tons)	847	729	731	803	952	986	1,054	1,172	*1,516*
Bacon and Ham (thousand tons)	139	98	115	194	225	215	*285*	257	256
Fish landed (thousand tons)	633	695	*722*	709	630	700	684	660	633
Underwear (millions)	114	109	155	166	156	140	124	*178*	165
Pullovers, Jumpers, etc. (millions)	25	29	33	42	64	57	59	75	71
Socks and Stockings (million pairs)	320	267	310	446	491	*504*	423	471	478

The latest year, 1954, shows the highest production in the case of Gas, Electricity, Refined Petrol, Pig Iron and Steel, Newsprint and Paper, Bricks, Ships, Diesel Locomotives, all types of Motor Cars and Motor Cycles, Television Sets, Rubber Footwear, Gloves, Spirits, and Home-killed Meat. The highest output was reached in 1951 for Under-wear and Pullovers, etc.; in 1952 for Coal, Matches and Bacon and Ham; in 1951 for Cotton and Rayon Cloth, Tractors, Radio Sets and Socks and Stockings; in 1950 for Woollen Cloth; in 1949 for Rail Steam Locomotives, and Non-rubber Footwear; in 1948 for Fish landed; and in 1946 for Beer. These figures deal with production and not with home consumption: they include exported products, but exclude imported supplies. We shall come later to the figures of consumption (see p. 79) and to those of imports and exports (see pp. 175 ff.).

Industrial Production since 1946. The general index of *manufacturing* production has risen each year since 1946, except in 1952, when it fell by 6 points. The recovery in 1953, however, carried it only 2 points beyond the level reached in 1951, whereas in 1954 there was a further rise of 10 points. Comparing 1954 with the base year, 1948, we find the sharpest rise in Chemicals (66 per cent), followed by Vehicles (55 per cent), Paper and Printing (55 per cent), and Gas, Electricity and Water (42 per cent). The combined group Engineering, Shipbuilding and Electrical Goods (40 per cent) also rose by substantially more than the average manufacturing increase of 33 per cent. On the other hand Mining and Quarrying (10 per cent), Building and Contracting (11 per cent), Textiles and Clothing (16 per cent), and Food, Drink and Tobacco (16 per cent) lagged well behind the average increase.

By far the largest increase in any branch of production was in petrol refining, which increased between five and sixfold (and nearly tenfold from 1946) as a consequence of the building of large new refineries, partly with American capital. The other prodigious increase was in television sets—from 91,000 in 1948 to 1,206,000 in 1954. The output of private motor-cars nearly doubled between 1948 and 1953, more than doubled between 1947 and 1953, and increased faster than ever in 1954. On the other hand, that of boots and shoes, after falling in 1951–2, rose fairly sharply in 1953, but fell back again in 1954.

Production: International Comparison. How do these estimates of the course of industrial production in Great Britain compare with those which have been made for other leading industrial countries? In drawing comparisons we must of course bear in mind that there is no uniform method of making the estimates and that there is room for considerable discrepancies on that account. Still, the estimates probably give a tolerably acceptable picture of broad trends. (See Table 51.)

Look first of all at the first and last columns. The last column shows the size of the estimated increase in industrial production in each

TABLE 51

Index Numbers of Industrial Production in certain Countries,
1938 and 1948–54

(1948 = 100)

	1938	1948	1949	1950	1951	1952	1953	1954	1954 as per cent of 1938
United Kingdom	86	100	106	114	117	114	121	129	150
United States	46	100	92	108	115	119	129	120	261
Western Germany	159	100	143	180	216	213	251	282	177
France	90	100	109	111	125	131	127	139	154
Belgium	82	100	100	102	118	114	114	124	151
Canada	52	100	102	108	115	119	127	125	240
Japan	228	100	129	142	193	213	261	278	122
Sweden	67	100	104	108	113	111	111	115	172
Yugoslavia	63	100	112	115	111	111	122	139	221

country over the whole period 1938 to 1954. The United States and
Canada both show far higher increases than have been reached in any
other country for which estimates are available.[1] These two countries
have been foremost during the past two decades in the development of
industrial techniques; and in both cases war served as a stimulus to
higher output and involved no such destruction of productive capacity
as occurred in the belligerent countries—above all, in the Soviet Union.
As against this, it has to be borne in mind that the United States—
and to a less extent Canada—were suffering from considerable unemployment and under-use of resources in 1938: so that the comparison
between that year and 1954 gives a rather exaggerated impression of
the advance. Next in order comes Yugoslavia, whose industry was very
underdeveloped in 1938, and where a very great effort has been made
since 1945 to expand industrial production under an ambitious, indeed
too ambitious, Economic Plan. Western Germany holds the fourth place
—a remarkable feat in view of the very low level to which industrial
production fell at the end of the war. Then comes Sweden, which
escaped devastation and has been able to achieve on the whole a steady
advance.

Next come, quite close together, France, Belgium and the United
Kingdom, each with an increase of about 50 per cent between 1938 and
1954. Of these three, Great Britain suffered the least devastation of
productive resources during the war, but had to undertake the most

[1] There is no well assured estimate for the Soviet Union; but Soviet output of
producer goods stood in 1950 at 205 per cent of that of 1940, and of consumer goods
at 123 per cent. The target for 1955 involved an additional increase of 80 per cent in
producer goods and of 65 per cent in consumer goods over 1950; and the Economic
Commission for Europe regarded these as likely to be achieved. These figures relate
only to industrial production.

difficult transformation from wartime back to normal production. Belgium was the most depressed of the three in 1938.

In the last place stands Japan, which was the most adversely affected of all immediately after the war, and had the biggest recovery to attempt after 1945.

Turn now to the last column but one, which records the advances made not over 1938 but over 1948—the first post-war year for which it is possible to present even roughly comparable estimates. In terms of this measure of post-war recovery the leading places are occupied by Western Germany and Japan, both advancing rapidly from very low levels.[1] Next come France and Yugoslavia, which have both devoted high proportions of their national incomes to new capital investment. The next place is held by the United Kingdom, which is well ahead of Belgium, and also well ahead of both the United States and Canada. The American countries came out highest in the previous comparison, because their advance had been continuous from 1938. They do not show so rapid an expansion since 1948 as any of the other countries except Sweden, partly because they were not confronted with the same urgent pressure to re-build their economies in order to protect their standards of living. In actual amount, the United States has been increasing its production most rapidly of all; but not in percentages, which give a better clue to the development of productivity, as against total volume of output.

It will be noticed that no country except Western Germany and Japan[2] has kept up a continuous year by year advance since 1948. The United States suffered a setback in 1954, from which it subsequently recovered. The United Kingdom, Belgium and Sweden all experienced a fall in 1952, after the spurt caused by the Korean crisis; and Yugoslavia's advance was checked at the same time. In France the setback came in the following year, 1953. Canada, like the United States, fell back in 1954, though only to a small extent.

In general, then, the United Kingdom appears to have increased its total output since 1938 in much the same proportion as France and Belgium, but very much less than the United States and substantially less than either Sweden or Western Germany. Since 1948, its increase has been rather faster than that of the United States, but not so much faster as to go far towards catching up the vast arrears of growth between 1938 and 1948. British industrial output has risen since 1948 rather faster than that of Belgium or Canada, and considerably faster than that of Sweden, but less fast than that of France and very much less fast than that of either Western Germany or Japan.

The Rate of Increase. The increase of industrial production in Great Britain between 1948 and 1954 was at an average rate of 4 per cent per

---

[1] Followed by the Soviet Union with an increase of 89 per cent from 1948 to 1952.
[2] And the Soviet Union.

annum—nearly twice the average rate estimated for the period before 1914, but by no means comparable with the rates achieved by the Soviet Union since the 1930s, with the American advance during the second world war, or with the German recovery since 1945. The slackened rate of advance in 1951 and the actual decline of 1952 put Great Britain seriously back; but in 1953 and 1954 advances of more than 6 per cent were achieved under favourable world conditions. Even this rate of advance, however, was inadequate to provide both for increased consumption and for adequate investment.

Output and 'Labour Cost'. Physical productivity, measured in terms of output, is of course not the same thing as cost of production. Costs can rise or fall, not because productivity changes, but because of alterations in wages, salaries, rates of interest, taxes falling on production, or any other factor which makes a unit of output dearer or cheaper to produce. In the Government periodical, *Bulletin for Industry*, figures have recently been published showing, for the main branches of the economy, the percentage changes from 1948 to 1954 in physical output, measured in terms of constant prices, in the total bill for wages and salaries taken together, and in the 'labour cost' for each unit of output —'labour cost' being taken as including salaries as well as wages. In the accompanying table I have added to the published figures a further calculation for wages only, excluding salaries. It will be observed that in all the groups for which this separate calculation can be made the increase in wages and salaries together has been steeper than for wages alone, and that wage-costs per unit of output show a smaller percentage rise than wage- and salary-costs taken together. This is doubtless the effect, at any rate in part, of the employment of a higher proportion of salaried persons in technical and administrative posts—a concomitant of the application of more scientific methods. But the additional figures, though less appropriate for measuring the change in 'labour costs' in the widest sense, give a more correct impression of what has been happening to wages and to wage-costs over the past six years. The separate figures for wages are derived from the current Blue Book on National Income and Expenditure, published in 1955.

Output and 'Labour Cost' in Different Sectors. It will be seen from the table that over the whole economy, including service occupations as well as physical production, output is estimated to have risen by 20 per cent between 1948 and 1954, while the bill for wages and salaries together rose by 52 per cent, and that for wages alone by 48 per cent. This meant an increase of 27 per cent in total 'labour cost' per unit, and of 23 per cent in wage-cost. But the figures differed substantially from one section of the economy to another. For all manufacturing industries, taken together, output rose by 33 per cent, wages and salaries by 60 per cent, and wages alone by 58 per cent; but 'labour

The Value Product of Industry and its Distribution, 1948 and 1954

	Year	Gross Product £ million	Gross Product 1948 = 100	Wages Paid £ million	Salaries Paid £ million	Other Payments £ million	As percentage of Gross Product — Wages	As percentage of Gross Product — Salaries	As percentage of Gross Product — Wages and Salaries
Agriculture, Forestry and Fishing	1948	642		224	17	401	34.9	2.6	37.5
	1954	760	118.5	257	28	475	33.8	3.7	37.5
Mining and Quarrying	1948	383		311	20	52	81.2	5.2	86.4
	1954	549	143	435	30	84	79.3	5.5	84.8
Manufacturing	1948	3,722		1,752	563	1,407	47.1	15.1	62.2
	1954	5,902	158.5	2,775	934	2,193	47.0	15.8	62.8
Building and Contracting	1948	656		455	64	137	69.4	9.8	79.2
	1954	950	145	652	103	195	68.6	10.8	79.4
Gas, Electricity and Water	1948	209		79	33	97	37.8	15.8	53.6
	1954	363	174	123	60	180	33.9	16.5	50.4
Transport and Communication	1948	828		392	155	281	47.3	18.7	66.0
	1954	1,170	141	534	220	416	45.6	18.8	64.4
Distributive Trades	1948	1,393		651		742	—	—	46.7
	1954	1,944	140	1,024		920	—	—	52.7
Insurance, Banking and Finance	1948	282		210		72	—	—	74.5
	1954	471	167	322		149	—	—	68.4
Other Services	1948	927		471		456	—	—	50.8
	1954	1,304	141	758		546	—	—	58.1
Public Administration and Defence	1948			163 *	229	80			—
	1954			228 †	314	113			—
Public Health and Education	1948			48	194	15			—
	1954			443		37			—
Domestic Service	1948			113					—
	1954			100					—
Services to Non-Profit-making bodies	1948			72					—
	1954			67					—
Rent of Dwellings	1948					348			—
	1954					544			—

* Add Forces Pay £233 m.   † Add Forces Pay £335 m.

cost' increased by only 20 per cent and wage-cost by 19 per cent. The public utility services showed a still greater increase in output—42 per cent—and in the wages *plus* salary bill—64 per cent; but the wage bill rose by only 56 per cent, 'labour cost' by only 15 per cent, and wage-cost by only 10 per cent. Transport and Communication, with a much lower increase in output—24 per cent, showed an even smaller increase in 'labour cost'—12 per cent—and again only 10 per cent in wage-cost alone. This was largely because their wage and salary bills had risen much less than those of manufacturing or public utilities, whereas these latter had spent much more capital on mechanization and had thus been able to sustain larger advances in wages and salaries.

As compared with all these groups, the mining and quarrying and building and contracting groups increased their output at much less than the overall rate of increase. Their wage and salary bills rose faster than those of transport, but less fast than those of the manufacturing and public utility services. Their 'labour costs' per unit, and also their wage-costs, showed the biggest increases among the industrial groups —30 per cent and 27 per cent for mining and quarrying, and 32 per cent and 30 per cent for building and contracting, as against the overall averages of 27 and 23 per cent.

For the remaining group for which particulars are given—Distribution—it is not possible to separate the wages bill from the salaries bill. This group shows less than the overall average increase in output, measured in terms of the volume of goods sold. Its wage *plus* salary bill shows the next highest percentage rise after the public utility services, and its 'labour cost' per unit is up by 40 per cent—by far the highest recorded for any group. This looks the most unsatisfactory record of all, indicating excessive development of distributive outlets and slow progress with mechanization—for example, self-service and mechanical computing.

Output and Investment. The figures as a whole are somewhat disquieting. It may be useful to set beside them the figures of gross investment in the shape of fixed capital formation in each of the groups concerned. These figures show gross investment—that is to say, they include replacements and renewals of existing capital as well as additional formation of fixed capital (see p. 107). They therefore reflect not only the rate of capital expansion, but also the varying rates at which capital assets wear out or become obsolete, and are actually replaced, in the different groups. Nevertheless, they throw some light on the extent to which the increase in output has involved capital investment in the branches of the economy concerned.

In studying these figures it should be borne in mind that the amounts of capital involved differ greatly from group to group. They range in 1948 from £346 million for manufacturing to a mere £20 million for building and contracting and £30 million for mining and quarrying, and in 1954 from £584 million for manufacturing to £55 million for the building and £84 for the mining group. Thus, a big percentage rise does not necessarily mean a very big total. Nevertheless, certain things stand out—the consistently low level of investment in transport and communication; the low level in mining and quarrying up to 1952, and thereafter the rapid increase; the steadily rising level in the public utility services; the more chequered record of the distributive trades, from which goods transport by road cannot be disentangled; and the check to manufacturing industry in 1952 and 1953.

TABLE 53

Fixed Capital Formation by Industry Groups, 1948–54

(1948 = 100)

	1949	1950	1951	1952	1953	1954	1954 actual amounts £m.	Total 1948–54 actual amounts £m.
Manufacturing Industry	114	133	153	162	163	168	584	3,155
Mining and Quarrying	120	113	120	163	213	280	84	333
Building and Contracting	110	115	165	215	225	275	55	241
Electricity, Gas and Water	125	142	159	173	191	217	300	1,528
Transport and Communication (except Road Goods Transport)	110	108	104	107	138	142	275	1,568
Distribution and Road Goods Transport	118	140	145	136	159	175	198	1,095

It is of course impossible to give figures showing the total values of fixed capital in these groups; and it is also impracticable to show how much of the gross investment has been required simply to offset depreciation and obsolescence of existing fixed assets. The whole question of capital accumulation is discussed in a later section (see p. 99). Here we are concerned only with the relation between fixed investment and the movement of output and of 'labour costs'. It will be seen that both the mining and the building groups show very large increases in gross investment in 1953 and 1954, combined with only small increases in output and with considerable rises in 'labour costs'. This may, of course, be due in part to the time-lag before investment shows its effects on output.

'*Labour Costs*' *and Profits.* The only further comparison that seems to be practicable is between the increase in the bills for wages and salaries and that in gross profits of companies before allowing for depreciation. These figures do not, of course, cover the public sector of the economy, or the sector carried on by unincorporated businesses or by sole traders.

They are, however, of some significance when they are set beside the figures of wages and salaries.

TABLE 54

Gross Company Trading Profits by Industry, 1948–54

(1948 = 100)

	1949	1950	1951	1952	1953	1954
Manufacturing Industry	104	126	143	119	132	—
Building and Contracting	120	114	126	129	166	—
Distributive Trades	105	115	139	125	130	—
All Non-nationalized Companies	103	120	142	126	134	146

Figures for the separate groups are not available for 1954, and those for the groups not cited are rendered incomparable by nationalization measures affecting them. It will be seen that, up to 1954, gross company profits rose by 46 per cent as compared with a rise of 48 per cent in the total wages bill and 52 per cent in wages and salaries combined, but that in 1951 company profits were up by 42 per cent and the wages bill by only 22 per cent. Then came the setback to profits in 1952 and 1953, while the wage bill continued to rise, followed by sharp increases in both in 1954. The whole question of profits and their relation to wages will be considered further in later sections (see pp. 232 and 246).

TABLE 55

Labour Costs, 1948–54

Percentage Increases over 1948

	1949	1950	1951	1952	1953	1954
Manufacturing Industry:						
Output	7	16	21	15	23	33
Wages	6	13	25	33	45	58
Wages and Salaries	7	14	27	36	48	60
Wages per unit of output	0	2	3	15	18	19
Wages and Salaries per unit of output	0	− 2	5	18	20	20
Mining and Quarrying:						
Output	3	4	8	9	9	10
Wages	2	2	14	31	34	40
Wages and Salaries	3	4	16	34	38	43
Wages per unit of output	− 1	− 2	5	20	23	27
Wages and Salaries per unit of output	0	0	7	23	27	30
Building and Contracting:						
Output	5	5	1	3	10	11
Wages	6	7	15	23	32	43
Wages and Salaries	7	9	18	25	36	47
Wages per unit of output	1	2	14	19	20	30
Wages and Salaries per unit of output	2	4	17	21	24	32

TABLE 55 (*continued*)

	1949	1950	1951	1952	1953	1954
Electricity, Gas and Water:						
Output	7	16	24	27	32	42
Wages	6	14	25	37	46	56
Wages and Salaries	10	20	34	46	55	64
Wages per unit of output	− 1	2	1	8	11	10
Wages and Salaries per unit of output	3	3	8	15	17	15
Transport and Communication:						
Output	6	9	13	17	21	24
Wages	5	8	20	25	28	36
Wages and Salaries	5	9	22	29	32	39
Wages per unit of output	− 1	− 1	8	7	6	10
Wages and Salaries per unit of output	− 1	0	8	10	9	12
Distribution:						
Output (quantity of sales)	5	9	6	3	10	16
Wages and Salaries	9	16	30	38	44	62
Wages and Salaries per unit of output	4	6	23	34	31	40
Whole Economy:						
Output	5	9	11	10	15	20
Wages	5	10	22	30	38	48
Wages and Salaries	6	12	26	34	42	52
Wages per unit of output	0	1	10	20	20	23
Wages and Salaries per unit of output	1	3	14	22	23	27

Agricultural Production. Turning to agriculture alone, we find for the United Kingdom as a whole an increase in total output of about 55 per cent over the pre-war average in 1953–4, but of only about 52 per cent for 1954–5, the 'years' for this purpose beginning on June 1. The very bad summer in 1954 seriously affected output in many respects, and substantially reduced farmers' incomes (see p. 226). The adverse effects of the bad weather were taken into account in determining the level of the various price-guarantees to farmers at the annual and special price reviews of 1955. Since these were settled in March farmers have enjoyed the benefit of the exceptionally fine summer, which has yielded a substantial increase in total output.

Table 57 (overleaf) gives the figures of acreage and production for the main crops for the pre-war period (averaged) and for certain years since 1946–7. It also gives the figures of livestock production for the same years. It will be seen that, on the estimate for 1954–5, the total acreage tilled, though nearly 3 million acres up on the pre-war average, was nearly 1½ millions lower than that of 1946–7—involving a correspondingly higher acreage available for grassland. The Government, in its advice to the farmers in 1955, commented that this acreage was not being fully utilized for livestock production, and advocated the maintenance of a high level of ley farming as against permanent grassland.

TABLE 56

Crop Yields per Acre (*tons per acre*)

	Pre-war average	1946–7	1951–2	1952–3	1953–4	1954–5
Wheat	0·89	0·95	1·09	1·14	1·20	1·14
Barley	0·82	0·89	1·02	1·02	1·13	1·09
Oats	0·81	0·81	0·92	0·96	0·99	0·95
Potatoes	6·74	7·15	7·89	7·93	8·39	7·80
Sugar Beet	8·18	10·37	10·68	10·38	12·71	10·40

TABLE 57

United Kingdom Agricultural Production
(Years beginning 1st June)

	Pre-war average	1946–7	1951–2	1952–3	1953–4	1954–5
Crop Acreage thousand acres:						
Wheat	1,856	2,062	2,131	2,030	2,217	2,457
Rye	16	55	54	56	68	44
Barley	929	2,211	1,908	2,281	2,226	2,063
Oats	2,403	3,567	2,857	2,882	2,840	2,588
Mixed Corn	97	458	836	838	804	602
Potatoes	723	1,423	1,050	990	985	945
Sugar Beet	335	436	425	408	415	437
Total Tillage, inc. other crops	8,907	13,300	12,118	12,261	12,304	11,834
Crop Production thousand tons:						
Wheat	1,651	1,967	2,316	2,307	2,664	2,783
Rye	10	39	47	50	66	39
Barley	765	1,963	1,939	2,334	2,521	2,244
Oats	1,940	2,903	2,616	2,772	2,821	2,440
Mixed Corn	76	350	804	830	845	555
Potatoes	4,873	10,166	8,284	7,848	8,260	7,325
Sugar Beet	2,741	4,522	4,534	4,236	5,275	4,521
Livestock Products thousand tons:						
Beef and Veal	578	537	617	583	632	783
Mutton and Lamb	195	141	147	172	170	208
Pigmeat	435	208	477	589	627	781
Milk (million gallons)	1,563	1,665	2,014	2,053	2,170	2,177
Eggs	385	322	464	494	526	532
Wool: Clip	34	27	29	31	33	34

It also drew attention to the need for improvement in permanent grass-land and for better management of grassland generally, in order to reduce the cost of livestock production and to allow more to be met out of home-produced output of feed.

The decline in the tilled area since 1946–7 has been mainly in land used for oats and potatoes. Land under wheat and mixed corn showed increases; and the decline in respect of barley was not very great. In comparison with the pre-war position there is a substantial increase in the area under each type of crop. Yields too were rising. Table 56 shows the figures of yields of some main crops for the years shown in Table 57.

Meanwhile, the output of livestock products had been following a more chequered course. Milk production rose during the war and continued to rise fairly sharply thereafter; whereas consumption of liquid milk showed some decline after 1951. The supply of both beef and mutton declined during the war years; but whereas production of beef and veal fairly soon recovered and then considèrably surpassed the pre-war level, that of mutton and lamb remained below the pre-war level right up to 1955. Production of pigmeat, reduced by more than 50 per cent below the pre-war average in 1946–7, not merely increased thereafter but shot ahead at an embarrassing rate, at costs a long way ahead of those of imported supplies: so that the Government reduced the price guarantees both in 1954 and again in 1955, output having risen sharply despite the earlier reduction. In 1955 the Government was pressing the farmers strongly to improve quality and to reduce cost, and was saying categorically that no further rise in output could be afforded. Egg production, which was below the pre-war average in 1946–7, also rose rapidly thereafter, but not so as to outstrip demand, though costs also increased.

Farm Income and Efficiency. The Government, in its statement of March 1955, estimated that net farm income amounted in 1954–5 to about £280 million as against £320½ million the previous year, during which weather conditions had been favourable. It reckoned that if 1954–5 had been a year of 'normal' weather, the net income would have been £312 million: in other words, the bad season cost the farmers about £32 million. If weather had been normal in 1953–4, net farm income would have been £306½ million instead of £320½. In other words, farm efficiency had increased as in previous years, and 'the industry's net income on a normal weather basis' had been maintained in spite of the reduction made in price guarantees in 1954. It was estimated that the value of the rise in efficiency was about £25 million on this basis for commodities covered by the annual price review, and about £30 million for the entire industry.

This was the basis for the price review of 1955. The broad policy was to encourage more production of beef and veal, and also of mutton and lamb if costs could be reduced; to procure a steady continuing improvement in crop yields, and to cut down the need for imported feeding stuffs by encouragement of ley farming and improvement of grassland, and by greater economy in the use of concentrated feeding stuffs. In order to achieve this, it was deemed necessary to offer the industry certain increases in guaranteed prices to meet that part of the rise that could not be met by improved efficiency, and also to take account of the after-effects of the losses due to the bad weather of 1954. The Government accordingly increased the subsidy on lime used, and on nitrogen and phosphates, and also the grants for ploughing and the subsidies on calves and ewes. They also raised the standard prices for fat cattle and for fat sheep and lambs, but removed those for fat cows. They reduced the price guarantees for pigmeat, but increased those for hens' eggs and for milk. Guaranteed prices for wheat and rye were left unchanged, whereas those for barley, oats, potatoes and sugar beet were raised. The total cost of the support given by the Government to agriculture was reckoned at nearly £250 million for 1954–5.

Farm Grants and Subsidies in relation to Output. The increase in agricultural output has thus been secured only at high cost, both to the consumers in rising prices and to the taxpayers in grants and subsidies. The course of food prices is considered in a later section (see p. 219). In this section we are dealing mainly with the question of production, and not save incidentally with its cost. Output and cost, however, are interconnected. For example, the formula which allows higher prices for feeding stuffs to be automatically reflected in higher guaranteed prices gives the producer no incentive to reduce his consumption of this expensive import, which has risen in cost by £55 million during the past two years. As Mr. E. M. H. Lloyd pointed out in his articles published in *The Times* on July 20 and 21, 1955, the present system of guaranteed prices, instead of being used to promote efficient farming, seems to be based mainly on assuring farmers of whatever is deemed to be a 'proper remuneration' for their services, and has become a matter of bargaining on this issue between the farmers and the Government. In effect, the entire industry is treated as if it were a single gigantic farm, and no account is taken of the varying needs of differently placed farmers or kinds of farming. Mr. Lloyd pointed out that in fact the major part of the existing subsidies goes to the bigger farmers—the 'top third'— most of whom would be making quite good incomes without them— and that their total effect is to distort as well as to increase output, and also to increase costs. His conclusion is that the subsidies on cereal and milk production should be either abolished or substantially reduced, and that, in order to help the smaller farmers, reductions in the subsidies on pigmeat and eggs should be accompanied by an extension of direct grants designed to promote efficiency.

CHAPTER SIX

CONSUMPTION

No people can afford to consume the whole of its current product, either directly or by way of exchange. A part of what is produced has to go in replacing worn-out or obsolete capital goods; for if this is not done, production will be bound to fall off. Nor is this only a matter of making good actual wear and tear: it is usually one of replacing the worn-out instruments of production with better ones, wherever there have been advances in productive techniques. A country which depends largely on imported food and materials especially needs to keep its capital goods up to date; for otherwise it will not be able to sell its exports in a competitive world market.

Consumption and Investment. Moreover, if the pace of technological advance is swift, many capital goods will need to be replaced well before they are physically worn-out; and accordingly, the swifter the development of techniques is, the larger will be the proportion of current output needing to be diverted from consumption to investment. Nor must we forget that every increase in population carries with it the need for more capital goods to supply the larger number of consumers, or that, broadly speaking, the more highly developed the standard of living is, the more capital goods, as well as consumers' goods, are required—more houses, roads, places of entertainment, and so on, as well as more food, clothing, furnishings, and other goods of everyday consumption. The demand for capital goods competes with the demand for consumers' goods; but the need for more of both advances simultaneously.

When, for any reason, a country has failed, over a period, to create enough new capital goods to maintain its efficiency and keep pace with the advances made in other countries, there is need for it, in order to regain its position, to divert a larger than normal proportion of its current product from consumption to investment. The same need arises if, although it has kept consumption down, it has applied a large part of its product to such uses as armament-making, which makes no contribution to greater welfare either immediately or later. Great Britain during the war invested heavily in the types of industry that could be used for making munitions of war, and let other kinds of investment fall badly into arrears—for example, not only houses but also capital equipment in the textile and other consumer industries.

After the war, only a part of the investment made in war industries could be converted to peace-time uses. The rest had to be written off, save to the extent to which it was deemed to be needed for re-armament in the cold war; and attention had to be transferred to the building up of new supplies of capital goods that could be used for meeting home needs or for providing exports to exchange for necessary imports.

It was accordingly desirable after the war, not only to increase total output as far as possible, but also to keep total consumption within limits that would not interfere with a high rate of investment in new capital goods. This was not easy to do, for a number of reasons. In the first place, people who had put up with severe restrictions on their consumption during the war were eager to be free of these restrictions and to spend money on enjoying themselves. Secondly, it was felt to be desirable not only to keep in being the welfare services that had been developed during the war, but also to put these services on a permanent footing and to provide new ones—especially a comprehensive Health Service and a better provision for the aged and incapacitated. The development of the social services was in itself a factor making for increased current consumption, both of medical and hospital services and of everyday commodities, by those whose incomes were increased by cash benefits. There was also more spent on education, both in salaries to teachers and through keeping young persons longer at school; and this too meant more consumption.

In these circumstances, investment could be carried to an adequate level only by damping down other kinds of consumption. This meant continuing heavy taxation on the larger incomes; but it meant also keeping a tight hold on the growth of other incomes, such as wages. Under the prevailing conditions of full employment the Trade Unions, if they had chosen to use their economic power to the full, could have exacted much higher wages than they actually attempted to secure. It would have been bad policy on their part to do this, because what matters to their members is not how many pounds a week they receive but what their money will buy. If they had forced wages up higher, prices would have risen too; for either there would have been too little investment to maintain productive efficiency or the investment could have been secured only by inflationary means. Trade Union leaders were well aware of this and therefore fell in with the Labour Government's requests to show 'restraint' in pressing wage-claims. It was, however, difficult for them to explain their attitude to their members, who saw prices and profits rising, despite wage-restraint, because of the real scarcity of all sorts of goods. The Government made rather half-hearted attempts to induce business men to accept a parallel policy of 'dividend-restraint' and to plough back a large part of their high profits into capital accumulation by means of reserves; and for a time this policy had some effect. But in the long run both 'wage-restraint' and 'dividend-restraint' were largely thrown over; and wage-workers and shareholders both set out to get all they could. Even then, however, most of the Trade Union leaders continued to commend restraint as far as they dared and to accept arbitration awards made by arbitrators who believed in the need to keep wage-advances within fairly modest limits.

In fact, total consumption had to be kept down, because of sheer shortages of consumers' goods or of the means of bringing them from abroad. It was therefore in the last resort a matter of deciding what kinds of consumption to check. Rationing, though increasingly unpopular, was used by the Labour Government as a means of ensuring 'fair shares' in supplies of necessaries that were physically scarce; but as the problem came to be less that of sheer physical shortages than that of finding the money to buy supplies from abroad the 'consumer-resistance' to rationing grew stronger; and it had to be gradually given up. Its place, under the Conservatives, was taken by 'rationing by the purse'—that is, by letting people buy all they wished, and could afford, at prices which compelled them to limit their demands. This involved considerable hardship for those who were least able to increase their incomes—for example, those living on fixed incomes or pensions and those employed persons who had no strong Trade Unions behind them. It therefore cancelled a part of the benefits conferred by the development of the social services and led to demands—which had to be granted in part—for higher social service benefits. It also led to pressure from shareholders for the payment in dividends of a higher proportion of profits, at the expense of the accumulation of capital through business reserves. In one way or another, the Government was able to do a great deal to hold total consumers' expenditure in check, and to ensure the provision of funds for investment. But to-day there is considerable dissatisfaction with the ways in which this is being done and with the effects on the relative distribution of consuming power.

For recent years there are reasonably accurate figures showing the total expenditure on the various kinds of consumption; but there are, unfortunately, no comparable figures for the pre-war period, and no detailed comparison is possible for any year before 1946. The figures of actual consumers' expenditure are of course expressed in market prices and therefore give, in themselves, no indication of the amounts consumed. It is therefore necessary, if we want to get a notion of the changes in physical consumption, either to discover the actual quantities consumed—which is possible in some cases, but not in all—or, failing this, to re-express the figures in terms of the prices prevailing at one particular time; and the official statistics use for this purpose the prices of 1948. We thus get a rough idea, not only of what consumers have spent on, say, meat or tobacco, but of the quantities of these things they have consumed from year to year. There is, however, one important qualification. Market prices are affected not only by costs of production but also by taxation—for example, on alcohol or tobacco—or by subsidies paid out by the Government in order to keep down the prices of certain necessary foods—such as bread and milk. The importance of these latter—subsidies—has fallen greatly in recent years. Figures based on the prices of a particular year—1948—take them as they were in that year and do not take account of changes in them from year to year.

Consumption. Between 1946 and 1954 total consumers' expenditure in the United Kingdom increased from £7,178 million to £11,854 million —by 65 per cent. This increase was largely due to rising prices: if the goods and services consumed in each year are re-valued at the prices prevailing in 1948 the increase is only from £8,251 million in 1946 to £9,467 million in 1954—less than 15 per cent for a population which had risen by 1 per cent. Let us consider first the make-up of actual consumers' expenditure at current market prices over these years, and then try to get an idea of the amounts consumed by eliminating the factor of changing prices. We shall then need to make a further correction in order to eliminate the high tax element in certain types of consumers' expenditure, by re-valuing the various items again—this time at 'factor cost'.

Here, first of all, is a break-down of total expenditure by consumers at current market prices under a few broad heads. (See Table 58.)

It will be seen that in one case actual money expenditure by consumers has not risen at all since 1946, and that in one other it has sharply decreased. These are domestic service and income in kind. As we saw (on p. 23) the number of families that can afford to keep private servants has fallen sharply since the 1930s. It continued to fall up to 1953 by more than enough to offset the increase in wages and other emoluments, but increased slightly in 1954, when expenditure on it regained the level of 1951. Income in kind means mainly the produce of gardens and allotments, which increased greatly during the war and then fell away rapidly till 1950, since when it has risen again, but not nearly to the 1946 level. Expenditure on entertainments shows practically no change since 1946, partly because of the growth of entertainment in the home, and partly because this type of expenditure was at a high level during the war, when alternative outlets for spare cash were few. In both 1946 and 1954 it was nearly three times as large as in 1938. Expenditure abroad—mainly by tourists—fell off after 1947, mainly because of restrictions on the supply of foreign currency, but rose considerably in 1951 and again in 1954.

At the other end of the scale by far the largest increase is in expenditure on private motoring, which has risen sharply every year since 1949, and shows a total rise of 215 per cent since 1946. Household goods come next, with a rise of 136 per cent—partly on account of making good war arrears, but largely due to the building of new houses. Then comes

Consumers' Expenditure at Market Prices, 1938 and 1946-54 (£million)

	1938	1946	1947	1948	1949	1950	1951	1952	1953	1954	1954 as per cent of 1946
Food	1,285	1,816	2,104	2,265	2,471	2,734	2,987	3,282	3,559	3,810	210
Alcoholic Drink	285	735	761	838	781	772	803	808	828	842	115
Tobacco	177	602	689	764	753	766	800	821	837	855	142
Housing	518	665	729	766	816	837	889	926	989	1,056	122
Fuel and Light	197	278	298	324	332	353	388	423	447	486	175
Household Goods	288	397	498	561	641	732	809	782	840	936	236
Clothing	446	638	736	902	1,013	1,063	1,099	1,064	1,064	1,129	177
Books, Newspapers, etc.	64	104	121	127	134	142	148	158	177	179	172
Chemists' Goods	—	104	116	121	130	135	144	149	153	161	155
Other Goods	—	199	218	238	240	236	255	256	262	270	136
Private Motoring and Cycling	141	139	167	127	169	206	237	300	373	438	315
Travel	167	305	329	357	362	356	384	416	437	439	144
Communications	29	54	56	58	59	62	68	72	77	81	150
Entertainments	64	183	174	180	175	177	183	186	184	187	102
Domestic Service	121	117	115	113	105	103	100	99	99	100	85
Other Services	407	608	648	648	614	631	681	710	737	761	125
Income in Kind	17	126	73	55	49	49	62	73	77	78	62
Expenditure Abroad	34	121	123	94	105	116	152	149	146	169	140
Deduct Foreign Tourists' Spending in U.K.	− 43	− 13	− 21	− 33	− 44	− 65	− 85	− 104	− 117	− 123	—
Total	4,394	7,178	7,934	8,505	8,905	9,405	10,104	10,570	11,168	11,854	165

food, with an increasing expenditure every year resulting mainly from rising prices, including the effects of subsidies being withdrawn. Clothing, fuel and light, and books and newspapers come next, in that order. All these figures relate to actual spending at current market prices and not to quantities consumed. Total consumers' expenditure at market prices rose by nearly 6 per cent in 1953 and by more than 6 per cent in 1954.

It will make matters clearer if we now re-express these figures so as to show the proportion of total consumers' expenditure directed to each of the groups. In order to bring out the changes I have given in italics the figures for the year in which this proportion was highest for the various forms of spending. It will be noted that food, housing, fuel and light, and private motoring were all at their highest points in 1954, whereas alcoholic drinks, travel, entertainments, income in kind, domestic service, and tourist expenditure abroad were all relatively highest in 1946. Expenditure on books and periodicals was at its highest relative level in 1953.

Here then are the figures, expressed as percentages of total consumers' expenditure year by year.

TABLE 59

Percentage Distribution of Consumers' Expenditure
at Market Prices, 1946–54

	1946	1947	1948	1949	1950	1951	1952	1953	1954
Food	25·6	26·9	26·9	27·9	29·2	29·5	31·0	*32·1*	*32·15*
Alcoholic Drink	*10·1*	9·3	9·55	8·8	8·45	8·25	8·15	7·85	7·10
Tobacco	8·5	8·8	*9·1*	8·5	8·25	8·0	7·85	7·55	7·21
Housing	8·35	8·1	8·1	8·1	7·6	7·55	7·5	7·55	*8·91*
Fuel and Light	3·9	3·8	3·85	3·75	3·8	3·9	4·0	4·05	*4·10*
Household Goods	5·6	6·4	6·7	7·3	7·9	*8·1*	7·5	7·6	7·9
Clothing	9·0	9·4	10·7	*11·5*	11·45	11·0	10·2	9·6	9·5
Books and News-									
papers	1·5	1·55	1·5	1·5	1·5	1·5	1·5	*1·6*	1·5
Chemists' Goods	*1·5*	*1·5*	1·4	*1·5*	1·45	1·45	1·4	1·4	1·4
Other Goods	*2·8*	*2·8*	*2·8*	2·7	2·5	2·55	2·5	2·4	2·3
Private Motoring									
and Cycling	1·8	2·0	1·4	1·8	2·1	2·25	2·8	3·3	*3·7*
Travel	*4·3*	4·2	*4·3*	4·1	3·9	3·85	3·95	3·9	3·7
Communications	*0·75*	0·7	0·7	0·7	0·7	0·7	0·7	0·7	0·7
Entertainments	*2·6*	2·2	2·1	2·0	1·9	1·8	1·8	1·65	1·6
Domestic Service	*1·6*	1·5	1·3	1·2	1·1	1·0	0·95	0·9	0·85
Other Services									
(incl. Insurance)	*8·8*	8·6	8·1	7·3	7·2	7·3	7·3	7·1	6·4
Income in Kind	*1·8*	0·9	0·65	0·55	0·5	0·6	0·7	0·7	0·7
Expenditure Abroad	*1·7*	1·6	1·1	1·2	1·25	1·5	1·25	1·2	1·4
Deduct Foreign									
Tourists' Expendi-									
ture in U.K.	−0·2	−0·3	−0·4	−0·5	−0·7	−0·85	−1·0	*−1·05*	−1·04

Both sets of figures so far given in this chapter relate to consumers' expenditure at current market prices. The next table, by re-valuing consumers' purchases at the prices prevalent in 1948, embodies an attempt to eliminate the factor of changing prices and to show changes in the total quantities concerned, except that it makes no correction to allow for changes in taxation and subsidies affecting these prices. This table is more fully itemized than those preceding it: the fuller particulars relating to the preceding tables can be found in the Blue Book on National Income and Expenditure for 1954.

We see from these tables that, in terms of constant prices, total consumers' expenditure was higher in 1954 than in any previous year and was next highest in 1953 and after that year in 1950, with substantial drops in both 1951 and 1952. Apart from a small drop in 1948 there was a substantial advance each year from 1946 to 1950. Expenditure on food has followed the same pattern, except that there was a small increase instead of a drop in 1948. But the composition of the food budget has changed. Fish consumption reached its highest point in 1947 and has since declined rapidly, except for an increase in 1951 and again in 1954. Consumption of potatoes and vegetables also reached its peak in 1947 and thereafter fluctuated without again approaching the same level. The peak for bread and cereals came in 1949, followed by drops in 1950, 1952, 1953 and 1954. The peak reached in 1950 was surpassed only in 1954, and has not been reached since for either meat and bacon, oils and fats, or dairy produce. Of these there was a recovery in meat and bacon in 1952 and 1953, and a further advance in 1954 brought consumption to a record level. Oils and fats and dairy produce both continued to decline in 1951 and 1952, and made only smaller recoveries in 1953 and 1954. As against this, 1954 was the year of highest consumption for sugar, preserves and confectionery, fruit, and non-alcoholic drinks. Of these, the sugar group rose in 1947, 1949, 1951, 1953 and 1954, but fell in 1948, 1950 and 1952. Fruit rose each year up to 1949, and again in 1951, 1953 and 1954, but fell in 1950 and again in 1952. Beverages showed the same fluctuations.

These are not altogether the characteristics of an economy advancing steadily in wealth and prosperity, even though the total was considerably higher in 1954 than in any previous year.

The total increase between 1946 and 1954 was rather less than 15 per cent, and of this more than half took place in two years—1953 and 1954—when the increases were over 4 per cent. The next largest increase was $3\frac{1}{2}$ per cent in 1947, which was followed by a small decrease the next year. Then came rises of 2 per cent in 1949 and in 1950, succeeded by actual falls of 1 per cent or more in 1951 and in 1952. These last reflect the inflated prices of imports during the Korean crisis, as well as the greater resources devoted to re-armament. The reduced

TABLE 60

Consumers' Expenditure at 1948 Market Prices, 1946–54
(1) Food, Drink and Tobacco

(£million)

Food:	1938	1946	1947	1948	1949	1950	1951	1952	1953	1954
(a) Household Expenditure										
Bread and Cereals		332	349	358	*362*	351	357	351	342	331
Meat and Bacon		366	350	326	340	436	369	403	433	*468*
Fish		90	*95*	91	79	64	71	65	58	63
Oils and Fats		60	61	71	82	*87*	83	75	77	83
Sugar, Preserves and Confectionery		159	197	190	217	212	246	240	297	*318*
Dairy Products		325	319	350	383	*394*	379	360	374	379
Fruit		110	160	173	178	170	189	166	183	*203*
Potatoes and Vegetables		241	*276*	267	272	266	271	271	259	269
Beverages		95	99	101	105	104	102	106	111	*112*
Other Manufactured Food		86	*88*	78	81	91	101	*104*	97	95
Total		1,864	1,994	2,005	2,099	2,175	2,168	2,147	2,231	*2,321*
(b) Other Personal Expenditure		227	256	260	265	274	*278*	274	267	272
Total Food	2,196	2,091	2,250	2,265	2,364	2,449	2,446	2,421	2,498	*2,593*
Alcoholic Drink:										
(a) Beer	601	*632*	608	577	549	545	552	549	552	540
(b) Wine, Spirits, Cider, etc.	281	239	277	261	257	281	294	288	299	*321*
Total	882	871	*885*	838	806	826	846	837	851	861
Tobacco:										
(a) Cigarettes	543	*776*	674	638	616	629	659	671	686	704
(b) Other	137	*132*	121	126	124	116	109	111	108	107
Total	680	*908*	795	764	740	745	768	782	794	811

Here are the corresponding figures for other forms of consumers' expenditure:

TABLE 61

Consumers' Expenditure at 1948 Prices, 1946–54

(2) Non-Food Goods (£*million*)

	1938	1946	1947	1948	1949	1950	1951	1952	1953	1954
Housing	661	708	744	766	802	804	809	809	827	*853*
Fuel and Light:										
Coal	*195*	137	139	140	138	144	145	143	143	147
Electricity	32	65	71	75	76	82	93	94	96	*104*
Gas	60	76	*80*	79	78	78	*80*	79	78	79
Other	31	29	31	30	30	32	32	32	32	*35*
Total Fuel and Light	318	307	321	324	322	336	350	348	349	*365*
Durable Household Goods:										
(a) Furniture and Furnishings	*355*	175	224	250	296	326	289	266	299	331
(b) Hardware, Radio and Electrical Goods	203	200	231	229	241	267	281	261	297	*338*
Total D.H.G.	558	375	455	479	537	593	570	527	596	*669*
Other Household Goods:										
(a) Matches	15	11	13	14	15	*16*	15	14	14	14
(b) Soap and Detergents	56	42	41	45	58	69	68	68	78	92
(c) Other Cleansing Materials, etc.	27	23	23	23	23	24	24	25	25	26
Total O.H.G.	98	76	77	82	96	109	107	107	117	*132*
Clothing:										
(a) Footwear	142	131	155	178	186	*190*	165	157	158	167
(b) Other—Men and Boys	272	194	217	250	264	*282*	248	228	223	231
(c) Other—Females and Infants	524	400	444	474	518	531	488	489	510	*534*
Total Clothing	938	725	816	902	968	*1,003*	901	874	891	932
Recreational Goods:										
(a) Books and Periodicals	81	109	121	127	129	*130*	129	127	129	129
(b) Other	—	93	98	99	103	101	99	99	105	*108*
Total Recreational Goods	—	202	219	226	232	231	228	226	234	*237*
Chemists' Goods	—	116	129	121	133	139	135	134	144	*154*
Other Goods	—	121	131	139	144	130	119	116	137	*154*

CONSUMPTION

TABLE 62

Consumers' Expenditure at 1948 Prices, 1946–54
(3) Services and Totals (£*million*)

	1938	1946	1947	1948	1949	1950	1951	1952	1953	1954
Private Motoring and Cycling	279	154	177	127	168	191	195	221	279	*333*
Travel: Railway	79	*116*	115	108	101	96	97	104	110	111
„ Other	168	199	228	249	262	259	255	259	275	*277*
Total Travel	247	315	343	357	363	355	352	363	385	*388*
Post, Telegraph, Telephone	45	55	56	58	57	59	64	62	64	*67*
Entertainments: Cinema	—	*120*	107	112	104	102	100	96	94	93
Other	—	65	66	68	70	69	72	*73*	71	70
Total Entertainments	116	*185*	173	180	174	171	172	169	165	163
Domestic Service	264	*123*	118	113	101	95	89	83	80	80
Other Services	*734*	657	680	648	582	574	579	580	587	593
Income in Kind not included elsewhere	29	*145*	78	55	47	44	52	54	56	53
Deduct Foreign Tourists' Expenditure in U.K.	− 81	− 15	− 22	− 33	− 43	− 60	− 73	− 84	− 93	− 96
Expenditure Abroad	71	*132*	109	94	100	98	118	109	109	125
Total Expenditure in U.K.	8,493	8,119	8,425	8,411	8,593	8,794	8,709	8,629	8,961	*9,342*
Total Expenditure in U.K. and Abroad	8,564	8,251	8,534	8,505	8,693	8,892	8,827	8,738	9,070	*9,467*

consumption did not prevent the balance of payments from going badly wrong in 1951 (see page 196).

Over the whole period up to 1953 consumption, as measured in actual market prices, had risen in about the same proportion as total production. Only in 1954 did the rise in consumers' expenditure out-run the increase in the gross national product. Till 1954, despite the difficulties, a high proportion of output had been withheld from the consuming public and had been either invested or spent on armaments. The attempt simultaneously to build up capital resources and to spend heavily on re-arming involved a severe strain on the economy—so severe that the armament programme, after being increased to a fan-tastic level, had to be cut because of sheer inability to carry it into effect.

There had been, in effect, between 1946 and 1953, only a fairly modest increase in total consumption measured in fixed prices, though more than enough to balance the rise in population, which was only 3 per cent from 1946 to 1954, as against nearly 15 per cent for consumption. What we most want to know is how the rise, such as it is, has affected different sections of the population—rich and poor, wage-earners and profit-makers, children and old-age pensioners, for example.

There is, however, no way of breaking up the statistics of total con-sumption by classes or social or income groups as the basis for a fully comprehensive analysis. We have, indeed, for the period up to 1953 the annual reports of the National Food Survey Committee, based on a sample enquiry which is probably broad enough to give its general estimates a fair amount of validity in respect of food and nutrition. The Committee does not, however, cover any forms of expenditure other than food. For its general estimates it accepts the figures given in the annual Blue Book on National Income and Expenditure, which have been used so far in this section; but it then proceeds to break up its sample of 11,395 households, including 36,756 persons or 3·23 per household, studied in 1953, on the basis of a rather elaborate sampling method which aimed at getting roughly the correct proportions from very large towns, other towns, and rural areas, from the various regions of Great Britain, and from different social classes or income groups. The method used cannot be described here in detail, but seems to be reasonably satisfactory. The details can be found in the report, *Domestic Food Consumption and Expenditure*, 1953.

The report opens with a comparative account of the supply of the main foods per head of population in 1953 (and provisionally in 1954), as compared with 1947, 1952, and the average of the pre-war years 1934–8. The supplies are given in lbs. The main figures are shown in Table 63 (overleaf).

This table shows remarkable changes in food consumption per head since the 1930s. In 1953 butter consumption had been nearly halved, and margarine consumption more than doubled. Consumption of meat

CONSUMPTION

TABLE 63

Supplies of Principal Foods (lbs. per head) in certain years

	1934–8 (average)	1947	1952	1953	1954 (provisional)	Change per cent 1952–3	Change per cent 1930s–1953
Dairy Products (except Butter) as Milk Solids	38·3	48·7	51·5	52·3	52·7	+ 2	+ 36
Cheese (included above)	8·8	10·5	7·7	9·2	10·0	+ 19	+ 5
Meat (edible weight)	110·0	82·0	84·6	92·9	103·1	+ 10	− 15
Fish, Poultry and Game (edible weight)	32·7	36·3	28·2	25·6	25·6	− 9	− 22
Eggs (shell egg equivalent)	28·3	20·9	26·6	28·3	28·7	+ 6	− 0
Oils and Fats:							
Butter	24·7	11·2	10·9	13·2	14·2	+ 21	− 47
Margarine	8·7	14·9	19·3	17·8	19·4	− 8	+ 104
Lard and Cooking Fats	9·3	7·4	11·0	9·7	10·1	− 12	+ 4
Other Edible	9·9	4·6	8·7	10·0	11·9	+ 5	+ 1
Total (Fat content)	46·9	33·9	45·1	45·6	50·1	+ 1	− 3
Sugar and Syrups (Sugar content)	104·6	85·0	90·7	100·6	111·1	+ 11	− 4
Potatoes	181·9	284·1	237·8	222·1	220·8	− 7	+ 22
Pulses, Nuts, etc.	9·5	7·9	9·4	10·6	11·8	+ 13	+ 12
Fruit and Tomatoes (fresh equivalent)	137·4	132·4	123·1	132·9	137·2	+ 8	− 3
Other Vegetables	107·0	114·0	100·9	99·7	99·1	− 1	− 7
Cereal Products	210·1	240·2	219·5	208·6	201·3	− 5	− 1
Tea	9·3	8·5	8·5	9·5	9·8	+ 12	+ 2
Coffee	0·7	1·6	1·5	1·3	1·4	− 13	+ 86
Total Calories per Day	3,000	2,880	2,950	3,000	3,120	+ 2	0

was down by 15 per cent, and of fish, game and poultry by 22 per cent; whereas consumption of dairy products other than butter had risen by 36 per cent and that of potatoes by 22 per cent. Tea consumption had barely changed, whereas coffee consumption, very small in the 1930s, was up by 86 per cent, though still only one-seventh of that of tea. Consumption of cereal products had hardly changed, and that of sugar and sugar products had fallen, though only by 4 per cent. Egg consumption was just back at the pre-war level. Fruit and vegetables, other than potatoes, had fallen away, though not very heavily, whereas pulses and nuts showed an increase. Cheese (included in dairy products) was up a little: the total supply of fats showed a small decline per head.

If we look at the post-war years only, we get a different picture. The total intake of calories has been rising, but did not surpass the pre-war level till 1954. Consumption of meat and eggs, which had been heavily reduced, has been rising, and so has that of sugar products and that of tea. Dairy products, of which supplies were rising even during the war, have continued to rise, but at a decreasing rate. Butter supplies have tended to rise, but not continuously: margarine supplies have fluctuated. Total fat supplies, seriously down during and just after the war, have improved. Consumption of cereal products, which increased under war conditions, has been falling away. There is evidently some tendency to revert to the pre-war pattern, but with more milk and margarine and much less butter, rather less meat and much less fish, rather more sugar and sugar products by 1954, about the same amount of fruit, more potatoes and pulses, but fewer other vegetables, rather more tea, and much more coffee. What is at first sight most surprising here is the fall in butter, meat and fish and the size of the increase in potatoes. The big rise in dairy produce, other than butter, is significant, but less surprising.

Of course, patterns of consumption in recent years have been considerably affected by rationing, by limitations on imports, and by government policies in relation to agriculture, including subsidies and price guarantees (see p. 77), which have influenced supplies. Meat and bacon were de-rationed only in July 1954, butter and other fats only in May 1954, and sugar and tea only in the autumn of 1952; and in several cases the weekly ration was substantially lower in 1951–2 than in 1950—for example, meat, butter, and to a less extent tea. From 1950 to 1952 the energy value of consumption per head fell, to rise again in 1953 and 1954. Rationing by order, as it was removed, was replaced by 'rationing by the purse', which affected the pattern of 'free' consumption. The proportion of total consumers' expenditure devoted to food was about the same in 1938 and in 1951—29·8 and 29·9 per cent respectively—but rose thereafter to 31·4, 32·2 and 32·6 per cent in the three years after 1951. Retail food prices increased by 38 or 39 per cent from 1950 to 1954, and household expenditure on food by 48 per cent (see section on prices, p. 219). Even in 1952—a bad year—average intake of essential nutrients was well above the minimum level recommended by the British Medical Association's Committee on Nutrition in 1950, though there was a deficiency of 1 per cent in total energy value. Protein intake was 4 per cent above the B.M.A. minimum, calcium 8 per cent above, iron 6 per cent, and the essential vitamins considerably more than adequate by this standard. In 1952 more than half the total energy value—52·9 per cent—was derived from carbohydrate, as compared with 12·6 per cent from protein and 34·5 per cent from fat. In 1953 the proportion derived from fat had risen to 36 per cent, mainly at the expense of carbohydrate, but with a slight fall in the protein proportion as well.

In 1953, urban households consumed more per head than rural

households in the case of meat, fish, potatoes and other vegetables, fruit and tea, whereas rural households were ahead of urban in respect of milk, cheese, eggs, sugar and preserves (taken together), and cereal products. In respect of fats and of sugar as distinct from preserves there was not much difference. If expenditure is taken instead of quantity consumed, rural households spent less on milk and eggs, though they consumed more. Total household expenditure on food averaged 23s. 3d. a week in towns and 20s. 9d. in the rural areas, with an overall average of 22s. 8d., as compared with 20s. 8d. in 1952. The rural diets showed on the whole a rather better energy value and nutrient content than the urban, with small deficiencies in fat and vitamins, and also in animal protein.

The Food Survey's analysis of consumption by Social Class is based on a fourfold division into income groups, based exclusively on the income of the head of the household, *plus* a further group consisting of old age pensioners alone. The income classification, which was altered in 1953, was based that year on dividing lines at £15, £9 and £6 a week, as against £13, £8 and £4 10s. in previous years. £6 in 1953 was described as 'the approximate minimum wage for an adult male in full-time employment'. Class D—under £6—thus represents broadly the less skilled or less well paid manual workers and also households lacking an able-bodied male adult earner; Class C—from £6 to £9—the main body of more skilled manual workers; Class B—£9 to £15— the highest paid groups of manual workers and the rank and file of the white-collar workers, though some of the latter fall into Class C; and Class A, the upper and middle classes. In 1953 6 per cent of all the households studied were in Class A, 23 per cent in Class B, 40 per cent in Class C, and 31 per cent in Class D, including the old age pensioners. If the older income classification had been adhered to, the percentages for 1953 would have been 9, 32, 36 and 23. In 1950, on that basis, they were actually 3, 13, 58 and 26.

On the revised basis of 1953, average weekly expenditure on food per head in that year was as follows: Class A, 26s. 9d.; Class B, 23s. 4d.; Class C, 22s. 3d.; Class D (excluding the old age pensioners) 21s. 11d.; Old Age Pensioners, 20s. 11d.—with a general average of 22s. 8d. These totals are exclusive of food obtained without direct purchase— e.g. from gardens or allotments, or from employers. If an estimate for these is included the deviations from the general average of money value of food consumed work out at + 21 per cent for Class A, + 3 per cent for Class B, − 2 per cent for Class C, − 3 per cent for Class D (excluding the pensioners), and − 9 per cent for the Old Age Pensioners. The sharpness of the difference between Classes A and B is notable, but it is less than in 1950 or 1951, when the excess was 29 per cent on the old classification of incomes. Had that classification been adhered to, it would have been 18 per cent for 1953.

It is interesting to see how the pattern of consumption differed from Class to Class. Here are the figures for the main food groups in 1953.

TABLE 64

Domestic Food Consumption, by Social Class, 1953

(oz. per head per week, or other unit where mentioned)

	Class A	Class B	Class C	Class D (except O.A.P.)		O.A.P	All Classes
				(with earners)	(without earners)		
Milk and Cream (pints)	6·07	5·24	4·97	4·71	5·52	4·98	5·07
Cheese	2·58	2·40	2·50	2·60	2·42	2·60	2·50
Meat	36·31	32·17	31·79	32·84	32·34	31·54	32·34
Fish	8·44	6·24	5·87	6·52	7·41	6·86	6·30
Eggs, Hens' (number)	4·81	4·22	3·90	3·69	3·49	3·20	3·97
Fats	9·93	10·44	10·57	10·39	10·37	10·63	10·48
Sugar and Preserves	19·34	18·67	18·70	18·32	18·71	19·30	18·67
Vegetables (exc. Potatoes)	35·97	32·86	31·75	31·95	34·74	31·15	32·67
Potatoes	50·32	63·16	66·85	64·50	53·95	55·63	64·17
Fruit and Tomatoes	41·60	30·12	24·51	22·92	26·55	18·56	26·53
Cereals	69·30	78·85	85·55	87·18	77·90	82·79	82·77
Beverages	3·57	3·23	3·33	3·49	3·78	4·45	3·41

It seems worth while to re-express these figures as percentages of the general average for each group.

TABLE 65

Domestic Food Consumption by Social Class, 1953

(per cent of general average of all classes)

	Class A	Class B	Class C	Class D (except O.A.P.)		O.A.P.	All Classes
				(with earners)	(without earners)		
Milk and Cream	120	103·5	98	93	109	98	100
Cheese	103	96	100	104	97	104	100
Meat	112	99·5	98·5	101·5	100	97·5	100
Fish	134	99	93	103·5	117·5	109	100
Eggs, Hens'	121	106·5	98	93	88	80·5	100
Fats	95	99·5	101	99	99	101·5	100
Sugar and Preserves	103·5	100	100	98	100	103·5	100
Vegetables (exc. Potatoes)	109·5	100	96·5	97	105·5	94·5	100
Potatoes	78·5	98·5	104	100·5	84	87	100
Fruit and Tomatoes	157	113·5	92·5	86·5	100	70	100
Cereals	83·5	95	103·5	105·5	94	100	100
Beverages (non-alcoholic)	104·5	94·5	97·5	102·5	111	130·5	100

Class A shows the largest excesses above the average in fruit, fish, eggs and milk, and falls a long way below the average in consumption of potatoes and cereals, and 5 per cent below it in fats (though well above the average for butter alone). Class B does not deviate from the average by more than 10 per cent except for fruit (+ 13·5), or by more than 5 per cent except for eggs (+ 6·5) and beverages (— 5·5). Class C is within 10 per cent of the average in all cases, and more than 5 per cent below it only for fish and fruit. Class D is here broken up into two groups—those with and without a principal earner; and there are sharp divergences between the two. The 'with earner' group broadly represented the low-paid manual workers: it is $5\frac{1}{2}$ per cent above the average for cereals, but $13\frac{1}{2}$ per cent below it for fruit, and 7 per cent for milk and eggs, the remaining divergences being under 5 per cent. The nonearner D group, which represents an average household of only 1·8 persons as against 3·1 for the earner D group, shows a high consumption per head of fish, beverages, milk and vegetables, and a low consumption of eggs and potatoes, and also of cereals. Finally, the old age pensioners are a long way above the general average in respect of beverages (mainly tea) and of fish, but are 30 per cent below it for fruit, nearly 20 per cent for eggs, and 13 per cent for potatoes.

In comparison with the 1930s, the gaps between the classes have certainly narrowed a great deal; but exact measurement is not possible. The Survey notes some tendency for them to widen again in the early 1950s, though not by a great deal. General comparison is not possible except in terms of money expenditure; and in this respect the gap had narrowed between 1950 and 1953. For Class A the excess over the average expenditure had fallen from 29 per cent in 1950 to 18 on the old and 21 on the new classification in 1953, and for Class B from 12 to 1 and 3 per cent. For Class D (excluding the pensioners) it had fallen from 7 to 3 per cent on either reckoning, and for the Old Age Pensioners it had remained unchanged at — 9 per cent. Class C showed a change from — 2 to — 3 per cent on the old reckoning, but remained at — 2 per cent on the new.

Of course, the figures of consumption take no account of the quality of the food bought, as distinct from its weight or nutrient value. The figures of spending, on the other hand, do take account of this factor. In terms of calories Class C, followed by Class D as a whole, was ahead of Class B, which in turn was ahead of Class A; but Class A led in animal protein, in total fat intake, and in vitamins, except Vitamin B: it was lowest in carbohydrate intake.

Size of family or household and age composition were found to be more important than Social Class in determining food consumption and spending on food. Households of 2 adults without children in 1953 spent on the average 31s. a week per head on food where both were under 55 years of age, but only 25s. 10d. where either was over 55.

Households with 2 adults showed a falling average as the number of children increased—23s. 11d. with 1 child, 20s. 1d. with 2 children, 17s. 4d. with 3, and 15s. 6d. with more than 3. In such households with 4 or more children, the average child got under 40 per cent of the quantity of fresh green vegetables consumed by each adult in the younger childless households, only 40 per cent of the fresh fruit, only half the meat or eggs, and only 77 per cent of the milk, as against 90 per cent of the potatoes and 86 per cent of the bread. These large-household children were 7 per cent below the B.M.A. requirement for protein, and 13 per cent for calcium, and only just up to it in total energy value. They did, however, get enough vitamins and just enough iron. In both protein and calcium they were worse off in 1953 than in 1950 or 1952.

Much more valuable information than I have space to give here is to be found in the Food Survey's reports, to which readers wanting more facts are referred. There is unfortunately no comparable analysis of other kinds of consumption; and we have no means of breaking up the statistics of total consumption by class or other groups. Other things being equal, one would expect any approach towards equalization of incomes to increase the proportion of income spent on consumption, because the poor, when their purchasing power rises, may be expected to spend rather than save most of the increase. Clearly the decreases in fixed price spending on consumption in 1951 and 1952 meant some worsening in the position of the poorer consumers; but how much, the statistics do not allow us to say. Nor can we say at all accurately how the increases of 1953 and 1954—respectively £332 million and £397 million at 1948 prices—were distributed between richer and poorer consumers.

Most figures relate to total consumption, and little use can be made of them for estimating the differing fortunes of the various classes and income groups. It is, however, undoubtedly significant that fixed price expenditure on private motoring continued to advance in 1951 and 1952, and made great leaps in 1953 and 1954, whereas the figures for food fell in both 1951 and 1952, and those for furniture and furnishings did the same and were in 1954 still only a little above the 1950 level. The figures for clothing tell the same story, though women's clothing, unlike men's, recovered a good deal in 1953 and 1954. The decline in domestic service is of course part of a long-term trend, intensified by full employment. Further consideration of this matter must be left till we come to consider incomes and earnings of various types (see pp. 221 ff.).

The figures I have been using so far in this chapter are taken from the Blue Books on National Income and Expenditure, or from the *Food Surveys. The Economic Survey for 1955*, published in March 1955, gives somewhat different figures for the years 1951 to 1953, and adds a much less detailed estimate for 1954, both in terms of consumers' expenditure at the prices of 1948. Here is the Table from the *Survey*.

TABLE 66

Consumers' Expenditure at 1948 Prices, 1951–4

(*£million*)

	1951	1952	1953	1954	Per cent change from	
					1952–3	1953–4
Food	2,446	2,421	2,498	2,593	+ 3	+ 4
Drink and Tobacco	1,573	1,573	1,604	1,632	+ 2	+ 2
Rent, Rates, Water, Fuel and Light	1,038	1,034	1,055	1,085	+ 2	+ 3
Household Goods	677	634	713	786	+ 12	+ 10
Clothing and Footwear	901	874	891	932	+ 2	+ 5
Other Goods	482	476	515	545	+ 8	+ 6
Cars and Private Motoring	180	204	259	308	+ 27	+ 19
Travel	352	363	385	388	+ 6	+ 1
Other Services	1,021	999	999	1,029	—	+ 3
Total	8,670	8,578	8,919	9,298	+ 4	+ 4

Some of these changes are of course connected with relaxation and abolition of rationing, and with easier supplies.

Beer consumption declined each year up to 1950, and again in 1952: it increased slightly in 1953, but fell off in 1954. Consumption of wines and spirits rose in 1947, fell in 1948 and 1949, rose again in 1950 and 1951, declined a little in 1952, and then rose, reaching its peak in 1954. Tobacco consumption was at its peak in 1946, fell sharply in 1947 and less sharply in 1948 and 1949, and then rose slightly in 1950 and more substantially in 1951, 1952, 1953 and 1954, but failed to regain the 1946 level. The figures for drink and tobacco are of course affected by taxation, to which we shall come later (see p. 296).

Turning now to non-food goods we find that housing expenditure at constant prices rose fairly fast up to 1949 and thereafter changed but little until 1953 and 1954, when it again rose sharply. Expenditure on fuel and light increased sharply in 1951 and 1954; but whereas the maximum was reached in 1954 for coal and in 1947 and 1951 for gas, for electricity there was a continuous rise from 1946 to 1954, which was also the peak point for other fuel (mainly oil).

For furniture and furnishings the highest expenditure at fixed prices was in 1954; but 1950 was not much behind. Up to the latter year there had been a continuous rapid rise, due largely to the making good of war arrears. Then came sharp falls in 1951 and 1952, followed by a substantial recovery in 1953, which however stopped some way short of the 1950 level. For other durable household goods, including radio sets and electrical goods, there were rises in 1947, 1949, 1950, 1951, 1953 and 1954, but falls in 1948 and 1952. Other household supplies also reached their peak in 1954, after a continuous rise except for a small setback in 1951 and 1952.

For all types of clothing taken together, the peak year was 1950. For footwear the advance was continuous up to 1950, but was followed by a sharp fall in 1951 and a smaller fall in 1952, with hardly any recovery in 1953, but more in 1954. Men's and boys' clothing followed the same course up to 1950 and fell sharply in 1951 and 1952 and less sharply in 1953, but recovered to some extent in 1954. Women's and girls' clothing, on the other hand, after rising up to 1950 and falling abruptly in 1951, recovered a little in 1952 and rose substantially in 1953 and again in 1954.

For books and periodicals there was a considerable rise in 1947, followed by smaller rises up to the peak in 1950. Then came small declines in 1951 and 1952 and a small increase in 1953. There was no change in 1954. For other recreational goods there were advances up to 1949, followed by small declines in 1950 and 1951, no change in 1952, and rises in 1953 and 1954.

Chemists' goods rose in 1947, 1949, 1950, 1953 and 1954—the peak year—but fell in 1948, 1951 and 1952. Other goods—too various to be itemized—followed much the same course, with increases in 1947, 1948, 1949, 1953 and 1954, but falls in 1950, 1951 and 1952. Their peak too was in 1954.

Finally we come to fixed price expenditure on services, as distinct from goods. Private motoring, as we saw, increased each year, save for a sharp fall in 1948. Much the biggest increases were in 1953 and 1954—the peak year. Travel expenditure at fixed prices was at highest levels in 1953 and 1954, having risen each year up to 1949, declined in 1950 and 1951, and then risen very slightly in 1952. But for rail travel only the peak years were 1946 and 1947, followed by declines in 1948, 1949 and 1950, no change in 1951, and increases in 1952, 1953 and 1954. Postal and telephone services reached their peak in 1954, after showing only small increases up to 1953, except in 1951. Entertainment was at its highest in 1946: it fell sharply in 1947 and less sharply in 1949, 1950, 1952, 1953 and 1954, with small rises in 1948 and 1951. Included under this head is fixed price expenditure on the cinema, which fell each year from 1947 to 1954. Domestic service expenditure also fell continuously up to 1953, and was unchanged in 1954. The large miscellaneous group of other services, including education and health, showed the highest fixed price spending in 1947, followed by 1946. It fell in 1948, 1949, 1950 and 1951, and then rose slightly in 1952, 1953 and 1954.

The residue of income in kind—e.g. from gardens and allotments—fell off very rapidly after 1946 up to 1950, and then increased in 1951 and, slightly, in 1952 and 1953. It then fell off again in 1954.

British tourists' activities abroad were affected by currency regulations. They were highest in 1946, fell in 1947 and 1948, rose in 1949, fell in 1950, rose again in 1951, and then fell again in 1952 and 1953. There was a considerable rise in 1954.

It is none too easy to draw general conclusions from these changes. It is significant that, whereas fixed price expenditures totalling £3,800 million reached their peak in 1954, others totalling £1,100 million did so in 1950.

Difficult though it is to relate the changes in consumption at all accurately to the fortunes of particular groups or classes, there is no doubt at all about their general effect. In the 1930s it could be said without question that more than a quarter of the total population was living below the Rowntree 'human needs' standard and at least 15 per cent below the much lower Bowley 'poverty line'. In 1954 the latter type of absolute privation had almost ceased to exist as a serious social problem, though there were still many households which fell short of the more generous Rowntree standard. The maintenance of full employment, the relative rise in the wages of the less skilled workers, and the improvement of the social services had all played their parts in this dramatic change. Children's allowances, though inadequate, had materially improved the condition of the bigger families; and old age pensions, supplemented in many cases by National Assistance (see p. 325), had gone some way towards eliminating sheer physical privation among the elderly. There were still gaps in the social services needing to be filled: the position in respect of both children's allowances and old age pensions was still markedly unsatisfactory. Nevertheless, a truly revolutionary change had taken place in the condition of the bottom quarter, or third, of the population; and, broadly speaking, this change had been generally accepted, to the extent that no major political party dared contest it openly.

We shall come back later to this great question of standards of living, when we discuss the changes in incomes and their distribution in relation to changing prices (see p. 221). At this point, we are chiefly concerned with the changes in total and average consumption and with the problem of reconciling higher total consumption with the maintenance of investment at a level high enough to meet the needs of a period of unprecedentedly rapid technological development.

CHAPTER SEVEN

INVESTMENT

OUT of the current product, including the net return on investments abroad, a society needs to make provision both for current consumption of goods and services and for 'investment'—that is to say, for the renewal of the supply of instruments of production and the provision of new ones and for the accumulation of stocks of materials and work in progress and of durable consumers' goods, such as houses. A society can, of course, live beyond its means to the extent to which it is receiving net gifts from abroad, or is using up and not replacing either existing instruments of production or stocks of materials, etc., or again is borrowing from foreigners or foreign Governments and using the proceeds to meet current expenditure. Normally, however, societies spend on consumption less than they produce, by applying a part of their resources to the provision of new additional instruments of production, after providing for the depreciation and obsolescence of those already in use. They must, indeed, do this on a considerable scale if their productive capacity is not to fall off rapidly; for not only are instruments of production continually wearing out or becoming obsolete, but also changes in demand at home or abroad are continually calling for new kinds of instruments or for an increased supply of some kinds as against others. Moreover, if population is increasing, or if, even for a stationary population, standards of living are to improve, it is needful to provide not only enough new productive assets to replace those which are discarded for any reason, but also an increase in the total usable supply. These forms of provision are called 'investment': 'gross' investment includes that which is needed to keep productive capacity intact by replacing discarded assets: 'net' investment is that part of 'gross' investment which goes beyond this requirement and increases total productive capacity.

The Sources of Investment. These definitions and distinctions are easy enough to make in theory; but it is a much harder task to express them in definite amounts so as to show what proportion of current national income is being actually invested, either 'gross' or 'net', at any particular time. 'Gross' investment is indeed a good deal easier to estimate than 'net' investment. Broadly speaking, it is made up of four elements, one of which cancels itself out. These include, first, the savings made by persons, companies, corporations and public authorities out of their current receipts—personal savings, company profits not paid out in dividends, the surpluses of corporations, including allocations for the amortization of debts, similar allocations by public authorities, including local authorities, and any budget surplus accruing from taxation—all these being reckoned 'gross', i.e. before making any provision for depreciation of existing capital assets or for appreciation in the value of accumulated stocks or work in progress. The second item is in the first instance negative: it consists of the sums levied as taxes on capital—e.g. death duties—which re-appear as assets of the Government and thus cancel out. The third item is made up of sums received from abroad as gifts—e.g. aid from the United States—as distinct from interest and dividends on foreign investments, which have already been included in the first group. This third item is called in the National Income Blue Book by the name 'capital transfers'. The fourth and last item, which may be either positive or negative, consists of the provision made by trading agencies, including the Government, for appreciation or depreciation in the value of stocks of goods.

Disinvestment in Wartime. During the war Great Britain lived much beyond its national income. The Government was spending vast sums on war services and was using a large part of the national man-power for non-productive purposes, such as military service. There was, of course, some capital investment in the war industries and some employment of labour and other resources in patching up houses and other buildings damaged in air raids, or in clearing away debris. But much of the capital investment was uneconomic: it was designed to meet immediate war needs and its long-run value was highly problematical. Meanwhile, other industries, deemed less essential for war purposes, were allowed to run down their capital equipment without the normal expenditure on renewals and repairs: so that they emerged after the war with their productive assets largely worn out or obsolete. Over the same period, in order to meet the cost of goods and services supplied by overseas countries to aid the war effort, large masses of British-owned assets abroad were sold or mortgaged; and in addition Great Britain incurred big debts to overseas countries for goods and services that could not be paid for at once.

Lease-Lend. During the later stages of the war the strain was relieved in some measure by the institution of Lease-Lend, under which the United States supplied war materials without immediate charge, leaving the payment to be settled when the fighting was over, and both the United States and Great Britain ceased to charge one another for goods supplied, for example, to American forces in the United Kingdom or to British personnel in the United States. But for Lease-Lend it would have been impossible for this country to sustain its war effort at the required level; and the abrupt termination of the system by the United States as soon as hostilities ceased involved a serious crisis in the British balance of payments.

The Wartime Fall in Exports. The difficulties of the war years were greatly aggravated by the sharp fall in British exports, due partly to the diversion of current production to meet the needs of war and partly to the difficulties in the way of procuring the materials required by the export trades. By 1943 the volume of British exports had fallen to less than one-third of the pre-war volume. It rose a little during the first three-quarters of 1945, largely as a result of shipments for relief purposes; but it is broadly the case that Great Britain emerged from the war with only about one-third of the volume of exports sent out in 1938, and accordingly unable to meet out of its own current production more than a fraction of the cost of indispensable imports. The consequence was that further debts had to be allowed to pile up, and that in 1946 Great Britain was forced to incur fresh liabilities under the terms of the loans negotiated with the United States and Canadian Governments. Here are the figures of the money value and volume of British exports during the war period, as compared with those of 1938:

TABLE 67

British Exports, Value and Volume, 1938 and 1939–45

	Value (£million)	Index of Volume
1938	471	100
1939	440	94
1940	411	73
1941	365	56
1942	270	36
1943	233	29
1944	258	30
1945 (Jan.–Sept.)	272	42*

* Including relief shipments.

Shipping Losses. Capital losses during the war included a large part of the merchant navy, sunk in submarine warfare. The merchant fleet consisted in September 1939 of 17·7 million deadweight tons of general shipping and 4·4 million tons of tankers. By the middle of 1945 the total tonnage had been reduced to 15·6 million tons of general vessels and 3·8 million tons of tankers; and of these 3·4 and 0·1 million tons were ships lent under Lease-Lend and returnable to the lending countries. The total British-owned tonnage had thus fallen to 12·2 and 3·7 million tons—15·9 million as against 22·1 million in 1938. No less than 15·2 million tons of general shipping and 2·8 million tons of tankers had been lost during the war, and had been only in part replaced by new acquisitions of 13·1 and 2·2 million tons, including those under Lease-Lend. Moreover, many of the vessels built during the war were

none too suitable for normal use, as speed of construction rather than
quality or economic value had been the guiding consideration.

These shipping losses put a further strain on the balance of payments, as they both reduced Great Britain's earnings from shipping
services and involved expenditure in hiring foreign vessels.

Sale of Overseas Investments. Sales of British overseas investments,
or non-renewal of such as were repaid, during the war amounted in all
to £1,118 million, not including the British holdings in the United States
that were deposited as collateral for the loan made to Great Britain
through the Reconstruction Finance Corporation. These lost overseas
investments, which were requisitioned from their owners by the Government and sold to meet overseas liabilities, were made up as follows:

TABLE 68

Proceeds of Sale or Repatriation of British Overseas Investments, 1939–45

(*£million*)

Sterling Area		United States	203*
Dominions	201	Canada	225
India, Burma and Middle East	348	South America	96
Colonies and other Sterling		Rest of World	30
Area Countries	15		
Total	564		554
		Grand Total	1,118

* Excluding collateral deposited for Reconstruction Finance Corporation loan.

In consequence of these capital losses British net revenue from overseas investments was reduced to less than £100 million as' against well
over £200 million before the war.

Wartime Debts. Over the same period, Great Britain's external debts
were piling up at a great rate. They amounted to less than £500 million
at the outbreak of war; but by June 1945 they stood at £3,355 million, of
which by far the greater part consisted of unfunded short-term loans,
formally due for early repayment, but in practice clearly incapable of
being paid off in the circumstances of 1945. This immense total indebted-
ness was distributed as shown in Table 69.

It will be seen that the largest parts of this debt were owed to sterling
area countries, above all India and the British Colonies and Dominions,
which provided vast quantities of war supplies without immediate payment. Debts to America took for the most part other forms, and were
kept down by the operation of Lease-Lend.

Loss of Foreign Reserves. There was also a big loss of gold and dollar
reserves. These stood at £864 million in August 1938, but had been
reduced to £605 million a year later. By October 1945 they were down

TABLE 69

Outstanding United Kingdom Debts, June 1945 (£million)

Due to Dominions	384	Due to American Countries	303
India, Burma and Middle East	1,732	European Countries and	
Other Sterling Area Countries	607	Dependencies	267
		Rest of World	62
Total	2,723		632
		Grand Total	3,355

to about £453 million—a loss of £411 million since 1938. Thus, in all, Great Britain had incurred a loss of overseas assets, including gold and dollar reserves held on behalf of the Sterling Area as a whole, amounting to about £4,200 million.

Disinvestment at Home. All these losses reacted adversely on the British economy. They reduced British income from overseas and at the same time increased the amounts payable from Great Britain to overseas countries. But at the same time extensive disinvestment had been going on at home, on account of the failure to keep industrial equipment up to date and of the actual destruction of capital assets by submarine warfare and air bombardment. About 4,000,000 homes were damaged by enemy action; and of these 210,000 were totally destroyed and another 250,000 rendered uninhabitable. The estimated sum required to make good war damage to property of all sorts, at 1945 prices, was £1,450 million, or about £860 million at 1938 replacement costs. To this must be added the large arrears of maintenance of houses and other buildings, and also the arrears of normal replacements in industry. These last alone were estimated to have reached a total of £885 million by the end of 1944, simply for accumulated arrears of expenditure to make good depreciation and obsolescence. Total disinvestment at home and abroad, exclusive of private disinvestment in deterioration of dwellings and household goods, was reckoned at £7,300 million, or about one-quarter of the estimated total capital wealth of Great Britain in 1945.

The Wartime Deficit. In 1944, it was estimated, Great Britain was spending at the rate of 53 units of its national income on war services, for every 57 units spent on consumption. These two figures add up to more than 100, because 10 units out of every 100 were being derived not from the current national income but from disinvestment.

The figures given in the foregoing paragraphs are derived from the White Paper, *Statistical Material Presented during the Washington Negotiations*, which was submitted to the United States Government while Great Britain was negotiating for a post-war loan and for a settlement of Lease-Lend obligations. They formed the background for these discussions, which resulted in the United States Loan of 1946.

Post-war Borrowing. Great Britain thus emerged from the war very much poorer in capital assets than it had been in 1939, and with huge arrears of investment to be made up out of a reduced productive power. There was evident need, unless the country was to be plunged more and more deeply into debt—and who would go on lending it the money in any case?—for an abnormally high rate of capital investment until the arrears had been worked off, and therefore for continued restriction of consumption. Actually, in 1946 and 1947, further debts had to be incurred to overseas countries while peace-time productive power was being re-built. There were adverse balances of payments in respect of current transactions amounting to £298 million in 1946 and £443 million in 1947; and during these years Great Britain borrowed £856 million from the United States and £235 million from Canada. Only in 1948 was the external current account balanced, and only in 1950 did a substantial surplus appear—to be wiped out by a heavy deficit in 1951.

By 1948 an intensive effort had been made both to restore productive capacity by means of large investment and to restrict imports to what could be afforded without incurring further debt. From this point it is possible to follow the course of investment year by year from the figures given in the annual Blue Books on National Income and Expenditure.

Gross Investment from 1948. Here, from 1948 onwards, are the estimates made in the National Income Blue Book of the sums *available* each year for 'gross' investment. That a sum is available for investment need not mean that it is actually invested: the process of investment is distinct from that of 'saving' a sum of money, even if certain ways of defining 'savings' and 'investment' involve a necessary equality between them. Fortunately, it is not necessary here to enter into the complications of these definitions—only to point out that we are at present dealing only with what is available, and not with what is actually invested.

TABLE 70

Gross Capital Formation, 1948–54

(Funds available for Gross Investment (£million))

Gross Savings:	Persons	Com-panies	Public Corpora-tions	Central Govern-ment	Local Authori-ties	Residual Error	Tax and Dividend Reserves, etc.	Total
1948	84	916	59	520	71	− 20	181	1,811
1949	122	939	84	581	77	− 18	28	1,813
1950	99	1,228	118	662	79	20	184	2,390
1951	284	1,135	143	590	68	− 4	521	2,737
1952	785	859	144	348	71	38	16	2,261
1953	902	1,092	169	155	109	27	72	2,525
1954	860	1,243	203	237	109	− 5	228	2,870

TABLE 70 (*continued*)

Gross Capital Formation: Forms of Investment, 1948–54 (£*million*)

	Persons	Companies	Public Corporations	Central Government	Local Authorities	Residual Error	Tax and Dividend Reserves, etc.	Total
Taxes on Capital:								
1948	− 215	—	—	215	—	—	—	—
1949	− 254	—	—	254	—	—	—	—
1950	− 190	—	—	190	—	—	—	—
1951	− 194	—	—	194	—	—	—	—
1952	− 159	—	—	159	—	—	—	—
1953	− 165	—	—	166	—	—	—	—
1954	− 183	—	—	—	—	—	—	—
Capital Transfers (net receipts):								
1948	116	73	4	12	29	—	—	234
1949	105	58	42	− 60	44	—	—	189
1950	97	43	3	7	18	—	—	168
1951	68	39	5	− 47	14	—	—	79
1952	59	33	5	− 72	12	—	—	37
1953	54	43	6	− 81	24	—	—	46
1954	41	24	6	− 51	14	—	—	34
***Less* Provision for Stock Appreciation:**								
1948	− 59	− 200	− 42	− 24	—	—	—	− 325
1949	− 39	− 170	—	9	—	—	—	− 200
1950	− 63	− 440	− 29	− 118	—	—	—	− 650
1951	−112	− 465	− 80	− 93	—	—	—	− 750
1952	− 10	22	6	32	—	—	—	50
1953	− 7	44	6	32	—	—	—	75
1954	− 20	− 52	− 8	5	—	—	—	75
Total Funds Available for Gross Investment:								
1948	− 74	789	71	723	100	20	181	1,720
1949	− 66	827	126	784	121	− 18	28	1,802
1950	− 57	831	92	741	97	20	184	1,908
1951	46	709	68	644	82	− 4	521	2,066
1952	675	914	155	467	83	38	16	2,348
1953	784	1,179	181	271	133	27	72	2,647
1954	701	1,215	201	374	123	− 5	228	2,837

Investment from 1948. The Blue Book next goes on to estimate the amount of actual investment that took place during these years. This gross investment includes provision for the replacement of worn out and obsolescent means of production. It is made up of five items. The first is Fixed Capital Formation at home—i.e. the acquisition of new real capital assets of every sort and kind. The second is the Value of any physical increase in stocks or work in progress, as distinct from changes in value of the pre-existing quantity of such assets. The third— a balancing item—is Net Borrowing from Tax Reserves, and the fourth —also negative—Net Borrowing from Dividend and Interest Reserves. Finally comes the complex item, Net Acquisition of Financial Assets (e.g. gold and currency reserves) *plus* Net Overseas Investment. These together give the total of Gross Investment.

TABLE 71

Gross Capital Formation, 1948–1954

(Forms of Investment (£million))

	Persons	Companies	Public Corporations	Central Government	Local Authorities	Residual Error	Tax and Dividend Reserves, etc.	Total
Home Fixed Capital Formation:								
1948	226	519	180	105	376	—	—	1,406
1949	236	554	264	111	387	—	—	1,552
1950	241	614	288	123	412	—	—	1,678
1951	267	610	359	152	463	—	—	1,851
1952	291	604	409	192	543	—	—	2,039
1953	351	649	484	207	614	—	—	2,305
1954	434	709	537	182	590	—	—	2,452
Value of Physical Increase in Stocks and Work in Progress:								
1948	35	212	− 10	− 62	—	—	—	175
1949	30	49	33	− 47	—	—	—	65
1950	41	− 24	− 15	− 212	—	—	—	− 210
1951	70	426	4	75	—	—	—	575
1952	− 15	− 62	51	76	—	—	—	50
1953	42	64	− 25	44	—	—	—	125
1954	46	356	− 59	− 118	—	—	—	225
***Less* Net Borrowing from Reserves:**								
1948	− 23	− 139	− 19	—	—	—	181	—
1949	− 74	51	− 5	—	—	—	28	—
1950	− 60	− 115	− 8	—	—	—	184	—
1951	− 67	− 425	− 29	—	—	—	521	—
1952	47	− 25	− 38	—	—	—	16	—
1953	24	− 78	− 18	—	—	—	72	—
1954	− 72	− 173	− 17	—	—	—	228	—
Net Acquisition of Financial Assets *plus* Net Overseas Investment:								
1948	− 312	197	− 130	680	− 276	− 20	—	139
1949	− 258	173	− 166	720	− 266	− 18	—	185
1950	− 279	357	− 173	830	− 315	20	—	440
1951	− 224	98	− 266	417	− 381	− 4	—	− 360
1952	352	397	− 267	199	− 460	38	—	259
1953	367	544	− 260	20	− 481	27	—	217
1954	293	323	− 294	310	− 467	− 5	—	160

INVESTMENT 107

Distribution of Investments, 1945–1954. The next Table in the Blue Book breaks up the figures of home formation of fixed capital into a number of groups, as follows:

TABLE 72
Gross Formation of Fixed Capital by Type of Asset, 1938 and 1947–54
(*£million*)

	1938	1947	1948	1949	1950	1951	1952	1953	1954
Road Vehicles	47	126	138	161	155	161	168	185	212
Aircraft	1	6	8	12	8	7	10	10	10
Ships	22	91	71	70	67	57	54	91	86
Railway Rolling Stock	14	23	28	29	31	33	27	37	48
Plant and Machinery	181	360	494	554	633	732	765	815	853
New Housing	180	333	342	332	331	372	489	619	636
Other Buildings and Works	194	195	279	345	402	435	481	509	563
Fees and Stamp Duties	17	39	46	49	51	54	45	39	44
Total	656	1,173	1,406	1,552	1,678	1,851	2,039	2,305	2,452

TABLE 73
The same at 1948 Prices

	1938	1947	1948	1949	1950	1951	1952	1953	1954
Road Vehicles	100	140	138	158	147	129	119	138	160
Aircraft, Ships, Railway Rolling Stock	98	127	107	109	99	83	69	100	102
Plant and Machinery	402	398	494	533	582	610	567	595	614
New Housing	474	355	342	327	315	318	388	491	497
Other Buildings and Works	451	210	279	339	379	354	362	380	411
Fees and Stamp Duties	34	42	46	47	48	51	41	37	42
Total	1,559	1,272	1,406	1,513	1,570	1,545	1,546	1,741	1,826

Investment by Trades and Industries. Then comes an alternative break-up by industries and trades. This is given both in terms of actual money and, for wider groups only, in fixed prices of 1948. Here are the figures at the actual prices of each year.

TABLE 74

Gross Formation of Fixed Capital by Industries and Trades, 1948–1954 (£million)

Industry or Trade	1948	1949	1950	1951	1952	1953	1954	Total 1948–53	Total 1948–54
Agriculture	84	81	79	86	80	83	87	493	580
Coal Mining	24	30	27	29	42	57	75	209	284
Oil Refining	6	18	32	34	40	34		164	—
Chemicals	33	42	54	67	70	72		338	—
Iron and Steel	32	42	49	55	54	54		286	—
Engineering, Ship-building and Electrical Goods	52	52	55	64	72	74		369	—
Vehicles	22	22	29	33	38	37		181	—
Other Metal Trades	27	29	29	30	32	31		178	—
Textiles, Leather and Clothing	49	61	63	62	44	51		330	—
Food, Drink and Tobacco	48	51	60	65	68	71		363	—
Paper and Printing	23	22	24	30	29	26		154	—
Bricks, Pottery, Glass, Cement, etc.	19	18	19	18	20	19		113	—
Other Manufacture and Mining and Quarrying	23	24	28	28	28	24		155	—
Building and Contracting	20	22	23	33	43	45	55	186	241
Electricity, Gas and Water	138	173	196	219	239	263	300	1,228	1,528
Railways	41	44	45	46	42	55	64	273	337
Shipping	63	61	60	53	50	86	81	396	477
Other Transport (except Road Goods)	53	65	61	49	52	54	57	388	445
Posts, Telephones, Radio and Broadcasting	38	44	46	53	65	75	76	319	395
Road Goods Transport *	15	17	15	16	152	173	195	895	1,090
Distribution and other Trading Services	97	115	141	146					
Other (M. of Supply, Forestry, Fishing)	19	20	21	25	34	37	37	158	195
Total, Industry and Trade	929	1,061	1,179	1,297	1,374	1,495	1,559	7,335	8,894
New Housing	342	332	331	372	489	619	636	2,497	3,133
Education and Child Care	28	45	57	69	79	81	83	359	442
Health Services	13	16	17	18	20	20	21	104	125
Other Public Services	43	49	55	64	68	76	81	308	359
Total (incl. Fees and Stamps)	1,406	1,552	1,678	1,851	2,039	2,305	2,452	10,887	13,339

* For Road Goods Transport Vehicles only, the following are the figures for each year from 1948 (in £m.)—71, 75, 75, 81, 83, 93, 106. For Public Road Passenger Transport Vehicles the corresponding totals are 33, 38, 35, 24, 21, 18 and 20, and for Passenger Cars 34, 48, 45, 56, 64, 74 and 86.

It will be seen that new housing alone accounted for nearly a quarter
—about 23½ per cent—of total gross capital formation during the years
1948–54, with a total investment of £3,133,000,000. Next in magnitude
came the electricity, gas and water services, with £1,528,000,000, of
which no less than £1,059,000,000 was in electricity supply services.
Besides these two, the rest look modest—agriculture with £580,000,000;
coal mining with £284,000,000; railways with £337,000,000; shipping
with £477,000,000; education and child care with £442,000,000; building
and contracting with £241,000,000; other transport (including road
goods transport) with about £550,000,000; and health services with a
mere £125,000,000. Figures for the various manufacturing industries
are not yet available for 1954; but up to 1953 iron and steel accounted
for £295,000,000, and oil refining for £164,000,000. The total investment in oil refining—partly financed by the earnings of American oil
companies in the United Kingdom—is impressive; for the consequent
increase in refining capacity, see p. 65. Beside these large totals, the
total government expenditure up to 1954 on research and development
under the Ministry of Supply of £163,000,000, which includes atomic
development, looks modest. The gas industry, with £276,000,000, has
taken a great deal more.

Investment as a Proportion of National Income. What proportion of
gross national income does this gross investment represent? Here are
the comparative totals:

TABLE 75

Gross National Income and Gross Capital Formation, 1948–54

(£million)

	1948	1949	1950	1951	1952	1953	1954
Gross National Income	10,379	11,099	11,666	12,785	13,861	14,805	15,718
Gross Fixed Capital Formation	1,406	1,552	1,678	1,851	2,039	2,305	2,452
Fixed Capital Formation, percentage of Gross National Income	13·5	14·0	14·4	14·5	14·7	15·6	15·6

When gross capital formation is expressed in terms of 1948 prices,
instead of at the actual prices of each period, the effect is as shown in
Table 76 (overleaf).

On this reckoning, new housing again comes to nearly a quarter of
the total, with a rapidly rising trend after 1951. Manufacturing industry
accounts for just over a quarter, and transport and communication for
just under 12 per cent. Gas, electricity and water services exceed 11 per
cent. Agriculture, rather surprisingly, takes only 5 per cent, and mining

Gross Fixed Capital Formatio

	1938	1948	1949
Agriculture, Forestry and Fishing	27	90	85
Mining and Quarrying	18	30	35
Manufacturing		348	384
Building and Contracting	469	20	21
Distribution and Other Services*		113	130
Gas, Electricity and Water	143	138	168
Transport and Communication†	208	194	208
New Dwellings	474	342	327
Social Services	85	41	60
Other Public Services	101	44	48
Legal Fees, Stamps, etc.	34	46	47
	1,559	1,406	1,513

* Including road goods transport.

and quarrying less than 2½ per cent. The Social Services, including Health and Education, take rather more than 4 per cent. It is unfortunate that figures for the separate kinds of manufacturing industry are not available.

It will be seen that the proportion of gross fixed capital formation to gross national income has been slowly but continuously rising. If we take instead of fixed capital formation the larger figures of gross investment in all its forms, the percentages of gross national income become the following:

TABLE 77

Gross Investment as percentage of Gross National Income

1948	1949	1950	1951	1952	1953	1954
16·5	16·2	16·4	16·2	17·0	17·9	18·0

For 1938 gross capital formation was estimated at £845,000,000 out of a gross national income of £5,175,000—a proportion of roughly 16·0 per cent. Even if these figures are not entirely comparable with those of the post-war years, there seems to have been no great change in the proportion invested until 1952.

Stocks of Goods and Work in Progress. Finally, account has to be taken of changes in stocks and work in progress, in respect of both quantity and value.

ttry Groups at 1948 Prices (£million)

1950	1951	1952	1953	1954	Total 1948–1954	Per cent Total
79	74	61	63	65	557	5·0
31	30	37	47	61	271	2·4
427	438	416	417	422	2,852	25·5
22	27	32	32	40	194	1·7
147	132	110	128	146	906	8·1
182	181	178	194	217	1,258	11·3
198	172	158	199	201	1,330	11·9
315	318	388	491	497	2,678	24·0
69	71	74	76	76	467	4·2
52	51	51	57	59	362	3·2
48	51	41	37	42	312	2·8
1,570	1,545	1,546	1,741	1,826	11,187	100

† Excluding road goods transport.

TABLE 78

Changes in Stocks and Work in Progress 1948–54

(£million)

	1948	1949	1950	1951	1952	1953	1954
Increase or Decrease in Total Value	500	265	440	1,325	—	50	300
Value of Increase in Physical Assets	175	65	− 210	575	50	125	225
Stock Appreciation Value	325	200	650	750	− 50	− 75	75
Total Value of Stocks, etc.					7,200	7,500	

This last total of the value of stocks held and work in progress includes £1,792,000,000 for the metal and vehicle industries, about £900,000,000 for wholesale and £657,000,000 for retail distribution, £830,000,000 for agriculture and forestry, £592,000,000 for textile, leather and clothing, £447,000,000 for the food, drink and tobacco trades, £376,000,000 for government trading bodies, £206,000,000 for the chemical industries, £218,000,000 for government strategic stocks, £119,000,000 for electricity, gas and water services, £103,000,000 for mines and quarries, and about £1,260,000,000 for other industries and services.

It will be seen that movements of stocks are very unstable, in terms both of values and of physical quantities. The very large increase of the latter in 1951, accompanied by a sharp rise in the value of existing stocks, which had begun in 1950, stands out as a highly disturbing factor. It was of course closely connected with the great price changes, especially in raw materials, accompanying the Korean War (see p. 215).

CHAPTER EIGHT

CAPITAL

THERE is no reliable way of estimating the total amount of capital in existence in Great Britain at any particular time, though a very rough estimate of £30,000 million was made in 1945 in connection with the negotiations for a loan from the United States (see p. 194). The value of the assets belonging to individual persons is ascertained normally when they die, if they die leaving more than a very limited amount; and by comparing the value of estates passing at death from one year to another it is possible to get some idea of the rate at which the money value of property is rising or falling. But since 1946 estates of less than £2,000 in value have not been liable to estate duties, and particulars have ceased to be collected about them. In consequence of this change the number of estates on which death duties have been paid fell from 153,000 in 1938–9 to 69,000 in 1952–3, whereas the total yield of the duties rose from £77 million to £164 million. The comparison however tells us little; for the rates of duty had been altered substantially between the two dates.

Joint Stock Companies. The only other set of figures that even appears to throw any light on the total value of capital assets relates to the capital of joint stock companies. In 1938–9 there were in existence 149,000 companies with a total nominal paid-up share capital of rather more than £6,000 million. By 1954 the number of companies had risen to nearly 284,000 and their total capital to nearly £6,661 million. Thus, the number of companies had increased very greatly, and the total capital very little. This was partly because, whereas the process of converting private businesses into companies had continued at a rapid rate, a considerable section of the larger companies had been removed by nationalization from the company category and had been turned into public concerns—for example, in coal-mining, steel, various forms of transport, electricity and gas. The number of new companies registered was about the same in 1938 and in 1953, but rose in 1954. It had increased considerably in 1946 and 1947 and had then fallen back gradually to the pre-war level. The numbers of companies going out of existence were also much the same in 1938 and in 1953 and 1954.

These figures are, however, almost valueless as clues to the real amount of capital engaged in joint stock enterprises; for they represent not the real money value of the shares in question but the nominal value of these shares. Even in the case of newly issued shares this nominal value may not coincide with the real value, for shares can be issued at prices above or below the par value nominally assigned to them. In the case of shares already issued, the nominal bears no regular relation at all to the real value. If a company does well, the market value of its shares rises: if it does badly, the market value falls. Moreover, the price put on shares in the capital market is affected by changes in current rates of interest and in the value of money. Some companies, when they do well, issue bonus shares and thus alter their nominal capital so as to bring it into closer relation to the real value; but others do not. Some which do badly undergo reconstruction in which they write down their nominal capital to a lower figure: others do not. The nominal capital accordingly gives no clue to the real or market value of the capital.

Stock Market Values. In the case of most public companies an attempt to compute the real value can be made by taking account of the prices at which their shares are bought and sold in the stock markets. But of the 284,000 companies on the register in 1953 fewer than 11,500 were public companies whose shares could be freely bought and sold. The remainder were private companies with fewer than fifty shareholders, and their shares were marketable only under legal restrictions and were not quoted on the stock exchanges. It is true that the 11,500 public companies had a total nominal capital of nearly £4,200 million, as against a total of £2,473 million for the 272,000 private companies; but there is no way of discovering whether the two groups of nominal capital were or were not similarly related to the respective real values. We can only say that between 1945 and 1954 the average value of a representative sample of ordinary shares of public industrial companies increased by 31 per cent and that by January 1955 the increase was 54 per cent, practically the entire increase having taken place during 1953 and 1954, and most of it during 1954. In the case of preference shares there had been between 1945 and 1954 a fall in average value of about 20 per cent—a natural consequence of rising prices which reduced the value of fixed dividend returns. The average yield in income of ordinary shares had risen from 3·76 per cent in 1945 to 5·4 per cent in 1954, and on preference shares from 3·89 per cent to 4·84 per cent. None of these comparisons can be carried back to 1938.

We are therefore without the means of telling either what is the total real capital in existence at any particular date, or how it changes from one year to another. We can only take the estimated national income at one date and convert it into 'capital' by reckoning its capital value as equivalent to so many years of income, and then compare this total with that for another year, arrived at by the same method. This, however, clearly adds nothing to our knowledge derived from the figures of income.

Depreciation. In studying capital, then, it is necessary to get away from total figures and comparisons between them and to consider instead how holdings of particular kinds of capital have been changing. It is also possible, within broad limits, to estimate the extent of new capital accumulation in a particular year, but not so as to set against it the amount of depreciation of existing capital and so to arrive at any reliable estimate of the net increase in capital assets. For, though estimates can be made for depreciation of existing capital in certain forms, there is no way of estimating the extent to which capital assets are losing their value for other reasons.

Gross Capital Formation. As we saw in the preceding section, estimates of Gross Capital Formation are now presented annually in the Blue Book on National Income and Expenditure. According to these the total saving out of income, before allowing for depreciation and without taking account of any change in the value of stocks in hand, amounted in 1954 to £2,837 million. Of this, £701 million consisted of savings by individuals, £1,416 million of allocations to reserves by companies and public corporations, and £497 million of savings by government and local government authorities. Out of the savings by individuals the Government took £183 million in taxation. £2,452 million of the total took the form of formation of new fixed capital assets, made up of £434 million in individual investments, £709 million in company investment out of reserves, £537 million of investment by public corporations, £182 million of investment by the Government, and £590 million of investment by local authorities—a large part of it in new houses. A further £300 million represented increased value of stocks of goods and work in progress, and a further £160 million net overseas investment or acquisition of financial assets such as gold or dollars. As we saw (page 105) the total figure for gross investment in 1954 in all forms was £2,837 million—the highest figure so far reached. The comparable figures for previous years were as follows:

	£m.		£m.
1948	1,720	1952	2,348
1949	1,802	1953	2,647
1950	1,908	1954	2,837
1951	2,066		

In the earlier years individual, as distinct from corporate, savings made less than no contribution to this total, as taxes on capital exceeded individual savings: only from 1952 onwards did such savings make a significant positive contribution.

Net Capital Formation. I have made it clear that all the available figures refer to *gross* capital formation before provision has been made for depreciation of existing capital assets. It is unfortunately not possible to say how much needs to be deducted in order to arrive at a *net* total after allowing for depreciation. The Blue Book on National Income did formerly include certain figures relating to depreciation; but these did not cover all types of capital assets and included only the sums provided explicitly for depreciation in business accounts and allowed by the Inland Revenue for taxation purposes. They amounted to the following totals for the years for which figures are available:

Depreciation (mainly Incom

	1938	1946	1947
Professional Persons	1	3	4
Farmers (Vehicles and Machinery)	10	24	28
Sole Traders and Partnerships:			
(a) Initial Allowances	—	11	11
(b) Annual Allowances	13	19	34
Companies:			
(a) Initial Allowances	—	97	85
(b) Annual Allowances	142	148	206
Public Corporations	3	5	23
Central Government (Trading)	10	23	26
Local Authorities	8	14	18
Total	185	341	435

These figures are considerably lower than those which were given in earlier issues of the Blue Book up to 1951, when they were discontinued till 1954. In any event, whenever they have been estimated, a warning has been given that they must not be taken as representing total depreciation and obsolescence, and that it is not legitimate to deduct them from the estimates of gross capital formation for the purpose of arriving at a net figure for the real addition of capital in each year.

All that can be shown is what proportion of the current product has been devoted to either renewing or increasing the capital stock and has thus been withdrawn from current consumption. On this basis the figures shown in Table 80 (overleaf) are arrived at.

ances), 1938 and 1946–54 (£*million*)

1948	1949	1950	1951	1952	1953	1954
6	8	9	9	7	8	9
31	35	42	49	57	63	64
12	20	23	26	9	10	12
28	29	28	26	30	34	36
95	183	232	237	112	100	144
208	222	242	255	279	320	371
72	96	109	127	144	161	167
28	32	34	32	36	37	40
10	8	8	10	8	8	10
490	633	627	671	682	741	853

The main reason for the high percentage of capital formation in 1951 is that large additions were made to stocks of materials bought at very high prices after the onset of the Korean crisis.

TABLE 80

Proportion of National Product devoted to Gross Capital Formation, 1946–54

(£million)

	1946	1947	1948	1949	1950	1951	1952	1953	1954
(1) Gross National Product	8,783	9,364	10,379	11,099	11,666	12,785	13,861	14,805	15,718
(2) Consumers' Expenditure	7,178	7,934	8,505	8,906	9,405	10,104	10,570	11,168	11,854
(3) Public Expenditure on Goods and Services	2,291	1,743	1,761	1,977	2,067	2,439	2,893	3,083	3,099
(4) Gross Capital Formation									
(a) Fixed	905	1,173	1,406	1,552	1,678	1,851	2,039	2,305	2,452
(b) Increased value of stocks	−54	309	175	65	−210	573	50	125	225
(5) Total	851	1,482	1,581	1,617	1,468	2,424	2,089	2,130	2,677
5 as per cent of 1	9·7	15·8	15·2	14·6	12·6	19·0	15·1	14·4	17·0

CHAPTER NINE

THE PUBLIC SECTOR

SINCE 1945 there have been big developments in public ownership of essential industries and services. The State has taken over the Bank of England, the coal mines, the railways, the waterways, a large section of road transport, civil aviation, wireless communications, the supply of electricity and gas. The main part of the steel industry and a section of road transport have been first nationalized and then handed back—in the latter case only in part—to capitalist ownership and management. The local authorities have lost their electricity and gas undertakings to the State, but have greatly expanded their activities in house-ownership. The hospitals have become a public service, and most medical and dental practice has been brought under public auspices. The State has become in effect a great employer of labour, with millions of workers employed in the new public services.

The Public Corporations. The State, however, does not directly employ these workers or conduct the industries and services in which they are engaged. The parts of the economy that have been taken into public ownership have for the most part been entrusted to the care of what are called 'Public Corporations', which administer them under general directions given by Ministers and ultimately by the Government as a whole. These Corporations are appointed bodies: their members are chosen by the Ministers concerned. They do not—or are not supposed to—represent any particular interests: the choice is supposed to rest on their personal suitability for the jobs they have to do. There are, however, various provisions which oblige Ministers, in making the appointments, to consult bodies specially concerned and to include persons possessing certain special kinds of competence—for example, familiarity with labour problems. In practice, on all industrial Corporations there are members who were formerly Trade Union or Co-operative officials; but such persons, unless they hold only part-time positions on the Corporations, have to give up their official connections with the bodies for which they used to work. For example, Lord Citrine had to renounce his Trade Union office and Lord Rusholme to leave his post at the Co-operative Union. These severances were indeed unavoidable, unless the members of Public Corporations had been appointed only for a limited period, without the possibility of renewal. No man can give full-time service to each of two masters.

Forms of Public Management. There has been much debate on the question whether it was the right course to put the nationalized industries under Corporations of this type, rather than place them directly under a Minister, as is done in the case of the Post Office. The latter would have meant in practice administration by Civil Servants; for save by accident no Minister will be competent to manage a nationalized service, or can give the time needed in addition to carrying out his parliamentary duties. The third alternative would have been to hand over the administration not to Corporations appointed by Ministers on grounds of personal capacity but to representative bodies chosen by agencies having a special interest—for example, Trade Unions or professional institutions. Or, of course, there could have been Corporations of a mixed character—partly appointed and partly representative. Many Trade Unions, in urging nationalization, had demanded representation on the bodies that would be set up to administer the nationalized industries on the public behalf. It was largely Herbert Morrison's opposition that decided the Labour Party against any element of representation on the Public Corporations set up by the Labour Government after 1945. He argued forcibly that it was necessary for the administration to be in the hands of men who would consider exclusively the general interest and would have no special axe to grind, and that a man would be put in an impossible position if he were made responsible at one and the same time to two masters—the State and the particular body to which he owed his appointment.

The Question of Workers' Control. Against this view it was urged that the workers employed in industry had a democratic right to participate in controlling it. No one suggested that they had a claim to exclusive control as against the general body of consumers. But it was argued that either the control should be shared by representatives of producers and consumers, each group nominating some members, or the control function should be divided, so as to assign power in some matters to producers' representatives, while leaving others in the hands of the consumers or of the State. The latter would, in such an event, be the arbiters of policy, deciding in the general interest what the nationalized services should set out to do, while the producers' representatives would be responsible for the actual execution and day-to-day running, which are of closest concern to the workers employed.

The contests inside the Labour movement between the advocates of rival methods of nationalization were fought out mainly in the 1920s and early 1930s; and the advocates of Public Corporations without workers' representation carried the day in the Labour Party, though the Trade Unions remained doubtful. The controversy died down in the 'thirties, during the depression; and there had not been time for it to revive when the Labour Government came to power immediately after the war. The Morrison method was then applied almost without opposition, on the plea that only disinterested managers could be relied on to carry through the fundamental technical changes that were felt to be necessary. Workers' representation, it was urged, would mean working-class conservative opposition to economic change. Nor were the Trade Unions, satisfied with having a Labour Government in full power, inclined to oppose the methods which its leaders favoured. The National Coal Board was set up in the form which Mr. Morrison wanted; and with minor variations the same plan was followed as other industries and services were taken over. In the case of transport, in which the Labour Government hoped to bring about a co-ordination of competing services, the new high administrative authority was called a 'Commission' rather than a 'Board', and separate 'Executives' were established under it for Railways, London Transport, Road Passenger and Road Goods Transport, Docks and Waterways, and other special services. But the principle remained the same; nor was it affected when the Conservatives abolished the separate 'Executives' and put all the nationalized transport services directly under the Transport Commission. The only important deviation from the normal pattern was in the case of gas, which was put under a number of regional Boards co-ordinated by a national Gas Council representative of the regional bodies.

The Extent of Socialization. The total effect of these nationalization measures, in the industrial field, was to transfer to public employment more than two million workers, made up of the following groups (in terms of the numbers employed in May 1954):

TABLE 81
Numbers Employed in Nationalized Industries, 1954

Coal Mining	875,000
Electricity Supply	148,000
Gas Supply	382,000
Railways	529,000
Road Transport, Goods	178,000
Civil Aviation	29,000
Total	2,141,000

This total does not include Steel, which employs about 250,000 workers, but was not completely nationalized, or the Post Office, which was nationalized long ago. Nor does it include the 640,000 employees of the medical and dental services, the great majority of whom were incorporated in the National Health Service, or any of the 660,000 persons engaged in the teaching service. It also omits the 624,000 persons in the administrative service of the Central Government and the 751,000 similarly employed by local authorities. If these are included, the total number of persons in public employment comes to not far short of six millions—between a quarter and a third of the total number of persons employed. The armed forces and auxiliary services accounted in 1954 for a further 830,000. In industry proper, including transport but not communications, the 'public sector' accounts for about two millions out of nearly fourteen millions, or one-seventh.

These figures give some idea of the extent of socialization in the British economy to-day. With steel de-nationalized, there is no major manufacturing industry in public hands—only a few scattered groups, in arsenals and dockyards and in railway construction shops. But the industries taken over—mines, electricity, gas, and transport—are key industries, of vital importance to the entire economy.

The Public as Customer.   Apart from the industries and services that are under public operation there are a number in which the State and the local authorities play a vital part as principal customers. Building operations are carried on mainly by private firms—though a number of local authorities run their own 'direct labour' departments; but a large share in the industry's output is produced to public order—houses and public buildings, roads, bridges, and industrial buildings for the nationalized services. The metal and chemical trades are recipients of a great volume of public orders, especially for armaments. During and for a time after the war the range of government custom was much wider. Many foodstuffs were bought by government agencies, which re-sold them to the consumers; and there were immense military contracts for clothing and other supplies. Some of these types of public buying have disappeared and others have been much contracted as the wartime controls have been done away with. Government control of materials and man-power, and therewith of production, has been swept away over a wide field. Nevertheless, state intervention in industry remains much more pervasive than it was in 1939, largely because of the need to restrict imports and stimulate exports in order to safeguard the balance of payments. Agriculture in particular, under a continuing system of subsidies designed to stimulate high production, remains largely subject to government influence in deciding between alternative uses of the land.

The Financial Policies of Socialized Industry.   The general principle adopted for the nationalized industries was that they should be so conducted as to cover their costs out of revenue, not necessarily year by year, but taking one year with another. These industries were acquired by purchase from their previous owners, who were paid in stock bearing fixed rates of interest. The payment of this interest became a charge on each nationalized service, which was thus put in the position of making a 'loss' unless it was able to cover payment for the use of capital as well as running expenses out of its receipts; and in some cases there was a further requirement to pay back capital at a fixed rate out of current revenue. What is called a 'loss' on a nationalized industry is thus something essentially different from a loss incurred by a joint stock company, which has most of its working capital in the form of shares. Shareholders cannot be paid dividends except out of profits; and the company is not held to be losing unless it is unable to meet out of revenue the interest on its borrowed capital—debentures as distinct from shares. The compensation paid to the dispossessed owners of nationalized industries gave them a guaranteed in place of an uncertain and conditional return; and the new Public Corporations were faced with the necessity of earning a substantial profit if they were not to be regarded as making a 'loss'. If they do show a 'loss', in this special sense, it is carried forward against their future earnings, and they are under instruction to recover it from the public, if they can, by raising their charges or in any other way open to them.

Wages under Public Ownership. Many workers in the nationalized industries resent this situation, which they hold is used as an argument for keeping down wages. Although the Public Corporations are supposed to be responsible for their own labour relations and for fixing the wages and salaries of their staffs, in practice every big wage dispute in which they become involved brings in the Government as the finally responsible party. No Public Corporation could lock-out its employees without government support; and the Trade Unions concerned, if they fail to secure reasonable terms from the Corporation, will almost inevitably appeal for its 'last word' to the Government, with which the last 'last word' is bound to lie.

Financial Results of Public Ownership. The fortunes of the various Public Corporations in the matter of surpluses and losses are set forth in Table 82 (overleaf).

Thus, the combined financial results for the five groups showed losses up to 1951, but on a diminishing scale, and surpluses for 1952 and 1953, on a rising scale, followed by a serious decline in 1954. The fortunes of the different enterprises, however, have varied greatly. British Airways (including both B.O.A.C. and B.E.A.) have shown losses in every year except 1952, when the operating figures broke even. These 'losses' are of course partly due to the fact that the Corporations have to operate a number of uneconomic services and to adapt themselves to government requirements.

At the other end of the scale, the British (now Central) Electricity Authority has recorded substantial surpluses in all years, with a peak surplus of nearly £19 million in 1954. On a more modest scale, the Gas

TABLE 82

Financial Results of Nationalized Industries 1947–54

(£million. + = Surplus. − = Deficit)

	1947	1948	1949	1950	1951	1952	1953	1954
National Coal Board	−23·3	+1·7	+9·5	+8·3	−1·8	−8·2	+0·4	−3·8
Central Electricity Authority	—	+4·4	+7·2	+6·3	+2·9	+7·5	+13·2	+18·8*
Combined Gas Boards	—	±0	±0	+1·6	+1·4	+2·3	+2·1	+2·5
Transport Commission	—	−4·7	−20·8	−14·1	+0·1	+4·5	+4·2	−11·9
Combined British Airways (operating)			−9·7	−9·2	−5·5	±0	−1·1	+0·3
			−13·8	−7·1	−2·9	+6·1	+18·8	+5·9

* £10·5 million transferred to special reserve fund for renewals of plant.

Council has been able from 1950 onwards to report regular surpluses on the combined operations of the Regional Gas Boards.

The National Coal Board and the Transport Commission have had much more chequered careers. The N.C.B. after a big deficit in 1947 showed a small surplus for 1948 and larger surpluses for 1949 and 1950, only to meet with a renewal of 'losses' in 1951 and 1952 and then barely to square its accounts for 1953. For 1954 it showed a 'loss', due entirely to the high cost of imported coal, which, some think wrongly, is debited to the N.C.B.

The Transport Commission showed a 'loss' in 1948 and much heavier 'losses' for 1949 and 1950. It then appeared just to turn the corner in 1951 and did appreciably better in 1952 and 1953, but plunged back into a heavy 'loss' in 1954.

The figures here given mostly relate to financial years, not necessarily to calendar years. They have been entered under the years within which the greater part of their own financial year falls. It must be borne in mind that in most cases the word 'loss' is to be understood in the special sense already mentioned: it relates to the position after payment of interest on capital.

Where there are deficits on the working of these industries, they are carried forward to be met, if practicable, out of the surpluses of future years. Only British Airways have been in receipt of a direct subsidy from the Government, at the rate of £1·5 million a year. This was for-gone in 1952–3, when the operating account balanced.

Financial Considerations in Public Enterprise. Obviously, the surpluses and deficits of the nationalized industries are not to be judged as if they were the profits and losses of ordinary business concerns. The purpose of publicly operated industries is not to make all the profits they can, but to serve the public interest as well as possible while endeavouring to meet their costs, including interest charges, taking one year with another. Indeed, if a clear conflict arises between meeting costs and serving public needs, preference has to be given to adequacy of service. It has further to be borne in mind that both the coal mines and the railways were in very bad condition when they were taken over, and that the bodies responsible for them have usually not been able to raise their charges at the same time as their costs have risen. There has been a lag between rising costs and increased receipts; and this factor accounts for a substantial part of their difficulties. In the case of transport services there is the further handicap that the projected co-ordination of rail and road services has not in fact been carried through, and that the railways have suffered seriously as a result.

Replacement Reserves and Self-financing. Particular interest attaches to the Central Electricity Authority's decision to allocate more than half of its record surplus of 1954 to a special reserve fund, earmarked for meeting the high cost of replacing plant as it wears out or becomes obsolete, and to its declared intention of continuing this policy, as far as it can, in future years. The Authority's decision was based partly on the increasing cost of replacements under modern technical conditions, but also no doubt partly on the fear of being restricted in respect of capital borrowings in the open market. Lord Citrine, in announcing the new policy, added that it might be necessary to raise charges for electric current to a sufficient height to provide a substantial contribution for this purpose, and to endeavour to make the industry 'self-financing' to a greater extent than it has been hitherto. This, of course, is not a matter that concerns electricity alone. In all industries, whether publicly or privately owned, costs of capital renewals are rising, not only because of higher prices, but also because up-to-date equipment is more costly in real terms than that which it replaces. No doubt, the new plant is also as a rule more productive; but it is a question in what proportion the higher gross investment costs ought to be met by borrowing or out of gross profits. In privately owned industries, higher placings to profit reserves are demanded as means of footing more of the bill for gross investment; and in the same way the Central Electricity Authority is now treating a large part of its current surplus, not as a reserve to be set against possible future losses, but as a contribution to expected high capital costs in future years. The question has become much more urgent because of the 'credit squeeze' of 1955, which is forcing the C.E.A. to reduce its programme of rural electrification and to seek other means of economizing on current costs. Other Public Corporations are not in a position to follow its example by creating special reserves; for this can be done only when there is a surplus to be drawn upon. The C.E.A.'s action is nevertheless significant: it is a recognition of a long-term element in costs for which provision needs to be made in advance if the enterprise is to maintain its value. It is simply a particular aspect of the high investment needs of the British economy—needs which have been explained at a number of points in this volume (see especially p. 79).

Joint Consultation in Public Services. Although the principle of workers' representation on the Boards of the nationalized services has been rejected, the various Nationalization Acts contain provisions requiring the Boards to set up systems of joint consultation with their employees and the Trade Unions concerned. The machinery for this has been built up in each service both nationally and locally and at the workplace level. Each industry has devised its own system or, as in the case of the railways, has taken over and developed a system already in existence. On the whole, the methods of joint consultation that have been adopted—and the similar method used in the Post Office—appear to have worked reasonably well. They apply, not to wage-rates, which are dealt with by ordinary Trade Union bargaining with arbitration or reference to the Government as a last resort, but to conditions of work and service, including many matters that can be dealt with only at a local or workplace level. There is no great difference between these methods of consultation and those which have been instituted by a good many firms under private ownership; but they are applied generally and as a statutory right. They do not of course amount to any sort of 'workers' control' or meet the claim to participate in management of nationalized industries; for the responsible Boards have always the last word and are not obliged to accept the representations made by the workers' nominees.

The Effects of Public Ownership. How much difference has the socialization of a substantial fraction of the British economy made to the workers employed, to the consumers, and to the dispossessed owners of the capital assets transferred to public ownership? The State is under an obligation not to be a notably bad employer by current standards; but it does not recognize any obligation to pay better than the more advanced private firms. Direct comparison with such firms is not easy, because in the main the State has taken over entire industries, so that there are no private firms left in them to furnish a basis for comparison. Nor, under conditions of full employment, is it easy to estimate the advantage represented by the greater security which public employment as a rule confers. In the main, in respect of wages, hours, and other standard conditions, the Public Corporations have inherited the traditional structure of conditions established under private enterprise, but, in making changes after nationalization, have tended to level up rather than down where variations existed previously. In the case of the mineworkers, wages and conditions have been substantially improved; but it should be borne in mind that mining wages were abnormally low before nationalization and that without these improvements it would have been sheerly impossible to maintain an even barely adequate labour force. Railwaymen have complained again and again that the bad financial position of the railways has been made an excuse for paying unduly low wages; and despite recent advances this grievance has not been wholly removed. In general, wages in the public sector are not notably higher than in the most nearly comparable industries still under private ownership, as can be seen by studying the statistics given in the section on wages in this book (see pp. 223 ff.).

Nationalization and the Consumer. As for the consumers, it is even harder to say what the effects of public ownership have been. The special Consumers' Councils established to advise the Public Corporations have been almost entirely ineffective, as indeed they were bound to be unless they were equipped with their own independent expert staffs. The annual reports published by them are tenuous and jejune; and it is clearly not intended that they should exercise any real power. Protection of the consumers' interests, as far as it exists at all, is provided mainly by Parliament and by pressure of public opinion. Whenever a Public Corporation increases its prices there are complaints; but these are apt to come much more loudly from consuming industries than from the general public. Some critics have argued that basic industries such as coal-mining and railways, which affect the cost-structure of many industries as well as the private citizen's costs of living, ought to be run deliberately at a loss, and that the policy laid down in the Nationalization Acts of seeking to make each service pay its way is bad. It remains true, however, that even after recent price-increases coal is cheaper in Great Britain than in most other countries; and there is no evidence that the prices of other publicly owned services have been put unduly high in relation to working costs. The real question is whether enough has been done to bring costs down by the use of improved methods; and this is largely, though not entirely, a matter of the amount of capital expenditure on modernization of equipment. We have seen in a previous section the sums devoted to fixed capital formation in the main industries and services in recent years (see p. 73). These seem to indicate that an unduly low priority has been given so far to both mines and railways; but it has to be borne in mind that there has been an overall shortage of capital for economic development and that it has not been easy either to decide between rival claims or to increase the total investment at the cost of restricting current consumption. There are some who contend that out of the inadequate supply of new capital too much has been devoted to housing and too little to industry as a whole; but the housing shortage has been, and remains, acute, and any diversion of resources away from house-building would have been very unpopular. The Conservatives, who usually favour industrial investment, actually increased house-building when they returned to power; and it is not easy to suggest forms of investment that could properly have been cut in order to transfer capital resources to the public industrial sector. The plain fact is that capital investment as a whole has been unduly low largely as a consequence of the heavy expenditure on re-armament (see p. 306).

Compensation. As for the former owners of the socialized services, there has been some fall of income, coupled with greater security, as a result of the transfer to public ownership. It can, however, by no means be taken for granted that, if these services had remained in private hands, their owners would have continued to earn the profits earned in past years. Indeed, one reason for nationalizing both coal-mines and railways was that there seemed no chance of their being carried on at a level compatible with public need under private ownership: so that the dispossessed owners may well have fared better in their new status as bondholders than they could have done if they had been left to themselves. On the whole the terms of compensation appear to have been tolerably fair, even on the assumption that the capital-owner is entitled to a value equivalent to what is taken from him.

The Efficiency of Public Enterprise. Finally, there is the question of efficiency—that is, of the relative efficiency of public and private enterprise. It is, I think, equally absurd to contend either that all public enterprises are inefficient or that all are more efficient than large-scale capitalist businesses. Neither public nor private operation as such affords any guarantee of efficient management. In certain cases monopoly, whether public or private, makes possible productive economies that are unrealizable under competitive conditions; and in such cases the State, unlike the private monopolist, is unlikely to cancel these advantages by resorting to restrictive practices in order to increase profits beyond a reasonable level. There is no evidence that the ordinary worker works harder or less hard for a public than for a private employer—at any rate when the former is a Public Corporation such as the National Coal Board or the Transport Commission. The case for nationalization, at any rate of the type actually adopted since 1945, is not that it will induce the employees to work harder than before, but rather that it can be used to bring about better organization of production and to secure a better application of scarce capital resources to the more urgent tasks. Even if the Conservatives, instead of the Labour Party, had been in office after 1945, they could hardly have escaped the necessity of nationalizing, in some form, both the coal mines and the railways, and probably the gas and electricity services as well. At all events, they have shown since 1951 no desire to undo the work of their predecessors in these fields of enterprise.

The Future of Public Enterprise. There has been so far no opportunity of testing by experience the effects of nationalizing a major manufacturing industry. The experiment with steel was cut off abruptly before it had gone beyond a preliminary stage; and in no other branch of manufacture has the experiment been even attempted. The Labour Party, if and when it returns to power, seems likely to take over the major part of the chemical industry, and possibly others, as well as to reverse the denationalization of the main branches of iron and steel manufacture. It is, however, clear that even if these and some other industries can be taken over in much the same way as the services already in public hands, considerably different methods will be needed if it is decided to extend socialization over a much wider field, into branches of manufacture at present in the hands of numerous competing private firms. The methods suitable for this wider application of public ownership and management have not yet been at all fully worked out. The Labour Party, in its discussions with the leaders of the Co-operative Movement, has recognized Co-operative ownership as a satisfactory alternative form of social ownership, but has reached no decision concerning the extent to which it can, or should, be applied. Nor has it done much towards exploring other alternative forms of socialization.

In effect, what has happened is that public ownership has become securely established within the limited field to which it now applies, but that, even within the Labour Party and among its electoral supporters, enthusiasm for general nationalization, at any rate in its present form, has noticeably waned. This has come about largely as a consequence of full employment, which has both weakened anti-capitalist feeling and, by making capitalist profits more secure and easier to earn, enabled private businesses to offer improved conditions. While these circumstances continue, strong public pressure for extensive further schemes of nationalization is unlikely to make itself felt; for doctrinaire Collectivism is out of fashion, and outright Socialists provide only a small fraction of Labour's electoral support—or even of its leaders. These are plain facts, whether they are to be welcomed or not. They largely explain the very moderate emphasis on further nationalization in the Labour Party's programmes of recent years.

CHAPTER TEN

FUEL, POWER AND TRANSPORT

I T came, I think, as a great shock to many people that Great Britain ran short of coal during the war; and, even to-day, many of us are inclined to blame the National Coal Board for a continuing shortage which offends our sense of fitness. We have heard so often that British industrial supremacy has been based on coal; and we have been used in the past to having not merely enough of it for ourselves but a large surplus for export to other countries. To the layman, nothing in the 1930s suggested that we were at all likely to be faced before long with a scarcity of supplies. Were there not very many thousands of skilled miners eating their hearts out in unemployment, and very many pits producing a great deal less than the output for which they had been designed? The problem seemed to be one of surplus capacity, not of scarcity, actual or impending. Whatever we might run short of, coal seemed highly unlikely to be ungettable in quantities ample to meet our needs.

Coal in the 1930s. And yet the seeds of the present deficiency were being sown in those very years of 'redundant' capacity. The conditions of redundancy were discouraging young people from entering so depressed an industry, and capitalists from investing their money in it. Old pits were wearing out, and were not being replaced; and ageing pits were not being renovated by the provision of more up-to-date equipment. No doubt, progress was being made with mechanized haulage and mechanized coal-getting; and the newer pits in the better placed coalfields were doing tolerably well, even in the bad times. But, by and large, the coal industry was running down; and because, even so, it could easily provide all the output for which it could find markets, hardly anyone was bothering to do anything about its future. When war came, bringing with it both the need for more coal and a sharp reduction in the labour force for getting it, the effect was not that a national effort was made to put the industry into proper order; for that would have required both an increased labour force and a heavy capital investment that seemed impossible under war conditions. Instead of reorganization, what happened was a concentration on getting as much coal as could be got at once without new investment, by working the easiest seams to the fullest possible extent, at the price of making coal harder to get in the not distant future.

The Coal Question after the War. When the war ended, it was quite impracticable to hand the industry back to private operation. The colliery owners had not the capital needed for restoring it to health; nor had they any prospect of raising the money from the investing public. If they had been left to carry on as best they could, either there would have been a quite appalling shortage of coal as the high-cost pits were forced to close down or the price of coal would have risen to a crippling height for consumers so as to fit it to the needs of profit-making operations by the marginal concerns. But neither a sharp fall in supplies nor a sharp rise in coal prices could have been suffered without sheer disaster. The high-cost pits had to be kept at work because their output was needed until new pits could be constructed to replace them; and coal prices had to be kept to a level which would clearly not allow them to cover their costs. At the same time, costs had to be raised in order to prevent miners from flocking away to other jobs and to attract new recruits under the prevailing conditions of full employment. This made it indispensable to base prices on a pooling of costs over the entire industry; and the only workable way of achieving this, and of providing the resources needed for reorganization, was to make the mines public property and to bring them under unified public administration.

Thus, the coal mines were nationalized, not simply because the Labour Party won the General Election of 1945, but because they had to be, as a matter of sheer economic necessity. Nationalization, however, could not at all quickly repair the damage the industry had suffered, however efficiently the new administration did their job. It could not have done so, even if there had been more miners available and if there had been no difficulty in supplying all the capital that was needed or in turning the money supplied into actual new equipment. Sinking new pits—especially modern pits to get at deep-lying coal—is a lengthy business; and so is any substantial modernization of existing pits. The more easily got coals have been worked, and in many cases worked out, already. New supplies must come in the main either from thinner seams at high cost or from deep seams which can be reached only by heavy expenditure of capital. Moreover, work on modernizing existing pits, while it is going on, interferes with current production, and involves diversion of man-power from current coal-getting to work which will yield output only after a considerable interval.

The Coal Board's Problem. Accordingly the National Coal Board was faced, on 'vesting day', with a very intractable problem. More coal was urgently needed; but so was more immediately unproductive work designed to maintain and increase future supplies. There was also a call for new capital goods which the machinery-making industries were very ill-equipped to supply; for they had been used, both before and during the war, to a low level of demand for mining machinery, and many of the types of equipment most needed were not being made in Great Britain at all, or only on a very small scale. Despite the acute shortage of dollars, a good deal of machinery had to be bought from the United States, until home production had been given time to expand; and the claims of the coal industry, both for money capital and for the actual capital goods it needed, were keenly competitive with the claims of other industries and services and with the need to increase exports in order to improve the adverse balance of payments.

Coal Supplies since Vesting Day. Even if the National Coal Board had been all-wise—which it was not—acute coal shortage could not have been avoided. Under war conditions total output had fallen from 240 million tons in 1937 and 227 million in 1938 to less than 183 million in 1945. In 1946 output rose to nearly 189 million tons, including nearly 9 million tons of opencast coal; and in 1947—the first year of nationalization—it improved to 197½ million, of which 10¼ million were opencast. Thereafter, up to 1954, the yearly totals were as follows:

TABLE 83

Coal Supplies, 1947–54

(*million tons*)

	1947	1948	1949	1950	1951	1952	1953	1954
Mined	187·2	197·6	202·7	204·1	211·9	214·3	212·5	214·9
Opencast	10·3	11·8	12·5	12·2	11·0	12·2	11·7	10·1*
Total	197·5	209·5	215·2	216·3	222·9	226·5	224·2	225·0
Imports	0·7	0·1	—	—	1·2	0·3	0·6	3·0
Exports and Overseas Bunkers	5·5	16·3	19·4	17·1	11·7	15·1	16·9	16·3

* Exclusive of screening losses.

The supply of mined coal rose each year up to 1952 and again in 1954, after a decline in 1953. Opencast supplies were more erratic, reaching their peak in 1949; but in this case it should be borne in mind that screening losses were excluded from the total in 1954. Total supplies were highest in 1952, and only a little coal was imported that year; but since then imports have risen sharply, to 3 million tons in 1954 and to 5·7 million during the first half of 1955. In March and April, and again in June and July 1955, imports actually exceeded exports, and in June exports and bunkers combined. It will be seen that in 1954 mined output was nearly 28 million tons higher than in 1947, but that most of this improvement had occurred by 1951. The greatest difficulties of the Coal Board have been during the past three or four years: the greatest of all in 1955, when the Board had not only to meet rapidly rising costs of production but also to face an unprecedentedly big bill for the losses on imported coal resulting both from the large increase in imports and from much heavier freight charges, especially from the United States. There were many who held strongly that the Coal Board ought not to be required to bear the loss on imported coal, which accounts for a large part of its monetary deficit, and that this charge should be borne directly by the Exchequer. But, even if this were done, the seriousness of the situation would remain. What is needed is a large increase in home output, in order both to meet home needs and to provide a substantial surplus for export. Until this can be achieved the Government has decided that exports must be cut down as much as possible; but this involves serious dangers, as foreign countries which are suppliers of imports from Western Europe want British coal in exchange and may send their goods elsewhere if it is not forthcoming.

Coal and Atomic Power. The position, then, is serious. It has led already to considerable efforts to replace coal by oil. This, however, involves heavy investment in refining plant and cannot at most be more than a palliative. It has also, no doubt, influenced the Government's decision to embark on an extensive plan for the generation of fuel from atomic energy in place of coal. The projects announced in February 1955 involved an investment of £300 million over the next ten years in building twelve atomic power stations, of which the first two were intended to come into productive operation in 1961. In June 1955 it was announced that a further six stations were to be built. Costs per unit of power supplied seemed likely to be neither much higher nor much lower than those of generation based on coal; but future costs are of course extremely uncertain, and no one can tell whether the new source of power will prove in the long run to be cheaper or dearer than the old. Nor will the new projects go at best more than a little way towards supplementing coal-based supplies. The combined output of the 12 stations announced in February 1955 will only be equivalent to that of between 5 and 6 million tons of coal—only two or three per cent of total coal consumed. Thus, it seems quite improbable that in the near future nuclear energy can displace coal as the principal source of power, or that it will become less necessary to develop coal production to the fullest possible extent. We may be on the verge of a revolution in the sources of fuel supply that will utterly transform the world's economy; but this cannot happen very fast and it would be highly unwise to reckon on it till we are sure and know more about the comparative costs.

Capital Investment in the Coal Mines.   £300 million over ten years—or even £450 million, if we put the cost of each of the 6 additional stations at the same level as that of the first 12—is not a very large sum—only £30 million—or £45 million—a year. It compares with a gross investment in the coal industry which has totalled £284 million from 1948 to 1954, with a peak of £75 million in 1954 alone—and with a total fixed investment of more than £2,400 million in that year in the economy as a whole. It is far below investment in the development of electric power, which from 1948 to 1954 totalled £1,059 million and amounted to £211 million in 1954. Even in oil refining, the total investment from 1948 to 1954 has been £164 million. It seems clear that the coal industry will need rapidly increasing sums in the coming years if it is to meet the urgent needs of the economy. Each year the exhaustion of old pits involves a loss of output of from 3 to 4 million tons, which have to be made good by new developments. This largely explains the slow progress made by the Coal Board in expanding total output; for there has not yet been time for most of the larger schemes either of new sinkings or of re-development of existing collieries to come into operation. The other main difficulty is the shortage of man-power in the coal industry. Despite intensive efforts to recruit young workers and substantial improvements in wages and conditions of work, the Coal Board has been struggling all the time to maintain an adequate labour force. In 1938 the coal industry, then still badly depressed, had 782,000 wage-earners on its books. By 1946 it had fewer than 700,000, and after a rise to 724,000 in 1948 the number fell again below 700,000 in 1950 and 1951. It then recovered to 716,000 in 1952 and 717,000 in 1953, but fell again, on a slightly changed basis of reckoning, to 707,000 in 1954 and to 703,000 in July 1955. Actual employment, reduced by sickness, accident, strikes and other causes of absence, was much less. It too reached its peak in 1948, when it averaged 661,000: thence it fell to 626,000 in 1950, recovered to 647,000 in 1952, but again fell away, on a revised basis of enumeration, to 618,000 in 1954. From January to April 1955 it was rather better, averaging 638,000; but then it fell again into the summer decline. Meanwhile, output per manshift, which was 1·0 tons in 1945 and 1·03 in 1946, rose under the Board to 1·21 in 1951 and again in 1953, and reached 1·23 tons in 1954, when it was 3·26 for shifts worked at the coal-face as against 2·76 in 1946.

Refashioning the Coal Industry. In the light of these facts and figures, how much has the Coal Board been to blame for the coal shortage? There is certainly a good deal to be said on its behalf. It has increased both total output and output per shift despite the shortage of man-power and the need to divert workers from production to development work which interferes with it, and despite the fact that, with the exhaustion of the more easily worked coal, it has to operate under ever-increasing difficulties. It has done this despite the fact that its capital expenditure during the early years was far too low to allow the accumulated arrears of the 'thirties and of the war years to be overtaken, and also despite the fact that there has not yet been time for its major capital schemes to come into productive effect. As Mr. E. F. Schumacher pointed out in his remarkable address to the N.C.B. Summer School at Oxford in 1955, collieries can be divided for purpose of study into four groups—dying pits, pits scheduled to carry on without major reconstruction, pits scheduled to undergo such reconstruction, but not having yet completed it, and pits where reconstruction has already taken full effect. Of these four groups, between 1952 and 1954, the first showed a loss of output of 3·6 million tons, or nearly 15 per cent; the second increased output by nearly a million tons, or 1·2 per cent; the third increased output by a million tons, or 1 per cent; whereas in the fourth group the rise of nearly a million tons represented an increase of 10 per cent. Clearly reconstruction, where there has been time to complete it, is proving its value. The only criticism that can be made is that it is not proceeding fast enough. To this Mr. Schumacher replies that it is very difficult, for physical reasons, to speed up colliery construction or reconstruction, and that in any case the effect of more rapid capital development would be to reduce immediate output. This is not a complete answer; but it has considerable force at the present time. What can fairly be criticized is the low rate of capital development during the Board's first few years, which eased difficulties for the moment at the cost of adding to them in the longer run.

The Problem of Man-power. As for the man-power position, part of the problem is the high rate of wastage. In 1954 the total number of new entrants to the industry was 60,786 and the total loss of man-power 61,033. Of the entrants 20,363 were juveniles under 18, another 16,760 adults over 18 not previously employed in the mines, and 23,663 re-employments of workers who had been out of the industry. Of the losses, deaths and retirements accounted for 9,989, sickness and accident for 10,394, dismissals for 3,266, and other causes—mainly voluntary leaving for other kinds of employment—for 37,384. Despite improved wages, work in the mines was showing itself unattractive, not only, or even so much, to juvenile entrants as to those who had already entered it, but could easily, under conditions of full employment, leave it for less onerous and irksome jobs. The situation was very different in the 'thirties, when recruitment and continuance were alike maintained by the difficulties of finding work elsewhere. It is even doubtful how much effect further improvements in wages and conditions would have on the coal industry's ability to get and keep an adequate working force. Mechanization may make the physical toil less; but it adds greatly to noise, and many of the older miners dislike it. The young ones may for the most part mind it less; but it is a very long-term problem indeed to bring about general changes in the amenities of work in the mines, and it seems pretty certain that it will continue to be unattractive for a long time to come in the majority of pits, whatever efforts may be made to improve matters. Perhaps, in the long run, the increase in mechanization will so reduce the numbers of miners needed as to bring demand into balance with supply. But that is a long way ahead, and may not occur at all if the distaste for mining grows stronger. In that event, there will be no alternative to further improvements in wages and other conditions large enough to increase supply to the required extent. This, however, raises a further difficulty. Probably most miners would prefer shorter working shifts, no Saturday work, and longer paid holidays to more money. Indeed, the National Union of Mineworkers is already making just these claims. But to grant them would mean a fall in output which could not be speedily made good. Some day, all these claims will clearly have to be met. The only real question is, How soon?

Training for Management. The Fleck Report of 1955 on the operation of the coal industry under public ownership was strongly critical of the Coal Board's organization and methods of work, particularly in the field of labour relations, but also on account of the failure of its members to work together effectively as a team. To say that the difficulties now facing the industry are largely not the Board's fault is by no means to exonerate it altogether. It is however at least doubtful whether the Fleck Report was right in urging that the coal industry ought to be run in most respects in the same way as a privately owned large-scale business. Nor did the Report wholly maintain this; for it insisted that the coal industry must in future make provision for the training of its own administrators right up to the highest levels, and put stress on the need for intensified development of such training. This, to a substantial extent, the Board has actually been trying to do with its 'Ladder Plan', designed to open opportunities for promotion to those in its employment. It is clearly one important function of any industry which becomes a huge mono-polist employer to ensure such opportunities and to see that full advantage is taken of them. A management recruited at every level, up to the highest, from within the industry, on a foundation of really democratic opportunity to acquire the requisite qualifications, is the only possible foundation for good human relations in all its parts. It is not, however, a guarantee of such relations; for men who have risen from the ranks are often highly unsympathetic to those who have failed to rise, and in the coal industry in particular there is a very long tradi-tion of bad human relations to be overcome. Despite nationalization and the elimination of private profit, the ordinary miner is still highly suspicious of 'management' and disposed to resent the increase in technical and administrative staff which is a necessary consequence of more scientific methods of mining and management. This attitude will take a long time to change; nor will it change of itself, or without a real alteration in the attitude of the managers themselves. Employment in a publicly owned industry should be radically different from employment even by a good capitalist firm. It should involve a real partnership in control—not merely a consultation which means something or nothing according to the spirit in which it is worked. Real partnership involves real responsibility, which at present neither is management ready to concede, nor labour to accept. That, however, is a problem not for coal mining alone, but for nationalized services as a whole. Something has been said of it already in the preceding section.

The Prospective Demand for Coal. Coal, at present, is the source of nine-tenths of the power used in Great Britain, including of course the coal used in generating gas and electricity, and to a small extent, oil fuel. Even if the use of atomic power develops fast, it is unlikely for a long time to do so fast enough to prevent the rising total demand for power from requiring more rather than less production of coal. In 1954 gas and electricity undertakings used between them 1,287,000 tons of coal a week, as against about 14,000 tons of oil. Nor does hydro-electricity provide more than a tiny fraction of the total supply of current.

Oil as a Source of Power. This, of course, does not mean that oil is not a very important source of power. Imports of crude petroleum have increased from 568 million gallons in 1938 to 7,267 million gallons in 1954, whereas imports of refined petroleum have fallen from 2,636 million gallons to 1,759 million, the decline in refined imports being due largely to the big expansion in home refining capacity since the Persian supplies were cut off. The shift to crude imports has of course affected the cost of imported supplies, which nevertheless increased from £47 million in 1938 to £312 million in 1954—between six and seven times as great, as against a less than threefold increase in quantity. This high cost is a notable anomaly. The major part of British and of West European—oil supplies now come from the Middle East, where the cost of production is very low. In 1952 it was only about 35 cents a barrel as against a selling price of $1.75. But the price is regulated by the eight huge concerns—mainly American and British—which control most of the supply so as to equal the cost of crude petroleum in the Gulf of Texas, less costs of transport thither and also less the American protective duty. The American costs being many times as high as those of the Middle East, the companies operating in the latter region make colossal profits, which they share, mainly on a 50/50 basis, with the rulers of the Middle Eastern States. Thus Great Britain pays a grossly inflated price for its supplies—a fact which has been brought out recently in a special report on petroleum prices in Europe prepared by the United Nations Economic Commission for Europe. The American oil interests, fearful of the effects of free competition on home production of crude petroleum, are strongly opposed to bringing down prices in the Middle East; and the high prices also suit the British oil interests, though not the consumers. They also, of course, suit very nicely the Middle Eastern rulers, to whom they bring immense revenues. There are thus very powerful forces ranged against any attempt to bring this singular instance of monopoly pricing to an end. In the negotiations with the Persian Government, which have led to a partial re-opening of the Persian oilfields, the British and American oil companies acted together; and they are now partners in the marketing and refining of the Persian supplies. The British Government is itself the major shareholder in the British (formerly Anglo-Iranian) Petroleum Company; but it does not appear disposed to take any action that would involve it in a dispute with the American oil companies; and accordingly the anomaly remains.

Electricity.   Electricity provides each year a growing proportion of the total supply of energy. Current generated by authorized undertakings, excluding generating stations owned by transport concerns, has risen from 24,372 million units (KWH) in 1938 to 72,920 million in 1954, and coal and coke used from 15 to nearly 40 million tons. There has been heavy investment in power stations (see p. 109), totalling £1,059 million from 1948 to 1954. The Central Electricity Authority, unlike the Coal Board, has been able to work at a clear profit, after meeting interest charges, and has shown a net surplus of £41½ million up to 1954. In 1954 the C.E.A. announced its intention of raising its generating capacity by 50 per cent over the next six years, and estimated its further capital requirements up to 1959 at not less than £1,275 million, of which it proposed to provide about £375 million out of its own resources. This was before the Government announced its plans for the building of atomic power stations, which are intended to be under the management of the C.E.A.

Gas.   The production of gas has also expanded, though less fast than that of electric current. Production in 1938 averaged weekly 6,700 million cubic feet, and in 1954 11,290 million, including gas bought by gasworks from coke-ovens and other sources, but not other coke-oven or producer gas. The gas industry used in 1954 rather over 27 million tons of coal and about 525,000 tons of oil fuel. Like electricity, the gas industry has shown a surplus after meeting interest charges, but on a more modest scale. Up to 1955 its accumulated surplus amounted to £11 million, which was probably no more than barely enough to meet the high and rising cost of impending capital renewals.

The Fuel Outlook.   In sum, the fuel and power problem of Great Britain is essentially still that of coal—both of getting enough and of continuing to get it at reasonable cost. The prospect of atomic power ousting coal from its dominant position is still remote and problematical. It may, as some hope and believe, become the means of abolishing want over all the world; or, remaining the monopoly of the richest countries, it may widen instead of narrowing the gap between them and the less advanced. Short of ending poverty it may become the means of rescuing mankind from the disastrous consequences of having squandered the natural resources of fuel on which its very existence at present depends. In conjunction with the development of electronics and automatic factory control it may, one fine day, make human labour a drug in the market—with what consequences to social structure who will dare to predict? It may—or it may not: whether or no, its large-scale development and diffusion will take time; and for a substantial time to come the economic life of Great Britain will continue to depend on coal and on the power to get it at costs that will not price British exports out of the world market. Accordingly, there is no room at all for regarding the advent of atomic power as exempting us from doing everything that can be done to lift the coal industry out of its pressing difficulties, both by enabling it to attract and hold the labour force it needs and by supplying it with the capital without which it cannot be expected to do its work efficiently.

The Problems of Transport: Road and Rail.   The problems of transport are closely related to those of fuel because transport services are heavy fuel consumers. Aviation, both civil and military, and road transport alike depend upon oil: railways on coal either directly or as the main source of electricity: shipping on both coal and oil. These, except railways, are all expanding services; and even railways, though they are shedding branch lines and losing goods traffic to the roads, remain the essential carriers of heavy materials and of a high proportion of the total volume of goods transported by land. We have seen in the preceding section (see p. 124) the financial difficulties that beset the nationalized railway service in face of road competition, mainly in the form of transportation by producers' and traders' own vehicles rather than from the separate road transport industry; and we shall have something to say later (see p. 362) about the problems of traffic congestion in relation to town and country planning and about the growth of private motoring during the past two or three years.

The problem, baldly stated, is this. How can we, without killing or maiming an altogether excessive number of persons, best arrange for the convenient and economical transport of the passengers and goods that require to be moved from one place to another? Can this be done best by allowing the different kinds of transport agency to compete freely one with another, subject only to such regulations as are necessary in order to keep down accidents and limit extreme congestion?

Or does the situation demand such co-ordination of some or all of the transport services as will considerably restrict the consumers' choice in the interest of cheaper and speedier movement? I have omitted shipping from this summary statement of the problem because the questions which arise in connection with it are for the most part different from those affecting inland transport, though of course coastwise shipping, on its small scale, belongs rather with the inland services.

In arranging for the nationalization of a large part of the inland transport services the Labour Government recognized the need for some measure of co-ordination by making them all subject to a single Transport Commission; but this Commission was set up not as a managing but as a supervisory authority, and each service was put into the hands of a separate Executive and was in effect administered quite apart. This arrangement has since been altered by sweeping away the separate Executives and giving the Transport Commission much greater authority to control the subordinate administrations of the various services. But, as against this, a part of the original plan—nationalization of public passenger transport by road—has for the most part never been put into effect, and a sector of the road goods transport service—but by no means the whole of what was taken over—has been handed back to private enterprise. Moreover, the sector of road goods transport that was left unaffected by nationalization—the carriage of their own goods in their own vehicles by producing or commercial firms—has been growing most rapidly of all and has become responsible for the most intractable problems of road congestion.

The Railways.   Take first the railway problem. The total number of passenger journeys on the British railways, excluding the London Transport undertaking, has fallen from 1,237 million in 1938 to 991 million in 1954. Of these totals, however, 77·8 million only were at full fares in 1938, as against 253 million in 1954, largely because cheap monthly return tickets ceased to be issued in May 1952. Average receipts per journey, of all types, rose from about $11\frac{1}{2}d$. in 1938 to about $2s. 3\frac{1}{4}d$. in 1954. The total of freight traffic, in tons carried, rose only from 5·1 million tons weekly in 1938 to 5·44 million in 1954; but the rise in ton-miles was much greater, from 320 million weekly to 424 million. Coal and coke, which accounted for nearly half the total, showed similar variations, and so did general merchandise and also mineral traffic. Average hauls were thus longer than before the war because of the loss of more short-distance traffic to the roads. They rose from under 60 to about 74 miles. Average receipts per ton-mile increased from $1\frac{1}{2}d$. to $2\frac{3}{4}d$.

The Transport Commission as a whole, we have seen, incurred a serious deficit in 1954, after showing surpluses, over and above interest charges, in 1952 and 1953. For the railways alone, excluding railway operated road services, net traffic receipts, before paying interest, but after provision for maintenance and renewals, fell from £35 million in 1953 to £16½ million in 1954. Total interest charges falling on the Commission in respect of all its services amounted in 1954 to £52·4 million as compared with £50·4 million the previous year; and there were additional charges of nearly £3 million in each year for redemption of capital, calculated at 3 per cent to replace the money value of the stock issued in compensation to the railway companies over a period of 90 years. Over the entire period since the various services were taken over the Transport Commission had accumulated by the end of 1954 a total deficit of over £39 million; but the proportion of this attributable to the railways cannot be exactly stated. Apart from interest and redemption charges, railway traffic accounted for 66 per cent of the Commission's total receipts, and for 67 per cent of its total working expenses. Of the working expenses attributable to railway traffic—£419 million in all —£171 million, or 41 per cent, were for maintenance and renewals of rolling stock, permanent way and buildings, as compared with £141 million, or 34 per cent, for train operation and £94 million, or 22 per cent, for other traffic expenses, leaving a residue of rather more than £12½ million, or 3 per cent, for general railway expenses. Maintenance costs were thus very high, even apart from major schemes of development or reconstruction. Most of the capital investment in British Railways since 1948 (see p. 108) has gone into maintenance and renewals rather than into new developments. Only towards the end of 1954 did the Transport Commission, which is now the responsible authority, issue its plan for the modernization of the railway service, at an estimated cost of £1,200 million; and even this is no more than a first instalment of what is needed to bring the system as a whole thoroughly up to date.

The Railway Development Plan.   What most struck the general public when this plan was announced was the sentence of extinction passed on the steam locomotive. It will take a long time to replace the existing 19,000 steam locomotives by the new Diesel and electric types, of which many fewer will be needed; but it is now clear that the familiar and traditional 'steam-engine' is on the way out, after more than a century of outstanding success. It is to be discarded because, though it is relatively cheap to build, it is a heavy consumer of high-cost fuel and has very high maintenance costs and is often out of service as soon as it begins to get old—and also because it is a great spreader of dirt and uses a great deal of skilled man-power. Various kinds of Diesel engine will largely take its place; for though electrification is to be extended, the present plan includes only one or at most two major projects of main-line electrification—from Euston to Birmingham, Manchester and Liverpool and/or from King's Cross to Leeds. There are also lesser electrification projects, mainly in the South-East and perhaps on Clydeside; but for the present most of the railway track will continue to be operated by other means. The capital cost of conversion is too high except where traffic is very dense: what will happen later will depend on how the railways fare in their competition with the roads and on the total volume of traffic, as well as on relative costs of construction and operation.

No less important than the impending change in the means of locomotion is the more complete revolution contemplated in the freight-wagon. The very low speed of most railway freight trains is due largely to the fact that 85 per cent of all the wagons now in use have no continuous power brakes and therefore depend on the braking power of the engine. As speedily as possible all these out-of-date wagons are to be replaced: they are largely a legacy from the period when most wagons were privately owned by coal and other concerns. The change will make it possible, by speeding up freight trains, not only to ensure speedier delivery of consignments but also to run more other traffic over the lines with a great deal less delay, thus reducing both costs and time taken for passengers as well as goods.

A further essential part of the modernization plan is the improvement of stations, marshalling yards, and permanent way. In this last there will be no comprehensive change. The old lines will stay except for the closing of uneconomic branch lines; but a good deal will be spent on cutting out particularly bad obstructions. Passenger stations are in very many cases obsolete and need complete re-planning; and this is even more the case with goods terminals and marshalling yards, which are mainly a legacy from the days of many separate railway companies and were for the most part planned to suit conditions utterly different from those which now exist. A very large part of the cost of transporting freight on the railways consists not of the cost of running the ton-miles required but of time and equipment spent on shunting, transhipment, and sorting out, with all the burden of clerical work these manoeuvrings involve. The power of the railways to compete with the roads as carriers of general merchandise depends on drastic cutting of these costs; and this is impracticable without major reconstruction. Other possibilities are appearing with the development of new methods of signalling and of automatic train-control by electronic devices; but these for the most part fall outside the range of the 1954 plan.

The Problem of Equipment.   One big problem raised by the plan is that of getting the supplies of new equipment which it requires. The railways' existing construction and repair shops have great traditions in the building and maintenance of steam-locomotives and other rolling stock, and will need to shift over to the new types and considerably to adapt their methods and equipment. This they should be able to do,

but not without making large demands on the heavy engineering industries, whose services are also in great demand elsewhere, both for
exports and for home capital projects. The pace at which the railways
can be economically transformed is substantially governed not only by
their rivalry with other forms of investment for the money they require,
but also by the competitive nature of their demand for actual capital
goods. Reduced expenditure on armaments would do much to lessen
this strain; and, in the longer run, the effect of expanding and modernizing railway engineering might well be a recovery of world leadership
in this field, leading to a big expansion of export trade.

Rail Charges.   Freight accounts for nearly three-quarters of the total
annual turnover of British Railways, and passenger traffic for not much
more than a quarter. It is therefore even more on success in holding, or
even re-capturing, freight traffic than on attracting more passengers
that the solvency of the system depends. But of course both are needed;
and it is especially important for the railways to develop efficiently their
suburban passenger services, which are most threatened by road transport, public and private. In respect of freight, there is no road threat to
the bulk of the heavy traffic, which, in the form of coal, coke and
minerals only, accounts for as much revenue as all other freight combined. The loss of freight traffic has been in general merchandise and in
parcels; and in this field the great question is whether road and rail
are to continue, as they have done so far for the most part under
nationalization, as competing services or are to be somehow co-ordinated in the hope of reducing total costs. Under the Transport Act of
1953 the railways have obtained much greater freedom than they have
had in the past to fix their own charges, subject to certain maxima, as
suits them best, and to adopt flexible rates which were formerly excluded as involving discrimination. This, however, only improves their
power to compete: it does nothing of itself to reduce total costs. When
the main inland transport services were nationalized, there were many
who hoped that this would lead to a system of uniform charges for
carrying goods from one place to another, the method of transport
being left to a combined rail-road service to determine on grounds of
relative cost. But nothing of the sort occurred, even while British Road
Services were operating as universal carriers for those who did not
transport their own goods in their own vehicles.

British Road Services.   Indeed, really effective co-ordination was
hardly practicable in face of the rapid increase in 'C Licence' traffic
competing with both British Railways and B.R.S. It is true that the railways did something to develop their own auxiliary road services; but
in 1954 these brought in a gross revenue of little more than £12 million
—with an operating deficit of nearly £2 million—as compared with a
B.R.S. revenue of £72·7 million, yielding a surplus of £8·7 million. This

latter was a fall from over £80 million of receipts the previous year, resulting from the partial denationalization of B.R.S. The Conservatives having now abandoned their attempt entirely to disband B.R.S. and to hand the whole road goods service back to private enterprise, the Transport Commission will continue to operate a considerable road fleet in conjunction with the railway service; but it is still quite uncertain how far it will make an attempt to co-ordinate the two. It can indeed do but little in this respect, now that the scope of B.R.S. has been substantially reduced and commercial road competition restored over a part of the field. B.R.S.'s stock of motor vehicles fell from 35,849 at the end of 1953 to 25,442 a year later, nearly 10,000 having been sold under the Transport Act; and in addition 1,093 vehicles were discarded from service as against 648 new vehicles acquired. B.R.S. remains a substantial enterprise, mainly in the field of long-distance haulage; but it is now only a small provider in relation to the total number of goods vehicles on the roads, which was nearly a million at the annual census of 1954, exclusive of 45,000 agricultural vans and lorries.

It has been estimated, on the basis of a sample survey made in 1952 by the Ministry of Transport, that at that time about 900 million tons of traffic in all were being carried by road, as compared with 300 million tons by rail. Of the road traffic, 540 million tons were being carried by holders of 'C Licences', which accounted for three-quarters of the total of miles run and for 54 per cent of total ton-mileage. About 90 million out of the 900 million tons travelled by road for upwards of 40 miles; and this included a growing amount of heavy goods, such as specialized plant and machines, largely carried by firms owning their own lorries. But of course the major part of the 'C Licence' traffic consisted of loads of various kinds of branded and proprietary consumers' goods.

The Growth of Road Traffic.   Road goods vehicles, however, number less than one-fifth of the total number of mechanically propelled vehicles using the roads. At the census of 1954 these totalled 5,775,000, and of them 3,100,000 were private cars and 1,139,000 motor-cycles or tricycles. There were 110,000 public passenger vehicles, including taxi-cabs, and 346,000 agricultural tractors and engines, 18,000 ambulances and fire-engines, and a residue of 28,000 other motor vehicles. By far the greatest rate of increase was in private cars, of which new registrations more than doubled—from 188,000 to 387,000—between 1952 and 1954, whereas new registrations of goods vehicles rose only from 7,181 to 9,453 and those of public passenger vehicles from 5,388 to 5,544. But of course the goods and public passenger vehicles were on the average much bigger than the private cars and caused road congestion out of proportion to their numbers. As compared with 1938, the total number of motor vehicles had risen in 1954 by 87 per cent, private cars by 60 per cent, public passenger vehicles by 14 per cent, road goods vehicles by

105 per cent, and motor-cycles and tricycles by 147 per cent. The roads, as we shall see (see p. 362), had undergone no adaptation to fit them for taking this increase in use.

Other Services under the Transport Commission.   The remaining inland services operated by the Transport Commission are certain provincial and Scottish road passenger services, the road and rail services of London Transport, the docks, wharves and harbours, and the inland waterways. The first two of these, with receipts of £51·3 million and £70·5 million in 1954, both showed operating surpluses, of £5 million and £2·3 million respectively. The docks, wharves and harbours owned by the Commission, with receipts of £18·5 million, also showed an operating surplus, of more than £2·5 million. The waterways, with receipts of less than £1 million, showed an operating deficit of £80,000. In many of the motor bus companies the Transport Commission had only a minority holding, rising in some cases to one-half; but in other cases, including the big Tilling Group and the Scottish Group, it was the sole owner; and the figures cited above refer only to these concerns. Road passenger transport is indeed still at a halfway stage between public and private enterprise, and seems likely to remain so for the present. London Transport, on the other hand, was already for the most part nationalized before the war, and has retained larger powers than other services subject to the Transport Commission since the reorganization of 1953. It is undeniably a highly efficient service, as far as the roads allow it to be so. The major part of its receipts—£49·5 million out of £68 million in 1954—come from road services; but its rail services provided nearly half of its operating surplus in 1954, and in 1953 its road services showed a small operating deficit. In the case of docks and harbours, the Transport Commission is again only one operating agency among a number, and has in the main inherited the docks that were previously under railway control. It has no footing in London, Liverpool, Manchester, or a number of other big ports: its largest dock enterprises, in terms of length of quays, are at Hull, Swansea, Cardiff, Southampton and Grimsby. Nor does it control the major Scottish ports. Its power to improve port conditions is therefore limited; and in fact progress has been relatively slow.

The Future of the Canals.   As for the inland waterways, which now carry only about 13 million tons of goods a year, most of the existing mileage is definitely uneconomic, though some canals can still work at a fair operating profit. In April 1955 a Board of three members, chaired by Lord Rusholme of the Transport Commission and set up by that body a year earlier, presented a report in which they urged that 771 miles of waterway should be closed as of no commercial value, that 994 miles should be maintained at an adequate standard of efficiency for the present—though some of these might need to be closed later—and that only 336 miles, which are already carrying a considerable traffic, should be developed and modernized. The Board also recommended that the Caledonian and Crinan Canals and a number more in Scotland—all of them uneconomic—should be handed over by the Transport Commission to the Secretary of State for Scotland and, in effect, no longer regarded as commercial concerns. This report provoked an outcry from the 'canal-fanciers' organized in the Inland Waterways Association; but it is difficult to see how the Board could have reached, in general, any other decision. The trouble with a large part of the canals is that they are too narrow to take craft which can operate economically, and that the costs and difficulties of general widening would be prohibitive. Moreover, some of the essential canal links have gone out of use already, and could hardly be restored. The canals scheduled for restoration include most of the main network in the Midlands, Lancashire and Yorkshire, with the exception of the southern section of the Oxford Canal and some in the East Midlands; but most of these are to be only maintained, and not re-developed. The principal re-developments are planned for Yorkshire, from Leeds and Sheffield to the Humber or the Trent—for the Gloucester to Stourport route, the Nottingham–Trent route, and in the area north of London. These are all existing *broad* canals, capable of taking the bigger barges now regarded as essential; whereas the canals of the West Midlands and those linking London and the South to the Midlands and the North are all narrow and could be modernized only at an immense cost. The wish to do more than the report proposes is understandable, but mainly sentimental. It could not be satisfied except by diverting scarce capital from much more pressing projects. Within fairly narrow limits, the canals can continue to play a useful part: as a major factor in inland transport, they have had their day; and it has been a long day, as most of them were built between 1760 and 1830 at latest. If more than one-third of them must now be retired from economic use, that is no good reason why many of them should not continue, at quite low maintenance costs, to beautify the countryside and to serve as amenities for the canoe-lover and the fisherman. Clearly, however, it is not the business of the Transport Commission to maintain them for such uses as these.

Shipping. Shipping, except a section of coastwise shipping, was unaffected by the nationalization measures of the later 'forties. It remains a privately owned industry, mainly in the hands of big companies. Even in 1954 the British merchant fleet, exclusive of tankers, had not quite regained its pre-war size. Taking only vessels of more than 1,600 gross tons, the 13 million gross tons of 1938 were down to 12·4 million tons in the middle of 1955, and the smaller vessels from 783,000 to about 580,000. Gross tanker tonnage, on the other hand, had risen from just over 3 million tons to well over 5 million, making a total rise from 16·3 million to well over 18 million. These figures exclude tonnage registered in Commonwealth countries, other than Great Britain, which has increased considerably since before the war—from 1,231,000 gross tons in 1939 to 1,944,000 at the end of 1953. Total entrances and clearances in overseas trade were both rather smaller, in net tons, in 1954 than in 1938; but entrances with cargo were up and entrances in ballast down, whereas clearances with cargo were down, and clearances in ballast up. The 1954 figures were, however, much bigger than those of any previous post-war year. Here are the actual figures for 1938 and onwards from 1945.

TABLE 84
Shipping Clearances, 1938 and 1945–54
(in millions of net tons)

	1938	1945	1946	1947	1948	1949	1950	1951	1952	1953	1954
Entrances:											
With Cargo	68·4	28·9	33·9	42·7	50·6	54·9	57·5	63·6	64·2	69·4	71·4
In Ballast	23·5	26·7	16·4	11·6	12·8	12·2	13·7	14·7	17·4	17·9	18·2
Total	91·9	55·6	50·4	54·4	63·4	67·1	71·2	78·3	81·6	87·3	89·6
Clearances:											
With Cargo	58·9	13·4	21·1	24·0	35·8	41·5	45·3	43·6	47·0	50·2	50·2
In Ballast	33·3	42·4	30·3	30·7	28·6	26·1	27·0	34·9	35·1	37·4	39·9
Total	92·2	55·8	51·5	54·7	64·4	67·7	72·2	78·5	82·1	87·6	90·1

Shipping freight rates fluctuate greatly, even over short periods. The Chamber of Shipping's index for tramp shipping on voyage charter, based on the average rates of 1948, fell by more than 30 per cent by October 1949 and was still more than 25 per cent down in June 1950. Then it began to rise steeply, and in May 1951 was at more than twice the rate of 1948. It then fell, but rose again to 90 per cent above 1948 in October 1951. Thereafter it declined sharply, and by June 1952 was actually 1 per cent lower than in 1948, and in August 20 per cent lower. By the end of the year it was back at the June level. A new index, with different weighting, based on the 1952 average, was then introduced, and for 1953 this showed an average fall of 22·5 per cent below 1952. In June 1954 it was at about the same level as the 1953 average. Time-charter rates showed similarly large movements, falling from 184 in January 1952 (1952 average = 100) to 54 in December, averaging only 60·6 in 1953 and 64·2 in June 1954. These figures are of course greatly affected by the price-boom of 1950–1, arising out of the Korean war scare, which I have needed to mention so often in this book. By the middle of 1955 there had been another sensational rise. Voyage charter rates, which had averaged 14 per cent below the 1952 average in 1954, had risen to 30 per cent above it, and time-charter rates were at 146 as compared with the 1954 average of 71·7. Shipping, in effect, was enjoying a boom only less sensational than that of 1951.

Civil Aviation. I come finally to civil aviation. Something was said in the preceding chapter about the nationalized air corporations— B.O.A.C. and B.E.A. Here what concerns us is civil aviation as a whole, or rather all scheduled services conducted by British air-lines, but not services operated by foreign lines to or from Great Britain. For all such services, the mileage flown by civil aircraft was nearer five than four times greater in 1954 than in 1938: the number of passengers carried had risen more than tenfold and the tonnage of freight carried twenty-fivefold. Passenger miles had increased from 4·5 million a month to nearly 126 million, and freight ton-miles (in short tons of 2,000 lb.) from 91,000 to 2,685,000. The bulk of these services were international: only 15 million passenger miles and 65,000 freight ton-miles were attributable in 1954 to domestic services. The following table shows the general course of development.

TABLE 85

United Kingdom Airways: Growth of Scheduled Services, 1938 and 1946–54

	1938	1946	1947	1948	1949	1950	1951	1952	1953	1954
Number of Flights (thousand)	91·4	89·6	114·1	102·1	113·9	131·3	138·8	158·8	177·6	180·
Average Length (miles)	140	369	346	433	388	368	378	366	347	32
Miles flown (millions)	13·2	33·0	39·5	44·2	44·3	48·3	52·5	58·1	61·2	58·
Passengers carried (thousand)	219	423	586	713	921	1,156	1,415	1,733	2,154	2,43
Freight carried (thousand short tons)	2·8	4·6	5·7	9·1	15·8	21·7	37·4	34·8	62·9	72·
Mail carried (thousand short tons)	3·5	3·0	3·4	4·8	5·9	7·3	8·9	9·5	9·8	10·

These figures, though impressive in themselves, of course leave Great Britain an immense way behind the United States, where in 1954 freight ton-miles were ten times and passenger miles nearly fourteen times as many as for the British services. France too was a little ahead of Great Britain in 1954, when the British Air Corporations were going through a difficult time after the withdrawal of the *Comet* aircraft from service as the sequel to several unexplained disasters.

Although the quantity of freight carried by air nearly doubled between 1951 and 1954 and rose eightfold from 1948 to 1954, it remains insignificant in relation to the amount of freight carried by sea, and will clearly remain so, at least for a long time to come. Air transport is too expensive for use except by armies or for quite exceptional kinds of goods, such as bullion or newspapers, or of course letters. Even for passengers it costs too much to be used except for important business or for luxury travel, or for persons journeying at the public expense. Civil aviation is still to a large extent a by-product of military aviation, and could not stand on its own feet without public subventions, at any rate for research and development, if not for actual operation of services.

CHAPTER ELEVEN

MANUFACTURING INDUSTRIES

WE saw, in the section dealing with production (p. 64), the extent to which manufacturing production as a whole is estimated to have risen in recent years and also how the total output of a number of important products has been changing. The outstanding fact is the relatively rapid increase in the industries engaged in the making of metal goods—of engineering in its numerous branches and especially of vehicle-making, and also of the light metal trades. We saw also, in an earlier section, how the proportion of man-power employed in these groups has increased—first, of course, during the war, which made immense demands on them, but also subsequently, in connection both with home investment and consumption and with the development of the export trades.

It is unfortunately not possible to estimate with any accuracy to what extent the total output of these industries has changed since 1938. The latest pre-war Census of Production relates to 1935; and thereafter no Census was taken until 1948. Since then, Censuses have been taken each year; but the full reports take a considerable time to prepare, and at present no complete figures are available for any year after 1951, though a good many figures for particular industries or products can be found in the annual *Economic Surveys* or in special reports on particular trades. A number of these figures have been cited already, on pp. 65 ff. The *Economic Surveys* also give a general account of annual changes in output in the main branches of industry and add a very general estimate of changing productivity per worker over industry as a whole.

As the total output of industry can be estimated only in terms of money value (see p. 58), the Censuses of Production can provide a total only of money values and not of quantity. They provide in fact two final figures, one of 'gross output' and the other of 'net output' after deduction of the cost of materials and fuel consumed. In 1935, for manufacturing industries only, the Census of Production showed a gross output of £2,900 million and a net output of £1,226 million, exclusive of the output of firms too small to be included. This output was produced by a man-power of 5,376,000 persons, including working employers. If all the smaller firms had been included, the man-power would probably have approached 6 million; but it is not possible to say how much the additional output would have been worth. For all industries covered by the Census—including, for example, mining, building and contracting as well as manufactures—gross output was £3,542 million and net output £1,640 million, produced by 7,297,000 persons out of an estimated total of 8,130,000 engaged in the industries concerned.

By 1948 both the money value of output and the numbers employed had increased, the former by much more than the latter, because of greatly increased prices. For manufactures only, gross output had risen to £10,029 million, and net output to £3,770 million, produced by 6,715,000 persons out of an estimated total of 7,144,000 engaged in the industries concerned. For all the industries covered, gross output was £12,396 million and net output £5,038 million; and the producers of this output numbered 9,335,000, out of 10,161,000 in the industries in question. Thus, net output had risen in money value by nearly 208 per cent in manufacturing industry, and by 207 per cent for the whole range included in the Census. Over the same period wholesale prices, measured by the old Board of Trade index, had risen by about 148 per cent. By this very rough measure, the increase in physical output was of the order of 40 per cent. Per person employed net output in manufacturing industry had risen in money value from £228 in 1935 to £561 in 1948—that is, by 146 per cent—in about the same proportion as prices. British manufacturing industry as a whole had just about recovered to its pre-war level of productivity per person—no more.

Thereafter, as we have seen, the index of manufacturing production rose till in 1951 it reached 21 per cent above the 1948 level, only to fall to 15 per cent above that level in 1952, but to recover to 23 per cent above it in 1953 and to 33 per cent in 1954. The rate of increase was, however, very different for different branches of manufacture. In 1954 for the metal, engineering and vehicle group as a whole it was 37 per cent, for the chemical trades 66 per cent, and for paper and printing 55 per cent, whereas for textiles it was only 17 per cent, for clothing 14 per cent, for food, drink and tobacco 16 per cent, and for pottery 9 per cent. Within the metals group, the vehicle trades showed the largest increase—55 per cent—and the miscellaneous group the smallest—11 per cent. For all the industries covered by the index, including mining and building, the increase was 29 per cent.

Most industries felt the effect of the recession of 1952; but only textiles—4 per cent below 1948—and leather—14 per cent below—dropped below the 1948 output. The metals group as a whole just maintained its 1951 output—22 per cent above 1948—and so, within the group, did the vehicle trades—at 24 per cent. Only the food, drink and tobacco trades and the brick and cement trades produced more in 1952 than in 1951—8 per cent as against 5 per cent above 1948 for the first, and 21 per cent as against 15 per cent for the latter. During the first half of 1955 the general index for manufacturing industry averaged

41 per cent above 1948, as against 33 per cent for 1954, and the general index as a whole 37 per cent, as against 29 per cent.

Thus, over the whole field, the increase since 1948 is substantial, though not, as we have seen (see p. 68), comparable with what has been achieved recently by countries such as Western Germany and Japan, or even France, which have been recovering from much more serious dislocation during and after the war, or with what has occurred in countries which have been advancing almost continuously since 1939, such as the United States and Canada. There are, however, serious exceptions to the general improvement.

The cotton industry is the only major industry that has experienced really serious unemployment since 1945. This occurred in 1952–3, when the export demand suffered a large decline, and the number of unemployed operatives rose for a time to more than 80,000, in the spinning and weaving branches together. Much more serious, however, has been the long-term decline of the industry from its former position of Great Britain's most important export trade. This decline began as early as the slump which followed the first world war, by which it was largely occasioned; indeed, it was threatened a good deal earlier, as the countries of Asia developed their own manufacturing production. The decline, received at first almost with incredulity by most of those engaged in the industry, persisted through the inter-war period and was intensified in the 1930s. India had gained the right to protect its own manufactures by tariffs; and the colonial markets were preserved in face of strong Japanese competition only by tariffs which were unfair to the very poor colonial consumers. The second world war resulted in a further decline, despite the limits it imposed on Japanese competition; and the cotton industry emerged into the post-war world further reduced and much more dependent on the home market than it had been for at least a century.

This, indeed, was practically bound to occur. The industry is one which, where it uses modern techniques of large-scale production, is suitable for development in areas where labour is cheap; for these techniques greatly reduce the need for highly skilled workers. Consequently Lancashire, with its skilled and relatively well-paid labour force, was placed at a severe disadvantage in meeting the demand for cheap, standardized cotton cloths; and this disadvantage, confined at first to the coarser cloths, soon spread to the medium 'counts' and even to the finer. Exports of cotton piece goods, which had exceeded 3,000 million *linear*[1] yards in 1913, had been halved by the middle 'twenties and had fallen still further by 1938, when they amounted to 1,368 million *square*[1]

---

[1] It is not my fault that the statistics oscillate between linear and square yards, usually without the possibility of converting the one into the other. Luckily, in this case, the difference hardly matters, as we are concerned with orders of magnitude, rather than with fine differences.

yards; and by 1948 they had been reduced to not much more than 761 million *square* yards, equal to the 766 million *linear* yards shown in the accompanying Table. This figure represented a recovery from the war years, and it was bettered during the next three years, 1949–51. But thereafter the decline was renewed and persisted through 1954. Meanwhile output, after falling very heavily in 1952, picked up again as the home market improved, but was still, in 1954, a long way below that of 1951. Unemployment declined mainly because operatives continually drifted away to more promising occupations: so that, whenever demand revived for a time, the cotton industry presented the paradox of a declining industry that was short of man-power.

Its decline was due in part, but not for the most part, to the rapid development of man-made fibres. Though the output of rayon yarn was almost doubled between 1948 and 1954, it was only about half as large in the latter year as that of cotton yarn; and to a considerable extent the cotton industry itself made use of the new fibres in producing mixed yarns and piece goods, and also for weaving rayon fabrics. Rayon, in effect, became a co-operating as well as a competing factor. The cotton industry's chief difficulty was that it had been built up under conditions which made economic certain forms of equipment—the spinning mule and the non-automatic loom—requiring the use of highly skilled labour, and that in order to adapt it to more automatic methods almost complete re-equipment would have been needed. Even if this had been practicable, Lancashire, by adopting the new methods, would have forfeited the gains from its skilled labour force without being able to reduce wages to a level competitive with those of the countries accustomed to lower living standards, or to prevent the exclusion of its products by high protective tariffs. In these circumstances, investors were quite unprepared to subscribe the capital which thorough re-equipment would have called for. The plain fact is that the cotton industry could not afford to modernize its methods; but it is more than doubtful whether it could have kept its prosperity even if it had been able to do so. There is no valid reason to-day why Great Britain should be the centre of the world's manufacture of cotton goods. It has no decisive natural or acquired advantage for this; and it has the disadvantage that the industry in its modern forms can be widely developed on a basis of cheap labour.

This, of course, does not mean that the industry is doomed to die out in Great Britain. There are branches of it that still call for high skill; and there is a home market most of which it is likely to keep. It will, no doubt, go over more and more to the use of man-made fibres; and it will for some time retain even a substantial market for exports. But its great days are over; and it cannot for long hope to maintain its position of artificial privilege in the British colonies and dependencies.

The woollen industry, which cotton ousted from its predominance in

the course of the Industrial Revolution, is much better placed for survival, but suffers from much short-term instability. In 1938 it exported
a total square yardage of 88 millions; and in 1948 it bettered this record
by nearly 30 per cent. In comparison with the cotton industry it was
well nourished by wartime demand. In 1950 it reached a new export
record of 127 million square yards; but thereafter it fell away rapidly,
to less than 100 million in 1954. In that year it suffered an especially
heavy loss of trade in Canada, where the home woollen industry was
also depressed.

If long-term trends are considered, the woollen industry too has lost
ground as an exporter. On the average of the years 1909-13 exports of
woollens and worsted piece goods amounted to nearly 226 million

TABLE 86

Textile Production and Exports, 1948-54

	1948	1949	1950	1951	1952	1953	1954
Production:							
Rayon: Staple Fibre (million lb.)	86	117	173	176	127	202	228
Rayon: Continuous Filament Yarn (million lb.)	148	171	198	217	156	217	220
Cotton Yarn (million lb.)	890	918	954	968	673	777	841
Spun Rayon and Mixed Yarn (million lb.)	60	71	98	109	98	157	155
Woven Cotton Cloth (million linear yards)	1,900	2,005	2,123	2,202	1,691	1,829	1,994
Woven Rayon and Mixture Cloth (million linear yards)	500	587	707	759	601	754	781
Woollen and Worsted Yarn (million lb.)	501	528	556	501	455	535	539
Woven Wool Cloth (except blankets) (million sq. yards)	414	439	450	418	378	412	414
Exports:							
Woven Cotton Piece Goods (million linear yards)	766	903	815	858	715	707	631
Woven Rayon and Mixture Cloth (million sq. yards)	—	171	197	218	152	177	175
Woven Wool Piece Goods* (million sq. yards)	114	116	127	119	98	105	99

* Excluding carpets and blankets.

square yards, as against the 127 million of 1950 and the 99 million of 1954. In this case too, manufactures have developed in many countries, especially in Europe and America; and the competition of man-made fibres has made itself increasingly felt.

Both the textile and the clothing industries were badly depressed in 1952, but recovered substantially the following year. In 1954 the home market improved further, but exports dropped off. Any check to domestic personal and household expenditure would hit them hard unless they were able to increase overseas sales; and the prospects of this do not appear to be good in view of increasingly keen competition and the continuing development of production in other countries, especially on a foundation of man-made fibres. In the United States the output of rayon and staple fibre rose between 1938 and 1954 from 10,800 metric tons to 41,000, and in Western Germany from 4,100 to 15,800. In the United Kingdom the increase was from 5,100 to 16,900 metric tons. As against this, United States output of wool yarn rose only from 21,800 metric tons to 23,200 and W. German output from under 4,000 to 8,800, while the British output fell from about 21,500 to 20,400. The position of the textile and clothing industries will be discussed further in the section dealing specifically with external trade (see p. 175). In respect of the home market, something has been said already in the section dealing with consumption (see p. 79).

Of other manufacturing industries not much need be added to what has been said in previous sections. The development of the printing and paper industries has been remarkable, especially as it has occurred in spite of sharply increased prices. Imports of newsprint were kept down by rationing of supplies up to 1954, because of high dollar cost: even in 1954 they were running at only 27,300 tons a month, as against 37,200 in 1938, and other imports of paper and board were also slightly down. But in 1955 they rose considerably, after rationing had been removed. Imports of wood pulp were still below the pre-war level in 1953, but rose rapidly in 1954 and 1955. Total paper imports cost over £33 million in 1953, and over £51½ million in 1954, and wood pulp of all kinds cost £67·8 million and £86·6 million, as compared with £14·8 million for paper and £14·2 million for wood pulp in 1938.

The British steel industry was the only manufacturing industry included in the nationalization plans of the Labour Government of 1945; and, in face of strong opposition, the nationalization Bill was held up by the House of Lords and was not finally enacted until 1949. Moreover, the date when it was to come into operation was postponed till after the General Election of 1950. When that Election had resulted in the return of the Labour Government to power, with a greatly reduced majority, the Government took steps to put the Act into effect and took over the ownership of the firms producing crude steel, including their finishing departments. The Conservatives, however, maintained their opposition, and announced their intention of repealing the Act when they returned to power. On winning the General Election of 1951, though with only a small majority, they proceeded to carry out this intention, by offering for sale the nationalized firms in a series of transactions by which they were re-constituted as joint stock companies with shares sold in the open market. This meant in effect that the big capitalist steel concerns re-acquired their old properties before there had been time for the government-appointed Iron and Steel Corporation to do much about them, and that the nationalized part of the industry passed back into the hands of the cartel—the Iron and Steel Federation—which had dominated it for a long time past. The Labour Party in turn announced that it would re-impose nationalization when it came back to power; but its second defeat, in the General Election of 1955, has made this intention inoperative up to the present—though it still stands as part of the Party's programme.

The case for nationalizing the greater part of the steel industry, which I argued in a pamphlet published in 1948,[1] rested on the crucial importance of steel as a basic industry for the entire group of metal-using industries and services, and on the undesirability of leaving such an industry in the hands of a cartel liable to abuse its power by adopting restrictive practices and especially by preferring to keep production and productive capacity at unduly low levels in order to keep prices high. The Iron and Steel Federation was accused, in its relations with the pre-war continental Steel Cartel, of having preferred to safeguard its monopoly of the home market—and to a substantial extent the sterling area market as well—to attempting to push exports in the rest of the world, where they had fallen off seriously in the 1930s. It was also accused, even in relation to the home and sterling area markets, of undue restriction of its capacity and of planning for too low a level of future production. This question had become much more serious after 1945, when it had become indispensable to raise total British exports to a much higher level—the more so because it was clear that this expansion would need to take place above all in the metal and metal-using industries. Steel production had actually expanded during the earlier war years, under pressure of military demands. It was just under 10,400,000 tons of ingots and castings in 1938, and 12,142,000 in 1944. But in 1937 it had already reached almost 13 million tons—a figure not reached again until 1943, nor, after that year, until 1948, when it was greatly surpassed. It actually declined in 1944 and 1945, when large quantities were imported from the United States under Lease-Lend—mainly because of coal shortage and in order to save shipping space by importing finished steel rather than the bulkier ingredients for making it.

After the war there was an acute shortage of steel, not only in Great

[1] 'Why Nationalize Steel?', *New Statesman and Nation*, 1948.

Britain but also in continental Europe. Here are the figures of production for the leading countries from 1937 onwards.

TABLE 87

Steel Production in Leading Countries 1948–54

(*million metric tons*)

	United Kingdom	U.S.A.	Germany	France and Saar	Belgium and Luxemburg	Italy	Czecho-slovakia	Poland
1937	13·2	51·4	19·8	10·3	6·4	2·1	2·3	1·5
1938	10·6	28·8	22·7	8·8	3·7	2·3	1·9	1·4
1944	12·3	81·3	18·3	4·9	1·9	1·0	2·5	—
1945	12·0	72·3	—	1·7	1·0	0·4	1·0	0·5
			W. Germany					
1946	12·9	60·4	2·6	4·7	3·6	1·2	1·7	1·2
1947	12·9	77·0	3·1	6·4	4·6	1·7	2·3	1·6
1948	15·1	80·4	5·6	8·5	6·4	2·1	2·6	2·0
1949	15·8	70·7	9·2	10·9	6·2	2·1	2·8	2·3
1950	16·6	87·8	12·1	10·5	6·2	2·4	3·0	2·5
1951	15·9	95·4	13·5	12·4	8·1	3·1	3·3	2·8
1952	16·7	84·5	15·8	13·7	8·1	3·5	—	—
1953	17·9	101·3	15·4	12·7	8·3	3·5	—	—
1954	18·8	80·1	17·4	13·4	7·8	4·2	—	—
Increase 1954 over 1937	5·6	28·7	−0·5*	3·1	1·4	2·1	—	—
per cent	42	56	—	30	22	100	—	—

* Western Germany only, 1954 over 1938.

In 1946, with West German output down from nearly 18 million metric tons in 1938 to little more than 2½ million, with the combined production of France and the Saar, Belgium and Luxemburg, and Italy down from nearly 15 million metric tons in 1937 to 9½ million, and with British production still below that of 1937, though well above 1938, only the United States could help to fill the vacuum; and the dollar shortage ruled out large purchases from that source. The effect was seriously to retard European production of capital goods based on steel, as well as of consumers' supplies, and to open a large market in Europe, as well as elsewhere, for British goods as fast as British steel output could be increased. In 1948 British steel output did expand considerably; but the rate of increase was much slower in 1949 and 1950, and in 1951 there was a fall. In 1952 output was barely higher than in 1950; but it increased faster in 1953 and rather more slowly in 1954.

Behind these changes in output lay a tough struggle. In 1946 the Iron and Steel Federation produced its plans for the development of the industry under private ownership. It proposed to base its capital works on an output of about 15½ million tons, and a total output capacity of 16 million tons, both these targets to be reached at the end of a six-year programme in 1953. Of the higher total, 13 million tons was meant to be for the home market, and 3 million for export. These were, no doubt, totals well above the actual figures of 1937—when production was rather under 13 million tons; but they were utterly inadequate in relation to post-war needs. Indeed, in the event the actual output of 1949 was higher than the Federation's target for 1953, and by 1953 output was more than 2 million tons higher. Faced with the threat of nationalization, the Federation was forced to mend its pace; but this was done much more by slowing down the disuse of obsolescent capacity than by increasing new construction. The Federation had estimated for the scrapping of 3 million tons of existing blast furnace capacity out of 7·3 million, and of 4 million tons of steel furnace capacity out of 14 million. But in practice the immediate demand was too high to allow high-cost capacity to be scrapped at anything like these rates. The blast furnaces, which were in the worse condition of obsolescence, were largely replaced; but much old steel plant remained at work, and accordingly costs stayed high.

In 1948, still under private ownership, the industry reviewed its plans and decided on a target of 18 million tons to be reached by the middle 'fifties. But the rate of construction of new plant was barely increased, though the original estimate of capital cost—£168 million—was, by no less than £142 million, owing to rising cost of plant. One important factor in making higher output possible without more new construction was extensive use of imported scrap, largely from Germany. During the brief period of public ownership there was no time for the thorough review that was clearly needed of the revised plan of 1948; but in 1952, after the decision to denationalize, the Iron and Steel Federation laid before the new Government a revised plan based on an expected need for an output of 21 million tons by 1957–8. Even this was soon seen to be inadequate, and early in 1955 the new Iron and Steel Board which has replaced the Corporation raised the target output to 22½ million

T/

British Steel Su

	1937	1938	1944	1945	1946
Output of Crude Steel	12,984	10,398	12,142	11,824	12,695
Imports of Steel (ingots)	1,482	975	1,668	173	484
Exports of Steel (ingots)	2,407	1,985	240	674	2,302
Producers' Stocks (tonnage)	—	—	1,684	1,224	1,067
Home Use (ingots)	12,059	9,238	14,341	12,260	11,831

tons by 1958, plus a margin of capacity able to meet, if need be, a still greater demand. This latest target is made up of 19½ million tons to meet home demand, including demand arising from industries producing further manufactured steel goods for export, and 3 million for direct export of steel not further processed in Great Britain. The actual figures for the British steel industry are shown in Table 88.

Observe particularly the large fluctuations in imports, which have been affected both by the fortunes of the coal industry and by considerations arising out of the balance of payments and the availability of American aid. Observe too the considerable fluctuations in producers' stocks, and the relative steadiness of the total home consumption. As we saw, home production has increased each year since 1945, except 1951, when it fell off substantially. The biggest increases were from 1947 to 1948, when the industry was facing the prospect of nationalization and was trying to demonstrate that it was not necessary, and from 1952 onwards, after the return to private ownership; but the latter increases were due rather to the general development of the economy than to the changes in ownership, which had hardly affected production.

All this shilly-shallying about targets has arisen out of the reluctance of the steel producers to run any risks of losing the advantage of a seller's market. They have consistently under-estimated requirements in the hope of keeping prices high and investment profitable, and have preferred keeping high-cost capacity at work to expanding new construction. They have indeed been able to argue that the rate of new construction cannot be speeded up without further expansion of the industries which supply the requisite plant and machinery—industries for the most part already fully employed. This expansion, however, could have been started away back in 1945-6: that this was not done has held back the whole course of development in subsequent years. As things have turned out, the steel industry has not felt the need, in its own interest, actually to apply a restrictive policy. It has been able to sell all it has been able to produce, at prices kept up by the high costs of the less efficient plants. From 1948 to 1953, steel consumption in the

8 and 1944–54 (*thousand tons*)

1947	1948	1949	1950	1951	1952	1953	1954
12,724	14,877	15,533	16,293	15,638	16,418	17,609	18,517
461	502	1,092	556	525	1,774	1,113	468
1,733	1,986	2,360	3,153	2,611	2,557	2,756	2,896
797	805	1,012	959	556	683	962	811
12,608	13,842	14,606	14,247	14,762	15,938	16,040	16,593

United Kingdom rose at an average rate of 3·2 per cent per annum: the revised plan of 1955 contemplates an average rise of 4·5 per cent up to 1958. This, it is estimated, will suffice to allow the steel-using industries to expand their own output at an average annual rate of 5 per cent.

Obviously, the raised targets for steel production have been influenced considerably by rearmament. But the main demand for steel comes from the investment programmes of other industries and services, which in 1953 used 10 million tons out of a total consumption of 15·65 million. Defence services took directly less than 1·5 million and consumers' goods rather less: the remainder went to the exporters of processed steel goods. Clearly, the vehicle, canning, and miscellaneous metal goods industries have been increasing their consumption of steel at an annual rate much above 5 per cent—probably 10 per cent is nearer the mark. But, as against this, defence expenditure is not expected to go on rising: indeed, it should clearly fall. Investment demand, on the other hand, is likely to, and should, rise fast (see pp. 99 ff.); and it is to be doubted whether the pace now contemplated for the increase of steel output is high enough. If steel consumption in Great Britain had continued after 1937 to rise at the same rate as it actually rose between 1927 and 1937, it would have been actually over 20 million tons in 1947, when it was in fact under 13 million. The figure of less than 20 million tons for 1958 looks, on this basis, still quite astonishingly low.

But, of course, cost is an important factor; and it is highly uneconomic to keep obsolete plant in use because there is no other way of meeting current demand. To do this actually curtails demand, because of the high prices it requires. A nationalized industry would be able to hold prices down by averaging costs over better and worse plant, until it could replace the obsolescent capacity with new low-cost equipment. It would also be free from the temptation to keep supplies low in order to exact a monopoly price.

Nationalization did not last long enough to have any noticeable effects in practice. But the terms on which the denationalized properties have been sold back to private enterprise indicate a high level of confidence in the prospects of the industry. Whether this confidence rests on the prospect of reviving the old monopolistic practices it is not easy to say. So far, the steel industry has been under no temptation to restrict its output; but it remains to see what will happen to steel prices in the event of a recession. In place of the pre-war continental steel cartel, the British industry is now face to face with the Schuman Plan European Coal and Steel Community, which in some respects closely resembles the old cartel. The Community, to be sure, is formally pledged not to resort to restrictive practices; but one does not know how binding that pledge would be if the tide of demand were to ebb. The British industry has kept out of the 'Schuman' Community because it wants to keep its special position in the sterling area market; but it has come of late into much closer relations with the Community, and no one can say yet how much closer still the links will become.

Nationalization, while it lasted, took for the iron and steel industry a form considerably different from the common pattern. It applied, for one thing, not to the entire industry, but only to the firms, necessarily large, which produced pig-iron or crude steel. As many of these firms, which were taken over entire, were also makers of finished and semi-finished products, nationalization did extend well beyond crude steel production; but a substantial part of the industry was left in private hands. Moreover, the firms taken over were not 'scrambled' into a single great concern, or even into a number of regional concerns. They were left intact, names and all, with merely a change—now reversed—in the ownership of their capital. This made it the easier to pass them back to private ownership; but the special form of nationalization was not, of course, adopted with that in view. It was indeed clear that the model of a huge public corporation, administering a whole national industry, was not suitable for steel, or for that matter for most manufacturing industries. The Iron and Steel Corporation, had it endured, would no doubt in course of time have done a fair amount of re-arrangement, so as to re-group the existing firms into more economic units. But this was not allowed to happen, though it is probably not unlike the model that will be followed when and if other large-scale manufacturing industries are transferred to public ownership.

CHAPTER TWELVE

MONEY AND BANKING

MONEY is the common measure that is applied to all the kinds of things that are bought and sold, as a convenient means of measuring their relative value and terms of exchange. Very broadly speaking, the more money there is, the higher will prices tend to be, and vice versa. But it is not at all easy to say how much money does exist at any particular time. We can say how much purchasing power at any given price level is represented by all the coins and notes in circulation or lying in the banks; but a great many purchases, including most big ones, are made not with coins or notes but by means of cheques written on bank accounts; and, in the world of to-day, deposits in banks are the main form in which money is held. Cheques usually change hands only once; but both coins and notes and bank deposits circulate again and again. The more frequently they change hands, the more work they do in financing purchases in any given period: so that when we are considering the relation between money and prices we need to take account of what is called the 'velocity of circulation' as well as of the amount of bank deposits, coins and notes. The main aim of monetary policy in this connection is, or should be, to ensure that the means of payment are adequate to maintain full employment, but not so plentiful as to cause an inflationary rise in prices.

The Circulation of Currency. The amount of currency in existence—that is to say, the total money value of all the coins and notes available for use—is easily ascertained with reasonable accuracy. It is made up first of the coins in the hands of the public or of the banks, and secondly of all the bank or Treasury notes similarly held. These latter are nowadays nearly all issued by the Bank of England; but there are still small amounts issued by the Scottish and Northern Irish banks. The figures are shown in Table 89.

It will be seen that the money value of notes and coins held by the public (see the final line of the table) is more than three times as great as in 1938, and that the value of bank notes has risen in much the same proportion. This is much the same as the rise in wholesale prices between 1938 and 1954, and indicates some fall in the relative supply of currency, as the quantity of goods exchanged had substantially

TABLE 89

Currency Circulation, 1938 and 1945-54

(*£million*)

	1938	1945	1946	1947	1948	1949	1950	1951	1952	1953	1954
Coin	73	128	138	145	158	170	156	151	151	155	159
Notes (Bank of England)	529	1,311	1,403	1,450	1,313	1,315	1,329	1,383	1,476	1,570	1,662
Notes (Scottish and N. Irish)	29	81	84	86	78	80	80	83	90	98	104
Notes and Coin in Banks:											
Bank of England	45	28	46	68	60	50	46	41	42	41	34
Other Banks	144	228	238	253	250	266	274	284	305	321	339
Notes and Coin in hands of											
Public	446	1,263	1,340	1,361	1,239	1,248	1,244	1,291	1,370	1,462	1,551
Ditto as percentage of 1938	100	283	300	305	278	280	281	292	310	331	351

increased. This is of no great significance: it only indicates that a larger proportion of transactions are made to-day without the use of coin or notes—that is, mainly by cheque.

Bank Money.   The main source of information about payments made by cheque is the return of bank clearings—that is, of the volume of cheques dealt with through the London Bankers' Clearing House or through the provincial Clearing Houses. These returns do not cover all cheque payments, as when a customer of a particular bank writes a cheque in favour of another customer of the same bank there is no need for it to pass through the Clearing House, which exists for the purpose of setting off and thus cancelling out claims of one bank upon another. Nevertheless, the Clearing House figures give a reasonably good account of the ups and downs of money payments, apart from transactions in coin or notes. They include, however, not only payments arising out of the buying and selling of current output but also those concerned with capital transactions—among them, purchases

TA

Bank Clearings,

	1938	1945	1946	1947	1948
London Clearing House:					
Town	33,862	38,710	50,060	52,672	57,424
Other	5,749	28,234	18,951	20,657	22,786
Provincial Clearing Houses	1,258	1,030	1,258	1,413	1,737
Total	40,868	67,974	70,270	74,743	81,947

and sales of shares and stocks in companies and other financial holdings. It is therefore necessary, not only to take account of cheques in the total amount of bank clearings but also, as far as possible, to break up the total so as to distinguish between purely financial transactions, in which ownership of money or of capital assets merely changes hands, and industrial transactions, in which some part of current output is bought and sold. This cannot be done at all completely; but the volume of what are called 'Town' clearings is generally taken to indicate the volume of financial, including speculative, business, whereas that of 'Metropolitan' and 'Country' clearings gives a better indication of the volume of industrial transactions. The difference is important because whereas normally all current output, except what is kept in stock, changes hands soon after it is put on the market, there can be big variations in the number and proportion of capital assets that change hands in any particular period, such as a year. When speculation is prevalent, the volume of stock exchange business rises sharply, with no necessary accompanying change in the volume of current industrial business.

Table 90 shows the relevant figures of bank clearings in recent years.

Here again, the total volume in 1954 was more than three times that of 1938; but up to 1953 the increase was much greater in the 'Other' (Metropolitan and Country) clearings than in the 'Town' clearings. This indicates a high level of industrial activity, with a lower level of purely financial and speculative dealings. There was, however, a sharp rise in 'Town' clearings in 1954, when the daily average rose from £307 million to £368 million as a consequence of the speculative boom in equity share prices. The rise in 'Other' clearings was much smaller, from £96 million daily to £102 million.

945–54 (*£million*)

1949	1950	1951	1952	1953	1954
62,604	69,548	80,687	82,438	94,070	112,923
23,456	24,693	28,086	28,146	29,303	31,365
1,886	2,076	2,284	2,053	2,140	2,346
87,946	96,317	111,057	112,637	125,513	146,634

Deposits and Advances. Bank clearings are made against bank deposits—that is, against sums standing to the credit of bank customers, including loans and advances made to them by the banks. The next significant set of figures is that relating to the total volume of deposits held by the banks. Here we have to use the figures published by the London Clearing Banks, which cover the main volume of deposits throughout the country. They are divided into 'current' and 'deposit' accounts, the former bearing no interest and to be freely drawn upon at any moment, whereas the latter can be drawn upon only after notice and carry a small rate of interest payable to the depositors. Here are the figures:

TABLE 91

London Clearing Bank Deposits and Advances, 1938 and 1945–54

(£million)

	1938	1945	1946	1947	1948	1949	1950	1951	1952	1953	1954
Deposits											
Current Accounts	1,244	3,127	3,377	3,690	3,850	3,940	3,979	4,095	3,961	3,995	4,141
Deposit and other	1,033	1,566	1,720	1,959	2,062	2,034	2,036	2,067	2,122	2,261	2,354
Total	2,277	4,692	5,097	5,650	5,913	5,974	6,014	6,162	6,083	6,256	6,495
Advances to Customers	976	768	888	1,107	1,319	1,440	1,603	1,822	1,838	1,732	1,804

It will be seen that total deposits in 1954 were well under three times those of 1938, whereas deposits on current account were well over three times greater; deposit accounts had nearly doubled. Advances to customers had not even doubled; for, despite the greater volume of business, firms were in a position to finance more of their activities out of their liquid assets, without calling for loans from their banks. Most businesses had large reserves of liquid capital, which had not been locked up in buildings or machinery, and were available to finance current transactions. They were keeping, in proportion to the money value of their current activities, less in deposit accounts, which usually increase in periods of economic depression.

Who Borrow from the Banks?   A further set of figures shows the broad distribution of bankers' loans and advances among the various kinds of borrowers; but these figures cannot be carried back to 1938. See Table 92 (overleaf).

It will be seen that industries and types of business differ greatly in their dependence on loans from the banks. Coal-mining and transport, for example, make hardly any use of them; but, despite nationalization, public utility services use them to a substantial extent. The largest single group of advances is to individuals and professional persons, including private overdrafts: such advances can of course be used for a wide variety of purposes, but they cannot be further analysed. In 1953 the next largest group was agriculture and fishing, which has more than doubled since 1947. Farmers are commonly not in a position to finance the period between production and receipt of payment out of their own resources, and therefore depend a good deal on bank advances. Third in order come advances to financial concerns, including stockbrokers, who however account for only a small fraction of the total. Retail trade comes next, with large demands for financing the period of turnover. It is followed closely by engineering, which has been expanding very rapidly in recent years. Then come the food, drink and tobacco trades, closing the list of those accounting for more than £100 million.

It will be observed that the total of bank advances rose very sharply in 1951 and 1952. This was mainly a consequence of the sharp rise in the prices of materials, which suddenly swelled the cost of acquiring and holding stocks and affected most those businesses which are large buyers of imported materials. Thus, advances to the textile trades rose from £66 million in 1950 to nearly £100 million in 1951, and in engineering the increase was from £93 million in 1950 to £150 million in 1952. Financial advances also rose sharply in 1951, because of the sudden rise in prices.

Bank Investments and Short-term Loans.   Apart from advances to customers, the banks hold their resources mainly in investments and in bills—especially Treasury Bills, which are the sums on loan by them

TABLE 92

Distribution of Bank Advances

(£million)

	1946	1947	1948	1949	1950	1951	1952	1953	1954	1955 (August)
Advances to—										
Agriculture and Fishing	73·7	89·0	115·4	137·2	163·6	190·4	198·9	200·3	213·7	242·8
Coal Mining	9·6	8·2	7·1	6·0	5·6	4·2	2·2	1·8	1·8	1·2
Chemicals	8·6	15·0	19·7	18·5	22·0	26·3	35·1	25·9	27·0	31·2
Iron and Steel	15·5	14·3	17·1	23·5	21·8	17·3	30·9	55·0	48·8	28·9
Non-ferrous Metals	2·3	3·1	3·1	3·5	6·2	6·0	5·3	4·6	6·3	9·0
Engineering	62·5	82·3	112·4	109·6	93·1	109·5	150·0	153·6	137·7	166·5
Textiles	24·9	30·6	44·0	47·9	65·9	99·4	94·8	81·3	88·6	108·0
Food, Drink and Tobacco	59·4	75·1	81·7	101·3	121·0	142·7	158·1	132·5	133·6	154·2
Building and Contracting	42·9	56·1	60·6	61·9	64·1	70·6	66·4	60·9	61·3	75·9
Building Materials	6·0	9·5	12·4	12·6	14·2	18·0	20·2	17·1	17·7	24·0
Shipping and Shipbuilding	10·5	15·1	16·9	16·2	15·5	15·8	11·7	16·0	16·5	23·9
Other Transport and Communications	9·9	12·6	15·4	16·8	16·7	16·9	20·0	17·6	18·1	21·5
Public Utilities	8·4	12·7	23·0	25·2	64·8	74·8	96·4	86·6	120·5	207·0
Retail Trade	68·4	102·3	138·9	159·2	180·1	207·1	189·4	169·6	176·9	188·5
Financial	81·8	102·0	107·5	130·4	164·6	206·6	183·0	185·5	202·9	235·6
Local Government	71·9	78·8	85·9	88·2	90·9	91·7	78·0	78·3	89·0	94·1
Entertainment	25·2	24·6	31·2	33·6	31·2	28·4	25·4	21·7	21·1	22·2
Personal and Professional	261·4	321·1	365·9	400·0	419·4	434·3	402·2	366·7	374·3	397·7
Unclassifiable and Miscellaneous	53·2	76·2	96·3	102·8	123·2	160·3	162·5	140·8	146·2	228·2
Total	896·2	1,128·6	1,354·6	1,494·4	1,683·9	1,920·3	1,930·5	1,815·8	1,902·0	2,260·4

to the Government. They have also substantial sums lent out for short periods to bill brokers, discount houses, and other dealers in short-term credit. The banks' holdings of bills and short-term money market loans constitute, together with their cash holdings and their balances at the Bank of England, their more liquid assets. If they wish to reduce their total liabilities, they can at any time call in some of these short-term loans and hold the sums in cash or in the Bank of England. This has been the banks' customary method of restricting the supply of loan money when they are fearful of the outlook or consider it necessary to combat inflationary tendencies. Table 93 (overleaf) shows the figures of the London Clearing Banks' holdings of investments, bills, and other assets, apart from their advances to customers, which have been dealt with already.

Bank Assets and Reserves.   It appears from this table that the banks have made only small additions to their capital since 1938, though their deposits have greatly increased. On the other side of the account their cash reserves, including balances with the Bank of England, form a smaller proportion of their total assets than in 1938; and since 1947 they have kept the proportion about steady at rather more than 8 per cent. On the other hand, their next most liquid asset, money at call or short notice, was from 1947 onwards a higher proportion of total deposits than in 1938—7 per cent in 1954 as compared with 6·6 per cent in 1938. It had been considerably higher between 1949 and 1952. If cash and money at short call are added together the combined proportion to deposits becomes 17·2 per cent in 1938 as against 15·1 per cent in 1954. It was over 17 per cent in 1950 and 1951, during the price-boom. Bills discounted are also fairly liquid, and count as part of the banks' second line of defence when they wish to reduce their liabilities. They represented in 1954 a substantially higher proportion of total deposits than in 1938—18·5 per cent as against 12·3 per cent. For the intervening years comparison is complicated by the introduction of an alternative method of government borrowing direct borrowing from the banks by means of 'Treasury Deposit Receipts'—which have now been discontinued. These partly took the place of government borrowing by means of Treasury Bills during and shortly after the war, and were then gradually allowed to run off. In all, there has been a great increase in government borrowing in the short-term money market; and to-day Treasury Bills are a very much larger proportion of the banks' total bill holdings than they used to be, as against Trade Bills used chiefly for the financing of international trade.

Bank Investments.   The least liquid of the banks' assets are their investments, which in the past have tended to rise in times of depression, when the demand from industry and trade for advances falls off. To-day, however, investments are a higher proportion of deposits than

TABLE 93
Assets and Liabilities of London Clearing Banks
(£million)

	1938	1945	1946	1947	1948	1949	1950	1951	1952	1953	1954
Liabilities:											
Capital and Reserves	139	144	146	148	149	153	154	156	156	161	169
Deposits	2,277	4,692	5,097	5,650	5,913	5,974	6,014	6,162	6,083	6,256	6,495
Assets:											
Cash and Balances with Bank of England	241	492	523	473	486	496	497	511	505	509	528
Cash and Balances as percentage of Deposits	10·6	10·5	10·3	8·4	8·2	8·3	8·3	8·3	8·3	8·1	8·1
Balances with other Banks	60	141	165	186	199	202	203	232	226	232	256
Money at Call or Short Notice	151	206	300	450	473	510	550	569	529	472	457
as percentage of Deposits	6·6	4·4	5·9	8·0	8·0	8·5	9·1	9·2	8·7	7·6	7·0
Treasury Bills discounted	280	188	457	723	744	914	1,298	1,228	957	1,156	1,119
Other Bills discounted									105	63	87
Bills as percentage of Deposits	12·3	4·0	9·0	12·8	12·6	15·3	21·6	19·9	17·4	19·5	18·5
Treasury Deposit Receipts	—	1,811	1,492	1,308	1,284	983	430	247	7	—	—
as percentage of Deposits	—	38·6	29·3	23·1	21·7	16·4	7·1	4·0	0·1	—	—
Investments	637	1,156	1,345	1,474	1,479	1,505	1,505	1,624	1,983	2,163	2,321
as percentage of Deposits	28·0	24·6	26·4	26·1	25·0	25·2	25·0	26·4	32·6	34·6	35·7
Advances to Customers	976	768	888	1,107	1,319	1,440	1,603	1,822	1,838	1,732	1,804
as percentage of Deposits	42·9	16·4	17·4	19·6	22·3	24·1	26·7	29·6	30·2	27·7	27·8
Acceptances, etc.	118	104	153	233	248	259	307	468	427	336	349
Total Assets or Liabilities	2,536	4,942	5,397	6,032	6,311	6,387	6,476	6,787	6,667	6,754	7,014

they were in 1938—35·7 per cent in 1954 as against 28 per cent in 1938. This rise is counterbalanced by a fall in advances from 42·9 per cent of deposits in 1938 to 27·8 per cent in 1954. This is largely a result of the increased ability of businesses to finance their current transactions out of their own liquid resources; for this forces the banks to find more outlets for their funds in the holding of long-term securities, though the latter tend to be less profitable when interest rates are at a moderate level.

Bank Rate and other Rates of Interest.   Actually, interest rates were kept low for some time after the war, especially while Mr. Dalton was at the Exchequer. They were then allowed to rise, and have risen considerably in recent years. Bank Rate—that is, the re-discount rate of the Bank of England—was 2 per cent in 1938 and after a brief rise in 1939 was back at that figure till November 1951, when it was increased to 2½ per cent. In March 1952 it was raised sharply to 4 per cent; but it then came down to 3½ per cent in September 1953 and to 3 per cent in May 1954. The rates for day-to-day money, which stood at ½ per cent in 1938 and after a rise to 1 per cent during the war came back to ½ per cent from 1945 to 1951, shot up to 2 per cent in 1952–3 and then fell to 1¾ per cent in 1953–4 and to 1¼ per cent by June 1954. Treasury Bill rates, which were fractionally over ½ per cent in the first half of 1938, were over 1 per cent by 1945 and then fell back to a little over ½ per cent till towards the end of 1951, when they shot up to 1 per cent and within a few months reached nearly 2½ per cent, falling back in the middle of 1954 to rather over 1½ per cent. These changes reflect monetary policy affected by problems of the balance of payments and the desire to combat inflation and exaggerated speculative activities. They are also closely related to the movement of prices and yields of securities. Thus British 2½% Consols gave a yield of nearly 3·4 per cent in 1938 and of 3·75 per cent in 1954, as against 4·23 per cent in 1952; whereas the average yield on industrial ordinary shares was 5·4 per cent in 1954 and 6·46 per cent in 1952. Unfortunately, no valid comparison can be made with 1938 or other years before 1950.

Blaming the Bankers.   When economic conditions are bad and unemployment rife, it is a time-honoured practice to blame the bankers and to cry out that all would be well if they would provide the advances needed to pay wages to the workless and so restore their lost purchasing power. There is indeed no little substance in these complaints as applied to the 'orthodox' financial policies of the past. But in post-war Britain there has been no unemployment for which the bankers could be called to account. Banks, with government encouragement, have indeed restricted their advances, and rates of interest have been raised in order to discourage borrowers; but little or no unemployment has resulted from these measures. The only serious unemployment since 1945 occurred in the textile industries—especially cotton—in 1952; but no one as far as I know blamed this on the bankers. The problem of the post-war years has been one of too little, not too much, labour; and when full employment already exists further easing of the conditions for borrowing leads not to increased employment but to rising prices and wages, which must react either on exports or on the rates of exchange. Sir Stafford Cripps and Mr. Gaitskell, and then Mr. Butler, were in turn attacked for stiffening up the conditions against borrowers and thereby reducing the demand for labour; but none of them in fact reduced it below the available supply. Such temporary recessions as there were in the British economy arose out of events that took place elsewhere, especially out of slackening in American demand. The blame for them cannot be put either on the bankers or on the Government, which has been since 1945 in effective control of banking as well as of budgetary policy.

Credit Policy and Inflation.　Even when the leaders of the cotton industry were most alarmed about the outlook, their main demand was not for more credit but for government measures to control foreign— particularly Japanese—competition and to secure improved openings in overseas markets. A more 'liberal' credit policy could not but have, by raising British prices, worsened a balance of payments problem that was already serious enough. The devaluation of the British currency in 1949 was the necessary sequel to the failure to check inflationary tendencies during the preceding years, after matters had been brought to a head by the astonishingly unwise decision to restore free transactions in currency. This decision precipitated a run on the reserves which could be checked only by devaluation; but devaluation would have been necessary in any event.

Devaluation.　The devaluation of a currency in terms of gold and of other currencies based on gold involves that the country which resorts

T.

Official Exchange Rates

	1938	1945	1946	1947
£1 = U.S. dollars	4·89	4·03	4·03	4·03
= French francs	170·65	203·89	480·0	480·0
= Belgian francs	144·65	176·63	176·63	176·63
= Swiss francs	21·37	17·35	17·35	17·35
= Swedish crowns	19·40	16·90	15·77	14·49
= £ Australian	1·25	1·25	1·25	1·25
= £ New Zealand	1·244	1·244	1·244	1·244
= Canadian dollars	4·92	4·45	4·24	4·03

to it has to pay more of its own money to buy any given quantity of imports from those other countries, unless they devaluate their currencies to an equal extent. In 1938 the £ sterling was worth $4.89: by 1945 it was being held at an official value of $4.03 only by an elaborate system of restrictions on changing pounds into dollars, aided by a series of manoeuvres by the monetary authorities in London and New York. It was held at this nominal value until September 1949, but only at the cost of the development of a black market in which pounds were changed for dollars at much less favourable rates. Then, the official rate was reduced abruptly to $2.8 to the £1; and there, or thereabouts, it has remained ever since. It has not, however, been easy to sustain even this rate in face of the keen demand for dollars. Black market rates have appeared from time to time, when the supply of dollars has been reduced by changes in American policy; and the outlook is still uncertain. The 'right' rate, at which there would be no pressure on either the pound or the dollar, depends on American policy fully as much as on British—which is the chief reason why it would still be most unwise to return to free convertibility of pounds into dollars at a fixed rate of exchange.

Foreign Exchange Rates. The British devaluation of 1949 caused a number of other countries to devalue their currencies to a greater or less extent and this caused a whole series of shifts in relative currency values. The official figures of exchange, as they were in 1938 and have been from 1945 onwards, are given in Table 94.

It will be noted that Canadian dollars have followed much the same course as U.S. dollars in relation to the £ sterling, but, after reaching the same sterling value in 1947 and 1948, fluctuated a little during the following years, ending up in 1954 as slightly more valuable than U.S. dollars. Swiss francs have risen steadily in value in relation to sterling, but have been virtually stable in relative value since 1950.

45–54 (Average of Year)

1948	1949	1950	1951	1952	1953	1954
4·03	3·68	2·80	2·80	2·79	2·81	2·81
879·7	1,053·1	980·0	979·7	981·5	982·8	981·6
176·63	166·49	140·00	139·97	139·76	140·12	140·04
17·35	15·90	12·25	12·24	12·20	12·19	12·22
14·49	14·49	14·49	14·48	14·49	14·52	14·53
1·25	1·25	1·25	1·25	1·25	1·25	1·25
1·155	1·004	1·004	1·004	1·004	1·004	1·004
4·03	3·76	3·04	2·95	2·73	2·77	2·73

Belgian francs were depreciated in relation to sterling from 1945 to 1949, but had thereafter an appreciably greater value in sterling than in 1938. French francs fell rapidly from 1945 to 1949 and then appreciated slightly after the British devaluation, but were in 1954 worth only between one-fifth and one-sixth of their 1938 exchange value. Swedish crowns gained in sterling value during the war and up to 1947, but have since been practically stable in relative value. Australian pounds have kept the same ratio of depreciation in terms of the British pound as they had in 1938; but the relative value of New Zealand pounds was increased in 1948-9, and this improvement has been maintained.

We shall have to consider the implications of these shifts in currency values when we come to deal with the problems of the international trade and the balance of payments. They are set down here because they are matters of banking and financial practice and policy. The regulation of rates of exchange is primarily a matter for the Government, acting through the Exchange Equalization Fund and using the nationalized Bank of England as its second instrument. The other banks have no control over it because their money-making powers are governed by the Bank of England, which can increase or reduce at will the money resources at their disposal. As the Bank of England is now a government agency, it is the Government that settles monetary policy with an eye on the foreign exchanges and especially on the demand for dollars in exchange for sterling. To this we shall come back later (see pp. 193 ff).

CHAPTER THIRTEEN

EXTERNAL TRADE

THE United Kingdom is, among the nations, the most dependent of all on foreign trade. Needing to import not only a large proportion of its supplies of food but also most of the raw materials for its industries, it must export a considerable fraction of its manufactured products in order to meet the cost of necessary imports. Moreover, as many of its exports are made largely of imported materials, exports must meet the cost of these imports as well as of those which are retained for consumption at home. The only important raw material of which there has usually been a considerable surplus available for export is coal; and in recent years it has even been necessary on occasion to import coal, though not on a scale equal to that of continuing exports.

British Exports and Imports. In 1954, exports of United Kingdom goods totalled £2,673,000,000 in value, as compared with £2,584,000,000 in 1952 and £2,582,000,000 in 1953. These totals are 17·2 per cent, 19·0 per cent, and 17·7 per cent of the gross national domestic product of these years. Imports were valued at £3,379,000,000 in 1954, as compared with £3,447,000,000 in 1952 and £3,343,000,000 in 1953—21·8 per cent, 25·1 per cent, and 23·1 per cent of gross domestic product. These are *c.i.f.* values, including cost, insurance and freight: the totals *f.o.b.* (free on board at the port of departure) were £3,007,000,000 in 1954, £2,946,000,000 in 1952, and £2,889,000,000 in 1953. Of these imports, goods to a value of £101,000,000 were re-exported in 1954, the corresponding values being £144,000,000 in 1952 and £105,000,000 in 1953. The visible adverse balance, with imports valued *c.i.f.*, was £605,000,000 in 1954, £749,000,000 in 1952, and £655,000,000 in 1953. These deficits were met partly out of the net receipts of income from abroad, including both returns on owners' investments and gifts from the United States for defence services, and partly out of the receipts from 'invisible exports', such as shipping and financial services.

Table 95 (overleaf) gives the figures for the value of imports and exports since 1947, with four pre-war years for comparison.

The Trade Gap. Table 95 (overleaf) is in terms of money value. During the four years 1951–4 total imports cost more than three times as much as in the four years 1935–8. As against this, exports of United

T

Value of the External Trade of the

	1935	1936	1937	1938
Imports: Total	755·5	847·2	1,027·2	919·0
Food, Drink, Tobacco	353·0	379·3	428·9	428·1
Basic Materials	207·3	242·6	307·4	240·2
Minerals, Fuels and Lubricants	34·9	38·6	49·6	47·3
Manufactures	156·1	181·2	234·8	195·7
Exports of U.K. Products: Total	426·1	440·9	522·0	471·4
Food, Drink, Tobacco	30·0	34·5	37·4	35·1
Basic Materials	27·3	27·5	32·6	23·2
Minerals, Fuels and Lubricants	39·2	36·6	47·1	45·4
Manufactures	316·7	329·0	390·9	354·3
Re-exports: Total	55·0	60·4	74·5	60·8
Food, Drink, Tobacco	12·5	11·6	13·1	12·2
Basic Materials	29·1	32·9	36·9	30·3
Minerals, Fuels and Lubricants	1·5	1·6	1·8	0·8
Manufactures	11·9	14·3	22·7	17·4
Transhipments under Bond	25·5	29·0	37·3	32·5
Visible Adverse Balance	274·4	346·1	430·7	386·8

Kingdom goods were worth five and a half times as much, but re-exports only 50 per cent more during the later period. The effect was that the visible trade gap had doubled; but a part of this rise was due to the abnormally high import figures for 1951.

T.

Index Numbers of Volume of the Ex

(1938

	1935	1936	1937	1938	1947*	1947†	1948
Imports: Total	93	99	105	100	70	89	93
Food, Drink, Tobacco	—	—	—	—	—	95	96
Basic Materials	—	—	—	—	—	85	87
Fuels	—	—	—	—	—	74	91
Manufactures	—	—	—	—	—	87	95
Total, Retained	93	99	105	100	72	88	92
Exports: U.K. Products, Total	103	104	113	100	99	62	78
Exports: U.K. Manu- factures	—	—	—	—	—	64	79
Re-exports: Total	104	103	107	100	37	126	—

* Based on valuation in terms of 1947 prices.

dom, 1935–38 and 1947–54 (£million)

1947	1948	1949	1950	1951	1952	1953	1954
1,798·4	2,075·4	2,277·5	2,606·5	3,901·9	3,477·0	3,344·9	3,378·9
798·4	875·1	966·0	1,026·5	1,291·1	1,205·6	1,316·1	1,330·6
539·9	646·5	726·6	909·4	1,522·0	1,144·9	1,054·5	1,024·5
105·2	158·6	149·1	197·0	315·7	338·6	314·8	329·2
329·5	370·6	413·6	456·4	757·6	767·9	641·5	679·8
1,141·8	1,578·3	1,787·4	2,174·2	2,581·6	2,584·2	2,582·0	2,774·2
63·4	91·8	95·3	132·3	157·6	154·9	149·3	157·3
39·1	45·0	50·1	89·2	108·4	81·9	96·7	101·1
10·7	52·5	69·9	77·1	69·8	125·5	147·7	152·2
988·8	1,344·2	1,524·9	1,827·6	2,195·4	2,141·4	2,098·4	2,171·0
59·2	60·6	58·0	84·7	127·0	143·9	105·4	100·8
7·6	9·6	11·7	14·5	17·3	21·3	24·9	26·9
42·6	40·4	37·2	56·7	90·8	95·0	55·6	46·8
3·1	1·7	1·4	1·4	2·3	0·6	1·4	2·7
5·9	8·8	7·8	12·1	16·6	27·0	23·5	24·3
55·4	94·5	94·5	136·7	217·4	168·2	152·5	—
597·4	436·5	432·1	347·6	1,093·3	748·9	657·5	503·9

The Volume of Trade. In terms of quantities of goods imported and exported the situation was considerably different. The figures for the pre-war and post-war periods are unfortunately not fully comparable; but the discrepancy is not great enough seriously to upset the comparison.

of the U.K., 1935–38 and 1947–54
= 100)

1949	1950	1951	1952	1953	1954	1953 1938 = 100 (approx.)
100	100	112	103	112	114	87·5
104	100	110	98	111	108	—
95	100	104	92	103	102	—
91	100	135	134	148 ·	167	—
106	100	128	123	119	130	—
100	100	113	101	112	114	—
86	100	101	95	98	104	150
88	100	103	94	94	99	—
—	100	105	144	117	109	—

† Based on valuation in terms of 1950 prices.

Thus, by 1947, the volume of British exports had almost recovered the level of 1938, but was still considerably behind that of 1937; whereas the volume of imports was almost a third lower than in 1938, and actually a third lower than in 1937, and re-exports had fallen off by 63 per cent. By 1954 imports were 28 per cent greater in volume than in 1947, and exports 68 per cent greater; but re-exports had fallen away to not much more than a third of the volume of the pre-war years.

Britain's Need for Imports. The exceptional dependence of the United Kingdom on imports is mainly a consequence of high industrialization, which has allowed a large population to become concentrated in a small country and has thus made it dependent on imported food supplies as well as on imported materials. At an earlier stage, the United Kingdom was well supplied with home resources of many of the most essential materials . . . especially coal and iron, on which its rapid industrial development during the nineteenth century was largely based. Of timber it was short from an early period; and it ran short of wool about the middle of the century. All its cotton had to be imported, and also a substantial proportion of hides and skins. Silk and silk goods headed the list of imported manufactured consumers' goods; and in 1850 chemicals accounted for the largest value among imports, after grain, cotton, sugar and tea. By the end of the nineteenth century grain was still the most costly import; but meat had risen to the second place, with cotton standing third and timber fourth. Then came wool, sugar and butter—all close together—and then fruit, leather and tea. Despite falling prices net imports rose from £259,000,000 in 1870 to £386,000,000 in 1896, when average prices were lowest. By 1913 they had increased to a value of £659,000,000. The great rise in prices during and after the first world war brought net imports to £1,710,000,000 in 1920. Thereafter the value fell away with falling prices; it was £958,000,000 in 1930 and, after a fall during the great slump of the early 1930s, was back at £958,000,000 in 1937, falling again to £858,000,000 in 1938. In 1954, as we have seen, it was £3,278,000,000.

The Bill for Imports. We have now to see what the main items in this huge bill for imports are. In 1954 foodstuffs accounted for £1,254,000,000 and tobacco for £76,700,000. The principal items were—

TABLE 97

Imports of Foodstuffs (values), 1953

	£million		£million
Meat and Meat Preparations	256	Coffee, Cocoa, Tea and Spices	217
Cereals and Cereal Preparations	176	Sugar and Sugar Preparations	103
Fruit and Vegetables	204		
Dairy Products; Eggs and Honey	161		
	Other Food and Drink	£136,000,000	

Then came the basic materials, to a total value of £1,024,000,000. The main items in this group were:

TABLE 98
Imports of Basic Materials (values), 1953

	£million		£million
Wool and other Animal		Pulp and Waste Paper	87
Hair	198	Rubber	51
Wood and Cork	155	Other Textile Fibres	36
Metal Ores and Scrap	137	Hides, Skins and Undressed	
Cotton	126	Furs	44
Oil Seeds, Nuts and Kernels	68	Crude Fertilizers, etc.	36

The third group—Mineral Fuels and Lubricants—with a total value of £329,000,000, consisted mainly of petroleum and petroleum products, valued at £312,000,000.

Fourthly, we come to the manufactured goods, many of which were further processed in the United Kingdom. They consisted indeed quite largely of semi-manufactured industrial materials. The total value of the group as a whole was £680,000,000; and the biggest items were as follows:

TABLE 99
Imports of Manufactured Goods (values), 1953

	£million		£million
Non-ferrous Metals	174	Misc. Textile Goods	30
Chemicals	102	Iron and Steel	28
Machinery, other than		Road Vehicles and Aircraft	24
Electrical	75	Cotton Yarns and Goods	22
Paper, Board, etc.	52	Leather, Leather Goods and	
Wood and Cork Manufac-		Dressed Furs	21
tures (except furniture)	39		

Other Manufactured Goods   £98,000,000

All these figures are for *retained* imports, excluding re-exports. They also exclude postal packages (£11,000,000) and live animals not for food (£7,000,000).

Import Prices. The maintenance of full employment calls for a large and steady supply both of basic materials and of foodstuffs, because it increases total demand. Fluctuations in import values are affected, not only by changes in consumption, but also by fluctuations in prices and by the extent to which stocks in the United Kingdom are being accumulated or depleted. As we saw (page 117), there were particularly violent changes in raw material prices after the outbreak of the Korean war; and the total cost of imports was at the same time swollen by stock accumulation, especially of strategic goods. The bill for retained imports of non-ferrous metals, after rising fairly steadily from £77,000,000 in 1947 to £103,000,000 in 1950, shot up suddenly to nearly £159,000,000 in 1951 and almost £202,000,000 in 1952, before falling back to £151,000,000 in 1953 and rising again to £174 million in 1954. For iron and steel the rise was even more sensational, from £14,000,000 in 1947 and £37,000,000 in 1951 to £116,000,000 in 1952—and then down to £61,000,000 in 1953 and a mere £28 million in 1954. Imports of machinery also doubled in cost between 1950 and 1952, and paper imports rose threefold in cost from 1950 to 1951. Chemical imports also more than doubled in cost from 1949 to 1951. For the effect of changes in stocks see page 61.

Despite the high cost of imports, the quantities imported were in the aggregate always considerably below those of the years before 1939. Even in 1951 and in 1953 they were down by about an eighth from the level of 1938. British exports, on the other hand, had been in recent years a long way above those of the years before 1939—in 1953 they were in volume more than 50 per cent above those of 1938 when weighted by post-war prices. This points to great efforts both to dispense with replaceable imports and to expand the export sector of home industry.

The Composition of British Exports.   British exports consist to an overwhelmingly preponderant extent of manufactured goods. In 1954, out of total exports (excluding re-exports) valued at £2,673,000,000, manufactures accounted for £2,171,000,000. Outside the manufactures group the only big items were petroleum and its products (£84,000,000), coal (£68,000,000), wool (£63,000,000), drink (£46,000,000), sugar and sugar preparations (£33,000,000), and tobacco (£22,000,000); and most of them except coal owed a substantial part of their value to manufacture in the United Kingdom. Of the groups classified as 'manufactured goods', the biggest items in values were in 1954 as shown in Table 100.

It will be seen at once how greatly preponderant are the products of the metal, engineering, vehicle and kindred industries in the total of British exports. Five of the six leading groups belong to this category, and all five were ahead of the cotton industry, which formerly held the leading position, and had done continuously from the Industrial Revolution. In all, 9 out of the 20 groups belong to the metal goods category; and the value of these 9 groups of exports amounted in 1954 to £1,358,000—more than half the total for exports of all kinds. As against this, the 5 textile and clothing groups added up to only £370,000,000, to which may be added a further £74,000,000 for textile materials—mainly re-exported after processing.

Changes in Exports.   This is a really remarkable change from the pre-war situation, even if we take 1937, the most favourable pre-war year, rather than 1938 as a basis for comparison. A glance at the table

TABLE 100

Exports of British Manufactured Goods (values), 1937 and 1954

(£million)

	1937	1954	Increase per cent
Machinery, other than Electrical	44	408	828
Road Vehicles and Aircraft	25	307	1,128
Chemicals	33	204	518
Electrical Machinery and Appliances	18	170	845
Other Metal Manufactures	23	145	530
Iron and Steel	37	137	270
Cotton Yarns and Goods	62	112	81
Woollen and Worsted Yarns and Goods	27	83	207
Miscellaneous Textile Goods	29	90	210
Non-ferrous Metals	13	56	331
Miscellaneous Mineral Manufactures (non-metallic)	9	59	555
Clothing, Footwear, Travel Goods	14	45	222
Rail Vehicles	6	44	633
Ships and Boats	4	50	1,150
Synthetic Fibre Yarns and Goods	5	40	700
Rubber Goods	6	32	433
Paper, Board, etc.	8	33	312
Scientific Instruments, Watches, Clocks, etc.	3	31	933
Sanitary Goods, Buildings and Furniture	3	22	633
Leather Goods	7	17	143
Other Manufactured Goods	15	82	447

shows that, in terms of money value, the exports of 1954 were in three cases ten times or more those of 1937, and in two other cases nine times; and all these increases were in the metals and vehicles group. Of course, a large part of this rise was due to higher prices: the prices of all exports rose on an average by about 224 per cent between 1937–8 and 1953–4. But even after allowance has been made for price changes, the rise in exports of metal goods and vehicles remains very remarkable. It was, of course, made possible by the heavy concentration on the development of these industries during the war, and by the large accumulation of arrears in the supply of capital goods, motor-cars, and many other kinds of metal goods, as well as by the huge losses of shipping suffered during the war. It was, indeed, quite impossible, during the years after 1945, for more than a fraction of the total demand for many of these goods to be supplied; and sellers were largely free to pick and choose between competitive customers. Nevertheless, even in a seller's market, the expansion of British exports of metal goods was remarkable; for it involved keeping home consumers waiting for a great many goods they were eager to buy.

Quantities of Exports. In some cases it is impossible to give the actual

	1936	1937	1938
Food, Drink and Tobacco:			
Fish and Fish Products (thousand tons)	227	201	219
Potatoes „ „	32	56	53
Sugar and Sugar Confectionery „ „	362	335	370
Beer (thousand bulk barrels)	325	341	281
Spirits (million proof gallons)	8·5	9·5	9·1
Tobacco (million lb.)	37	43	40
Raw Materials and Fuels:			
Wool, Raw, Tops, Noils, etc. (million lb.)	150	122	103
Coal (million tons)	34	40	36
Coal, bunker „ „	12	12	10
Petroleum, refined (million gallons)	110	118	118
Manufactured Goods:			
Chemicals, Sodium Compounds (thousand tons)	382	466	355
Chemicals, Soaps „ „	38	41	37
Ammonium Nitrate and A. Sulphate „ „	232	317	330
Rubber Tyres and Tubes (millions)	8·9	8·2	6·0
Paper and Board (thousand tons)	206	216	172
Woollen Yarns (million lb.)	47	41	35
Woollen, etc., Fabrics (million sq. yards)	114	118	88
Cotton Yarns and Thread (million lb.)	167	175	136
Cotton Fabrics (million sq. yards)	1,916	1,921	1,368
Art Silk Fabrics „ „ „	64	78	59
Linen and Hemp Fabrics „ „ „	89	83	52
Jute Fabrics „ „ „	122	137	84
Felt Base, Lino and Oil Cloth „ „ „	26	29	25
Cement (thousand tons)	690	716	760
Glass and Glassware „ „	44	52	51
China and Domestic Pottery „ „	27	23	24
Finished Steel „ „	1,568	1,876	1,324
Machinery, other than Electrical „ „	226	266	274
Machinery, Electrical „ „	31	34	44
Radio Sets and (from 1947)			
Radiograms (thousands)	56	69	85
Rail Locomotives (number)	463	377	458
Rail Carriages and Trucks (thousand tons)	28	33	38
Rail Vehicle Parts „ „	48	52	71
Motor Cars, New (thousands)	51	54	44
Motor Vehicles, Commercial, New „	3	4	3
Motor Chassis with Engines, New „	27	41	35
Motor Cycles and Tricars, New „	20	25	20
Pedal Cycles (millions)	0·5	0·8	0·6
Ships, Steam and Motor (thousand gross tons)	109	77	177
Leather Footwear (thousand dozen pairs)	368	394	374
Knitted Underwear (thousand dozen)	1,006	1,021	808
Hats and Caps „ „	763	717	594
Books and Periodicals (thousand tons)	28	29	28

1947	1948	1949	1950	1951	1952	1953	1954
60	90	94	68	74	65	57	62
55	89	70	56	95	61	96	132
278	597	580	771	750	702	687	727
110	205	254	221	275	267	285	248
7·6	8·8	9·6	11·0	12·4	13·1	14·7	15·2
52	45	47	43	51	47	45	41
85	107	129	167	113	127	148	152
1	10	14	14	8	12	14	14
4	5	5	4	4	3	3	2·5
75	44	95	259	750	1,267	1,762	1,944
257	413	379	524	603	508	437	545
18	28	43	44	66	63	55	60
326	318	330	336	319	503	427	349
6·5	10·9	8·5	10·0	11·7	9·7	9·5	12·4
104	128	180	259	254	212	250	277
14	21	29	35	27	25	28	25
75	102	106	117	109	92	96	91
37	71	96	84	80	45	52	52
533	761	904	815	852	712	709	637
106	144	172	197	218	152	177	175
46	44	38	49	50	39	47	47
30	33	26	37	34	28	23	26
18	41	31	39	45	32	34	43
888	1,584	1,889	1,881	1,970	2,130	1,995	1,850
94	126	144	151	168	126	133	144
36	43	43	48	48	38	33	37
1,199	1,355	1,637	2,251	1,828	1,793	1,918	2,114
409	480	524	732	758	629	524	505
69	75	100	112	109	115	111	105
406	308	295	280	479	428	320	311
941	1,025	1,066	929	972	1,046	942	962
50	34	59	65	41	54	81	68
98	125	153	136	113	124	135	95
126	194	219	343	309	276	264	316
23	36	44	73	67	61	51	57
43	70	87	125	129	100	98	119
55	75	65	74	92	70	63	70
1·4	1·8	2·2	2·1	2·7	2·8	2·0	2·1
197	416	463	452	634	460	372	475
504	433	328	463	518	398	455	427
1,995	2,270	1,666	1,252	1,266	934	970	809
501	395	432	500	627	352	437	460
13	14	16	20	23	24	28	32

quantities of United Kingdom products exported in recent years. In Table 101, for example, are some of the main items, beginning with the non-manufactured categories.

In this table, note again the very great increases in Vehicles, Machinery and Refined Petroleum, and the sharp falls in Coal and Cotton Goods.

Sources of Imports. Of total United Kingdom imports in 1954, an amount valued at £1,737,000,000 came from countries in the British Commonwealth, including Ireland, and an amount valued at £1,642,000,000 from other countries. Of exports of British goods, a value of £1,477,000,000 went to Commonwealth countries, and £1,256,000,000 to other countries. Thus 51·4 per cent of imports came from Commonwealth countries, which took 53 per cent of all British exports. As compared with these proportions, in 1937, only 38·3 per cent of imports came from Commonwealth countries, but 48·3 of United Kingdom exports were consigned to them. Thus in 1954 the United Kingdom derived its markets for a much higher proportion of its total exports from the Commonwealth area than in 1937; but the proportion of total exports sent to the Commonwealth, though it had increased, had risen much less than the proportion of imports. This is partly the sequel to what happened during the 1930s, when exports to Commonwealth countries were maintained much better during the depression than exports to foreign countries. It is also in part the outcome of the high post-war demand all over the world for the products of the steel, engineering and vehicle industries, and of the difficulties which most countries faced in buying such goods from the dollar areas. (For the whole balance of payments problem see page 193.)

In the table on page 187 will be found a list of the countries from which the United Kingdom drew the largest value of imports in 1937 and 1954, and on page 188 of those to which it sent the largest value of exports. 1937 has been chosen in preference to 1938 as giving a fairer picture of pre-war conditions. It will be seen that in both years the three leading countries as sources of imports were the same, and in the same order, but that the Argentine fell from fourth place in 1937 to fourteenth in 1954, mainly because of the big decline in meat supplies from that source. New Zealand, with its alternative supply of meat and its dairy produce, rose from sixth to fourth place. India came fifth in both years, and Denmark seventh; but in 1954 the sixth place was taken by the small area of Kuwait, recently developed as a source of oil when the Persian supply was cut off. Germany, which held the eighth place in 1937, was only fifteenth in 1954, including East as well as West Germany; but the Germans were rapidly climbing back after their eclipse at the end of the war. Their place in 1954 was taken by Sweden, which rose from eleventh to ninth. Holland was tenth in both years; but the Soviet Union, twelfth in 1937, had dropped to the twenty-third place in 1954. In the remainder of the list of 25 countries, the Dutch West Indies, Egypt, Japan, Poland and Persia, which figured in it for 1937, had been replaced in 1954 by Kuwait, Nigeria, Northern Rhodesia, Italy and Iraq.

Export Markets. There had been even more considerable changes in the principal markets for British exports. At the head of the list in 1937 was the Union of South Africa; but by 1954 Australia had not merely risen from second to first place but was a very long way ahead of all the rest. South Africa was still second in 1954, but not much ahead of the United States, which had ousted India from the third place. India had fallen from third to sixth, whereas Canada had risen from fifth to fourth, and New Zealand from ninth to fifth. Germany, sixth in 1937, was eleventh in 1954; Ireland was seventh at both dates; France fell from eighth in 1937 to fourteenth in 1954. The Argentine, ninth in 1937, dropped right out of the list in 1954; Denmark rose from eleventh to tenth place, and Holland from twelfth to eighth. Besides the Argentine, Egypt, Brazil, China, Poland and the Channel Islands dropped out; and Italy, Pakistan (previously included in India), Kenya, Southern Rhodesia, Switzerland and Venezuela took their place. The Soviet Union was not in the list for either year. Japan was among the suppliers of imports in 1937 only, and was not among the customers in either year.

'Dollar' and other Imports. It is to be noted that, despite the post-war scarcity of dollars, two 'dollar countries'—the United States and Canada —have kept their places at the head of the list of United Kingdom suppliers. From Canada, in 1954, came more than two-thirds of the United Kingdom's total imports of wheat, at 60 per cent of the total cost: the next largest supplier was the United States, followed closely by Australia, with the Soviet Union a very long way behind. Canada also sent more than half the barley, and the United States more than half the maize. The biggest suppliers of meat in 1954 were New Zealand, Denmark, Australia and the Argentine—in that order. New Zealand also led in dairy products, followed by Denmark and, at a long distance, by Australia. For fruit and vegetables, the United Kingdom paid most to Australia, South Africa, Italy, Spain and Holland—in that order; for crude sugar, most to Australia, Mauritius, Cuba, the Dominican Republic and Jamaica—also in that order; for coffee, to Kenya and Uganda, and then Brazil; for cocoa, to the Gold Coast and to Nigeria; for tea, to India and Ceylon; for feeding stuffs, to the Argentine; for alcoholic drinks, to France, to Eire and to Spain; and for tobacco, to the United States, followed at a long distance by Southern Rhodesia.

Raw Materials. Turn now to raw materials. Hides and skins came from many sources—the United States and the Soviet Union leading the rest by a short head. Oil seeds, nuts and kernels came mainly from Nigeria—with the rest almost nowhere. Rubber came preponderantly from Malaya—£35,000,000 out of £50,000,000. Timber came mostly from Canada, Sweden and Finland, with the Soviet Union some way behind. Pulp came from Sweden most of all, followed by Norway and Canada. Of wool, Australia was by far the largest supplier: then came New Zealand and, at a long distance, South Africa. For cotton, nearly three times as much was paid to the United States as to any other country: next in order came the Sudan, Brazil and Egypt. The United States also led in the supply of fertilizers and crude minerals other than fuel. Iron ore came in mainly from Sweden and in the second place Algeria; nickel ore from Canada; bauxite from Australia; tin ore from Bolivia and on a smaller scale Nigeria; manganese ore from India and the Gold Coast; zinc ore from Australia; oils and fats from Nigeria.

Of fuels, coal—an exceptional import—came in from Belgium and the United States; petroleum much the most from Kuwait, imports from which cost four times as much as from the next largest source, Iraq. Next stood the Dutch West Indies, and then the United States, Venezuela and Bahrein. Kuwait and Iraq were the main suppliers of unrefined oil.

Manufactured Imports. Of manufactured goods chemicals cost more than £100,000,000, with the United States leading, and accounting for a quarter of the total cost. Western Germany and France held second and third place. Dressed leather and furs came mainly from India; manufactured timber mainly from Finland, Sweden and France; paper in nearly equal values from Canada—mainly newsprint—and from Sweden, followed by Finland and Norway. Cotton manufactures, of which imports were growing, came mostly from India, Belgium and Japan; and synthetic fibre fabrics and yarns from Italy, followed by France and Western Germany. Other textile imports came chiefly from India.

Iron and steel came from many sources, mostly in small amounts. The United States headed the list. Copper was imported mainly from Northern Rhodesia, followed at long distances by Canada and Chile; nickel from Canada; lead from Australia; zinc from Canada. Of fully manufactured goods imported machinery came chiefly from the United States and Germany, with Switzerland a long way behind. Electrical machinery came most largely from Holland, with the United States well behind. Imported road vehicles and aircraft were mainly from Canada and the United States—in both cases fairly small totals.

TABLE 102

British Imports (values): Principal Sources

(*£million*)

	1937		1954
U.S.A.	114·1	U.S.A.	282·9
Canada	88·8	Canada	272·9
Australia	71·7	Australia	236·8
Argentine	59·8	New Zealand	176·9
India	58·2	India	148·6
New Zealand	49·9	Kuwait	134·8
Denmark	36·6	Denmark	124·5
Germany	36·1	Sweden	116·9
Holland	32·0	Holland	109·7
U.S.S.R.	29·1	Nigeria	107·6
Sweden	26·2	Eire	103·3
France	25·6	France	97·2
Belgium	22·7	S. Africa	84·4
Finland	22·4	Argentine	81·1
Eire	21·1	Germany (E. and W.)	79·3
S. Africa	17·9	British W. Indies	60·0
Dutch W. Indies	16·6	Finland	59·0
Egypt	14·3	N. Rhodesia	58·9
Malaya	13·1	Belgium	52·9
Japan	11·8	Italy	52·6
Ceylon	11·6	Malaya	52·4
Norway	11·6	Iraq	44·5
British W. Indies	11·2	U.S.S.R.	41·8
Poland	10·8	Norway	41·7
Persia	10·4	Ceylon	40·5

The Terms of Trade. These figures make plain the extreme dependence of Great Britain on imported materials for keeping its industries at work. No major industry could maintain its production without these imports; and any stoppage of supplies would confront the British people with mass unemployment as well as with starvation. This makes the country particularly vulnerable to submarine or other warfare directed against shipping: indeed, the Germans clearly reckoned on this both in 1914 and in 1939. In times of peace, it also gives Great Britain an evident interest in the cheapness of materials as well as of foodstuffs in the world market—cheapness, that is to say, in terms of the manu-factured goods which Great Britain chiefly exports. The fewer manu-factured goods it takes to pay for each unit of imports, the more goods Great Britain can afford to import, or the more of its own products it can afford to use at home instead of selling them to customers overseas.

This truth, however, is not unqualified; for the more of their food-stuffs and materials the overseas countries have to provide in exchange for each unit of manufactured goods, the fewer such goods can they

TABLE 103
British Exports (values): Principal Destination
(£*million*)

	1937		1954
S. Africa	41·4	Australia	277·8
Australia	37·5	S. Africa	156·2
India	35·8	U.S.A.	149·8
U.S.A.	31·4	Canada	131·9
Canada	27·6	New Zealand	126·0
Germany	21·6	India	114·9
Eire	21·6	Eire	100·6
France	21·4	Holland	99·8
New Zealand	20·2	Sweden	93·0
Argentine	20·0	Denmark	82·1
Denmark	16·9	Germany	72·1
Holland	15·0	Norway	68·5
Sweden	13·0	Malaya	65·4
Malaya	11·6	France	64·3
Belgium	11·1	Italy	59·0
Norway	8·9	Belgium	54·6
Egypt	7·8	Nigeria	48·8
Nigeria	7·3	Pakistan	45·9
Brazil	7·0	British W. Indies	41·1
British W. Indies	6·2	Gold Coast	33·9
Finland	6·0	Kenya	33·8
China	5·9	S. Rhodesia	33·3
Poland	5·7	Finland	31·7
Gold Coast	5·6	Switzerland	26·8
Channel Isles	5·5	Venezuela	25·4

afford to buy. High prices for British exports mean low sales, even apart from their effect in directing custom to alternative suppliers. So much of Great Britain's overseas trade is with countries that are mainly producers of foodstuffs and materials that this is a most important point. It is to Great Britain's advantage that the buyers of British goods should be prosperous and should have a high purchasing power. Yet if they do have this, as a consequence of high prices for their own products, the 'terms of trade' (see p. 199) go against Great Britain, and more British goods are needed for buying any given quantity of imports.

Great Britain has therefore a mixed interest—which may be called an interest in 'fair' relative prices for what is imported and what is sold overseas. But what are 'fair' prices? Are they the prices that yield equal returns to each unit of land, capital or labour applied to production? Or, if not, what meaning can we attach to the notion of fair exchange? Land, capital and labour, used in conjunction one with another, are on the average more productive in some countries than in others, as they are in one farm, mine or factory than in another in the same country.

TABLE 104

Exports of British Products, 1954. Chief Destination of Certain Products

£million	Total Exports	To U.S.A.	Other Chief Customers
Whisky	39·1	20·9	
Wool	63·2	6·2	Canada 5·3, W. Germany 5·2, India 4·9
Coal	59·1	—	Denmark 11·5, Eire 7·9, Italy 6·4, W. Germany 5·3
Petroleum	84·2	—	Denmark 10·8, Eire 8·3, Norway 6·7, Holland 6·6
Chemicals	203·8	7·1	Australia 17·2, India 15·1, S. Africa 9·7, Holland 7·6
Rubber Manufactures	31·9	0·3	Denmark 1·8, Nigeria 1·4, Sweden 1·4
Paper and Board	33·5	1·7	Australia 9·4, New Zealand 2·9, S. Africa 2·7
Woollens and Worsteds	83·4	9·2	Canada 11·0, W. Germany 7·7, S. Africa 6·2, New Zealand 5·7
Cotton Goods	112·0	2·4	Australia 20·1, S. Africa 11·8, New Zealand 7·0, Nigeria 6·3
Synthetic Fibre Goods	40·1	—	Australia 11·7, New Zealand 4·3, S. Africa 4·0
Other Textile Goods	89·8	10·1	Australia 19·0, New Zealand 9·0, S. Africa 6·4, Canada 6·2
Iron and Steel	136·9	3·3	Australia 20·0, New Zealand 10·9, Canada 8·6, India 5·9
Non-ferrous Metals	55·8	6·8	W. Germany 6·2, Australia 4·2, Sweden 3·3, Holland 3·2
Metal Manufactures	145·4	5·0	Holland 16·8, Australia 12·6, S. Africa 11·3
Machinery, other than Electrical	407·8	15·0	Australia 47·0, S. Africa 28·7, India 28·0, Canada 18·7
Machinery and Appliances, Electrical	170·1	2·7	S. Africa 18·0, Australia 17·5, India 14·8, New Zealand 9·8
Rail Vehicles	44·4	—	S. Africa 9·2, Australia 5·1, Kenya 3·5, India 3·1
Motor Cars, New	109·1	11·2	Australia 15·3, New Zealand 12·8, Sweden 12·7
Road Goods Vehicles	27·6	—	Australia 4·3, New Zealand 1·4, Kenya 1·0
Cycles	18·2	4·7	Nigeria 1·5
Motor Cycles	8·0	1·0	Australia 1·1
Ships and Boats	50·4	—	Norway 17·7, Liberia 13·2, Panama 2·8
Clothing and Footwear	44·7	6·0	Canada 4·3, Australia 3·8, New Zealand 2·9, S. Africa 2·3
Postal Packages	85·4	6·0	S. Africa 6·3, Canada 5·9, Eire 5·9

Evidently buyers will not be prepared to pay more for the products of a particular country because they have cost more land or capital or labour to produce, if there are on the market alternative supplies produced under more favourable conditions. Prices cannot correspond to productive costs in a particular country or establishment: they depend broadly speaking on what is needed to elicit an aggregate production corresponding to the demand. This in turn is affected by the size of the wages that have to be paid to attract the required labour, or the price of land, and on the rate of interest required to attract the requisite investment of capital.

Trade and Productivity. Broadly speaking, in many of the less advanced countries labour is very plentiful and cheap, whereas capital tends to be scarce and dear. Such countries use large quantities of labour in relation to the amount of invested capital, and would be able to produce very cheaply if their labour were efficient as well as cheap. But in practice shortage of capital lowers its efficiency: nor have the workers in these countries been inured to the steady pace of work that is characteristic of advanced capitalist production. Accordingly, they are often unable to produce at as low a cost as other countries where wages are much higher. Their standards of living are low partly because their productivity is low.

There may, however, be a second reason; for their productivity, measured in terms of the money value of their products, is low partly because their products are sold at low prices. Historically, the countryman's labour has usually been valued less highly than the industrial worker's; and this low historical valuation has affected the relative selling prices of agricultural and industrial products. Country workers, moreover, usually find it more difficult than industrial workers to improve their incomes by combination; and it is usually harder for the rural than for the industrial entrepreneur to establish any sort of monopoly. Accordingly, there has been a tendency, historically, for the townsmen to out-bargain the country-dwellers and to establish 'terms of trade' favourable to the towns. Only when, for any reason, foodstuffs or primary materials become scarce in the world's markets can the countrymen get some of their own back on the town-dwellers—and this is most likely to happen in times of war, or of war's immediate aftermath. For, in war, the land may undergo devastation and many of the cultivators may be made forcibly into soldiers; and it may also become difficult to transport the country products to the places where they are needed. In such circumstances, the relative prices of foodstuffs and primary materials may rise sharply; and in such cases the highly industrialized countries may find the 'terms of trade' turning against them.

The Terms of Trade before and after the War. This, as we shall see in the next section, occurred in the case of Great Britain after 1939. In the 1930s the prices of both foodstuffs and materials fell to abnormally low levels, owing both to the decline in industrial demand and to the difficulty which agricultural producers find in adjusting their output at all quickly to changes in demand. These low prices mitigated the effects of the slump of the 1930s on Great Britain, by making the terms of trade abnormally favourable—though they also restricted the demand for British exports. After the war, however, there was a world scarcity of many foodstuffs and materials, and their relative prices rose. Great Britain had then to use every possible effort to expand its exports in order to meet the higher cost of essential imports. In 1950–2, during the Korean crisis, the position was greatly aggravated by the forcing-up of prices of many essential materials, not only because the immediate demand for them was increased by rearmament, but also because, in view of the possible imminence of another world war, the United States, and other countries to a smaller extent, began 'stock-piling'—that is, building up stocks of potentially scarce materials of strategic importance. This led to a very sharp rise in the prices of such materials, greatly aggravated by speculative buying in anticipation of still higher prices to come. The 'terms of trade' then moved against the purchasing countries; and the primary producers experienced a sudden affluence. Agricultural prices were much less affected: the benefit accrued chiefly to the suppliers of materials important for war purposes, such as metals, wool and oil, and minerals such as sulphur.

Britain's Interest in Overseas Development. In these circumstances, the British balance of payments deficit, which had disappeared in 1948, recurred in an aggravated form; and the effort to expand exports had to be redoubled in order to redress the trouble. Great Britain has a strong immediate interest in the industrialization of the less advanced countries; for its exports now consist largely of capital goods, the market for which depends on industrial development. It is sometimes argued that, in supplying such goods to the less developed areas, Great Britain is only raising up new competitors against its own industries; but this view of the matter is mainly mistaken. For a long time to come, the more these areas develop their own productiveness, the better markets will they be for the goods of the advanced countries. They will hardly be in a position for a long time to come to proceed far along the line of producing for themselves the more intricate and expensive kinds of machinery which they need both for electrification and irrigation projects and for building up their own manufactures of consumer goods. No doubt the Soviet Union, with its gigantic Five Year Plans devoted largely to the expansion of the heavy industries, appears to contradict this argument; but the Soviet Union is highly exceptional both on account of its size and because it has had to concern itself largely with the development of its military power. It is to be hoped that other countries will not need, as they increase their productive resources, to waste a large part of their output on preparation for war, at the expense of their consumers' standards of living. If they avoid this, their industrialization will be able to take the shape of increasing the output of consumers' goods for their home markets and of producing more materials and surplus foodstuffs for export, with the aid of imported machinery. This is the more natural line of development for countries which have abundant man-power but are short of capital; and if world tension can be eased this is the most probable course of economic growth in the under-developed areas, as well as the most advantageous both for their peoples and for those of the more advanced countries.

Colonial and Dominions Development.   In Great Britain's case this is the right line of development especially in relation to markets in the British Colonies and Dominions. The economically backward countries can most increase their wealth and their standards of living, not by attempting to spread their scarce capital resources over the whole field of industry but by concentrating each on a relatively few kinds of output, in order to achieve the economies of large-scale production, and to devote a considerable fraction of their investment to the improvement of the conditions of agriculture and transport. Such forms of advance will make them not so much competitors as better customers of Great Britain and other relatively advanced countries, but will be thwarted if each country is seeking to build up its military power rather than to raise its people's standard of living.

Great Britain, then, needs to do all it can to help the less developed countries—and particularly those in the Commonwealth—to improve their productivity and therewith their standards of living by building up the efficiency of the types of production for which they are best suited. This involves not only loans to these countries to speed up their advance but also outright gifts, such as are already being made on an inadequate scale under the Colonial Development Acts. The release of a substantial part of the productive effort which Great Britain has been directing to war production would make possible a much more generous policy of economic aid in the world 'war upon want'; and Great Britain would in the not distant future reap a rich harvest in the increased purchasing power of the under-developed areas and from their demand for those kinds of capital goods which British industry is best adapted to supply.

CHAPTER FOURTEEN

THE BALANCE OF PAYMENTS

A COUNTRY'S balance of payments is made up of the difference between the total sum of money accruing to it or to persons resident within it in payments from other countries or persons resident in them, on the one hand, and on the other the total sums which it or its residents pay to recipients abroad during a given period. The balance of payments, in this sense, is made up of two elements which it is desirable to distinguish. Most payments are made in settlement of debts arising out of current transactions, such as payments for goods imported or for the use of shipping and payments of interest or dividends in respect of capital assets owned by persons or institutions outside the areas in which the assets are located, or similar interest payments on public debts. But there is a second class of international payments representing capital transactions—loans from persons or Governments to persons or Governments in different countries. Loans of capital from one area to another increase the immediate international purchasing power of the borrowing area, but decrease it correspondingly when and if the loans are repaid and also, while they are current, involve the debtor country in payment of interest to the lending area.

Current and Capital Transactions. Transactions of this second kind, not arising out of current transactions, are usually excluded in calculating what is called the 'balance of payments' in discussions of current trends. When a country is said to be in deficit on its balance of payments what is usually meant is that its receipts from abroad in respect of current transactions are not large enough to meet its current outgoings. In one sense, a country's international receipts and payments must always balance; for every international monetary transaction involves an exchange of one country's money for another's. But this balance may be reached only by selling assets abroad previously owned by the country or its nationals, or in the opposite case, by a 'surplus' country lending money to, or buying capital assets in, a 'deficit' country. Thus, in these days, the United States and its citizens have every year a surplus of receipts from abroad over payments due to be made abroad; and a balance is achieved only because they give or lend this surplus to foreigners without any, or at any rate without an equivalent, immediate return.

Changes in the British Balance. Up to 1914 Great Britain had normally a large current surplus, which was absorbed by British overseas investment. This surplus disappeared during the first world war and was thereafter painfully rebuilt, but never to the pre-war level in terms of real values. The great depression of the 1930s led to the reappearance of a small deficit, which was made good by selling assets held abroad or by repatriating foreign loans as they fell due. During the second world war, the British current deficit became very large. It involved the sale to foreigners of large amounts of British-owned assets, especially in the United States, and also, even after the introduction of 'Lease-Lend' had removed the main burden of payments due to the United States, the piling-up of heavy debts to other countries, such as India, which supplied goods needed for war purposes without immediate payment in full. Great Britain emerged in 1945 with a big current deficit due to the fall in export trade and to the loss of many foreign assets. The immediate difficulty was met mainly by borrowing from the United States and Canada; and within a few years, by means of an export 'drive' combined with severe restrictions on imports into Great Britain, this deficit was wiped out and a small surplus again achieved.

The Dollar Shortage. When this had been done Great Britain would have been able again to pay its way, had each national money been freely exchangeable into any other. But this was not the case. There was, in particular, a world shortage of dollars, as other countries wanted to buy from America—and from the United States in particular —goods to a higher total price than the Americans wanted to buy from them. It was thus possible for a country, such as Great Britain, to have enough foreign money, of a sort, to meet all its bills out of current receipts, and yet to be unable to do this because some sorts of money— e.g. francs—could not be changed into dollars. It therefore continued to be necessary for Great Britain to restrict purchases that needed to be paid for in dollars even when the British current balance of payments again showed a surplus as against the rest of the world as a whole.

The Sterling Area. There is a further complication. Great Britain is the centre of a group of countries, mainly members of the British Commonwealth, and together constituting what is called the sterling area. The countries within this area, instead of managing independently their own international finances, make use for this purpose of the Bank of England, with which they keep their accounts. Instead of holding their own reserves of gold or foreign currencies in order to meet claims falling upon them, they hold balances in the Bank of England which they replenish by paying in their receipts from other countries and draw upon for making their foreign payments. The Bank of England has therefore to be ready at all times to meet their claims for foreign money and is helped to do so by the sums of such money it receives from them. This involves regular consultation between the Commonwealth and British Governments, in order to ensure that the Commonwealth countries' needs are met, but are not allowed to reach a level at which the Bank of England could not provide the requisite finance.

Thus, the balance of payments of Great Britain incorporates many transactions to which Great Britain is a party only in an indirect way; and for certain purposes it is necessary to reckon in terms of the balance of payments of the sterling area as a whole. We can, however, for the moment disregard this complication and consider only the British balance of payments as it is affected by payments due to and from Great Britain and its inhabitants.

Components of the Balance of Payments. The principal components of the British current balance of payments in this sense are as follows. First, the payments made to Great Britain for its exports of goods and, on the other side of the account, the payments made by Great Britain for imports, including those which are subsequently re-exported either in the same state or as altered by manufacturing processes performed on them in Great Britain. British exports are usually valued *f.o.b.*— that is, at their estimated value when leaving a British port, excluding the cost of transmitting them from the port to their foreign destination. British imports, on the other hand, are valued *c.i.f.*—that is, so as to include the cost of getting them to a British port, but to exclude any duty payable on their admittance to Great Britain. Thus, if the goods imported and exported were of equal value as goods, the imports would appear from the figures to be worth more, because of the inclusion of insurance and freight charges.

'Invisible' Items. Secondly, account is taken of the payments made for shipping services, as far as they have not been included in the cost of imports. If goods leaving this country are carried in foreign vessels, the owners have to be paid for their services; and if British ships carry foreign goods from one foreign port to another, the British owners are paid for this service. In addition, British ships incur expenses in foreign ports for supplies bought abroad, and payment must be made for these. Similarly with air transport. The practice in presenting the figures of the balance of payments is to extricate the amounts received and paid out in these ways and to include only the difference between them as a credit or debit item in the total account.

Thirdly, payments are made across national frontiers for certain financial services, such as insurance. If foreigners place insurance business in Great Britain they pay for this service and receive whatever payments fall due to them under the relevant policies; and if British persons or businesses place insurance abroad the position is reversed. Here again, an estimate is made of the difference between what falls due

TABLE 105

United Kingdom General Current Balance of Payments, 1946–54

(£million)

	1946	1947	1948	1949	1950	1951	1952	1953	1954
Debits:									
Imports (f.o.b.)	1,082	1,560	1,794	1,978	2,383	3,491	2,946	2,889	3,007
Shipping	141	170	178	191	180	280	296	243	256
Interest, Profits and Dividends	100	93	103	106	117	178	208	226	258
Travel	42	76	66	75	85	104	83	89	101
Migrants' Funds, Legacies and Private Gifts	− 16	35	34	21	− 5	14	15	4	9
Government:									
(a) Military	374	209	113	110	100	126	141	141	147
(b) Colonial Grants	10	7	10	16	18	17	28	24	29
(c) Relief, etc., Grants and Admin.	103	62	49	48	{16 / 31}	18 / 31	19 / 29	21 / 29	19 / 28
Total Debits	1,836	2,212	2,347	2,545	2,925	4,259	3,765	3,666	3,854

Credits:	1946	1947	1948	1949	1950	1951	1952	1953	1954
Exports and Re-exports (f.o.b.)	917	1,145	1,602	1,841	2,250	2,748	2,826	2,671	2,815
Shipping	169	205	255	282	321	412	401	367	388
Interest, Profits and Dividends	162	186	192	200	271	307	295	285	293
Travel	13	21	33	42	61	75	80	88	95
Government: (a) Grants	164	129	96	35	—	14	17	3	—
(b) Other	113	83	170	176	29	24	28	57	54
Other (net)					293	272	256	310	319
Total Credits	1,538	1,769	2,348	2,576	3,225	3,852	3,903	3,781	3,964
+ Defence Aid	—	—	—	—	—	4	121	102	50
Total, including Defence Aid	1,538	1,769	2,348	2,576	3,225	3,856	4,024	3,893	4,014
Balance Credit	—	—	—	31	300	—	259	217	160
" Debit	298	443	1	—	—	403	—	—	—

to Great Britain in respect of such services and what is paid out; and this difference is entered as a credit or debit item in the account.

Fourthly, there is British capital invested or lent abroad, and foreign capital invested or lent in Great Britain. Estimates are made, not of the amount of capital involved, but of the payments of interest, dividends or other incomes made in respect of it to or from Great Britain; and, once more, the difference appears as a credit or debit. Repayments of capital previously lent or invested are excluded in estimating the current balance of payments.

Fifthly, there are certain special government items, including especially the cost of maintaining British armed forces, embassies and consular services outside Great Britain and, on the other side, similar costs incurred in Great Britain by other countries; and with these are reckoned any payments made by one Government to another except on account of capital loans.

Sixthly, citizens of one country may make gifts to citizens of another country—for example, remittances to and from emigrants. In addition, tourists and other travellers spend money in the countries they visit and usually need to draw this money from their own country. All these payments enter into the balances of the countries concerned, and are estimated and cancelled out, leaving the differences to accrue as credits or debits in the total current account.

The British Balance in 1954.   It is now time to present the actual figures arrived at by this process of calculation. In 1954 the total balance of current payments for Great Britain was estimated at £160 million on the right side—i.e. current receipts exceeded current payments by that amount. British exports and re-exports of goods were valued at £2,815 million; and imports at £3,007 million—an adverse balance of £192 million. Government expenditure abroad added £169 million to the deficit; but favourable balances on the remaining items totalling £471 million provided a total favourable balance of £110 million, to which was added a sum of £50 million given as 'Defence Aid' by the United States.

These figures are only provisional, and it seems best to set out for more detailed study the figures for the previous years as well. (See Table 105.)

This table relates only to current transactions; it excludes capital transactions. It will be seen that after the heavy deficits of 1946 and 1947, a bare balance was recovered in 1948 and 1949, and a substantial one in 1950. The serious deficit of 1951 was due mainly to the sharp rise in prices which followed the outbreak of the Korean crisis: it was aggravated by heavy buying of imports at high prices as attempts were made to build up stocks in anticipation of possible world war. A favourable balance was regained in 1952 at the expense of severe restrictions on imports: the terms of trade, which had been very unfavourable in 1951, improved again, and the favourable balance was maintained, though at falling levels, in 1952 and 1953.

The Terms of Trade. By 'terms of trade' is meant the relation between the average prices of imports and exports. The 'terms' are favourable to a country when the proceeds of an average unit of exported goods will buy a large quantity of imported goods, or, in other words, when export prices rise faster, or fall less, than import prices. Heavy American purchases of imports of raw materials forced up the prices of such goods in 1951, without a corresponding rise in the prices of manufactured goods, which Great Britain chiefly exports. If the average value of both imports and exports in 1950 is taken as 100, the corresponding figures for 1951 were 133 for imports as against 117 for exports. The terms of trade moved from 1 to 1·13: it took 113 units of exports to buy the imports 100 units would have bought the previous year. Indeed, the position was worse than these figures indicate; for the terms of trade had already worsened seriously in 1950, after remaining practically stable in 1947, 1948 and 1949. After 1951 the situation gradually improved again. Here are the figures for the years 1947–54.

TABLE 106

United Kingdom Terms of Trade, 1938 and 1947–54 (1950 = 100)

	1938	1947	1948	1949	1950	1951	1952	1953	1954
Import Prices:									
Food, Drink and Tobacco	—	82	89	90	100	115	120	115	120
Basic Materials	—	70	81	84	100	161	137	113	111
Fuels	—	72	88	84	100	119	129	108	100
Manufactured Goods	—	83	87	87	100	130	137	118	114
Total	30	77	86	87	100	133	129	114	114
Export Prices.									
Manufactured Goods:									
Metals	—	82	91	95	100	117	135	131	129
Engineering Products	—	83	90	93	100	111	123	125	125
Textiles	—	84	93	95	100	128	122	109	111
Other	—	89	97	95	100	119	126	117	109
Total		84	92	94	100	117	125	122	119
Total	38	84	92	95	100	117	124	120	117
Terms of Trade	79	92	93	92	100	113	105	96	97

It will be seen that even in the years 1947–9 the terms of trade were much less favourable than in 1938. Detailed figures for the various classes of imports and exports are not available for the pre-war period. From 1947–9 both import and export prices rose, but not so as to upset the relation between them. In 1950, however, and much more in 1951, import prices rose much faster than export prices, and in the case of basic materials, which enter largely into the cost of exports, the prices of 1951 were practically double those of 1948, whereas the prices of exported manufactures were up by not much more than one-third. At the peak period for prices of imported materials the discrepancy was even greater. Thereafter raw material prices came down rapidly, whereas the prices of manufactured exports continued to rise in 1952. By 1954 basic materials were only 11 per cent above the prices of 1950, whereas manufactured exports were 19 per cent higher in price. The terms of trade had improved from 113 in 1951 to 96 in 1953 and 97 in 1954, but they were still not so favourable as in 1947–9 and much less favourable than in 1938.

The prices of foodstuffs—Great Britain's main import apart from raw materials—rose much less in 1951, but moved upwards again in 1952 and, after a brief fall in 1953, yet again in 1954. As against this, the prices of manufactured exports also rose in 1952, but thereafter fell away, so that the terms of trade, after improving in 1953, made no further improvement in 1954. The volume of British exports, however, after a setback in 1952, began to improve in 1953 and advanced more rapidly in 1954.

The Capital Items.   So much for the bare facts concerning the balance of current payments and the terms of trade in relation to it. We have now to consider the capital items, which have so far been left out

TABLE 107
United Kingdom Balance of Payments, 1946–54
Investment and Financing Account
(*£million*)

	1946	1947	1948	1949	1950	1951	1952	1953	1954
Grants to U.K.	—	30	138	154	140	43	—	—	—
Investment (−), Borrowing (+) by U.K.	+324	+ 21	− 20	−378	− 86	−322	− 86	−200	−152
Increase (+) or Fall (−) in Sterling Liabilities	+ 28	+240	−174	+190	+221	+338	−348	+223	+ 79
Increase (−) or Fall (+) in Gold and Dollar Reserves	− 54	+152	+ 55	+ 3	−575	+344	+175	−240	− 87
Balance	298	443	1	−31	−300	+403	−259	−217	−160

of account. These 'capital' items include, first, loans and investments of British capital abroad and, on the other side, loans and investments of overseas capital in Great Britain; secondly, capital grants by way of gift to Great Britain or by Great Britain to countries overseas; thirdly, deposits of funds in Great Britain by countries belonging to the sterling area, and withdrawals of such deposits; and fourthly, additions to or subtractions from the reserves of gold and dollars held by Great Britain as the international banker of the sterling area as a whole. The position in these respects is set out summarily in Table 107.

In this table, the grants represent mainly United Kingdom receipts under the Marshall Aid plan and other outright capital gifts. Investment consists of capital investments in, or loans to, overseas countries, including the countries of the British Commonwealth: borrowing consists of loans or investments from overseas to the United Kingdom. The figures for each year represent the net total, after setting off borrowings against investments.

Sterling Liability.   Sterling liabilities consist of sums held on deposit in the United Kingdom on behalf of countries in the sterling area: for example, the proceeds of sales of colonial or other sterling area exports are paid in to the Bank of England and are then drawn upon by the countries concerned. If these countries draw out less than they pay in, the sterling liabilities of the United Kingdom increase, but for the time being the money can be used for meeting the United Kingdom's financial obligations: whereas, if the sterling area countries draw out more than they pay in, the United Kingdom's sterling debt is reduced, but more has to be paid out currently to meet the demands of the sterling area. Finally, if gold and dollar reserves increase, the United Kingdom has to pay for the increase out of its current receipts, whereas a decline in the reserves means that a part of them has been used to meet current charges.

The Balance of Capital Transactions.   In 1946 and 1947 the United Kingdom was a net borrower on capital account. It borrowed money, chiefly from the United States and Canada, and used the borrowed money to meet its current deficit. But whereas in 1946 direct borrowing was the main method of meeting the current deficit, in 1947 the main contributions came from a sharp increase in sterling liabilities—that is, in effect, borrowing from the rest of the sterling area—and from a drawing upon gold and dollar reserves. By 1948 the current account approximately balanced, and investments and loans made by the United Kingdom exceeded direct borrowings. Capital grants under Marshall Aid made a substantial contribution and largely offset a decline in sterling liabilities, due to repayments to India and other countries which had built up large sterling credits during the war. There was, however, a further substantial fall in gold and dollar reserves. In 1949, when there was for the first time an appreciable favourable balance on current account, overseas investment by the United Kingdom reached considerable proportions and was financed partly by a sharp increase in sterling liabilities and partly by Marshall Aid grants from the United States, so that there was no significant change in gold and dollar reserves. In 1950 the favourable balance on current account rose very sharply, and the excess of overseas investment over borrowing sharply declined. Sterling balances again increased greatly and foreign aid was again on a large scale. The effect was that gold and dollar reserves rose very rapidly. The situation, however, changed greatly in 1951, when the rise in prices due to the Korean crisis upset the current balance, which moved from a favourable figure of £300 million to a debit of £400 million. There was also, that year, a sharp fall in foreign aid, as Great Britain ceased to receive help under the Marshall Plan. Overseas investment was a great deal higher than in 1950; and, despite a very large increase in sterling liabilities, there was a heavy drain on gold and dollar reserves. The following year, 1952, the deficit on current account gave place to a substantial surplus. Overseas investment fell sharply; and there was a large decrease in sterling liabilities, as the sterling area countries drew on the balances they had accumulated in 1951 during the period of very high prices for materials. These drawings had to be met in part by payments out of the gold and dollar reserves, which fell in 1951 and 1952, taken together, by nearly as much as they had risen in 1950. In 1953 there was again a substantial favourable balance on current account. Investment increased during the latter part of the year. Sterling liabilities also rose, and the United Kingdom was able to use the increase for adding to its gold and dollar holdings. Finally, in 1954, with a smaller balance on current account and with net overseas investment also at a lower level, a further rise in sterling liabilities made it possible to add further, though only to a much smaller extent, to gold and dollar holdings.

Thus, apart from the state of the current account, the main factors determining the United Kingdom's supply of means of international payment have been capital loans and gifts, mainly from America, and deposits of sterling made by the countries of the sterling area; while the demand upon sterling has depended on the level of overseas investment, and the final balance has been struck by drawing upon, or adding to, gold and dollar reserves.

Overseas Investment. In a sense, a country's ability to invest capital abroad depends on its possession of a surplus on its current account; for clearly, in the absence of such a surplus, it can invest or lend only by borrowing the wherewithal. In recent years, United Kingdom investments abroad have averaged about £200 million a year, mainly in the countries of the British Commonwealth. A considerable part of this investment has been possible only because of the continued increase of sterling liabilities—that is to say, because the countries of the Commonwealth have drawn out less than they have paid in to the combined funds of the sterling area. Thus, in a sense, the United Kingdom has been lending the Dominions and Colonies their own money, which they remain entitled to draw upon in future years. Of course, a substantial part of their holdings is needed as a reserve against their own currencies as long as they continue to keep their reserves in sterling instead of building up gold and dollar holdings of their own, but it is none the less true that, were they for any reason to draw heavily upon their sterling balances, the United Kingdom would be faced with a serious difficulty in respect of its balance of payments and particularly with an awkward drain on gold and dollar reserves.

The Supply of Dollars. In this general account of the balance of payments problem, nothing has been said so far about one very important special aspect—the shortage of dollars. It is fully possible for a country such as Great Britain to have at one and the same time a favourable total balance of payments and an acute scarcity of one or more particular means of payment, such as gold or dollars. This would not be the case if each national currency could be freely exchanged for any other at a fixed rate. But this is not the position to-day and cannot well be unless the United States is prepared greatly to increase its purchases of foreign goods without a corresponding expansion of its exports. Ever since 1945 most countries have been eager to increase their purchases of dollar goods up to the very limit of their ability to find means of paying for them. There has been a world scramble for dollars; and the shortage of them has been met only in part by large gifts, as well as loans, from the United States to other countries—particularly to Western Europe. Without these gifts and loans the war-devastated countries of Europe would have been unable to buy the foodstuffs needed to maintain their peoples or the materials needed to keep their industries at work. Even with the help of American loans and gifts it has remained necessary for most countries to put strong restrictions on purchases of goods that have to be paid for in dollars and on the right to obtain dollars in exchange for their national currencies.

Regional Balance of Payments. In order to see how this works out in practice we need to break up the total figures bearing on the balance of payments into a series of separate regional accounts, so as to show the different situations in the main groups of countries. For this purpose, the relevant groupings are, for the United Kingdom, first the Rest of the Sterling Area (Known as 'R.S.A.'); secondly the Dollar Area, including Canada as well as the United States and a number of other countries; thirdly, the European countries which together make up the area covered by the Organization for European Economic Co-operation

(O.E.E.C.); fourthly, the rest of the Western Hemisphere; and fifthly, other Non-sterling Countries.

If we break up the figures of the British balance of payments into these five groups we get the following results, in respect of current as distinct from capital payments:

TABLE 108

United Kingdom Current Balance of Payments by Regions, 1946–54

(£million)

	1946	1947	1948	1949	1950	1951	1952	1953	1954
Balance of Current Transactions with:									
Dollar Area	−301	−510	−252	−296	− 88	−436	−174	− 8	−101
Rest of Western Hemisphere	− 24	− 65	− 38	+ 62	+ 26	+ 5	+ 91	− 23	− 2
O.E.E.C. Countries	+ 80	+ 6	⏐ 88	− 16	+115	−197	− 27	+105	+ 31
Other Non-sterling Countries	− 17	+ 11	− 42	− 8	− 35	−101	− 4	− 16	− 29
Rest of Sterling Area	− 28	+127	+254	+293	+287	+335	+379	+173	+269
Non-territorial Organizations	− 8	− 12	− 9	− 4	− 5	− 9	− 6	− 14	− 8
Total	−298	−443	+ 1	+ 31	+300	−403	+259	+217	+160

Here we see that, every year since 1947, the United Kingdom has had a large surplus with the rest of the sterling area—that is, has sold to these countries much more than it has bought from them—whereas there has been every year except 1953 a large deficit in relation to the dollar area. There has been, in most years, a surplus on the United Kingdom's dealings with the O.E.E.C. countries; but in one year, 1951, there was a big deficit. For the other groups the position has varied from year to year, but not enough to offset the preponderance of the three principal groups.

To find the dollars needed to meet the deficit with the dollar area, the United Kingdom has not been able to convert its surplus on transactions with other areas into dollars; for these others have for the most part no dollars to spare. It has been necessary to obtain dollars direct from the United States or from other dollar countries by way of loans or gifts, or, where these have fallen short, to draw on gold reserves. It has also been necessary, in order to reduce the deficit, to impose special restrictions on purchases from the United States and other dollar countries, and to endeavour to replace dollar imports by finding alternative sources of supply in countries to which payment can more easily be made. Such replacement is in many cases very difficult, either because the imports needed are produced mainly in the dollar area or because other producing countries have no adequate surpluses available for export.

Sterling Area Finance. As we saw, Great Britain acts as the reserve banker for the entire sterling area. Such countries as Australia, New Zealand, India and the British Colonies, instead of holding their own reserves of gold or dollars to finance their external transactions, hold sterling, on the understanding that they will be provided, through the Bank of England, with such dollars and other foreign money as they need to pay for their imports of dollar and other foreign goods or to meet other external obligations that cannot be settled directly in sterling. In order to be able to meet these claims, Great Britain needs to hold larger amounts in gold or dollars than would be required in their absence; and it possesses these sums through the payment to it of debts owing from other countries to the countries included in the sterling area. As dollars are scarce, the sterling area countries cannot be left free to draw them out of the gold and dollar reserve pool just as they please. There have to be understandings between them and Great Britain concerning the amounts they can draw at any particular time; for otherwise Great Britain might be faced with demands for gold or dollars that either could not be met at all or could be met only at the cost of serious depreciation in the gold and dollar value of the British pound. The other countries included in the sterling area recognize this necessity and take measures—for example, by limiting their imports—to reduce their demand for gold or dollars when it threatens to get out of control. Australia, for instance, has several times drastically cut its imports when they were becoming excessive in relation to the sterling area's capacity to pay.

It suits the sterling area countries to hold their reserves in sterling rather than to build up gold and dollar reserves of their own, because pooling makes it possible to manage with a smaller total reserve. Canada, however, is not a member of the sterling area because of its very close economic relations with the United States and because the Canadian dollar is also a scarce currency. Canada, as well as the United States, has made large loans to Great Britain since the war in order to help it to buy Canadian wheat and other products and to finance such purchases by other members of the sterling area.

The up and down movements of the United Kingdom's gold and dollar reserves are thus the outcome, not only of the British balance of payments, but of the combined balances of the sterling area as a whole. Great Britain loses or gains gold or dollars not only as a result of its own surplus or deficit but also as a result of the transactions involving payments in gold or dollars of all the countries which are members of the area. The British gold and dollar reserve is not Great Britain's exclusive property: it is in effect the common property of the sterling area countries; and over and above their share in it these countries hold large amounts in sterling deposits in London. These deposits, as far as they arise out of current transactions, can be drawn upon freely at any time; but a large part of them represents debts incurred by Great Britain during the war, and can be repaid only gradually. The countries which own these deposits do not wish to draw on them to more than a limited extent; for they desire to hold permanently big balances in London as a reserve against their own currencies; though, if Great Britain had been in a position to pay, some of them would have desired a more rapid liquidation of those which represent accumulated war debts, and are not the product of current international transactions. A further part of the deposits, belonging chiefly to the Colonies, represents the proceeds of sales of colonial produce abroad at prices which would have swollen colonial purchasing power had they been paid over in full to colonial consumers. In order to check such spending and to build up reserve funds to meet a possible decline in the Colonies' future receipts, the Colonial Governments, through specially established Marketing Boards, have been holding back part of the sum accruing from these sales and have accumulated them in reserves for future spending. Great Britain has thus in effect been borrowing large amounts of money from the Colonies, and has been using this money to finance the sterling area pool as a whole, but is of course under an obligation to repay it to the Colonies when it is needed either to finance colonial investment or to prevent a fall in standards of living should the prices of colonial produce suffer a reverse.

The Sterling Debts. Table 109 (opposite) shows the total amount of Great Britain's sterling liabilities—that is, of the amounts standing in London to the credit of the other sterling area countries, *plus* the sterling holdings of countries outside the sterling area. The amounts held by the non-sterling area countries are relatively small. They represent short-term funds left in London by foreigners who either expect to have payments to make in sterling or, in certain cases, prefer to hold temporarily unused resources in sterling rather than in their own currencies.

Colonial balances, it will be observed, have more than doubled since 1945, whereas the balances standing to the credit of other sterling area countries have fallen by well over £100 million, chiefly as a result of the paying off of a part of the accrued war liabilities, especially to India. Outside the sterling area, British liabilities have fallen substantially, unless one includes debts to 'non-territorial organizations' such as the World Bank and other agencies of the United Nations—in which event there has been a slight increase. Total liabilities have risen by nearly £600 million between 1945 and 1954.

TABLE 109
United Kingdom Sterling Liabilities, 1945-54
(£million. End of Year)

	1945	1946	1947	1948	1949	1950	1951	1952	1953	1954
Balances held by:										
British Colonies	454	504	510	556	582	754	968	1,076	1,103	1,189
Other Sterling Area Countries	2,008	1,924	1,787	1,809	1,771	1,980	1,825	1,604	1,832	1,864
Total Sterling Area	2,462	2,428	2,297	2,365	2,353	2,734	2,793	2,680	2,935	3,053
Dollar Area Countries	34	33	18	19	31	79	38	34	62	61
Rest of Western Hemisphere	163	212	235	135	80	45	57	6	40	27
O.E.E.C. Countries	412	424	480	370	439	395	409	321	305	304
Other Non-sterling Countries	623	632	573	531	514	492	514	394	366	378
Total Non-sterling Area	1,232	1,301	1,306	1,055	1,064	1,011	1,018	755	773	770
Non-territorial Organizations	—	26	388	398	576	577	566	567	509	514
Total	3,694	3,755	3,991	3,818	3,993	4,322	4,377	4,001	4,217	4,337

European Payments Union. In addition to these financial relations, the United Kingdom has been in recent years a member of the European Payments Union—an organization established for the purpose of clearing debits and credits between the countries of Western Europe, so as to facilitate inter-European trade and to provide for short-term loans between the countries concerned. Under E.P.U. there is now an arrangement whereby a country which is in deficit on its current transactions with the others has to pay off part of its deficit in gold or dollars, leaving the remainder to be carried over as a debt in its own currency. The United Kingdom has piled up a substantial deficit in E.P.U.—that is to say, it owes the other E.P.U. countries a large amount, due to be paid in course of time in their own currencies or in gold or dollars. Under the current arrangement, which is at present under revision, a part of this accrued debt is being paid off by instalments. Here are the actual figures showing the United Kingdom's position in E.P.U.:

TABLE 110

United Kingdom Position in European Payments Union, 1949–55

(*£million*)

	1949–50	1950	1951		1952		1953		1954		1955
	July–June	July–Dec.	Jan.–June	July–Dec.	Jan.–June	July–Dec.	Jan.–June	July–Dec.	Jan.–June	July–Dec.	Jan.–June
U.K. Surplus	48	170	47	—	—	85	51	—	53	6	39
U.K. Deficit	—	—	—	385	154	—	—	21	—	—	—
	July 1949–Dec. 1950		Jan.–Dec. 1951		Jan.–Dec. 1952						
*Credit Received (−) or Granted (+)	+88		−281		−18		+21	−10	+26	+4	+19
*Gold Paid (−) or Received (+)	+13		−74		−51		+29	−10	+26	+4	+19

* In respect of period indicated.

Thus, in 1951–2 the United Kingdom accumulated large deficits in respect of its transactions—including those of the rest of the sterling area—with the other E.P.U. countries; but these deficits were substantially reduced in the latter part of 1952 and in 1953–4. In all the United Kingdom paid £135 million in gold to E.P.U. and received from it £68 million—a net gold loss of £67 million. Up to June 1954 the United Kingdom owed a debt to E.P.U. of £173 million.

Gold and Dollar Reserves. These gold payments were only a minor factor in affecting the total amount of the United Kingdom's gold and dollar reserves, which were chiefly determined by the sterling area's position in relation to the dollar. The amount of these reserves can be best expressed in dollars, as the dollar value of sterling was reduced to $2·8 = £1 in 1949. Here are the figures from 1945 to 1954.

TABLE 111

United Kingdom Gold and Dollar Reserves, 1939 and 1945–54
(million U.S. $. End of year)

1939	2,680	1948	1,856	1952	1,846
1945	2,476	1949	1,688	1953	2,518
1946	2,696	1950	3,300	1954	2,762
1947	2,079	1951	2,335	1955	2,120

The gold and dollar reserves were thus back in 1954 at roughly the same amount, in dollars, as they stood at in 1939; but in pounds they stood at a higher value because of the lower relative value of sterling. They had been built up substantially since their sharp fall from $1,912 million in March 1949 to $1,340 million in September of that year—when the pound was devalued—and since their still sharper fall from $3,867 million in June 1951 to $1,685 a year later, during the Korean war crisis. After the recovery of 1953–4 reserves slipped back seriously in 1955; and in relation to the value of the transactions for which they formed the basis they were, in 1955, a long way below what they had been before the war. At only £757 million at the end of 1955 they were a long way under a quarter of Great Britain's sterling liabilities; and they were subject to some pressure as a result of current balance of payment difficulties. There was indeed some talk in 1955–6 of further possible devaluation of sterling; but any such intention was promptly contradicted by the Government. The reserves as they stood were adequate to withstand small pressures: there was clearly no prospect of building them up to a height at which they would be able to resist a major upset in the balance of payments.

CHAPTER FIFTEEN

PRICES AND COST OF LIVING

EVERY money transaction involves two parties—a buyer and a seller—of whom normally the one wants to buy as cheaply as he can and the other, not always to sell as dearly as he can, but to sell at the price he considers likely to yield him the greatest advantage. The buyer, taking quality into account, always prefers the lowest price he can find: the seller has often to take account of the fact that the higher he puts his price, the less of his goods or services he is likely to be able to sell. If the demand is what is called 'inelastic'—that is to say, if upward and downward movements of prices have little effect on sales, he will favour a high price: the more 'elastic' it is, the more disposed will he be to reduce his price, provided it is still enough to yield some surplus over costs of production. It has often been said that the prices of necessaries tend to be 'inelastic', and those of luxuries 'elastic'; but this is only broadly true, and the line between luxuries and necessaries is hard to draw. There are many things of which a limited amount is a necessary, but a larger amount a luxury; and what is regarded as necessary in some places is not so in others, or at other times. Necessaries beyond the barest minimum are indeed conventional: they vary with the current standard of living. Nor is anything, except water, an absolute necessary; for all other goods there are possible substitutes—for example, rye for wheat, or cotton for woollen clothing. It is, however, broadly true that demand for the cheaper conventional necessaries in any time and place tends to be inelastic and the demand for many luxuries elastic—which means that monopolists can make a bigger pile by cornering the supply of something it is difficult for consumers to do without than by cornering the supply of something most people have to do without in any case. It is, however, usually difficult to corner the supplies of really indispensable commodities—or the consequences of monopoly would be much more serious than they actually are.

Wholesale Prices. Prices are broadly of two kinds—wholesale and retail. Wholesale buying occurs most often where the purchaser intends to re-sell what he buys, either in the condition in which he bought it or after processing it or using it as a material or ingredient in some form of manufacture. But wholesale transactions occur also in the case of 'collective' buyers who do not mean to re-sell—for example, when the

Government buys military supplies or a hospital food and drugs for its patients. Nevertheless, the typical form of wholesale buying and selling takes place between commercial concerns in connection with the processes of production and distribution. Sometimes a finished commodity changes hands several times at wholesale prices before reaching the retail market; and usually the ingredients or components of which finished goods are made are bought and sold at wholesale prices, often more than once, before the goods assume a finished form.

All these wholesale prices have two aspects. They are costs to the buyer; but to the seller they are means to recouping his own costs and to making a profit over costs. Similarly the retail prices at which finished goods and services are finally bought and sold are costs of living to the buyers, but means of recouping costs and of profit-making to the retailer. All prices, then, have this dual nature, as costs and as gross receipts. The lower retail prices are, the more goods and services a given income will command. The higher all prices are, the more money the sellers have towards meeting their costs and towards achieving a profit.

Prices of Services: the 'Price' of Money. Wages and salaries are also prices—the prices of different sorts of labour. They are costs to the employer of labour, and incomes to the manual and non-manual employees. Money too has its 'prices'—the interest which has to be paid by borrowers for command of it over time. But incomes in the form of profits are not costs: they are the result of selling above cost. Nor are fee-earners' incomes costs, except to the buyers. They are the return for certain kinds of labour which are sold, not at a contractual price, but by independent entrepreneurs who seek a profit which is largely payment for work done, though it may contain an element of return on capital as well.

Second-hand Prices Most finished goods are sold either for consumption or for use as capital goods, and are not meant to be sold more than once after they have reached their market—though they can be. But there are important categories of finished goods that are quite often sold again and again—for example, houses and motor-cars. There are 'second-hand' prices, as well as prices for new goods; and the prices of second-hand goods bear much less relation than those of new goods to their original costs of production. The costs that affect their prices are those of currently produced new goods, with allowance of course for any deterioration in use-value since they were new. Similarly, stocks and shares, as well as any kind of physical property, can change hands a number of times; and, whereas the sellers of current products usually wish to dispose of them quickly, in order to avoid storage costs and risks of deterioration, there is no such pressure on the owners of goods already sold for use to sell them over again. In any accounting period, only a fraction of durable second-hand goods or of titles to ownership, such as stocks and shares, actually change hands; and the proportion doing so varies greatly from time to time. It is greatest in periods of rapidly changing prices and especially when speculation is rife; and it constitutes the most uncertain element of all in the price-structure.

Producer and Consumer Attitudes.   Consumers naturally prefer low prices—other things being equal. But most consumers are producers as well, and do not want the prices of the goods they sell, or on which their wages depend, to fall. It would suit them best if other prices fell, and their selling prices stayed up—unless indeed the effect were so to diminish sales as to increase unit costs and throw many of the producers out of work, as will usually happen if the demand for their wares is elastic. Producers, though they are also consumers, are apt to prefer high prices, even if in fact they reduce the size of the market, because a fall in takings is immediately evident to them, whereas any advantage from lower prices is widely dispersed and less easily appreciated.

Price History.   Moreover, falling prices are closely associated, historically, with depressions, and rising prices with periods of boom. Prices rose sharply round about the middle of the nineteenth century, when Great Britain was entering on its period of most rapid economic advance. They fell in the 'Great Depression' of the later 'seventies and continued to fall nearly to the century's end. Then they rose again, to the accompaniment of the industrial recovery that culminated in 1913. The next year, the other great force that affects prices came into play. There was a terrific rise during the war and immediately after it, the peak being reached in 1920. From that point, to the accompaniment of severe unemployment, prices fell sharply and continued to fall through the 'twenties, though at a slower rate. On this fall was superimposed the catastrophic fall in the early 'thirties—the period of the world slump. In the middle 'thirties there was a gradual recovery of prices—and a fall in unemployment. Then followed the very sharp rise in prices during the second world war, with unemployment virtually non-existent; and this time the rise continued after the war, and has continued up to the present time—and there has been no slump such as ensued upon the first war, though eleven years have passed since the fighting ceased. No wonder the producers, above all the wage-earners, have learned to associate prosperity with rising and depression with falling prices and living costs.

None the less, the workers as consumers have a strong interest in low prices; and the Co-operative movement is accustomed to express this aspect of their attitude. It is 'consumer', just as the Trade Unions are 'producer', minded. There is accordingly an ambiguity in the working-class attitude, with Trade Unionists pressing for higher wages and Co-operators demanding action against monopolists who keep prices high. These attitudes are, of course, not necessarily inconsistent. They represent differences of emphasis, rather than of opinion; and Co-operators are no more pleased than other sellers when their margins are cut. Trade Unions, for their part, have refrained from using the opportunities created by full employment to push wage-claims to a point at which the advantage of higher money wages would clearly be cancelled by inflation. Producers and consumers, being largely the same persons, cannot finally will opposite things, though they may see some consequences more plainly than others. From the combined standpoints there is much to be said for stable prices, which allow room for wage-advances as productivity improves and are not unsatisfactory to the housewife where she can feel assured that particular prices are not being maintained by anti-social monopolies (see pp. 254 ff.).

The Price of Houses.   The period since my previous book was published has been one of rising prices, both wholesale and retail, and also of rising wages and other incomes and of rising prices for most kinds of second-hand goods. There has, however, been one notable exception to the general trend. The retail prices of second-hand houses have risen much less than the prices of any other important class of goods. They have been artificially held down by legislation in the case of the smaller houses; and this has been made easier by the fact that large numbers of new houses have been made available at subsidized rents. The owners of second-hand houses, almost alone, have been denied the chance of profiting by the scarcity of dwelling space and by the high costs of new building. This has been frequently denounced as a gross injustice; but not even a Conservative Government has so far dared to 'set the landlord free', in face of the certain consequences upon public opinion among the tenants who have reaped the advantage. Recent legislation has indeed tempered the wind to the shorn landlord; but the sharp fall in the proportion of the national income derived from rent gives ample evidence of the disadvantage suffered by the owners of second-hand 'working class' or near-working-class dwellings.

The Threat of Higher Rents.   In October 1955, however, in conjunction with Mr. Butler's autumn budget, Mr. Sandys brought forward proposals designed to abolish altogether the general government subsidy on house-building and to limit the subsidy in future to schemes of slum-clearance and a few other special cases. At the same time Local Authorities which had not already adopted differential rent schemes were strongly urged to do so, in such ways as would limit rent subsidies to tenants able to prove special need. Mr. Sandys argued that on this basis Local Authorities would find it financially practicable to continue house-building without exchequer subsidies. He also announced that it was intended to amend the Rent Acts so as to allow rents hitherto restricted to be increased; but the Government's precise proposals in this respect have not yet been made public. Evidently the new policy foreshadows sharp increases in rent for many tenants of old as well as new houses. The subsidies on houses already built are not affected; but the rents of such houses may be, wherever the tenant is regarded as able to pay more. The general rise in interest rates and also the less favourable terms announced by Mr. Butler for capital loans to Local Authorities will of course have a serious effect on the 'economic rent' of new houses. Indeed, the new proposals threaten to provoke a serious crisis in the field of housing and greatly to intensify the demand for higher wages to meet the expected increase in the cost of living. They are being strongly resisted by the Labour Party and the Trade Unions, which see in them the greatest threat made since 1945 to working-class standards of life.

Subsidies and Prices. There are other instances in which market prices have been prevented, by means of subsidies, from rising as they would have risen had they been left to the working of unrestrained competition. The subsidies designed to keep down the prices of necessary foods during and after the war are the outstanding example. But in these cases the price-reduction was not made at the expense of the owners of the means of producing the goods in question. The owners were compensated by the subsidies, which enabled them to sell their goods at the lower prices without forfeiting their profits; and the cost of the subsidies was borne by the general body of consumers through increased taxation. It is thus the case that a large number of landlords were unfairly treated, *in comparison with other owners of property.* They were so treated, because there was felt to be no alternative at a time when it was impossible to provide new houses to meet the unsatisfied demand. Had there been no rent control, landlords would have been in a position to raise house-rents almost without limit, and there would have been disastrous results, above all to those tenants who would have been without means of raising their incomes to meet the higher costs, but also among the main body of working-class tenants, who would have been forced to struggle for larger wage-advances. The landlords of existing houses could be victimized because they were merely passive recipients of rent: the suppliers of bread and other current necessaries could not, because they would have been forced to retaliate by giving up production.

Rents and Rates. House-rents, then, have so far formed a notable exception to the general course of price movements. There are no figures which enable us to measure exactly how these particular prices have moved; for the index number of house-rents compiled by the Ministry of Labour includes new (mainly subsidized) houses as well as second hand houses. Nevertheless, its movements furnish some indication of the trend. The index of the combined cost of working-class rent and rates rose by no more than 8 per cent between 1939 and 1948, when the old index was discontinued; whereas the cost of living as a whole rose by 31 per cent. There was a further rise of 4 per cent for rent and rates in the new index between 1947 and the beginning of 1952, and then a sharper rise in the further revised index—20 per cent up to June 1955. The cost of rent and rates increased by 5½ per cent from 1952 to 1953, by 3 per cent from 1953 to 1954, and by a further 3 per cent to April 1955. These rises were due partly to the growing numbers dwelling in new houses built since the war, and partly to rising rates; but they also represented some gain to landlords of the older dwellings.

Recent Price Movements. It is now time to turn to consideration of the more general price movements of recent years—a task which is made difficult by the changes that have been introduced in the official methods of measurement. As we saw, the method of reckoning changes in retail prices and costs of living has been altered twice since the war —in 1947 and again in 1950; and a new index of wholesale prices was instituted in 1950, on the basis 1949 = 100.

Indexes of Wholesale Prices. There are two main sets of index numbers showing changes in general prices. The main wholesale price index, originally based on 1930 = 100, is here shown on a basis of 1938 = 100. It has fluctuated as follows since 1945:

TABLE 112

Wholesale Prices (Old Index) Yearly Averages, 1938 and 1945–54

(1938 = 100)

	1945	1946	1947	1948	1949	1950	1951	1952	1953	1954
All Articles	167	173	189	216	227	259	315	323	323	325
Food and Tobacco	162	163	169	186	202	227	254	292	315	315

Since 1950, this index has been supplemented by a new itemized index, with revised composition and weighting, based on June 1949 = 100. Some selected figures from this new index are given in Table 113 overleaf.

Speculative Price Movements. What stands out above all else in these figures is the very sharp rise in certain commodity prices in 1951, as a consequence of the speculative price movements and the increased American buying which followed the outbreak of the war in Korea. The figures given, being annual averages, fail to show the peak rises in particular months; but they are spectacular enough. The average price of rubber rose practically fivefold between June 1949 and 1951, and the prices of raw cotton and wool and of zinc more than doubled. Copper, nickel, lead and tin prices nearly doubled, the price of sulphur rose by

TABLE 113

Wholesale Prices (New Index) Yearly Averages
(June 1949 = 100)

	1945	1946	1947	1948	1949	1950	1951	1952	1953	1954	Rise from 1946–1954 (per cent)
Industrial Materials used in:											
Manufactures (non-food)	—	—	—	—	—	139	193	162	146	143	—
Mechanical Engineering	76	83	94	97	101	113	134	150	146	150	81
Building and Civil Engineering		83	94	101	102	106	126	134	130	131	58
House Building		84	94	101	102	105	123	131	129	131	56
Output of:											
Coal	—	—	—	—	—	100	110	122	130	135	—
Chemicals	—	—	—	—	—	109	124	138	143	147	—
Iron and Steel	—	—	—	89	97	101	113	136	140	141	—
Rayon	—	—	—	—	—	104	130	132	131	130	—
Hosiery	—	—	—	—	—	107	139	114	114	115	—
Clothing and Footwear	—	—	—	—	—	104	125	115	114	114	—
Commodities:											
Cotton	—	—	—	—	—	157	223	172	141	155	—
Wool	—	—	—	—	—	196	252	148	171	161	—
Hides and Skins	—	—	—	—	—	129	168	103	112	106	—
Rubber	170	155	119	124	114	325	499	283	199	198	28
Softwood	—	—	—	—	—	96	143	158	144	145	—
Sulphur	—	—	—	—	—	114	175	194	174	160	—
Copper	—	66	111	114	113	152	187	221	218	213	223
Nickel, Refined	—	85	85	92	112	161	194	203	215	217	155
Aluminium	—	82	87	91	106	126	138	173	174	173	111
Lead	—	58	104	116	126	130	197	165	115	120	107
Zinc	—	55	90	103	112	153	220	192	101	104	89
Tin	—	57	75	96	106	131	190	169	129	126	121
Cement	—	—	—	—	—	99	122	129	127	130	—
Soap	—	—	—	—	—	99	108	116	109	106	—
Cotton Yarn	—	—	—	—	—	142	205	154	124	135	—
Worsted Yarn	—	—	—	—	—	174	230	140	159	154	—
Carpets	—	—	—	—	—	131	171	148	159	164	—
Boots and Shoes	—	—	—	—	—	107	131	124	122	123	—
Tobacco	—	—	—	—	—	100	101	102	102	102	—
Paper and Board	—	—	—	—	—	100	181	174	141	142	—
Rubber Tyres and Tubes	—	—	—	—	—	123	180	169	142	140	—

75 per cent. In some cases the increases continued into 1952—for example, for copper and nickel and sulphur; but in most they were lower in 1952 than in 1951, and in many the fall continued in 1953 and 1954.

In the case of coal, iron and steel and chemicals, there was a continuous rise from 1949 to 1954.

These price movements greatly affected the terms of trade—that is, the relation between the average prices of imports and exports. Here are the figures of these prices and of the terms of trade from 1947, with comparative figures for 1938.

TABLE 114

Import and Export Average Prices and Terms of Trade, 1938 and 1947–54
(1950 = 100)

	1938	1947	1948	1949	1950	1951	1952	1953	1954
Import Prices:									
Total	30	77	86	87	100	133	129	114	114
Food, Drink and Tobacco	—	82	89	90	100	115	120	115	120
Basic Materials	—	70	81	84	100	161	137	113	111
Manufactures	—	83	87	87	100	130	137	118	114
Fuels	—	72	88	84	100	119	129	108	100
Export Prices:									
Total	38	84	92	95	100	117	124	120	117
Manufactures	—	84	92	94	100	117	125	122	119
Terms of Trade*	79	92	93	92	100	113	105	96	97

* Ratio of Import to Export Prices.

This table again brings out the sharpness of the rise in the prices of imported materials in 1951, and shows the consequent serious worsening of the terms of trade. The terms of trade had already worsened in 1950; and in 1953 and 1954, though better, they were still substantially worse than in 1947–9, and very much worse than in 1938. In other words, more exports were needed to pay for any given quantity of imports than either before 1950 or, further back, than in 1938. This, of course, connotes an improvement in the terms of trade of the countries which are mainly exporters of primary products. This matter has been discussed already in the section dealing with the balance of payments (see pp. 193 ff.).

Agricultural Prices. Table 115 deals with the prices of agricultural products in England and Wales. These prices are affected by various subsidies paid to farmers, whose receipts from this source are included. The retail prices of fertilizers sold to farmers are also given in the table.

Retail Prices and Costs of Living. The movement of retail prices and of the cost of living is less erratic than that of wholesale prices. It is not possible to make a direct comparison between pre-war and present

TABLE 115

Agricultural and Fertilizer Prices, 1938 and 1945—54

(1936–8 = 100)

	1938	1945	1946	1947	1948	1949	1950	1951	1952	1953	1954
All Products	102	197	207	241	249	260	270	296	306	312	301
Cereals and											
Farm Crops	93	198	198	214	238	239	250	283	279	283	263
Livestock and											
Livestock											
Products	104	192	208	233	252	267	281	310	323	331	318
Fruit, Veg. and											
Glasshouse											
Products	111	204	211	302	244	259	249	254	273	275	281
Wheat	100	202	192	205	244	250	273	289	296	313	262
Fat Cattle	106	164	173	203	223	233	238	257	283	299	311
Fat Sheep	86	171	184	225	252	260	270	291	309	314	306
Bacon Pigs	102	195	216	255	218	325	370	412	437	456	335
Poultry	105	187	237	287	283	294	312	360	334	300	299
Eggs	104	212	233	249	270	285	290	311	317	312	284
Milk	107	202	217	234	246	261	275	293	309	314	311
Butter	106	127	120	108	104	115	144	186	211	249	360
Wool	75	152	150	150	212	224	269	606	459	468	467
Fertilizers	—	—	—	—	—	—	112	158	183	172	172
Feeding-stuffs,											
Maize meal	100	150	151	156	163	253	355	432	453	453	425

retail prices, as the old working-class Cost of Living Index was discontinued in June 1947, when it was replaced by a new Interim Index of Retail Prices. This in turn was replaced by a new Interim Index in 1952; but the figures can be carried forward with approximate corrections on the older basis (June 1947 = 100).

Here, to begin with, are the figures of the old Cost of Living Index, which had become seriously misleading on account of changes in the pattern of expenditure long before it was discontinued in 1947.

TABLE 116

Old Cost of Living Index, 1938–47

	1938	1939	1940	1941	1942	1943	1944	1945	1946	1947
All Items										
(July 1914 = 100)	156	158	184	199	200	199	201	203	203·5	203
All Items										
(Sept. 1939 = 100)	101	102	119	128	129	128	130	131	131	131
Food ,, ,,	102	102	119	122	117	120	122	123	122	117
Clothing ,, ,,	100	103	137	177	192	169	166	167	166	166
Food and										
Light ,, ,,	99	101	115	125	129	134	141	149	152	155
Rent and										
Rates ,, ,,	99	100	101	101	101	101	101	102	103	108

This Index was replaced after 1947 by the Interim Index of Retail Prices. This was revised in 1952; but for general purposes the all-items figures can be treated as continuous from 1948, on the basis June 1947 = 100.

TABLE 117

Interim Index of Retail Prices, 1948–55

(June 1947 = 100)

	1948	1949	1950	1951	1952	1953	1954	1955	1956 Jan.)
All Items	108	111	114	125	136	140	143	149	153

The estimates for the various groups have to be given separately for 1947–51, and for 1952 onwards.

	June 1947 = 100				January 1952 = 100				Approximate Rise from June 1947– June 1955
	1948	1949	1950	1951	1952	1953	1954	1955 (June)	
Food	108	114	123	136	105	111	114	125	69
Clothing	109	118	120	138	98	96	96	96	42
Household Durable Goods	108	108	112	132	99	96	95	96	31
Fuel and Light	111	113	116	128	101	106	111	113	58
Rent and Rates	99	100	101	103	102	108	112	115	20
Misc. Goods	110	112	113	128	102	101	100	101	39
Services	105	105	108	118	104	108	111	115	43
Alcoholic Drink ⎱ Tobacco ⎰	109	108	105	106	⎰101 ⎱100	101 100	102 100	103⎱ 100⎰	10

What stands out here is the sharp rise in food prices, which has been continuous since 1947, and has of course been affected by the continuing reduction in subsidies. The cost of fuel and light has also risen by more than the average, whereas alcohol and tobacco, already taxed very heavily in 1947, show the smallest increase, and rent and rates the next smallest. Clothing, which had risen most in price in 1951, has declined a little since then, as have furniture and furnishings.

Working-class Costs. If we treat the successive cost of living indexes as forming a single series, we arrive at a figure of 91 per cent as representing the total rise between 1939 and 1954. This, however, is seriously misleading because the increase up to 1947 was greatly underestimated. I do not pretend to be able to say what the figure should be; but I feel sure the correct answer is nearer 150 per cent than 100 per cent. Of particular importance in recent years has been the rapid increase in the cost of food—roughly 78 per cent between 1947 and the beginning of 1955. This has been due partly to the rise in the cost of imported food after the pound was devalued in 1949 and partly to the withdrawal of subsidies since 1951. Till quite recent years a notable feature of working-class cost of living has been the diminishing proportion of total incomes spent on food. This was marked between the wars; and as a result of the subsidies the trend continued during and after the war, only to be sharply reversed during the past few years. As we saw, food, together with drink and tobacco, represented, despite the high taxes on the two latter, 44 per cent of total consumers' expenditure in 1946, and 47½ per cent in 1953. For food only the percentages were 25·5 and 32. Expenditure on alcohol and tobacco had fallen from 18½ per cent to 15½ per cent of the total, despite the large tax element included in the cost. High food prices were again becoming a big working-class grievance, and a means of encroaching on the gains of the Welfare State, especially among those who had to exist not on wage-incomes, but on fixed allowances. In this respect at any rate, there had been grave relapse from the policies of the immediate post-war years. It was sought to justify the change on the ground that it was part of the policy of 'liberating' the economy from 'controls' which distorted market relations; and it was indeed a return to the jungle law of the market. Whether or not its effects can properly be described as 'liberation' is another matter. Workers with strong Trade Unions to back them might be able, by collective bargaining or in the last resort by strike action, to maintain their real incomes. But this was done at the expense of those who were less able to look after themselves—most of all at the expense of pensioners whose incomes were not adjusted to the changed conditions of living.

NOTE: A new Index of Retail Prices, with a revised weighting, was introduced early in 1956, on the basis, January 17, 1956 = 100. By April 1956 the new index stood at 103, equivalent to 158 on the basis June 1947 = 100. The weights for the new index were as follows (old weights at 1956 prices in brackets);—Food 350 (432); Alcoholic Drink 71 (69); Tobacco 80 (80); Housing 87 (73); Fuel and Light (55) 73; Durable Household Goods 66 (55); Clothing and Footwear 106 (84); Transport and Vehicles 68; Services 58; Transport *plus* Services 126 (94); Other Goods 59 (40). These weights add up to 1,000 in each case.

CHAPTER SIXTEEN

INCOMES

A PERSON'S income is the sum of money which falls due to him or her during a particular year. Out of it, unless he is using up capital, or drawing on past savings, or is able to mortgage the future by borrowing, he needs to pay his taxes and rates, to cover his personal and family expenditure, and to make such savings as he may think fit or has contracted to make under a superannuation scheme or insurance policy. Income may be derived from ownership of property or investments, from earnings, or from public social service payments— or of course from private gifts. Some income may be received in kind, e.g. by domestic servants or from allotments or by miners in the form of free coal. In the case of the larger incomes a considerable proportion of gross receipts has to be paid in direct taxes, whereas the recipients of the smaller incomes pay chiefly in indirect taxes and compulsory insurance contributions, at least part of which increases the cost of what they buy. It is usual to distinguish between gross incomes, before taxation, and what are called 'net incomes', from which income tax and surtax, but not local rates or insurance contributions, have been deducted.

Distribution of Personal Incomes by Sizes. Table 118 (overleaf) shows, for the years 1948, 1949 and 1953, the distribution by sizes of such personal incomes as can be assigned to particular ranges of size. It excludes income which cannot be so assigned, as well as all income in kind except that of domestic servants. It also excludes interest on National Savings, Co-operative dividends, and some forms of income derived from social service payments. It further leaves out of account all income accruing not to individuals but to such corporate agencies as charities or insurance funds. Incomes of husband and wife are counted as a single income.

Incomes and Prices. In considering this table it is of course necessary to bear in mind the sharp rise in money incomes and prices between 1938 and 1949. This accounts for the great increase in the number of incomes over £250 between these dates and for the increased numbers in each group above £250, except the highest of all. The rise in incomes and prices continued after 1949, but on a smaller scale. As will be seen, on the average direct taxes took 7·1 per cent of personal incomes in

TA

Distribution of Personal Inc

Incomes before Tax	1938				1949		
	No. of Incomes	Gross Income	Income Less Direct Taxes	% of Income Retained	No. of Incomes	Gross Income	Income Less Direct Taxes
	(000)	£m.	£m.		(000)	£m.	£m.
Up to £250	—	2,613	2,609	99·8	12,050	1,952	1,923
£250–£500	1,890	631	611	96·8	9,980	3,480	3,312
£500–£750	390	234	212	90·6	2,130	1,260	1,137
£750–£1,000	149	127	110	86·6	560	480	395
£1,000–£1,500	130	157	130	82·8	400	480	363
£1,500–£2,000	53	90	72	80·0	150	255	181
£2,000–£3,000	46	112	87	77·7	118	284	188
£3,000–£5,000	33	126	91	72·2	68	225	145
£5,000–£10,000	18	123	78	63·4	33	224	99
£10,000–£20,000	6	76	39	51·3	9	117	35
Over £20,000	2	87	30	34·5	2	70	9
	—	4,376	4,069	93·0	25,500	8,857	7,787
Unallocated Personal Income	—	696	—	—	—	1,718	—

1938, 12·0 per cent in 1949, and 10·4 per cent in 1954. The recipient of an income of rather over £3,000 kept three-quarters of it in 1938, as against a recipient of under £1,500 in 1949 and roughly £2,000 in 1953.

Sources of Personal Incomes. We have next to see from what sources personal incomes are derived. The four main sources are employment; self-employment; rent, dividends and interest; and social insurance payments. Employment yields incomes in the form of wages, salaries, and the pay of the armed forces; and it is customary to treat employers' as well as employees' contributions to social insurance and to superannuation funds as forms of employee income deducted at source.

Self-employment yields incomes to professional fee-earners, to farmers, and to businesses conducted by individuals or partnerships as against joint stock companies. Rent, dividends and interest explain themselves; and finally come social insurance benefits and other grants of income from public funds.

The figures for these forms of income in 1938 and from 1946 to 1954 are shown in Table 119. (See pages 224–5.) The same data, expressed as percentages of total personal incomes in each year, are shown in Table 120. (See pages 224–5.)

It will be seen that the share of employment in the creation of

1949, 1953 and 1954

% of Income Retained	1953				1954			
	No. of Incomes	Gross Income	Income Less Direct Taxes	% of Income Retained	No. of Incomes	Gross Income	Income Less Direct Taxes	% of Income Retained
	(000)	£m.	£m.		(000)	£m.	£m.	
98·5	8,410	1,568	1,560	99·5	8,540	1,440	1,432	99·4
95·2	9,240	3,435	3,315	96·5	8,690	3,280	3,158	96·3
90·2	5,215	3,140	2,951	94·0	5,900	3,575	3,364	94·1
82·3	1,360	1,150	1,036	90·1	1,750	1,475	1,335	90·5
75·6	600	720	599	83·2	700	840	699	83·2
71·0	190	325	246	75·7	210	360	274	76·1
66·2	145	349	244	69·9	161	388	272	70·1
56·9	89	333	197	59·2	96	360	212	58·9
44·2	40	266	121	45·5	41	275	124	45·1
29·9	9	125	38	30·4	10	128	39	30·5
12·9	2	72	11	15·3	2	69	11	15·9
87·9	25,300	11,483	10,318	89·9	26,100	12,190	10,920	89·6
—	—	2,101	—	—	—	2,354	—	—

personal incomes rose until 1951 and was almost stationary in 1925 and 1953, but increased a little in 1954. Income from both wages and salaries followed this course; whereas income from self-employment accounted for an almost unchanging proportion up to 1949 and thereafter fell away, while rent, interest and dividends took a declining share from 1948, but declined very slowly after 1950. Farmers' earnings rose sharply from 1946 to 1949, but took a very slightly smaller share from 1950 to 1953, and fell quite sharply in 1951. Professional earnings represented an almost stable proportion up to 1950, and then fell, though not very heavily, up to 1952. Thereafter, their share remained stable. The share of private traders fell each year up to 1953, and hardly changed in 1954. Insurance benefits and other social service payments showed a falling tendency up to 1951, and then increased their share in 1952 and 1953, but fell away in 1954. Forces' pay declined sharply in its proportion up to 1949, but rose to and maintained a higher level in 1951 and 1952, and then fell back slightly in 1953 and 1954. In general, the movements were favourable to wages and salaries and unfavourable to rent, interest and dividends, up to 1951, but not thereafter; but the counter-tendency had gone only a little way by 1953 and was partly reversed in 1954.

	1938	1946	1947
Wages	1,920	3,270	3,710
Salaries	910	1,625	1,765
Pay of Forces (cash and kind)	66	577	395
Employers' Contributions (National Insurance)	54	84	113
Employers' Contributions (Other)	72	131	161
Total from Employment	3,022	5,687	6,144
Professional Earnings	118	178	199
Farmers' Earnings	69	229	247
Other Sole Traders and Partnerships	460	747	794
Total from Self-employment	647	1,154	1,240
Rent, Interest and Dividends	1,128	1,286	1,364
Insurance Benefits and Public Grants	275	672	682
Total Personal Income	5,072	8,799	9,430

	1938	1946	1947
Wages	37·9	37·2	39·4
Salaries	17·9	18·5	18·7
Forces' Pay	1·3	4·3	4·2
Employers' Contributions (National Insurance)	1·1	1·0	1·2
Employers' Contributions (other)	1·4	1·5	1·7
Employment Total	59·6	64·6	65·1
Professional Earnings	2·3	2·0	2·1
Farmers' Earnings	1·4	2·6	2·6
Other Sole Traders and Partnerships	9·1	8·5	8·4
Self-Employment Total	12·8	13·1	13·1
Rent, Interest and Dividends	22·2	14·6	14·5
Insurance Benefits and Public Grants	5·4	7·6	7·2

nd 1946–54 (*£million*)

1948	1949	1950	1951	1952	1953	1954
4,160	4,385	4,580	5,080	5,405	5,730	6,170
1,980	2,130	2,290	2,575	2,755	2,890	3,095
233	223	230	287	320	331	335
157	197	199	205	218	244	248
188	215	244	274	308	332	352
6,718	7,150	7,543	8,421	9,006	9,527	10,200
213	228	238	235	239	247	263
305	346	339	365	404	406	378
810	826	835	876	892	939	1,004
1,328	1,400	1,412	1,476	1,535	1,592	1,645
1,240	1,281	1,320	1,439	1,535	1,605	1,678
704	744	755	785	909	1,000	1,021
9,990	10,575	11,030	12,121	12,985	13,724	14,544

es by Sources, 1938 and 1946–54

1948	1949	1950	1951	1952	1953	1954
41·6	41·5	41·5	41·9	41·6	41·8	42·4
19·8	20·2	20·8	21·2	21·2	21·2	21·3
2·3	2·1	2·1	2·4	2·5	2·4	2·3
1·6	1·9	1·8	1·7	1·7	1·8	1·7
1·9	2·0	2·2	2·3	2·4	2·4	2·4
67·3	67·7	68·5	69·5	69·4	69·4	70·1
2·1	2·2	2·2	1·9	1·8	1·8	1·8
3·0	3·3	3·1	3·0	3·1	3·0	2·6
8·1	7·8	7·6	7·2	6·9	6·8	6·9
13·2	13·2	12·8	12·2	11·8	11·6	11·3
12·4	12·1	12·0	11·9	11·8	11·7	11·5
7·1	7·0	6·8	6·5	7·0	7·3	7·0

The Changing Distribution of Incomes. There are unfortunately no exactly comparable figures for any year before 1946. The nearest approach is to be found in the National Income and Expenditure White Paper of 1955, which gives revised estimates for 1938 of the sources of personal incomes derived from the various forms of work or ownership of property—and also of insurance benefits and payments from public funds. This estimate shows payments for employment as 59·6 per cent, payments for self-employment as 12·8 per cent, and payments for ownership as 22·2 per cent of the total, as against 70·1 per cent, 11·3 per cent, and 11·5 per cent in 1954. A substantial part of the re-distribution as between payments for work and payments for ownership had taken place during the war; but the trend continued to operate right up to 1954, though it was in suspense between 1951 and 1953.

These estimates of course relate to gross incomes, before taxation

T<

Farming Revenue, Expenditure and Net In

	1937–8	1945–6	1946–7
Farm Revenue:			
Crops	43·5	157·5	149
Fat Stock	89	115·5	120
Milk and Milk Products	80·5	176·5	190·5
Eggs and Poultry	39	58·5	68·5
Horticultural Products	33·5	95·5	108
Other Products	9	18·5	11
Production Grants, etc.	5·5	13·5	15·5
Increase in value of Stock and Work in Hand	7·5	17·5	6
Total	306·5	652·5	668
Farm Expenditure:			
Labour	66	180·5	209
Rent and Interest	43	47·5	50
Machinery Expenses	18	64·5	70
Feeding Stuffs	78	43	34
Fertilizers	8	27·5	28
Other Expenses	37	79·5	84
Total	250	442·5	475
Net Farm Income	56·5	210	193

has been taken into account. As we saw, direct taxation on the bigger incomes became much heavier during and after the war, though it has been relaxed since 1951. But it must also be borne in mind that the number of direct taxpayers has been very greatly increased, and that indirect taxation has risen greatly on commodities of popular consumption. For some account of the effects of these developments see page 297.

Farmers' Receipts, Costs and Incomes. The 1955 Annual Abstract of Statistics includes a new table giving an estimate of farmers' incomes in recent years. The figures given for farmers' net incomes do not tally with those of the Blue Book on National Income and Expenditure, cited on page 77, presumably because net, as distinct from gross, income has been reckoned on a different basis, and because the latter are for calendar years, whereas the new table is for years ending in May.

7–8 and 1945–6 to 1954–5 (£million)

1947–8	1948–9	1949–50	1950–1	1951–2	1952–3	1953–4	1954–5 (provisional)
147	189·5	175	196	199·5	187	241·5	212
123	154·5	189·5	228	283·5	337·5	370·5	403
209·5	242·5	274·5	283·5	299·5	318	340	330·5
82	102·5	126·5	135	144·5	161	150	148·5
121·5	111	114·5	96	113·5	123·5	116	126·5
12	24	18·5	19	33	28	33	27
17	27	32	30	35	50·5	57	58
44	27	42	31	50·5	29·5	25	30·5
756·5	877·5	972·5	1,018·5	1,159	1,234	1,333	1,336
224·5	236·5	239·5	243	255	264·5	275	278·5
50·5	53	57	60	65·5	69	73·5	77
83	87	97·5	115	135·5	151·5	155·5	157·5
43·5	61·5	113·5	142·5	177·5	187	270	289·5
33·5	36·5	41·5	51	50	65·5	65·5	65
94	107·5	116	135·5	149·5	159·5	173	188·5
529	582	665	747	833	897	1,012·5	1,056
227·5	295·5	307·5	271·5	326	337	320·5	280

Distribution of Product by Industry Groups. We can next consider the distribution of incomes in the different parts of the economy. The proportion of the total product that is paid out in wages and salaries varies greatly from industry to industry. Wages take a much larger proportion in mines and quarries than anywhere else—79·3 per cent in 1954, as compared with a mere 33·8 per cent in agriculture, forestry and fishing. Building and contracting also show a high proportion of wage-payments —68·6 per cent in 1954. The mining and building industries are alike in using a high proportion of manual labour to other factors of production. In both, however, the proportion of gross product paid out in wages was smaller in 1954 than in 1948. Indeed, most branches of production showed this falling tendency, though in the manufacturing industries the fall was too slight to be clearly significant. Salaries, on the other hand, were low in the mining group, only the agricultural group showing a smaller proportion of the product paid out in this form. The cause in the latter case was the prevalence in farming of small-scale production by working farmers, with little scope for salaried employment. In the case of mining, the main cause was the relatively small employment of scientific and technical staffs. Transport and communication services had the highest proportion of salary-payments— 18·8 per cent—followed by the public utility services—16·5 per cent— and the manufacturing group—15·8 per cent. In most groups the proportion of the product paid in salaries increased between 1948 and 1954, mainly because of increased use of technical and administrative specialists. For some groups it is not possible to draw a clear line between wages and salaries. This holds good for the distributive trades, in which the combined proportion paid out in wages and salaries rose from 46·7 per cent in 1948 to 52·7 per cent in 1954. Miscellaneous services showed a similar rise, from 50·8 per cent to 58·1 per cent, whereas in the group covering financial services the combined proportion fell from 74·5 per cent to 68·4 per cent, probably on account both of growing mechanization and of relatively small advances in wages and salaries. For the last five groups shown in the table no corresponding proportions can be given, as they have no commercial product that can be compared with the sums paid out to the employees.

The table shows, in addition to the amounts and proportions paid in wages and salaries, the change in the gross product between 1948 and 1954. It will be noted that the group showing the greatest percentage increase is that of the public utility services, followed by the financial group, and then by the general manufacturing group. Agriculture, which experienced bad harvests in 1954, shows the lowest increase. Most of the other groups come fairly close together, with increases ranging from 40 to 45 per cent.

In the service groups for which there are no figures of 'gross product' wage and salary payments have increased most of all in the health and education group, mainly as a consequence of the institution of the National Health Service. Defence payments have also risen sharply, because of re-armament. Wage-payments for domestic service on the other hand have fallen between 1948 and 1954; and so have wage and salary payments in the small 'non-profit-making' service group.

The Effects of Full Employment. One very important reason for the relative improvement in wage-incomes is full employment. Since 1945— and indeed during the war also—most wage-earners have been drawing incomes for fifty-two weeks in the year—and full-time incomes at that. The number of hours worked as part of the standard working week has been reduced in many occupations; but the number of hours actually worked has changed but little, because of overtime working. Actual hours worked by adult males have increased, whereas those worked by women and juveniles have been reduced. But in general more of the hours of employment are now paid for at higher, overtime rates. This benefits the worker; and it is a further advantage that he is much less liable to be stood off, or put on short time, in some weeks, and thus to sustain a cut in his annual earnings. Full employment of course benefits other persons besides wage-earners; but the benefit is most certain and direct in their case. The owner of capital reaps an advantage from having his capital goods fully employed; and the fee-earning professional is also benefited by more regular work. Those who do not gain in this way are the recipients of fixed incomes—holders of debentures or preference shares, pensioners and recipients of social service benefits in general.

Personal and other Incomes. The word 'income' is commonly used with reference to 'personal incomes'—i.e. those distributed to individuals or to bodies which pass them on to individuals or consume them as services to individuals—for example, charities and educational establishments. But by no means the whole of the 'national income' is in fact distributed in this way. A large fraction of the profits made by business firms, instead of being paid out in dividends to the shareholders, is kept back and accumulated in reserves, which are either invested by the firm in capital goods, or used as working capital in the business, or lent to or invested in other businesses or in government funds. These sums are in fact needed to provide for the renewal of worn-out or obsolete capital assets and are only in part available for the creation of additional capital goods. They form, however, equally with incomes distributed to individuals (personal incomes) part of the gross national income—that is to say, the total product of the year's work.

In 1954 the gross national income was reckoned as £15,718 million, and the total of personal incomes as £14,544 million—a difference of £1,174 million. The gross trading profits—before meeting interest charges—of joint stock companies, public corporations, and other public trading enterprises amounted to £2,892 million and payments of dividends and interest by companies and public corporations to £1,035 million. The undistributed incomes of companies and corporations, before providing for taxes, amounted to £2,447 million. Thus, the major part of corporate profits was not directly converted into personal income, though shareholders were free to convert a further part by selling off some of the shares they held. Personal income is not the only form in which owners of capital get a return on their property: they also become the owners of the reserves, which will yield them higher incomes in future years. It is therefore misleading to take the figures of distributed incomes quite at their face value as indicating how much wage- and salary-earners on the one hand and owners of capital on the other are getting out of the annual product. Even after the costs of depreciation and obsolescence have been met, a substantial amount accrues to the owning classes in the enhanced value of their property through the accumulation of business reserves. How much cannot be said; for as we have seen there is no valid way of estimating how much of gross profit should be assigned to meeting the costs of depreciation and obsolescence (see p. 116).

Spending, Saving and Investment.   Incomes are meant for spending, either on consumption or on investment, or on meeting the current cost of public services. If a recipient of income simply saves his money, and no one else spends it, the effect is to withdraw from the market a part of the demand that is needed to enable the producers to recover their costs and to realize normal profits. This involves a deficiency of used purchasing power which reacts on prices and becomes a cause of unemployment. But fortunately it is often not at the individual's discretion whether his income is used or not. If he simply puts it into a bank and leaves it there, without investing it, the bank, finding itself with so much more on its hands in deposits, can lend out more than it otherwise could and can thus put the idle money back into circulation —provided it can find additional borrowers. So no harm is done by mere hoarding, unless borrowers are scarce, as they are apt to be in times of economic depression. When business is active, someone spends the money, even if its owner does not; whereas in bad times hoarding makes depression a great deal worse, especially when corporate businesses join the ranks of the hoarders and pile up deposit accounts in the banks instead of using their full resources to finance production.

This is the danger of hoarding to which Keynes drew attention in the 1930s, when he was urging action to restore full employment. Since 1939 his remedies for this particular vice of the capitalist system have not needed to be invoked. Full employment has existed almost continuously in Great Britain, not because it has been stimulated artificially, but because every worker has been needed to make good war losses and arrears and to maintain exports to meet the cost of indispensable imports.

Therefore, incomes have been more regular as well as bigger; and it has been quite difficult even for relatively inefficient firms to fail to pay their way. Bankruptcies and compulsory windings-up of companies have become few, and the insecurities of competitive business have been greatly reduced. This is not altogether an advantage; for it means that a proportion of labour is wastefully and inefficiently employed. But it acts as a considerable stabilizing influence on incomes and simplifies the task of the tax-gatherer as well.

CHAPTER SEVENTEEN

WAGES

THE wage a worker gets depends partly on the *rate* at which he is paid by the hour, day, week or month, or sometimes by the unit of output, partly on the number of hours he works, and partly on any special allowances he receives, for example for overtime, nightshift or week-end work or as a piecework payment or bonus over his standard rate. In a rather small number of establishments, he also gets a share in profits, either as part of a co-partnership scheme under which he holds shares in the enterprise or without such shareholding participation. In most occupations there are nowadays standard rates of wages, agreed upon by collective bargaining or by arbitration; and in quite a number there are legal minimum rates, fixed under the Wages Councils Act or under special legislation. In most cases overtime, nightshift and week-end work are paid for at special rates higher than the rates for the standard week; and in a good many there are bonuses for specially skilled or important groups of workers. The 'annual wage', which has been coming to the front in the United States, is not found in Great Britain except among salary-earners; but in a good number of cases there is some form of 'guaranteed week', often of less than the standard number of hours worked; and in a good many others there is a distinction between 'established' and 'unestablished' workers, the latter being liable to more summary dismissal than those reckoned as belonging to the 'establishment'.

The Effects of Full Employment. Since the earlier version of this book was written, paid holidays—of a week or in some cases a fortnight—have spread over the greater part of industry. Wage-incomes have also become much more regular as a consequence of full employment. There has been since 1940 little short-time working or 'standing-off', except for a short period in some of the textile trades. Shortage of workers has meant regular work for most, with only brief intervals, or none, in changing from one job to another. There have been no 'depressed' industrial areas, like those which persisted through the inter-war period.

This has meant a very great advance in the worker's feeling of independence, and a considerable change in the conditions of workshop discipline. Employers and supervisors are for the most part no longer

in a position to play the petty tyrant, even if they would, for fear of
losing their employees and not being able to replace them. There has
been a considerable spread of arrangements for joint consultation at the
establishment level, not only in the nationalized industries, where they
are compulsory (see p. 229), but also in privately owned industries;
and where the firms take such arrangements seriously, industrial relations have in many cases substantially improved, though there has been
no change in their essential character.

Improved Position of the Less Skilled.   There has been a marked improvement in the position of most of the less skilled workers. As far
as wage-rates are concerned this is due mainly to the granting of
advances at flat rates rather than as percentages of the existing rates—
a method which narrows the real 'differentials' between the skilled and
less skilled grades. This narrowing has led to some difficulties, especially
of late, with the skilled workers protesting against the inadequacy of
the rewards for the higher types of work—as in the case of the railway
locomotive drivers' strike in 1955. In some cases, however, means have
been found of rewarding the more skilled workers, or some of them,
with special bonuses and allowances over and above the standard rates.
This method has been used especially in the engineering and kindred
trades, in which it took hold during the years of war. A considerable
number of skilled workers, however, are still left with a grievance over
narrowed differentials; and the Trade Union movement is in a quandary
concerning its attitude to this matter, because some Trade Unions
represent mainly skilled, some mainly less skilled workers, and some
both together, and they tend accordingly to take different views. There
is general sympathy for the improvement in the position of the lower-
paid grades: the only question is whether the narrowing of wage-
differences has gone too far.

Wage-rates and Earnings.   There has been some tendency for piecework and other forms of 'payment by results' to spread over a wider
field; but this has been less marked than many people expected, partly
because in many kinds of mass-production the pace of work is largely
set by the machine and the individual worker has little control over
it. These conditions have led, in some cases, to the development of
systems of 'group' piecework or collective bonus on output paid to a
whole working group. In many cases too 'oncost' workers and supervisors are now paid bonuses on the output of the groups they attend.
In general, weekly earnings have tended to rise faster than wage-rates
in most forms of manufacturing industry. On the whole, women's
earnings have risen more than men's, and those of juveniles most of all.

Wages and Salaries.   Wages and salaries form a larger fraction of the
total of personal incomes (see p. 224), than they did before the war.

The 'salaries' group of course includes many very highly paid managers and administrators, scientists and technicians, as well as less exalted groups of non-manual workers; but there are unfortunately no figures which make it possible to separate the higher from the lower. On the whole it would appear that the lower grades of salary-earners have improved their position less than the main body of manual workers. This is certainly the case in some branches of the public service, except possibly at the lowest levels of all.

The Distribution of Incomes by Sources. The general estimates of the distribution of 'personal income' between wage-earners, salary-earners, and other income groups are as shown in Table 122.

The Share of Wages. It is evident from these figures that the share of wages in the total of personal income and in the gross national product rose sharply between 1938 and 1946 and continued to rise up to 1948. Thereafter, in relation to the total of personal incomes, it did not vary much up to 1953, but rose substantially in 1954. As against this, the share of salaries rose between 1938 and 1946 and thereafter continued to rise up to 1951, but showed little change between 1951 and 1954. If wages, salaries and the pay of the armed forces are taken together we get a bigger increase up to 1946, because of the rise in forces pay, and then a continuing increase up to 1951, followed by a slight fall in 1952–3 and a small rise in 1954. Comparing 1938 with 1954, we find that wages have risen from 37·9 to 42·4 per cent of the total of personal incomes, whereas salaries have risen from 17·9 to 21·3 per cent. Wages, salaries, and forces pay combined have risen from 59·6 to 70·2 per cent.

These increases certainly mean a big improvement in the distribution of the national income to the advantage of the wage-earners, even without taking any account of re-distribution through the social services. The wage-earners, taken as a group, are both relatively and absolutely better off in terms of money income, as well as from the receipt of improved social services and benefits. The major part of this improvement, however, occurred during the war, and not as a consequence of the Labour Government's policy after 1945. Labour policy improved the social services, but did not, as far as can be told from the figures, greatly affect the initial distribution of incomes between wage-earners and other groups.

Wage Statistics. We can now turn to the available data concerning wages, not as a share in the national income, but in themselves.

Wages. There are two main ways of estimating wages and wage-changes. One of these is in terms of actual earnings and the other in terms of standard rates, usually for a week of so many working hours. Neither of these sets of data is available for the whole employed population or even for all manual workers. Standard wage-rates exist for

	1938	1946	1947	1948	1949	1950	1951	1952	1953	1954
Wages	1,520	3,270	3,710	4,160	4,385	4,580	5,080	5,405	5,730	6,170
Salaries	910	1,625	1,765	1,980	2,130	2,290	2,575	2,755	2,890	3,095
Pay of Armed Forces (cash and kind)	56	577	395	233	223	230	287	320	331	335
Total of above	3,022	5,687	6,144	6,718	7,150	7,543	8,421	9,006	9,527	10,200
Other Personal Incomes	2,050	3,112	3,286	3,272	3,425	3,497	3,700	3,979	4,197	4,344
Total Personal Incomes	5,072	8,799	9,430	9,990	10,575	11,030	12,121	12,985	13,724	14,544
Wages—per cent of above	37·9	37·2	39·4	41·6	41·5	41·5	41·9	41·6	41·8	42·4
Total National Product	5,125	8,783	9,364	10,379	11,099	11,666	12,785	13,861	14,805	15,718
Wages—per cent of above	37·1	37·3	39·7	40·1	39·5	39·3	39·7	39·0	38·7	39·2
Salaries—per cent of total Personal Income	17·9	18·5	18·7	19·8	20·2	20·8	21·2	21·2	21·2	21·3
Wages, Salaries and Forces Pay per cent of total Personal Income	59·6	64·6	65·2	67·3	67·6	68·4	69·5	69·4	69·4	70·2

many, but not for all occupations; and statistics of average earnings cover mainly manufacturing industries and are compiled for broad groups, including skilled and less skilled workers together. The Ministry of Labour publishes twice each year a study of average earnings in a large number of industries, each study covering only a single week. Figures of average earnings, compiled in different ways, exist for a few industries not covered by the Ministry of Labour's surveys. The same Ministry issues annually a survey of wage-*rates* covering a larger field and distinguishing the standard rates for the various types of skilled and less skilled workers; and the Trades Union Congress issues a monthly survey of wage-*rates* fixed by statutory Wages Councils for trades subject to statutory wage-regulation.

Average Earnings. It is easiest to begin with the figures of average weekly earnings, which relate to one week in April and one in October of each year. The statistics cover, besides all manufacturing industries, the following groups: Mining and Quarrying (except Coal), Building and Contracting, Gas, Electricity and Water, some branches of Transport (but not Railways, London Transport or British Road Services) and the industrial services of National and Local Government. Separate figures are shown for men over 21, youths and boys, women over 18, and girls, as well as general averages covering all these. There are accompanying figures for average hours actually worked, including overtime. The statistics are available for 1947, with comparative figures for October 1938; and hourly as well as weekly earnings are given. There are also general averages for the whole of the industries covered by the returns.

Here, first, are the general figures of average weekly earnings for each return since April 1947 and for October 1938. (See Table 123.)

The rises have been continuous, except on one occasion (1948–9) for youths and boys, and on one occasion (1951–2) for girls. By April 1949 men's earnings had risen by 100 per cent above those of October 1938. Youths' and boys' average earnings had more than doubled by April 1948, and women's and girls' by April 1947; and the general average had more than doubled by October 1947. By April 1955 the increases over October 1938 averaged 215 per cent for men, 249 per cent for youths and boys, 246 per cent for women, and 287 per cent for girls, with a general average increase of 242 per cent. The adult men's earnings had risen least, and the girls' most, despite the fact that the average hours worked by men had risen from 47·7 a week to 48·9, whereas the girls' hours had fallen from 44·6 to 42·7. Hours worked by youths and boys had also fallen, from 46·2 to 45·0, and women's hours from 43·5 to 41·9. In calculating women's earnings each part-time worker is reckoned at one-half.

Earnings by Industries. These general averages conceal substantial

TABLE 123

Average Weekly Earnings in Certain Industries

		Men over 21	Youths and Boys	Women over 18	Girls	All Workers
1938	Oct.	69/–	26/1	32/6	18/6	53/3
1947	April	123/5	47/4	67/4	40/2	103/6
	Oct.	128/1	51/10	69/7	43/9	108/2
1948	April	134/–	57/2	72/11	48/4	114/–
	Oct.	137/11	58/9	74/6	49/5	117/4
1949	April	139/11	58/6	77/2	50/3	119/4
	Oct.	142/8	60/1	78/9	51/8	121/9
1950	April	145/9	61/5	80/6	51/10	124/1
	Oct.	150/5	63/9	82/7	53/5	128/–
1951	April	160/2	66/11	87/4	55/11	136/2
	Oct.	166/–	69/1	90/1	57/11	141/1
1952	April	173/7	71/9	92/2	57/9	147/3
	Oct.	178/6	74/11	96/4	60/9	151/11
1953	April	185/11	77/7	100/3	62/6	157/7
	Oct.	189/2	78/11	102/5	64/11	160/1
1954	April	197/8	82/–	105/3	65/10	166/6
	Oct.	204/5	85/7	108/2	69/5	171/9
1955	April	217/5	90/11	112/5	71/6	182/3

differences in the fortunes of workers in different industries. Here, for selected dates, are the average weekly earnings of men and women, in the various industries included in the returns. (See Table 124 overleaf.)

In 1938 much the highest-paid group of adult men was in the printing and paper industries, followed by Government Industrial Establishments and by the huge metal, engineering and shipbuilding group, and then by such Transport as was included in the returns. The lowest-paid group for men was in textiles, largely a women's industry, and the next lowest in mining and quarrying (excluding coal). Then came gas, electricity and water services, and then brick-making, pottery and glass. The range of average weekly earnings, taking skilled and less skilled together, was from 84s. 3d. in printing and paper to 57s. 3d. in textiles: more than half of the 16 groups lay between 60s. and 67s. For women much the highest group was Government Industrial Establishments, followed by transport and leather, and then by paper and printing. The lowest group was gas, electricity and water, and the next lowest bricks, pottery and glass. Of the 14 groups, excluding mining and building, in which hardly any women were employed, 3 showed average women's earnings of less than 30s., 2 more of less than 32s., 3 more of less than 33s., 2 more of less than 34s., and the remaining 3 less than 35s. The general averages were 69s. for men and 32s. 6d. for women. The average

TABLE 124

Average Weekly Earnings of Men over 21 and Women over 18, in Certain Industries

	MEN					WOMEN				
	1938 Oct.	1946 Oct.	1951 Oct.	1954 Oct.	1955 April	1938 Oct.	1946 Oct.	1951 Oct.	1954 Oct.	1955 April
Stone, etc., Mining, Quarrying	60/-	112/8	165/3	194/5	207/1	—	—	88/2	108/8	113/4
Treatment of Non-metal Mining and Quarrying Products	66/5	123/3 ⎫	173/2	209/9	230/10	29/8	67/5	86/6	103/-	113/-
Bricks, Pottery and Glass	63/2	119/11 ⎬	169/-	206/-	216/10	27/10	58/4	88/11	106/5	111/10
Chemicals, Paints and Oils	69/3	119/11			221/6	32/8	64/-	90/10		120/8
Metals, Engineering and Shipbuilding	75/-	132/9	176/7	*	*	33/4	70/7	95/11	*	*
Textiles	57/3	110/-	162/10	196/9	199/6	31/9	63/7	86/1	112/-	112/5
Leather, Furs, etc.	64/1	118/8	157/7	191/3	194/6	34/11	65/9	86/-	103/1	105/5
Clothing	64/3	114/9	151/8	184/3	190/11	32/9	63/-	85/10	104/2	107/9
Food, Drink, Tobacco	65/3	112/6	154/6	185/6	194/3	32/11	60/7	92/4	100/4	105/9
Woodworking	66/3	119/1	163/1	202/9	200/7	33/8	67/11	93/1	114/3	111/8
Paper, Printing, Stationery, etc.	84/3	126/7	187/5	227/7	236/6	34/1	60/9	80/8	109/9	112/8
Building, Contracting, etc.	66/-	110/7	161/-	198/7	214/1	—	61/9	89/1	94/3	98/8
Miscellaneous Manufacturing	69/1	129/5	177/10	214/8	224/7	31/9	68/5		105/2	109/-
Transport, Storage, etc. (part)	70/-	115/2	157/2	189/1	205/11	34/11	84/2	117/4	139/7	151/11
Gas, Electricity and Water	63/1	105/11	142/6	187/4	204/7	27/8	55/8	78/3	103/1	111/1†
Government Industrial Establishments †	75/3	116/6	—	157/4	163/8	44/9	76/4	—	96/4	98/3

* For 1954 and 1955 this total is broken up into groups, as follows: for men, Metal Manufacture 228s. 6d. and 242s. 7d., Engineering, Shipbuilding and Electrical Goods 215s. 7d. and 231s. 11d., Vehicles 225s. 9d. and 241s. 7d., Precision Instruments and Jewellery, etc., 210s. 4d. and 220s. 1d., and other Metal Goods 215s. 7d. and 229s. 11d. The corresponding figures for women are: 114s. 2d., 116s. 7d., 123s. 8d., 113s. 7d., and 106s. 11d. for 1954 and 120s. 8d., 123s. 10d., 131s. 6d., 119s. 8d., and 112s. 1d. for 1955.

women's wage, in the occupations covered, was 47 per cent of the average man's.

In April 1955, the metal manufacturing group, not shown separately in 1938, occupied the top position for men, followed by the paper and printing group. Then came the vehicle group, also lumped in with metals and engineering in 1938. Next came engineering and shipbuilding, bracketed with the miscellaneous metal trades. At the other end, National and Local Government services—a new grouping—were at the bottom, and next came clothing, followed by food, drink and tobacco. The range was from 228s. 6d. to 157s. 4d. Out of 19 groups, 4 showed average earnings above 230s., 10 others above 200s., 4 more above 190s., and only 1 of less than 190s. For women much the highest group was transport, at 151s. 11d. Next came vehicles, at 131s. 6d., engineering, at 123s. 10d., and metal manufacture, at 120s. 8d. At the bottom were National and Local Government services, at 98s. 3d., followed by building and contracting, at 98s. 8d. Out of 19 groups, 2 were under 100s., 5 more under 110s., 8 more under 120s., 2 more under 130s., 1 more at 131s. 6d., and the remaining 1 well under 150s. The general averages had risen to 217s. 5d. for men and 121s. 5d. for women—by 215 and 246 per cent respectively. The women's average earnings were rather less than 56 per cent of the average man's, although the men's average working week had increased by rather more than an hour, whereas the women's had fallen by an hour and a half.

Wage Differentials. These figures tell us nothing of the relative earnings of skilled and less skilled workers, who are grouped together in each industrial category. There has been no full study of this matter of 'wage differentials' for skilled workers, except in terms of standard *rates* of wages as distinct from actual *earnings*. There is, however, some very useful information in a series of articles published in the *Bulletin of the Oxford University Institute of Statistics* over the period 1951–4, and written mainly by Mr. K. G. J. C. Knowles. These articles were concerned with rates of wages as well as with earnings; but for the present I am concerned only with earnings. The first of these articles (June 1951) dealt with engineering. It showed skilled workers earning in July 1938 an average of 88 8s. a week, as against 61·1s. for labourers and 74·6s. for semi-skilled male workers. Time-workers and workers paid by results are grouped together. Actually the latter earned more—14·6 per cent more for skilled, 9·9 per cent for unskilled, and 19 per cent for semi-skilled workers. On the average, the unskilled earned 68·8 per cent of the average earnings of the skilled, and the semi-skilled 83·9 per cent. The article then gives comparative figures of earnings for January 1948. By then skilled men averaged 146·6s. a week, the unskilled 115·8s., and the semi-skilled 135·1s. Workers on payment by results averaged, if skilled, 6·8 per cent more than time-workers, if unskilled 9·8 per cent, and if semi-skilled 20·4 per cent. The unskilled averaged 79·1 per cent of the skilled average, and the semi-skilled 92·2 per cent. There had been a marked narrowing of the differentials paid for skilled work.

A second article (November 1951) dealt with shipbuilding, and compared June 1940 with January 1950. It showed unskilled workers on time work as earning 78 per cent of the earnings of skilled workers in 1940, and 80 per cent in 1950, after a rise to 85 per cent in 1944. Skilled workers on payment by results earned 32 per cent more than skilled time-workers in 1940, but only 20 per cent more in 1950. For unskilled workers no figures were available for 1940: for 1950 the excess of earnings was 32 per cent.

A third article on dock workers' earnings (September 1952), had little bearing on the question of differentials; but a fourth, dealing with London Transport (August 1953), embodies some interesting information. On the Underground Railways in 1938 the average weekly earnings were 105s. 5d. for motormen, 83s. 4d. for guards, and 58s. 8d. for station men and women. By 1951 these earnings had risen to 187s. 2d., 157s. 5d., and 131s. 10d. In 1938 guards averaged 79 per cent of the motorman's average, and station workers between 55 and 56 per cent. In 1951 these percentages had become 84 and 70 per cent. Actually, the station men averaged 141s. 8d., and the women 128s. 5d.—which brought the men to nearly 76 per cent of the motormen's earnings, and the women to nearly 69 per cent. On London omnibuses drivers averaged 94s. 2d. in 1938, and conductors 87s. 6d.—a differential of only 7 per cent. By 1951 the figures were 157s. 3d. and 150s. 3d.: the differential had fallen to 4½ per cent. For trams and trolleybuses, on the other hand, the differential between drivers' and conductors' earnings was only 6d.—82s. 7d. as against 82s. 1d.—in 1938, but had risen to 8s. 3d. in 1951—157s. 9d. as against 149s. 6d., or from ½ per cent to over 5 per cent. These were differences similar to those on the Underground between men and women employed as conductors.

The latest article in the series, dealing with earnings in the boot and shoe industry (February 1954), throws light mainly on differentials between pieceworkers and day workers, and between men and women, rather than on differential payments for skill. It shows, for October 1938, average earnings of 60s. 5d. for men and 35s. 8d. for women on day work, and for men and women on piecework of 67s. 7d. and 40s. 4d. . . . the women getting respectively 59 and nearly 60 per cent of the men's average. In May 1953 the corresponding sums were 156s. 8d. and 92s. 11d. for time-workers and 199s. 5d. and 118s. 2d. for pieceworkers: the women's earnings were again 59 and nearly 60 per cent of the men's.

Wage-rates. These figures, useful though they are, are clearly inadequate to provide a basis for any generalization about the relative earnings of skilled and less skilled workers. But what further information there is about differentials relates mainly to relative *rates* of wages as distinct from earnings; and data about wage-*rates* tend to lead to an overestimate of the narrowing of differentials, as many—though by no means all—skilled workers are in receipt of special bonus over and above their standard rates, or are in a position to add more largely to their earnings by means of piecework payments than most unskilled workers—though not than many who are semi-skilled. Before we come to *rate*-differentials, we must say something of the position in relation to wage-rates generally.

In most manual occupations, and in some branches of non-manual work, there are to-day standard wage-rates fixed by collective bargaining or arbitration, or minimum rates fixed by statutory Wages Councils or similar bodies. One big exception, especially in the engineering and kindred trades, is that there are no generally applied standard rates for many semi-skilled occupations, whose members are paid at varying rates intermediate between those of skilled workers and labourers. In many cases, the rates for semi-skilled work are in fact also settled by collective bargaining or arbitration, or by Wages Councils; but only in the case of statutory regulation are they usually settled nationally. The national data about wage-*rates* relate mainly to skilled workers and unskilled workers and differ from the data about earnings in that they are based not on whole industries but on particular occupations or kinds of work, showing separately the various types of skilled workers in each main industry.

Index of Wage-rates. The Ministry of Labour publishes regularly three sets of figures relating to rates of wages—an index of wage-rates for all the main industries and services taken together; an annual volume giving details of a large number of wage-rates in force in particular occupations; and a monthly estimate of the current changes in wage-rates in each main industrial group and of the number of workers affected by them. The general index of wage-rates has been published only since June 1947, though broad annual estimates were made for earlier years. The figures for the end of each year since 1947 are as follows:

TABLE 125

Index of Wage-rates, 1947–54 (June 1947 = 100)

	1947	1948	1949	1950	1951	1952	1953	1954
Men	103	107	109	113	125	132	136	142
Women	103	109	112	116	130	138	143	148
Juveniles	106	110	113	118	132	143	149	155
All Workers	103+	107	109	114	126	134	138	146
Rise per cent each year	—	4	2	4½	10½	6	3	6

At June 1947 the index, based on September 1939 = 100, stood between 166 and 167.

For earlier years from 1938 the end-of-year estimates, with September 1939 as 100, were as follows:

	1938	1939	1940	1941	1942	1943	1944	1945	1946	1947 (Nov.)
All workers	99–100	103–4	116	126–7	132–3	139–9	145–6	153	165	173

Rates and Earnings. Comparison with the movement of average earnings (see p. 237) makes it clear that weekly earnings have been rising considerably faster than wage-rates over the whole period. In April 1954 average earnings for all the workers covered by the Ministry of Labour's survey were 213 per cent higher than in October 1938, whereas average rates of wages for a wider range of occupations had risen only by 145 per cent. Between October 1947 and April 1954 the rise in average earnings was 54 per cent, and in wage-rates 53 per cent: so that the divergence between the movements of rates and earnings clearly occurred before 1947—in fact, during the war.

Earnings in other Industries. In addition to the industries covered by the Ministry of Labour's surveys, figures of weekly earnings are available for certain other groups of workers. Permanent employees at the docks and some road transport workers are included in the figures already cited for Transport. For dock workers generally average weekly earnings in the first week of May 1954 were 219s. 2d., and for April 1955 were 261s. For the three months April–June 1955 they averaged 246s. weekly. The corresponding figures for the last week in April 1947 and for the months April to June 1947 were 149s. and 152s. 11d. No comparable figures exist for earlier dates.

For coal-mining, statistics of earnings are compiled on a basis of earnings a shift, as well as weekly earnings. For the last week in April 1955, the average for all male workers, including juveniles, was 253s. 9d. and for men over 21 years of age 266s. 8d. Earnings a man-shift for all males for May 1954 were on the average 46s. 6d. | about 2s. 2d. for the value of allowances in kind. In 1947, over the whole year, the corresponding figure for cash earnings was 27s. 8d., and in 1948 31s. 9d. Allowances in kind were valued at 1s. 2d. a shift in 1947 and at 1s. 4½d. in 1948. In 1938 the average cash earnings of colliery workers of all ages were only 55s. 9d., and allowances in kind were valued at 2s. 2d. a week. The average number of shifts worked was 4·96 a week in 1938 and 4·71 in 1954.

On the railways, in March 1954, engine drivers earned on an average 220s. 3d. as compared with 165s. 3d. in April 1949. Firemen averaged 182s. 8d. in March 1954 and 135s. 8d. in April 1949, and cleaners

150*s*. 3*d*. and 109*s*. 9*d*. Guards, at the same dates, averaged 183*s*. 3*d*. and 139*s*. 11*d*., passenger porters 158*s*. 6*d*. and 117*s*. 6*d*., and goods porters 155*s*. 8*d*. and 109*s*. 11*d*. For all grades, except officials, the average earnings were as follows:

TABLE 126
Main Line Railway Workers' Average Earnings
(March or April)

	1939	1945	1947	1954	1955
Wage-grades	68/9	116/10	123/6		
Men, Clerical and				188/2	—
Supervisory	93/3	143/6	140/8		
Women	—	82/8	87/4	115/7	—
Youths and Boys	28/10	42/3	46/2	73/3	—
Girls	—	48/8	43/6	61/10	—

No figures for 1955 are yet available.

For agriculture, average weekly earnings for the year April 1953 to March 1954 were 142*s*. 6*d*. for men, 94*s*. 5½*d*. for women and girls, and 88*s*. 5*d*. for youths. For the half-year ending in March 1955 the corresponding figures were 150*s*. 2*d*., 96*s*. 5*d*., and 90*s*. 5½*d*. For the year 1947–8 the corresponding figures were 100*s*. 11½*d*., 67*s*. 9*d*., and 64*s*. 11½*d*. For 1938 average *annual* earnings of farm workers of all grades and types have been estimated at £92·3 in England and Wales, £84·1 in Scotland, and £54·7 in Northern Ireland, with an overall average of £87·8, or 36*s*. a week on a 52-week basis.

Wages. Finally, here are a selection of wage-*rates*, extracted from the Ministry of Labour's annual report on *Standard Time Rates of Wages and Hours of Labour*. Figures in brackets are *hourly* rates. The rates shown are either minima or standard rates, wherever possible separately for 'labourers' and for skilled workers.

TABLE 127
Wage-rates in Certain Industries, 1950 and 1955

Men		1950	April 1955
Agriculture, E. & W.	Minimum	94/–	127/–
Coal Mining (Underground), G.B.	rate	115/–	27/9 a shift
(Surface), G.B.	,,	100/–	24/5 a shift
China Clay	,,	91/–	127/–
Brickmaking (Labourers), E. & W.	,,	(2/2½)	(2/11½)
Pottery (Labourers)	,,	93/8	100/10 + 6¼%
Cement Manufacture			
(Labourers)	,,	(2/2·7–2/4·3)	(3/3½–3/4·3)
(Most craftsmen)	,,	(2/11)	(4/3¾–4/4½)
Fine Chemicals (Labourers)	,,	98/–	137/–
(Process workers)	,,	108/–	144/–
Heavy Chemicals (Labourers)	,,	(2/3½–2/4½)	(3/2¾–3/3½)
(Skilled workers)	,,	(2/11½)	(4/–)
Light Castings (Labourers)	,,	95/6	137/7
(Moulders)	,,	114/1½	162/11½

TABLE 127 (continued)

Men		1950	April 1955
Engineering			
(Labourers, most areas)	Standard	92/– – 93/–	132/10
(Fitters, most areas)	rate	107/– – 108/–	155/10
Shipbuilding (Labourers)	,,	92/–	133/–
(Craftsmen)	,,	109/–	158/–
Constructional Engineering			
(Labourers)	,,	(2/3½–2/5)	(3/5½)
(Craftsmen)	,,	(2/8–2/9)	(3/11–4/–)
Railway Shopmen (Labourers)	,,	69/–	103/6
(Most craftsmen)	,,	110/–	157/6
Vehicle Building (Labourers)	,,	(2/4)	(3/2½)
(Craftsmen)	,,	(2/9)	(3/7½)
Electrical Cable-making			
(Labourers)	,,	92/7	132/–
(Craftsmen, top grade)	,,	106/4	150/4
Hollow-ware	General Minimum	(2/0½)	(2/7)
Cotton			
(Preparing) (Labourer)	Minimum	95/6	118/9
(Spinning) (Mule spinners)	rate	95/6–107/6	167/2
(Weaving) (4-loom weavers)	,,	74/2	95/4
(Weaving) (6-loom weavers)	,,	81/8	105/–
(Weaving) (Maintenance mechanics)	,,	135/–	174/5
Wool Textiles, Yorks (lowest rate)	,,	97/1	120/5
(Fully skilled spinners)	,,	121/5	150/5
(Pattern weavers)	,,	98/11–103/7	122/7–128/3
Silk	,,	95/–	124/–
Jute	,,	89/6	117/1
Textile Dyeing, etc.	,,	92/6	128/5
Carpets	,,	96/7	130/–
Leather	,,	(2/2)	(2/10½)
Tailoring, Ready-made	,,	(1/11½)	(2/7)
(Cutters)	,,	(2/4–2/6)	(2/11½)
Shirt-making	,,	(2/1½)	(2/9)
(Cutters)	,,	(2/5–2/7)	(3/0½)
Boot and Shoe Manufacture	,,	108/–	140/–
Repairing	,,	95/–	125/–
Glove Manufacture	,,	(2/1)	(2/10½)
Flour Milling (Labourers)	,,	96/– – 106/–	133/6–140/–
(First roller men)	,,	116/– – 132/–	161/– – 180/–
Baking	,,	(1/10½–1/11½)	(2/7½–2/8½)
(First hands)	,,	(2/2½–2/4)	(3/– – 3/1)
Biscuit Manufacture	,,	100/–	130/–
(Machinemen)	,,	115/–	150/–
Cocoa, Chocolate and Sugar			
Confectionery	,,	100/–	137/–
Tobacco	,,	100/– – 108/–	134/6–143/–
Sawmilling (Labourers)	,,	(2/1½–2/3)	(3/1½–3/2½)
(Skilled sawyers)	,,	(2/7–2/9)	(3/6–3/7)
Furniture (Labourers)	,,	(1/6¾)	(3/5)
(Skilled workers)	,,	(2/9)	(3/10)
Paper-making (Labourers)	,,	(2/2)	(3/–)
(Craftsmen)	,,	(2/7½–2/8¼)	(3/9¼–3/10½)
Wallpaper making (Labourers)	,,	111/–	138/2
(Craftsmen)	,,	121/– – 147/10	161/8–194/11
Printing			
(General assistants)	,,	102/6–126/–	141/6–144/6
(Hand compositors, jobbing)	,,	122/– – 131/–	169/– – 174/6
(Hand compositors, morning news)	,,	145/– – 156/–	193/– – 199/6
(Bookbinders)	,,	122/– – 131/–	169/– – 174/6
Rubber (Labourers)	,,	(2/1½)	(2/11½)
(Skilled)	,,	(2/3½–2/4½)	(3/2½)
Building (Labourers)	,,	(2/3½–2/6½)	(3/4–3/5½)
(Craftsmen)	,,	(2/9–3/–)	(3/10½–4/–)
Domestic Engineering			
(Mates)	,,	(2/4½)	(3/6)
(Craftsmen)	,,	(2/11¼)	(4/0½)

TABLE 127 (continued)

Men		1950	April 1955
Electrical Installation			
(Mates)	Minimum	(2/5–2/6½)	(3/2¾)
(Craftsmen)	rate	(3/– – 3/1)	(4/0½)
Gas Supply (Labourers)	Standard	(2/3–2/4½)	(3/2¼–3/3¾)
(Gas fitters)	rate	(2/9–2/11)	(4/– – 4/1½)
(Craftsmen)	,,	(2/11–3/–)	(4/0¼–4/1½)
Electricity Supply (Labourers)	,,	(2/4¾)	(3/3¾)
(Electricians)	,,	(2/11)	(4/1)
Water Supply (Labourers)	,,	(2/4–2/5)	(3/3¾)
Docks (Dockers—*daily*)	Minimum rate	(18/– – 19/–)	(26/–)
Railways (Porters, passenger)	Standard	96/– – 99/6	135/–
(Guards)	rate	101/– – 113/6	144/– – 160/–
(Engine drivers)	,,	124/– – 138/–	175/– – 195/–
(Firemen)	,,	103/– – 117/–	145/– – 164/–
(Cleaners)	,,	96/–	133/– – 135/–
Trams and Buses (Labourers)	,,	98/6	131/– – 131/6
(Drivers)	,,	101/6–107/6	141/– – 145/–
(Conductors)	,,	97/6–103/6	137/– – 140/–
Road Haulage (Labourers)	Minimum	94/– – 98/–	134/– – 136/–
(Drivers)	rate	95/– – 114/–	135/– – 157/–
Shipping (Able Seamen)	Standard	112/– + food	141/2
(Ordinary Seamen)	rate	86/4 + food	109/1
Post Office	Minimum		
(Postmen at 21)	rate	90/– – 94/–	125/– – 129/–
(Telegraphists at 21)	,,	92/– – 97/–	127/– – 131/–
(Telephonists at 21)	,,	92/6–94/6	125/6–129/6
Retail Food Distribution			
(Shop assistants at 24)	,,	92/– – 98/–	121/6–127/6
(Co-op. at 23)	,,	108/– – 111/–	140/– – 144/–
Milk Distribution			
(Roundsmen at 21)	,,	92/– – 94/6	124/– – 130/–
Local Authorities Non-trading	Standard		
Services	rate		
(General)	,,	97/– – 113/–	128/6–131/6
(County roadmen)	Minimum	94/– – 97/–	132/2–135/2
Fire Service (at 19)	rate	131/–	177/–
Cinemas (Lowest paid attendants)	Standard rate	76/9–86/–	100/6
Hotels (Barmen)	Minimum	90/– – 93/–	117/– – 120/–
(Waiters)	rate	100/– – 103/–	117/– – 120/–
Laundries	,,	(2/0)	(2/8)
Hairdressing (Men's)			
(hairdressers after 1 year)	,,	95/–	126/6

CHAPTER EIGHTEEN

PROFITS

UNEARNED incomes from property reach individuals mainly in four forms—rent, interest, dividends and bonus shares. Rents are received by owners of land and buildings from the occupiers of these capital assets. Interest is the return on money lent by its possessors to borrowers—Governments, national or local, business firms, or individuals. Dividends are the sums paid out of business profits to the owners of share capital, as distinct from bonds or debentures. Finally, bonus shares represent a capitalization of profits placed to reserve, in the form of a writing-up of the nominal value of the share capital held by investors in the business. Where businesses are carried on by partnerships or individuals and not as companies no dividends are declared: the owners directly receive whatever profits are made, and can leave any part of them they please as capital in the business, or spend it, or invest it elsewhere.

'Marginal' Firms. Under what used to be regarded as normal conditions, businesses were continually disappearing because they were unable to cover their costs out of their receipts. It used to be regarded as natural and desirable that the less efficient firms should be driven out of existence by the competition of more efficient rivals. But under the conditions of full employment that have prevailed since the war, relatively few businesses have been crushed out in this way. Demand has been high enough to enable even the less efficient to carry on in most cases; and profits have been relatively easy to earn. Full employment has been of benefit not only to the employed workers but to their employers as well.

Profits, Interest and Rent. The forms of income we are concerned with in this section are mainly interest and profits—including shareholders' dividends and sums allocated to business reserves. It will, however, be convenient to include rent as well, in order to deal with all the forms of income that are derived mainly from the ownership of property. It is true that a part of what is called 'profit' is attributable to work as well as to ownership; for when a person works in his own business there is no way of telling how much of the return he gets should be attributed to his labour as distinct from his ownership. The farmer, the small non-company business, and the professional receiver of fees all work for

TABLE 128

Incomes derived from Ownership of Property alone, or from such Ownership combined with Personal Effort, 1938 and 1946–54 (£million)

	1938	1946	1947	1948	1949	1950	1951	1952	1953	1954
Rent of Land and Buildings	470	440	473	473	500	540	573	621	673	744
Gross Profits of Companies	690	1,475	1,689	1,790	1,839	2,123	2,472	2,176	2,323	2,560
Gross Profits of Public Enterprise	74	108	154	228	266	341	380	321	376	445
Incomes from Self-Employment:										
(a) Professional Incomes	118	178	199	213	228	238	235	239	247	263
(b) Farmers' Incomes	69	229	247	305	346	339	365	404	406	378
(c) Private Traders' and Partnership Incomes	460	747	794	810	826	835	876	892	939	1,004
Total	647	1,154	1,240	1,328	1,400	1,412	1,476	1,535	1,592	1,645
Grand Total	1,881	3,177	3,556	3,879	4,005	4,416	4,901	4,653	4,964	5,394

TABLE 129

Rent, Interest and Profits and Incomes from Self-employment, 1938 and 1946–54 (1938 = 100)

	1938	1946	1947	1948	1949	1950	1951	1952	1953	1954
Rent	100	94	101	101	106	115	122	132	143	158
Gross Company Profits	100	214	245	259	267	308	358	316	337	371
Gross Profits of Public Enterprise	100	146	208	305	360	461	514	434	508	602
Professional Incomes	100	151	169	181	193	202	199	202	209	223
Farmers' Incomes	100	332	358	442	502	491	530	586	589	548
Private Traders' and Partnership Incomes	100	162	173	176	180	181	190	194	204	218
Total	100	169	189	206	213	235	260	247	264	287

what they get, but regard their incomes as a reward for their labour and their ownership jointly. It is therefore impossible to say how the total national income is divided as between payments for work done and payments for the use of things owned, other than a man's own labour. We can only make the somewhat different distinction between wage-and-salary incomes on the one hand and on the other incomes derived from property, with or without an element of work combined in operation with it. Here are the broad totals of incomes of the latter kind (Table 128), followed by the same incomes, re-expressed as percentages of their amounts in 1938 (Table 129). (See previous page.)

Relative Changes in Recent Years. These are really remarkable figures. Even in 1954 the landlords' gross money return was only 58 per cent higher than in 1938, whereas company profits had risen by more than 270 per cent. Professional earnings were up by 123 per cent and private traders' profits by 118 per cent, whereas farmers' incomes had risen by 448 per cent and had been still higher in 1952 and 1953. The astronomical rise in the profits of public enterprise by 502 per cent is of course misleading, for it reflects a great enlargement in the scope of such enterprise. All the figures need deflating to allow for the changed value of money; but it is simpler to relate them to the change in the national income as a whole. This rose by about 204 per cent between 1938 and 1954 (see p. 224): so that all the groups except landlords, professionals and private traders increased their relative shares—the smallest rises being those of the professionals and the sole traders, and much the biggest that of the farmers, followed by that of company profits.

All these are gross figures, before making provision for depreciation of capital and prior to direct taxation. They do not represent the incomes retained by the recipients: nor do they in all cases represent incomes actually distributed to individuals. They include the large amounts of company profits that were not distributed in dividends, but placed to reserve. They also include interest on borrowed money, as well as profits in a narrower sense.

Distributed Profits, Interest and Rent. We may now turn to the figures of income actually distributed in the form of rent, interest and dividends, excluding reserved profits. These have been as follows:

TABLE 130

Rent, Interest and Dividends distributed to Persons, 1938 and 1946–54

(*£million*)

	1938	1946	1947	1948	1949
Total Distributed	1,128	1,286	1,364	1,240	1,281
per cent of 1938	100	114	121	110	114

	1950	1951	1952	1953	1954
Total Distributed	1,320	1,439	1,535	1,605	1,678
per cent of 1938	117	128	136	142	149

Comparison with 1938 must be made with care, as the Government has changed its method of reckoning these amounts. The White Paper of 1949 gave a figure of £1,109 million for 1938 as compared with £1,446 million for 1946. But the latest Blue Book on National Income gives the figure for 1946 as £1,286 million, and there are similar discrepancies for later years. This is presumably because the revised figures omit certain dividends and interest distributed not to persons but to institutions. It will be seen that the increase in *distributed* incomes from interest and dividends remained very small up to 1950, but has been more considerable in recent years. It still, however, remains small in relation to the changes in most other forms of income.

If, instead of the total sum distributed in rent, interest and dividends, we consider only the distributed profits of joint stock companies, a very different picture emerges. The total trading profits earned by companies, excluding those nationalized since 1948, but including profits earned by British companies operating abroad, rose from £796 million in 1938 to £2,034 million in 1948 and to £2,918 million in 1954. Out of these amounts were paid in dividends and interest £608 million in 1938, £626 million in 1948, and £888 million in 1954, and in addition £7 million in 1938 and £69 million in 1954 were added to dividend reserves. In 1948, on the other hand, such reserves were drawn upon to the extent of £21 million. These totals, however, need to be broken up in order to give a correct impression of what has happened. Here are the figures showing how the payments of dividends and interest have been divided between different kinds of property owners. (See Table 131 overleaf.)

The most significant contrast offered by these figures is between the fortunes of preference and ordinary shareholders. The preference shareholder differs from the bondholder in that he receives not guaranteed interest, but only a share in profits, if they are made. His share, however, is limited: so that he participates little if at all either in increased profits beyond the fixed limit or in the rise in share values resulting from profitable trading. Indeed, if current interest rates rise, preference shares usually fall in market value. In 1954, in view of these conditions, preference shareholders as a group were actually receiving a smaller sum than in either 1938 or 1948—85 or 88 per cent of the sums paid in these years. Ordinary shareholders, on the other hand, received in 1954 66 per cent more than in 1938 and 51 per cent more than in 1948, and the larger part of this rise occurred in 1953 and 1954. In addition, in 1950, 1952, 1953 and 1954 very large sums were put into special dividend reserves for future distribution mainly to ordinary shareholders. If these are added to the amounts distributed to ordinary shareholders, the rise from 1938 to 1954 becomes 81 per cent, and from 1948 to 1954 78 per cent.

The remaining figures are of less significance. Debenture interest is of course affected, though slowly, by changes in current interest rates

Dividend and Interest Payments by Joint S

	1938	1946	1947	1948	1949
Debenture Interest	61	48	47	35	28
Preference Share Dividends	121	128	129	117	103
Ordinary Share Dividends	360	356	386	395	391
Co-operative Dividends and Interest	29	43	44	43	44
Building Society Interest	24	21	22	25	29
Other Interest (Bank, etc.)	13	17	19	11	12
Additions to Dividends Reserves	7	30	7	−21	2

as well as by the amount of new borrowings and repayments. Building Society interest is affected more rapidly and Co-operative interest rather slowly. In general, preference shares are held by the less wealthy shareholders, and financiers and active business people are the chief holders of ordinary shares. Because of the divergent fortunes of the two, there have been shifts into ordinaries both by private persons and by trusts and institutions, such as educational bodies, which have been able to widen their investment powers. But the main tendency is for increases in ordinary dividends, reflected in stock market values, to benefit the wealthier as against the smaller property owners. The actual figures on which the percentages given in the preceding table are based show that between 1948 and 1954 the sums actually distributed to ordinary shareholders increased by more than £200 million and that nearly all this increase occurred from 1951 onwards. The same trend towards higher ordinary dividends and higher stock market values for ordinary shares continued through the first half of 1955, until it was checked in the summer by the growing difficulties of the economy, manifested chiefly in a more adverse balance of payments (see p. 196). The average value of 'equities'—i.e. ordinary shares—increased as shown in Table 132 for yearly and half-yearly periods from 1950.

Thus share values, after rising to a peak in 1951, fell back substantially in 1952 and were still below this peak, though again rising, through 1953. Only in the opening months of 1954 was the 1951 peak surpassed; but during the first half of 1955 values were 35 per cent above those of the second half of 1951, and in July 1955 no less than 48 per cent above the earlier peak. With both higher share prices and higher dividends, average yields had changed much less. From 5·85 per cent in 1950 they fell to 5·61 in 1951, rose to 7·16 on the average of 1952, and then fell to 6·92 in 1953, to 6·19 in 1954, and to 5·98 for the first half of 1955. In 1938 the average yield was 6·19 per cent, but in panies, etc., 1938 and 1946–54 (£million)

1950	1951	1952	1953	1954	1954 as percentage of 1938	1954 as percentage of 1948
31	36	41	46	50	82	234
104	104	102	102	103	85	88
403	459	445	507	597	166	151
46	45	43	45	46	159	107
32	35	40	48	54	225	216
12	14	43	51	38	292	346
44	3	45	56	69	986	—

TABLE 132

Average Prices of Equity Shares, 1950–55

(1938 = 100)

		Prices		Yield per cent
1950	First Half	131		—
	Second Half	140		5·74
	Whole Year		134	5·85
1951	First Half	150		5·61
	Second Half	156		5·71
	Whole Year		155	5·61
1952	First Half	133		7·00
	Second Half	126		7·31
	Whole Year		128	7·16
1953	First Half	133		7·03
	Second Half	146		6·79
	Whole Year		138	6·92
1954	First Half	166		6·45
	Second Half	200		5·90
	Whole Year		183	6·19
1955	First Half	212		5·98
	July	231	—	5·94

1937 only 5·10. It had risen above 8 per cent only in one ill-starred year
—1931—and in only two other years since the series started in 1925 had
it averaged more than 7 per cent. These two years were 1930 and 1952.
Yields, of course, tend to rise in bad times, when confidence falters, and
to fall when stock market prices improve.

Profit Reserves. The explanation is, of course, that since the war joint
stock companies, instead of paying out high dividends corresponding to
their big profits, have placed a larger part of these profits to reserve.

Such reserves are the property of the shareholders no less than the dividends they receive; but they appear not as personal incomes but as additions to the capital market value of the shares. Any shareholder who wishes to turn this appreciation in the value of his property into current income has only to sell some of his shares in order to receive payment in cash, which he can then either spend on current consumption or re-invest elsewhere. It is doubtless the case that, as many shareholders value direct present income more highly than potential future income, the market value of shares may rise less than the amount of profit placed to reserve would logically justify; but there is no way of measuring to what extent this actually occurs.

The amounts of profit made by companies, but not distributed, including sums to cover depreciation, have been as follows:

TABLE 133

Gross Undistributed Profits of Companies, including Depreciation
1938 and 1946–54

	1938	1946	1947	1948	1949
Amount	378	1,110	1,409	1,659	1,647
Per cent of 1938	100	294	373	439	436

	1950	1951	1952	1953	1954
Amount	2,061	2,260	1,804	2,037	2,221
Per cent of 1938	545	598	477	539	588

The contrast with the preceding table is immediately evident. There are two reasons for the greatly increased appropriation of profits to reserves. One is that renewals and extensions of capital goods have to be made at current prices, which are now much higher than before the war, so that more has to be allocated to cover depreciation. The second reason is that much the easiest way of providing new real capital for companies is to do so directly out of reserves, instead of distributing the money in dividends and then borrowing it back. The Government has strongly urged dividend limitation on this and other grounds, as correlative to 'wage-restraint'. But the essential difference is that the worker who forgoes an increase in wages has no claim on the future, whereas the shareholder who accepts a low dividend receives in place of it an addition to the real value of his capital.

If we now put together the figures in the two tables as far as they relate to company profits and to interest payments we see that, whereas gross company profits rose by 271 per cent between 1938 and 1954, distributed profits, including interest, rose by only 46 per cent. It was largely through this difference that the rate of investment was kept high enough to meet the more urgent needs of industry for new capital. As we saw earlier, corporate saving has replaced private saving as the main source of new investment. This, however, still leaves the ownership of the new capital in the hands of the investing classes.

The Rise in Profits. According to a different calculation made by the London and Cambridge Economic Service the total amount of company profits rose by 201 per cent between 1938 and 1953, and the average rate of dividend from 9·8 per cent to 17·2 per cent in 1954. The dividend rate had been rising substantially, though not continuously, from 1946, when it stood at 12·4 per cent. Here are the figures for the subsequent years:

TABLE 134

Average Dividend Rates, 1938 and 1946–54

1938	1946	1947	1948	1949	1950	1951	1952	1953	1954
9·8	12·4	15·5	14·6	14·5	14·9	17·8	16·5	15·8	17·2

In 1954 they were almost back at the level of the boom year, 1951.

The Sources of New Investment. In the past it was an assumption of orthodox economists that the main source of new investment would be found in the incomes of well-to-do persons, though substantial amounts would accrue through the savings of poorer provident persons who were laying aside resources for old age or in life insurance policies. Already well before 1939 this assumption had become unreal. There had been a large increase in savings of the latter type; but a larger and larger proportion of 'savings' was being provided through the accumulation of company reserves. There was also a growth of compulsory saving by the workers through state insurance for contributory pensions. The rich, as individuals, were no longer an important element in capital accumulation: they saved not as individuals but mainly as shareholders in joint stock concerns. This tendency has been accentuated since the war; and there has also been a very rapid growth not only in compulsory insurances but also in pension schemes financed by joint stock companies on their employees' behalf—especially for the more highly paid salaried employees. For a further analysis of the post-war sources of capital accumulation see pages 99 ff.

CHAPTER NINETEEN

MONOPOLIES AND RESTRICTIVE PRACTICES

IT is an undoubted fact that there has been in recent years a very rapid spread of monopolistic and restrictive trade practices in Great Britain, both in industry and in commerce and indeed in agriculture as well. This decrease in the extent and degree of competition characteristic of capitalist economies is due mainly to two causes—the development of techniques which put a high premium on large-scale production and specialization and the great extension of state control over the economy in both world wars. The technological factors have in many instances restricted the possibility of low-cost production to very large firms, so that only a few potentially competing firms are able to exist. This condition of 'oligopoly'—few sellers confronting many buyers in the market—necessarily makes monopolistic practices easier to put into effect, because it is easier for a few than for many rival businesses to come to terms. The other factor—the extension of state control in wartime—has operated largely by bringing rival firms together to deal with the Government on collective lines; and groups thus formed have shown a marked tendency to hold together and to continue their efforts to 'regulate' their trades even when the government 'controls' have been removed. A third factor favouring capitalist combination is to be found in the severity of economic depressions between the wars. It is true that combinations formed in relatively prosperous times tend in many cases to break down during periods of depression: nevertheless the conditions of depression engender keen desires to combine for mutual protection, and signs of reviving business activity usually give the signal for renewed attempts to establish regulative combinations on an ever-increasing scale.

What is 'Monopoly'? The word 'monopoly' is commonly given a wide meaning in current economic discussions, to cover not only cases in which a single seller or combine of sellers completely controls or dominates the market but also those in which such a seller or combine is powerful enough to exert a considerable influence on the conditions of supply. It is sometimes distinguished from 'oligopoly', in which a few sellers share the market between them, with or without any formal understanding or agreement about the terms of sale. Let us leave 'oligopoly', in this sense, aside for the moment, and consider 'monopoly', in the wide meaning mentioned above.

'Monopoly' has two main forms. One arises where a single firm or a closely integrated group of firms holds a dominant position in the supply of a particular commodity or type of goods and is able to exert a significant influence on market conditions. The other arises where a number of firms which share the total market combine to form a cartel and seek, without complete fusion of interests or pooling of profits, to regulate trade in the goods concerned either by agreeing on common price policies or by concerted limitations on output or by controlling the conditions of sale or by discriminating between sales agencies—or indeed by any method they regard as likely to further their common interests.

The first of these kinds of monopoly has at any rate the advantage that it affords the maximum of scope for large-scale production and specialization and facilitates the pooling of technical 'know-how' and patent rights, thus contributing to the possibility both of low-cost output and of standardization. Monopolies of this type are in a position to cut out a large number of useless varieties of product and, where servicing is needed, to provide better facilities than are usually within the reach of competing producers, except the very largest. They can reach a very high level of both technical and business efficiency, provided they are successful in overcoming the dangers of bureaucracy and over-centralization and in devising flexible structures of management and maintaining effective contact between management and the elaborate research organizations they are in a position to set on foot.

Single Firms and Combines. The nucleus of a monopoly of this type usually consists either of a single firm which has expanded far beyond its original limits or of a combination in which a number of previously competing firms have been integrated into a single business under unified central control. Such businesses, whatever their origins, often embrace a considerable number of legally distinct joint stock companies, with separate but interlocking directorates subject in matters of high policy to a single central directorate, which may be that either of a holding company conducting few or no operations of its own or that of the chief among the operating companies constituting the 'concern'. The essence of this type of business is that it works under the guidance of a central plan and that, however much day-to-day autonomy it may allow to the directorates and managements of its constituent units, the control of high policy is in the final resort unified under a common direction. Outstanding examples of such 'concerns' in Great Britain are Imperial Chemical Industries and Unilever, each of which has under its aegis, not only many different establishments with their separate managements but also a considerable number of separately registered companies, some of them with many establishments under their control —for example, Nobel Industries and I.C.I. Metals in the case of Imperial Chemicals, and Lever Brothers and Vandenberghs in the case of Unilever. Some of these separate companies are concerned with particular kinds of production; whereas others may have been set up to handle the affairs of the concern in particular export markets or to handle branches of distribution.

I.C.I. and Unilever. Both I.C.I. and Unilever are outstanding giants in their own branches of production, with no competitors in their home markets at all nearly approaching them in size. There are other chemical manufacturers and other makers of soap and margarine; but they are small in comparison with the two giants, which effectively dominate the market. But both I.C.I. and Unilever produce, in addition to the kinds of goods in which their primacy is undisputed, other kinds in which they do not hold a similarly exclusive pre-eminence. They are makers of a wide range of products; and in some fields they are in direct competition with other huge concerns—for example, I.C.I. with Courtaulds and other makers of synthetic textile fibres, as well as with the older types of textile manufacture, and Unilever with Co-operative soap-making and with other producers of margarine. The great integrated business 'concern' is seldom limited to the making of a single group of products. Usually, it has thrown up many subsidiary activities in the course of extending its control, either in acquiring ownership of industries which provide it with essential materials or in seeking to find means of utilizing the by-products or waste products of its main manufacturing activities. It thus becomes a monopolist or near-monopolist in some of its fields of action, but not in all, and finds itself entering into relations and perhaps business agreements with firms and trade associations in many different branches of production, and probably in a number of countries. This is especially the case where it depends on patent rights and other exclusive processes, about which it has to negotiate continually with its rivals in other countries as well as at home. It is not simply a monopolist: even more essentially it is a giant, stretching out its hands into many kinds of enterprise and of necessity in constant close relations with its own Government and with the Governments of other countries in which it operates or markets its wares.

The Organization of Giant Concerns. The problems of organizing such giant enterprises are formidable. Fully as much as nationalized businesses they are confronted with the difficulty of reconciling central planning and financial control with the need to encourage decentralized responsibility and initiative. At the centre they need to make some sort of choice between 'functional' and 'general' directive and administrative structure, to decide how to relate the technological to the administrative and financial aspects, and to take steps to ensure that their central staffs keep closely in touch with the managements of their main establishments. Usually they seek to provide for a constant interchange of key personnel between the centre and the branches, both at home and abroad; and they are also much concerned with building up the right relations between research and executive staffs. The most important tasks confronting the central directors are apt to be largely financial or to be concerned with relations with Governments or with other industries. On the financial side investment is the most important problem of all. It is the centre that must finally control investment policy, deciding between rival demands for capital expenditure on the renovation or extension of plants, the starting of new ventures, the carrying of the results of research to the stage of productive development, the acquisition of related firms or of an 'interest' in them, and the scrapping or sale of branches which are failing to show satisfactory results—not to mention decisions about the proportion of profits to be distributed as dividends or held back in reserves, or about the starting or extension of pension and superannuation schemes for employees. These decisions often take the form of preparing prospective 'budgets' for the various branches of the concern and of keeping these 'budgets' under constant review—the so-called method of 'budgetary control'.

Monopolies, or giant concerns, of this type, being legal persons by virtue of their status as companies, can act as persons without necessarily having to combine with any other person or organization; and so can their subsidiaries, when they are organized as companies too. Thus, in fields where such concerns exist, a large amount of regulative or restrictive action can be taken without the need for any form of agreement among different businesses. The Monopolies Commission, in its most recent report on restrictive practices, recognizes that many of these are operated not by combines consisting of a number of firms, but by single concerns which impose them on dealers in their products unilaterally and by direct corporate decision. The question thus arises whether projected legislation for the prevention or regulation of such practices should apply only where they are imposed by cartels or trade associations including a number of firms, or should extend also to similar practices operated by single firms important enough to be in a position to exert monopolistic pressure on their own.

Cartels and Trade Associations. Let us turn now from the single giants, such as I.C.I., to the other main form of monopolistic structure—the trade association or cartel. The giant concern, as we have seen, is seldom a monopolist in the strict sense of controlling directly the entire output even of its main products—though it has usually a monopoly, based on patent rights and exclusive processes, of a number of branded varieties. The trade association or cartel, on the other hand, usually, though not always, aims at including all the producers of, or traders in, a particular group or groups of goods and, in proportion to its success in this respect, approaches being a monopolist in the strict sense. The giant concern is usually to a considerable extent *vertical* in structure, combining a series of successive processes and products under its control. The cartel or trade association is more often *horizontal* in essence, bringing together all producers of, or dealers in, a particular kind of product at a particular stage of production or marketing. Its essential aims are to work out and enforce a common code of practice for the trade as a whole, sometimes with a view to the enforcement of standards of quality, but more often in order to regulate selling prices or conditions of sale, to fix or allocate output, and sometimes to take the business of selling out of the hands of the constituent firms and transfer it wholly or partly to a common marketing organization. The members of the cartel or association bind themselves to observe the rules which it lays down and usually agree to accept certain penalties for failing to do this. Because of the difficulty of enforcing such agreements in courts of law, which are usually reluctant to sanction collective practices that are in 'restraint of trade', resort is often had to extra-legal methods of enforcement. For example, the associated firms may be required to deposit considerable sums of money in the hands of an agent of the association, who is authorized to draw upon them in cases of breach of the agreements. Extra-legal methods are also used to punish non-members who do not abide by the association's rules—for example, dealers in their products who re-sell at prices or under conditions unacceptable to the association, or break 'exclusive dealing' arrangements by selling the products of firms outside its ranks. The penalties in such cases may be either the boycotting of the offending dealer by withholding further supplies or the forfeit of rebates to which he is entitled as long as he observes the association's rules.

Extra-legal Coercion.   There has grown up under the auspices of the trade associations a large body of extra-legal coercion by what are in effect private courts conducted by the trade associations concerned. These 'courts' operate chiefly against dealers—largely retailers who have failed to keep the rules laid down by the associations, especially those laying down fixed or minimum re-sale prices to the public. The dealer who finds himself deprived of further supplies from the firms forming the association may be utterly unable to remain in business unless he can get the boycott removed—which usually involves at the least complete submission to the association's orders, and sometimes severe penalties as well. All this takes place without any reference to the regular courts of law: the association administers its own private 'law' and is able to enforce obedience by means of its economic power.

Re-sale Price Maintenance.   Such practices raise two questions—first, that of the legitimacy of 're-sale price maintenance' and of other rules laid down by the associations, and secondly that of the legitimacy of the extra-legal structures set up by them for purposes of enforcement. On the first point, the associations have put forward a number of arguments. Unlimited freedom for the dealer to charge what prices he pleases leads, they say, to price-cutting which upsets trade conditions and is unfair to dealers who abide by the rules. It is reasonable, they say, in the case of many standardized and branded products, for the manufacturer to fix the retail selling price and the margin to be allowed to the dealer, which should be set at a level just adequate to cover distributive costs *plus* a sufficient profit. But, of course, distributive costs actually vary a great deal between one dealer and another and are often difficult to isolate where the dealer is trading in a variety of products. Why should not the low-cost dealer be allowed, if he thinks fit, to undercut his competitors by passing on some of his advantage to the public in lower re-sale prices? This raises two issues—one where the dealer can actually make a profit on the transaction at the reduced price, and the other where he thinks it worth while to re-sell a particular product at a loss in the hope of attracting customers to buy other goods at his shop. Goods sold at a loss for this purpose are commonly known as 'loss leaders'; and the practice has undoubtedly been growing as a form of competitive advertising.

Manufacturers, and also some dealers, take objection to these practices, for a number of reasons. Dealers who are prepared to accept the associations' rules naturally object to being undercut, not only by their competitors in the same specialized line of business but even more by department or multiple firms which are better placed for making use of particular products as 'loss leaders'. They even demand sometimes that only specialized firms shall be allowed to handle the goods in question and claim that it is illegitimate or unfair trading for department or 'general' stores to enter their special field. Short of such legalized trade monopoly, they claim that uniform retail prices provide the only real security against unfair competition. Manufacturers, for their part, fear the effects of undercutting on the prices they will be able to charge the dealers for their wares, and, when they engage in national advertising of branded products, wish to be in a position to advertise standard retail prices at which their goods can be bought by the public at any retail outlet.

Discriminative Dealing. The fixing of retail prices by the manufacturer or group of manufacturers leaves open the prices at which they themselves supply the dealers. Such prices are seldom the same for all dealers: they usually involve quantity rebates on large orders and sometimes special rebates for 'exclusive dealing'—that is, where the retailer agrees to deal only in the products of a particular manufacturer or group. Such rebates make it possible for the successful retailer with a large market for a particular product to reduce his costs and to re-sell, if he wishes and is allowed to, at a lower price. But this the manufacturers who have adopted 're-sale price maintenance' will not let him do. The public is thus charged more than would yield some retailers an adequate return; and this is said to be justified because a lower price would make it impossible for the higher-cost retailers to remain in business. A further factor is that costs of transport from the manufacturer's depot to the retail store necessarily differ greatly from case to case: so that a retail price that is adequate in some places is excessive in others; but the manufacturer may prefer a standard retail price which is uniform everywhere and leaves this factor out of account.

The Net Book Agreement. Among re-sale price maintenance agreements of longest standing is the Net Book Agreement operated by the Publishers' and Booksellers' Associations. Under this convention, the bookseller retails books at net prices fixed by the publisher and receives a standard discount, usually with special terms for quantities either of single books or sometimes of a number of titles. There are special terms for certain classes of books—notably for school textbooks, which are commonly bought in quantity. There are also different rates of discount for regular booksellers, who keep shops, and for book agents, who supply their customers by post, and for libraries. This arrangement was started in order to check price-cutting by booksellers, particularly by general and department stores which used certain books as 'loss leaders'. Such practices were said to prevent the 'legitimate' bookseller from carrying adequate stocks; and a further reason advanced for the system was that authors' royalties are usually reckoned as a percentage of the retail price. One effect of the agreement has been to encourage the growth of book clubs, which supply their members at special prices, with royalties reckoned at a lower rate in consideration of the increased sales.

Other Instances of Price Maintenance. Another well-known instance of 're-sale price maintenance' is that of the best-known brands of chocolate, and yet another that of the standard brands of tobacco and cigarettes. New motor-cars too are sold at retail prices fixed by the manufacturers; and so are a wide range of branded products. In such cases the prices are most often fixed by each manufacturer for his own products, with or without consultation with other manufacturers; whereas the conditions of discount and rebate are more often laid down collectively by associations either of manufacturers or, in some instances, of wholesale dealers. In some cases, conditions of sale as well as retail prices are prescribed by the individual manufacturer and differ from one firm to another; but there is a marked tendency towards standardized conditions of re-sale, even where the retail price itself is fixed by each producer on his own account.

Retail trade in branded products is honeycombed with restrictive agreements of these types; and there is not in practice a great deal of difference between those operated by single big firms and those which are enforced under the rules of trade associations, though both lawyers and critics of monopoly are apt to regard them differently. It is in no way unlawful for an individual or for a joint stock company to act 'in restraint of trade'; whereas an association so acting may fall foul of the law in either of two ways. In the extreme case it may be regarded as a 'criminal conspiracy' and may expose those who practise it to the danger of prosecution. In practice, however, this seldom happens; for the 'restraint' becomes criminal only when the courts hold it to be unreasonable and anti-social, and this they have become very reluctant to do. What is more likely to happen is that the courts will regard a particular practice, not as criminal, but as so tainted by its 'restraint' of trade as to render any agreement to enforce it unworthy of being sustained at law. Accordingly, trade associations and similar groups commonly take pains to draw up their agreements in such forms as will not require any appeal to law for their enforcement, and use, as we saw, extra-legal means of enforcement by economic power.

Proposals of the Monopolies Commission. The question that then arises is whether the law should be so altered as to make these practices, or some of them, definitely illegal, and to void any agreements made in pursuance of them. The recent report of the Monopolies Commission on Collective Discrimination expresses the conclusion of a majority of its members that a number of practices should be definitely outlawed, with the proviso that it should be open to any group desirous of maintaining them to appeal to a publicly constituted tribunal for an exception to be made in their case. As against this, the minority argues against any general prohibition, but proposes a system of compulsory registration of restrictive agreements and of disallowance of such as are found, after special enquiry, to operate to the disadvantage of the public. In view of the number and complexity of the agreements involved, it would inevitably take a very long time to enquire fully into all of them; and it seems probable that the effect of the minority's proposal would be to leave the great majority of them in effective existence for a long time to come, even if some were to be ultimately disallowed. The Government, however, when the question was debated in Parliament in July 1955, refused to commit itself to act on the recommendation of the majority, promising only to introduce legislation for compulsory registration of a limited range of practices and to set up some sort of tribunal before which those wishing to use such practices would have to prove their case.

Conflicting Views on Price Maintenance. There is undoubtedly in business circles strong opposition to any general ban on such practices as 're-sale price maintenance', even if exceptions are to be allowed. Those who make use of restrictive practices would naturally prefer, if they cannot be left entirely alone, to remain free to continue them subject only to the possibility of disallowance of a particular practice in a specific instance and after specific enquiry. They would wish the burden of proof that a practice is anti-social to rest on their critics rather than to be called on to show that their practices are in conformity with the public interest. Against this view are ranged on the one hand the advocates of unrestricted competition, including many Liberals, and on the other both the Labour Party and the Co-operative movement, which suffers seriously from their imposition by capitalist suppliers. The Co-operative movement is itself a considerable producer, without holding any position of monopoly. It needs to buy extensively from producers of branded goods in order to meet its members' demands. But its long-established practice of using its surplus to pay its customers 'dividends' on their purchases runs counter to the regulations imposed by many trade associations, especially by those carrying on systems of 're-sale price maintenance'. On many goods in which they deal the retail Co-operative Societies are absolutely prevented from paying 'dividends'; and in not a few cases they are unable to obtain any supplies at all from the manufacturers concerned. The Co-operative movement is accordingly one of the principal bodies calling urgently for legislation to outlaw restrictive practices in the consumers' interests.

'Rings'. The forms of restriction so far discussed in this section do not stand alone. Another familiar method is found chiefly in the building and allied industries, in which it is not uncommon for all the firms invited to tender for a particular contract either to submit practically identical offers or in some cases to arrange among themselves which firm is to send in the lowest estimate and to be allowed to get the contract. This type of collusive tendency is commonly called a 'ring'. It seems to be used particularly against municipalities and other public bodies in relation to housing schemes or public works involving the use of structural steel. The leading municipalities have recently been driven by their experience of this device to demand legislation for its prevention; but here again the Government seems to be unwilling to act. The chief excuse offered for such evidently anti-social behaviour is that the preparing of contract specifications involves a great deal of work and that it is wasteful for a number of firms to be put to this expense. It is also argued that building firms, if they are allowed to share out the available work, can operate under stable conditions and can thus afford to offer continuous employment to their labour force—which is an advantage because regular employment is likely to produce better

quality production than can be got with a continually shifting body of workers. There is some force in both these contentions; but it is manifestly dangerous to allow the building industry in effect to settle its own prices and to render the competition between firms merely nominal. If the work is to be shared out, instead of being left to the operation of competitive tenders, the body making the decisions and fixing the contract prices should be some impartial authority, and not a 'ring' of firms with a common interest in high prices.

Monopolistic Competition. As we saw, the word 'monopoly' is commonly used in a wide sense, to include not only cases in which a single firm or a closely integrated firm holds exclusive control over the supply of a particular product or commodity or kind of service but also those in which a group of associated firms or a single firm controls a large enough part of the total supply to exert a marked influence on the conditions of sale. Cases of absolute monopoly are somewhat rare, unless the terms 'product', 'commodity', etc., are very narrowly defined. There is a sense in which every supplier who is the sole source of a particular branded or patented product can be described as a 'monopolist', even if he is in keen competition with rivals supplying rather different products that are fully adequate substitutes for his own—for example, motor-cars closely similar in type and price—but such situations are better described as instances of what has been called 'monopolistic competition' than of 'monopoly' properly so called. There is a group of marginal cases in which a single supplier, by virtue of some patent or secret process, holds a monopolistic advantage over potential competitors, so that they can in fact compete only by offering a less satisfactory product at a lower price; but usually, in cases of 'monopolistic competition', each of the main competitors holds some advantage over his rivals in some particular respect, and some buyers prefer one of the rival products and some another. In such instances real competition exists, and is usually carried on with the aid of expensive advertising of the merits of the rival products. This advertising becomes of course an element in the cost of production and increases the costs of the rival producers unless its effect is sufficient to increase total sales so as to enable producers to lower manufacturing costs to an equivalent extent.

The Arguments for and against Monopoly. The case usually advanced in favour of monopoly is that, by making possible production and specialization on the largest scale and thus enabling costs to be cut to the lowest practicable level, it can benefit consumers more than competition, which may make it impossible for the full economies of scale to be realized. It is also argued that complete pooling of patents and of all kinds of productive 'know-how' makes it possible to offer consumers a superior article to what can be produced where each firm guards its exclusive hold over particular kinds of 'know-how'. Even, however, where a monopoly possesses these advantages it does not follow that the benefit will be passed on to the consuming public. Even if a superior article is produced, too high a price may be charged for it; for it may suit the monopolist best to keep the price up even at some cost in restricting total sales. How far this will be the case will depend mainly on the degree of elasticity in the demand for the product in question— that is, on the effect on sales of a change in the selling price. There are always some kinds of goods for which demand is highly elastic and others for which it is little affected by relatively small price-changes— and indeed some where even large changes have little effect on the quantity that can be sold. Generally speaking, demand is least elastic for necessaries and most elastic for the less costly kinds of luxury or semi-luxury goods. There is, however, no clear distinction between necessaries and luxuries; for a 'luxury' may be, and often is, only a higher quality of a product of which some supply is a necessity, or even a larger quantity without variation of quality. There are, however, at any time some products which a great many persons would like to buy but cannot afford at all unless their price can be brought down below the existing level. Motor-cars are an obvious example. The private motor-car was for a long time a luxury available only to a very limited class of buyers. Henry Ford, by revolutionizing the conditions of pro- duction, put on the market a cheap car which attracted a great new buying public, not merely at once but so that there set in a continuous and rapid expansion in the demand and that every reduction in price brought in fresh groups of buyers. This occurred not only because the number of buyers of new cars rose, but also because the cheaper cars were oftener exchanged for new ones and in some cases buyers acquired a second or a third vehicle. There was also under these conditions a rapid growth of the market for second-hand cars, and many people who could not have afforded new ones became possessors of such vehicles, which at the same time competed with new cars and increased the demand for them by enlarging the total size of the motoring public.

Accessories and Servicing.   Of course, in this case, the size of the market depends not only on the prices charged for new cars and for necessary accessories such as tyres and spare parts but also on the cost of running a car—that is, especially, on the price charged for petrol and oil and on the quantities of these things consumed. The cheap car, if it is to attract the marginal buyers, needs to have low running costs and cheap repair and servicing facilities; and thus the demand depends not on the car manufacturer alone but also on the tyre-makers and on the sup- pliers of petrol and oil—who in fact follow a closely controlled common price policy—and on the policies of Governments in taxing, not only the cars themselves, but also anything else the motorist needs. Nevertheless, the cheap car, built for low petrol and oil consumption, is in itself an outstanding example of high elasticity of demand: so that even if its production were monopolized by a single firm or group of firms it would probably pay these firms better to keep prices down in order to increase sales than to attempt to extract monopoly profits by keeping prices higher than they need in order to cover their costs.

Monopoly under Conditions of Elastic Demand. This kind of high elasticity is found most in the case of relatively new products based on advancing technical knowledge. Rather similar conditions apply to a wide range of goods embodying techniques based on the use of electrical power—for example, refrigerators, radio and television sets, electrical heating appliances, and many other useful gadgets which, beginning as luxuries for the few, pass rapidly into wider and wider use. In these cases the most important factor is the attraction of additional buyers, rather than the increase in the quantities bought by those already accustomed to using the goods in question—though this of course counts for something too. In most such cases there are in the market alternative goods differing widely in quality and price—expensive motor-cars as against the cheaper mass-produced types, and so on; and the market may be highly elastic for the cheaper varieties, but much less so for the more expensive, so that it may pay the monopolist—if he exists—best to keep prices low for the one but not for the other. An elastic demand for the cheapest type of product usually means, however, a fairly elastic demand at any rate for the types not too much more highly priced, as many buyers who begin with the cheapest are eager to replace it with something rather better as soon as they can.

Oligopoly. In this case of 'popular' motor-cars there is no absolute monopoly. There is, indeed, keen competition between a limited number of suppliers, each producing their own 'models' in an endeavour to capture a larger share of the market. The scale of production required for effective competition at this level is, however, so great there can be room for only a few rivals; and in practice many of the smaller firms have been driven out of the cheap car market. Indeed, the existence of protective tariffs makes it practically impossible for the smaller countries to possess factories for the production of cheap motor-cars, except in some cases assembly plants owned by firms operating in the greater countries. A very big home market is indispensable, if only because of the very high capital costs of putting a new model on the market; and even the countries where demand is highest cannot economically have more than a few great firms engaged in this brand of production.

Such a situation is known by economists as 'oligopoly'—that is to say, one in which the sellers, being few, and each requiring a large market, can each influence the fortunes of the others to a considerable extent. A successful innovation or a sharp reduction in price by one supplier can react greatly on the sales of the others; and each is there-fore bound to watch very closely what the others are doing or pro-posing to do. This may lead them, despite their rivalry as sellers, to come together in some attempt to impose common rules on the market —for example, by agreeing to prescribe common conditions of sale, rules to be observed by dealers, and perhaps agreed terms of discount, either open to all dealers or such as to discriminate between dealer and dealer according to the quantities sold or where a dealer becomes an exclusive agent for the products of a particular firm. Producing firms may further fix, either alone or in agreement with their rivals, the prices at which dealers are to re-sell their goods to the public; and may penalize dealers who break these rules by withholding supplies or by supplying them only at a higher price. In the case of motor-cars, where the trade in second-hand vehicles is competitive with that of new, the manu-facturers of new cars may further attempt to regulate the prices payable for old cars or to adopt measures to increase the rate of scrapping. On the whole, however, where the total demand is highly elastic, it will usually suit manufacturers better to rely on increasing sales by keeping prices low than to charge high prices at the cost of reducing the quan-tities they can sell.

Monopoly under Conditions of Inelastic Demand. The situation is quite different where demand is inelastic. The classic case of inelasticity is that of bread in the wealthier countries, where changes in prices have usually not much effect on the quantity sold and may even at times have the paradoxical effect that the higher the price the greater the sale. This can happen only where the commodity in question is the cheapest means of satisfying an imperative need. If bread is cheap some consumers will be induced to spend more of their limited incomes on preferable but more expensive substitutes; whereas, if it is dear, they may be driven to give up some of these substitutes in favour of more bread, as still the cheapest means of satisfying hunger. This, of course, will not apply where bread is itself a more expensive substitute for some other kind of food, such as rice or potatoes. In the vast majority of cases, the cheaper a thing is, the more of it can be sold; but how much more will differ very greatly from one thing to another. Economists speak of elasticity of demand as being 'equal to unity' where a change in price leaves con-sumers spending the same sum of money on it as before; less than unity where a rise in price causes them to reduce their total spending on it, and greater than unity where a fall in price causes more money to be spent on the goods in question by the whole body of consumers.

Substitution. Instances of inelastic demand arise most where there is little possibility of substituting directly one kind of purchase for an-other. If I have to get to and from work and there is only one available form of transport, I must use much the same quantity whatever the price may be. If, on the other hand, I have the choice between bus and train, relative costs as well as convenience or comfort may influence my decision, and a demand for travel facilities which is inelastic in total may be elastic for each of the alternative suppliers. Substitution of one kind of purchase for another is an important element in the market economy under which we live and extends over a very wide field; for it is possible to substitute not only like for like but also unlike for unlike —for example, by deciding to keep a motor-car instead of living in a roomier house, or not to have another child in order to have more to spend on other things, or on children already born. There is indeed no limit to the range of substitution, except where some particular good or service must be got at any price within the buyers' ability to pay.

Obstacles to Monopoly. Where demand is relatively inelastic, the monopolist is under the strongest inducement to keep prices high in order to secure as large as possible a surplus over cost for each thing that he sells. But, fortunately for consumers, most things of this character are difficult to monopolize in anything like an absolute sense. Most real necessaries are produced by large numbers of business units, which find it difficult to combine unless their Governments help them to do so and are prepared to protect their combines against competition from abroad. This applies especially to the primary producers of foodstuffs, who in many countries are aided in respect of home markets by their Governments, not only by means of restrictions on imports but also through marketing schemes or even guaranteed prices. Such protection, however, cannot much help exporters who have to sell their goods in a competitive world market; at any rate unless a number of Governments and trade combines act together in order to influence world prices. Peasant producers and small farmers are apt to find combination particularly difficult, though certain outstanding cases of success are to be found in advanced agricultural countries—for example, the Co-operative Wheat Pools in Canada and the United States and the wide range of Co-operative selling agencies in Denmark.

The Conditions of Elastic Demand. Of course, elasticity is not something fixed, applying for good and all to some commodities and not to others. For each commodity the degree of elasticity of demand varies from time to time and may at any time be both low for small and much greater for big changes in price. A small change in the price of refrigerators or television sets may make little difference to the demand, whereas a big change may bring in or drive away a large amount of custom. Moreover, demand is of course affected not only by the prices charged but also by changes in the consumers' incomes. A fall in price may be accompanied by reduced demand if it occurs during a depression, or a rise by an increase if it coincides with a boom.

Does Monopoly 'Steady' the Market? The purpose of monopoly is by no means always mainly to increase prices, or even to prevent them from falling together with costs of production. Many monopolists claim that their main purpose is to steady the market by limiting the extent of price fluctuations, changing less than they could during a boom and more in a slump. Such claims, however, need to be closely scrutinized; for unless the demand is very elastic there will be a strong temptation to keep the average price at a level that yields an excessive profit. It may be true, even so, that in a few cases the monopoly price is lower than a competitive price could be, if it rendered inoperative the economies dependent on really large-scale production; but even a price conforming to this condition may be yielding the monopolist an exorbitant profit where these economies are great.

Difficulties of Controlling Monopoly. The existing methods of dealing with monopolistic and restrictive practices are beyond doubt very unsatisfactory. It takes a long time to conduct a thorough investigation into the practices of any particular trade; and the facts elicited by such a body as the Monopolies Commission are necessarily to a great extent out of date before its reports appear. Moreover, the practices are so widespread that not more than a few of them can possibly be studied in this way, the great majority being left uninvestigated and undisturbed. That is why the Commission in its most recent report recommended by a majority a general outlawing of certain prevalent practices, subject to the right of any trade association or similar body to put forward a plea of justification in its particular case. This would put the burden of proof on those using the practice, rather than on their critics; and it appears to be the only method likely to yield substantial results. Mere compulsory registration, without general disallowance of the practice in question, seems likely to be quite ineffective in checking abuses; for it would still leave on the Monopolies Commission or on any successor the onus of proving the anti-social effects of each particular instance of restriction. Surely there should be at least a general presumption that such practices as 're-sale price maintenance' and discrimination between dealers are usually contrary to the public interest, even if they may be justified in certain highly exceptional cases.

Collective and Individual Restrictions. The Lloyd Jacob Committee on Re-sale Price Maintenance, which reported in 1949, made a study of the following trades, all of which were administering collective schemes of this kind:

'Toilet and medicinal preparations, hairdressing and hairdressers' articles, grocers, cigarettes and tobacco, chocolate and sugar confectionery, stationery, books, hardware, bicycles and motor cycles, motor vehicles and accessories, electrical goods, electric lamps, radio valves, refrigerators and refrigeration equipment, and dental goods.'

This Committee in its recommendations drew a sharp line between schemes administered by a single manufacturer in respect of his own branded goods and collective schemes. It proposed that there should be no interference with schemes of the former kind, but that the Government, after 'consultations with the principal national organizations in trade and industry', should devise means of preventing trade associations from taking action 'to obstruct the development of particular methods of trading, to impede the distribution by another manufacturer of competitive goods, or to deprive the public of the benefit of improvements in distribution'. The Committee further proposed that steps should be taken 'to render illegal the application of sanctions which extend beyond the remedies open to an individual producer for any breach of resale price maintenance conditions'. Mr. Henry Smith, in his note of reservation, expressed his hostility to schemes operated by a single manufacturer as well as to collective schemes. He also expressed his opposition to the use of 'loss leader' methods, but recognized the difficulty of framing legislation to prevent it.

The Report on Collective Discrimination. As we saw, the Monopolies Commission, in its Report on Collective Discrimination, was working on both a narrower and a wider reference. It covered other practices besides re-sale price maintenance, but it was concerned only with collective practices, as distinct from those operated by single firms. Its general conclusion was that 'the general effect of each of these practices is against the public interest though . . . there may be special circumstances . . . where the use of some of them at any rate may be justified in the public interest'. The types of case in which these special circumstances might exist were described as including some in which 'final consumers are not able to judge the standard of service which it is in their interest to demand from distributors'—i.e. where considerations of safety are important. Other possible exceptions were to be found where an industry is of 'strategic importance' or 'peculiarly liable to competition from dumped imports'; where a system of common prices is found to be in the public interest; or where the arrangement is a necessary means of enabling smaller concerns in a trade to compete effectively with a very large concern in that trade which is itself resorting to restrictive practices. The Commission held, however, that in most such cases the required end would be better served by other means, such as safety legislation or tariff protection. It then proceeded to recommend general legislation prohibiting all the collective practices considered in its report, with provisions for the granting of exceptions and for the review of such exceptions, or of refusals to grant them, in the light of changed conditions. In an appendix there appeared a long list of goods which were found to be subject to one or other of the forms of collective restriction studied in the report; and it seems worth while to set out this list in full in order to indicate the very wide range of restrictive practices in the market for consumers' supplies.

TABLE 135

The Scope of Restrictive Practices

(Re-printed from Appendix 2 of the Report on Collective Discrimination issued by the Monopolies and Restrictive Practices Commission, June 1955)

In the course of our inquiry we have considered statements about arrangements affecting the supply or processing of the following goods which appeared to us to have some relevance to our report. We have not in all cases attempted to determine whether or not these arrangements were completely within our reference. Some of the arrangements affect only certain sections of the trade in these products and others are operated only in certain parts of the United Kingdom.

Agricultural Machinery.

Baths.
Bicycles and motor-cycles.
Biscuits.
Books.
Bricks.
Bright steel bars.

Carpets and rugs.
Casein plastic.
Cement.
Certain chemicals.
Chain link fencing.
Chocolate and cocoa.
Cinematograph films.
Confectionery.
Copper cylinders and boilers.
Cotton velvet.
Curtain rails.

Dampcourses.

Electrical goods (some).
Electric lamps.
Engineers' small tools.

Fertilizers.
Fibre building board.
Fine art publications.
Flat glass.
Flushing cisterns and copper balls.

Galvanized tanks.

Garage equipment.
Glazed and floor tiles.
Groceries.

Hand tools.
Hard fibre cordage.
Hardware.
Heating boilers and radiators (cast iron).

Jute goods.

Laboratory ware.
Lead sheet and pipes.
Leather and grindery for footwear repairs.
Lime.
Linoleum.

Mechanical clocks.
Medicinal and toilet preparations.
Memorials.
Metallic slide fasteners.
Millinery.
Motor vehicles and accessories.

Newspapers and periodicals.

Paint and paint materials.
Paper.
Petroleum products.
Pins, hair grips, etc.
Plasterboard.

TABLE 135 (*continued*)

Radiator blocks.	Steel conduit.
Radio batteries.	Steel mesh reinforcement.
Radio valves and cathode ray tubes.	Steel wire.
Refrigerators.	Surgical dressings.
Rubber footwear.	
	Tobacco and cigarettes.
Salt.	Typewriters.
Salt glazed pipes.	
Sanitary earthenware.	
Sanitary fireclay and other clayware.	Wallpaper.
Sports goods.	White fish.
Starter batteries.	Wines and spirits.
Stationery.	Wire rope.

It will be seen that among the goods included in this list are a wide range of household supplies and of materials and accessories used in building, many kinds of electrical goods, motor cars and cycles and accessories, petrol, medical, dental and toilet goods, tobacco and cigarettes, chocolates and confectionery, cinematographic films, fertilizers, books and periodicals, paper and stationery, sports goods, typewriters, and wines and spirits—to mention only some of the most important. Nor can it be assumed that the list is exhaustive, or that other supplies are subject to fully competitive conditions. It is evident that the tendencies inducing manufacturers, and in some cases traders, to enter into collective schemes involving restrictions on competition are very strong, and that there will need to be very stringent measures of prevention if any prohibition is not to be evaded by devices for circumventing the law.

The Case for Public Regulation. The case for regulative action is the stronger because it is highly desirable, in view of the general shortage of labour and productive resources, to prevent the waste of resources in the processes of distribution. As we saw (on p. 51), the distributive trades, which lost a good deal of labour during the war, have been re-absorbing labour rapidly since 1945. Since 1954 they have been employing more than 2,750,000 persons, as against 2,887,000 in 1939 and 1,927,000 in 1944. In 1939 and earlier years, with considerable unemployment in productive occupations, the size of the distributive labour force may have seemed not to matter greatly; but even then it involved an inflation of costs to the consumers' detriment. Under conditions of full employment it becomes imperative to do all that can be done to check the waste of labour in unproductive tasks. It is, of course, no worse to waste labour in distribution than elsewhere; but it will be agreed that the distributive trades are peculiarly liable to such waste, and that the tendency for retail prices to continue rising in Great Britain when they are stationary or falling in other leading industrial countries makes it particularly important to do all that can be done to reduce distributive margins and to check practices which tend to keep these margins unduly high. Especially is it undesirable to allow practices which prevent the granting of discounts or dividends on purchases to customers, and desirable to promote the development of 'self-service' as a means of economizing labour. In this field, as well as in respect of dividends on purchases, the Co-operative movement has been a notable pioneer; and it has suffered to a notable extent from the growth of restrictive methods, above all at the hands of the Proprietary Articles Association. It is also particularly necessary, at a time when housing is being extensively subsidized, to prevent all practices that artificially inflate the costs of house-building and house-equipment; and the high cost of the National Health Service indicates the need to prevent the exploitation of the public by unnecessarily high charges for dental, surgical, and other medical goods.

Can Control be made Effective? Admittedly, it is difficult, under a system governed by the quest for private profit, to devise effective means for the prevention of practices which serve the interests of groups of capitalist manufacturers or traders, especially in a situation of high demand which makes it easy to maintain restrictions because traders who are doing well under them have no great inducement for evasion. There has been long experience of 'trust-busting', especially in the United States; and the results have been none too encouraging, though the restrictionists have at any rate been kept busy finding new ways round the law. It is a further complication that Trade Unions, which are often accused of engaging in restrictive practices on their members' behalf, are apt to be sympathetic to forms of trade regulation which make it easier for them to bargain collectively with entire trades and make it less tempting to the 'private' trader to cut costs at the expense of wages and standard conditions of employment. This tendency, it should be noted, has not prevented the Labour Party from taking a strong line against restrictive capitalist practices; but it does lead Trade Unions, in certain cases, to look with favour on big firms which can afford to behave generously to their employees out of the high profits they are in a position to make.

Trade Union Restrictions. As for Trade Union practices of a restrictive kind, it is none too easy to distinguish those which form an essential part of the Unions' function of securing good wages and conditions from those which react unfavourably on production. Trade Unions seldom, if ever, impose direct limitations on what their members are to produce. Where such restrictions exist, they are usually imposed, not by the Trade Unions, but by groups of workers in particular establishments, often as retaliation against alleged attempts at undue 'speeding-up' or the introduction of fancy forms of incentive bonus or piecework payment. Trade Union restriction, properly so called, usually takes such forms as limitation of the number of apprentices or the attempt to secure a monopoly of a particular job or machine for properly qualified craftsmen. It is mainly a matter of the 'right to a trade'; and in face of changing technical conditions of production, it undoubtedly sometimes leads to anomalies which hamper employers in introducing improved methods. The effects, however, are often exaggerated: under conditions of full employment there is much less temptation to rigidity in enforcing trade rules and customs, though the fear of coming unemployment persists in many trades because of lively memories of the past. It is doubtless true that many workers produce, especially where industrial relations are bad, less than they could if they set out to do their utmost; but this is due much less to any formal restrictions on output than to a feeling of antagonism to capitalist profit-making and to a reluctance to be 'exploited' in the interest of shareholders who care little or nothing for the working conditions under which their profits are made. Full employment, by removing or reducing the fear of getting the sack, makes it easier for bodies of workers to keep their productive effort within what they regard as the limits of a 'fair day's work' and to obstruct changes favoured by technicians where these disturb established trade customs or threaten to make work more irksome or to undermine traditional forms of skill. The best way of keeping such tendencies in check is to give the workers concerned a sense that they are being both treated fairly in respect of wages and conditions and consulted in advance about changes that will affect their working lives. But, though many of the bigger firms have made a considerable success of joint consultation, some—and especially many of the smaller—hold back and insist on their exclusive 'rights of management', often to their own detriment. It would, of course, be folly to pretend that in such matters Trade Unions always behave reasonably—though to a great extent their leaders do. Nevertheless, the wholesale accusations sometimes made against Trade Unions of being the exponents of a restrictionism fully as damaging to the public interest as that of trade associations and capitalist monopolies certainly cannot be sustained. It is a necessary and legitimate function of the Trade Union to protect its members against unfair working conditions and against technical changes based on ignoring the human effects. Technicians are all too apt to leave this human factor out of account and to run into trouble through failure either to make their purposes understood or to be ready to consult the workers concerned before they finally make up their minds.

Private and Public Monopoly. So far, this chapter has been concerned with monopolies organized by private bodies, such as trade associations of various kinds. But of course monopoly exists also both in the nationalized part of the economy and in certain cases in which the

State has endowed groups of private persons with monopolistic powers. Legally sanctioned monopoly is of long standing in the public utility services—electricity supply, gas and water—where it would be in most areas impracticable to have rival undertakings covering the same territorial markets. Electricity and gas supply services have now been brought under national ownership—the one under a Central Electricity Authority with subordinate Regions, and the other under a number of regional undertakings, co-ordinated by a national Gas Council. Water supply services are also to a large extent publicly owned and administered by local government agencies conducted either by a single local authority or by a number acting together; but a residue of private ownership remains in this field. Such services, where they have not been taken over by the State, are operated under powers granted by Act of Parliament to the private or municipal bodies concerned, and are made subject to some measure of public regulation.

The Public Monopolies. In another chapter a brief account has been given of the nationalized services and of their working (see p. 119). With the exception of coal-mining and road goods transport these services are to a great extent 'natural' monopolies—forms of economic activity in which it would be clearly impracticable or wasteful to have rival undertakings in the field. In the case of railways, grouping by Act of Parliament in 1921 had created, well before nationalization, a considerable element of monopoly; and the companies acted closely together and under public regulation in fixing fares and freight charges. Public ownership, now that a substantial element of regional management has been introduced, is important chiefly in providing for centralized financial control, especially control of investment, and central planning of main-line services. In the case of goods transport by road, the Conservative Government has now (July 1955) modified its projects of de-nationalization, and British Road Services is to be allowed to maintain its trunk service intact, though considerable numbers of lorries have been re-sold to private operators, who are again free to offer competitive facilities. Whereas a complete return to private operation would have made impossible any co-ordination of road and rail services, allowing the operators to choose the most convenient method of transporting goods consigned to them, the retention of B.R.S.'s trunk service leaves such co-ordination practicable in part, should the Transport Commission decide in favour of it. The case for it appears to be strong, with a view to checking the growth of congestion on the roads and to procuring a fuller utilization of rail facilities and therewith an improvement both in the quality of service and in the financial results.

Pricing Policy in Public Enterprise. The institution of public monopoly raises important questions of pricing policy. Under the various nationalization Acts the Boards or Commissions to which the conduct of operations has been entrusted are required to do their best to carry on their enterprises in such a way as to cover their costs, including interest on capital, not necessarily each year but taking one year with another. This some of them are finding it difficult to do—especially the railways, which are in need of heavy capital expenditure for modernization and are faced with a form of competition in which road services are apt to 'cream' the traffic, leaving the railways to carry the less remunerative loads. Even if it were possible by raising charges to make the railways pay their way, this would not necessarily be the correct policy to follow; for it would inevitably drive yet more traffic away to the roads and thus render necessary even heavier expenditure on road improvement. The railways provide an indispensable service, which must be carried on whether it pays its way or not—though it is of course possible in certain cases to economize by closing unremunerative branch lines, and this is being done, sometimes in face of strong local opposition. Logically, the answer must lie in planned coordination of alternative forms of transport, and in setting gains in one sector against losses in another. This offsetting already exists under the Transport Commission, which controls the nationalized road services as well as the railways; but the necessary coordination between them has not yet been achieved, or even attempted.

The National Coal Board too has been in difficulties over finance; and in 1955 coal prices were sharply raised in the hope of wiping out its deficit. This deficit is at present swollen by the Government's decision that the Board must meet the loss on imported coal, which has had to be brought in to make up a shortage in home-produced supplies. It is impracticable, because of British trade relations with other countries, to eliminate coal exports, which are necessary to the economies of certain of Britain's national customers; and in view of this coal has had to be imported at high cost, especially from the United States. The Mineworkers' Union protects that it is unfair to charge the Coal Board with the losses thus incurred, and argues that the Treasury should foot the bill; but the Government has hitherto rejected this plea. In the long run, the solution must be found in increased home output of coal; but this is not easy to achieve, in face of the difficulty of enrolling enough mine workers, except as the outcome of extensive new investment in sinking shafts and improving colliery equipment. The price of coal is of course an important element in the costs of many other industries, as well as directly in the consumers' costs of living; and the reactions of higher coal prices on the export trades have to be carefully considered in deciding how much to charge. It should, however, be noted that coal, even after the price increases of 1955, is relatively cheaper in Great Britain than in the other leading coal-producing countries.

Under private ownership, failure to produce at a profit normally means the discontinuance of the uneconomic production, unless the State is prepared to provide a subsidy. Under nationalization it may be indispensable to maintain output produced at a loss, where the national interest requires this. To some extent such losses can be met by pooling, so that the more productive units pay for the less productive; but if losses occur on the pooled output as a whole they are bound to appear as a deficit in the accounts. Under the nationalization Acts such deficits are not borne by the Treasury: they have to be carried forward, to be wiped out, if possible, by surpluses in future years.

In nationalized services both price and wage policies become, almost of necessity, in the last resort matters for the Government. It is the Government that must decide whether national interests require the running of a particular service at less than an economic price; and wages form so important an element in running costs that it may depend on the wage-level whether a surplus or a deficit results. Normally, each Board or Commission is left to carry on its own wage-bargaining; but if a deadlock occurs, the Government is almost bound to be called on to intervene.

The Control of Public Monopolies. Nationalized services, unlike those in private hands, are not carried on with a view to maximum profit. They are required only to seek to pay their way, inclusive of interest charges and in some cases of provision for gradual amortization of capital. They are therefore under no inducement to charge monopoly prices in order to make unreasonable profits. They may, however, if they are inefficiently run, exploit the public by incurring inflated costs; and it is on this ground desirable that there should be some means of estimating their efficiency. This is not easy to do; for there are no other enterprises with which they can be directly compared: nor is it easy to find outside them experts who can be asked to pronounce authoritative judgment upon them. In the final resort it is the responsibility of the Ministers under whose direction the Boards or Commissions are placed to estimate how well they are doing their jobs and, in case of need, to reorganize or replace a defaulting authority. But sometimes the Boards themselves prefer to invite a special committee to investigate their affairs and report to them—as in the recent case of the Fleck Committee on the Coal Board. Boards are apt to resent outside investigations which they have not invited for themselves; and it is hardly practicable for each Ministry to maintain an expert staff equipped to conduct an all-round review of each Board's proceedings. Ministers are empowered under the nationalization Acts to issue policy directives to the Boards within their sphere of authority; but they have been for the most part reluctant to do this, for fear of being accused of bringing 'political' pressure to bear on what are essentially economic administrations. Ministers, however, can and do affect policy by changing the membership of Boards when the members fall due for re-appointment or re-placement; and they can at any time seek to persuade their Governments to introduce amending legislation.

Marketing Boards. The remaining category of public monopolies consists of the Marketing Boards established for a number of products under the Agricultural Marketing Acts. These Boards, which have large statutory powers of regulation, are quasi-public bodies; but they are chosen by the producers of the products concerned, and thus represent profit-seeking as against consumer or public interests. Strong objection has been taken to this type of arrangement, especially by the Co-operative movement, and it has been proposed that the Marketing Boards should be re-constituted so as to represent public and consumer, as well as producer, interests. Farmers, however, vigorously oppose such a system and, in the name of self-government, claim the right to make compulsory regulations for their own trades. During the war, the Marketing Boards became in effect agencies of the Ministry of Food, which with its wartime powers was in a position to exercise effective control; but the discontinuance of rationing control, followed by the merging of the Food Ministry with the Ministry of Agriculture, has altered the situation—for the latter Ministry can by no means be regarded as a satisfactory guardian of the consumers' interests. The whole question is closely involved with that of the subsidies paid by the State to farmers in order to stimulate high agricultural production and with that of the special conditions under which milk is supplied to schools and others as a part of the social services. Co-operators are pressing, with Labour support, for the establishment of a new Ministry charged especially with the safeguarding of consumer interests; but there is no likelihood of legislation on these lines as long as the present Government stays in power.

CHAPTER TWENTY

THE CO-OPERATIVE MOVEMENT

I N 1954 the consumers' Co-operative Societies of the United Kingdom
had a total membership of nearly 11½ millions and a total retail trade
of approximately £793 million. As compared with the previous year
their membership had increased by 2¼ per cent and the value of their
trade by 3·8 per cent. Their capital (share and loan) amounted to £285
million—a rise of about £2 million over 1953. They had reserves of over
£29 million, and a trading surplus of £47½ million, or nearly 6 per cent
on turnover. Since 1938 membership has increased by about three
millions, but the rate of increase has slackened off: in the later 'thirties
it averaged nearly 4 per cent per annum. Trade value has naturally
risen much faster, because of rising prices: in 1938 it was about £268¼
million, with a trading surplus of nearly £26 million, or nearly 10 per
cent of turnover. Co-operative Societies are thus trading on narrower
margins than they used to do, and this is reflected in lower dividends on
purchases. Average dividends indeed had been falling steadily in recent
years up to 1953, though there was a fractional increase in 1954. There
has been increasingly keen competition between the Co-operative
Societies and their principal rivals—the chain and department stores.
The average dividend in the £1, which was 1s. 8½d. in 1946, had fallen
in 1954 to 1s. 0¼d., and was only 9½d. in the Southern Section and 8d.
in the South-West, as against 1s. 6½d. in Scotland and 1s. 5¼d. in the
North.

Local Consumers' Societies. The British consumers' Co-operative
Movement consists of a large number of local retail Societies of widely
varying size, together with the big Wholesale Societies, English and
Scottish, and a number of federal trading bodies conducted by groups
of local Societies for particular purposes, such as baking, laundering,
coal and milk distribution, and funeral undertaking. In 1954 there
were 973 separate local Societies: the number had been falling steadily
because of amalgamations. In 1938 it was 1,085. In 1953 one Society—
London—had more than a million members, and ten others more than
100,000. Thirty more exceeded 50,000, while at the other end of the
scale there were 222 with fewer than 1,000, and 391 with fewer than
5,000. Small Societies were more frequent in the North of England and
in Scotland than elsewhere—these being the old centres of Co-operative

strength and showing strong resistance to amalgamation into bigger units. The great majority of Societies are local, in the sense of being confined to a single town and its neighbourhood; but there are some, such as Plymouth and Barnsley, that cover quite wide areas. In a number of big towns there is more than one Society. Greater London has several, besides the monster London Society, and so have Glasgow and Manchester. There is, however, a tendency for overlapping Societies within a town to amalgamate: a recent instance is Oldham, where two rival and long-established Societies have recently joined forces.

Co-operative Principles. Each local Co-operative Society is fully self-governing and determines its own policy, subject only to the acceptance of certain rules laid down for registration under the Industrial and Provident Societies Acts or as conditions of membership by the Co-operative Union. The general principles on which the Societies work are (1) open membership, which allows anyone to join and become a shareholder on the same terms as the existing members; (2) one member one vote, irrespective of the number of shares held; (3) democratic control by members' meetings, which all are entitled to attend; (4) payment of fixed, but variable, interest on capital; and (5) in almost all cases, but not compulsorily, payment of dividends on purchases to members, except in respect of goods covered by restrictive trade practices which do not allow such payments to be made. Almost all the local Societies are members of either the English or the Scottish Wholesale Society, which they jointly own and control through periodical meetings of delegates held at a few main centres. Similarly, the 'federal' Societies are owned and controlled by the local Societies which belong to them; but sometimes one of the Wholesale Societies also has a shareholding interest. Each local Society has an elected Management Committee and a salaried manager or managing secretary; and many have also a separate Educational Committee, with its own secretary, in charge of education and propaganda. Nearly all the larger and many of the smaller local Societies are also affiliated to the Co-operative Party, whose candidates join the Parliamentary Labour Party on election; and in many areas there are local Co-operative Parties or Political Committees, with their own membership drawn from the Societies' ranks.

Co-operative Democracy. On paper, no structure could easily be more democratic than that of the consumers' Co-operative movement. But, unfortunately, most of the members take little interest, and play almost no part in the affairs of their local Societies. It is rare for even one member in a hundred to be present at a members' meeting, and on the average only about $1\frac{1}{2}$ per cent take part in the voting for Management Committees and other elective positions. This apathy is found most of all in many of the very large Societies, and some of the smaller have considerably better records of attendance and voting. But overall the movement is carried on by a tiny minority, and the proportion participating has been falling as the membership has increased.

The reasons are not far to seek. A high proportion of members join a Co-operative Society not on principle but simply for convenience, and not a few of them deal with the Society only for a narrow range of goods, or even for one thing only, such as milk or coal. Many more take no interest in the working of their Society, as long as it seems to be giving them reasonable service; and if it does not they are far likelier to leave it than to go to the trouble of making a complaint. In some cases meetings have to be held at a considerable and inconvenient distance from the members' homes. A few Societies covering wide areas arrange for local meetings at or in connection with branch stores or groups of stores; and in a very few the meetings are held simultaneously in a number of places and the votes added together. This is done also in the Co-operative Wholesale Society, in order to avoid the cost of sending delegates to a single centre. It has the disadvantage that the central body of directors or managers, being represented at all the meetings, can usually prevail over any localized opposition or minority group, and that it becomes impossible to vary the agenda in order to meet local interests.

Co-operative 'Loyalty'. Leading Co-operators are well aware of this big defect in Co-operative democracy, and are continually striving to arouse more interest among the members, both in order to make the movement more really democratic and in the hope of stimulating trade by arousing a spirit of Co-operative 'loyalty'—that is, of inducing the members both to buy more goods at the 'Co-op' and to give preference to goods that are Co-operatively produced as well as distributed. The Wholesale Societies own and conduct a considerable number of factories for the production of goods that are in wide demand among the members. In 1953 the Co-operative Wholesale Society did a distributive trade of nearly £421 million, of which its own products accounted for a value of nearly £120 million. The corresponding figures for Scotland were £84 million and £27 million, and the Joint Wholesale owned by them in partnership produced a value of £17¾ million—mostly tea. This left a large proportion of total trade to be carried on in goods produced outside the movement; and local Societies also made considerable purchases without going through the Co-operative Wholesale channels. A substantial part of this trade is in branded proprietary goods, on many of which dividends cannot be paid. The Wholesales cannot economically establish their own factories except for goods for which they can secure a large and regular demand: nor would their present resources allow them to expand their production to more than a limited extent. They could no doubt draw in more capital or loans from the local Societies, many of which have large sums invested outside the movement; but in order to do this they would have to offer favourable rates of interest, and large-scale failures might lead them into very serious difficulties. In practice they are apt to be cautious in expanding production and particularly in entering new fields where they would be likely to encounter serious opposition. It has often been suggested that they should set up chains for multiple retailing on the lines either of Woolworth's or of Marks and Spencer; but it would be difficult to secure the approval of the local Societies for central management of such ventures, and without this they could hardly be carried on with commercial success.

The Range of Co-operative Trade.   The question is nevertheless of the greatest importance for the future of the Co-operative movement, which has been definitely losing ground of late in respect of the proportion of members' total income spent at the stores. The retail Societies, except a few of the largest, are still predominantly grocers, which have added a number of ancillary departments for dealing in other kinds of goods. At the time of the Retail Distribution Census of 1950, out of total Co-operative retail sales of £593 million, food accounted for £434 million and groceries alone for £283 million. The 'Co-ops' had about 12 per cent of total trade in all the goods covered by the Census; but their proportion in the food trades was 17 per cent, and in coal nearly 15 per cent, whereas in clothing it was only 6 per cent and in footwear under 7 per cent. For chemists' and photographic goods it was again 6 per cent and for furniture 6¼ per cent. These figures include all Co-operative sales of the goods in question, whether or not they were produced as well as distributed under Co-operative auspices.

For grocers' goods alone the Co-operatives made a better showing, with 24 per cent of the total, and for dairy products a still better— 34·6 per cent. For butchers' goods their proportion was just under 17 per cent; but for greengroceries, fruit, fish and poultry it was, only about 5 per cent, and for sugar confectionery, tobacco and newsagency a long way under 1 per cent. For books and periodicals it was almost nothing, and for jewellery, leather and sports goods a fraction of 1 per cent. In fact, not much short of half the total Co-operative retail trade was in grocers' goods alone, and the trade in all types of 'dry goods' added up to only 21 per cent of the whole.

Co-operatives, Department Stores and Multiples.   There is no reason to suppose that these proportions have changed greatly during the past four or five years. Despite the establishment of big central department stores by a number of local Societies, the impact made on the non-food trades has been small in relation to the potential market. The 'Co-ops'' clearest advantage is in those branches of trade in which there is a fairly steady, large demand for identical standard supplies week after week, so that the number of varieties needing to be stocked is limited and the risk of being left with unsaleable goods small. The 'Co-ops' have been much less successful in invading the markets for 'fashion' goods, where varieties are very many and demand is highly uncertain. Such firms as Marks and Spencer have overcome this problem by being able to place very large orders, sometimes at cut prices. This the Co-ops cannot do, as long as each local Society employs its own buyers and chooses what to buy from the whole range of available products outside as well as within the Co-operative movement. The most rapid advances in retail sales in recent years have been made neither by the Co-operative Societies nor by the privately owned department stores but by the multiple chains. Here are the figures showing the relative advance by the three types of large-scale retailer between 1950 and 1954.

TABLE 136

Board of Trade Index of Retail Sales, 1950-4

(1950 = 100)

	Department Stores	Multiple Shops	Co-operative Societies	Total
All Goods:				
1951	102	113	108	109
1952	99	121	118	117
1953	102	128	126	124
1954	110	137	131	131
Food and Perishables:				
1951	111	112	108	110
1952	113	124	123	123
1953	116	133	132	132
1954	124	138	135	136
Non-Food Goods:				
1951	102	114	109	109
1952	99	118	105	110
1953	101	123	107	114
1954	109	136	118	125

The relative gain of the multiple shops sector is clear. Even in the food trades the Co-operative Societies have barely kept abreast of the growth in total trade, and in the non-food trades, in which they were already far behind, they have lagged still further. They have indeed gained substantially in comparison with the department stores; but this is cold comfort.

Nor can it be regarded as unimportant that the Co-operative movement has little or no footing in many forms of supply on which consumers are coming to spend a higher percentage of their total incomes. In 1931 the average Co operator spent in England £29 8s., in Wales £34 1s., and in Scotland £47 5s., at the Co-operative stores—an overall average of £31 11s. for Great Britain as a whole. By 1938 the overall figure was actually lower—just over £31 6s. By 1946 it was £41 7s., and by 1954 £69—an increase a long way behind the rise in prices since 1938, partly as a consequence of more lukewarm Co-operators who used the stores only for a very limited range of purchases.

Total consumers' expenditure had increased over the period 1946–54 —from £6,111 million to £10,116 million—a rise of about 65 per cent (see p. 83). Over the same period average Co-operative expenditure per member had risen by 67 per cent; but this was due largely to the sharp rise in food prices as subsidies were reduced and the terms of trade altered to Great Britain's disadvantage (see p. 199). In view of full employment and higher working-class earnings (see p. 237), the Co-operative movement should have done better than this.

Obstacles to Co-operative Development. There is, however, great difficulty in breaking into many of the trades which are absorbing an increasing proportion of consumers' total incomes. In some countries, including the United States, the Co-operative movement has become a substantial supplier of petrol; but here the trade is too closely controlled for entry to be easy. Nor have the movement's small efforts to enter the amusement trades met with much success. Both cinemas and theatres are difficult to run except under the auspices of big national 'circuits'; and over a wide range of products—e.g. books and newspapers—the existence of powerful restrictive trade associations makes entry difficult. Considerable efforts have been made during the past year or two to increase Co-operative trade in 'dry goods'—particularly clothing, furnishings and furniture. There have been some successes; but they are still very limited and likely to remain so unless radically new methods are tried out on a big scale.

Is Co-operative Localism Out of Date? Here, as we have seen, one great obstacle to Co-operative development is the local basis on which the movement's organization rests. There would be a great deal to be said in favour of this if it meant real 'consumers' democracy'; but this, as we saw, can hardly be claimed in view of the widespread apathy of the membership. Some attempt has been made to overcome the movement's parochialism by introducing a plan of 'national membership' that allows Co-operators to make purchases at any 'Co-op' connected with the scheme and to receive from their own Societies dividends on their purchases at these Societies' local rates, whatever they may be. This is to the good as far as it goes; but its results have not been great. There have been other local arrangements allowing members of a group of Societies to make purchases at the general department stores maintained by the bigger in the urban centres, and to receive dividends on what they so buy. These too have not been without effect; but they do not yet come to a great deal. The Co-operative Wholesale Society, which already controls a number of retail branches either in Co-operative 'deserts' or in areas where the local Societies have got into financial difficulties, has for some time been pressing for greater powers to open branches in promising areas—for example, in new towns. But such projects meet with much opposition from the existing local Societies, which fear the C.W.S.'s competition or the effect in limiting their own expansion. In Scotland indeed the existence of a very scattered population, especially in the Highlands, has led to the S.C.W.S. being given much greater freedom to set up its own retail branches in such areas; and this form of expansion has met with considerable success. None of these measures, however, more than touches the fringe of the main problem, which is that of standardized large-scale buying and larger-scale manufacture by the Wholesales themselves. A Woolworth type or Marks and Spencer type of retail outlet cannot be successfully run except on a very large scale, with central control over stocks and buying; and this has so far been much too big an innovation for local Management Committees or local full-time officers to swallow.

Co-operation and the Consumer. The Co-operative movement, despite its limitations, is a most important champion of consumers' interests. The proportion of trade it controls in coal distribution, dairy products, groceries, and certain other key goods enables it to stand out against excessive prices and to put serious obstacles in the way of the growth of restrictive practices; and, even though most of its members take little or no part in its affairs, except as customers, it has a substantial power to mobilize opinion against the more bare-faced forms of extortion. Its influence in this respect would be much greater could it make more success in the field of journalism. The movement owns a Sunday newspaper, *Reynolds'*, but has done but little to build up a mass-circulation —which would require much more capital, as well as better journalism, than it commands at present. Its other principal 'popular' journals— *Co-operative News* and *The Scottish Co-operator*—are both too parochial to command much circulation outside the ranks of active committee-members and officials; and its less popular ventures—*Agenda* and *The Co-operative Review*—have only small circulations. It is impossible to procure a wide reading public for the day-to-day activities of the movement, for much the same reasons as account for the small proportion of members who take an active interest in its affairs. The only hope of changing this situation would be to sink a large amount of capital into establishing a first-class general newspaper and perhaps other journals appealing to the general body of working-class readers; but it seems improbable that this will be done in the near future, often though leading Co-operators have spoken of their desire to set up a daily newspaper of their own.

The Basis of Co-operative Finance. The Co-operative movement, perhaps rightly in its own interests, is not venturesome with its members' capital. It has always to bear in mind that this capital, subscribed by many thousands of relatively poor people, is withdrawable at any time, and that any serious run on it could place the movement in a very awkward predicament. As we saw, Co-operative share capital has been accumulating in recent years only at a modest rate, while loan capital has tended actually to fall. It is true that by no means the whole of this capital is actually being used to finance Co-operative trade. In 1952, out of nearly £212 million's worth of investments owned by the local Societies, nearly 59 per cent was invested in the Wholesale Societies and more than 9 per cent in other Co-operative bodies, including the producers' Societies and the Co-operative Building Society. The rest was mainly in government and local government securities and in the stock of public corporations—these three groups accounting for nearly a quarter of the total. 6·3 per cent was out in loans to members, and only one-half of one per cent was in joint stock companies of any kind. These figures do not include the investments held by the Wholesale Societies themselves or the £90 million of non-Co-operative deposits held by the two Co-operative Banks. It will, however, be seen that by far the greater part of the movement's capital is already tied up either in the local Societies or in the Wholesales. The Producers' Societies, though of some importance in a few branches of production—mainly boots, other clothing, and printing—have only a very small capital— under £1 million, exclusive of the shares in them held by local consumers' Societies.

Co-operatives under Rationing. While rationing was in force for a number of essential foods, the local Co-operative Societies held a number of ration registrations for certain articles substantially in excess of their total membership, but not nearly so many as they would have held if all members and their families had bought these goods at the Co-ops. In 1953-4 they held 14,105,000 registrations for sugar, 14,054,000 for butter and margarine, 14,009,000 for cheese, and 12,838,000 for bacon and ham. In comparison with 1946-7 they had increased their registrations by 16 per cent for sugar, 17 per cent for butter and margarine, 16·7 per cent for cheese, and 16 per cent for bacon and ham. In 1953-4 Co-operative registrations were approximately 28 per cent of all registrations for sugar, butter and cheese and about 25½ per cent for bacon. These figures are of course peculiarly favourable to the movement because they concern commodities in which it has a long tradition of successful trading.

The Co-operative Outlook. The outlook for the consumers' Co-operative movement is uncertain, not in the sense that it is in any immediate danger of losing its hold where it is well entrenched, but rather in the sense that its capacity to adapt itself to a changing pattern of consumers' expenditure cannot be taken for granted. Co-operative ownership is accepted by the Labour Party as a satisfactory form of social ownership in the fields of retail and wholesale trade and also in branches of production closely related to them; and if private trade were to be eliminated by 'socialization' from any section of these fields, Co-operation would obviously be called upon to replace it to a considerable extent, in preference to the opening of state or municipal shops. The Labour Party, however, seems to have no intention of launching in the near future any attack on the main branches of retailing or wholesaling of consumers' goods; and it appears likely that Co-operation will be left to grow by its own efforts, without special help from the State. In these circumstances its rate of growth cannot be very rapid. The great majority of Co-operative members make only a very small contribution to the movement's capital funds—often not enough to cover the additional costs of serving them. The bulk of share capital is held by a very small minority of the members, and no great effort has been made so far to attract additional resources in competition with such bodies as building societies and insurance companies, though in both these fields the movement does a quite substantial business of its own. There would indeed be considerable difficulty in present circumstances in the way of attracting large additional investments, even if the movement could make up its mind how to spend the money. As against this, its share capital shows a high degree of stability and should continue to do so as long as full employment persists. Serious and prolonged depression, however, might well mean considerable withdrawals of share capital as well as of loans, and would certainly check the movement's growth.[1]

[1] For a fuller discussion of the possibilities of Co-operative expansion see my book, *The British Co-operative Movement in a Socialist Society*, published in 1951.

Since the present volume was written the Co-operative movement has set up, with Mr. Hugh Gaitskell as chairman, an enquiry committee to review the whole question of Co-operative trading policy. This committee is due to report in 1958.

CHAPTER TWENTY-ONE

TAXATION

TAXATION has two main purposes—to meet the costs of government, and to re-distribute incomes, usually in the interests of the poorer citizens. It can be used for other purposes—to discourage or to encourage the consumption of particular kinds of goods or services, or to withdraw from the people what is deemed to be an excess of spendable income, and thus to prevent or check inflation. It could also be used as an aid to a policy of nationalization, by providing out of public revenue the capital funds needed for new investment, instead of leaving them to be provided out of personal or business savings. These, however, are subsidiary uses of the tax-gatherer's power. The two main uses are the financing of expenditure on such things as administration, armaments and other services conducted by the Government, as far as these last are not met by selling the products or services in question, and the redressing of such inequalities in the distribution of incomes as are felt to be either intolerably oppressive or regarded as such by the public opinion on which the Government depends.

Taxes, Rates and Contributions. In addition to national taxes in the strict sense, there are two other kinds of taxation of which we must take account. The first of these is local taxation—called in this country 'rates', which are levied on the owners of certain kinds of property. The second consists of compulsory contributions to various kinds of social insurance funds, which must be regarded as taxes because they are levied without any relation to the individual's prospects of benefiting by them and are used to meet a part or the whole of the cost of certain social services—usually only a part.

Subsidies. Subsidies are *negative* taxes, by which the Government adds to the incomes of its private citizens. The name is usually limited to subsidies which are paid out in order to increase certain kinds of production or to keep down the prices at which certain things can be sold; but in a wider sense subsidies include children's allowances, pensions, and other social service benefits.

Progressive and Regressive Taxes. Taxes are called 'progressive' when they bear more heavily on large than on small incomes, and 'regressive' in the opposite case. They are called 'direct' when they are levied on incomes or property, and 'indirect' when they are levied on commodities, so as to raise their prices to those who buy them.

Taxes on Capital. In a sense, all taxes have to be paid out of the current product except when they take the form of transfers of real capital assets from the citizens to the State. There is, however, a real difference between taxes, direct or indirect, that fall on the current incomes of the taxpayers and capital taxes, such as death duties, which are levied on the estates belonging to dead persons. The Government can live beyond its income not only by borrowing but also by using the proceeds of taxes on capital for financing its current expenditure, as distinct from its expenditure on capital investment.

The Burden of Taxation. It is often very difficult to say on whom the burden of a particular tax finally falls. For example, if a tax is levied on a commodity, such as tea, how far can the sellers of that commodity pass it on by raising their prices? Or again, if imports are taxed, how far can the foreigner be made to pay the tax? Such questions admit of no simple answers: the answers depend on the relative bargaining strength of the parties and vary from case to case and from time to time. Nor is it possible to say on whom the burden of inheritance taxes falls—on the dead person or on his heirs.

The Limits of Taxable Capacity. It used to be thought by most economists that there were narrow limits to the amount of taxation that could be levied without reducing the incentives to production. In our own day, however, the world has grown accustomed to levels of taxation that would formerly have been regarded as impossibly high; and there is no evidence that incentives have been in any way affected thereby, though some particular taxes may have affected incentives because rather of their nature than of their amount.

The Public Revenue. In 1953-4 the total 'ordinary' revenue of the United Kingdom was £4,368 million, as compared with £927 million in 1938-9. Almost all of this came from taxes, which were then between four and five times as great in money amount as before the war. These totals exclude both local rates and compulsory insurance contributions. Local rates amounted in 1953 to £436 million, and in 1938-9 to £217 million: they had only just doubled. National insurance contributions were about £75 million in 1938 and £588 million in 1952-3—a rise of not far short of 700 per cent. The sum of all these kinds of taxation was about £1,220 million just before the war and roughly £5,400 million in 1953—again an increase of between four and five times, compared with an increase of national income from under £5,000 million to between £14,000 and £15,000 million a less than threefold increase The greater increase in public expenditure and taxation was mainly accounted for by the growth of social services and by the heavier burden of armaments.

The principal sources of national tax revenue were taxes on incomes and taxes on expenditure. Lesser sources were insurance contributions and taxes on capital. Here, from the Blue Book on National Income and Expenditure, are the figures for these kinds of taxation from 1946 onwards, with the amount of local rates in addition:

TABLE 137

Tax Revenue of State and Local Authorities, 1946–54
(including Insurance Contributions)
(£million)

	1946	1947	1948	1949	1950	1951	1952	1953	1954
Taxes on:									
Income	1,716	1,495	1,595	1,780	1,795	1,907	2,154	2,096	2,125
Capital	143	164	215	254	190	194	159	165	183
Expenditure	1,282	1,478	1,703	1,655	1,722	1,907	1,893	1,936	2,016
Insurance									
Contributions	170	232	335	436	440	452	476	525	532
Local Rates	269	307	317	326	338	365	393	435	460
Total	3,580	3,676	4,165	4,451	4,485	4,825	5,075	5,157	5,316

Observe the very sharp rise in insurance contributions after 1946, as the new social services came into operation. Note also the fall in taxes on capital in 1950 and in 1952, as a consequence of tax changes, including the exemption of small estates. A further significant change is the increase of taxation on expenditure by 51 per cent between 1946 and 1953, as against a rise of only 22 per cent in taxes on income. It will be seen that local rates rose steeply after 1950—up to which point the increase had been relatively modest.

Income Tax. Of all taxes, income tax yields by far the greatest return —£1,740 million in 1954 as against £312 million in 1938, or more than five times as much. This big advance was due not only to higher rates of taxation but also the extension of the tax to include the great majority of adult wage-incomes under the system of 'Pay as You Earn' (PAYE). Since 1938 the number of incomes brought under review for income tax has more than doubled—from under ten to more than twenty million. Wage-earners whose earnings were high enough to bring them within the law were of course already subject to income tax in 1938; but the tax authorities had then to chase them individually in order to find out whether they were liable or not, whereas now employers are forced to make returns for all their employees and to deduct from wages or salaries such tax as they are due to pay. This both brings more incomes under review and practically prevents evasion of tax by employed persons. Moreover, the minimum income at which tax becomes payable has been reduced in real value, so that more of the poorer groups are to-day liable to tax.

Surtax. Closely allied to income tax is the surtax payable on the bigger incomes. This yielded £132 million in 1954, as compared with £59 million in 1938—a relatively modest increase. As standard rates of income tax were raised, the effect was to transfer a proportion of what was previously surtax to that tax, leaving less scope for special taxation of the bigger incomes. Here are the year-to-year figures of the yield of the two taxes for 1946, as compared with their yield in 1938:

TABLE 138

Yield of Income Tax and Surtax, 1938 and 1946–54

(£million)

	1938	1946	1947	1948	1949	1950	1951	1952	1953	1954
Income Tax	312	1,250	1,128	1,213	1,370	1,404	1,485	1,651	1,694	1,740
Surtax	59	75	81	99	110	114	125	128	130	132
Total	371	1,325	1,209	1,312	1,480	1,518	1,610	1,779	1,824	1,872

Changes in Income Tax and Surtax. In 1938–9 the standard rate of income tax was 5s. 6d. in the £1, having been raised from 5s. the previous year. Tax began to be levied at an income of more than £125 a year. In 1955, with the standard rate at 9s., the exemption limit was actually lower than in 1938–9, at £120 for single persons and £210 for married couples living together. Surtax payable in 1939, under the Finance Act of the previous year, was levied on incomes of £2,000 or over, at a rate rising from 1s. in the £1 on the first £500 over £2,000 to 7s. 6d. on income in excess of £20,000: in 1955 it still began at £2,000 at 8d. in the £1 and rose to 10s. on income in excess of £15,000.

The Burden of Taxes on Income. Clearly, what matter most in relation to both income tax and surtax are not the extremes, but the rates payable on the incomes nearer the middle. Here is a comparison of the amounts payable in 1938–9 and in 1954–5 by single persons whose incomes were all earned.

TABLE 139

Income Tax on Earned Income Payable by Single Persons,
1938–9 and 1954–5

	1938–9	1954–5
Income under £125	Nil	Nil
„ £200–£250	£5	£4 8s. 10d.
„ £500–£600	£56 12s. 6d.	£56 12s. 2d.
„ £1,000 £1,500	£166 12s. 6d.	£218 10s. 0d.
„ £2,000	£214 2s. 6d.	£568 10s. 0d.

Thus, the tax payable is the same or less up to an income of £500–£600, but is much heavier on incomes above this level—more than twice as much on an income of £2,000, though of course the purchasing power of such an income has been sharply reduced. There have been so many changes in the nature of the exemptions and allowances granted before arriving at the figure of taxable income as to preclude direct comparison. For surtax the comparable rates in the £1, levied on the excess income over £2,000, are as follows:

TABLE 140

Rates of Surtax, 1938–9 and 1954–5

Rates per £1	1938-9	1954-5
On the first £2,000	Nil	Nil
On the next £500	1/-	2/-
„ „	1/3	2/6
„ £1,000	2/-	3/6
„ „	3/-	4/6
„ „	3/6	5/6
„ „	4/-	6/6
„ „	4/-	6/6
„ „	5/-	7/6
„ „	5/-	7/6
„ „	5/-	8/6
„ „	5/-	8/6
„ „	5/-	9/6
„ „	5/6	9/6
„ „	5/6	9/6
„ „	5/6	10/-
„ „	5/6	10/-
„ „	5/6	10/-
„ £5,000	6/-	10/-
„ £10,000	6/6	10/-
„ £20,000	7/-	10/-
„ excess over the above	7/6	10/-

Incomes after Direct Taxes. Thus a person with £5,000 a year paid in surtax £306 5s. in 1938–9, and £512 10s. in 1954–5, over and above his income tax. The Blue Book on National Income and Expenditure shows the combined effects of income tax and surtax on incomes of various sizes in the following way, giving the proportion of income retained by the taxpayer after paying the two taxes. (See Table 141 overleaf).

Thus, the lowest class of all pays a slightly higher proportion of income in tax than before the war; but the groups with from £250 to £1,500 pay a smaller proportion, though the difference is tiny at an income of £1,000 to £1,500. All the groups with incomes over £1,500 pay a higher proportion in income tax and surtax than before the war. In 1954 a person paid about one-third of his income at £2,000, one-half at about £6,000, two-thirds at about £10,000, and 84 per cent at the

TABLE 141

Proportion of Income Retained after Payment of Direct Taxes on Income,
1938 and 1954

Range of Income	Total Amount Paid (£)		Proportion Retained	
	1938	1954	1938	1954
Under £250	4	8	99·8	99·4
£250–£500	20	122	96·8	96·3
£500–£750	22	211	90·6	94·1
£750–£1,000	17	140	86·6	90·5
£1,000–£1,500	27	141	82·8	83·2
£1,500–£2,000	18	86	80·0	76·1
£2,000–£3,000	25	116	77·7	70·1
£3,000–£5,000	35	148	72·2	58·9
£5,000–£10,000	45	151	63·4	45·1
£10,000–£20,000	37	89	51·3	30·5
Over £20,000	57	58	34·5	15·9

top level. In 1938 he paid one-quarter at rather over £3,000, one-third at well under £5,000, one-half at rather over £10,000, and nearly two-thirds in the highest range of all. Direct taxation has become much more progressive on the really big incomes, but much less so on middle-class as well as working-class incomes, which are of course the more considerably affected by the rise in indirect taxes.

Taxes on Profits. In addition to income tax and surtax there are certain other taxes on income of which we need to take account. These are the taxes on profits, which are levied not on personal incomes, but on the profits made by various kinds of business. Taxation levied on profits, other than income tax, is a newcomer to British public finance. It existed in 1938 only in the novel form of the National Defence Contribution, which brought in a mere £15 million. It was developed during the war years, and still more after the war, when it was deemed necessary to budget for a large surplus in order to check inflationary spending. Here are the figures for 1938 and for the years from 1944–54:

TABLE 142

Taxes on Profits, 1938 and 1946–54

(£million)

	1938	1944	1945	1946	1947	1948
Profits Tax	15	35	35	35	31	154
Excess Profits Taxes	—	482	440	356	255	129
Total	15	517	475	391	286	283

	1949	1950	1951	1952	1953	1954
Profits Tax	257	264	301	378	233	177
Excess Profits Taxes	43	13	—4	—3	39	76
Total	300	277	297	375	272	253

There have been many changes in these taxes and in the conditions under which they are collected. It will be observed that their total yield reached its peak in 1944, while hostilities were still proceeding, and that there were sharp falls in 1946 and 1947. Thereafter the total did not change very greatly until 1952, when it reflected the speculative movements of 1950-1, and it again fell sharply in 1953. Excess Profits Tax, imposed at the rate of 60 per cent in 1939, was stepped up to 100 per cent in the following year and remained at that level till 1946.

Business men usually complain strongly against taxes on profits, as distinct from taxes on those profits which are paid out in dividends. They regard profits which are held in reserve as entitled to favourable treatment as a means of encouraging investment; and they defend high profits as facilitating the accumulation of capital. Chancellors of the Exchequer, on the other hand, find the taxation of excess profits a simple and useful instrument of war finance and also a means of counteracting inflationary tendencies in time of peace. At the same time Conservative Chancellors especially are apt to be impressed by the argument that everything possible should be done to encourage private investment and on this account to be generous in granting tax remissions and allowances, especially where profits are applied to the building up of capital resources. It would take too much space to follow here the changes that have taken place in profits taxes since 1945. It must suffice to say that the conditions have been a good deal eased since the Conservatives came back to office in 1951. (For the actual movement of profits since 1945, see pp. 247 ff.)

It will have been noted that for 1951 and 1952 the yield of Excess Profits Tax was entered as a *minus* amount. This was because, after the discontinuance of this tax—or rather its merging in Profits Tax—repayments could be claimed by those who had paid in previous years more than was ultimately found to be due. In 1951 and 1952 such repayments actually exceeded receipts.

Taxes on Capital. Taxes on capital need to be considered in close relation to taxes on income, as they both belong to the category of 'direct' taxes. They consist mainly of death duties, levied on the estates of dead persons: the only other capital tax of which we need take account is the so-called 'Special Contribution' levied by Sir Stafford Cripps. This first became payable in 1948, but never yielded a large sum except in 1949. Later small payments were merely a gradual clearing off of arrears.

Death duties, unlike taxes on incomes and profits, have been fairly stable. Their yield did barely more than double between 1938 and 1952—which implies a decline in their real weight. After a fairly slow rise between 1945 and 1949, and little change from 1949 to 1951, they fell sharply in 1952 and showed only a small upward movement in 1953, but rose much more in 1954.

TABLE 143

Taxes on Capital 1938 and 1944–54

(£million)

	1938	1944	1945	1946	1947	1948
Death Duties	78	107	119	143	164	182
Special Contribution	—	—	—	—	—	33
	78	107	119	143	164	215

	1949	1950	1951	1952	1953	1954
Death Duties	190	184	191	157	165	183
Special Contribution	64	6	3	2	1	1
	254	190	194	159	166	184

Death duties, of course, transfer capital ownership from private persons to the State, which can use the proceeds either for public investment or to meet current expenditure. As the products of general taxes are not earmarked for spending on particular purposes, it is not possible to say for which of these purposes the sums raised by death duties are being used. We can only estimate how much of the Government's total spending should be regarded as capital epxenditure and, if we wish, treat the yield of death duties as a contribution to this investment.

Capital Formation by the Government.　Government capital accumulation, however, is not easily identified. Its gross amount is made up of the value of government-owned new buildings and other fixed assets, plus any increase in the value of stocks held by government trading or

TABLE 144

Gross Capital Formation by Government or its Agencies, 1946–54

(£million)

	1946	1947	1948	1949	1950	1951	1952	1953	1954
Fixed—By Government Trading Bodies	− 2	7	64	61	65	88	114	125	104
Fixed—by Other Agencies	108	88	41	50	58	64	78	82	78
Stocks—of Government Trading Bodies	− 97	−6	22	−24	−67	64	2	−23	−166
Stocks—Strategic	—	—	—	—	—	127	49	42	46
Deduct Sales of War Stores in U.K.	−102	−92	−60	−32	−27	−23	−7	−7	− 3
Capital Payments Abroad	—	—	11	117	108	15	—	—	—
	−93	−3	78	172	137	333	241	227	59

other agencies, plus any capital sums paid out by the Government as grants towards overseas development—mainly colonial. The gross figures of such government capital formation since 1946 are as shown in Table 144.

Capital Formation by Local Authorities and Public Corporations. These bear no relation to the total capital expenditure of public bodies, most of which does not fall on the Budget. They do not include the values of houses or other buildings erected by local authorities, or that of Post Office buildings; nor do they include the capital expenditure of public corporations. Actually, these two types of agency—local authorities and public corporations—accounted for the following gross amounts of capital formation.

TABLE 145

Gross Capital Formation by Local Authorities and Public Corporations, 1946–54

(*£million*)

	1946	1947	1948	1949	1950	1951	1952	1953	1954
Local Authorities:									
Housing	99	208	269	264	265	290	353	404	375
Trading Services	32	49	38	27	24	18	18	20	20
Other	20	41	69	96	123	155	172	190	195
Total	151	298	376	387	412	463	543	614	590
Public Corporations:									
Fuel and Power	—	—	161	119	237	176	303	371	339
Iron and Steel	—	—	—	—	—	34	48	38	—
Transport and Communications	—	—	2	48	17	90	83	29	81
New Towns, etc.	—	—	10	13	12	20	33	40	—
Raw Cotton Commission	—	—	36	10	31	11	−34	−52	—
Others	—	—	26	25	16	13	17	7	—
Total	—	—	235	215	313	343	450	433	—
Grand Total	151	298	621	602	725	806	993	1,047	—

Gross Formation of Capital by the Government. It is reckoned in the Blue Book on National Income and Expenditure that the Government, apart from the local authorities and the public corporations, showed a gross fixed capital formation of the following amounts.

TABLE 146

Gross Capital Formation by Government, 1946–54

(£million)

1946	1947	1948	1949	1950	1951	1952	1953	1954
106	95	105	111	123	152	192	207	182

If these amounts are added to the previous total, we get

257	393	726	713	848	958	1,185	1,254	—

Most of this was of course financed not out of budget or current local authority revenues, but by means of loans. (For further discussion of public formation of capital, see pp. 104 ff.)

Indirect Taxes: Customs and Excise. We can now turn from taxes levied on capital to 'indirect' taxes, of which by far the most important class consists of taxes on commodities—especially articles of consumption. The most familiar sub-group of such taxes consists of customs duties levied on imports; and with these must be considered individual excise duties. Customs and excise are sources of very considerable revenue. Some customs duties are levied mainly for revenue purposes, and others mainly for the protection of home industry or in order to keep down imports. Others, accompanied by excise duties, have besides the raising of revenue the purpose of limiting the consumption of certain things—for example, alcoholic drinks. Yet others, such as taxes on purchases in general, are mainly designed to reduce consumption by transferring part of the consumers' spending power to the State. There are also some duties that are levied, not on commodities, but on particular kinds of service, such as entertainment or betting. Here are the figures of public revenue from taxes of these types.

TABLE 147

Yield of Taxes on Expenditure: Customs and Excise, 1938 and 1946–54

(£million)

	1938	1946	1947	1948	1949	1950	1951	1952	1953	1954
Taxes on:										
Beer }	107	276	261	305	286	266	261	257	257	252
Wines and Spirits }		88	95	121	115	120	128	124	130	136
Tobacco	84	438	541	598	600	602	622	612	628	651
Purchase Tax	—	161	217	300	282	299	338	313	306	322
Entertainments	8	55	49	49	44	44	45	46	45	43
Betting	—	—	—	20	26	25	26	28	29	30
Others	138	147	179	171	166	228	333	375	393	410
Total	337	1,165	1,342	1,564	1,519	1,584	1,753	1,754	1,787	1,844

Some of these taxes fall very heavily on the luxuries of the poorer sections of the people. This applies especially to the taxes on beer and tobacco and on betting—though the betting tax is too small to have any great effect. Others have a progressive element—for example, purchase tax, from which many necessaries and goods of low price are exempted, or are taxed at low rates, and the taxes on entertainments. In general, however, this group of taxes bears heavily on those whose incomes are small—and is meant to do so; for because of the small numbers of the relatively rich, taxes on luxuries alone cannot yield very large revenue. It is particularly important to bear this aspect of taxes on expenditure in mind, because comparisons are often made between the proportions of taxes on incomes falling on the rich and the poor, as if these represented the total tax burdens falling on these categories of citizens. In fact, taxation as a whole is much less 'progressive' than such comparisons suggest, because of the high share of indirect taxes that falls on the less well-to-do.

Of course, the amounts raised by these taxes do not simply reflect the actual consumption of the goods and services on which they fall. The high taxes have had a substantial effect in reducing consumption. For the facts about quantities concerned see pages 86 ff.

These 'consumption' taxes together accounted in 1954 for nearly the same amount of revenue as was raised by income tax and surtax together —£1,844 million as against £1,872 million. The specially regressive taxes alone—on beer, tobacco and betting—accounted for £933 million.

In all, this group of taxes produces more than five times as much revenue as it did in 1938—a slightly greater increase than that in income tax and surtax together. The increase in the tobacco tax from £84 million to £651 million is particularly notable—it has risen by six and a half times, whereas the taxes on alcoholic drinks have risen only between threefold and fourfold. Purchase tax, the second largest contribution in 1954, is a new tax since 1939. The 'Other' element, made up mainly of duties on petrol and other imports, has risen only threefold, largely because imports have been deliberately kept down.

Motor Vehicle Taxes. The only remaining important tax on consumers' expenditure—not included in the foregoing totals—is the group of motor vehicle duties, which has increased as follows:

TABLE 148
Yield of Motor Vehicle Duties, 1938 and 1944–54

(*£million*)

1938	1944	1945	1946	1947	1948
35	28	35	46	51	50

1949	1950	1951	1952	1953	1954
54	59	64	67	72	77

This is the only tax in the group which has a substantial progressive element, and it has not much more than doubled, despite the great growth of motoring in recent years. It was at a low level during the war because the use of private motor-cars was then much restricted; but it remains low in spite of the post-war expansion.

Other Taxes. Of taxes in the narrow sense there remain only a small number, belonging to the general category of taxes on expenditure. These include Stamp Duties, mainly on transfers of property, cheques, etc., the surplus of revenue over expenditure of the Post Office, and a miscellaneous group which it would take too much space to analyse. Here are the figures:

TABLE 149

Yield of other Taxes on Expenditure, 1938 and 1946–54

(*£million*)

	1938	1946	1947	1948	1949	1950	1951	1952	1953	1954
Stamp Duties	21	36	51	59	53	53	63	53	55	72
Post Office Surplus	11	27	21	16	14	13	10	2	7	6
Others	−13	18	13	15	16	14	18	17	15	17
Total	19	71	85	90	83	80	91	72	77	95

Insurance Contributions. Finally, we must take account of the amounts raised in contributions to National Insurance, which are in effect taxes, falling partly on the workers and partly on employers, who treat them as an element in the cost of production and seek to pass them on in selling prices. The figures are as follows:

TABLE 150

Compulsory Insurance Contributions, 1938 and 1946–54

(*£million*)

1938	1946	1947	1948	1949	1950	1951	1952	1953	1954
109	170	232	335	436	440	452	476	525	532

The almost fivefold rise in this group is of course largely due to post-war legislation setting up a comprehensive 'Beveridge' scheme of Social Insurance (see p. 320). But it represents a further regressive element in the tax structure, as it is levied at a flat rate irrespective of the contributor's income.

Types of Government Expenditure. We have now to consider how much of the proceeds of all these taxes the Government itself expends on goods and services or on grants towards such spending by local authorities, and how much it passes back to the private citizen in the form of social service benefits—which must be to some extent set off against

the taxes which are levied on the main body of consumers. According
to the Blue Book on National Income and Expenditure, the Central
Government and the local authorities between them spent in 1954
approximately £3,100 million on goods and services, as distinct from
what they paid out to be spent by their employees or in 'transfers' of
income, through taxation, from one citizen or body of persons to
another. When the Government levies a tax, or the local authority a
rate, the mere doing of this does not take any goods or services off the
market: the effect is simply to transfer to the State or the local Council
a part of the taxpayers' incomes. The sums thus transferred have still
to be expended. When the State or a local authority uses some of this
purchasing power to buy goods or services, there are so many the less
such things left to be bought, unless indeed the public purchases are
for re-sale. When the money is used to pay public employees for their
work, the effect is similar: those who are employed by public bodies are
not available to work for others, and their labour is abstracted from
other forms of service—though here again we must distinguish between
the public employee who performs a public service that is not sold to
private purchasers and the public employee in, say, the Post Office,
for whose services the consumers are required to pay. The sums paid
for the carriage of letters and other postal services are part of the consumers' purchasing power: they come out of private incomes. So, in
conducting the Post Office, the State does not take any goods or services
off the market and does not need any tax revenue to pay the postal
workers' salaries, unless the Post Office is being run at a loss. As against
this, the salary of a judge or a Civil Servant does represent a form of
public consumption of productive resources. The State 'consumes' their
services, leaving less 'production' available to be consumed by private
persons.

Public Consumption of Goods and Services. Table 151 sets out the

TABLE 151

Current Net Expenditure on Goods and Services by Public Authorities,
1938 and 1945–54

(£million)

	1938	1945	1946	1947	1948
Central Government	461	4,572	1,823	1,220	1,233
Local Authorities	355	484	468	523	528
Total	816	5,056	2,291	1,743	1,761

	1949	1950	1951	1952	1953	1954
Central Government	1,437	1,507	1,814	2,206	2,350	2,312
Local Authorities	540	560	625	687	737	787
Total	1,977	2,067	2,439	2,893	3,083	3,099

total money value of the goods and services that are publicly 'consumed'.

The total rose tenfold for the Central Government between 1938 and 1945, and then fell by more than half in a single year. This was because in time of war the Government was using and 'consuming' the services of millions of persons in the armed forces and was also purchasing and consuming immense quantities of munitions. When hostilities ended and demobilization began, there was a rapid fall in these forms of public consumption; but the total remained more than three times as large as in 1938. It fell further in 1947, but thereafter rose again quite sharply, and by 1954 was five times as large as before the war. The local authorities, on the other hand, expanded their expenditure on goods and services but little—indeed, their *real* expenditure fell—during the war; and the subsequent increase was largely accounted for by rising costs

Public Expenditure on Goods and Services Analysed. In order to make the significance of these figures clear it is necessary to break down the totals and to show for what kinds of purposes the money was spent. It is not practicable to do this with the pre-war figures or with all those relating to later years. Such details as can be supplied are shown in Table 152.

Defence Expenditure. By far the biggest of these items is military expenditure, which in 1946–7 and again in 1954 accounted for more than half the total, after falling to a much smaller proportion between 1948 and 1950. It is re-armament that has been causing the Government to use up so high a proportion of the current national product, much more than the growth of social services. Health and Education together did not in 1954 use up much more than half as much; and all the other elements in the total were relatively small. Government itself is, in terms of the man-power it uses up, a relatively inexpensive service. Arms are the really insatiable devourers of men.

Let it be clear that these figures relate, not to total public spending, but only to such spending as directly uses up productive resources. They include such spending by local authorities, but do not cover spending by public corporations, which sell their wares to the consumers.

Total Government Expenditure. Total public spending, including transfers, is another matter. That of the Central Government and of the National Insurance Funds, taken together, has been as shown in Table 153 (pages 302–3) in the period under review.

Some of these items call for explanation. Subsidies are grants made in order to reduce prices, and also any losses on government trading. 'Other Pensions and Grants to Persons' include non-contributory and war pensions, national assistance, children's allowances, scholarships, and grants to non profit making institutions. 'Grants to Local Authorities' exclude capital grants. 'Grants paid Overseas' consist largely of

TABLE 152

Current Public Expenditure on Goods and Services by Types, 1946–54

(£*million*)

	1946	1947	1948	1949	1950	1951	1952	1953	1954
General Administration:									
Financial	—	—	—	—	54	59	64	68	71
Law and Order:									
Police	—	—	—	—	55	61	67	71	74
Other	—	—	—	—	15	16	16	21	23
Overseas Services	—	—	—	—	39	40	40	38	38
Defence:									
Military	1,560	930	734	762	820	1,090	1,445	1,570	1,520
Civil	—	—	—	—	2	8	22	24	20
Services to Persons:									
Education and Child									
Care	—	—	—	—	272	314	347	370	408
Health	—	—	240	410	458	475	489	501	516
National Insurance, Pen-									
sions and Assistance	—	—	—	—	51	55	61	63	64
Services to Industry and									
Trade:									
Agriculture, Forestry									
and Fishing	—	—	—	—	33	35	37	38	33
Industry and Commerce	—	—	—	—	17	21	20	21	23
Transport	—	—	—	—	12	10	11	10	10
Employment	—	—	—	—	16	17	17	17	17
Environmental Services:									
Roads and Public									
Lighting	—	—	—	—	84	91	100	104	110
Water, Sewerage and									
Refuse Disposal	29	32	34	36	38	40	45	48	51
Town and Country Plan-									
ning and Parks	—	—	—	—	27	31	33	33	34
Fire Service	4	4	11	14	15	16	18	19	19
Land Drainage and Coast									
Protection	—	—	—	—	5	5	6	11	12
Other	—	—	—	—	55	54	54	54	54
Total	1,291	1,743	1,761	1,977	2,067	2,439	2,893	3,083	3,099

colonial grants. 'Transfers to Capital Accounts' include war damage payments, re-funds of excess profits, and compensation payments to doctors and dentists.

Note the reductions in subsidies after 1949, as the Government gradually withdrew or reduced payments designed to keep down the cost of living. Note the rise in National Insurance benefits, despite the continuing low level of unemployment. This rise is due to the introduction of the comprehensive post-war scheme of insurance and to

Total Government Expenditure, in

	1938	1946	1947
Expenditure on Goods and Services	461	1,823	1,220
Subsidies	15	378	460
National Insurance Benefits	82	133	272
Other Pensions and Grants to Persons	41	504	368
Interest on National Debt	205	481	514
Current Grants to Local Authorities	162	244	264
Current Grants paid Overseas	—	105	56
Transfers to Capital Accounts	7	554	391
Total Expenditure	973	4,222	3,545
Surplus before Provision for Depreciation	−108	−865	−103
Total (met out of public revenue)	865	3,357	3,442

increased costs because of rising prices and benefit levels. The fall in other pensions and grants in 1947 and 1948 is a result of the transfer of some of these expenses to National Insurance. National Debt interest, which remained about stable up to 1950, increased thereafter as rates of interest in general were allowed to rise. Transfers to Capital Accounts fell after the main payments for war damage and re-funded excess profits had been made. The final figures 'Surplus' are a balancing item, corresponding to the surplus or deficit in the public accounts. Any deficit was of course financed not out of taxation but by borrowing.

'*Transfer*' *Incomes*.   Of the items in the table, some went to constitute what are commonly called 'transfer incomes', where the State, having raised money by taxes or compulsory contributions, pays it out not as a return for work but as spendable income for which no service is required in return. This category includes on the one hand the interest on the National Debt, which is payable mainly to businesses and institutions or to individual property-owners, and on the other hand pensions, benefits and allowances designed to redress excessive inequalities in the distribution of income. Transfers of the latter type amounted in 1954 to £964 million; but it must be borne in mind that towards this £532 million was received by the Government in national insurance contributions; so that the net relief to the poorer sections of the population was no more than £432 million — not including the actual goods and services provided under the National Health Service or otherwise.

:e Funds, 1938 and 1946–54 (£*million*)

1948	1949	1950	1951	1952	1953	1954
1,233	1,437	1,507	1,814	2,206	2,350	2,312
559	511	461	453	400	345	403
334	379	388	406	473	527	531
332	329	328	337	388	424	433
504	502	501	544	602	627	623
279	287	295	324	363	401	432
42	40	45	49	60	58	53
222	249	161	126	109	127	85
3,505	3,734	3,686	4,053	4,601	4,859	4,872
513	586	691	658	398	193	335
4,018	4,320	4,377	4,711	4,999	5,052	5,207

Total transfers were thus substantially larger, but were partly offset, as we saw on page 296, by the sharp rise in progressive taxation on such things as beer and tobacco.

Expenditure of Local Authorities. To the totals given in the preceding table must be added the total additional current expenditure of local authorities. As these authorities meet a part of their expenditure out of central government grants, this part must be eliminated in order to avoid duplication. The *total* current expenditure of local authorities in 1938 and from 1946 is shown in Table 154 (overleaf).

The sums shown in the last line but one of this table have already been included in the totals of the Central Government's expenditure. The local authorities met the rest of their current costs out of rates or income from property or trading services. The final line shows the amounts provided from these sources.

The Extent of Re-distribution of Incomes. We have now seen in enough detail both how taxes and compulsory contributions are levied and how the proceeds are spent or transferred both by the Central Government and by the local authorities. What we are not in a position to do is to estimate at all precisely to what extent public taxation and expenditure act as a means of re-distributing income between rich and poor. The National Health Service is used to some extent by all classes; and the National Insurance Services now extend in some degree to the whole population. We can, however, make a very rough estimate of the extent

TABLE 154

Total Current Expenditure of Local Authorities, 1938 and 1946–54
(£million)

	1938	1946	1947	1948	1949	1950	1951	1952	1953	1954
On Goods and Services	355	468	523	528	540	560	625	687	733	787
Housing Subsidies	23	9	11	12	13	13	15	19	22	23
Grants to Persons	25	35	42	38	36	39	42	48	49	57
Debt Interest	68	61	61	62	66	73	83	98	116	127
Total Current Expenditure	471	573	637	640	655	685	765	852	920	994
Current Surplus before Depreciation	12	63	58	71	77	79	68	71	109	109
Total	483	636	695	711	732	764	833	923	1,029	1,103
Deduct Government Grants to Local Authorities	−162	−244	−264	−279	−287	−295	−324	−363	−401	−432
Total (Net)	321	392	431	432	445	469	509	560	628	671

to which incomes are transferred through the cash benefit social services, not precisely between rich and poor, but in ways which on the
whole benefit the poor more than the rich. But in order to do even this
we have to decide how to treat the compulsory contributions to National
Insurance, which are paid partly by the employed persons and partly
by their employers. The employed persons' contributions should clearly
be set against the benefits received, as no re-distribution is involved
where the insured are paying for the benefits. The employers' contributions raise more difficult issues. Either they so act as to reduce the
wages paid or they are passed on in higher prices—at any rate under
conditions of full employment. If their effect is to raise prices, they
amount in effect to deductions from the purchasing power of all classes
of consumers, and cannot be regarded as effecting transfers of income
from the rich to the poor. We must therefore deduct the whole of the
contributions from the benefits in order to arrive at the effective transfer
of incomes.

We have, moreover, to reckon with the other main form of income
transfer through taxation—the interest payments on the public debt.
So much of the debt is held by corporate bodies that it is quite impossible to estimate what effects the payment of interest has on the distri-

bution of incomes among individuals or classes. It is, however, clearly more likely to benefit the property-owning sections of the community than the rest.

Total re-distribution of *incomes* between rich and poor through the social services is, then, a good deal less than it is sometimes reckoned to be. It is the case that the poor, being many more than the rich, derive a much larger aggregate benefit from public expenditure on health, education, housing and other social services. But they also pay a much greater aggregate sum in taxation; and it would be an unprofitable exercise to start guessing how their total payments compare with their total receipts. After all, the healthfulness and educational attainments of the poor are advantages not only to the poor but to the whole community.

CHAPTER TWENTY-TWO

ARMAMENTS

EVERYONE is aware that re-armament for the 'cold war' has imposed crushing burdens on the British economy, as on those of many other countries. The British Government's expenditure on the so-called 'Defence' services has not of course reached the fantastic heights to which it rose during the war; but it is immensely higher than it was even during the years of active re-armament before 1939. In order to appreciate the magnitude of the strain it is necessary to carry the comparison back to the beginning of the 1930s, before Nazism had come to power in Germany. In the 1930s military expenditure was as follows:

TABLE 155

Defence Expenditure, 1929–30 to 1937–8

(£million)

1929–30	1930–1	1931–2	1932–3	1933–4	1934–5	1935–6	1936–7	1937–8
113	110	107	103	108	114	137	186	262*

* Including £65 million under the Defence Loans Act of 1937.

By the year 1937–8 expenditure had much more than doubled within a very few years. If it had stayed at the level of 1931–2, just before the Nazi *coup*, nearly £160 million would have been released for other uses.

Defence Expenditure in Recent Years. For the years from 1946 onwards it is more convenient to use the figures of the White Papers and Blue Books on National Income and Expenditure, which relate to calendar years. These show the following totals, omitting the years of actual war:

TABLE 156

Defence Expenditure, 1938 and 1946–54

(£million)

	1938–9	1946	1947	1948	1949	1950	1951	1952	1953	1954
Military	382*	1,560	930	740	770	820	1,090	1,445	1,570	1,520
Civil	—	15	9	4	2	2	136	76	76	77
Total	382	1,575	939	744	772	822	1,226	1,521	1,646	1,597

* Including £128 million under the Defence Loans Act.

In the last full year of war, 1944–5, Defence expenditure reached a total of £5,125 million—which was more than the entire national income before the war. In 1945–6 it dropped to £4,410 million, and in 1946–7 to £1,653 million. In 1948, when it reached its lowest point, it was still almost twice as large as in 1938–9, and seven times as large as in the early 1930s. From that point it started to rise, fairly slowly at first and then at immense speed from 1951 onwards. By 1953 it was more than twice as large as it had been in 1949 and more than four times what it had been in 1938–9. That is to say, it had risen fourteen-fold since the early 1930s. As a proportion of gross national income, it was about $7\frac{1}{2}$ per cent in 1938–9 and about $10\frac{1}{2}$ per cent in 1953. There was a small decrease in 1954.

The Effects of Re-armament. Every country spends the major part of its national income on current consumption, and has then to meet the cost of replacing its worn-out or obsolete equipment in order to keep its productive power intact. Added to these claims are the need for new investment to increase productive power—and the cost of armaments. As people do not willingly reduce their consumption there is direct competition between the claims of investment and those of the armed forces. In the circumstances that existed after 1945 this competition was exceptionally severe. A high rate of investment was urgently needed to make good war damage, especially to houses and other buildings and to merchant shipping, and to re-equip industry for its post-war tasks. Re-armament expenditure struck directly at the funds which would normally have been devoted to investment and made it necessary to take special measures to restrict consumption, so as to prevent investment from being all but wiped out. This need lay at the back of the Government's repeated appeals for wage-restraint and dividend-limitation; and the restrictions on private expenditure needed to be particularly severe because public expenditure on consumption through the social services was being rapidly increased.

Moreover, the heavy expenditure on arms required the services of just those branches of industry which were most needed for other purposes—for re-equipping industry and for re-expanding export trade to find the means of buying indispensable imports. When, under American pressure, the scale of projected defence expenditure was twice drastically increased in 1950 and 1951, it soon became apparent that the additional strain was past all bearing. The choice had to be made between letting exports fall, with disastrous effects on the balance of payments, and slowing down the projected rate of expenditure on arms by spreading the expansion over a longer period. The Conservatives had reluctantly to accept the latter alternative when they were back in power because any other course would have meant immediate disaster. But even when this had been done, the actual expenditure on the armed services remained a crippling burden on the whole economy.

Re-armament and Manpower. Nor is the cost of armaments limited to the money expense. They take men away from useful production or service at the most important period of their lives, interrupting their training for civilian employments and often getting them into bad ways. 'Scrounging' has always been the vice of armies; and, except in time of actual warfare, there is little about military service to encourage the civic virtues—except in the eyes of those who regard enforced discipline and passive obedience as virtuous forms of behaviour. In 1938, when military conscription was already in force, the total strength of the armed forces and their auxiliary services was 382,000, including about 1,000 women. In 1953 it was 866,000—an increase of 126 per cent. By 1956, it was a good deal lower—773,000 in March, with another 6,000 on release leave but not yet back in civil employment. The women numbered 17,000 out of this total.

Thus, enough workers to man a major industry—for example, the coal mines or the railways—are being kept out of such employment by the claims of military service. This is not the place to argue whether Governments have been right in devoting to warlike purposes so large a share in this country's limited resources of man-power and productive capacity. That is a political issue which falls outside the scope of the present volume. It is, however, pertinent to point out how great is the burden which the 'cold war' imposes on us. It hampers industrial recovery; it limits both production and consumption; and last but not least, it is the most formidable obstacle in the way of our playing our part in the great 'War upon Want', in which we should be taking an important place in furthering productive advances in the less developed countries—above all, in the colonies still under our rule. Our capacity to invest—or to make gifts—for these purposes is disastrously limited by the strain on our balance of payments that the 'cold war' imposes. Could we rid ourselves of this heavy burden, the 'War upon Want' would have the foremost legitimate claim on the productive power that would thus be set free.

CHAPTER TWENTY-THREE

THE SOCIAL SERVICES

THE more the public authorities spend on social services, other than cash benefits, the smaller will the immediate incomes of the private consumers tend to be. This does not apply to cash benefits, which transfer purchasing power from one person to another, but do not use up goods and services, beyond the costs of administration, so as to leave less to be consumed according to the citizen's personal choice. But it does apply to all services that use up productive resources. However well the money is spent, it has to come out of what would otherwise be available to increase private purchasing power.

Social Services and Freedom of Choice. Therefore, if we consider that on the whole freedom of choice is a good thing, we should always be asking how far it is desirable to push social service expenditure on goods and services at the cost of limiting the consumers' freedom. Of course, this does not mean that the social services which have this effect are even a necessary evil; but it does mean that all such expenditure needs strong reasons to justify it, and that there is a danger that ardent social reformers may wish to carry it too far. It is not enough for a social service to be a good thing in itself: to be justified, it has to promise better results than leaving the money it costs in private hands, after making allowance for the loss of consumers' freedom it involves.

How Much Communal Living? Of course, this view can be questioned. It can be argued, for example, that we should be better off if we lived much more communally than we do, taking our meals at public messes, residing in communal buildings, and having our children looked after and brought up communally rather than in private houses. In present-day Britain, however, most people certainly do not wish to live in that way. Most married couples prefer small houses, if they can get them, to flats, and, though they like going to a restaurant well enough now and then, prefer to take most of their meals at home rather than at a communal dining-hall with their neighbours. There has indeed been a great growth in recent years in the number of industrial and business canteens at which employees can get their midday meals on working days; but the reason for their spread is much less a desire to feed in company than the greater difficulties of travel between home and work-place. The same reason partly underlies the development of school meals, though in this case there is more weight behind the desire to ensure that the children are properly nourished—which cannot be guaranteed even where the parents can afford it. Moreover, in the case of factory and other canteens, people pay for the food they consume, and do not receive it as a 'free' social service—though many of them may in fact get it at less than the full cost.

Some day, perhaps, people in general will wish to live more in common than they do now. But there are few signs of such a desire—which can indeed hardly develop far in a society divided into classes and groups whose social habits differ as widely as ours, both in the meals taken and the times they are taken at and in countless other respects. Much life in common implies a society without such divisions, which the development of the Welfare State has so far done nothing to abolish, though it has narrowed some of the gaps—especially in the matter of clothing and mass-entertainment. The British are an indivi-dualistic and a 'family' people, traditionally favourable to the economy of the small private household and preferring to spend 'their own' money to having it spent for them—unless for very cogent reasons. The social services have expanded, not because the ordinary citizen likes collective spending for its own sake, but because their absence was felt to involve intolerable social evils; and their development has taken largely the form of cash benefits rather than of benefits in kind because the recipients in general prefer the money, which they can spend as they please, to goods and services chosen for them, whether they prefer them or not.

The Cost of Social Services.   In the financial year 1953–4—the latest for which full particulars are available, public authorities, national and local, in Great Britain spent £1,926 million on the social services, in-cluding health, nutrition, housing, education and child care as well as national insurance and assistance, family allowances, and pensions of all sorts except those of public servants. Of this total, nearly half—£941 million—was paid out in grants to persons and thus involved mainly income transfers and not public consumption of goods and services. More than £98 million went on administration: the rest—£887 million—covered those services which take the form of benefits in kind. Among the cash benefits the highest cost was that of pensions. The figures for both types from 1949–50 are as shown in Table 157.

The expenditure on the second group of services includes some cash grants to persons, but consists mainly of services in kind. Total cash grants to persons were £700·4 million in 1949–50, £712·5 million in 1950–1, £752 million in 1951–2, £896·1 million in 1952–3, and as we saw, £940·9 in 1953–4.

TABLE 157

Current Public Expenditure on Social Services, Great Britain

(£million)

	1949–50	1950–1	1951–2	1952–3	1953–4
National Insurance (total)	403·1	406·2	431·0	512·0	539·6
Retirement Pensions and Widows over 60	248·3	247·9	274·1	314·4	332·9
Other Widows' Benefits and Guardians' Allowances	22·0	22·3	24·5	28·5	30·9
Sickness Benefits	65·6	68·6	63·3	79·2	85·0
Maternity Benefits	8·5	8·6	8·4	8·7	10·5
Death Grants	1·6	2·6	2·5	2·7	2·8
Unemployment Benefits	14·4	12·6	11·4	22·5	22·1
Industrial Injuries Benefits	12·1	14·2	16·3	21·3	24·8
Administration	25·8	25·0	27·1	30·4	30·6
Extended Unemployment Benefit	5·5	5·2	4·1	4·9	—
Non-contributory Old Age Pensions	27·0	25·0	23·8	22·6	20·3
National Assistance	63·0	75·6	88·7	115·9	121·3
War and Other Service Pensions	81·8	79·1	77·5	84·7	84·3
Family Allowances	62·7	63·7	65·0	89·2	105·7
Total of above Cash Benefits excluding Administration	612·5	625·4	674·1	794·6	—
Rehabilitation Services	1·7	2·8	3·4	2·8	3·1
Nutrition Services	62·7	60·9	68·1	78·1	75·9
Education Services	282·1	295·8	341·9	368·2	389·6
Child Care Services	13·6	16·6	18·6	20·2	21·1
National Health Services	406·3	434·7	446·2	487·0	470·3
Housing (net) Services	67·6	70·7	74·5	84·8	94·8
Total of above	834·0	881·5	952·7	1,014·1	1,054·8

National Insurance Payments. In the first group, a large part of the cost of National Insurance services was, of course, met out of contributions: government grants to the Insurance Funds were as follows:

TABLE 158

Government Grants to Insurance Funds

(£million)

	1949–50	1950–1	1951–2	1952–3	1953–4
National Insurance Fund	135·7	139·8	104·5	65·3	70·0
Industrial Injuries Fund	6·0	6·0	6·0	6·2	6·6

National Assistance. A large part of the expenditure on National

Assistance went to old people, by way of supplement to pensions. Here are the main heads for this and other services.

TABLE 159

National Assistance Payments

(*£million*)

Grants to:	1949–50	1950–1	1951–2	1952–3	1953–4
Old Persons	21·8	28·3	33·0	48·2	51·7
Unemployed Persons	4·5	5·3	5·0	7·7	8·0
Sick Persons	11·6	13·5	16·9	20·8	21·1
Others	11·3	13·3	16·0	19·3	19·1
Administration	3·5	3·8	4·4	4·9	5·5
Grants for Local Authority Services and their Administrations	0·4	0·4	0·4	0·5	0·5
Total	53·1	64·6	75·7	101·4	105·9

The Problem of Pensions. The National Insurance Funds, thanks to low rates of unemployment, have been building up substantial reserves. The main Insurance Scheme opened in 1948 with a balance of £801 million taken over from previous schemes and by the end of the financial year 1952–3 held in its central Reserve Fund more than £1,090 million, besides an accumulated balance in its current fund amounting to nearly £308 million; and the Industrial Injuries Fund held a further balance of £96 million. Vast though these sums may seem, they are not enough to meet the claims that will fall on the main fund as the number of old persons increases and as more persons become entitled to benefits from 1959 onwards. Faced by the prospect of sharply rising costs, the Phillips Committee proposed in 1955 to raise the standard ages for receipt of state pensions by three years, to 68 for men and 63 for women; and a variety of other proposals have been put forward, including reduced rates of pension during the first so many years of receipt, differentiations between those who retire from work and those who remain in full-time or part-time employment, and so on. But, heavy as the cost of pensions threatens to be, there seems to be no good reason for denying them to anyone who is or will become entitled to them under the existing law, or for failing to adjust them to changing costs of living. If by improved medical and other services old people are enabled to live longer, the community is under an obligation to enable them to live tolerably well; and it would be quite unfair to penalize the old simply because they are coming to be a higher proportion of the total population.

In March 1955, a Special Correspondent of *The Times*, in discussing the Report of the Phillips Committee, made certain calculations of the probable future cost of old age pensions. The exact cost cannot of course be estimated, above all because it is unknown what will happen to the cost of living. Nor is it possible to estimate how large a proportion of national income old age pensions will be, even in terms of fixed prices for the means of life. The following calculations were made with no allowance for price changes in estimating either the national income or the probable cost of pensions. They are alternatives, based on different sets of assumptions. On Assumption A. the average worker's *real* output and income will be 25 per cent higher in 1979 than they were in 1953. Pensions are taken at the new rates announced in 1955. On Assumption B. *real* output and income will be up by 50 per cent, and insurances and assistance payments—and contributions—will be up by 25 per cent. Moreover, both Assumptions include estimates of the cost not only of state old age pensions but also of superannuation payments made under private schemes. These latter, largely because of their favourable treatment under income tax law, have been spreading very rapidly in recent years, and are continuing to spread. Assumption A. takes them as likely to cover 10 million workers by 1979, whereas Assumption B. raises the coverage to 13,750,000.

The estimates rest on the calculation that between 1953 and 1979 the number of potential old age pensioners will have risen by 38 per cent, and that the actual number of National Insurance pensions will be up by 76 per cent because of the inclusion of classes of persons not at present eligible, but due to become so under the existing law. These figures rest on the assumption that the actual average rate of retirement will remain as it was in 1953. On these alternative Assumptions the *Times* Correspondent made the following estimates of prospective costs:

TABLE 160

Prospective Cost of Pensions and Superannuation Benefits for Old People in 1979 compared with Actual Cost in 1953 (£*million*)

	1953	1979 Assumption A.	Assumption B.
Total Outlay:			
National Insurance Pension	334	800	1,000
Superannuation Schemes	144	600	950
National Assistance	72	40	50
Tobacco Tokens	14	30	30
Total	564	1,470	2,030
Proportion Falling on:			
Taxes or Rates—N.I.	107	460	575
Superannuation	105	190	255
Assistance and Tobacco	86	70	80
Total	298	720	910

Thus, before another twenty-five years are out, social provision for the needs of old age, including both state and occupational pensions, will be absorbing anything from just under £1,500 million to more than £2,000 million, according to the assumption on which the estimate is based. On the larger assumption, occupational pensions will by then be costing not much less than state pensions; and a large part of the cost of these two will be falling on public funds as long as employers' contributions to such schemes continue to be allowed as costs and thus escape taxation. On the other hand, a large part of the cost of state pensions will continue to be paid for, not out of taxation, but by compulsory contributions, which are in effect a poll tax entirely unrelated to ability to pay. The total burden falling on taxation within twenty-five years will have risen from under £300 million to well over £700 million and perhaps to more than £900 million.

The Burden of Old Age. In 1953 about 4¼ per cent of the total of personal incomes was transferred to the aged by means of state and occupational pensions combined. By 1979 it seems likely that state insurance pensions alone will take 4½ per cent of the enlarged total of personal incomes, whatever it may be, and that the total cost of state and occupational pensions will have increased to 8 or 9 per cent. This is the approximate magnitude of the relative expenditure on maintenance of the old Great Britain must expect to face unless it alters its policy to their disadvantage. Stated in this way, the prospective burden looks a good deal less formidable than when one looks only at the sums of money likely to be needed. It has, however, to be borne in mind that the money cost will be higher if prices continue to rise—but also that this may not involve an increase in the *real* cost; for higher prices will swell the national money income as well as the social service budget.

Occupational Pensions. In view of the above figures it is obviously unrealistic to consider state pensions, financed out of contributions and taxes, without considering also the huge sums that are being piled up as reserves in private funds for occupational pension schemes. The growth of this type of pension has been very rapid indeed in recent years. This type of pension began mainly in the Civil Service. Before 1939 such schemes covered only about 1,500,000 persons—chiefly public employees. By 1953 they covered about 2,500,000 public and about 5 million other employed persons. Under many of these schemes pensions began at lower ages than under the state scheme; and of course most of those who are eligible for them will draw state pensions as well from the statutory ages. One effect of these occupational pensions is to encourage early retirement, both before and at 65. At the latter age, for men, the rate of retirement is much higher in occupations with such schemes than in other occupations. If we wish to encourage more persons to remain at work beyond the state pensionable age, in order to spread the task of production over a greater number of people, we are certainly not going about the matter the right way in making it financially easy for business firms to start their own superannuation schemes.

The Age of Retirement.   It is true that under the state scheme a person who stays on at work instead of taking his pension at the statutory age becomes entitled to a rather higher pension when he does retire. This costs the State and the Insurance Fund nothing; for the cost is covered by what is saved in payments to those who do not retire. There are, however, a good many people who think it a mistake to make the receipt of state pensions depend on actual retirement, or to make deductions where persons over the retiring age continue to work part-time. The old person, it is urged, should receive the state pension as a right, whether he or she retires or prefers to go on working. It does not appear that the increments that can be got by staying at work after the standard retiring age have any appreciable effect on the proportion who do retire; and it is doubtful whether payment of the full pension irrespective of retirement would have much effect either. The Phillips Committee, as we saw, favoured raising the minimum age for receipt of pensions by three years for both men and women. Others have suggested that the ages should remain as they are, but that state pensions should be paid at lower rates to men between 65 and, say, 70 and to women between 60 and, say, 65; while yet others urge two rates of pension, one for those who retire and another for those who remain at work. All these proposals are designed to reduce the cost falling on state funds; for it is recognized that it will not be easy to put most of the increase on to compulsory contributions. But it is also argued that pensions should be withdrawn or reduced in respect of those still capable of work.

Is it, however, really necessary to economize at the pensioners' expense? It is indeed highly desirable to help those who wish to stay at work, and are capable of doing so, not to retire prematurely But, as most people will agree, the right way of achieving this is to take more steps to provide jobs old people are capable of doing, rather than to mulct them in order to drive them into carrying on with work which may be unsuitable and quite possibly detrimental to their well-being. It is not as if Great Britain were threatened with a sharp fall in the proportion of the population belonging to the groups of 'working age'. As we saw (on p. 45), this is not the case, and will not be for some time to come. As against more old people there are likely to be relatively fewer children than in the past, especially now that the post-war bulge in the birth-rate appears to be at an end. It is for the old people's own sakes, and not mainly in order to save public money, that steps should be taken to render it easier for those who wish to stay at work after reaching the standard retiring age.

The Basis of Occupational Pension Schemes. In considering occupational pensions it is necessary to bear in mind that at present they benefit most those groups of the working population that are relatively well-paid—especially public and other salaried employees and the employees of relatively prosperous industries and businesses. As they spread, this may be less the case; but it is also a very important fact that, whereas state pensions are paid at flat rates, irrespective of previous incomes, occupational schemes are almost always based either on average earnings over the period of employment or on the earnings of the final years of work. The latter type, based on final earnings, of course works out much more favourably than the former in periods of rising prices: so that Civil Servants, for example, fare much better than university teachers under the existing arrangements. But it has to be remembered that under both types of scheme the State is in effect subsidizing through tax remissions the higher pensions at higher rates and is thus benefiting the better-off partly at the expense of the worse-off as well as of those who get no occupational pensions at all, but have to contribute more to taxation in order to make up for the remissions.[1]

National Insurances. National Insurance, which began in 1911 as a social service confined to the working class and not even covering the dependants of employed workers, has now become universal. Not only all employed persons, irrespective of the size of their incomes, but also the self-employed and the non-employed pay compulsory weekly contributions, though not at the same rates, and become entitled to benefits, the range of which differs from one of these groups to another. In the case of employed persons the employer also contributes and of course charges up his contributions as a trading expense. These various contributions provide the bulk of the Insurance Funds' income; but a contribution from the Exchequer is added to them and, partly offsetting this, the Insurance Fund makes a contribution towards the cost of the National Health Service. In 1952–3 the Exchequer grant to the main National Insurance Fund was about £65·3 million, and to the special Industrial Injuries Fund £6·2 million. In the same year the National Insurance Fund paid about £41 million towards the cost of the National Health Service, and the following year £41·2 million. Thus, the net contribution of the State to National Insurance is quite small: the main cost falls on the insured contributors and on the firms which employ those of them who are 'employed persons'. On the other hand the bulk of the cost of the National Health Service is borne by the Exchequer, which also meets the entire cost of National Assistance services and of statutory Children's Allowances—except those payable as benefits under National Insurance.

[1] See on this whole question of the social effects of occupational pension schemes the excellent Fabian Research study, *New Pensions for the Old*, by Brian Abel-Smith and Peter Townshend.

Rates of Contribution to National Insurance. National Insurance contributions, and also benefits, are at flat rates for each category of contributors, whatever the size of their normal incomes. They differ for employed, self-employed, and non-employed persons, and also for men and women and for adults and juveniles. Here are the rates of contribution as they stood in the middle of 1955:

TABLE 161

National Insurance Weekly Contributions, 1955

	Men over 18	Males under 18	Women over 18	Girls under 18
A. Employers' Contributions (in respect of employed persons only)	6/–	3/6	4/11	2/10
B. Insured Persons' Contributions:				
Employed Persons	6/9	3/11	5/6	3/3
Self-employed Persons	8/5	4/10	7/2	4/3
Non-employed Persons	6/6	3/9	5/2	3/1

The above amounts include the following contributions to the Industrial Injuries Fund, in respect of employed persons only:

Employers	6d.	3d.	4d.	2d.
Employed Persons	5d.	3d.	3d.	2d.

Married women, even if they are at work, are not required to pay contributions except for the Industrial Injuries Scheme, though they are entitled to certain benefits on account of their husbands' payments. They can, however, if employed or self-employed, elect to pay at the regular rates in order to draw more and larger benefits in their own right.

Contributions are usually paid by means of stamps stuck to the insured person's insurance card. Self-employed and non-employed persons are required to stamp their own cards week by week. In the case of employed persons, however, the stamps are affixed by the employer as a statutory duty, and he deducts the employee's contribution from the wage or salary paid. Big firms, however, can arrange to pay by other methods, which save the labour of a great deal of stamp-licking; but they too deduct the employee's contribution from his wage or salary.

As we saw, National Insurance contributions brought in a total revenue of £457·4 million in 1952–3, as compared with an Exchequer contribution of £72 million. Employers' contributions were £218 million in 1952 and £244 million in 1953—say, about £225 million for 1952–3. The remainder—say, £232 million—came from the insured persons themselves, and thus involved not a transfer of income from class to class, but only a re-distribution among the contributors themselves, irrespective of their several abilities to pay. The employee's contribution is in effect a poll-tax, levied on both rich and poor at the same rates within each group of contributors. It is thus a highly regressive and unfair kind of tax, unless the National Insurance Scheme is regarded as a kind of service for which the recipient is expected to pay almost at the market rate. Of course, some insured persons draw out much more than they pay, and others much less. There are many whom it would not pay to insure unless the State compelled them, and others on whom the scheme confers an undoubted benefit. But this depends mainly not on their incomes but on their health and expectation of life and on their liability to unemployment. The scheme, as far as it depends on the insured persons' contributions, is a vast arrangement for compelling them to meet collectively the cost of their own social security.

Employers' Contributions. The employer's contribution raises more difficult issues; for who really pays it? It is a cost of production, which the employer in profit-making business will seek to pass on to his customers. It is also a tax on employment, which adds to the cost of employing labour and may be reflected in the payment of a reduced wage or salary. If it is passed on to consumers, it raises the cost of living and falls on the general public very roughly in proportion to their consumption. If it causes lower wages or salaries to be paid, it becomes in effect an additional poll-tax on the employed persons. It is impossible to state dogmatically which of these two things will chiefly happen: it will depend on such factors as the state of employment and the state of demand, which vary from time to time and from case to case. Of course, employers who employ not for profit but for direct service cannot pass on the cost to the public: they must either recover it by paying lower wages or meet it themselves. It seems most plausible, if a choice has to be made, to regard the employers' contribution as mainly a deduction from wages and salaries and, on this basis, to argue that most of the cost of National Insurance is borne by the insured contributors.

Insurance Benefits. What are the benefits that insured persons receive in return for these payments? Broadly speaking, employed persons are entitled to any or all of the benefits provided under the Acts. Self-employed persons do not get either unemployment or industrial injury benefits, but are entitled to all the rest. Non-employed persons get the same benefits as the self-employed, except that they do not get either sickness benefit or a maternity allowance. Eligibility for benefits depends, however, except in the cases of industrial injury benefit and guardian's allowances, on the number of contributions actually paid by the insured person in question—on his 'contribution record'. Benefits are paid in various ways. Unemployment Benefit has usually to be collected personally at the local Employment Exchange. Sickness and Injury Benefits, and also Maternity, Home Confinement and Death Grants are usually paid through the post in the form of drafts cashable at any Post Office. Other benefits, including Retirement Pensions, are usually paid by means of Order Books with coupons cashable weekly at a particular Post Office chosen by the recipient. Persons in National Health Service hospitals, who get their maintenance free of charge, have their benefits reduced after the first eight weeks, in most cases to 7s. 6d. a week after 12 months in the hospital and by smaller amounts in the meantime.

Sickness Benefits.   Apart from Pensions and from benefits under the Industrial Injuries Scheme, the most important benefits are Sickness Benefit and Unemployment Benefit. Sickness Benefit is at the rate of 40s. a week for both adult men and unmarried women from 18, *plus* 25s. for each adult dependant, 11s. 6d. for the first dependent child, and 3s. 6d. for other dependent children. These other children are, of course, also entitled to Children's Allowances apart from the National Insurance Scheme. *Insured* married women get 25s., but may get 40s. if they have invalid husbands or are living apart from their husbands, and not getting financial help from them. Insured persons under 18 get 23s. a week, unless they have adult dependants—in which case they are entitled to 40s. *plus* the dependant's allowance.

Unemployment Benefit.   Unemployment Benefit is at the same rates as Sickness Benefit, except that an *insured* married woman gets 30s. instead of 25s. a week. Both benefits are available only to those who have paid at least 26 contributions since they last became insured, and the rates of benefit are reduced for all who have paid fewer than 50 contributions during the previous contributor year, and nothing is payable if there have been fewer than 26 such contributions. Sickness Benefit is payable for an unlimited period while the illness continues, provided the insured person has paid in all 156 or more contributions; but Unemployment Benefit is limited in normal cases to 180 weekdays, though it can be extended to as much as 492 days for persons with a very high record of contributions in relation to benefits previously drawn. Further Unemployment Benefit becomes payable only after payment of 13 further contributions while in employment. Insured persons can receive Unemployment Benefit only while they are fit and available for work; and those who have lost work through a trade dispute may be disqualified, as may, for up to 6 weeks, anyone who loses a job by his own fault or leaves one without proper cause, or anyone who refuses either a suitable job that is offered or a course of training.

Supplementation.   The availability of Unemployment Benefit is thus a good way short of complete; and those who are disqualified can get public help only by applying for National Assistance. However, when employment is 'full', or nearly so, the great majority of unemployed persons are entitled to benefit at the standard rate and can in cases of proven need seek supplementation from the Assistance Board. This provision for supplementary payments has become in practice much more important than was intended when the National Insurance Act became law. Lord Beveridge, in his celebrated Report on Social Insurance, had recommended a standard rate of Disability (i.e. Sickness or Unemployment) Benefit of 24s. for a single person and 40s. for a married couple at an assumed cost of living level 25 per cent above that of 1938. Actually, in mid-1955, the official cost of living index was 47 per cent above that of June 1947. As we saw (see p. 219), no direct comparison is possible on the basis of the official figures between 1947 and any previous year; but the old official index put the increase between September 1939 and 1947 at 31 per cent—which was generally regarded as a serious under-estimate. Putting these figures together would bring the total rise from 1939 to 1955 up to about 93 per cent, which is clearly much too little. Even on the inadequate basis, the Beveridge rates would need to be raised by at least 55 per cent: so that his 24s. would become 37s. This, however, would be much too little to meet the rise in living costs of those at the lower levels; and the present 40s., or 65s. for a married couple, is all too little for tolerable maintenance. In June 1955, minimum rates for the lowest grades of adult males in trades regulated by Statutory Wages Councils (see p. 243) were in many cases over £6 a week and practically nowhere under £5 10s. This helps to explain why supplementation by the Assistance Board has proved necessary in so many cases; but there are many who do not get or claim supplementation and manage to exist on the statutory benefits only by using up small savings or getting help from relatives or other private sources. Still worse is the plight of those who are not qualified to receive benefit at the full rates.

Maternity and Widows' Benefits. The remaining benefits under the National Insurance Acts include a *Maternity Grant* of £10, a *Home Confinement Grant* of £4 for babies born at home or outside a public institution, and a *Maternity Allowance* of 40s. a week, usually for 18 weeks starting eleven weeks before the expected confinement. This last is payable only to employed women who are *personally* insured in addition to their husbands. Here again there are conditions about the contributions that must have been paid to entitle a mother to claim these benefits. Next come *Widows' Benefits*—a *Widow's Allowance* of 55s. a week for 13 weeks only, plus supplements of 11s. 6d. for the first and 3s. 6d. for other dependent children. Widows with dependent children, after exhausting this allowance, can draw *Widowed Mothers' Allowance* at 51s. 6d. for the widow and the first dependent child, *plus* 3s. 6d. for further dependent children; and in this case there is no time limit. If, however, the widow is at work, her allowance is reduced by 1s. for each 1s. earned over 60s., subject to a minimum payment of 40s. a week. There is also a *Widow's Pension* of 40*s*. payable only where the widow is unable to support herself and after she has exhausted her claim on the foregoing benefits. This too is reduced by 1*s*. for every 1*s*. of earnings over 40*s*. a week. In certain cases widows who are not eligible for the pension can draw a basic pension of 10*s*. a week, but only if they were married before July 1948 and if their husbands were insured under the old Insurance Scheme. Widows' benefit rights depend on the payments made by their husbands, and can be reduced or disallowed where these fall below certain fixed levels.

Next comes *Guardian's Allowance* at 18*s*. a week for persons who take charge of the maintenance of orphan children at least one of whose parents was insured. No Family Allowance is payable in respect of children on whose behalf this benefit is being paid. Then there is *Death Grant* at £20 in the case of adults and less for children, with reduced rates or no payment at all for elderly persons born before certain dates. Death Grant is payable to the survivor in the case of a married couple, or where there is no survivor to whoever bears the funeral expenses.

Retirement Pensions. Finally there are *Retirement Pensions*, of which something has been said already (see p. 315)—the least satisfactory and yet the most expensive element in the entire scheme. These pensions are payable at 65 for men and at 60 for women, but only on condition of retirement from regular work. At over 70 for men and over 65 for women, pensions become payable without the retirement condition. Wives who are not personally insured are eligible for retirement pensions as well as those who are personally insured. By continuing at work between 65 (60 for women) and 70 (65 for women) higher pensions can be earned. The standard rates of pension are £2 a week for a single person and £3 5*s*. for a married couple: the maximum that can be earned by staying at work till 70 (or 65 for women) is £2 15*s*. for single persons and £4 10*s*. for married couples. If both husband and wife are personally insured, the standard rate for the two becomes £4, or if they work till 70 and 65 respectively £5 10*s*. These Retirement Pensions are not open either to persons who were already over pensionable age in July 1948 or to late-age entrants to insurance.

There are provisions for the drawing of Retirement Pensions by persons who continue to do a limited amount of paid work. The pension is reduced for men between 65 and 70 and for women between 60 and 65 by 1*s*. for each 1*s*. earned above 40*s*. in a week.

Industrial Injury Benefits. Industrial Injury Benefits come under a separate scheme, though the contributions to both are collected together (see p. 317). *Injury Benefit* required by reason of work accident or industrial disease is at the rate of 67*s*. 6*d*. for an adult, plus 25*s*. for an adult dependant, 11*s*. 6*d*. for the first dependent child, and 3*s*. 6*d*. for other dependent children. For young persons it is 50*s*. 8*d*. at 17 and

33s. 9d. for those under 17. It is payable for a maximum of 26 weeks, after which the insured person, if still disabled, can fall back on Sickness Benefit. There is also Disablement Benefit, payable only after the 26 weeks, and depending on the degree of the disablement. The rate for adults varies from 67s. 6d. for total down to 13s. 6d. for 20 per cent disablement, the degree being assessed by a medical board. To this benefit certain supplements can be added in special cases—for example in case of permanent unemployability a supplement of 40s. a week, *plus* allowances for dependants, a Constant Attendance Allowance, up to a maximum of 30s. a week, and a Special Hardship Allowance up to 27s. 6d. a week. There is also a Hospital Treatment Allowance, which raises the benefit to 100 per cent while the injured person is in hospital. The scheme also includes a Widow's Benefit for the widows of persons dying as a result of industrial accident or disease. This is at the rate of 55s. a week for 13 weeks and thereafter at rates varying from 45s. to 20s. a week. In addition, Dependants' Allowances are payable in respect of the children of such victims of industrial casualty.

Children's Allowances.   This is the wide range of benefits payable under the National Insurance Acts as they stood in mid-1955. Outside the Insurance Scheme are Children's Allowances for families with more than one dependent child, at the rate of 8s. a week. These are usually payable by order books, cashable weekly at a Post Office. National Assistance too stands outside the Insurance Scheme, and so does the National Health Service, except for the payments made towards its cost out of the National Insurance Fund (see p. 316). War Pensions too are administered entirely apart from National Insurance.

The 'Five Giants'.   Regarding the Insurance Scheme as a whole, the first thing to be noted is the vast improvement over the conditions that existed in the 1930s. Although Lord Beveridge's proposals have not been fully implemented, his general position—insistence that the social services should be so designed as to provide as nearly as possible complete minimum protection against what he called the 'five giants'— has been broadly accepted as the basis of post-war legislation. In the 1930s Health Insurance both failed to cover the dependants of insured workers and provided benefits admittedly quite inadequate for subsistence; and there was no National Health Service providing free consultant services and hospital treatment and maintenance. Unemployment Insurance, though it had already been extended to include dependants' allowances and had burst its financial banks to throw off the unavoidable auxiliary of Unemployment Assistance, was still hedged round with conditions which seriously limited its scope and drove most of the long-unemployed sooner or later under the irksome rule of the family means test. Pensions on a contributory basis were available only for employed persons; and the non-contributory Old Age Pension at

70 was admittedly quite inadequate in amount. There was no Industrial Injuries Scheme—only a most unsatisfactory system of Workmen's Compensation administered by the Insurance Companies, which resulted in injured persons being constantly driven into accepting lump-sum settlements greatly to their disadvantage. Public Assistance, to which great numbers of the sick and the partially disabled, and also not a few of the long-unemployed and their families, were compelled to resort, was still under local authority administration, with conditions varying greatly from area to area, and a good deal of the old 'poor law' stigma still remaining, though it had been nominally removed. The evils of the pre-war structure were heavily accentuated by the severe depression in certain areas, where large numbers of workers barely subsisted year after year without hope or prospect of a job. But, apart from this aggravation of its evils, it was fundamentally wrong and muddled because there was no general structure of social security: only a hotch-potch of separate schemes which fell a long way short of covering the ground.

The Post-war Structure of Social Services.   The new post-war structure is not fully unified. Children's Allowances are still mainly administered apart from National Insurance, though they are now in the hands of the same Ministry. What used to be the Unemployment Assistance Board has broadened out into the National Assistance Board, covering a much wider field; but the Assistance Scheme is still separate from the Insurance Scheme and has been forced by the inadequacy of the latter to assume much wider functions than were intended when the new scheme was drawn up. The National Health Service too is quite apart from the Insurance Scheme, and under a separate Ministry. In general, however, the post-war scheme does at least make sense and does set out to cover most of the basic needs. Its main weaknesses are the inadequacy in many cases of the fixed benefits and pensions and of the statutory Children's Allowances, the regressive nature of the tax-contributions on which the insurance part of it is based, and the absence of any clear principle determining how much of the total cost is to be met by contributions from insured persons and employers and how much out of general taxation.

Is the Insurance Method the Best?   The merit of the insurance method is generally held to be that it confers statutory rights to benefits upon the insured and does not leave them at the mercy of changing ministerial or administrative decisions. This advantage could, however, be preserved without the necessity of so regressive a form of taxation as the present contributory system involves—for example, by instituting a Fund based on a graduated social security tax on incomes. As we saw, at present neither do contributions bear any relation to ability to pay, nor benefits any relation to more than absolutely basic needs. Under some foreign systems, including the German, both contributions and benefits vary with the normal earnings of the insured; and thus families accustomed to higher standards of living both pay and receive more. It has often been proposed that this system should be adopted in Great Britain, for the services financed mainly out of contributions; but there is everything in favour of treating really basic needs as having a prior claim and for making sure these needs are met before attempting to provide more for those who are normally better paid. Moreover, it would be hardly practicable to introduce discrimination into those services which are financed out of general taxation; and this would mean that those who paid more and got more under the insurance schemes would experience a sudden drop when they had to go over to National Assistance. It is no doubt the case that under the present system those who are normally better paid suffer a sharper fall in income when they fall into unemployment or disability; but this seems preferable to failure to make adequate provision for universally basic needs.

The Rent Problem.   A special difficulty does however arise over rents, which vary greatly from family to family both according to the quality of the accommodation and according to inequalities produced largely by rent control. The question of rent allowances in determining needs has been the most difficult of all for the Assistance Board in its task of supplementing social security payments to bring incomes up to a level adequate to cover basic needs. It would be quite impracticable to require highly rented applicants for help to move into cheaper quarters—which most of them would be unable to find; but to fix rent allowances at a common basic level would mean that the highly rented families would get too little to cover even their most essential other needs. The problem is indeed insoluble until it becomes possible for rents to recover a nearer approximation to the quality of the accommodation, and for the scandal of over-rented 'furnished' accommodation to be put an end to; and even if this were done it would still be impracticable to compel applicants for assistance to move into the cheapest dwellings, or to standardize rent allowances completely without leaving many families short of the incomes requisite for meeting basic needs.

Other Forms of Insurance.   The flat-rate system of benefits, apart from this complication about rents, leaves those who are normally better paid to supplement public social security provision by private insurance or saving. Over and above the weekly insurance contribution, a large proportion of the poorer classes, as well as many of the better-off, contribute to sick funds of various kinds through Friendly Societies and Insurance Companies; and statutory Death Grants also are extensively supplemented by private payments. The institution of a comprehensive National Insurance System has naturally led to some decrease in the number of members enrolled in the Friendly Societies, which fell from about 8½ millions in 1938 to 6,700,000 in 1952 and had been falling fairly slowly year by year from 1944. Despite the changed value of money, the Friendly Societies paid out a little less in sickness benefits in 1952 than in 1938 and only a little more in death grants. The Insurance Companies, on the other hand, had in 1952 a premium income from 'industrial business' nearly twice as great as that of 1938, and paid out more than twice as much in claims; and their accumulated industrial assurance funds stood at £746·5 million at the end of 1952 as compared with £359 million in 1938. The Collecting Societies too had approximately doubled their previous incomes and their claims payments. The decline thus affected chiefly the traditional types of Friendly Society, with a social as well as a purely commercial character. Membership of the Friendly Society 'Orders' with branches fell from 2,861,000 in 1938 to 1,792,000 in 1952, and that of Societies without branches from 5,630,000 to 4,923,000. The figures as a whole, however, indicate a high maintenance of voluntary insurance supplementary to the state system of minimum provision.

The Assistance Board. On the other hand the returns of the National Assistance Board show that the number of persons needing their help to supplement National Insurance benefits more than doubled between the starting of the new Scheme in July 1948 and the end of 1953. The figures for the various forms of supplementation, as well as for the Board's activities in other fields, are as shown in Table 162 (overleaf).

Thus, at the end of 1954, more than 1¾ million persons were receiving weekly National Assistance, and 1,262,000 of these were getting it to make up for the recognized inadequacy of National Insurance benefits. Most of the latter—1,001,000—were contributory pensioners; and the total number of old age pensioners receiving assistance was 1,158,000, as against only 168,000 in respect of sickness, injury and unemployment benefits combined. The other big contingents consisted of widows and of persons not required to register for employment—that is to say, persons unfit for ordinary work—who numbered 327,000—and there were about 90,000 blind or tuberculous persons under special schemes. Evidently, the greatest defect of the Insurance Scheme was its failure to provide adequately for the needs of the aged. Of course, in many cases the need for National Assistance arose out of the ineligibility of the persons in question for insurance payments, and not out of their inadequate amount. Only about one-quarter of the main group of pensioners were also getting Retirement Pensions under the Insurance Scheme, and one-fifth of the unemployed were getting Unemployment Benefit. The average payments, on a household basis, ranged from an average of 14s. 8d. a week to those getting Retirement Pensions to 43s. to those not receiving any pension or insurance benefit. The average was 19s.

TABLE 162

Assistance Board. Numbers of Persons receiving Weekly Allowances, 1948–54

(*thousands*)

	1948 July	End of Year						
		1948	1949	1950	1951	1952	1953	1954
In Supplementation of:								
Retirement Pensions	412	473	534	651	737	825	903	1,001
Sickness and Injury Benefits	60	64	73	90	96	109	114	138
Widows' Benefits	70	79	86	95	85	94	99	93
Unemployment Benefit	10	19	29	37	33	58	47	30
Total	552	636	722	873	950	1,086	1,162	1,262
Non-contributory Old Age Pensions	61	71	81	90	108	141	146	157
Other Assistance to Persons on Ordinary Scale:								
Not required to register for Employment	148	208	248	271	288	308	317	327
Required to register	24	33	36	38	32	43	46	50
Assistance on Special Scale (included above):								
Blind Persons	39	43	44	47	50	52	53	55
Tuberculous Persons	18	20	26	31	34	36	36	34
Grand Total	842	1,011	1,157	1,350	1,462	1,667	1,761	1,885

for recipients of non-contributory Old Age Pensions, 20s. 7d. for those getting Widows' Pensions, 21s. 10d. for those receiving Sickness or Injury Benefits, and the same for those with Unemployment Benefit. National Assistance thus provided both for those not eligible for insurance benefits and for those inadequately covered by them. Action is clearly needed to reduce greatly the size at any rate of the latter group.

The Advance since 1939. When all has been said by way of criticism, the advance upon conditions in the 1930s remains most remarkable. The nation has accepted, even if it has not fully implemented, the responsibility for a minimum standard of social security for all its citizens. It has been able to do this without really serious difficulty because there has been full employment, which has both greatly reduced the numbers needing help and provided more productive workers to contribute to the maintenance of those unable to work. Nor should it be left out of the reckoning that, if private 'charity' has declined, there has been a rapid growth both of private superannuation schemes conducted by business firms (see p. 314) and of business expenditure on other forms of 'welfare'. These developments have all something to do with the improvement in general health conditions (see p. 373); but they have above all done a great deal to reduce the unhappiness caused both by absolute privation and by the sense of complete dependence and unwantedness, especially among the elderly, as well as to give the children of the poorer families a better time and an improved chance in life.

The Poverty Line. In 1951 Seebohm Rowntree published in collaboration with G. R. Lavers his third study of poverty in the City of York. The main purposes were to discover, first, how the proportion of working-class persons and families living below the 'poverty line' had changed since 1936—the date of his second survey—and secondly to estimate how the situation had been affected by such factors as the growth of social security legislation, food subsidies, industrial pensions outside the state schemes, and increased work for wages by married women. On the first of these points his one-in-nine sample investigation showed a very great reduction in the number and proportion of those below the 'poverty line', which was calculated on the basis of a minimum diet of sufficient nutritive value and a minimum expenditure on such things as clothing, fuel and light, household sundries, and other necessary purchases. He found that the minimum income required, in addition to rent and rates, for a family of man, wife, and three dependent children under these very stringent conditions came in 1950 to just over £5, of which £2 7s. 4d. was for food, £1 7s. 9d. for clothing, 7s. 7d. for fuel and light, 6s. for household sundries, and 11s. 6d. for all other expenditure except on rent and rates. Calculations were also made for households of different composition. Rent and rates were found to vary too widely for average figures to have real meaning; and accordingly the sums actually paid were deducted from the incomes in calculating whether persons or families were above or below the 'poverty line'. Direct taxes and insurance contributions deducted from earnings were also excluded from income.

On this basis, Rowntree found that the number of individuals living below the 'poverty line' had fallen from 17,185 in 1936 to 1,746 in 1950, or from 31·1 per cent of the working-class population to 2·77 per cent. If families are taken instead of individuals, the numbers in 1950 were 846, or 4·66 per cent. When the causes of poverty are studied for the two years, a further remarkable difference emerges. This is shown in the following table:

TABLE 163

Causes of living below the 'Poverty Line' in York, 1936 and 1950

(*per cent of those in poverty*)

	1936	1950
Unemployment of Chief Wage-earner	28·6	Nil
Inadequate Wages in regular employment	32·8	1·0
Inadequate Earnings of other Workers	9·5	Nil
Old Age	14·7	68·1
Death of Chief Wage-earner	7·8	6·4
Sickness	4·1	21·3
Miscellaneous	2·5	3·2

Thus, whereas in 1936 unemployment and inadequate earnings in regular work were the chief causes of poverty, with old age a long way behind, by 1950 the first and second of these causes had virtually disappeared, and old age was the principal factor in more than two-thirds of all the cases. Sickness also accounted in 1950 for a greatly increased proportion of the poverty; and these two causes between them covered nearly 90 per cent of the total.

Rowntree then went on to calculate how much of the decrease in sheer poverty was due to social legislation. He calculated that, if the social services had been the same in 1950 as in 1936, the percentage of working-class individuals living in 'poverty' would have been 22·18 instead of 2·77, and of families 24·73 instead of 4·64. The absence of food subsidies would have put 13·74 of the individuals and 16·59 of the families below the line, whereas that of family allowances would have increased the percentage of individuals only to 5·97 and that of families to 6·46. The difference in this case is of course due to the very high proportion of old people among the very poor.

The results of this survey confirm what has been said already—that there has been a really remarkable improvement at the bottom levels, but that the numbers of old people living under very bad conditions was still in 1950 much too large for complacency about the working of the social services. It is no minor matter to find, in a city of roughly 100,000 inhabitants, and a not unprosperous city at that, more than 1,700 persons and nearly 850 families still below the very low 'poverty line' used as a basis for the calculations. In 576 out of these 850 families the main cause of the 'poverty' was old age. In only 9 was it low wages —so much of the difference being attributable to full employment and to the increase in the earnings of the less skilled workers.

CHAPTER TWENTY-FOUR

EDUCATION

SINCE the earlier version of *The Condition of Britain* was published, the British educational system has been greatly altered by the Butler Education Act of 1944 enacted under the Churchill Coalition Government during the war. This Act, which is still a long way short of being fully in force, has for the first time laid on local education authorities a comprehensive duty to provide for the education of all children and young persons short of the university level, and has also extended their responsibility for adult education and for the granting of 'major awards' to students at Universities and other places of higher education. The Universities themselves are still left outside the purview of the Ministry of Education: state aid to them, which now accounts for the major part of their revenue, is administered by a specially appointed University Grants Committee, acting directly under the Treasury. For the rest, apart from certain kinds of adult education conducted by voluntary bodies, each local education authority has a statutory duty to prepare comprehensive plans of education for its area and to secure the approval of the Ministry or the Scottish Educational Department for its proposals.

Education controls the Public System. Nevertheless, the new structure does not cover every type of school. The so-called 'public' schools remain for the most part outside it, together with the preparatory schools which lead up to them, and a large number of other 'independent' schools, ranging from the so-called 'modern' or 'progressive' schools based on newer educational ideas to a host of mainly lower middle class schools carried on for private profit. The 1944 Act gave the Ministry and its Scottish equivalent power to inspect *all* schools and to close any that failed to bring themselves up to a tolerable standard; but this power has not yet been exercised, though most of the preliminary inspection has been done. Some 'public' and 'independent' schools submit their affairs to inspection voluntarily, and some receive from the Ministry what is called 'direct grant' from public funds; and in many other cases the local education authorities pay the fees of boys or girls attending schools they do not directly control, or have a number of 'reserved places' in such schools for their nominees. Broadly speaking, however, the 'public' schools and the other 'independents' remain outside the general system of public education and carry on the old tradition of the 'two nations', providing schooling for children of parents belonging to the 'superior' classes. Actually, despite the fact that all education in the state-provided schools is now free of charge to the parents, the 'public' schools have been crowded ever since 1945 by the children of parents who think it worth while to pay high fees in order to give their children what they regard, in some cases as a better education, but in many others as education that offers superior social advantages.

Public and 'Public' Schools.   The non-state schools, however, no longer have any monopoly of the higher types of education. The local authorities own and administer a large number of grammar schools and higher technical schools which provide education up to the level of university entrance and indeed of competition for university scholarships—not to mention the new 'comprehensive' schools which set out to cater for boys and girls of all types. There are also a large number of 'controlled' and 'aided' schools which fall mainly within the state system, though they keep a certain measure of independence. There is no clear line of demarcation between 'public' schools and 'state' schools. Nevertheless, the greater 'public' schools, with their high ratios of teaching staffs to pupils and, for the most part, their high standards of equipment, form, because of their high charges and their endowments, a continuing preserve of the wealthy; and they carry along with them a large number of lesser 'public' schools, many of which have little to recommend them except their 'snob' appeal, or in some cases their conduct under religious auspices—Catholic or Protestant, or in some cases Jewish.

County and Voluntary Schools.   Even within the domain of state schooling, the 1944 Act has left in being the old distinction between 'provided' and 'non-provided' schools. A large number of primary schools, especially in rural areas, are still under the auspices of the Church of England; and the Roman Catholics conduct many similar schools, largely in poorer urban areas. In these 'voluntary' schools, the entire cost of the actual teaching is met by the local education authorities from public funds: the contribution of the 'providing' bodies is limited to a share in the costs of upkeep for buildings, and even a part of this is borne by the public. The Coalition Government deemed it impracticable to face the Roman Catholic and Church of England opposition to the complete taking-over of their schools, and accordingly the 'dual' system remains as a legacy from the past, though some schools, especially Church of England schools, have been handed over to the local education authorities, where the providing bodies were unable to raise even the small funds needed for keeping control, and some others—

mostly small—are being closed and amalgamated with near-by schools under full local authority auspices.

Primary and Secondary Education. 'Primary' education now normally ends at 11+; and all normal schooling beyond 11 is ranked as secondary. This means that a host of former 'elementary' or 'senior elementary' schools have been transformed into 'secondary' schools, though they may be housed in inadequate premises and none too well equipped with teachers capable of the higher types of work. Indeed, not a few 'all-age' schools, catering for pupils at both the 'primary' and the 'secondary' stage, still survive, though these are being gradually replaced.

'Secondary' education, then, begins for most children at 11+, though many of the 'technical secondary' schools have a higher age of entrance, up to 13. The 'dual' system extends to public secondary as well as primary schools taken over from the old structure; but the local authorities have a higher proportion of secondary education wholly under their control. The main difference, apart from finance, between the 'county' and the 'voluntary' schools is that in the latter the providing bodies' approval is needed for staff appointments and denominational religious teaching is allowed.

The Eleven Plus Examination. The greatest defect of the present system is that it makes the whole future of most children, as far as it is affected by education, depend almost entirely on the result of a single examination taken at the age of eleven; for on the results of this examination it depends whether a child can gain entrance to a grammar or technical school. This is not merely unfair to late developers: it is staking far too much on a single test. If 'comprehensive' schools existed as the general practice, this evil would mainly disappear; for even if the children were graded into separate streams on entry, mistakes would be easy to rectify and there would be no need for a change of school. As against this, removal from one school to another involves great difficulties and is liable to be obstructed by teachers who are reluctant to lose their best pupils or, equally, by parents who object to having their children 'de-graded': so that exclusion from or admittance to a grammar or a technical school at the critical age is very liable to be final. In some areas, secondary modern schools are attempting to meet the problem by developing 'grammar-school' forms; but this is unusual, nor is it a satisfactory substitute for correct choice of school where the 'comprehensive' principle is not being applied. If 11+ is accepted as the right age for the transition to secondary education, adequate means must be found for correcting wrong choices at later ages; and everything possible ought to be done to lessen the importance to the child of a single test imposed at so early an age.

Types of Secondary Schooling. 'Secondary' schooling is of three kinds, within the public system—'grammar', 'technical' and 'modern'. This, however, does not mean that each kind need be conducted in a separate school. Apart from the new 'comprehensive' schools, of which there are still only a very few, many schools provide more than one kind of schooling—'grammar' and 'technical', for example, or 'technical' and 'modern'. The separate 'technical' schools are the least numerous: the 'secondary modern', which are in practice a residue—that is, what remains after selection for other types—are by far the most numerous.

The General Certificate of Education.   An important feature of the new post-war structure is the introduction of the General Certificate of Education, which has replaced and extended much further than the old School Certificate. Both these examinations have been organized at two levels—'ordinary' and 'higher' or 'advanced'; but whereas in 1938 only 77,000 sat for the ordinary School Certificate and only 13,000 for the higher School Certificate, in 1954 there were more than 212,500 candidates for the ordinary General Certificate and more than 49,000 who offered one or more subjects at the 'advanced' level.[1] The General Certificate seems capable in time of becoming a general school-leaver's qualification—though there are some who, mistakenly in my view, advocate the institution of a different Certificate at a lower level designed for pupils from secondary modern schools—and the increase in the numbers entering for the 'advanced' level is of particular significance. There has been much controversy about the age at which pupils should be allowed to take the examination, as well as about standards. In 1953 pupils under 16 were admitted for the first time on the recommendation of the Headmasters or Headmistresses; and this change seems to have worked well and to have been widely welcomed.

The Teachers.   The Education Act of 1944 had large effects on the teaching profession. It transformed (without altering them) a great many former 'elementary' into 'secondary' teachers—continuing a process which had begun under the pre-war 'Hadow' system. Therewith, it broke down the old barrier between 'elementary' and 'grammar-school' secondary teachers, and constituted all 'secondary' teachers as a single group. This led to much grumbling among the more highly

---

[1] In 1954, 58 per cent of the boys and 64 per cent of the girls were successful at the ordinary level—making 61·3 per cent in all. At the advanced level 70·6 per cent succeeded, and another 16·1 per cent were awarded passes at the ordinary level. Here again the girls secured a higher percentage of advanced passes than the boys—72·6 per cent as against 69·2 per cent. But, whereas at the ordinary level the entries were 466,000 for boys and 360,000 for girls, at the advanced level there were 81,000 boys' and 32,000 girls' entries. These totals exceed the figures given in the text, because they relate to subject entries and not to the number of candidates. 1,644 boys and 553 girls received nominations for State Scholarships as a result of the examination; and in all there were nearly 21,900 boy and 6,341 girl entrants who took papers in the G.C.E. at the still higher level required of candidates for such scholarships.

qualified 'grammar-school' teachers, who felt they were losing both differential income and status; and various expedients were adopted to allow teachers carrying on the more advanced types of work to receive special supplementary allowances. The problem, however, has not yet been fully solved, at any rate in the case of particularly scarce types of teaching ability, such as teaching of science and mathematics. There is so large a demand in industry for persons holding scientific qualifications that the schools have found difficulty in attracting enough recruits of adequate quality; but there are obvious objections to paying teachers in these fields more than equally qualified teachers of other subjects. It was inevitable and right that the institution of 'secondary education for all' should carry with it in general equality of pay and status for all secondary teachers, subject only to special payments to university graduates and to allowances for posts of special responsibility or need for higher attainments than the ordinary.

The teaching profession, despite this partial equalization, continues to be organized for the most part in accordance with the old lines of division. In England and Wales, but not in Scotland, the 'grammar-school' and 'technical' teachers are organized apart from the general run of 'primary' and 'secondary modern' school teachers, who are mostly in the National Union of Teachers. In the 'grammar' schools, including the 'public' and other 'independent' schools outside the state system, the teachers have their own associations of Assistant Masters and Mistresses—note the name—and of Headmasters and Head Mistresses; and principals and teachers in technical institutions too have associations of their own. The existence of 'public' schools outside the state system makes it difficult to assimilate the teachers' organizations to the new pattern, and helps to preserve 'snob' differences in spite of the growth of higher state education.

Implementing the Butler Act. It was indeed evident from the first that it would take a long time to transform the practical working of the British educational system so as to bring it into conformity with the intentions of the Butler Act. School buildings had to be taken over as they were; for it was impracticable to set about replacing them on any considerable scale in face of the need for additional accommodation for the considerably increased number of children. Nor could teaching staffs be replaced, except gradually, or additional teachers of the required quality be provided in sufficient numbers, though something was achieved by an Emergency Training Scheme for those coming out of war service. These factors put powerful obstacles in the way of achieving the 'parity of esteem' for all kinds of 'secondary' education that the Butler Act was nominally designed to bring about; and there was the further difficulty that 'parity of esteem' was the very last thing wanted by most parents who sent their children to supposedly 'superior' types of school, or by most teachers in such schools. The new system had to make its way in face of very powerful social as well as political opposition; and in practice the larger number of children needing education forced the authorities to give most of their attention to the provision of additional school places, rather than to altering the character of the education supplied. It is, indeed, evident that 'parity of esteem' is unattainable as long as a rival structure exists side by side with the public structure of education, though something can be and is being done to raise the quality and prestige of the 'secondary modern' type of school.

The Principle of Equal Opportunity. The most important principle laid down in the Butler Act was that no child should be deprived by the poverty of its parents of the opportunity to benefit by the higher types of education. But this too is very difficult to achieve in practice, not only because of differences in home environment, but also because the facilities for the higher types of schooling are very unevenly spread over the country: so that it is much harder to obtain entry to a 'grammar' or 'technical' school in some places than in others—though it must be added that standards in such schools may be low in some areas where 'places' are relatively abundant. These disparities can, no doubt, be gradually removed as new building becomes easier; but even so it will remain harder to provide full opportunities in rural areas than in towns and above all in the remoter and more thinly populated areas. In many cases the problem can be solved with the aid of the school bus; but in others the only way of providing the opportunities needed is by sending the children away to boarding-school or to a specialized technical institution. This is expensive, and the burden falls largely on the areas whose authorities are least able to bear it.

Day-schools and Boarding-schools. 'State' schools are mainly dayschools, whereas the 'public' schools include a high proportion of boarding-schools. 'Public' boarding-schools do not usually draw on a clientele that lives in a particular area: they are 'national' or at least 'regional' in their appeal. The 'public' schools, however, include also a large number of day-schools, such as St. Paul's and Manchester and Bradford Grammar Schools; but these too usually draw their pupils from the areas of a number of local education authorities and cannot be brought within the local school system without changing their character for the worse. Their assimilation to the state system would have to be achieved by bringing them in nationally, or at least regionally, either on the lines of the national recognition already accorded to the 'direct grant' schools, most of which are indeed in the 'public' school category, or by establishing some regional school authority co-ordinating the local authorities over wider areas. Even 'regionalization' would not meet the case of the great 'public' boarding-schools, such as

Winchester and Eton, which are essentially national and provide education of a high quality the nation cannot afford to do without, and should seek to make available to any suitable pupil, irrespective of the parents' income or social status. Some believers in the 'public' school system favour 'democratizing' it by opening entry to a limited number of 'free' pupils drawn from the classes now shut out; but this is an objectionable solution because it would result in practice in turning such pupils into 'gentlemen' and 'ladies' and taking them out of their class instead of diminishing class inequality. There are, indeed, some who advocate filling most, or even all, places in the 'public' schools with local authority nominees; but most of those who favour the 'public' school system are against this, on the ground that it would utterly alter their character and destroy their distinctive value.

Local education authorities are empowered to provide boarding-school education for those who need it, and they do so in special cases, but usually by paying the fees for pupils to attend 'non-provided' schools. They do, however, in some areas, have boarding-schools of their own for handicapped children. There have undoubtedly been great advances in the treatment of children suffering from physical or mental handicaps—especially in drawing finer distinctions between the merely 'sub-normal' and the 'mentally deficient'; but there is still a widespread shortage of 'special' schools and special classes in ordinary schools, and only slow progress is being made in catching up with modern methods.

Secondary Modern Schools. For normal children there have been many successful experiments in the better 'secondary modern' schools, which are less subject to examination pressure than either 'primary' or 'grammar' schools. Education in music and the arts has made large strides—especially in music, where general standards of appreciation have risen greatly in recent years. There is, however, a very wide spread between the best and the worst 'secondary modern' schools, in respect both of premises and of teaching. The newer schools are immensely better equipped than the older, and have been able to attract imaginative teachers; whereas the old 'elementary' traditions linger on in many of the pre-war schools.

Grammar School Places. More children are staying on past the age of 15 in the 'secondary modern' schools and past 16 in the 'grammar' schools. But as long as finding a 'grammar' school place continues to depend largely on locality, as well as on suitability, there will be many children leaving school prematurely because they have been wrongly placed. There is also still much to be done towards increasing the numbers who stay at school beyond sixteen. The 'comprehensive' school is capable of making an important contribution in this respect; but difficulties in finding suitable sites, as well as largely political opposition to the 'comprehensive' principle, retard the development of schools of this highly desirable type, of which the London County Council has made itself the outstanding advocate.

The Advance since 1944 and its Limitations. In general, there can be no reasonable doubt that education has made big advances under the 1944 Act, though it will be a long time before its provisions take full effect. Nor is there any doubt concerning the improved appearance and health of the main body of school-children—a consequence mainly of full employment and better living standards at the bottom income levels. School-feeding, though it still falls a long way short of covering the whole school population, has also made an important contribution. There is, to a great extent, a changed and more hopeful attitude in the schools, among both pupils and teachers; and further advances in this respect can be confidently expected as it becomes possible to replace the less satisfactory buildings and the less teachable among the older teachers and heads. Education is becoming more democratic, as well as more efficient, as far as the preponderant state sector is concerned. It cannot, however, become fully democratic as long as the 'snob' sector remains apart, not only because its existence perpetuates snob values, but also because many of the 'independent' schools are of low educational and cultural quality—though of course the quality of the best among them is very high.

The Cost of Public Education. Public expenditure on education has risen sharply since the 'thirties; but it will have to rise a good deal more in the near future if full effect is to be given to the terms of the Butler Act. In particular, the building needs of education are very high, and much more will need to be spent in order to bring structures and equipment up to modern standards. This applies not only to schools but also to Technical Colleges and other places of 'further' education; and over and above this the entire problem of County Colleges for part-time education up to 18 has still to be tackled. The Universities, on the whole, have been treated with reasonable generosity; but they too need more buildings, especially for hostels and for scientific and medical teaching. The number of university students has increased sharply since the 1930s—some think too much and at the expense of proper standards. I see no real evidence, however, that standards have fallen off; and it seems reasonable to suggest that, as the secondary schools keep more of their pupils beyond 16, there will be an increased number of suitable candidates for university and other forms of higher education. It is quite unproven that the limits have been exceeded, or even nearly reached, of the number of boys and girls whom an adequate secondary education can render fit for university or other higher studies. Indeed, the recent report on Early Leaving goes a long way towards proving that this view is wrong.

Adult Education. There is also plenty of room for a further expansion of 'adult' education, both under the auspices of local authorities mainly in the vocational and recreational fields and under those of Universities and voluntary bodies, such as the Workers' Educational Association, in the field of 'liberal' studies. These types of education have been growing; but there have been some uncertainties about the quality of some of them, and they have been badly hampered by lack of funds. Fortunately the Report of the Ashby Committee has pronounced strongly in favour of the types of education supplied in the 'liberal' field by the Universities and the W.E.A., and some of the financial obstacles to growth have recently been removed or reduced. There is, however, still some danger that too little effort may be made to develop the higher types of adult education, such as the three-year 'tutorial classes' conducted by the Universities in partnership with the W.E.A.; and there is also a danger that, in the interest of administrative tidiness, the voluntary bodies may be denied the freedom they require to adapt their provision to the widely varying needs of different groups of students.

The Quality of Education. In the following pages an attempt is made to give a quantitative account of what has been happening in the field of education since 1945. It must, however, be borne in mind that this is a field in which statistics can tell only part of the story. What matters, fundamentally, is fully as much the quality of education, and the purposes animating it, as the numbers receiving it, or the institutions through which it is carried on. People often speak as if education should be the great innovating force guiding men and women towards a more cultured and more democratic way of life; but in practice education is bound to take its colour mainly from the institutions and attitudes prevalent in the whole society. It must direct its teaching to the opportunities in fact open to pupils and students; and in this sense it must be largely 'vocational', even when it is concerned with the most 'liberal' studies. Nor can it escape the effects of differences in home environment, though it may seek to minimize them. As long as there is a 'class' society, class divisions will of necessity be in some degree reflected in the schools, and full 'parity of esteem' will continue to be an unattainable ideal. This does not prevent the schools from so acting as either to aid or to counteract the tendencies in society making for a reduction of social inequality; but it limits their achievement to what can be made consistent with the conditions of living that actually confront the pupils when they leave school. Let us now turn to the quantitative aspects.

The Child Population. In 1939, when the second world war began, there were fewer children in the United Kingdom than there had been at

the time of the Census in 1931. But by 1954 there had been a reversal
of the position.

TABLE 164

Number of Children under 14 in United Kingdom, 1931, 1939, 1953
and 1954

(*thousands*)

	1931	1939	1953	1954
Under 1 year	713	701	781	787
1 and under 2	700	690	762	774
2–4	2,119	1,986	2,417	2,334
5–9	3,897	3,341	4,205	4,258
10–14	3,746	3,576	3,367	3,464
	11,175	10,294	11,532	11,617

Thus, the number of children under 15 had risen by more than a
million and a quarter since 1939, but was only about 400,000 greater
than in 1931. Children of school age (5–14) numbered 7,643,000 in
1931, only 6,917,000 in 1939, and 7,722,000 in 1954. Only in 1954 did
the numbers in these age-groups pass the 1931 figure as the bulge in
the birth-rate reached school age. As we have seen, the number of live
births reached its peak in 1947, when it exceeded a million. It then fell
to 793,000 in 1952, and was 804,000 in 1953 and 795,000 in 1954—
nearly 16 per 1,000 of total population, as compared with an average
of 15·3 in the years before 1939.

The Demand for School Places.   This meant that in 1954 the number
of children needing *primary* schooling (5–11) was well over a million
higher than it had been in 1939, whereas the secondary school population under 15 was still appreciably smaller, but certain to rise sharply
during the next few years. Accordingly, during the years immediately
after the end of the war the most pressing problem confronting educa-
tionalists was that of providing schools and teachers for a rapidly increasing entry to the primary schools, in the knowledge that the same
problem would arise within a few years at the secondary stage. This
provision had to be made under the conditions laid down in the Butler
Education Act of 1944, which prescribed a system of secondary schooling for all normal children from age 11 to age 15, but left open the kinds
of school in which this provision was to be made. It is still supposed by
some that the Butler Act made provision for three distinct types of
secondary school—grammar, technical and modern—between which
the children were to be sorted out at the age of 11+ according to their
several aptitudes. But in fact the Education Act contains no such requirement: it leaves the matter open as between the provision of
secondary schools of different kinds and that of 'comprehensive' schools

designed to cater for all types of normal children, with internal arrangements for specialization to meet varying interests and capacities.

The School Building Problem.   In practice, as it would have been impossible to build at once more than a limited number of new schools, and as most of the available building resources had for the time to be devoted to providing additional primary school accommodation, it was necessary for the most part to make do with the existing secondary schools, including large numbers of former elementary schools which had been converted to secondary use before the war when, under the Hadow reorganization plan, secondary education for all was being introduced at the age of 11+. This meant that the existing pattern of selective grammar schools for a small proportion of the total number of children, of technical schools for a still smaller proportion, and of 'modern' schools—some new, but largely old elementary schools converted to secondary use—for the great majority was unavoidably continued. Indeed, in not a few cases secondary education continued to be provided in the higher forms of old elementary schools—'all-age' schools—which were still used for the younger as well as for the older children. Even in 1954 among schools maintained by local education authorities there were still in England and Wales 3,957 of these 'all-age' schools, with 694,000 pupils, as against 3,480 'modern' secondary schools, with 1,167,000, and 1,181 grammar schools, as well as 164 direct grant schools aided by the Ministry of Education, with 518,000 and 88,000 pupils respectively. Technical schools numbered only 300, with 85,000 pupils; and schools combining either grammar and technical, or grammar and modern, or technical and modern elements numbered but 77, with 37,000 pupils, and 'comprehensive' and 'multilateral' schools but 16, with 15,000.

It must, however, be borne in mind in considering these figures that, because of the 'bulge' in the number of births, attention had to be concentrated during the early years of the new Act on providing additional primary schools, so that the intensive provision of new secondary schools to meet the 'bulge' when it reached the secondary stage has only now begun. That is why the controversy about 'comprehensive' schools has only become really lively during the past two years or so. Whether replacement is by 'comprehensives' or by secondary schools of different types, the 'all-age' schools, except a very few, will soon be gone, and the supply of new secondary places will be largely increased. Even now the surviving 'all-age' schools are mostly either very small or under sectarian auspices.

Direct Grant and 'Efficient' Schools.   The figures cited in the preceding paragraph exclude schools, except 'direct grant' grammar schools, not maintained by local education authorities, some of which receive 'direct grants' from the Ministry of Education. At the beginning of

1954 these 'direct grant' schools numbered 317, with 100,000 pupils, of whom 88,000 were in grammar schools. Other schools, not grant-aided but certified by the Ministry as 'efficient', numbered 1,324, with 249,000 pupils—61,000 in secondary schools and 113,000 in schools with both primary and secondary departments. They include a considerable number of the so-called 'public' schools which cater chiefly for the children of the wealthier classes; but as we have seen there are other 'public' schools, including some of the most famous, which remain wholly outside the system of truly public education and are neither grant-aided nor inspected by the Ministry. As far as I know there are no figures showing the numbers of children attending 'public' or other (e.g. preparatory) schools which are quite outside the main educational system.

Infant and Junior Schools. Within the public system in January 1954 local education authorities in England and Wales maintained, in addition to the 3,957 'all-age' schools already mentioned, the following schools for infants and juniors at or preceding the primary level.

TABLE 165

Numbers of Maintained Infant and Junior Schools, 1953

	Schools	Pupils (000's)
Junior Schools without Infants	4,174	1,265
,, ,, with Infants	9,785	1,419
Infant Schools	5,585	1,176
Nursery Schools	457	23
Special and Hospital Schools	591	47
	20,602	3,930

There were also a small number of schools of these types which received 'direct grants' from the Ministry of Education, as follows:

TABLE 166

Numbers of Direct Grants of 'Efficient' Nursery and Primary Schools, 1953

	Schools	Pupils (000's)
Nursery Schools	20	1
Special and Hospital Schools	121	9

and there were in addition a number recognized as efficient but not receiving grants from public funds. These were as follows:

Primary Schools	690	75
Nursery Schools	9	0·3

Schooling before and after Fifteen. All these schools taken together provided for 6,302,000 children aged 5–14, out of a total population of

6,540,000 in the age-group; and 6,041,384 of these children were in schools maintained by local education authorities, whereas 70,811 were in direct grant schools and 189,551 in other schools recognized as efficient. As against these figures, out of 2,274,000 young persons aged 15–18 only 316,459 were in schools maintained or grant-aided or recognized as efficient—232,201 in maintained, 27,817 in 'direct grant', and 56,441 in other 'efficient' schools. The proportions still at recognized schools from 15 onwards were as follows:

TABLE 167

Proportions of Young Persons remaining at School after 15, by Ages, 1953

(*thousands*)

Age	Persons in Age-groups	Pupils at L.E.A. Schools	Per cent	Pupils at all Recognized Schools	Per cent of total
15 +	578	135	23·4	172·2	29·8
16 +	571	59	10·3	85·8	15·0
17 +	565	27·7	4·9	43·1	7·6
18 +	560	10·2	1·8	15·3	2·7

Thus, nearly 30 per cent of all children stayed at school beyond 15, but only 15 per cent beyond 16, and only half this proportion beyond 17. Of those at school between 15 and 16, the great majority—78·5 per cent—were at schools maintained by local education authorities, whereas of those between 16 and 17 the other schools provided for not far short of one-third, and of those between 17 and 18 for about one-third. At all ages a majority of those still at school were in schools maintained by the L.E.A.s.

All the above figures relate only to England and Wales. For Scotland the statistics are not fully comparable, as they exclude schools recognized as 'efficient', but not in receipt of grants from public funds. In March 1953 there were in Scotland 818,527 pupils in schools managed by local education authorities and 14,753 in other grant-aided schools. Of the former 574,977 were in primary schools or departments, and 229,522 in secondary schools or departments: of the latter 6,423 were in primary and 7,697 in secondary schools or departments. Special schools accounted for 9,841 children under L.E.A.s and 497 in other grant-aided schools; and nursery schools for 4,187 and 136.

County Schools and Denominational Schools.   In England and Wales, out of 29,603 primary and secondary schools and departments maintained by local education authorities, 17,743 were 'county' schools unconnected with any particular religious denomination. 8,422 were Church of England schools, 1,885 Roman Catholic, and 505 of other denominations. Here are the respective numbers of pupils and the average for each type of school.

TABLE 168
Maintained Schools, by Types, 1953

	Number of Schools or Departments	Number of Pupils (000's)	Pupils per School or Department
Junior and Infant Schools:			
County	11,907	2,908	244
Church of England	6,616	745	113
Roman Catholic	855	186	218
Others	166	22	132
All Age Schools:			
County	1,554	303	195
Church of England	1,543	187	121
Roman Catholic	801	194	242
Others	59	9	153
Secondary Schools:			
County	4,282	1,582	370
Church of England	263	67	255
Roman Catholic	229	63	275
Others	280	110	393
Total:			
County	17,743	4,793	270
Church of England	8,422	1,000	119
Roman Catholic	1,885	443	235
Others	505	140	277
	28,555	6,376	223

The Church of England schools were in general much smaller than those of other types, being largely village schools. Secondary schools were on the average considerably larger than primary schools.

The School Leavers. As we saw the majority of children cease full-time education at the age of 15. In the year ending on July 31, 1954, out of nearly 390,000 who left secondary schools in England and Wales at 14 or 15 only about 3,000 boys and 6,600 girls did so in order to proceed to some other form of full-time education. Of 62,000 who left at 16, only 1,100 boys and 3,200 girls, and of the 17,100 who left at 17, only 1,400 boys and 2,750 girls continued full-time education elsewhere, whereas of the 20,000 who remained at school after 18, as many as 14,300 went on to other forms of full-time education—8,400 to Universities, 5,000 to Teachers' Training Colleges, and the rest to Technical Colleges, Art Schools and other institutions of higher education. In all 9,428 (6,938 boys and 2,490 girls) left to enter Universities and nearly 6,500 to enter Teachers' Training Colleges.

Teachers and Pupils. To teach the 6,376,000 pupils in maintained primary and secondary schools the local education authorities in

England and Wales in 1953 employed 232,699 teachers—one for every 27·4 pupils. In junior and infant schools the number of pupils for each teacher was higher—32·3—whereas in secondary schools it averaged only 20·6. In Roman Catholic schools of all types it was 27·8, in Church of England schools 22·6, and in County schools 23·7. More than half the total number of pupils were in schools which had more than 30 for each teacher: for almost a quarter the number exceeded 35, and for 231,000 it was over 40. Out of 129,000 classes in primary and infant schools about 36,000 had 30 or fewer pupils on the register, nearly 52,000 between 30 and 40, and more than 41,000 more than 40. Even in secondary modern schools, out of 38,000 classes, 17,900 had between 30 and 40, and nearly 2,600 more than 40, and in grammar schools, out of 18,700 classes, more than 7,500 had more than 30. In primary and infant schools there were actually 1,150 classes of more than 50. There were nearly 1,000 small schools which had only a single teacher, and another 4,211 with only two.

In 1954 the number of teachers in primary and secondary schools maintained by local education authorities in England and Wales was about 231,000—88,600 men and 142,600 women. This teaching force was made up as follows:

TABLE 169

Number of Teachers in Maintained Schools by Qualifications, 1953

	Men	Women	Total
Graduates or Equivalent	24,012	16,809	40,821
Uncertificated Qualified	387	8,197	8,584
Others—Qualified	63,951	113,110	177,061
Non-qualified	229	4,515	4,744
	88,579	142,631	231,210

These figures exclude teachers in schools not maintained by local authorities, even if they receive grants from public funds. They also exclude teachers engaged in 'special' schools or in 'further' or university or adult education. For Great Britain as a whole, the Census of 1951 showed a total of nearly 357,000 teachers of all types.

The Training of Teachers. The majority of teachers in schools maintained by local education authorities are trained in special Training Colleges under L.E.A. auspices. A minority, employed mainly in secondary education, are university graduates trained as teachers in University Training Departments. In England and Wales, the number admitted for training in Universities or permanent Training Colleges in 1954–5 was approximately 15,360—4,500 men and 10,850 women. The number who successfully completed courses of training in 1953–4 was 13,812—4,258 men and 9,554 women. Of these 1,520 men and

1,222 women were university graduates or held equivalent qualifications. The majority of the others completed two-year courses at Training Colleges.

It is of interest to compare the numbers being trained in recent years with those of 1938–9—the last pre-war year.

TABLE 170

Number of Teachers Trained, 1938–9, 1952–3 and 1953–4

	1938–9	1952–3	1953–4	1954–5
Admitted to training courses:				
Men	2,203	4,707	4,504	4,506
Women	4,705	10,463	10,492	10,856
Total	6,908	15,170	14,996	15,362
Successfully completing courses:				
Men	2,128	4,410	4,258	—
Women	3,993	9,686	9,554	—
Total	6,121	14,096	13,812	—

Thus, the regular supply of trained teachers has been more than doubled. During the years 1945–1951 a special Emergency Teachers' Training Scheme was in operation in order to build up the supply of teachers, which had been depleted during the war years. Under the scheme more than 23,000 men and nearly 12,000 women were recruited to the teaching profession. The scheme was wound up in 1951, when the increased intake of the regular Training Colleges was deemed adequate to meet the need. It should, however, be noted that there have been special difficulties in the way of securing a sufficient supply of suitable teachers because the trainees have had to be drawn from age-groups born when the birth-rate was particularly low.

It will be seen that of the 231,000 teachers in L.E.A. primary and secondary schools only 40,800 had graduate or equivalent qualifications —rather more than one in six. Of the 13,800 who completed their training in 1953–4 roughly 2,740 were graduates or the equivalent— approximately one in five. It should however be noted that a substantial proportion of the graduate teachers in grammar schools not maintained by L.E.A.s enter on their professions without special training in teaching method.

Part-time Continued Education. Those who cease full-time schooling at 15, or at any later age, may continue their education by attending part-time or evening courses of study in institutions for Further Education provided or aided out of public funds. In England and Wales, in 1952–3, rather more than two million students, about equally divided between the sexes, recorded nearly 206 million student hours in such establishments. This total includes 59,000 full-time students, who accounted for 50 million student hours; 372,000 part-time students, accounting for 58·5 million hours; and 1,860,000 evening students, accounting for 97 million hours. A large part of this Further Education was vocational. Out of 48,000 full-time students in 'Major Establishments', other than Art Schools, 37,400 put in more than 32 million hours at courses on specifically vocational subjects, as compared with 10,800 students and 8½ million hours for courses of a 'general educational nature'; and many of the latter had also a vocational use. Of part-time day students, who numbered 371,500, vocational courses in the strict sense accounted for 295,000, and more general courses for over 76,000. 335,000 of these students were attending 'day-release' courses—that is, courses for which they were released by employers— 269,000 for specifically vocational and 66,600 for more general courses. 'Day-release' was for the most part confined to a limited range of occupations. Of the 269,000 taking vocational courses, engineering alone accounted for 130,000, the other main subjects being related to building and contracting (41,000), mining (26,000), commerce and professions (24,000), pharmacy and medicine (10,000) and chemicals (11,000). No other group exceeded 6,000. These figures exclude art and craft students (11,000 full-time, 2,000 part-time), most of whom were taking largely vocational courses. These included 13,000 'day-release' students. All these figures involve some duplication, where students were attending more than one course.

Evening Classes.   Much larger numbers of students attend one or more evening classes after their day's work. In this case it is impossible to give, even approximately, the number of individuals concerned, as large numbers enter for more than one course of study. Nor is it possible to say how many of those who entered dropped out without finishing the courses, though the numbers so failing are known to be high. All that can be done is to list under the main groups of subjects the numbers of classes and entrants and the total student hours recorded. See Table 171 (overleaf).

Adult and Workers' Education.   In addition to these courses provided by local education authorities there is the movement of non-vocational Adult Education carried on chiefly by the University Extra-mural Departments and the Workers' Educational Association. These bodies organize Tutorial Classes, which extend over three or more winter sessions, one-year and shorter classes, and summer and week-end schools. In 1953–4 Universities, mainly in partnership with the W.E.A., organized 906 Tutorial Classes with 13,936 students, 1,089 one-year classes with about 19,000 students, and 1,813 shorter courses with about 54,000 students. In addition the W.E.A. organized 401 one-year classes with 6,300 students and 2,750 shorter courses with 52,000 students; and there were a few organized by other bodies with grant

TABLE 171

Evening Classes in Major Establishments (including Schools of Art), and in Evening Institutes, England and Wales, 1952–3

(the figures following the plus (+) sign are for Art Establishments)

Subject Group	Number of Classes	Number of Entrants (000's)	Student Hours (000's)
English	9,877+72	214+1	4,938+31
Languages (other than English)	4,977+2	91+0	2,556+1
Social Sciences	3,230+3	60+0	1,459+1
Mental and Moral Sciences	241+1	4+0	118+1
Mathematics	13,980+51	278+1	8,865+29
Natural Sciences	7,968+1	132+0	4,902+0
Art	1,596+2,745	33+59	845+1,981
Handicrafts and Recreational Subjects	15,485+1,084	301+19	8,891+720
Music, Elocution, Theatre	5,651+48	125+1	3,984+30
Physical Culture	11,651+7	325+0	7,166+1
First Aid and Hygiene	767	16 —	285 —
General Courses	294+41	7+1	177+25
Agriculture and Fishing	605	10 —	198 —
Nautical	32 —	1 —	18 —
Mining and Quarrying	838 —	15 —	447 —
Building, etc.	9,614+1,673	129+30	5,132+1,150
Woodworking	2,610+63	39+1	1,516+37
Quantity and other Surveying	480+12	6+0	233+5
Architecture	195+349	4+6	158+242
Structural Engineering	486+14	7+0	307+4
Glass, Pottery, Brickmaking	120+90	2+1	59+37
Chemical Industries	450+9	6	0	192+4
Engineering, etc.	15,982+8	270+0	11,044+5
Textiles	812+55	11+1	339+34
Clothing Manufacture	912+117	14+2	502+59
Furniture	206+301	3+5	93+208
Food Processing	583+11	8+0	322+6
Other Manufactures and Trades	187+156	2+4	99+127
Printing and Book Trades	1,121+1,096	20+17	672+628
Professional Occupations	3,234+34	50	0	1,327+14
Commerce and Management	1,879+1	30+0	854+0
Clerical	14,943+1	328+0	8,563+0
Wholesale and Retail Trade	619+117	10+2	267+65
Public Health	149 —	2 —	58 —
Transport	238 —	4 —	85 —
Personal Services	569+28	9+1	373+27
Needlecraft	23,588+1,181	414+21	12,927+776
Child Care and Nursing	242 —	4 —	72 —
Cookery	4,942+49	84+1	2,677+28
Other Domestic Subjects	474 —	10 —	228 —
Other Subjects	640+5	17+0	453+3
Total	158,646+8,987	3,037+167	91,186+5,993

aid from the Ministry of Education. There were also of course many adult classes carried on by other bodies without any aid from the Government—for example, the numerous courses—mostly short—conducted by the National Council of Labour Colleges or by individual Trade Unions, the latter chiefly for the benefit of their branch officers, committee-members and shop stewards.

The Universities. There are in Great Britain 19 degree-granting Universities and 3 independent University Colleges recognized by the University Grants Committee. These had in 1952-3 approximately 81,500 full-time students—a fall of nearly 4,000 from the peak total of 1950-1, but a rise of more than 30,000 over 1938-9. In 1954-5 nearly 70 per cent of the total income of the Universities came from Treasury grants dispensed by the U.G.C. and amounting to about £28 million, inclusive of grants to teaching hospitals and agricultural colleges. Of other income, nearly 13 per cent of the total came from fees, $4\frac{1}{2}$ per cent from endowments, and $3\frac{1}{2}$ per cent from local authority grants.

Much the largest University is London, with 18,199 full-time students in 1952-3. Next was Cambridge, with 7,839, followed by Oxford, with 6,878. Glasgow, Edinburgh, Wales, Manchester and Durham had each between 4,000 and 5,000; Birmingham and Leeds exceeded 3,000; Bristol, Liverpool, Nottingham and Sheffield had between 2,000 and 3,000; Reading, Aberdeen and St. Andrews between 1,000 and 2,000; Hull, Southampton and the University Colleges of Exeter, Leicester and Stoke-on-Trent had fewer than 1,000 each. Certain Universities were made up of a number of constituent Colleges situated in different areas: thus, the University of Wales is composed of four regional Colleges in Aberystwyth, Bangor, Cardiff and Swansea, the University of Durham of Colleges in Durham and Newcastle-on-Tyne, and the University of St. Andrews of Colleges in St. Andrews and Dundee. Oxford and Cambridge are confederations of Independent Colleges; and London is composed of a number of largely independent Colleges and 'Schools', mostly specializing in particular fields. London University includes University College, with 2,615 full-time students, King's College, the London School of Economics and Political Science, the Imperial College of Science and Technology, each with from 1,600 to 1,800, and 15 Medical Schools and Colleges with over 6,000, as well as a number of smaller societies. Of University status, though not strictly Universities, are the Royal Technical College of Glasgow, with 1,200 full-time students, and the Manchester College of Technology, with 654.

In addition to the 81,500 full-time students there were in 1952-3 a total of 15,855 part-time university students, of whom about 3,500 were reading for degree or diploma courses and about 4,800 were engaged in research or other advanced work, the remaining 7,600 being 'occasional' students taking intra-mural courses not leading to a degree or diploma. These figures exclude extra-mural students taking technical or other courses under university auspices: these numbered 81,500 in 1952–3.

University Students: the Range of Studies. The U.G.C. classifies students as follows, under broad headings of subjects studied:

TABLE 172
Numbers of University Students by Subject Groups

	Students	Per cent of total		Students	Per cent of total
Arts	34,916	42·8	Technology	9,993	12·3
Pure Science	17,001	20·9	Agriculture and		
Medicine	13,511 ⎫	19·9	Forestry	2,279	—
Dentistry	2,715 ⎭		Veterinary Sciences	1,059	—

University Teachers. The Universities and University Colleges employed a total teaching staff of 9,098, including 1,297 Professors. These figures exclude 929 teachers employed at Oxford and Cambridge by the separate Colleges. Research workers not employed in teaching departments are also excluded.

University Finance. University income in 1952–3 totalled £29·7 million, of which £21·7 came from public funds. The largest public grants went to London (£6·7 million): Cambridge received £1·4 million, Oxford £1·2 million, and Manchester, Wales, Edinburgh and Glasgow each just over £1 million. The percentage of total income derived from public funds, including local authority grants, was 73·2.

In addition to grants made from public funds to the Universities many students receive scholarships or other grants from the Ministry of Education or the Scottish Education Department or from local education authorities. In 1953–4 there were current 9,896 scholarships awarded by the Ministry of Education and by the Scottish Education Department, 30,630 awards for university study made by local authorities in England and Wales, and 5,046 in Scotland. There were also in England and Wales 14,408 awards by local authorities for higher non-university education, and 5,088 in Scotland. Of these the great majority were 'major' awards, designed to cover as far as necessary the entire cost of education and maintenance. This is a very great advance on what existed before the war. In 1935–6 only 41 per cent of full-time university students received any sort of assistance either from public funds or from university or school scholarships or from grants made by other bodies. By 1946–7 this proportion had risen to nearly 68 per cent and by 1952–3 to more than 70 per cent. Moreover, in most cases the grants were much larger both absolutely and as a proportion of the total cost of education and maintenance.

State Scholarships and other Awards. The present arrangements for

State Scholarships and local authority awards have in part replaced the special arrangements for public aid to university students under the Further Education and Training Scheme which provided for persons with war service to continue their higher education at the public expense. Up to the end of 1953 there had been 86,362 awards under this scheme (80,097 to men and 6,265 to women), and of these 65,793 had been brought to successful completion. 15,605 had been terminated unsuccessfully or prematurely: others were still uncompleted.

Degrees and Diplomas. In 1952–3 British Universities granted 10,180 first degrees with honours and 6,755 ordinary first degrees. They also granted 2,758 first diplomas, as well as 2,646 higher degrees and 4,096 higher diplomas. Of the first degrees 8,006 were in Arts subjects, 4,329 in Pure Science, 1,882 in Medicine, 161 in Dentistry, 1,941 in Technology, 568 in Agriculture and Forestry, and 48 in Veterinary Science.

Technical Colleges and National Certificates and Diplomas. Side by side with these university degrees and diplomas, large numbers of students at Technical Colleges and similar establishments are working for National Certificates and National Diplomas with a vocational basis. These are awarded at two levels, 'ordinary' and 'higher', the Diplomas after full-time and the Certificates after part-time study. In 1954 Diplomas were awarded at the ordinary level to 361 and at the higher level to 248 students, all in either engineering or building subjects. In the same year, there were awarded to part-time students 12,443 ordinary and 6,941 higher National Certificates, more than 9,000 of the former and 4,800 of the latter in various branches of engineering, and 1,154 and 637 in building, the next largest group being in chemistry, with 912 ordinary and 502 higher Certificates. Much larger numbers enter each year for the technical examinations of the City and Guilds Institute, which examined more than 82,000 candidates in 1953. The Royal Society of Arts too is an important examining body in many fields. There are also many vocational examinations conducted by professional bodies. Indeed, all these vocational courses and qualifying examinations, as well as the numerous Art Colleges conducted under local authority auspices, constitute, side by side with university education, vital elements in the national system of recruitment for the professions and business techniques and provide extensive opportunities for spare-time and part-time students who have to earn their livings at the same time as they are qualifying for higher types of work.

Educational Building. Educational development, we saw, has been badly hampered since 1945 by the difficulties in the way of new building. These involved a high degree of concentration on the provision of additional primary school places, and particularly affected 'further' education except where it was closely related to the needs of industry.

It can be seen from the accompanying table that approval of educational building projects was seriously retarded after 1949, when the £ sterling was devalued and an economy campaign was instituted. The retardation continued up to 1953, when the financial situation was a good deal easier and the value of 'approvals' rose sharply; and there was a continued rise in 1954, together with some relaxation on the ban on building for non-technical further education. In spite of these shifts in policy, the total value of work completed rose each year; but this was partly an effect of rising prices. The value of buildings under construction at the end of the year was actually highest in 1951, when new

TABLE 173

Educational Building, Great Britain, 1946–54

Primary and Secondary Schools: Great Britain

	Projects Approved (£000)	New Places Provided Primary (000's)	Secondary
1946	15,014	18·5	11·7
1947	26,389	21·5	56·0
1948	18,104	29·8	114·0
1949	58,055	79·5	76·4
1950	42,936	97·5	48·8
1951	45,578	128·0	46·0
1952	36,443	155·1	48·1
1953	53,063	192·6	97·1
1954	59,385	158·0	88·0
	354,967	880·5	580·7

All Educational Building

	Projects Approved (£m.)	Contracts Completed (£m.)	Under Construction at end of year (£m.)
1946	19·5	4·4	8·6
1947	32·2	10·0	21·7
1948	25·1	13·8	37·9
1949	73·6	21·4	76·3
1950	54·1	31·2	94·3
1951	58·2	38·6	122·7
1952	44·4	49·7	116·9
1953	61·8	60·1	115·3
1954	69·8	65·6	118·0
	438·7	294·8	—

approvals were relatively low. This was accounted for by the time-lag between approval and the actual completion of the work.

In all, between 1946 and 1954, building work for education was approved to a total value of nearly £439 million, and contracts had been completed to a value of nearly £295 million—average rates of £49 million and £32½ million a year. This is a small appropriation in relation either to the size of the building industry or to the needs of education. The total output of the building and civil engineering industries was valued at £657 million in 1948 and at £950 million in 1954; and the total current public expenditure on education and child care, including that of local authorities, was £273 million in 1950 and £408 million in 1954. On the other hand, real public capital expenditure on goods and services for education and child care was only £25 million in 1948 and £74 million in 1954, as against £298 million and £375 million for new houses. That the health services, at £9 million and £18 million, were even worse served does not make the position of education any less serious.

The Financing of Public Education. We must now seek to show how much the public educational services have been costing in recent years, where the money comes from, and how the expenditure is made up. Here, to begin with, are the figures of total cost of educational services conducted by local education authorities, thus excluding the cost of university and certain other kinds of education, and the sums spent on education by private persons, of which only a rough estimate can be made.

TABLE 174

Finances of Local Education Authorities, England and Wales, 1945–6 to 1953–4

(£million)

	1945–6	1946–7	1947–8	1948–9	1949–50
Expenditure from:					
Rates	60·9	70·9	78·1	85·8	92·5
Specific Exchequer Grants	82·4	97·5	113·6	132·3	145·0
Total	143·3	168·4	191·7	218·1	237·5

	1950–1	1951–2	1952–3	1953–4	1954–5
Expenditure from:					
Rates	97·6	114·7	123·3	130·1	142·1
Specific Exchequer Grants	149·7	177·2	194·6	203·9	234·1
Total	247·3	291·9	317·9	334·0	376·2

Thus 42½ per cent of the cost was borne by local rates in 1945–6, and 38½ per cent in 1953–4; but, even so, expenditure out of rates had more than doubled. Total expenditure had increased each year, and bade fair to go on increasing fast as the Butler Act was put more fully into effect. This, in view of the objections to increasing local rates, was bound to involve higher Exchequer grants in some form.

The main heads of expenditure were as follows:

TA

Itemized Expenditure of Local Education Autho:

	1945–6	1946–7	1947–8
Primary and Nursery Schools	59·8	65·3	69·2
Secondary Schools	34·5	40·3	46·1
Special Schools	1·7	2·0	2·1
Further Education	6·2	7·9	9·5
Training of Teachers	0·6	2·2	3·5
Medical Inspection and Treatment	4·3	6·2	8·1
Aid to Pupils	2·8	4·2	5·6
Administration and Inspection	6·7	8·5	10·1
School Milk and Meals	10·8	14·5	18·1
Employers' Superannuation Contribution	3·9	4·1	4·3
Other Services	4·4	6·2	8·3
Loan Charges	7·6	7·0	6·7
Percentage met from Rates	42·5	42·1	40·1

Expenditure on 'secondary' schools has increased faster than expenditure on primary schools despite the bigger increase in the numbers in primary schools (see p. 338), because the process of turning old 'elementary' schools into 'secondary modern' schools has been continuing and involves higher costs per pupil. Spending on 'secondary' education may be expected to rise more steeply during the next few years, as the post-war bulge in births moves through the secondary stage. Other big increases are for 'special' schools, where again much more still needs to be done, for 'further education', and for aid to pupils, which have taken on quite a new aspect under the Butler Act. Indeed, one of the most unsatisfactory aspects of the present educational system is the insignificant expenditure on maintenance allowances for those who remain at school beyond the minimum leaving age. The conditions for qualifying for such allowances are now utterly obsolete, with the result that very few are being paid—and even those at an absurdly low rate. If we really wish to encourage longer stay by those capable of benefiting by higher education who now leave early, grants will have to be made available on a much more generous scale than at present.

Another field in which it will be necessary to increase public spending greatly is that of technical and higher technological education. More and more industries are passing into a stage at which they depend on mathematical and scientific techniques and need to employ larger proportions of technically trained executants as well as of higher technologists. The Government has already announced its recognition of this need, and may have published its plans before this book appears. It can be taken as certain that the problem cannot be solved without a sharp rise in expenditure.

and and Wales, 1945–6 to 1954–5 (£*million*)

1948–9	1949–50	1950–1	1951–2	1952–3	1953–4	1954–5
77·4	81·4	84·8	101·5	110·1	115·3	126·5
53·9	58·3	60·9	73·6	78·9	83·4	91·6
2·6	3·2	3·6	4·6	5·2	5·6	6·2
11·4	13·7	15·1	18·5	20·0	21·6	23·7
4·0	4·4	4·1	4·5	4·9	5·0	5·6
6·6	5·6	5·8	6·3	6·9	7·4	8·1
6·6	8·5	10·8	13·0	14·5	15·7	16·8
11·4	12·1	12·3	13·9	14·5	14·9	15·8
22·0	25·0	22·9	24·5	27·9	25·4	36·7
4·7	4·9	5·2	6·5	7·0	7·2	8·1
10·4	12·2	12·1	13·1	12·9	13·9	15·1
7·0	8·1	9·1	11·9	15·1	18·6	22·0
39·4	38·9	39·5	39·3	38·8	39·0	37·8

Expenditure on school milk and meals has also increased considerably, but needs to rise further; and training of teachers, back mainly under the local authorities since the termination of the emergency scheme, is both due to cost a good deal more because of the recent decision to improve maintenance grants and in need of great further expansion. Most people will agree that the courses ought to last over three years rather than two in order to be really effective; but, apart from the higher cost, the present obstacle to lengthening the period of training is that it would mean an acute shortage of teachers in the opening phase, and would thus render more difficult both reduction in the size of classes and the promised raising of the leaving age to 16. Clearly the best time for raising the age will come when the bulge has passed out of the secondary schools; and, if this occasion is missed, it may not be easy soon to find another. The conflict between these three claims presents indeed a very awkward problem; but, whatever the priorities given to them, the increased costs of all three will have before long to be met. Total costs rose by about 150 per cent from 1945–6 to 1953–4, but were still only a fraction of the cost of armaments.

The Financing of Education in Scotland. The above figures, as we saw, relate only to England and Wales. The Scottish figures are presented in a slightly different form: See Tables 176–7 (overleaf).

Scottish expenditure has risen rather more sharply than English— by more than 200 per cent since 1938–9. Exchequer grants were in 1953–4 four times as large as in 1938–9. Expenditure from rates, as in England and Wales, more than doubled between 1945–6 and 1953–4. The percentage of total expenditure met out of rates, which had been much the same as in England and Wales in 1945–6, has since become

TABLE 176

Finances of Local Education Authorities—Scotland, 1938–9 and 1945–6 to 1954–5 (£million)

	1938–9	1945–6	1946–7	1947–8	1948–9	1949–50	1950–1	1951–2	1952–3	1953–4	1954–5
Receipts from:											
Rates	6·5	9·2	9·5	9·1	10·4	10·4	10·7	13·1	14·6	15·2	16·4
Exchequer Grants	7·2	12·7	14·2	17·8	19·2	21·1	22·1	25·4	27·0	28·8	32·5
Fees	0·2	0·2	0·2	0·2	0·2	0·2	0·2	0·2	0·3	0·3	0·3
Other Sources	0·1	0·2	0·2	1·4	1·5	1·5	1·7	2·0	2·1	2·2	2·2
Total	14·0	22·2	24·1	28·6	31·2	33·2	34·8	40·7	44·0	46·5	51·4

TABLE 177

Itemized Expenditure of Local Education Authorities—Scotland, 1938–9 and 1945–6 to 1954–5 (£million)

	1938–9	1945–6	1946–7	1947–8	1948–9	1949–50	1950–1	1951–2	1952–3	1953–4	1954–5
Teachers' Salaries	8·9	14·3	14·8	15·3	16·3	16·9	17·8	21·7	23·2	24·1	26·2
School Maintenance	2·3	3·4	4·0	5·2	5·8	6·4	6·5	7·3	7·9	8·3	8·5
Administration	0·4	0·6	0·7	0·8	0·9	1·0	1·0	1·2	1·3	1·3	1·3
Aid to Students	0·2	0·5	0·7	1·5	1·9	2·1	2·3	2·5	2·5	3·1	3·3
Other Services	1·2	2·6	3·2	5·0	5·4	5·9	6·1	6·9	7·5	8·0	9·5
Loan Charges	0·9	0·9	0·8	0·8	0·9	0·9	1·0	1·2	1·5	1·9	2·2
Percentage met from Rates	47·3	42·0	40·0	34·0	35·1	33·0	32·7	33·9	35·2	34·5	33·6

appreciably less. Aid to pupils shows the same very sharp rise. The other items cannot be directly compared, because of the different basis on which the figures are computed.

The Sources of University Finance. In addition to the sums spent by local education authorities, the main heads of public expenditure on educational services are for Universities and for special kinds of research—above all, medical and agricultural research. Here are the figures of total university expenditure, excluding that of the separate Colleges of Oxford and Cambridge. They include the Scottish Universities.

TABLE 178

Income and Expenditure of Universities, Great Britain, 1938–9 and 1945–6 to 1953–4

(£million)

	1938–9	1945–6	1946–7	1947–8	1948–9	1949–50	1950–1	1951–2	1952–3
Income from:									
Endowments	1·0	1·2	1·2	1·2	1·2	1·3	1·3	1·3	1·3
Government Grants	2·4	5·1	6·9	9·4	10·8	14·1	15·8	17·1	20·7
Local Authorities	0·6	0·7	0·7	0·8	0·9	1·0	1·0	1·0	1·1
Fees	2·0	2·3	3·0	3·5	3·7	3·9	4·0	3·8	3·8
Other Sources	0·7	1·0	1·2	1·4	1·5	1·8	2·1	2·4	2·9
Expenditure on:									
Teaching Salaries	3·3	4·5	6·0	7·1	8·2	10·5	11·9	12·5	13·2
Maintenance	0·8	1·2	1·5	1·8	2·1	2·3	2·7	3·0	3·6
Administration	0·6	0·9	1·2	1·4	1·6	1·9	2·1	2·3	2·2
Other Expenses	2·1	3·4	4·3	5·6	6·1	7·0	7·6	8·5	10·1
Total Expenditure	6·8	10·0	13·0	16·0	18·0	21·8	24·3	26·4	29·0

Total expenditure rose more than fourfold between 1938–9 and 1952–3, whereas income from endowments rose by less than one third and income from fees was not quite doubled. Grants from local authorities too were less than doubled; but government grants increased more than eight times, and by 1952–3 accounted for well over two-thirds of total income, with practically no increase in public control. The University Grants Committee, operating directly under the Treasury, was scrupulous in limiting its interference with the freedom of the Universities to spend their money, including its grants, as they chose, limiting itself to advice and to asking the Universities to submit their development plans for consideration before the amounts of grant were determined. The Universities have, of course, endeavoured to adapt their plans to fit in with urgent national needs; but they have been left remarkably free from pressure in view of the high proportion of their costs now borne out of public funds.

These figures leave out of account public grants to Universities for capital expenditure, which too have been on a considerable scale, though they have not fully enabled the Universities to provide adequate accommodation for their increased number of students. Between August 1947 and July 1953 the total sums given in non-recurrent grants, mainly for building, were well over £40 million.

CHAPTER TWENTY-FIVE

HOUSING AND ROADS

HOUSING has been one of the most difficult of all post-war problems. As we saw, rents were controlled during and after the war for most working-class houses; and the rents landlords were allowed to charge were a long way below those at which newly built houses could be let at an 'economic' rent. Had such rents been charged, few working-class tenants could have afforded to pay them without suffering a serious fall in their standards of living in other respects; and accordingly most new house-building was subsidized by the Government, so as to limit the financial burdens falling on the local authorities which were the main direct providers. Even with the rents of new houses reduced by these subsidies, a big gap appeared between these rents and those of older houses subject to rent control. The costs of house-building rose very sharply during and after the war, despite the keeping down of interest rates during the immediately post-war years. The building industry had lost a large part of its labour force during the war years: in 1945 the numbers engaged in building and civil engineering were down to 722,000, as compared with 1,310,000 in 1939. By 1948 they had risen to 1,450,000, only to fall back a little in subsequent years. At the beginning of 1955 the figure was 1,421,000.

The Cost of House-building in Labour and Money. On this body of workers there were many urgent claims. But for some time after 1945 productivity remained low. Before the war it used to be reckoned that an average 'working-class' house could be built with the equivalent of an average building worker's labour for a full year; but after 1945 output was a long way below this level.

Between 1938–9 and 1949 the cost of building a standard '1947-type' house rose from £518 to £1,346, or by 160 per cent, as compared with 140 per cent in 1947. Labour cost did not rise at all between 1947 and 1949, because of improved efficiency; but the cost of materials and overheads rose sharply. Man-hours for standard houses fell between 1947 and 1949 by about 13 per cent. But up to 1947 the decrease in productivity had been serious. It was estimated that in 1947 the average number of man-hours needed for building a 'council' house rose by 45 per cent, and added about £150 to the cost. This meant a decline of nearly one-third in output per man hour.[1] By 1955 most of this decline

[1] These figures are taken from the Reports of the Committee on The Cost of House-building, published in 1948 and 1950 by the Ministry of Health.

had been made good; but houses were still very expensive in relation to pre-war costs. Interest rates and prices of materials were both high; and subsidies were still necessary both because economic rents would have taken too big a slice of working-class incomes and because they would have created much too wide a gap between the rents of new and old houses unless all the 'controls' had been removed.

Housing Subsidies: Differential Rents.   There were some who argued that this should be done, and that the State should withdraw all subsidies, except perhaps for slum-clearance, and should leave all other rents to find their economic level. But no Government dared follow such a policy, which would have meant a big rise in the rents of old houses and would have at once set on foot widespread wage-movements to meet the increased cost of living. Some local authorities tried to meet the difficulty by instituting schemes of differential rents for their tenants, either granting rent rebates to the poorer tenants, especially those with large families; or, in addition, charging higher rents to those better able to pay. But these schemes, which varied greatly from place to place, affected only a small minority of house-occupiers. The omission of the usual periodical revaluation of houses for the determination of rates payable was an additional factor in keeping down the inclusive rents charged for the older houses.

The Effects of Rent Control.   As we saw earlier, the proportion of personal incomes spent on rent and rates fell sharply as a consequence of 'controls' and subsidies. Those who argued that rents should be allowed to rise to an 'economic' level argued that the policy of subsidies was diverting too much labour to house-construction, by offering its product below cost price, at the expense of delaying other necessary building. This, they said, meant that the community was spending on house-construction more than consumers would have wished to spend had they been charged the full cost. But the Conservative Party, far from taking this view, criticized the Labour Government for providing too few houses, and promised an increase to 300,000 new houses a year; and after 1951 the rate of house-construction did actually rise by stages to this level.

Households and Earners.   At the time of the Census of 1951 there were in Great Britain 13,312,000 occupied dwellings, as compared with 10,272,000 at the Census of 1931. These were occupied by 14,481,000 households, of which 10,974,000 consisted of married persons. 1,556,000 of the households consisted of a single person, and 3,998,000 of only two persons. 8,228,000 included no children under 16 years of age, and in 3,080,000 there was but one such child. In 3,008,000 there were from two to four children under 16, and in 166,000 five or more such children. In 6,784,000 households there was but a single earner: 3,808,000 had two earners, and 1,857,000 three or more. 2,032,000 had no earner among the members. Of the 13,312,000 dwellings occupied by private households, 3,662,000 consisted of four rooms, and 4,351,000 of five rooms. 1,721,000 had only three rooms, and 949,000 one or two rooms. 1,592,000 had six rooms, and 767,000 seven or eight. Only 270,000 had more than eight rooms. 717,000 dwellings were occupied jointly by two households, and 164,000 by more than two.

Housebuilding since 1945. These dwellings were of very different ages and standards of accommodation and amenity. During the years from 1934 to 1939 new houses were being built in Great Britain at an average rate of 358,000 a year—a five-year total of 1,790,000. Between 1941 and 1944 total new house-building fell to an average of 11,200, and in 1945 it was lower still. Thereafter it gradually recovered, though not quite to the level reached in the 1930s. Total new house-building from 1946 onwards was as follows:

TABLE 179

New Houses completed in Great Britain, 1946–54

(*thousands*)

	Permanent Houses		Total	Temporary Houses		Total
	E. and W.	Scotland		E. and W.	Scotland	
1946	51·1	4·3	55·5	70·9	12·1	83·0
1947	127·5	12·1	139·6	34·4	12·0	46·4
1948	206·4	21·2	227·6	10·7	7·5	18·2
1949	171·8	25·8	197·7	—	—	—
1950	172·4	25·8	198·2	—	—	—
1951	171·9	22·9	194·7	—	—	—
1952	209·0	30·9	240·2	—	—	—
1953	279·2	39·5	318·9	—	—	—
1954	309·0	38·6	347·6	—	—	—

Thus, from 1946 up to the end of 1954, the number of new permanent houses built totalled 1,919,400, to which must be added 148,000 temporary houses built in 1946–8 and about 3,000 permanent houses built in 1945. The years 1939–45 provided only 323,000 in all.

Houses built before the War. Prior to 1934 the annual rate of building had been appreciably lower than it was during the next five years. From 1924 to 1928 the average number of new houses built was 202,000— 1,010,000 in the five years. From 1929 to 1933 it was 228,000—1,140,000 in the five years. Thus, from 1924 to 1954 inclusive the total number of new permanent houses built was about 6,182,000. Adding about

300,000 houses built between 1919 and 1923 we get a total of about 6½ million new permanent houses built since the end of the first world war—roughly half the number existing in 1954. As the rate of building for some time before 1914 was very low, many of the other half are of considerable age and of standards a long way below what would now be regarded as tolerable. But in face of continuing shortage of accommodation it has been impracticable to demolish even very unsatisfactory old dwellings.

Public and Private Building. Of the houses built since 1945, the great majority have been erected by local authorities with financial help from the national Exchequer. 1,462,000 new houses have been built in this way, in addition to 9,500 war-destroyed houses re-built, and 1,200 new houses built by local authorities in Scotland without Exchequer grants. Over the same period 333,000 new houses in all have been built by private owners, with or without Exchequer aid; and 36,000 war-destroyed houses have been privately re-built. From 1945 to 1951 the Labour Government gave a high preference to public house-building: of the houses built for private owners 187,000 were erected between 1952 and 1954.

By the end of 1954 the local authorities in Great Britain had built since the end of the war approximately 1,100,000 new houses, not including more than 8,000 war-destroyed houses re-built. Other public agencies and housing associations had built about 86,000, and about 308,000 had been built for private owners, again excluding more than 35,000 war-destroyed houses re-built. Here are the detailed figures:

TA
House-building by Types of Ag

	1945	1946	1947	1948
Local Authorities (new houses)	1·8	22·3	94·2	188·3
„ „ (re-buildings)	0·1	2·8	3·2	2·1
Private Owners (new houses)	1·0	27·3	31·5	20·4
„ „ (re-buildings)	0·0	2·9	9·4	12·3
Others	—	0·2	1·4	4·5
Total	2·9	55·5	139·7	227·6

Public and Private Building since 1951. Total house-building, after reaching 227,600 in 1948, was lower during the three following years as a result of increased priority for other kinds of construction. Under the Conservatives it was given a higher priority, and total construction of houses rose sharply in 1952 and 1953, and again in 1954. There was, however, a much sharper rise after 1951 in private than in local authority building, the rate of private building being nearly three times higher in 1953 than in 1951, and more than four times as high in 1954, whereas local authority building, after rising in 1953, declined slightly in 1954. The figures relate throughout to houses completed and not to work begun; but broadly the figures of work begun tell the same story, with a rise in 1954 to 106,800 privately built houses and a fall in local authority houses to 207,300. Northern Ireland is excluded throughout. The figures also leave out temporary houses.

Arrears of Building. This amount of construction since 1945 leaves large arrears still to be overtaken, especially in respect of replacement of obsolete dwellings. As we saw, the total number of occupied dwellings recorded in the Census of 1951 was 13,312,000; but at least a quarter of these were old, and considerably more sub-standard by modern reckoning. There is no risk of the building industry lacking full work for a long time to come: as we have seen, many other types of buildings, besides houses, are needed for the development of the social services, as well as for industry and recreation. Many of the new housing estates —not to mention the older ones, which are in many cases even worse provided—are short of buildings needed for community purposes.

Building and Civil Engineering: Road Accidents. Moreover, building work is to some extent competitive with civil engineering in its demand on labour; and here again there are huge arrears to be overtaken. Road maintenance and construction have utterly failed to keep pace with the rapid increase in the number of vehicles on the roads, including the

1945–Dec. 1954 (*thousands*)

1949	1950	1951	1952	1953	1954	Total
165·2	163·5	162·6	193·2	238·8	235·0	1,464·9
0·8	0·2	0·0	0·1	0·1	—	9·4
20·3	24·8	21·0	33·6	62·1	90·6	332·6
5·5	2·5	1·4	0·8	0·8	—	35·6
5·9	7·1	9·7	12·5	17·0	22·0	80·3
197·7	198·2	194·7	240·2	318·8	347·6	1,922·9

formidable increase in big lorries, which are a terrible cause of obstruction. The toll of road accidents runs higher and higher because of this neglect; and there is besides the prodigious waste of time in congested urban areas and the general slowing down of traffic despite the greater speed of which road vehicles are capable. Road accidents were fewer during the war, when there were severe restrictions on the use of petrol; but they have increased again and in 1954 exceeded the 1938 total. Here are the essential figures:

TA!

Road Accidents in C

	1938	1944	1945	1946
Total Casualties (000's)	233·4	130·9	138·3	162·5
Deaths	6,648	6,416	5,256	5,062
Serious Injuries (000's)	50·8	33·5	32·5	36·6
Licences current (000's)				
Private Cars	1,944	755	1,487	1,770
Goods Vehicles	497	452	477	563
Public Service Vehicles	97	97	105	111
Motor-cycles and Tricycles	462	124	309	462

Thus, total casualties fell by 44 per cent between 1938 and 1944, while the number of private cars in use fell by more than 60 per cent and that of motor-cycles by nearly three-quarters—whereas goods vehicles fell by only 9 per cent. Total casualties again reached the 1938 level only in 1954; whereas private cars returned to it in 1947, and, increasing each year, were 60 per cent above it in 1954. The growth in goods vehicles was much greater: the 1938 number was well exceeded in 1946, and had more than doubled by 1953. Motor-cycles too were back at the 1938 number in 1946, and had more than doubled by 1952. The record of deaths is rather better: in 1944 it was nearly as high as in 1938; but it has been well below these levels ever since—lowest in 1948, but still then the cause of more than 4,500 deaths, as compared with more than 5,000 in both 1953 and 1954.

Of the 1954 casualties, pedestrians suffered 61,381, pedal cyclists 49,295, motor-cyclists and their passengers 52,531, and other drivers and their passengers 75,074. Of those killed in 1953 pedestrians numbered 2,233, of whom 602 were children; pedal cyclists 720, including 126 children, motor-cyclists 1,048, and others 1,087, including 69 children. Those seriously injured included 9,681 children.

The Growth of Motor Traffic. New private cars registered in 1954 numbered 387,276 as against 295,073 the previous year and a mere 110,634 in 1948. The 1938 total was 272,192. But the new registrations of motor-cycles and tricycles, which were only 45,041 in 1938, had risen to 141,066 in 1953 and 168,720 in 1954. New registrations of goods vehicles rose from 68,604 in 1938 to 102,243 in 1953 and 113,436 in 1954.

Expenditure on Roads. Thus, by 1955 an immensely greater volume of

traffic was using the roads. Expenditure, however, had risen in the aggregate only from £58·3 million in 1938–9 to £86·0 million in 1952–3 and
£90 million in 1953–4. Of the 1954 total £63·4 million went on main-

ain, 1938 and 1944–54

1947	1948	1949	1950	1951	1952	1953	1954
166·2	153·4	176·8	201·3	216·5	208·0	226·8	283·3
4,881	4,513	4,773	5,012	5,250	4,706	5,090	5,010
35·7	33·1	43·4	48·8	52·4	50·4	56·5	57·2
1,944	1,961	2,131	2,258	2,380	2,508	2,762	3,100
674	772	848	900	938	968	1,000	
120	134	139	141	140	136	119	110
528	559	654	752	848	949	1,037	1,139

tenance and minor improvements, and only £7·7 million on new construction and major improvements, the remaining £19 million being absorbed by administration and road cleaning. Trunk roads, paid for
entirely out of national funds, accounted for £10·6 million for maintenance and construction; other classified roads for £11·3 million, and
unclassified roads for £19·2 million. In 1954 the total mileage of public
roads in Great Britain was 187,000 as compared with 179,630 in 1938.
Trunk roads, however, had risen from 4,459 to 8,270 miles.

The Question of Motorways. It was abundantly clear by 1956 that a
large programme of road construction and improvement was long over-
due. One great question was whether in addition to ordinary construction there should be built a new system of through 'motorways',
adapted for long-distance traffic, and perhaps reserved for such traffic
and partly maintained by tolls levied on the users. But apart from this
possibility much needed to be done to relieve the congestion in town-
centres by providing by-passes or alternative routes, to increase the
capacity of main roads by providing dual-carriageways, and to remove
bottlenecks. The Government had already announced a small programme in 1953; but its obvious inadequacy led to demands for further
action, and in June 1955 the Government made a further announcement, still for the most part in rather vague terms. It included, however,
the starting of work on a new motorway from London to Yorkshire,
to end in branches to Sheffield and Doncaster, and to relieve pressure
on the existing Great North Road. Only a section of this road—from
London to Dunchurch—was to be put in hand in the near future; and
even on this section building was not expected to start for about two
years, the interval being consumed in negotiations connected with the

acquisition of the land needed. The announcement also included a projected motorway of similar type from Preston to Birmingham; but no date for starting work on this was even mentioned. Another project was for a new crossing of the Firth of Forth, either by a bridge or by a tube moored to the bed of the Forth.

The Road Programme of 1954. In putting forward his plans, Mr. Boyd-Carpenter estimated that they would involve, apart from the cost of the projected motorways, an expenditure by the Treasury on improving trunk and classified roads of £8·25 million in 1955–6, and of £17 million, £30 million, and £42 million during the following three years. He also reckoned that in the fourth year of the plan local highway authorities would be spending roughly £35 million. Road maintenance, he said, as distinct from major improvements, would continue to cost the Exchequer about £30 million a year. He announced the intention to charge tolls in suitable cases for the use of the new motorways. No mention was made either of the long-debated Severn scheme or of the plan to build a new bridge across the Tamar.

The road problem is admittedly difficult, even apart from the problems of expense and the demand on man-power involved in it. Great Britain's towns were not made to carry anything approaching the volume of traffic that is already circulating, or failing to circulate, in them, or to find space for the ever-increasing number of parked vehicles. There have been many proposals for the construction of parking places underground or in multi-story buildings; but there is another school of thought which wishes to deal with the problem by means of restrictions rather than by providing increased facilities. Take the case of Oxford, where conditions are becoming almost intolerable because of road congestion. Traffic pressure on the High Street and other parts of the central area must be reduced somehow; but there is no way of doing this that is not open to grave objections. One school of thought, strong in the City, favours the making of new roads by-passing the centre of the City—one across Christ Church Meadow and another across the University Parks. Another section, strong in the University, bitterly resents these proposed desecrations and demands that Magdalen Bridge and the High Street be closed to all or most motor traffic and that by-passes be built further away from the City, which it is said should have its ancient peace restored to it. The plain fact, however, is that the major part of the congestion in Oxford is due, not to through traffic, but to local road-users who require to visit or to be in the central area, and can hardly be kept out of it unless there is to be a total prohibition of all motoring in Oxford—a barely conceivable solution because of the inconveniences it would cause. Yet no one can contemplate without dismay the spoiling either of Christ Church Meadow or of the Parks; and it has to be recognized that there is no really satisfactory solution.

Oxford is no doubt an extreme case, because the presence of so many beautiful and historic buildings makes it impracticable to provide alternative routes through the City by pulling down what gets most in the way. In many other cities, the problem is more one of cost, where there are few buildings whose loss need be regretted on aesthetic grounds. Clearly, a great opportunity was missed when the Government failed, at the end of the war, to take over all urban land in order to get the fullest possible freedom to re-build the central urban areas—especially those which had suffered seriously in the *blitz*. If this had been done, the cost would have been much less than it is bound to be if every demolition or road-widening involves complicated negotiations with a host of separate landowners and tenants.

CHAPTER TWENTY-SIX

TOWN AND COUNTRY PLANNING

THEORETICALLY, the whole area of Great Britain is now covered by town and country planning. In each Administrative County and County Borough, the local authority was required by the Act of 1947 to prepare a plan of development covering prospective changes in land-use over the next twenty years; and these plans now exist. They are, however, of widely varying value, and to a great extent it remains to be seen how far they will be acted upon so as to prevent socially undesirable development, and also how far public authorities will be prepared to face the cost of public developments of the right type, such as improved roads and better provision of service and amenity buildings in connection with new and old housing areas. A great opportunity was missed when the Government failed, after 1945, to nationalize the land, with due provision for non-disturbance of existing occupants save for good cause; for nothing short of this can bring about a right balance in the use of land or ensure that development follows lines consistent with public advantage.

Development Values. Instead of doing this, the Labour Government acted on the recommendation of the Uthwatt Committee and attempted to nationalize 'development value' without taking over the land itself. This meant that every owner of land who considered that his land possessed a potential value for a 'development' use different from its existing use—e.g. for building—was entitled to put in a claim for compensation for loss of 'development rights'. To meet such claims, the Government set aside a fund of £300 million, to be shared out as far as it would go in proportion to the claims recognized as valid by the tribunal set up for assessing them. Under the Act, all projects of land development were in future to require the sanction of the local Planning Authority—i.e. of the County or County Borough Council concerned; and any owner wishing to develop his land and having got permission was to be required to pay a 'development charge' corresponding to the increase in the land's value expected as a result of development. He would thus, where actual development took place, pay back what he had received in compensation for loss of development rights; but there was to be no compensation in respect of 'development values' coming into existence after the Act came into force, such values being regarded as rightfully accruing to the public rather than to the private owner of the land. It was intended that the £300 million should be paid out as soon as the proper value of the claims had been assessed, and that if the approved claims exceeded £300 million, each successful claimant should be paid so many shillings in the £1, so as to keep the total compensation down to that sum. In fact, the sum payable in the £1 would have been about 16s. if the scheme had been carried out, except for prior claims met in full. But before the scheme could be carried through the Conservative Government altered the law. The £300 million fund remained; but payments out of it were to be made only where actual development took place or where development claims were rejected as undesirable or inconsistent with the plans approved by the Planning Authorities. Where development was allowed, the sum due to the landowner was to be set off against the 'development charge' he would have to pay, so as to leave him neither better nor worse off— for he would get his compensation where development claims were refused and would profit by the development where they were granted.

The Case for National Ownership of Land. One reason for this change was the desire of the Government to avoid paying out at once a sum of £300 million, against which development charges could be recovered only gradually over many years. Another was that, whereas it had been intended and expected that, in view of the nationalization of 'development rights', land would change hands at prices representing only existing-use values, in fact land sales were taking place in many instances at higher prices, so that the total price, inclusive of 'development charges', was being artificially inflated. How much better it would have been for the public to acquire the land outright, and with it the power to ignore financial considerations arising out of divided ownership! For example, if privately owned land in a built-up area is taken over for a public park or playing field and building is thus driven further from the centre, the total commercial value of the land near the centre may fall, while the value of the new land needed for building rises—so that one owner's property loses, while another's gains, value. If both lots of land are publicly owned, no gain or loss need occur, and each parcel of land can be used for the most socially desirable purpose without giving rise to compensation claims. This obvious solution, however, was rejected as 'politically impracticable' and the way was opened to new speculation in land values despite the attempt to do away with it.

Under the revised arrangements now in force 'development charges' remain payable and compensation to owners of land must still be allowed where development is refused. This latter necessity deters Planning Authorities from refusing to allow development even where it is against the public interest; for if they refuse permission to develop there is naturally no 'development charge' to set off against what has to be paid. Moreover, in the past the 'betterment' charges which could be lawfully laid on the promoters of development schemes have proved very difficult indeed to collect. There were only three cases in all of successful collection under the pre-war Act. The situation should be better, now that 'development charges' can be set off against compensation payments; but the whole scheme is much too complicated to work easily or to ensure that development takes the right course.

The Rise of Town and Country Planning.   Town planning under Act of Parliament began in 1909, on a small scale. Town and country planning began only in the 1930s and covered up to the war only about 3 per cent of the total land area. It is a great advance that it has now become general; but it remains very difficult for local Planning Authorities to anticipate correctly the course of development over twenty years ahead, or to plan it rightly, especially as they have no positive control over the growth of local industry and employment. All they can do is to 'zone' certain areas for residential and others for industrial development and hope that the required factories will come their way—if they want them. The number of persons living in an area is bound to depend on the openings it offers for employment of different kinds—for men and women, and for workers of particular kinds and degrees of skill. But the Planning Authorities, though they can offer certain inducements to industrialists to establish factories, etc., in a particular area, cannot compel them to come or ensure a right balance of such as do come between different industries and types of work. Nor can they prevent an industrialist from moving elsewhere should he so decide. They have therefore to plan largely in the dark; and many of them, in order to be on the safe side, are apt to 'over-zone', especially by reserving unduly large areas for both housing and industrial development—far larger, in the aggregate, than the possible population of the whole country. As against this, some areas are determined to prevent development if they can, either in the hope of preserving local amenities, or in order to protect agricultural land, or to preserve local monopolies of demand for labour, or simply because they wish to remain 'select'. The power of such areas to prevent development has, however, been much reduced by the Act of 1947, which made the Counties, instead of the non-county boroughs and county districts, the Planning Authorities outside the County Boroughs.

The 'Trading Estates'.   Side by side with the extension of town and country planning in general have gone two special steps closely related to it—the development of Industrial Trading Estates and the establishment of New Towns designed to re-house a part of the 'overspill' of the great congested urban areas. The 'Trading Estate' movement began at Slough, as a legacy of the first world war, a big area that had been used for war purposes and subsequently for disposal of war stores being made the basis for a new factory area offering central facilities and expansible factory units. The movement developed in the 1930s chiefly as an attempt to attract new industries to the 'Depressed Areas', by offering facilities for hiring factory space or even getting factories built to suit the applicant's needs, as well as common services and the assurance of local supplies of labour. Supplemented by the work of the Nuffield Trust, which could offer subsidies to profit-seeking ventures, it achieved substantial, though limited, success, both in creating more demand for labour in the 'Depressed Areas' and in furthering a better balance between demands for labour of different kinds—e.g. for men's and women's labour in centres of heavy industry. After 1945 the 'Depressed Areas' were re-named 'Development Areas'; and the movement continued over a rather larger total area; but it has never covered most of the country or even of the industrial centres. In certain cases, however, as at Speke near Liverpool, and of course at Slough, there are Trading Estates set up not in Depressed Areas as such, but for the general furtherance of industrial expansion on lines which make it easier for businesses short of capital to get started in hired premises and with the aid of centralized services which reduce their capital costs.

New Towns.   Some of the 14 'New Towns' which have been established since 1945 are closely connected with Trading Estates—Newton Aycliffe and Cwmbrun. Two—Peterlee and Glenrother—are coalfield towns, intended to encourage counterbalancing light industries as well; and another, Corby, is a steel town, closely connected with the huge works established by Stewart and Lloyds. But the majority—8 out of the 14— are being built as 'dispersal' towns for Greater London, designed for industrial as well as residential dispersal at sufficient distances from London itself not to serve as mere dormitories or to become engulfed in the growth of the metropolitan built-up area. These 8 have a total planned population of rather more than 300,000, as compared with an actual previous population of rather under 100,000 in the areas concerned. Some of them cannot strictly be called 'New Towns': they are rather large planned extensions of existing urban areas, such as Basildon, Hemel Hempstead and Welwyn—this last being based on an earlier planned Garden City. Their planned populations range from 80,000 at Harlow and at Basildon to 25,000 at Bracknell and at Hatfield and, outside the London Region, to a mere 10,000 at Newton Aycliffe. What distinguishes the whole 14 is that they are being built, not, like Letchworth and the earlier Welwyn, by private societies or trusts, but under the auspices of publicly appointed Corporations—which, however, are not local authorities responsible for local public services, but capital-providing bodies more closely analogous to Investment Companies. In course of time the New Towns will of course acquire their own elected Councils; but for the time being they remain subject for purposes of local government to the authorities of the areas within which they have been set up and it falls on these authorities to establish schools and provide for other public services and also to share the task of house-building with the New Town Corporations and with private enterprise.

Actual Development in the New Towns.   Table 182 on page 372 presents a general picture of the development of the New Towns up to the end of 1953. Most of them had not by then advanced far towards the populations planned for them: the total increase over their previous population was under 75,000 out of a planned increase of about 480,000. They had only about 25,000 finished new houses, but there were nearly 14,000 building and another 13,500 were on the programme for 1954. The number of new shops varied greatly, partly because in some cases there were many already in existence: the number of new schools varied less; but provision seemed to lag behind outside the London Ring, except at Corby. The number of new factories and also their sizes varied a great deal, partly because in some cases houses were being built for people already in local employment. Total Corporation expenditure also varied much; but it must be borne in mind that these figures exclude all expenditure not borne by the Corporations, such as sums spent by local authorities and by every kind of private enterprise, including such expenditure on houses as well as on shops, factories, schools and other buildings. On the whole, the rate of building, especially for houses, was gathering momentum and seemed to be approaching its peak.

The Expansion of Existing Small Towns.   Originally it had been the intention to set up many more New Towns than are included in this list—especially away from the London Ring. Many projects, however, ran into difficulties—above all, in Lancashire—and were given up or postponed. There had been from the outset differences between the advocates of New Towns and those who preferred planned expansion of existing small towns with the co-operation of big towns needing to rid themselves of excess population; and from 1951 some of the emphasis was shifted to encouraging this simpler form of development. In highly industrialized regions it is usually very difficult to find suitable sites for brand-new towns; and the existing big towns did not look with favour on plans for removing populations to places a considerable distance away, in areas with different traditions and ways of living. It is a good deal easier in such cases to disperse population and employment from the big congested centres to small towns that can make room for more people. Unfortunately it is still easier not to disperse them at all, but either to allow the congestion to continue or merely to extend the built-up areas of the big towns further and further—which is what the New Towns were designed to prevent.

Amenities in the New Towns.   Clearly the New Towns, even if they reach their target increase of nearly half a million new inhabitants, will not make a major difference to the population structure. They are only one among a number of means of reducing the pressure in a planned way. It is an essential part of what is aimed at that they shall be both well planned, at not too high a density, and well equipped with service and amenity provisions and transport facilities as well as with houses and balanced openings for industrial employment. It is clear that, because of restrictions on building and non-productive capital expenditure, they have so far been starved of adequate provision for services and amenities and that there are considerable arrears to be made good in these respects. On the whole, building density in them has not been excessive, a common figure being 13 houses to the acre; but there appear to be very wide differences in the provision made for parks, playing fields, and other open spaces. Standards of public open space aimed at range from 2 acres for 1,000 persons at Basildon to 12·4 acres at Cwmbrun and 11 at Hemel Hempstead, with Stevenage, Crawley and Harlow all very low down at from 3 to 5 acres. There is obviously a danger that considerations of cost will lead to a low level of amenities and to a fall in housing standards—tendencies which should be strongly resisted.

Houses or Flats?   These dangers of course extend far beyond the New Towns. They arise out of the high costs of building and the recognized necessity of subsidies to render it possible on an adequate scale. There is also the familiar controversy between the advocates of single-family houses and those who favour a considerable amount of re-housing in blocks of flats. It appears to be beyond question both that in Great Britain most families prefer separate houses of their own, if possible with adequate gardens, and that such dwellings, though they use more land, are cheaper to provide than large tenement buildings. Moreover, saving of land by flat-building is often due largely to inadequate allowances of open space round them. In some cases, no doubt, such building is unavoidable; but in general the Town and Country Planning Association's strong preference for houses and private gardens seems to be basically sound and in accordance with the views of most of the prospective inhabitants. This strengthens the case for a vigorous policy of dispersal, either into New Towns or by the expansion of existing small towns possessing favourable situations. The additional encroachment on unbuilt land is in any event relatively small and can be largely kept away from really valuable agricultural land. If the ordinary family prefers a house of its own, why should it not have one—especially as the cost is likely to be lower?

TABLE 182
New Towns: Statistics, December 1953

	Date of Commission's Appointment	Area in Acres	Previous Population	Population, Dec. 1953	Planned Population	New Houses completed	Houses under construction	New Shops completed or under construction	New Schools completed or under construction	New Factories	Capital spent by Corporation only £000's
London Ring:											
Basildon	2/49	7,834	25,000	28,500	80,000	1,539	579	29	4	8	2,962
Bracknell	10/49	1,850	5,000	6,500	25,000	316	587	—	—	5	1,740
Crawley	2/47	5,920	10,000	18,000	50,000	2,975	2,362	76	9	31	10,500
Harlow	5/47	6,320	4,500	15,500	80,000	3,824	2,200	49	3	52	12,400
Hatfield	6/48	2,340	8,000	12,000	25,000	1,280	571	—	3	—	1,935
Hemel Hempstead	3/47	5,910	21,000	32,000	60,000	3,861	1,200	95	4	11	10,600
Stevenage	12/46	6,070	6,400	13,100	60,000	2,268	1,125	16	3	5	9,000
Welwyn	6/48	4,231	18,200	21,000	36,500	1,445	618	17	4	4	5,500
Others:											
Corby	5/50	2,500	14,000	19,500	40,000	1,713	550	59	4	2	1,350
Cwmbrun	11/40	3,160	12,000	14,000	35,000	1,043	979	6	1	3	1,750
E Kilbride	8/47	10,250	2,300	7,800	45,000	1,433	1,500	13	1	3	4,975
Glenrother	10/48	5,730	600	5,000	32,000	1,045	550	19	2	—	1,914
Newton Aycliffe	7/47	880	60	4,060	10,000	1,250	600	13	1	—	3,258
Peterlee	3/48	2,350	200	4,500	30,000	1,250	450	9	2	1	3,500
Total			127,260	201,460	608,500	25,242	13,871	401	41	125	71,384

CHAPTER TWENTY-SEVEN

HEALTH

SINCE *The Condition of Britain* first appeared in 1937 there has been an unquestionable improvement in the state of the people's health. This is due partly to improved medical knowledge and practice, including the advances in medical attention under the National Health Service, but also partly to full employment and to a better and more secure standard of living for the poorer sections of the people. Much remains to be done, especially in improved conditions for old people and in conserving and restoring the work capacity of those in whom it has become impaired by accident or disease; but the all-round improvement is great and the promise for the future good in most respects.

The Changed Age-structure. In assessing the extent of the advance it is necessary to take account of the changed age-structure of the population, which includes relatively fewer children and more elderly people than at any previous period. In 1954, out of every 1,000 persons in England and Wales, 225 were aged under 15, 125 from 15 to 24, 147 from 25 to 34, 140 from 35 to 44—making 637 under 45—142 from 45 to 54, 107 from 55 to 64, and 114 over 65; whereas in 1931 238 were under 15, 173 from 15 to 24, 160 from 25 to 34, 137 from 35 to 44—making 708 under 45—123 from 45 to 54, 93 from 55 to 64, and 74 over 65.

In Scotland the age-structure of 1954 was somewhat different. Out of every 1,000 there were 248 under 15, 139 between 15 and 25, 146 from 25 to 34, and 133 from 35 to 44—making 666 under 45. There were 134 aged 45 to 54, 98 aged 55 to 64, and 102 over 65. The Scots were a younger nation, with more children and fewer old people, but also with fewer in the groups of working age. In 1931 the Scottish proportions in each 1,000 were as follows: 270 under 15, 178 from 15 to 24, 152 from 25 to 34, and 126 from 35 to 44—making 726 under 45; and 113 from 45 to 54, 89 from 55 to 64, and 73 over 65. Then too Scotland had a higher proportion of children; but the difference in old people was smaller than in 1954.

The proportions of working age, taken as 15 to 64 for both sexes, were in 1954 for England and Wales 661 and for Scotland 650. In 1931 they were 686 for England and Wales and 658 for Scotland.

Improved Expectation of Life. As we saw (see pp. 1 ff.) these changes reveal the combined effects of a reduced birth-rate, modified by a sharp fall in infant mortality, and of a reduced death-rate in childhood and in adult life. It is not so much that the old tend to live longer as that the prospects of survival have improved from infancy and childhood through the middle years. A century ago the expectation of life for a male infant at birth was under 40 years: to-day it exceeds 67 years. But for a male aged 65 the improvement over a century has been only from 10·8 years to 12·0 years of further life. The old do not live much longer; but far fewer of the relatively young die prematurely. For girls aged 15–19 the death-rate has actually been halved since 1949, mainly because of the sharp fall in deaths from tuberculosis.

The crude death-rate per 1,000 of population in England and Wales fell only from 12·5 for 1936–40 to 11·4 in 1953. But this is misleading: when account is taken of the changed age-structure, there has been a fall in what is called the 'comparative mortality index' from 1·0 in 1938 to 0·81 in 1953. In the early 1930s the expectation of life at birth was 59 for males and 63 for females: in 1953, it was 67 and 72. The expectation at age 1 was 62 and 65: in 1953, it was 68 and 73.

Indices of Mortality. The following table shows the 'Comparative Mortality Indices' for certain diseases in England and Wales, taking 1938 to = 1·0.

TABLE 183

Comparative Mortality Indices for certain Diseases, 1931–39, 1940–9 and 1950–3

	1931–9	1940–9	1950	1951	1952	1953
Tuberculosis (all forms)	1·18	0·99	0·59	0·51	0·39	0·32
Typhoid and Paratyphoid	1·25	0·44	0·09	0·12	0·12	0·03
Dysentery	0·78	1·23	0·43	0·49	0·24	0·24
Meningococcal Infections	1·25	1·36	0·36	0·38	0·38	0·39
Cancer	1·0	0·99	1·01	1·01	1·01	1·01
Diabetes Mellitus	1·01	0·77	0·62	0·62	0·55	0·52
Pneumonia (all forms)	—	0·73	0·53	0·67	0·55	0·51
Influenza	2·46	1·15	0·71	2·87	0·31	1·14

Observe the almost complete elimination of typhoid as a cause of death: this applies also to diphtheria. Observe the very sharp fall in mortality from tuberculosis, dysentery, and meningococcal infections. Even in the case of diabetes, the mortality index has been practically halved. Contrast the failure to achieve any improvement in the case of cancer, which has actually worsened in the case of males. Mortality from influenza continues to fluctuate very widely from year to year, in accordance with the occurrence or non-occurrence of serious epidemics.

The figures for Scotland are not fully comparable; but there too the death-rate from respiratory tuberculosis fell sharply from 107 per 100,000 of population in 1914–1918 to 54 in 1939, 23 in 1953 and 20 in 1954. The death-rate from other forms of tuberculosis fell over the same period from 54 per 100,000 to 4 in 1953 and 2 in 1954.

Death from Infectious Diseases. Here are the numbers of deaths in England and Wales from the principal infectious diseases, with the death-rates per million inhabitants, comparing the average of 1940 to 1944 with 1953.

TABLE 184

Deaths from Principal Infectious Diseases: England and Wales, 1953 and 1940–4

	Number of Deaths 1953	Rate per Million Inhabitants 1940–4 (average)	1953
Tuberculosis, respiratory	7,913	563	179
„ other	989	113	22
Typhoid and Paratyphoid	5	2	0
Meningococcal Infections	291	36	7
Diphtheria	23	48	1
Gastro-enteritis	1,155	109	26
Influenza	6,465	198	147
Measles	245	18	6
Poliomyelitis	338	3	8
Whooping Cough	243	31	6
Post-abortive and Puerperal Sepsis	105	13	2

Of infectious diseases only poliomyelitis shows a worsened death-rate: in most other cases the improvement has been vast.

Child and Maternal Mortality. In addition to the fall in infant mortality from 53 for each 1,000 live births in 1938 to 27 in 1953 there has been a big reduction in the proportion of still births, from 38 for each 1,000 total births in 1938 to 22 in 1953. Deaths at ages 1–14 have also been sharply reduced, from 2·3 to 0·66 of all persons living; and maternal mortality, which for so long resisted all attempts to reduce it, has fallen from 3·24 to 0·75 for each 1,000 live births. In 1953, of 9 principal causes of death, diseases of the circulatory system still accounted for more than one-third of the total (36·2 per cent). Cancer came next (17·5 per cent); tuberculosis accounted for no more than 1·8 per cent.

The National Health Service. The improvement in general health conditions is obviously related to the creation since the war of a National Health Service available to the entire population, including general practitioner, specialist and hospital services. The cost of this service falls mainly on the Exchequer and is met out of general taxation, though a small proportion of the total is provided by a contribution from the National Insurance Fund. In 1953–4 the total expenditure on the National Health Service amounted to £503½ million for the United Kingdom as a whole: of this £74 million was derived from the Insurance Fund and £33 million from other sources, including patients' payments. The main cost was that of hospital, specialist and ancillary services, amounting to £311 million: general medical services cost £60 million, dental services £23 million, and pharmaceutical services nearly £47 million. Grants to local health authorities accounted for £22 million, compensation for loss of right to sell medical practices for more than £6 million, and central purchases of medical stores and equipment for £8 million.

Hospitals. In 1954 the hospital service in England and Wales employed a medical and dental staff of 11,106 full-time and 24,439 part-time persons. Other professional and technical staff, exclusive of nurses, numbered 15,555 full-time, 8,179 part-time, and 4,566 students. 4,803 of the part-time workers were chaplains: the biggest groups of full-time workers were 3,324 physiotherapists, 2,985 radiographers, 1,949 medical laboratory technicians, 1,173 pharmacists, and 1,217 occupational therapists. Full-time almoners numbered 935, and technical engineers of various types 1,346. Of other employees, administrative and clerical workers numbered 26,963, staffs of Regional Hospital Boards 1,973, and staffs of Blood Transfusion Centres 1,573. Nursing staffs in N.H.S. hospitals included 50,434 full-time and 10,058 part-time trained nurses, 48,174 student nurses, 10,438 full-time and 5,717 part-time assistant nurses, and 3,720 pupil assistant nurses. Other nursing staffs numbered 22,727 full-time and 13,358 part-time. Midwives and pupil midwives numbered 10,188, of whom 1,230 were part-time. These figures give a total nursing and midwifery staff of 144,551 full-time and 30,363 part-time. Hospital domestic staff accounted in 1952 for a further 131,825 full-time and 41,711 part-time employees. This gives, for England and Wales only, a total staff of 443,549 persons, 334,254 full-time and 109,295 part-time. There are a few thousands more in hospitals outside the National Health Service. In terms of persons employed the hospital service constitutes a major 'industry'.

The General Practitioner Service. Outside the hospital services, general medical practitioners working under the National Health Service in England and Wales numbered 19,300 in 1954, and to these must be added 1,504 practising as assistants, 296 trainee doctors, and 65 practising only in maternal medical services. 11,583 of the principals in general practice were practising in partnerships of two or more—9,543 of them in partnerships of two or three doctors. The average number of patients on the list of each principal (excluding assistants) was 2,293. In 1952 of 3,591 single-handed doctors in general practice in urban areas 526 had fewer than 500 patients on their lists, 393 between 500 and 1,000, 461 from 1,000 to 1,500, 534 from 1,500 to 2,000, 546 from 2,000 to 2,500, 488 from 2,500 to 3,000, 505 from 3,000 to 3,600, 114 from 3,600 to 4,000, and 24 more than 4,000. In rural areas, out of 985, 321 had fewer than 1,500, 453 had between 1,500 and 2,500, and 211 more than 2,500. In intermediate areas, out of 1,486, 427 had fewer than 1500, 535 between 1,500 and 2,500, and 524 more than 2,500.

The Health Service in Scotland. To the figures given in the foregoing pages for England and Wales must be added those for Scotland. The Scottish National Health Service employed in March 1954, 2,531 principal general practitioners and 272 assistants, and 1,168 dentists in general practice. Scottish hospitals had a medical and dental staff of 1,880 full-time and 1,123 part-time persons. Nursing staff numbered 19,953 full-time and 3,885 part-time; domestic staff 13,514 and 3,940; and administrative, clerical and other staffs 10,747, including part-time workers counted as one-half. Patients on doctors' lists numbered 4,915,000—an average of 1,753 to each doctor. Occupied hospital beds numbered 56,065. Of particular importance in Scotland were the arrangements for air transport of patients from the Highlands and Islands to centres where adequate treatment could be given.

Staffs and Training. The combined national health personnel for Great Britain in 1954 thus numbered well over 500,000—of whom about 384,000 were full-time workers. There was still, however, in 1956 a substantial shortage of staff. Hospital beds were out of use, despite the urgent demand for them, because there were too few nurses; and there was a prospect of an acute scarcity of dentists on account of heavy impending retirements. Medical and dental education have been considerably expanded. The British Universities had in 1952–3 a total of 13,511 full-time medical and 2,715 full-time dental students, as compared with 11,883 and 1,488 in 1938–9; but the increases were not enough. There were, however, difficulties in the way of more rapid expansion, in respect both of the provision of teaching staffs and of maintaining the standards of admission and examination. By far the biggest centre of medical education was London, with 5,630 doctors and 1,008 dentists in training. Glasgow came next, with 1,118 medical and 210 dental students, followed closely by Edinburgh, with 1,072 and 176. Wales had very small medical schools, and no dental schools at all. Oxford and Cambridge had only 348 and 542 medical, and no dental students. Medicine and dentistry together accounted in 1953 for just under 20 per cent of the total student population of the Universities, as against 26½ per cent in 1938–9. Expansion in these fields had not kept pace with the general growth of university education. No doubt, the long courses acted as a deterrent; for many of those coming out of military

service were eager to make a quick start at earning a living. But un-
questionably another factor was the reluctance of the academic doctors
and dentists to add large numbers to the medical and dental registers,
for fear of lowering status and remuneration.

The Postponement of Health Centres. The most serious failure of the
National Health Service, up to the present, has been the indefinite postponement of the proposed Health Centres, at which groups of doctors
were to be given facilities both for combined practice and for carrying
out on the spot many forms of diagnosis and treatment which at
present require hospital services. There has been some development
under the service of combined practice by partnerships, which make it
possible for doctors to specialize up to a point in sharing out general
practitioner's work; but this is a very different thing from providing
practitioners with well-equipped Centres, including proper auxiliary
staffs. One big reason why the provision of Health Centres has been
postponed has been shortage of building capacity in face of the urgent
demand for houses, schools, and industrial buildings. But another factor
has been fear of the cost; for even without the Centres the National
Health Service has turned out a good deal more costly than official
opinion expected it to be. Hence the attempts to reduce expenditure by
imposing charges for medicines and surgical appliances—not so much
in order to raise any great sums by these means as in the hope of
deterring the public from making some of the demands they would
make if the Service were to remain wholly free. These charges, when
they were first introduced, were argued for on grounds of financial
emergency and were said to be only temporary. But there seems to be
no present intention of remitting them.

Comparative Vital Statistics. Comparisons between the health conditions of Great Britain and those of other advanced countries are in
general none too favourable. The crude death-rates and rates of infant
mortality for a number of the leading countries in 1938 and in 1954
are as shown in Table 185.

Of all the countries given in the table, only Eire had a higher death-
rate in 1954 than the United Kingdom; but the infant mortality rate
was lower than those of all the others, except Sweden, New Zealand,
Holland and Australia. The United Kingdom birth-rate, after the post-
war bulge, had fallen back almost to the 1938 level, whereas in most of
the countries there had been a big rise. Only Italy, Western Germany
and Sweden showed a fall: the rises were very great in the United
States, Canada, Australia and New Zealand, and were substantial in
France and Switzerland. Infant mortality rates had fallen greatly in
every one of the countries. They had been more than halved in the
United Kingdom and Sweden, halved in Italy, and almost halted in
the United States, New Zealand and France. The United Kingdom,

TABLE 185

Birth- and Death-rates and Rates of Infant Mortality in Selected Countries,
1938 and 1954

	Birth-rate		Death-rate		Infant Mortality Rate	
	1938	1954	1938	1954	1938	1954
United Kingdom	15·5	15·6	11·8	11·4	55	26
U.S.A.	17·6	24·9	10·6	9·2	51	27
Australia	17·5	22·5	9·6	9·1	38	23*
New Zealand	18·0	24·7	9·7	9·0	36	20
Canada	20·7	28·5	9·7	8·1	64	36*
Eire	19·4	21·1	23·7	12·1	67	39*
S. Africa (white)	25·0	25·5	9·5	8·6	52	34
France	15·0	18·7	15·8	11·9	71	37
W. Germany	19·7	15·7	11·4	10·4	59	43
Switzerland	15·2	17·0	11·6	10·0	43	30*
Sweden	14·9	14·6	11·5	9·6	42	18
Holland	20·5	21·6	8·5	7·5	37	21
Italy	23·8	17·6	14·1	9·0	106	53

* 1953.

then, stood very well in respect of the improvement in the infant mortality rate, but much less well, comparatively, in terms of the general death-rate—though this too had been slightly reduced.

Mortality and Social Class. In the United Kingdom some disquietude was felt because the fall in death-rates appeared to have been spread almost evenly over persons belonging to different social classes, whereas one would have expected improved health services to bring greater benefits to the poorer than to the richer groups. The facts have not yet been fully investigated; but in respect of infant mortality an important piece of work has been produced by Dr. J. N. Morris and Mr. J. A. Heady, of the Medical Research Unit (see *The Lancet*, February 12 and March 12, 1955). From this source I take the following table. (See Table 186 on pages 380–1). The position improved in all classes, both before and after 1939. Between 1911 and 1939 it improved least in the top and bottom classes; and this trend continued between 1939 and 1950. The declines were much greater in mortality after the first four weeks than in neo-natal mortality; but broadly the same class-pattern appeared in both. There was no doubt less easy scope for improvement in the highest class; but it is notable that the second, or intermediate, class showed by all four tests the greatest advance of all, whereas the bottom class showed the smallest improvement between 1911 and 1939, but

TA]

Infant Mortality and S

Social Class of Father	Neo-natal Deaths per 1,000			
	1911	1939	Improvement per cent 1911–39	1949–50
Professional	26·8	18·9	29·4	13·5
Intermediate	34·8	23·4	32·7	16·0
Skilled Workers ⎫		25·4		17·8
⎬	39·6		33·0	
Partly Skilled Workers ⎭		27·7		19·9
Unskilled Workers	42·5	30·1	29·1	21·9
All Classes	39·1	26·4	32·4	18·2

rather more than the top class from 1939 to 1950. The skilled workers did better than the unskilled in both periods.

What, if anything, do these figures indicate? First and foremost, a big all-round advance. Secondly, a considerably greater advance among the skilled workers and the general run of blackcoats than among the unskilled, or even the less skilled workers. This makes it look as if, at any rate in the case of infant mortality, improved medical knowledge has been a bigger factor than better nutrition or environmental conditions. Admittedly, there is more study to be done before decisive proof can be reached; but so much at any rate seems highly likely to be a correct interpretation of the trend.

Occupational Mortality Rates. Occupational as well as class differences are of interest. Of all the groups studied, miners show the highest rates of infant mortality—both neo-natal and post-neo-natal. Their record is worse than that of builders' labourers, who came second to them in 1949–50. Teachers had the best record in 1911 and 1950—better even than professional workers; but they fell behind the professional group in 1939. Textile workers were second worst—after miners—in 1911, and were even worse than miners in 1939 in respect of neo-natal deaths, but not of others.

The Social Medicine of Old Age. At the other end of the scale of age, increasing attention has been given in recent years to what is called 'gerontology'—the social medicine of old age. The biggest developments in this field, as in most branches of field sociology, have been American; and Great Britain has definitely lagged behind both in investigation and in devising improved forms of treatment. The problem is much s of Father, 1911–50

	Post-neo-natal Deaths (4 weeks—1 year) per 1,000				
Improvement per cent 1939–50	1911	1939	Improvement per cent 1911–39	1949–50	Improvement per cent 1939–50
28·5	28·3	7·9	72·1	4·9	37·9
31·6	63·2	11·0	82·6	5·9	46·3
29.9		19·0		10·5	44·7
	85·8		75·2		
28·2		23·7		14·1	40·5
27·2	110·0	30·0	72·7	17·9	40·3
31·0	85·8	21·0	75·5	11·1	47·1

less one of helping old people to live longer than that of rendering them happier and more useful while they do live. It has two main aspects— that of providing the old with better living conditions, psychological as well as physical, and that of enabling them to work better and to continue their work longer where they are, or can be made, capable of doing so. The second part of the problem is closely connected with another—that of helping persons suffering from physical or mental handicaps to make the best of their resources by doing useful work up to the limits of their ability. This problem, of course, arises at all ages, but is apt to raise the most serious difficulties among those in or past middle age. If we are to spend more of our resources on helping the old, as we must do and are fully committed to doing, there is the greater need to make the fullest use of all the productive power we can muster, in order to spread the burden over a wider field.

Rehabilitation Services. As an outcome of war conditions increasing attention has been paid of late years to rehabilitation—first of all of war victims, but also of sufferers from industrial and other accidents and diseases, including nervous diseases. All the evidence goes to show that in such cases the best results are usually secured, not by devising special kinds of work to fit the disability, but by training the sufferers to work alongside normal employees—if necessary with specially adapted tools or machines, but in many cases without any special provision except for training. Where special workshops are set up for the disabled and these are subsidized to make up for their competitive disadvantage, there is often a temptation to take the employees' limited work capacity as a fixed datum and not to make any serious attempt to improve it. This criticism has been brought against the 'Remploy' factories for which the Government is responsible; and it appears that better results have been achieved where hospitals and training institutions have made the fullest use of physiotherapy and occupational therapy with the object of fitting men and women to return to suitable kinds of normal work. There are of course *some* sufferers who cannot be expected to become capable of such work; but their number seems to be much smaller than is often supposed. Even such workers will probably do best when their special workshops can be linked up with establishments of an ordinary commercial type, rather than segregated in an admittedly uneconomic sector.

Employment for Old People.   As far as old people are concerned, there is everything to be said for helping, but not coercing, those who are above the pensionable age and are still fit for work to remain in employment if they can find for themselves, or be found, suitable jobs. Although it is an ascertained fact that unemployment is heavier among elderly than among younger workers, this is much less because they are apt to lose their jobs than because they have greater difficulty in finding new ones. The Advisory Committee on the Employment of Older Men and Women found that in December 1952 the rates of unemployment for persons in the different age-groups were as follows:

TABLE 187

Rate of Unemployment analysed by Age-groups, December 1952
(*wholly unemployed only*)

Age-group	Unemployed per cent Males	Unemployed per cent Females
Under 20	1·2	1·5
20–39	1·5	2·0
40–49	1·4	1·8
50–54	2·0	2·5
55–64	2·9	2·7
		(to 59 only)

The same enquiry showed that the proportion of those unemployed workers who had been out of work for more than 13 weeks varied as follows:

TABLE 188

Duration of Unemployment, by Age-groups, 1952

Males		Females	
Under 20	12	Under 20	33
20–39	20	20–39	25
40–49	33	40–49	30
50–54	39	50–54	37
55–64	50	55–59	43

Here, the male percentages again rise with age, whereas among women the 'under 20' group has a higher percentage than either the '20–39' or the '40–49' group, and the percentages in the higher age-groups are lower than for men.

In Great Britain, there were in 1951, at the time of the Census, 2,175,000 males aged over 65, of whom 695,300 were returned as still 'occupied'. There were then 4,453,000 women over 60, of whom only 357,000 were 'occupied'. Men between 65 and 70 numbered nearly 867,000, of whom 422,400, or nearly half, were still 'occupied'; whereas out of 1,328,000 women aged between 60 and 65 only 191,000, or less than 15 per cent, were returned as 'occupied'. Of men over 70, numbering 1,308,000, the 'occupied' accounted for 273,000, or nearly 21 per cent, whereas for women aged 65 to 70 the corresponding figures were 1,153,000 and 103,600, or only 9 per cent.

CHAPTER TWENTY-EIGHT

LOCAL GOVERNMENT

LOCAL Government presents Great Britain with one of its most difficult and ever-present problems precisely because its reform is not a party question. Opinions on the subject cut right across ordinary party divisions and tend to vary according to the type of local authority with which the holder is most familiar. Most people, I think, have no settled opinions on the subject: the main body of those interested is made up of local councillors and aldermen and of officials, most of whom strongly uphold the claims of their own type of authority against all others. Thus, in the big towns, the County Borough type of local authority is strongly argued for on the ground that it covers the entire range of local government functions and avoids the conflicts that arise where two or more authorities are concerned with the administration of the same area. As against this view, County Councillors commonly defend the County Council as the indispensable representative of the town and country complex, co-ordinating the points of view of the villages and the smaller towns and preserving the villagers from being completely overshadowed by the town-dwellers. Urban District and non-county Borough Councillors usually insist on the need for the lesser urban centres to have their own local government apart from that of the countryside, and are in some cases eager to attain full County Borough status for their own towns, while in other instances they are content to share powers and functions with the County Councils. Finally, Rural District Councillors are usually keen advocates of allowing the country areas to have their own local authorities to protect them against the urban interests; and Parish Councillors urge the claim of the small local community to possess its own independent authority, even if its powers are bound to be rather small.

Conflicting Views on Reform. Whenever any project of local government reform is put forward all these groups rise in defence of the claims of their own type of authority, usually demanding for it some extension of its existing powers to other areas. Thus, many of the spokesmen of the County Boroughs urge that it would be a good thing to divide up the whole country, villages as well as towns, into a number of all-purpose authority areas like the existing County Boroughs. Many County Councillors argue that, in order to give the County Councils powers more nearly equal to those of the Councils of County Boroughs, the functions of County Councils should be enlarged so as to endow them with more control over the lesser authorities within their areas and to reduce the latter, at any rate for some purposes, to the position of executive bodies acting under County Council orders. Some even wish to abolish altogether the Rural District and Urban District Councils, leaving at most only local executives wholly subordinate to the Counties. Others wish, within the Counties, to replace the existing pattern of separate lesser authorities for town and countryside by County Districts each based as far as possible on a town and the country round about it. Some Parish Councillors demand the abolition of Rural Districts and an enlargement of the powers of the Parishes. At the opposite extreme all sorts of views are held about the best form of local government for the great 'conurbations'—that is, for regions in which a number of neighbouring towns have grown together into what is in essence a huge, populous super-town or city faced with many common problems there is no way of solving within the existing local government structure. In the biggest of all these conurbations, Greater London, the problem is at its worst; for any common government for the whole urbanized region is strongly opposed both by many of the outlying towns and by the County Councils from whose jurisdiction it would to some extent take them away. Some have even urged that Greater London, being they say too large to put under a single administration, should be cut up into a number of entirely independent County Boroughs, each with its own all-purpose administration.

Local Government Finance. Closely tied up with the question of local government areas is that of finance. The costs of local government are defrayed partly out of the proceeds of local rates on property—excluding exempted agricultural property—and partly out of grants made by the Central Government. It is generally agreed that local rates are a bad kind of tax, falling as they do most heavily on those who occupy certain kinds of property, such as dwelling-houses, shops, and other land and buildings not used for production in a narrow sense of the word. The value of the premises occupied often bears little relation either to ability to pay or to the services demanded of the local authority by the ratepayer. This did not matter so much when the costs of local government were low. It has mattered more and more as these functions have been enlarged, and especially since industrial properties were 'de-rated' by three-quarters in 1928–9 on the ground that rates constituted a charge on the cost of production and thus hampered British industry's competitive power. There have been many demands, particularly since 1945, for a reversal of the 'de-rating' policy put into force by Neville Chamberlain; but such proposals naturally provoke energetic protests from those who at present pay only very low rates, and politicians fear stirring up a hornet's nest by putting them forward.

The alternative course, of reducing rates by transferring a larger part of the cost of local government to the central Exchequer, is strongly opposed by Chancellors who are already in search of means to reduce national taxation, or at least to check its increase.

Party Attitudes to Reform. In face of these difficulties, neither the Labour Party between 1945 and 1951 nor the Conservatives since 1951 have made any real attempt to tackle the problem of local government reform. Labour had, indeed, an ambitious paper plan, prepared before it came to power, but made no attempt to put it into effect, on the plea that there were too many other matters calling for urgent attention and that Great Britain could not afford a major upset in its local government while it was engaged in a great effort to re-build its world position after the war. But undoubtedly another factor was that Mr. Aneurin Bevan, at the Ministry of Health, had more than enough on his plate with the problems of housing and the National Health Service to be able to attend to much else, and was doubtful besides what sort of reception any plan of local government reform would meet with, even in his own party. This latter consideration certainly weighs heavily with the Conservatives also: any party that seriously takes up the question seems likely to get more 'kicks than ha'pence'.

Moreover, it has to be admitted that the present situation of local government, though untidy and in many respects inappropriate, is by no means intolerable. It is a nuisance, but not a disastrous nuisance. In one instance after another, though the areas of local government no longer coincide with real areas of communal living and though communities are broken up by them into meaningless fragments, the essential tasks of local government nevertheless for the most part get tolerably well performed: so that few citizens have any keen sense of the shortcomings of the existing system or feel any enthusiastic desire for change. The disadvantages, however, though not intolerable, are real and substantial. It was largely on account of them that the Labour Government was induced, and was able without arousing serious opposition, to transfer to the central State's authority the administration of certain important services which had been to a great extent under municipal management—for example, the supply of gas and electricity and, at least in intention, local passenger transport by road. The local authorities found some compensation for the loss of these services in the big development of municipal housing which took place at the same time; but this does not make it less unfortunate that the unsuitability of the existing local areas for the conduct of key trading services should have led to the centralization under state control rather than to a reform in the structure of local government.

The Case for Regional Authorities. The plain truth is that the growth of towns beyond their municipal frontiers and the coming into existence of such major 'conurbations' as Greater London, Greater Manchester, Merseyside, Tyneside and Clydeside have created conditions which, in conjunction with the technological evolution of industry, call for the establishment of larger local authorities than at present exist. Each of these conurbations needs a co-ordinating regional authority of its own, even if it needs also smaller authorities within its area; and the same requirement is found, on a smaller scale, in and around many other big towns, especially in the more industrialized districts. Moreover, even where considerable towns have not grown one into another so as to constitute part of what is in effect a single major community, there are countless cases in which towns are cut off administratively from their suburbs, in which a high proportion both of their wealthier classes and of their workers live, in such a way that the outlying populations make no contribution to the cost of what are in essence services common to the whole area. The bigger urban authorities, for want of space within their own boundaries, are forced to build houses for their surplus populations in territory administered by other authorities; and many awkward financial and other problems arise.

Local Government in Rural Areas.   As for the alleged need to provide for the administration of rural areas apart from that of the towns, lest the point of view of the countryman fail to find expression, the plain fact of the case is that the widely scattered populations of the rural areas cannot economically provide for the administration of services such as communities have a right to expect, if they are cut off from their market towns and left to fend for themselves. In such a case they are forced to adopt areas so wide in geographical extent as to lack all sense of community and render truly democratic control impossible: the only solution lies in treating the town and the surrounding areas in which many of its workers and clients dwell as presenting a common problem and needing unified administration of major services—but so as to leave lesser services to be conducted by smaller neighbourhood units within the area of the major authority.

The Government of Large Cities and of other Areas.   The conurbations, and also the really big cities with the areas round them, are fully capable of conducting the major services of local government without having any larger administrative authority set over them. The case of the middle-sized and smaller towns and their surrounding areas is different. For them there is needed, in addition to a strong authority for each of them as a whole, with lesser authorities within it, some co-ordinating body capable of acting over a wider regional area, and of administering such common services as cannot be managed economically except on a large scale. This is the case for 'Regionalism'—for the constitution, for each conurbation or great city and for each conurbation of smaller centres of population, of a regional authority for the conduct of large-scale public services. Among these services are regional town and country planning and the execution of major projects connected with it, and the maintenance and improvement of roads, and of passenger transport services; and with these, in my view, should go the distribution as distinct from the generation of electricity, and the supply of gas and water. Regional authorities could also with advantage be put in charge of certain parts of the health service—particularly hospitals—and of education—particularly certain parts of technical and higher education, including the co-ordination of specialized technical instruction and the responsibility for such grammar schools as serve a regional rather than a local public.

Such projects are often opposed on the ground that in most parts of the country there is no tradition of regional, as distinct from local, community sentiment to build upon—which may be true in some areas, but is certainly not so in nearly all. The real objection rests much less on this basis than on the reluctance of local councillors and officials to hand over any of their powers to a major authority, and on the mutual jealousies between authorities of different types. In face of these obstacles, major changes in local government structure will have to be made if local government is not to suffer continuing erosion by the transference of more and more of its functions to the Central Government, which has already too much to do and has assuredly not found a satisfactory solution in the delegation of its authority to centrally appointed Public Corporations (see pp. 119 ff.).

The Case against De-rating: Sources of Regional Finance. Reorganization along regional lines would also ease the problems of local government finance, though it would not solve them by itself. In this matter, one urgent need is that of re-rating the properties de-rated between the wars. There is no valid reason why industrial property should escape bearing its share of local any more than of national taxation, or should be allowed to transfer its burdens to the local house-occupiers or to the occupants of commercial premises. De-rating is in effect a form of subsidy to industry that may have had something to be said for it during the inter-war depression, but is entirely indefensible under conditions of full employment such as have existed since the war. There are other respects in which the finance of local government calls for drastic amendment. Local rates are a tolerable tax only if they are kept low; yet it is undesirable that local authorities should depend much more heavily than they do on grants from the central Exchequer. Such dependence inevitably increases central control over local affairs; and local authorities, if they are to enjoy real independence, must have a sound reason for exercising due economy and making sure their citizens get good value for their money. It is therefore highly desirable to find new sources of local finance, not to the extent of abolishing local rates, but in order to supplement them with some other forms of local or regional taxation. I believe the right answer to lie in making the land, rural as well as urban, *regional* property or, till that is done, in making taxation of land values a source of *regional* rather than of national public income. This would leave it still necessary to come to the assistance of the poorer regions, either by some system of partial pooling or by grants from the central Exchequer. But it would at all events relieve the pressure on local rates without making local government still more dependent on grants from central funds.

When and whether these major problems will be tackled remains to be seen. In 1955 the Conservatives were making some vague indications that they hoped to take up the question of local government reform before long; but much hints have been heard often before, without anything coming of them. I shall believe in them only when a concrete scheme has been both produced and persisted in despite the clamour of opposition that any far-reaching proposal is certain to arouse.

Local Government as it is. We can now turn to a brief description of the existing structure. The local government of England and Wales is at present in the hands of two kinds of major local authorities—County Councils and County Borough Councils, which between them cover the entire country—and of a number of lesser authorities—Municipal Borough Councils, Urban and Rural District Councils, Parish Councils and Parish Meetings, all of which are within the areas administered by the County Councils. County Borough Councils, which exist for most large towns, are the sole authorities within their areas for general purposes of local government, whereas in other parts of the country authority is shared between the County Councils and the lesser bodies. In 1955 there were in England and Wales 83 County Borough Councils, 63 County Councils, 312 non-county Borough Councils, 568 Urban District and 475 Rural District Councils, and over 7,000 Parish Councils.

In Scotland the system is somewhat different. There are 33 County Councils and 197 Town Councils. But only 4 cities have Councils which are wholly independent of the County Councils within whose geographical areas they lie. The rest are divided into 68 Royal Burghs under charter, 14 Parliamentary Burghs, and 115 Police Burghs, with varying powers. Thirty of the larger are independent of the County Councils, except in respect of education and, in some cases, police. Within most counties there are District Councils, numbering 199, which receive delegated powers from the County Councils for areas outside the Burghs.

Tendencies towards Centralization. All these Councils are elected on a wide franchise—by over 30 million electors in England and Wales, and 3½ million in Scotland. In their present form they are the outcome

of more than a century of legislation which has radically transformed
the earlier structure of local government and has included the development of a system of grants in aid from the Central Government to
supplement funds raised locally through taxes on property. There has
been a continuous and immense extension of the functions and duties
of local government, corresponding to the extension of the activities
of the Central Government and involving a vast increase in the sums
expended by the local authorities. There has also been a tendency to
concentrate the tasks of local government in the hands of fewer bodies
by replacing *ad hoc* authorities responsible for particular services—
e.g. education and the Poor Laws—by *omnibus* authorities, and therewith some tendency to provide for the unification of administration over
larger areas. Of the existing types of local authority, County Councils
and County Borough Councils in England and Wales date only from
1888, and Parish Councils, in their present form, from 1894. Urban and
Rural District Councils, as sanitary authorities, date from the 1870s:
only Borough Councils, which were drastically re-modelled in 1835, go
back earlier than the nineteenth century and derive their powers in
part, not from parliamentary enactment, but from royal charters of
varying date. County administration, up to 1888, was in the hands not
of elected Councils but of centrally appointed justices of the peace.
The Poor Laws, prior to 1834, were administered by parish overseers
under the control of the county justices and, after 1834, were put under
the administration of locally elected Boards of Guardians subject to
strict central control of policy—until they were transferred, in 1929, to
the general authorities responsible for other forms of local government.
Education, which came under local government auspices only in 1870,
was in the hands from that year until 1902 of locally elected School
Boards and School Attendance Committees, but was similarly transferred in 1902 to the general local government authorities.

The Functions of Local Government.　To-day, local Councils are responsible for a very wide range of public services, mostly laid down by
Act of Parliament for the whole country—often with separate Acts for
England and Wales and for Scotland—but in some cases provided for
by local Acts applying only to particular areas. In some cases the
powers conferred by these Acts are not mandatory but adoptive or per-
missive, so that a local authority need not undertake them unless it
wishes so to do. Among the fields in which the Central Government
operates mainly through the local authorities as executants of social
policy are public health, education, housing and town and country
planning, police, water supply, highways and bridges, libraries and
museums, and child welfare; whereas the supply of electricity and gas
has been transferred from local to central control, with a large measure
of regional autonomy in the case of gas, and the local administration

of certain other services, notably those connected with the supply of labour, is carried on by the Central Government through regional and local offices maintained by the central government departments.

County Populations. Of English Administrative Counties (excluding the County Boroughs) one—London—had in 1953 a population of more than three millions. Two others—Middlesex and Lancashire—exceeded two millions, and four more—Essex, Kent, Surrey and the West Riding of Yorkshire—one million. Three more—Durham, Staffordshire and Cheshire—exceeded 750,000. Derbyshire, Hampshire, Hertfordshire, Nottinghamshire and Devonshire also had more than half a million inhabitants. 19 others had between 250,000 and half a million, and 9 more had above 100,000. Only the Isle of Ely, Huntingdonshire, the Soke of Peterborough, Westmorland, the Isle of Wight and Rutland had fewer than 100,000, the smallest of all being Rutland, with under 23,000. Geographically, including the County Boroughs, the most populous county was Lancashire, with 5,093,000, followed by the West Riding, with 3,574,000, and London, with 3,343,000. Geographically, Essex as well as Middlesex exceeded 2 millions, and Warwickshire, Staffordshire, Surrey, Kent, Durham, Cheshire and Hampshire all exceeded 1 million.

In Wales the most populous Administrative Counties were Glamorgan, with 736,000, and Monmouthshire, with 319,000. Carmarthenshire, Denbighshire, Flintshire and Caernarvonshire exceeded 100,000. The remaining 7 had fewer than 100,000, the smallest, Radnorshire, having fewer than 20,000. Geographically, only Glamorgan had more than a million.

In Scotland, excluding the 4 big cities—Glasgow, Edinburgh, Aberdeen and Dundee—the most populous County was Lanarkshire, with 529,000. Renfrewshire, Ayrshire and Fifeshire exceeded 300,000. No other County had more than 200,000. Five—Stirlingshire, Dunbartonshire, Aberdeenshire, Perthshire, and Midlothian—exceeded 100,000: the remaining 24 were less populous, 8 with more than 50,000 and 16 with fewer, down to Kinross with only 7,000.

Many of these Counties were clearly too small to be in a position to administer with full efficiency some of the major services entrusted to them, such as education and highway maintenance. A population of 100,000 can fairly be regarded as the minimum needed for this; but no fewer than 6 English, 7 Welsh, and 24 Scottish Administrative Counties fell below this minimum, and would have done so even if County Boroughs had been included—for there were none within their frontiers. The County is, however, a strong point of focus for local loyalties; and proposals to group neighbouring Counties for administrative purposes meet with lively opposition.

The County Boroughs. The County Boroughs, which are excluded from the Counties for purposes of local government, range in size from Birmingham, with over a million inhabitants, to Canterbury, with under 30,000. They include all the larger cities and real towns, but exclude some very populous areas which are in effect suburbs or satellites of greater centres. Each County Borough is responsible for the entire range of local services within its frontiers; but in many cases towns have grown beyond their municipal frontiers, so that the County Borough includes only a part of the population that really makes up the town. In other cases, as we saw, two or more neighbouring towns have grown together so as to constitute in effect, with their suburbs, a single 'conurbation', but remain separate municipally, each with its own Council. Thus, Manchester and Salford are separate County Boroughs, though they form part, with a number of other areas, of a 'Greater Manchester' conurbation. London, of course, exemplifies this development in an extreme form. The area counted in the Census as belonging to Greater London had in 1951 a population of 8,344,000, of whom only 3,346,000 were in the area administered by the London County Council, the majority living either in neighbouring County Boroughs, such as Croydon and West Ham, or in non-county Boroughs or Urban Districts falling within the Administrative Counties of Middlesex, Surrey, Kent, Essex and Hertfordshire. Some of these areas were very populous; but there was vehement opposition from the County Councils to the creation of new County Boroughs which would deprive them of important parts of their population and rateable value.

The Great Conurbations. The major conurbations, with their chief towns and populations, are as follows:

TABLE 189
Populations of Conurbations: 1951

Conurbation	Population 1951 (000's)	Chief Town	Population* 1951 (000's)
Metropolitan	8,344	London	3,346
West Midland	2,237	Birmingham	1,112
S.E. Lancashire	2,421	Manchester	703
Merseyside	1,382	Liverpool	790
W. Yorkshire	1,692	Leeds	505
Tyneside	835	Newcastle-on-Tyne	292
And in Scotland:			
Clydeside	1,758	Glasgow	1,090

The other principal cities in 1951 were as follows:

Sheffield	513	Bristol	442	Hull	296
Edinburgh	467	Nottingham	306	Bradford	293

* For more recent figures, see page 7.

The largest Welsh city was Cardiff, with 244,000 inhabitants. These figures exclude suburban populations living outside the municipal boundaries.

Income and Expenditure. During the financial year 1952–3 local authorities in Great Britain spent a total sum of nearly £1,783 million— £1,579 million in England and Wales and £204 million in Scotland. Of this total £568 million was for capital works financed out of loans— £498 million in England and Wales and £70 million in Scotland. Current expenditure was thus £1,196 million, made up of £1,062 million for England and Wales and £134 million for Scotland. These totals compare with an expenditure of £773 million in 1938–9.

The total income of local authorities in Great Britain was £779 million in 1938–9 and £1,783 million in 1952–3. For England and Wales only[1] the corresponding totals were £692 million and £1,579 million. Of this latter total, £502 million consisted of capital receipts, mainly from loans and central government grants. £336 million came from local rates and £385 million from central government grants. £78 million was derived from house-rents and £149 million from trading services (water supply, local transport, ports and docks, etc.). Total central government grants, including those of a capital nature, came to just under £395 million—a quarter of total gross expenditure, but well over a third of net expenditure after deducting receipts from trading services and from housing. Local rates levied on property were gener- ally recognized to be an unsatisfactory kind of tax, especially in view of the exemption of agricultural and part de-rating of industrial under- takings; for this exemption caused them to fall mainly on householders and occupants of commercial premises, whose rent-charges often had little relation to their capacity to pay. It is, however, regarded as essen- tial that local authorities shall have a source of revenue distinct from those of national taxation; and no satisfactory substitute for local rates has been found. It is widely held that full rating should be applied to the premises of productive undertakings, as it was until such premises were de-rated in 1928 on plea of trade depression.

The expenditure of local authorities in Great Britain, other than capital expenditure met out of loans, totalled £602 million in 1938–9 and approximately £1,196 million in 1952–3. Figures showing the allocation of this expenditure to particular purposes are not available for Scotland later than 1949–50. Accordingly, figures for Great Britain are given for this financial year, together with figures for England and Wales for 1952–3 in Table 190 (overleaf).

It will be seen that education is by far the most costly local ser- vice. It also attracts the highest allocated grant from the Central Government—£217 million in 1952–3 for England and Wales, and

---

[1] Itemized figures for Scotland are not yet available.

TABLE 190

Expenditure of Local Authorities on Principal Services (other than out of Loans for Capital Works), 1938–9, 1949–50 and 1952–3

(*£million*)

	1938–9 G.B.	1949–50			1952–3 E. and W.
		G.B.	E. and W.	Scotland	
Education	114·4	289·9	257·1	32·8	345·4
Libraries and Museums	3·5	9·9	8·3	0·6	10·7
Individual Health	—	34·7	32·1	2·6	42·9
Public Health:					
Sewage, etc.	23·8	43·3	38·3	5·0	47·0
Baths and Washhouses	3·5	6·4	5·5	0·9	6·3
Parks and Open Spaces	8·0	15·4	13·7	1·7	16·0
Maternity and Child Welfare	6·2	12·2	11·1	1·1	19·4
Hospitals and Dispensaries	21·6	—	—	—	—
Other Items	8·9	11·2	9·6	1·6	11·0
Lunacy and Mental Deficiency	16·5	—	—	—	—
Poor Relief	40·7	15·4	13·8	1·6	19·4
			(Nat. Assist.)		
Housing	52·4	96·0	80·8	15·2	122·2
Allotments and Small Holdings	2·2	2·8	2·8	—	3·0
Land Drainage, Conservancy, etc.	2·6	5·6	5·6	—	7·8
Highways, Bridges and Street Works	59·7	73·4	66·3	7·1	78·7
Public Lighting	6·8	10·3	8·5	1·8	11·0
Fire Service	3·4	14·9	13·8	1·1	17·9
Police and Justice	31·3	58·4	53·0	5·4	72·1
Civil Defence	4·8	1·5	1·5	—	3·3
Emergency Services	—	18·0	17·9	0·1	15·6
Water Supply	25·9	59·1	35·5	3·6	41·0
Gas Supply	22·9	3·8	3·8	—	—
Electricity Supply	61·5	—	—	—	—
Passenger Transport	30·4	59·4	49·9	9·5	60·3
Cemeteries	2·2	4·5	3·9	0·6	4·9
Harbours, Docks, etc.	15·8	28·5	25·4	3·1	29·5
Other Trading Services	7·0	20·6	20·3	0·3	19·6
Other and Unallocated	25·2	74·7	70·2	4·5	59·7
Total	601·7	949·4	849·1	100·3	1,062·3

£168 million for Great Britain in 1949–50. The government grants for this and other purposes have been as follows:

TABLE 191

Central Government Grants to Local Authorities, Great Britain, 1938–9, 1949–50 and 1951–2 (*£million*)

	1938–9 G.B.	1949–50 G.B.	1952–3 E. and W.
Education	60·5	168·0	197·4
Individual Health	—	16·1	19·8
Public Health and Child Welfare	3·0	7·8	10·3
Lunacy and Mental Deficiency	0·2	—	—
Poor Relief and National Assistance	—	0·5	0·4
Housing	17·7	31·5	31·7
Allotments and Small Holdings	0·9	0·8	0·8
Land Drainage and Conservancy	0·4	2·0	3·2
Highways, Bridges and Street Works	16·5	17·2	18·9
Fire Service	—	3·7	4·1
Police and Justice and Electoral Registration	14·3	27·1	32·1
Civil Defence	3·4	1·3	2·5
Other Emergency Services	—	10·4	7·6
Other Services	1·7	5·9	7·6
Unallocated Grants	54·3	51·1	58·2
Other Receipts	2·3	2·7	2·0
Total	168·5	346·2	395·2

In the field of capital expenditure, financed out of loans, the first place, both in 1938–9 and in recent years, has been taken by housing, which accounted for £67 million in 1938–9 and for £266 million in 1949–50 for Great Britain as a whole. For England and Wales only the amount in 1952–3 was £343 million. Education comes next, with nearly £16 million in 1938–9 and £56 million in 1949–50 for Great Britain and £58 million for England and Wales in 1952–3.

It will be seen that, whereas most forms of local expenditure have increased since 1938–9, local expenditure on certain Public Health services has decreased or even disappeared. This is, of course, a consequence of the institution of the National Health Service in 1948. As we saw (see p. 375) the major part of the cost of this Service falls on the National Exchequer.

Voluntary Service in Local Government. Local government requires the voluntary services of a host of unpaid workers, over and above the paid officials who serve it in full-time posts. First come the elected councillors and the co-opted members of certain bodies, such as local education authorities. These add up to a very large number when all types of local authority down to Parish Councils are taken into account. But there are many more—appointed members of Divisional or other Committees, representatives of local authorities on a host of bodies, from the Governing Bodies or Committees of schools to those who sit on their behalf as members of the Councils or Committees of voluntary bodies which they help or recognize. Widely varying amounts of unpaid service are called for from these participants in local government affairs. Even a mere seat on a major urban authority, plus the minimum of service on its committees, may make quite heavy inroads on a member's time; and the chairmanship of an important committee, if the office holder takes it seriously, may approach so nearly to a full-time job as to remove all possibility of earning a living by other work. Of course, the numbers on whom such extreme demands are made are relatively small; but the work grows continually, and it becomes more and more difficult to carry on a great deal of it and also to remain in full-time employment elsewhere, even if the employer does not object either because of real inconvenience caused by absences from work or on political grounds.

It is indeed a difficult matter to find enough really suitable persons to run the local Councils and committees and to fill all the other positions that need to be filled. A great number of working people are in effect disqualified, at any rate for the more exacting types of service; and there is a tendency for Councils to contain a high proportion of elderly retired persons, of wives who are relatively free from domestic duties, and of officers of bodies, such as trade associations or Trade Unions, which are prepared to release them for such public work. Of course, many of these persons are entirely suitable and make excellent public representatives; but their number tends to overweight the Councils with fairly elderly people, and difficulties in the way of regular attendance also discriminate against ordinary wage- or salary-earners, as distinct from Trade Union or Co-operative officials. A Council member, at any rate on the larger Councils, can do little unless he or she participates actively in the committee work; for it is in committee that the most important decisions are as a rule effectively made.

The Politics of Local Government. Nowadays, a party structure is to be found on almost all the main Councils—those of Counties and Boroughs—and on many of the lesser bodies. The principal contest at local elections is in most places between Conservatives and Labour, though Liberals keep a strong hold in some areas, mainly in the North, and the anti-Labour forces are sometimes called by other names, such as Ratepayers or Independents. There has been since 1945 a marked tendency for such groups to be taken over by the Conservatives, who have greatly extended their central effort in the local government field. But there remain groups of 'Independents' and single 'Independent' members who are Liberal rather than Conservative in sympathy. Many

of the Conservative gains recorded at local elections in recent years
have been at the expense not of Labour but of 'Independents' or 'Ratepayers' candidates whose organizations—and often personnel as well—
have been taken over by the Conservative Party.

Local Elections. Local government elections take place annually,
except for the London County Council and the London Metropolitan
Borough Councils, which have general elections every three years.
Elsewhere, the usual practice is for one-third of the Councils to be
elected each year: so that there is never a general election, and land-
slides are much less likely to occur. Party fortunes tend to fluctuate not
only in accordance with changes in public opinion but also according to
the party distribution of the vacated seats. In the great majority of
cases only a few seats change their party colour at any one time, except
in the 'general election' areas. In a good many instances, however, there
is so near a balance of parties that even a very few gains and losses can
change the balance of control. Aldermanic seats are in most cases distributed according to the strength of the parties; but sometimes, especially where control of a majority depends on them, the largest party
appropriates all or most of the vacant seats. The other party usually
complains loudly of unfair treatment, but would probably behave in
the same way if the boot were on the other foot.

Party Discipline. On most Councils, and especially on the less important, party discipline is a good deal less strict than it is in Parliament.
The London County Council comes nearest to being a lesser Parliament, and maintains a strict party control. In most Councils, however,
the day-to-day work is carried on mainly by committees, which are
usually composed in accordance with relative party strength and
carry on a substantial part of their administrative duties without party
questions seriously arising, save over major policy matters. Committee
chairmen are often, but not invariably, chosen by and from the predominant party or, sometimes, coalition of parties where no party
commands a majority of its own.

Councillors and Officials. Difficult problems sometimes arise over the
distribution of effective authority between elected Councillors and
officials. The officials, of course, are supposed to carry out the policy
of the elected Council, even if they personally disagree with it; and on
the whole they do this and perform their duties now at the beck of one
party and now at another's. Nevertheless, permanent officials, by virtue
of their detailed knowledge and practically complete security of tenure,
necessarily have a great influence on the application of policies to particular cases, which causes a high proportion of the everyday work.
Personalities here count for a great deal: a strong man as Town Clerk
or Education Officer, or in any other key position, can get great power

in his hands, especially if he is confronted by a weak, incompetent or inactive Chairman of Committee, or if the committee itself is of low calibre. As against this a strong Chairman with a reasonably safe seat on the Council can assert himself to great purpose in keeping the officials 'on their toes' and in advancing any cause approved by his party that he may have at heart.

County Council Problems. It is usually a good deal easier to find suitable members to sit on urban than on rural local authorities. The difficulty is most serious in the case of County Councils covering scattered rural areas; for attendance at meetings may involve long journeys and may even be impossible without the possession of a motorcar. It is impracticable for the larger Councils to confine their meetings to evenings, so as to avoid the need for absence from work; and much committee work has also to be done in the daytime, especially by the more important committees dealing with such matters as education and town and country planning, which require much detailed work.

Payments to Councillors. Up to 1948 the vast majority of Councillors neither received any payment for their work nor could receive any compensation for loss of earnings or even charge necessary travelling expenses. The exceptions were Mayors, and other Chairmen of large authorities, who usually received allowances for entertainment, County Councillors in Scotland, who received payments for both personal expenses and loss of earnings, and County Councillors in England and Wales, who could draw allowances for travel. Under the Act of 1948 Councils (except Parish Councils) are authorized to meet members' travelling expenses and to pay where necessary subsistence allowances and also compensation at a fixed rate for loss of wages. This has done a good deal to ease the difficulty; but it is still impossible for employed persons to serve unless their employers are prepared to grant them time off. Even now it is almost out of the question to serve on a major local authority without incurring expenses well beyond what can be claimed. There is less than no financial inducement to accept such service, except in the case of local business men who hope to profit by the contacts established through membership. In the vast majority of cases election is sought not for gain but either from desire to serve or on account of the local prestige and influence membership may carry with it. Despite this lack of financial inducements—or perhaps partly because of it—there seems to be very little corruption in British local government, at any rate beyond a certain amount of 'back-scratching', chiefly on the smaller town authorities. There is, however, a good deal of corporate selfishness, especially on Councils controlled by such dominant groups as farmers or local tradesmen.

Local Government Staffs. The municipal 'civil service' too has a high reputation for incorruptibility, though there are occasional lapses. In recent years conditions of service have become considerably better, and also more uniform; and the introduction of general superannuation schemes has made it easier to move from one authority to another up the ladder of promotion.

Apart from professionals, who have become steadily more important —lawyers, doctors, architects, surveyors, engineers, and so on—local government still recruits the great majority of its employees direct from school. The number of university-trained recruits is, however, slowly increasing, especially in the major authorities and particularly in the educational part of the service. The National and Local Government Officers' Association (N.A.L.G.O.) has played an important part in the development of qualifying examinations for various types of post, as well as in improving and standardizing service conditions.

Associations of Local Authorities. The local authorities have still no common organization representing authorities of all types. Each main type has its own association, such as the Municipal Corporations Association, the County Councils Association, the Association of Education Committees, and at a lower level the Associations of Urban and Rural District Councils and of Parish Councils. The London County Council, being *sui generis,* acts apart, but often works in consultation with other bodies. There are also professional associations of such persons as Town Clerks, Borough Treasurers, Borough Architects, Engineers, Medical Officers of Health, and so on, and of Directors and Secretaries of Education. The central associations of local authorities are regularly consulted by government departments on matters relating to local affairs and to the finance and structure of local government; and, as we have seen, on some matters, such as the reform of areas, they can be relied on to offer conflicting advice. Although these representative bodies have no formal constitutional standing, they are of great importance in practice as focusing points for opinion, and can exert considerable pressure on the Central Government when they know their own minds.

The Local Elections of 1955. In the most recent local government elections, held very shortly before the General Election of 1955, the Labour Party lost some ground in most parts of the country, but in most areas only to a small extent. In the County Council elections, Labour lost control of five Councils in England and Wales—Carmarthen, Essex, Lancashire, Staffordshire, and the West Riding; and in the Boroughs it gained 60 and lost 404 seats—a net loss of 344. Labour lost control in eight County Boroughs, but after the election still controlled 46 out of 83. Control was also lost in at least two non-county Boroughs. The Conservatives gained 346 seats as against 35 losses. These figures exclude new seats, where changes in structure had taken place. Of such seats Labour won 187 and the Conservatives 58. The Conservative head office estimated that 1,600 of their borough candidates had been returned, as compared with 1,338 Labour candidates, 55 Liberals, and 501 Independents. The returns for about 300 Urban Districts included 643 Conservatives, 1,142 Labour, 14 Liberals, and 798 Independents—a net gain of 97 for the Conservatives and of 35 for the Independents, and a net Labour loss of 134. The significant feature of the elections was that the trend was nation-wide, though the changes were mostly fairly small. In the boroughs the average poll was between 40 and 50 per cent; but there were big variations, from 80 per cent in Llanidloes to only 38 per cent in Merthyr. The Labour Party's most serious losses were in Lancashire and to a smaller extent in the West Riding.

The above figures are taken from *The Times* and differ somewhat from those issued by the rival parties. Such discrepancies always occur, partly because of incomplete coverage and partly because of uncertainties about the party allegiance of some of the elected candidates. The differences, however, hardly affect the general outcome: they arise chiefly in the smaller areas and concern largely the status of individuals who can be counted either as 'Independents' or as party men.

Local Election Issues. The previous year, 1954, was one of Labour gains somewhat exceeding the losses of 1955. Labour also made substantial gains in 1953, and much larger gains in 1952, when the seats contested in 1955 were last previously fought. In 1952 Labour had a net gain of 394 seats on County Councils and 641 in the Boroughs, so that the losses of 1955 fell a long way short of cancelling the gains then made.

In general it seems clear that most local elections, being on a party basis, turn much more on national than on local issues. The national machines of the two great parties pay ever-increasing attention to local contests and to some extent treat them as tests of the national movement of political opinion. In particular, the Conservative head office has greatly increased its activity in connection with local affairs, and has built up a powerful machine for this purpose as well as for parliamentary electioneering.

Party Strength in Large Towns and Counties. It would take too much space to show the electoral position in local government even for all County and County Borough Councils. I can give only a select list, with comparative figures of gains and losses in 1952 and 1955, and in the case of County Boroughs, for the intervening years as well.

TABLE 192

Local Government: Party Representation in Selected Areas, 1955, with Labour Gains and Losses for the Three Preceding Elections. Areas controlled by Labour in 1955 are in italics

	Composition of Council for 1955				Labour Gains or Losses			
	Labour	Conservative	Liberal	Others	1955	1954	1953	1952
Selected County Boroughs:								
Birkenhead	42	22	—	—	−2	+4	+3	+2
Birmingham	81	70	—	1	−11	+9	+4	+16
Bournemouth	3	51	—	6	−1	+2	+1	+2
Bradford	42	32	6	—	−5	+2	+1	+6
Brighton	22	51	—	3	—	+1	+5	+4
Bristol	70	—	—	42	—	+3	+2	+5
Cardiff	19	25	1	8	−1	+3	+1	+2
Coventry	41	22	—	1	−5	—	−1	+4
Derby	42	22	—	—	−2	+3	+2	+1
Hull	56	27	—	1	−2	+5	+1	+4
Ipswich	26	28	2	—	−3	+3	—	+4
Leeds	68	44	—	—	−3	+6	+7	+9
Leicester	37	27	—	—	−6	+4	+4	+6
Liverpool	74	80	2	4	−1	+2	+19	+13
Manchester	85	63	4	—	−4	+5	+4	+6
Newcastle-on-Tyne	30	2	—	44	−2	+2	—	+3
Norwich	37	23	3	1	−2	+2	—	+3
Nottingham	33	35	—	—	−5	+2	—	+2
Plymouth	44	36	—	—	−4	+4	+5	+7
Sheffield	71	29	—	—	−2	+2	+1	+3
Southampton	40	31	—	1	−2	—	+3	+2
Stoke-on-Trent	57	8	—	7	—	+1	—	+2
Sunderland	50	16	—	6	−2	+2	—	+2
Swansea	45	—	—	15	—	—	−1	—
West Ham	64	—	—	—	—	+1	—	—
York	23	26	—	2	−4	+8	+5	+9
Selected Counties.								
Cheshire	12	44	2	10	—			+7
Cornwall	4	—	—	68	+2			+1
Derbyshire	49	17	—	12	−2			+13
Devonshire	1	—	—	88	−1			+2
Durham	74	5	—	9	−2			+3
Essex	42	59	—	7	−9			+31
Glamorgan	58	—	—	8	−1			+2
Gloucester	15	20	—	30	−4			+6
Hampshire	5	13	—	52	−4			+1
Kent	17	60	—	3	−11			+23
Lancashire	46	71	—	4	−18			+30
Leicestershire	14	49	4	—	−4			+5
London	74	52	—	—	−14	—	—	+27
Middlesex	35	52	—	—	−6			+18
Monmouth	49	17	—	—	—			+3

LOCAL GOVERNMENT
TABLE 192 (*continued*)

	Composition of Council for 1955				Labour Gains or Losses			
	Labour	Conserva-tive	Liberal	Others	1955	1954	1953	1952
Norfolk	14	19	—	25	−10			+19
Northants	21	29	4	13	−2			+14
Northumberland	37	3	—	32	−3			+8
Notts	48	32	—	5	—			+1
Somerset	13	8	—	54	+1			+2
Staffordshire	28	12	1	29	−10			+5
Surrey	6	60	—	17	−7			+10
Warwickshire	15	31	—	17	−1			+6
Yorks. (W. R.)	44	38	2	12	−17			+15

CHAPTER TWENTY-NINE

PARTIES AND ELECTIONS

THE people of Britain are commonly reputed to be experts at the parliamentary game and are even apt to look down on others who are less expert. The British Parliament has been called, not quite accurately, the 'mother of Parliaments'; and certainly the British people are well accustomed to accepting the verdict of their General Elections, if not as the voice of God, at any rate as entitled to their respect and acquiescence. British elections, we are told, are 'free', and by means of them the electors choose the Governments they want and reject those they dislike or distrust. It is true that Rousseau described the British people as free but once every seven years; but he deemed them to be free at least so often—though in his day the freedom, as far as the right to vote was concerned, extended only to a small fraction of the whole. For what it is worth, it extends pretty widely now—in effect, to all, or to practically all adults of both sexes—though usually not more than four out of every five think it worth while to vote. In the General Election of 1955 the poll was smaller than that. Less than 77 per cent voted in the constituencies contested—more in some places but fewer in others—whereas in 1951 82·5 per cent voted, and in 1950 84 per cent. In 1945 only 76 per cent voted; but on that occasion the register of electors was abnormally bad because of the war. Anything over 80 per cent is reckoned a quite good poll: the 84 per cent of 1950 was unusually high. Between the wars, general election polls ranged from 80·6 per cent in 1924 and 74·6 per cent in 1935 to a mere 58·9 per cent in 1918, when the register was a great deal worse than in 1945. Before the first war, with a much smaller and exclusively male electorate, the proportions voting were higher—92·9 per cent in January 1910, 88·8 per cent in 1906, and 87 per cent in December 1910. All these figures omit the electors in uncontested constituencies, and represent votes cast and not the number of different individuals voting—i.e. an elector casting more than one vote is counted as more than one. This affects the earlier figures, for times when there was a good deal of plural voting. The business and university votes were swept away by an Act of 1948.

The Effects of Universal Suffrage. The extension of the franchise to include almost everybody makes it likely that there will be a higher percentage of abstentions, both because of the larger numbers to be sought out by canvassers and because the last groups to be enfranchised

403

are likely to include a higher proportion of the apathetic or uninterested. With the great increase in the numbers entitled to vote, the relations between M.P.s and candidates and their electors have necessarily changed. The candidate of to-day can make personal contact with only a small minority of his electorate; and it seems to be agreed that his personality, or even his personal popularity, makes much less difference than it used to do to his prospects of success. There is also much less chance for independents, or for adherents of small parties. Save under very exceptional circumstances, the major parties almost sweep the board. Even the once great Liberal Party has been almost eliminated. This, of course, is due partly to the nature of the electoral system. The single-member constituency, without provision for either second ballot or alternative vote, strongly favours the major parties; whereas proportional representation ensures the smaller groups of members corresponding to their total voting support. Liberalism is still the creed of quite large numbers of electors; but nowadays many Liberals must either vote for other parties or abstain where no candidates of their own are standing, and many others must know that, in voting Liberal, they stand no chance of getting their candidates returned.

The immense preponderance of the bigger parties is however by no means due wholly to the electoral system. It is also a consequence of the scale on which campaigning needs to be done. Now that relatively many fewer electors attend political meetings, centralized forms of electioneering count for much more than they used to do—newspapers, broadcasting and television, and the ability to pay for expensive electoral organization, for example. It is true that in 1955 audiences for both sound and television broadcasts were a good deal smaller than had been expected. Large numbers who had their sets on for other items turned them off without giving the politicians a hearing, or even a viewing. But this hardly affects the conclusion that centralized electioneering is of much greater importance than it used to be; for there was at least as notable a lack of response to local appeals of every sort. A high proportion even among those who voted were not deeply interested, or at all events did not feel it worth their while to pay much attention to affairs of the election. Whether this is to be taken as something exceptional or as a normal feature of latter twentieth-century politics is a moot point. There were in 1955 some special reasons why considerable numbers of electors should feel that it did not much matter whether they voted or not and why others should feel that nothing they heard would be likely to influence their votes. But it seems probable that, apart from this, there has been some growth of apathy in view of the more settled conditions of the past few years—and also perhaps some on account of more positive changes in voters' habits and interests.

The Growth of the Electorate. It is important to bear in mind how vast the growth in the numbers of electors has been. Half a century ago, despite the inclusion of the whole of Ireland, the electorate was not much more than one-fifth of its present size—about $7\frac{1}{2}$ millions as against 35 millions. The reform of 1918, which brought in the older women and the unenfranchised men, raised it from 7·7 millions in 1910 to well over 21 millions; and the inclusion of the younger women in 1928 carried it from nearly $21\frac{3}{4}$ millions in 1924 to not much under 29 millions in 1929. By 1935 it had grown, without further changes in the law, to 31·4 millions. In 1945 it was 33,194,000; in 1950 34,412,000; and in 1951 34,623,000. By 1955 it had reached 34,856,000. On that occasion, as compared with 1951, the Labour Party lost about $1\frac{1}{2}$ million votes and the Conservatives about half a million. In 1951 Labour polled nearly a quarter of a million votes more than the Conservatives and their allies: in 1955 they polled about 900,000 fewer.

Parties and Election Issues. How is this shift to be explained, and why was it so much at Labour's expense? The answer, I feel sure, is not to be found mainly in the rival party programmes: nor was it mainly a matter of the personalities of candidates or leaders. Something must be attributed to low turn-outs of voters in seats that were felt to be safe for the one party or the other; and the figures show that the safe Labour seats were affected by this more than those which were safely Conservative. But it seems pretty certain that a much more important factor making against Labour was the feeling that the country had surmounted most of its post-war difficulties and was in a tolerably prosperous condition—if only it could keep out of war. In respect of foreign policy there seemed to be little between the main parties, which were equally committed to the Atlantic alliance and to the re-arming of Western Germany—and also to the acceptance of atomic warfare. Most candidates reported that they were asked few questions about foreign policy, and that it had not been in their view an important election issue. It might have counted for rather more had not the election been fought at a time when international tension had been substantially relaxed by changes both in the Soviet Union and in public opinion in the United States; but even if more of the electors had been actively interested in foreign affairs it is not at all clear how their interest would have affected their votes, with both the main parties plainly desirous of keeping out of war.

Actually, foreign policy seems hardly to have counted, not because people are not afraid of war, but rather because the way they voted appeared almost irrelevant to the war danger. The issues that did count were mainly economic, and also mainly negative. Even in 1951 a high proportion of the electors had evil memories of the depression and unemployment of the 1930s, and many working-class electors voted for the party they regarded as most likely to maintain full employment.

But the proportion whose adult memories go back beyond 1939 is falling steadily; and it is doubtful if many voters were influenced by the Labour Party's appeal to them to "ask the dad" what things had been like in the bad old days. This was indeed a dangerous appeal for a progressive party to make; for the success of such a party is bound to depend greatly on how it strikes the young.

Parties and the Social Services. Of course, the difference between the 'thirties and 1955 was not only that of full employment and depression: it was also that of greatly improved and extended social services. The Conservatives, however, took care not to be caught on the wrong foot in this respect. Whatever some of their supporters would have preferred, they put themselves forward as no less good friends than the Labour Party to the claims of the social services—indeed, in respect of housing at least, as better friends, who had redeemed their promise to get more houses built. 'More houses' was indisputably a popular cry; for there are still a great many families unable to get a decent house, or even any house at all—not a few of them living in furnished rooms for which they have to pay exorbitant rents. In respect of other social services Labour was no doubt ready to offer rather more than the Conservatives—but, for financial reasons, not a great deal more; and the Conservatives were able to argue that the future of the social services would be safer in their hands than in their opponents' because it depended in the final resort on the country's economic prosperity, and this, they asserted, would be most assured by abstention from risky economic ventures, such as further nationalization or a re-imposition of 'controls'. They were in a position to say that conditions had become a good deal easier economically since they came back to power in 1951, and especially during the past two years; and their appeals to the electors not to upset things when they were going well were undoubtedly quite effective. A large part of the electorate was not ill-content with things as they were, and did not see how the Labour Party was likely to make them much, if any, better. There was a temptation on this score to vote for no change, or not to vote at all, on the ground that it did not make much difference which party held office.

This temptation applied more to potential Labour voters than to others because, on the whole, the working class is, strange as it may seem, the least discontented class. The wealthier classes resent both high taxation and the greater independence full employment has brought to their 'inferiors'. Most of them will vote Conservative in any case. But there is also a very considerable body of middle-class and even of near-working-class discontent with the social 'levelling' that has come about since 1939. There are many middle-class and 'intermediate' electors (see p. 34) who cling fast to their notions of social superiority, and resent the narrowing of 'differentials' and the 'coddling', as they regard it, of the working class; and these groups, not a few of whom voted Labour in 1945, have been steadily changing their allegiance since they have got what matters most to them out of the social services—the National Health Service, for example—and see more to fear than to hope for in their further growth.

The Question of 'Controls'. Among these sections of the electorate the Conservatives exploited with no little success the allegation that Labour, if returned to power, would re-impose 'controls' and rationing and undermine the consumers' right of choice. No matter how categorically the Labour Party repudiated all intention of re-introducing any sort of rationing, the accusation stuck; for the party could not and did not wish to deny its intention, if need arose, to use the weapon of 'control'. Now, as matters stand at present, 'control' as well as rationing is an unpopular cry. If the distribution of incomes moves seriously against the poorer households—as it has already moved a little—this may cease to be the case; but most people, including most members of the working class, dislike being 'controlled' and are always suspicious of 'controls' unless they feel confident they will not apply to themselves. The popularity of freedom to spend as one chooses may be illusory in cases of monopoly or where scarcity makes it easy to charge high prices; but 'controls' can become popular only when the sense of grievance at high prices and unfair shares is very strong, and in 1955 it was not very strong—though perhaps it should have been stronger than it was. At all events, on this issue the Labour Party did not effectively get its case across.

The Labour Programme in 1955. It has to be admitted that in 1955—as indeed in 1950 and 1951—the Labour Party's programme had rather a tired appearance. It seemed to consist rather of things left over from the substantial achievements of the years after 1945 than of new projects of equivalent appeal. Electors who troubled their heads about such things could be forgiven for finding it somewhat unimaginative and uninspiring. This is not at all to suggest that the Labour programme would have attracted more support if it had been more 'Socialist' or of stronger appeal to the Left. Indeed, it would most likely have alienated more support if it had been simply that. There is no evidence at all that many electors are in a mood to be inspired by proposals for further nationalization, or even by promises of more welfare which they doubt any Government's ability to make good. The trouble about the Labour programme of 1955 was not that it was too mild and reformist, but rather that it lacked both distinction and distinctiveness. In all probability, this was unavoidable as matters stood; for neither the party leadership nor the main body of the electorate was in an adventurous mood. The party had gone, by 1950, almost as far as it knew how to go in home affairs without causing a considerable upset, which it felt sure a majority of the electors did not want. This meant that what it could offer was bound to be at most only mildly attractive unless there was a large amount of real discontent with things as they were—and there was not. The Labour Party would have lost the election of 1955 whatever its programme had been—unless it had managed, by a miracle, to hit on something really novel and at the same time unalarming; and how was that to be done? It lost because the less politically minded electors, as well as the definite anti-Socialists, felt safer with the Conservatives in office, and because the more politically minded of its supporters did not find in it the inspiration needed to bring out all their reserves. It could not have won unless its opponents had handed success to it on a plate by some appalling blunder; and, far from doing this, they kept their heads—and their own 'wild men' in order.

The Electoral Outlook. What, then, is due to happen next? If on the world stage there is further progress towards détente and peaceable co-existence and if, further, no major depression ensues on the retreat from war, the Conservatives stand a good chance of consolidating and even of increasing their gains. A not too interested electorate suits their book as long as their policy is more that of arresting a further advance towards Socialism and equality than that of reversing in more than minor respects the accomplishments of the years since 1939. Their leaders are well aware that any attempt at major reversal would speedily arouse angry passions on both sides—among the main body of Trade Unionists and Co-operators and also among the instinctive reactionaries with whose support they cannot dispense, but who must be kept in order if they are not to upset the boat. Accordingly, the Conservative Government can be relied on for a time to abstain from obviously reactionary major measures and to side with the more progressive employers rather than with the less enlightened. And this will continue to put the Labour Party into a difficulty from which it cannot easily escape.

Of course, this forecast will not apply if the war danger, which has been receding, again grows worse, or if there is a major recession. Either of these events, or both, might bring Labour back to office with little effort of its own beyond taking its chances as they come. But what would Labour do then? Would it be able to avert the threat of war, which depends mainly on the Russians and the Americans, and not on either the Government or the people of Great Britain? And would it be able to restore full employment in a world dislocated by a major recession in the United States? To doubt this is not to blame the Labour Party; for either task might well prove beyond any party's power. Labour's greatest coming danger is the same as it was in 1929— that of winning office at a most unfavourable juncture, and then finding itself unequipped for facing the situation.

The Boundary Commission and its Work. I have tried to explain why the Labour Party went down to defeat in 1955, but by no means to ignominious defeat, as it did in 1931. I think everyone now agrees that, although the boundary changes made shortly before the 1955 election were on the whole unfavourable to the Labour Party, they had no major effect on the results of the election. That, however, by no means justifies the policy of the Boundary Commission. There is, no doubt, something to be said for the view that it is bad, in a supposedly democratic electoral system, for constituencies to differ very greatly in the number of their electors, and that some provision ought to be made for re-distribution to take account of changes in relative populations. If, however, re-distribution on grounds of population is carried at all far, it comes into direct conflict with another principle that is of no less importance—that, as far as practicable, M.P.s should represent, not mere aliquot parts of the whole population of Great Britain, or even of England, or Wales, or Scotland, but real local communities. It does no harm to split a large town into two or more constituencies; but it may do a great deal of harm to cut a ward or two out of a town and join them to a quite different community, and still more to keep shifting electors about from one constituency to another in pursuit of a merely arithmetical equality. Towns, and even country areas, are not made in sizes that fit neatly in with the requirements of equal electoral districts. Equal, or even nearly equal, electoral districts mean unreal constituencies, with M.P.s who scarcely represent them at all, but are merely party nominees, chosen in many cases without any regard for their local connections.

What is the Basis of Representation? No doubt the 'carpet-bagger', as he used to be called, is nowadays much too familiar a type to attract attention. To a very great extent, Great Britain had departed from the idea of M.P.s representing local communities long before the Boundary Commissions were set up with wide authority to carve the country up at will. The effect of their work, however, has been to aggravate what was already a growing evil and to make the M.P. more than ever a nominee of his party rather than the representative of a local community with a solidarity and an outlook of its own. There was a time when, at any rate in the counties and the bigger towns, M.P.s were primarily representatives of local feeling, albeit only of that of highly select bodies of voters. As against this, there were 'rotten boroughs' whose M.P.s represented only a dominant landowner or a highly corruptible local group of 'free-men'. In clearing out the 'rotten boroughs', may we not have gone too far towards the opposite extreme of denying local representation altogether and treating all electors as mere units in a single mass electorate: so that it ceases to matter where, or with whom, they vote? I feel that we have gone too far in this direction and that in doing so we are taking away an important part of the elector's rights and fostering just those evil features of mass-democracy which most of us profess to deplore. I think it more important that candidates should need to appeal to local communities with some feeling of identity than that each M.P. should have just so many persons entitled to vote for or against him.

I doubt, however, whether many electors, at any rate outside the constituencies affected by recent major changes, feel strongly about this, or are even conscious of the issue. To so great an extent have nation-wide appeals come to overshadow local concerns that, as we saw, it now makes little difference to a candidate's chances what sort of person he is or how far he has local connections. I am aware of the opposite danger of parochialism where local take precedence over national issues: what is needed is a balance between the two. But the tendencies towards mass party voting are in any case now so strong that it seems unfortunate they should be further strengthened by re-distributions that appear almost entirely to ignore the local aspect.

Moreover, a constituency, once established, has to be made as far as possible into a reality. It has to develop an electoral machine which relies on the service, voluntary as well as paid, of a host of helpers; and it is of the greatest importance that, for each party, these helpers should work together as a team. But how can they, if at any moment they are liable to be torn asunder—and required to re-adjust themselves to a new set of colleagues? Such re-arrangements weaken the local life of the parties and therewith increase the power of the central party machine. Party leaders may even prefer them on that account; but I am sure the effects are bad from the standpoint of democracy.

Difficulty of Measuring Gains and Losses. The extensive changes made in the constituencies shortly before the 1955 election make it impossible to reckon up gains and losses except over the country as a whole, or rather for England, Wales, Scotland, and Northern Ireland as a whole. There were too many constituencies in which it is impossible to describe the result as either a gain or a loss to a particular party. This, perhaps, does not much matter, save to the statistically minded; but for the statistician it is awkward enough. The effect of the re-distribution on the election as a whole has been variously estimated as having cost Labour anything from one to ten seats at most. It was certainly not a major factor in the Conservative victory; but this is not the point at issue.

The Two Main Parties. Let us turn now from the election to the parties by which it was mainly fought. Labour and Conservative candidates— including Liberal Nationals and other hybrids with Conservatives— were confronting each other in almost every constituency, with Inde- pendent Liberals intervening in fewer than a sixth of the contests and the smaller parties only here and there. The two big party machines were Conservative and Labour, both based on a mass membership, both employing considerable forces of full-time agents and staff, both directed by active central organizations, and both standing in somewhat uncertain relation to the parliamentary parties whose success they were endeavouring to promote. Both these parties have recognized leaders—recognized in these days by the Constitution as well as by the parties themselves. Each has a Cabinet when it is in office, and a sort of Shadow Cabinet when it is not. Each has its party meetings, at which its M.P.s debate on tactics and policy outside the sittings of Parliament; and each has an Annual Conference, representing its local organizations—and in Labour's case its affiliated Trade Unions as well—at which resolutions are passed and party policy reviewed, with somewhat uncertain effects on the behaviour of the parties in Parliament. Labour, unlike the Conservatives, subjects its leader to the ordeal of annual re-election; but it is not usually much of an ordeal. The Conservatives have been known to evict a leader: Labour has not, though, apart from Ramsay MacDonald, one at any rate of its leaders—George Lansbury—has evicted himself.

Both the main parties rest on a mass individual membership organized in local constituency associations or parties: and the Labour Party has in addition a large affiliated membership contributing to its funds through Trade Unions and other bodies. The National Union of Conservative and Unionist Associations has a subscribing membership of approximately three millions in its local associations—three times as many as it had at the end of 1946. It has made a series of big drives in recent years, and has succeeded in building up a remarkably effective local organization. The Labour Party had in 1953 an individual subscribing membership of just over one million and a total membership of just over six millions, including five million affiliated Trade Union members. This last figure does not include the whole membership of the Trade Unions affiliated to the Party, as some Trade Unionists contract out of paying the political levy and some Trade Unions pay, even apart from this, only on part of their membership. When the Labour Government repealed the Trade Union Act of 1927, thus restoring 'contracting-out' in place of the 'contracting-in' system established under that Act, the Labour Party's affiliated Trade Union membership rose suddenly from 2,635,000 in 1946 to 4,386,000 the following year. Its Trade Union membership in 1953 compares with a total of more than eight millions in the Trades Union Congress, the difference being due partly to some Unions belonging to the Congress but not to the Party and partly to payments on less than the full membership. Only 84 Trade Unions were in the Labour Party, whereas the Congress included 184; but most of the Congress Unions outside the Party were fairly small. The most important was the Civil Service Clerical Association, with about 150,000 members. A few big Unions, notably the

National Union of Teachers and the National and Local Government Officers' Association, belong to neither.

The Labour Party and the Trade Unions.   The local structure of the Conservative Party—and also that of the Liberal Party—rests on a basis of individual membership in the constituency organizations, whereas the Labour Party's is a mixture of individual and locally affiliated membership. Trade Union branches affiliate to the local Labour Parties in the same way as the national Trade Unions join the Party nationally, though there is no compulsion on the local branches to affiliate unless they wish to do so. Most of them do affiliate, and thus become entitled to send delegates to local party meetings; but attendance is often irregular and there is not much reporting back to the branches, except on special occasions. Even Trade Unionists who attend their Union branch meetings usually hear little at them about the Labour Party's proceedings, either national or local; and the majority of the members, who attend rarely or not at all, hear practically nothing. Trade Union affiliations to the local Parties do very little to keep the general body of the members in touch with Labour Party affairs. The Trade Unionist who is keen on Labour politics very often joins the local Party as an individual member, in addition to paying his political levy through his Trade Union. He is least likely to do this where his particular Trade Union holds a dominant position in the area, as is often the case in the coalfields; and in such areas the Trade Union branch or lodge may have a much closer connection with the local Party's work. Sometimes, however, in 'safe' Labour areas, there is very little local party activity except at elections.

The Local Party Machines.   The local Parties are concerned not only with parliamentary but also with local government elections; and there have been in recent years much closer connections between the two as local government has come to be conducted more on a party basis. Both party head offices have interested themselves to an increasing extent in local election campaigns, which have come to turn more and more on national rather than purely local issues. The Conservatives especially have paid ever-increasing attention to building up their Party for purposes of local as well as national electioneering; and the Liberals, almost driven out of municipal politics in many areas (see p. 401), have been doing what they can to hold on to their position in the relatively few places where they are still an important factor. In some other areas they have definitely combined with the Conservatives to fight the Labour Party.

The Communist Party.   The Communist Party, like the others, is organized on a basis of local branches; but it is nowhere strong enough to return even a single M.P. or to win a seat on a major County or

County Borough authority. It puts up a small number of candidates, both nationally and locally; but its polls are usually very small. In the General Election of 1955 most of its candidates forfeited their deposits. Communism has no hold on the main body of electors: its strength, such as it is, rests on small active minorities which have established an influence inside a few Trade Unions, especially at the factory level. As a political force it is negligible in both national and local affairs.

The Labour Party and the T.U.C. In the Labour Party, at the national Conference level, the Trade Unions, if they are united, can always out-vote the local Parties, which represent primarily the individual members. In recent years the local Parties, or rather the majority of them, have usually been well to the left of the Trade Union majority. Their left tendency has been reflected in the voting for the seats on the National Executive reserved for representatives of the constituency organizations: they have usually chosen a majority of 'Bevanites' or sympathizers with the left-wing, whereas the Trade Unions have elected a majority of right-wing members. As the Trade Unions elect 12 Executive members out of a total of 28, whereas the local Parties elect only 7, the remainder being 1 elected by the affiliated bodies other than Trade Unions, 5 women elected by the whole Conference, and the Treasurer, similarly elected, together with the Leader and the Deputy Leader of the Parliamentary Party, the majority of the Executive usually adheres to the dominant right wing. It usually includes a good number of M.P.s. In 1954–5 all 7 local Party representatives, 4 out of 5 women members chosen as such, and the three *ex officio* members were M.P.s, as against only 2 of the 12 Trade Union representatives. The same year, the 35 members of the Trades Union Congress General Council included only 2 M.P.s, both drawn from fairly small Trade Unions. The active Trade Union official to-day can no longer effectively combine service in Parliament with his Trade Union duties. The Trade Unionists on the Labour Party Executive tend on the whole to be drawn from the second line of Trade Union leadership, as the General Secretaries of the principal Unions prefer to serve on the T.U.C. General Council. Nominations for both bodies are under the control of the central Trade Union organizations; and the persons elected are practically always full-time Trade Union officials. Nor have 'rank-and-filers', even if they are well-known in their own areas, any chance of being chosen to serve on the Executive as nominees of their local Parties, as these seats go almost inevitably to national figures such as prominent Labour M.P.s.

The Conservative and Labour Organizations Compared. The Conservative Party's mass organization is less dominated than the Labour Party's by nationally known M.P.s or other public figures, largely because the Conservative National Union is essentially a federation of constituency organizations and has no block of nationally affiliated organizations corresponding to the Trade Unions. This, however, does not prevent the Conservative central organization, which is under the control of the Leader, from being dominated by parliamentary figures. In theory at any rate the final control of policy in the Labour Party rests with the Party Conference, of which the Executive is the agent; whereas in the Conservative Party power to determine policy is supposed to be in the hands of the Leader, and both the Parliamentary Party and the National Union are only advisory agencies. In practice, however, this does not make quite so much difference as the theoretical divergence would suggest. The Parliamentary Labour Party must 'accept' Conference decisions, but need not act on them immediately unless it thinks fit. The Leader and the Parliamentary Party can usually persuade the Executive, if not always the Party Conference, to do what they want; and in the Conservative Party the Leader, in taking decisions, has to consider carefully what the Party in Parliament will endorse. There is, however, a real difference between the two Parties, largely based on their different histories. The Conservative Party has always been primarily a parliamentary grouping, and has only in recent years developed a mass organization of electors. The Labour Party, on the other hand, began and developed in its earlier stages mainly as an extra-parliamentary mass movement, resting largely on the Trade Unions; and it still possesses many traces of its origins, even after becoming a great parliamentary force. Its active members throughout the country still think of it mainly as a mass organ of the working-class movement rather than in exclusively parliamentary terms. Nevertheless, a Party which has provided the basis for a Government and may at any time return to power is bound to conduct its activities mainly with an eye on parliamentary conditions and possibilities; and in such a Party the parliamentary element is bound to increase its relative influence.

Organizationally, the Labour Party's chief weakness is the tenuity of the links between it and the main body of Trade Unionists who contribute to its funds. In a situation in which most Trade Unionists play only a passive part in the affairs of their Unions, it would be too much to expect that affiliation through the Trade Union to the Party could result in a very meaningful relationship. The lack of active contact is chiefly a by-product of the 'membership apathy' which affects the Trade Unions themselves; and the remedy, if there is one, can be found only by discovering means of stimulating more widespread active participation in Trade Union affairs.

The Co-operative Party.   The Co-operative Party (see p. 279), though its nominal membership exceeds that of any other Party—it exceeded $9\frac{1}{2}$ millions in 1953—can hardly be regarded as a political party in the ordinary sense of the word. Although it is not affiliated nationally to the Labour Party, its candidates for Parliament stand as Labour candidates and, if elected, become members of the Parliamentary Labour Party. Some of them have held high office in Labour Governments. It contests only a small number of seats—38 in 1955, with 19 successes—and these are in areas where it is able to persuade the local Labour Parties to accept its candidates. Its M.P.s meet together as a group, but have no collective differences of importance from the rest of the Labour Party, though they naturally emphasize issues of particular significance to consumers. The Co-operative Party holds its own National Conference, and draws up its own Party Programmes, which require endorsement by the main Co-operative Congress convened annually by the Co-operative Union as the central body representing Co-operative bodies of every sort. It accepts the Labour Party's policy on such issues as socialization, while insisting on the recognition of Co-operative ownership as a legitimate form of 'social ownership'. The Co-operative Party is indeed politically well to the left of the main body of Co-operative opinion, though it is quite as strongly anti-Communist as the Labour Party itself. It is in effect not so much an independent political party as a wing of the Labour Party which keeps its separate organization both in order to press the claims of consumers and of Co-operation and because it would be far harder to draw the local Co-operative Societies into direct affiliation to the Labour Party. Such affiliation has been open to Co-operative Societies from the very beginning of the Labour Party; but only one big Co-operative Society—Royal Arsenal—prefers to conduct its political activities directly inside the Labour Party, and in this case only a small proportion of the membership subscribes to its Political Council. Elsewhere, most of the large Co-operative Societies adhere to the Co-operative Party; but such adhesion means little more than a small subscription and the possible formation of a special political section which members are free to join or not to join as they please. In practice, there is not a great deal of Co-operative political activity save in the areas where there are actually Co-operative candidates, adopted or in prospect, though a good many Co-operative Societies give some help to the Labour Party in elections.

Party Finances. Since 1950 the two main political parties have been fairly evenly balanced, with the Conservatives on the whole gaining ground in the parliamentary field. One cause of recent Conservative successes is undoubtedly much improved local organization, which is partly due to bigger financial resources. The Conservatives have full-time agents in many more constituencies than the Labour Party, which is continually short of funds. The Trade Unions, which supply the bulk of the money for central Labour Party expenditure, prefer to keep a substantial part of the proceeds of the political levies in their own hands for financing their own candidates. A high proportion of these candidates are successful, both because they mostly contest seats in which industrial Labour is strongly organized and because they provide adequate funds for maintaining local organization. The majority of Labour candidates, however, even if they are Trade Union members, are not put forward as official Union candidates. They stand as nominees and under the auspices of local Labour Parties, which have to find most of the money for both organization and election expenses. In both the Labour and the Conservative Party there are rules which limit the amount of money candidates are allowed themselves to provide, these rules having been adopted in order to prevent Parliament from being too much a rich man's preserve and to prevent rich men from virtually buying seats by offering to meet the bulk of the costs of organization and election out of their own purses. This, of course, does not prevent the average Labour candidates from being a good deal less wealthy than the average Conservative: nor has it seriously shaken the hold of aristocratic families and representatives of large-scale business over the Conservative Party. As against this, with the growth of the Labour Party into a body which contests almost every seat, the proportion of official Trade Union candidates has fallen off sharply, and it has become a good deal easier for the 'intellectuals' in the Party to get chosen as candidates. They have, however, in many cases to begin by undertaking hopeless fights, in the hope of being rewarded later by adoption for more promising constituencies. In the House of Commons the Trade Union M.P.s, including both official Union candidates and others, have a loose group of their own for the discussion of questions of policy; and this group includes a majority of the Party. It is not, however, very active; nor is there any substantial antagonism between the Trade Unionists and the 'intellectuals', who have no separate organization of their own, though most of them, as well as some Trade Unionists, belong to the Fabian Society as an extra-parliamentary Socialist organization.

Research and Discussion. Each Party has its own Research Department, attached to its central office, for collecting information and preparing reports on matters of policy for submission to the Party. Inside the Parliamentary Parties there are also groups of M.P.s interested in particular questions; and these meet for discussion and often invite outside speakers or experts to address them. The Conservatives have also, in the 1922 Committee, a general organization of back-bench M.P.s, which sometimes brings considerable pressure to bear on the leadership. The Labour Party has its regular general meetings of its M.P.s, which fulfil a somewhat similar purpose, but are more under the influence of the Party leadership—which takes part in them, with the Leader presiding. When the Labour Party is in office, its Parliamentary Party deals with the Government through a committee elected by it for this purpose, and this is replaced by a sort of 'Shadow Cabinet' when Labour is in opposition. Under the most recent arrangement, each member of this 'Shadow Cabinet' is charged with watching over a particular branch of parliamentary affairs and is not allowed to stray outside his special field of activity. This clearly increases the rigidity of 'party discipline', which has tended to grow stronger since the Parties in Parliament have become more evenly matched. Discipline is, on the whole, stricter in the Labour than in the Conservative Party, and has become considerably more stringent of late years. Abstention from voting is still allowed on grounds of conscience; but apart from this, M.P.s are under strong pressure to vote in accordance with the majority decisions of the Party meetings. Discipline was a good deal less strict between 1945 and 1950, when the Labour Government enjoyed a big majority. Its re-imposition and stiffening have provoked some protests; but there has so far been majority support for it, and even the Bevanites have usually obeyed the rules.

Problems of Parliamentary Democracy. There is, indeed, in the British House of Commons of to-day, very little room for the independent M.P., or even, save rarely, for the back-bencher who has a particular cause at heart. In 1955 there were even very few Independent or 'splinter-party' candidates. Apart from this, the legislative programmes of Governments make heavy demands on parliamentary time, and there is not much scope for Bills introduced by private M.P.s or even for debates which are not officially sponsored by a Party. Even questions have to be rationed, and can be questioned by the Party Whips; and access to debate, though it depends on catching the Speaker's eye or that of the Chairman of Committees, is not easy except for speakers put forward by their Party. The back-bencher still has plenty to do— indeed, more than ever—but chiefly as a cog in the wheel of the party machine. To a great extent, this is unavoidable in view of the pressure on parliamentary time and the near-equivalence of the principal Parties; but it is none the less regrettable. Some have hoped for a remedy by means of some form of regional devolution, involving the establishment of subordinate Parliaments or Assemblies for Scotland and Wales and perhaps for England either as a whole or through regional sub-division. There are small but active Scottish and Welsh Nationalist movements which demand the erection of secondary Parliaments for their countries; but the main parties frown on such aspirations, and it is doubtful whether they would in practice do much to relieve the central congestion, even if they are to be desired on other grounds.

Indeed, the best approach to decentralization is probably not through parliamentary devolution, but rather through the building up of some sort of regional structure more analogous to local than to central government structures, and centred upon regional town and country planning and economic development rather than on parliamentary issues. The consideration of such possibilities belongs rather to the section dealing with Local Government than to the present section of this book (see p. 384).

CHAPTER THIRTY

TRADE UNIONS

THE Trade Union movement, with a total membership of about 9½ millions, holds a position of great power and importance in economic affairs. Before the war, in 1939, it had about 6¼ million members; but by 1945 it was nearing 8 millions, and it reached 9 millions in 1950, out of a total working population, including employers and self-employed persons, of about 23 millions. It thus still includes less than half the total working population; but of course many of these are either boys and girls or grown-ups working not for wages or salaries but for other forms of income. Trade Unions have now come to include large numbers of 'black-coated' and professional workers; but a number of associations catering for the higher professional and business groups prefer not to be called 'Trade Unions', even if they perform certain analogous functions in regulating their members' remuneration and conditions of work. An outstanding example is the British Medical Association, which negotiates collectively on behalf of the profession and is very powerful: it resolutely refused to accept the status of 'employed persons' for its members who enrolled for the National Health Service, insisting on capitation fees rather than salaries and on freedom from being legally 'employed' by the health authorities. There are a great many professional bodies which, though they may seek to lay down standards for their professions, take no part in collective bargaining about salaries, or even about rates of payment in a wider sense; whereas others prescribe standard fees or attempt to lay down minimum salary rates for certain types of post. The main teachers' organizations, though they do not belong to the Trades Union Congress, are commonly regarded as Trade Unions because most of their members are employed salary-earners on whose behalf they negotiate about rates of payment and conditions of employment, chiefly nowadays through the various panels of the Burnham Committee; but such bodies as the Association of University Teachers are on the border line, though their methods approximate more and more to those of Trade Unions. The lesser professions have a host of associations which are marginal between Trade Unions and professional institutions: the chartered Institutes of Civil and other types of Engineers are definitely not Trade Unions and are not primarily concerned with pay or working conditions. Obviously, no clear line can be drawn; but it seems best to regard Trade Unions as essentially associations of *employed* wage- or

419

salary-earners which set out to bargain collectively about payment and conditions with the employers concerned.

Unions of Non-manual Workers. The main strength of the Trade Union movement still lies among the manual workers. But a quite substantial part of the affiliated membership of the Trades Union Congress is now made up of persons who are not manual workers in the ordinary sense. Taken broadly, the Unions made up of such persons number over 30, with a combined membership of nearly three-quarters of a million. The biggest are the Civil Service Clerical Association (148,000), the Transport Salaried Staffs Association (91,000), the Association of Engineering and Shipbuilding Draughtsmen (55,000), the Confederation of Health Service Employees (52,000), the Clerical and Administrative Workers' Union (46,000), and the National Union of Bank Employees (37,000). They also include the principal Unions of Actors, Variety Artistes, Cinema Technicians, Theatrical Employees and Musicians; those of Navigating and Engineer Officers in the merchant service, Radio Engineers, and Air Pilots; a number of other Civil Service Trade Unions besides the C.S.C.A.; the principal bodies of Insurance Workers; the National Union of Journalists; the Post Office Controlling Officers, as well as the main postal Trade Unions (which have not been included in the total given above); the Co-operative Officials; the Electrical Power Engineers; the Scientific Workers; and the Association of Supervisory Staffs, Executives and Technicians, which has its main membership in engineering and civil aviation. They even include a small body of doctors, the Medical Practitioners' Union, but not, as we saw, the B.M.A. Nor do they include either the Teachers' associations or the powerful National and Local Government Officers' Association, which is the principal Union for local government administrative employees. With this last, however, the T.U.C. acts jointly through a National Advisory Committee for Local Government Service; and it has also an Advisory Council for Non-manual Workers on which the non-affiliated National Federation of Professional Workers is represented.

The T.U.C. General Council. These 'non-manual' groups have been growing in relative importance in recent years; but the Trades Union Congress is still dominated by the big Unions made up mainly of manual workers, though some of them enrol non-manual workers as well. Its General Council of 35 members is elected so as to represent the 19 Trade Groups into which the affiliated Unions are divided, but by vote of the whole Congress. The method of election, however, gives virtually safe seats to the candidates of the biggest Unions—commonly their General Secretaries—and there is considerable continuity of membership from year to year. Where General Secretaries of big Unions do not sit on the General Council, the reason usually is that they have but recently assumed their posts (e.g. Mr. Tiffin), or, in a few cases, that they are Communists (e.g. Mr. Horner of the N.U.M.) or otherwise unacceptable because they have run foul of even more powerful Unions (e.g. Mr. Bryn Roberts of the National Union of Public Employees, which has built up its large membership in hot rivalry with the General and Municipal Workers).

The General Council of the T.U.C. is indeed a sort of federal cabinet, representing the principal Unions in each group through their leading officials. Its powers, however, are limited; for each affiliated Union jealously maintains its independent right to settle its own policy and manage its own affairs. The T.U.C. and its General Council are not negotiating bodies, nor have they any authority to lay down binding policies about such matters as wage-demands, or movements for a reduction of working hours. The most they can do is to advise, as they did in respect of wage-restraint after the war until the full Congress repudiated the policy against the wish of the Council. Each Union bargains independently with its members' employers, or sometimes joins with others in a bargaining federation covering a wider occupational field. Even where federations exist, their powers are often limited, and the constituent Unions bargain independently on some questions, or reserve the right to reject the federations' policies.

A 'National Wages Policy'? There have been since 1945 many proposals that the T.U.C. should adopt a 'national wages policy' and co-ordinate the claims made by the separate groups; but the General Council has always opposed such notions, partly on the ground that it lacks the requisite powers, but mainly because its members prefer to act independently through their own established negotiating machinery. There is indeed considerable doubt about the meaning of a 'national wages policy', which might involve the General Council, or even the T.U.C. itself, in adjudicating between the claims of different groups among the members—for example, about the degree of priority to be given to the claims of the worst-paid and about the proper amounts of the 'differentials' between skilled and less skilled workers in every industry. Such issues, as we have come to know from recent experiences, are sometimes very difficult to settle; and even if the Congress or its General Council were to be endowed under Standing Orders with the necessary powers, it is not easy to see how they could enforce their judgments on recalcitrant Unions. In effect, the only penalty open to them is to expel, or suspend from membership, an offending body; but a powerful Union, even if expelled from Congress, might well be in a position to go its own way with the support of its members.

More Power for the General Council. At the Congress held in September 1955 the General Council obtained from the delegates some enlargement of its powers of intervention in industrial disputes. The issue had been brought to the front as a consequence of the increase in the seriousness of stoppages of work earlier in the year; and the Government had conferred with the General Council as well as with the employers about possible means of avoiding strike action. There had even been talk in the newspapers of possible anti-strike legislation; but the Government had been wary of supporting any such project. What happened at the Congress was that the General Council was authorized to intervene at an earlier stage—in view of a threatened stoppage of work, without waiting for it actually to occur. The Congress also rejected a resolution which would have committed the General Council to support *all* demands put forward by its affiliated Unions, but took care not to give the Council power to settle any issue over the head of the particular Union concerned. It was pointed out that support of all demands might involve backing inconsistent claims—for example, in respect of wage differentials between skilled and less skilled workers; and there was clearly no readiness on the part of the Unions to hand over to the General Council any power to override their own members' opinions or to replace them as negotiating bodies. It is not easy to say at this stage how much difference, if any, the 1955 resolution will make to the effective authority of the General Council. It seems most likely to serve as a means of bringing in the Government, through the Council, at an earlier stage than hitherto, when the processes of collective bargaining in a particular industry look like breaking down. A suggestion by the Congress Chairman, Mr. Geddes of the Post Office Workers, that there should be set up some sort of appeals tribunal entitled to revise arbitration awards provoked strong opposition from many quarters, including the General Council itself. The Council is indeed clearly reluctant to be endowed with much larger powers, which it would have no effective means of enforcing against a recalcitrant Union.

Inter-Union Disputes. The General Council can, however, exert a considerable influence in disputes between Unions—which relate mainly to alleged 'poaching' of members or to invasion of a field of organization already occupied by another Union. The General Council's Disputes Committee is constantly dealing with cases of these kinds; and general rules to prevent 'poaching' have been embodied in the 'Bridlington Agreement', which has been recently invoked against the attempt of the Stevedores' and Dockers' Union—a London rival of the Transport and General Workers—to take over dissident groups of former T. and G.W. members at a number of Northern ports. The Stevedores, under pressure of suspension by the General Council, have been forced to give up these members and have been ordered to hand them back to the T. and G.W.U.—to which many of them are refusing to return. What will happen next is anybody's guess. The situation is complicated by the fact that it is impossible to get work at the docks without a Union card and that the dock employers, who recognize the T. and G.W.U., refuse to grant negotiating rights to a new body except in agreement with that Union.

This raises an awkward problem. The power of the Trade Unions would be undermined if it became easy to organize and secure recognition of rival Unions wherever an internal dispute arose; but as against this it is clearly illegitimate to treat men and women as if they were the property of the Union they have joined and could be handled to and fro between Unions regardless of their wishes. There have been somewhat similar cases previously—for example, in the coal mines after 1926, among the Clydeside dockers, and in the Post Office; but they have usually, though not always, ended in the return of the recalcitrants to the Union they had left. The National Union of Public Employees was not a 'breakaway' Union but a long-established small Union which organized a big recruiting campaign mainly among 'non-union' workers whom the General and Municipal Workers regarded as falling within their legitimate field.

Fortunately, really serious inter-union disputes are not very frequent; and usually the Disputes Committee is able to dispose of them without provoking a refusal to comply. Most of them arise in particular establishments where Trade Unionism is weak among a particular section of employees and a new Union, or one already enrolling other grades, comes in to take over the task of organization. Other cases occur where the workers in an establishment, or sections of them, have quarrelled with their Union Executives and seek to transfer their allegiance; and in such cases the Disputes Committee usually comes down on the side of the established Union, even if it has not been doing its job effectively, and orders the interloping Union to hand its new members back. Where particular Unions have established regular negotiating machinery with an employer, there are often agreements not to recognize rival Unions; and where the holding of a recognized Union card is virtually a condition of getting or keeping a job, this gives the Union head offices great power over their members, unless there is very deep and widespread discontent.

Compulsory Membership and the 'Closed Shop'. Trade Unions rest fundamentally on voluntary membership; but as they approach 100 per cent success in any particular field, they tend to become compulsory, either because the employer agrees to employ only Trade Unionists or because their members refuse to work with non-union men. Where this happens, the Unions lose as well as gain; for in achieving complete organization they also lessen the individual's feeling of responsibility for his Union and dilute their membership with apathetic or uninterested members, at the expense of its democratic quality. The Unions, however, can hardly be expected to stop short of the attempt to attain 100 per cent membership wherever they are strong, even if they do often stop short of the 'closed shop' in the strict sense, involving the employers' agreement to make membership a condition of employment. Even apart from the strength to be derived from inclusiveness, many workers feel it to be unfair that others should profit by the Unions' efforts to improve conditions without bearing their share in the cost; and many active Trade Unionists have a sense of loyalty which rests on more than a merely self-interested foundation and feel a strong moral disapproval of the non-unionist as a potential 'blackleg'. Such sentiments are probably less widespread than they were when the Trade Unions had to struggle hard to win recognition and establish collective bargaining. These rights are now very widely recognized, though there remain a number of firms—some of them quite large—which still stand out against recognition in the name of 'freedom of contract'. Nowadays, the larger of such firms, even if they reject collective bargaining, have usually to pay at least the Trade Union standard rates; and some of them pay more, in order to obtain freedom to settle their own conditions of employment. But in all the big industries, the great majority of firms are now 'Union' firms, at any rate to the extent of becoming parties to collective bargains and accepting their employees' right to join a Trade Union if they so desire.

Non-Unionists and 'In and Outs'. In spite of this, there remain a large number of non-unionists, even in most of the highly organized industries, especially among women and less skilled workers. A great deal of this non-unionism is less a matter of refusal to join than of simple failure to pay regular contributions. Less skilled workers, men and women alike, are continually in and out of Unions according to the effort put into collecting their contributions. The very high rates of membership turnover in the huge 'general' Unions are due less to continual recruitment of fresh individuals than to lapses followed by re-entry, especially where there has been a change of job. It is not easy to secure regular payment of small weekly contributions without the aid of paid collectors whose cost absorbs an appreciable proportion of what is paid. Where attendance at branch meetings is small, as it very often is among the less skilled, collection at such meetings is ineffective. It is more effective in such cases to collect at the workplace, through shop stewards or specially appointed collectors; but it is none too easy to discover an adequate number of reliable collectors. The Unions of skilled workers, with their higher contributions, have less difficulty; for there are usually friendly benefits that can be withheld from members who are in arrears, and it is worth the member's while to keep himself in good standing. Where such benefits are small, or even non-existent, there is much less inducement to pay regularly, even though the payments are small. This applies most of all to the big 'general' Unions, which present the problem of floating membership and member-apathy in the most acute form.

Voluntary Trade Union Service. Trade Unions, like other voluntary bodies, depend for their efficiency on an immense mass of unpaid, or barely paid, service. They are accustomed to paying small sums to their active members for undertaking certain duties and to meeting out-of-pocket expenses incurred in the course of Trade Union work; but a great deal of service is entirely unpaid—much more so than in the American Labour movement; and those who undertake such service do so mainly out of loyalty and belief in the value of Trade Unionism as a social institution. Trade Unions decline rapidly where they fail to enlist such service; but those most willing to undertake it are quite often left-wingers or rebels against authority, who are prone to fall foul of the directives of the Union officials or Executives. In many Unions there is a continual tussle between the Executives and the local militants, particularly at the establishment level; and it is in this connection that unofficial strikes most often occur. In a very few Unions the official leadership is in the hands of the left wing; and it is then the turn of the moderates to be discontented—for example, in the Electrical Trades Union or the Civil Service Clerical Association. Most Unions, however, are under moderate or right-wing leadership; and some of them have taken drastic action against malcontents, by suspending or winding-up rebellious branches or even by making rules formally excluding Communists from office. From such contests the head office usually emerges victorious, though in some cases unofficial strikes are subsequently recognized on appeal to a delegate Conference or special Appeal Court.

The Present Strength of Trade Unionism. It is now time to turn to the statistical aspects and to review briefly the essential facts of Trade Union membership and organization.

At the end of 1953 the Trade Unions of the United Kingdom had a total membership of 9,461,000, organized in 687 Unions. 17 Unions, each with more than 100,000 members, included more than two thirds of the total membership, and with a further 16 Unions, each with more than 50,000, included more than three-quarters. Thus, only about 2 million out of $9\frac{1}{2}$ were in the 654 Unions with fewer than 50,000, and half of these were in 39 Unions with memberships of between 25,000 and 50,000. By far the largest single Trade Union was the Transport and General Workers' Union, with a membership of more than $1\frac{1}{4}$ million.

The Largest Unions. The 15 largest Trade Unions affiliated to the Trades Union Congress were as shown in Table 193 (overleaf).

The two remaining Unions with more than 100,000 members were the National and Local Government Officers and the National Union of Teachers. Neither was affiliated to the Trades Union Congress.

TABLE 193

The Largest T.U.C. Trade Unions, 1954

	Membership 1953–4 (000's)	General Secretary 1955
Transport and General Workers' Union	1,259	A. E. Tiffin
Amalgamated Engineering Union	810	B. Gardner
N.U. of General and Municipal Workers	790	T. Williamson*
N.U. of Mineworkers	669	A. L. Horner
N.U. of Railwaymen	378	J. S. Campbell*
Union of Shop, Distributive and Allied Workers	339	J. A. Birch*
Electrical Trades Union	212	
Amalgamated Society of Woodworkers	196	J. F. MacDermott*
N.U. of Public Employees	175	B. Roberts
Union of Post Office Workers	161	C. J. Geddes*
Civil Service Clerical Association	148	G. F. Green
N.U. of Agricultural Workers	135	H. Collison*
N.U. of Printing, Bookbinding and Paper Workers	133	W. A. Morrison
N.U. of Tailors and Garment Workers	124	J. E. Newton*
Iron and Steel Trades Confederation	103	H. Douglass*
	5,632	

* Member of the T.U.C. General Council.

The Trades Union Congress returns show a further 18 affiliated Unions with more than 50,000 members. These are as follows:

TABLE 194

Other Large Trade Unions, 1954

	Membership 1953–4 (000's)	General Secretary 1955
Amalgamated Union of Building Trade Workers	95	G. H. Lowthian*
Transport Salaried Staffs Association	91	W. J. P. Webber*
Amalgamated Weavers' Association	86	L. T. Wright*
United Boilermakers' and Shipbuilders' Society	85	E. J. Hill*
N.U. of Boot and Shoe Operatives	84	L. Poole
Amalgamated Union of Foundry Workers	76	J. Gardner
N.U. of Dyers, Bleachers and Textile Workers	74	W. L. Heywood*
N.U. of Furniture Trade Operatives	72	A. G. Tomkins
National Society of Painters	70	S. Horsfield
Associated Society of Locomotive Engineers and Firemen	68	J. G. Baty*
N.U. of Seamen	62	T. Yates*
N.U. of Vehicle Builders	58	F. S. Winchester

TABLE 194 (*continued*)

	Membership 1953–4 (000's)	General Secretary 1955
Plumbing Trade Union	56	H. Kelly
Association of Engineering and Shipbuilding Draughtsmen	55	G. H. Doughty
Post Office Engineering Union	54	C. Smith
Typographical Association	52	F. C. Blackburn
Confederation of Health Service Employees	52	J. T. Waite
National Amalgamation of Card, Blowing and Ringroom Operatives	50	A. Roberts*
	1,240	

* Member of the T.U.C. General Council, 1954–5.

Total Membership. Total Trade Union membership has risen greatly since 1939, but the number of separate Trade Unions has fallen greatly, mainly as a result of amalgamations. Here are the figures for selected years since 1939:

TABLE 195

Total Trade Union Membership and Number of Trade Unions, 1939, 1945, 1950–4

End of Year	Number of Unions	Number of Members (*thousands*)		
		Males	Females	Total
1939	1,019	5,288	1,010	6,298
1945	781	6,237	1,638	7,875
1950	715	7,573	1,670	9,243
1951	710	7,706	1,775	9,481
1952	692	7,749	1,775	9,524
1953	687	7,701	1,760	9,461
1954	674	7,706	1,789	9,495

Female membership actually reached its peak in 1943, at 1,916,000, as a consequence of increased employment of women during the war. The peak for male membership was in 1952. The largest total increase in membership—11·8 per cent over the previous year—was in 1946, when many male workers returned from war service. From 1947 onwards the changes were relatively small.

Membership by Industries and Groups. It is not possible to break up total membership at all accurately by industries, both because of the large numbers enrolled in the two big 'general' Unions, which draw their members from many industries, and because the basis of organization varies. Some Unions, such as the Mineworkers and the Railwaymen, are broadly speaking 'industrial', whereas others are organized on a basis of craft or occupation, which may include persons working in a number of industries—e.g. Woodworkers, Painters, Engineers. Accordingly, the following table shows only the division into broad groups, some mainly industrial, but others occupational.

TABLE 196

Trade Union Membership by Industrial or Occupational Groups, 1954

(*thousands*)

	Male	Female	Total
General	1,768	310	2,078
* Metal, Engineering, Shipbuilding, Vehicles, Electrical, etc.	1,717	86	1,803
Coal Mining	819	20	839
Railways	510	30	540
* Building and Contracting	487	1	488
* Other Transport	384	58	442
* Local Government Service	310	131	441
Distributive Trades	239	154	394
National Government Service	238	121	359
Education	144	198	342
Paper and Printing	240	75	316
Cotton	69	150	219
Other Professional and Business Services	86	106	192
Other Textiles	87	86	173
Agriculture, Forestry and Fishing	140	8	148
Clothing	30	105	135
Manufactures of Wood and Cork	112	13	125
Insurance, Banking and Finance	74	19	93
Boots and Shoes	52	38	91
Theatres, Cinemas, Sports, etc.	61	25	85
* Food, Drink and Tobacco Manufacture	42	20	62
* Gas, Electricity and Water Supply	36	4	41
Pottery, Bricks, Glass, etc.	15	16	31
* Chemicals and Allied Trades	14	6	20
Leather and Fur	12	4	17
* Other Manufactures	10	3	13
* Other Mining and Quarrying	6	1	7
Other Services	2	—	2

* Considerable numbers assignable to these groups are enrolled in the general Unions.

Registered Trade Unions: Expenditure. The great majority of the bigger Trade Unions, and many of the smaller, are registered under the Trade Union Acts and make annual returns to the Chief Registrar of Friendly Societies. In 1953 there were 410 registered Trade Unions with a total membership of 8,323,000, leaving only about a million and a quarter unregistered. The registered Unions had in 1953 a total income of nearly £18 million derived from members' payments and nearly £2½ million from other sources, mainly investments. They spent rather more than

£17¼ million, leaving a surplus of about £3¼ million on the year. Their accumulated funds amounted to £70·7 million. The main items of expenditure were the following:

TABLE 197
Trade Union Expenditure, 1953
(£thousand)

Working Expenses	10,338
Superannuation Benefit	2,166
Sick and Accident Benefit	1,231
Other Benefits	973
Funeral Benefit	676
Political Fund	389
Dispute Benefit	258
Unemployment Benefit	172
Other Outgoings	1,111

Thus, almost 60 per cent of total expenditure was for working costs, 29 per cent for friendly benefits (superannuation, sickness, funeral, etc.), 2½ per cent for dispute and unemployment benefits taken together, and 2¼ per cent for political objects.

The remaining 6½ per cent was expended on other objects, including payments to federations and international grants to the International Confederation of Free Trade Unions and other bodies.

The Changes in Trade Union Costs. Trade Unions to-day spend a much smaller proportion of their resources than they used to on benefits. Unemployment has been slight in recent years, and there have been relatively few big industrial disputes. The growth of public social services has made it unnecessary for Trade Unions to increase their friendly benefits as much as they would have needed to do had the State made less provision. As against these savings, the costs of organization and negotiation have risen greatly, both because standards—including Trade Union salaries—have improved and because fuller recognition by employers has increased the work of collective bargaining. The income of £18 million from members averages not much more than £2 a year, or much less than 1s. a week, for each member. Of course, the amounts contributed differ greatly from one Trade Union to another. In the general Unions the minimum contribution is as little as 6d. or 7d. a week for men and 3d. or 4d. for women, whereas some of the Unions of highly paid skilled workers—e.g. compositors and cotton spinners—have contribution rates of several shillings a week, and pay high and numerous benefits in return.

Superannuation is a peculiarly expensive benefit, which only a few of the wealthier Unions can afford. It has, where it can be afforded, a big effect in stabilizing membership; but when a Trade Union gets into financial difficulties over it the result may be to deter new members from joining. Trade Unions have power, over and above their regular rates of contribution, to impose levies on their members in case of need, and the younger workers may be reluctant to pay substantial sums in order to provide pensions for their elders, at any rate where rates of pension have been put too high in relation to contributions. In these days, however, this seldom happens, except in declining trades. Most Unions are conservative in their financial methods and do not allow themselves to incur expensive obligations. Of course, a large-scale strike, if it lasts long, rapidly dissipates accumulated funds and may involve drawing on resources that are needed as a backing for other benefits. When funds have become depleted in this way, it is a common practice of the Unions of skilled workers to impose special levies in order to build them up; but Unions with low rates of contribution experience great difficulty in collecting additional levies. Luckily for the big 'general' Unions, disputes seldom involve more than a small fraction of total membership. The most recent occasion when funds were badly depleted was in 1926, on account of the General Strike and the much longer stoppage of the coal-miners. Total accumulated funds fell that year from £12½ million to £8½ million; but they were fairly soon built up again despite the depression of the early 1930s. They have indeed risen every year since 1933.

Trade Union Branches and District Councils. The basic unit for Trade Union membership is the branch, which varies greatly in size from Union to Union as well as from place to place. Some Unions divide their branches when they reach a certain size and may have a number of separate branches in the same town; whereas others, chiefly among the less skilled workers, prefer large branches, often with salaried full-time secretaries, and often including workers in different trades as well as in a number of establishments. Some Unions of varied membership have separate trade branches, whereas others prefer composite branches with or without special Trade Committees. In many Unions, especially among skilled workers, branches are based on place of residence rather than place of work, and this may make them unsuitable as bargaining agencies and prevent them from having any effective links with organization at the factory level. Other Unions base their branches on establishments, especially in the case of very big firms, and thus combine branch with factory organization. In other cases, organization in the establishments is in the hands of shop stewards or Works Committees, which often include representatives from a number of Unions. Usually, such bodies have no power to enter into collective agreements on the Unions' behalf, though they do often conclude works understandings within the limits set by collective agreements covering a wider field. Unions which have a number of branches in the same town or area often establish District Councils drawn from their branches and entrust the bargaining tasks to these Councils, on which shop stewards are sometimes given representation—as in the Amalgamated Engineering Union. Miners' 'lodges'—the equivalent of branches—are usually based on the colliery or pit; but small pits or collieries may be combined in a single 'lodge'.

In some Unions, where bargaining is highly centralized, District Councils take a different form. They cover much wider areas and are used not for negotiating but for recruitment of members and for other organizing functions. This is the position in the National Union of Railwaymen.

Shop Stewards and Works Committees. Many Union head offices are inclined to look askance at proposals to enlarge the powers of shop stewards or Works Committees. The shop steward was originally a minor Trade Union delegate with the function of checking Trade Union cards and seeking to enrol new members. He has developed gradually into a workers' representative whose task it is to take up workshop complaints and grievances and to conduct first-instance negotiations with the management, subject to his duty to call in Trade Union representatives if the matter cannot be amicably settled on the spot. General wage-rates and conditions of employment, save in the case of some very big firms, are usually laid down either in national agreements or in local agreements covering an entire area of the trade or industry concerned; and the functions of shop stewards and Works Committees are usually limited to negotiations within the overriding terms of such agreements. But in practice many big firms have ways of their own both in arranging the allocation of tasks and in paying for them—often by special bonuses over and above the standard rates; and a great many matters that are not fully covered by wider agreements arise in such establishments and need to be negotiated on an establishment or workshop basis. Where such conditions exist, an active Shop Stewards' or Works Committee may in fact exercise important bargaining powers; and Trade Union officials are often fearful of their factory representatives, especially where they have to act together with delegates of other Unions, entering into bargains which violate the terms of wider agreements or help to build up a 'loyalty to the firm', possibly at the expense of loyalty to the Union. Executives and officials are in addition often fearful of the establishment organizations coming under the influence of 'trouble-makers' and involving the Union in charges of breach of agreement, especially where unofficial strikes are called without going through the recognized stages of official negotiation. The difficulty about doing this is that such negotiations often take a very long time; and the workers on the spot, if they have a strong sense of immediate grievance, may not be prepared to wait, especially if they suspect the head office or the district officials of lukewarmness or opposition. It is, however, difficult to speed up official negotiations, above all where the employers wish to slow them down; and it is also impracticable to frame national or district agreements in such ways as to cover all the issues that may arise in each establishment concerned. The more mass-production develops, the more each vast factory tends to develop its own peculiar ways, and the more need there is for negotiation at the workplace level to supplement more general agreements.

National Agreements. Nowadays, there exist, for most important branches of production, either national agreements with provisions for local or regional variations, or national forms of negotiating machinery to which local or regional questions can be referred if agreement cannot be reached in negotiation at the lower level. In some cases there are both—some matters being dealt with on a national and others on a local or regional basis. The agreements in question are in some cases essentially procedural: they lay down the forms of bargaining and forbid strikes or lock-outs until the prescribed processes have been gone through. In such cases there are also secondary agreements embodying standard wage-rates and conditions of work. In other cases the procedures and the wages and conditions, including the conditions for varying them, are included in one and the same instrument. Some agreements provide for reference to arbitration where the parties fail to come to terms; and some include the appointment of an 'impartial chairman' who is either empowered to decide freely in case of deadlock or is bound to accept the full claim of one or other of the parties to the dispute. Even where no compulsory references to arbitration are laid down, the two sides may of course agree to submit their differences either to specially appointed arbitrators or to the Arbitration Court provided by the Government; and in practice much use is made of this body, though arbitration has ceased to be legally compulsory since the wartime regulations have been allowed to lapse. Big Trade Unions are usually very reluctant to call extensive strikes, save under extreme provocation, both on account of the cost and because most of their leaders are unwilling to hamper production for fear of upsetting the balance of international payments. Employers, too, are for the most part reluctant to declare lock-outs under conditions of full employment and of order books which require continuous production. Under these circumstances, such stoppages as do occur are in the majority of cases short and in many cases 'unofficial'—that is, unsupported by the Trade Union head offices, whose sanction is almost universally needed before any strike can be called in accordance with Union regulations.

Strikes and Lock-outs. The figures for disputes which have involved stoppages of work in recent years are as shown in Table 198.

In looking at these figures it should be borne in mind that they relate to a working force of well over 20 millions and to a Trade Union mem-

TABLE 198

Industrial Disputes, 1946–54

Year	Number of Stoppages beginning in year	Number of Workers Directly Involved (000's)	Indirectly Involved (000's)	Working Days Lost (000's)
1946	2,205	405	121	2,138
1947	1,721	489	131	2,389
1948	1,759	324	100	1,935
1949	1,426	313	120	1,805
1950	1,339	269	33	1,375
1951	1,719	336	43	1,687
1952	1,714	303	112	1,769
1953	1,746	1,329	41	2,157
1954	1,994	399	46	2,453
(provisional)				

bership of approximately 9 millions. The days lost have never amounted to more than about one-quarter of one day for each Trade Unionist, or to much more than one-tenth of one day for each member of the employed population. No doubt, some strikes cause inconvenience or dislocation extending far beyond the numbers involved; but as against this some of the days lost are made up for by more intensive work after the resumption. Strikes, unless they affect key groups or are prolonged, cause very little loss of production in relation to total output. The number of stoppages has indeed tended to be greater since 1945 than it was in the depressed 'thirties; but they have been on the average both smaller and shorter. There was some increase in 1953 and 1954, as compared with the immediately preceding years; but it was not large, though a few of the stoppages were highly inconvenient to the public— especially those which affected transport. It should also be remembered that in 1926—the year of the General Strike—the number of days lost exceeded 162 million, and in 1921 it nearly reached 86 million; whereas since 1945 it has never reached 3 million. Strikes and lock outs are no doubt a nuisance; but they are not a major factor affecting economic prosperity. In the four years after the first world war—1919–1922— more than 167 million days were lost by reason of them: in the four years 1946–49 the loss was only about 8 million days, though Trade Union membership had roughly doubled.

Joint Consultation. Something has been said in the section dealing with the nationalized industries concerning the development in them of methods of joint consultation between the Public Corporations and the Trade Unions. Outside this special field joint consultation has developed chiefly in the engineering and aircraft industries and in certain large firms and establishments in other industries. This development took place mainly during the war, in the form of Joint Production

P.-W.C.B.—F F

Committees with the function of smoothing away differences which were hampering output. It has worked well in some cases, badly in some, and neither particularly well nor ill in a large number. What has become evident is that it cannot work well unless the management takes it seriously and is prepared to consult, wherever possible, *before* rather than after making up its own mind. It is not real consultation merely to tell the workers' representatives that something has been decided upon, and that the management proposes to act upon it at a certain date. The throwing of such decisions at the workers' heads is much more likely to aggravate them than to promote harmonious working. Many managements, however, appear unable to appreciate this, or to recognize the need to solve their operational problems with real participation of those who will be called on to carry the decisions into practice and to experience the effects in their daily working lives. A further defect in many joint consultation schemes is that the management either fails to appoint to the joint committees the key persons who have the deciding voice in matters of policy or, if it does, allows a single individual to speak in its name, to the exclusion of other managerial or technological representatives, who are condemned to sit silent even if they have strong individual views on the questions at issue. Joint consultation should involve a pooling of ideas by all joint committee members rather than the presentation of collective propositions by either 'side'—unless the propositions really embody agreed judgments. Inevitably there will be some issues over which the management representatives take one view and the Trade Union representatives another; but there are also many matters in relation to which the problem is to find an acceptable arrangement that can be expected to work smoothly on a basis of general consent. For example, a group of technicians may have devised a method of re-arranging work or introducing new machines in order to increase productivity without taking due account of the effect of the projected changes on the demands made on the workers concerned, of whom some may be affected favourably and others adversely. It is fully possible that a free exchange of ideas among all concerned, including other managerial representatives or supervisors as well as the different groups of workers, may suggest a method of securing the desired output without the adverse consequences feared by some of the workers' spokesmen. Such a solution will be most unlikely to emerge if each side feels it has to speak with a single voice and to defend its point of view against the other without attempting to find a way round.

Conditions of Successful Consultation. This goes to show that joint consultation can be expected to work well only where those taking part in it recognize one another's point of view, and on a foundation of mutual trust between the parties—and, besides this, in an atmosphere that leaves every representative free to speak his mind. In the absence of these conditions, meetings of joint consultative committees are apt to become mere formal confrontations, at which nothing real is achieved. No doubt, the blame for failure does not always rest on the management. Workers' representatives can be exceedingly awkward, especially when they are defending some traditional workshop practice or when—rightly or wrongly—they distrust the management's sincerity. The workers' side of such committees can be captured by persons whose whole aim is to make difficulties and to stir up trouble; and the management has in such cases a difficult situation to meet and may lose patience and even throw over the entire attempt to work on agreed lines. There are, on the other side, managers who, though their intentions may be excellent, are dictatorial by temperament, or simply unable to make workers' representatives understand what they really mean. Even apart from the obstacles to success in joint consultation which arise out of divergent interests, there are big difficulties of human communication to be overcome. Nevertheless, real consultation is well worth the while of both the parties. Managements, under conditions of strong Trade Unionism and increasingly democratic attitudes among employees, have to find ways of making capitalist industry work as long as it continues at all; and these ways must involve a recognition of the workers' human right to a say in the conditions that affect their working lives. On the other part, the workers, even if they are hostile to capitalism, have to live under it, until it is replaced, and have a strong interest in doing so with as little avoidable unhappiness or irksomeness of labour as can be contrived. Joint consultation can be used to serve both these legitimate ends, and should be so used to the fullest possible extent.

There is a further aspect that needs to be taken into account. Joint consultation offers managements, if they choose to take it, an opportunity to explain frankly to the workers the financial and operational problems of their several businesses and to dispel misunderstandings which may adversely affect the spirit of the establishment and therewith the will to work well. Frankness in such matters is a necessary condition of success.

Consultation and Control. Joint consultation of itself of course does nothing to alter the fundamental relations between employers and employees. However it is worked, it leaves the final decision in the hands of the management and the workers with nothing to do save either obey the orders they are given or strike or abandon their jobs. Joint consultation does not involve, or even begin to carry with it, any sort of 'joint control' or real 'participation in management'. It is not even, as ordinarily worked, an extension of the field of collective bargaining, though it may develop along this line. Consultative Committees are expressly forbidden, where Trade Union collective agreements are in force, to negotiate about matters covered by such agreements, in order to prevent them from 'usurping' Trade Union functions. In practice, however, the line cannot easily be drawn; for there are many factors which affect earnings (as distinct from standard rates), and working conditions in a particular establishment cannot possibly be fully covered in general Trade Union agreements. On such matters negotiation has to take place on an establishment or workshop basis; and shop stewards are bound to be closely concerned. In some establishments there exist side by side a Joint Consultative Committee representing both management and workers and a Shop Stewards' Committee, representing only the workers; and the latter body deals with such matters of negotiation, while the former is confined to matters outside the scope of major Trade Union agreements. The line of demarcation is, however, often difficult to draw, and the attempt to keep the discussions separate may have unfortunate results. It is better, wherever possible, to combine both functions in the hands of the same persons by constituting the Shop Stewards the 'workers' side' of the joint body.

In other cases, separate Welfare Committees exist side by side with Consultative Committees and sometimes with Shop Stewards' Committees as well. This may or may not be a good arrangement. Consultative Committees are bound to discuss 'welfare' questions; but it does not follow that they are suitable bodies actually to administer 'welfare' services, such as works canteens, sports clubs, pension funds and other services. These are often best run by specially elected committees, or by a general Welfare Committee chosen entirely or mainly by and from the workers.

Changing Conditions of Collective Bargaining. In these days of mass-production and increasing automation based on scientific techniques, Trade Unions in many industries can no longer effectively serve their members by concentrating their attention on standard wage-rates and standard working conditions applicable to whole trades or regions. Both actual earnings and conditions of work depend increasingly on the methods and regulations adopted by the managements of particular factories, which involve different gradings of labour and arrangements of working tasks. Where such circumstances exist, increasing importance must be given to separate negotiations at an establishment level for the purpose of filling out and adapting the provisions of more general agreements. Trade Unions cannot afford to maintain bodies of full-time officials to undertake such negotiations, which have to be conducted mainly on the spot, by shop stewards or works delegates. Accordingly, it becomes an important matter for Trade Unions both to endow their workshop agents with authority adequate for this pur pose and to ensure that they receive adequate training for their tasks.

To an increasing extent, the Trade Unions are recognizing this latter need and are providing special short training courses for shop stewards and other active members, as well as longer courses for some of their junior officials. Such courses cover both technical matters and questions of 'industrial relations' in a broader sense. It is necessary for a Shop Stewards' or Consultative Committee to be able to understand such things as balance sheets and profit and loss accounts, and to grasp the implications of production plans and investment projects, as well as to master the essentials of committee procedure and to have a thorough knowledge of Trade Union agreements and policies. Joint consultation, we saw, does not give 'joint control'; but training in these matters improves the workers' power to participate in control when the time comes and strengthens the force of the claim to democratic industrial self-government. Only if Trade Unions take such tasks seriously and adapt their working methods to the conditions of modern productive techniques can they hope to exercise effectively, or to enable their members to exercise, the responsibilities that correspond to their greatly increased bargaining strength.

CHAPTER THIRTY-ONE

A SUMMING UP

How should one estimate the condition of a country which has made great advances towards the abolition of primary poverty, that has greatly improved in health and has made considerable strides forward in its educational provision, that has almost got rid of unemployment as a social problem, but that finds difficulty in paying its way internationally and has lost its old position of world leadership in international trade and investment? If one attends only to the present, ignoring the uncertainties of the future, the answer is not in doubt. Since the earlier version of *The Condition of Britain* was published in 1937 there have been immense improvements in the welfare of the people—above all in that of the poorer sections; and these material advances have carried with them great human gains in independence and self-respect, resting on more nearly equal human relations and on the acceptance of a narrower gap between richer and poorer groups. To anyone who accepts social equality as a desirable goal and hates the suffering caused by sheer privation and by the denial of a fair chance the achievement of the past two decades must give immense satisfaction, even if it still falls a long way short of his larger hopes. Even if this feeling of satisfaction is crossed by doubts and fears concerning the future, it seems unlikely that there can be, in the foreseeable time to come, any really substantial reversal of the trend towards social justice. The underdogs who have improved their status and condition will not easily submit to being thrust back into the ignominies of the old order; and even among the groups and classes that have lost some of their former superiority there are many who would not choose to regain it, even if they could, at the price of restoring the old iniquities. There is still plenty of selfishness and self-seeking in all classes; but all the same the assumptions of politics and economics have changed enough to put formidable obstacles in the way of a reversal of the general trend.

The Need for Increased Production. It is not, however, enough merely to survey the present state of the British people in respect of health, wealth, and the material means to well-being and to compare this state with things as they were in the 1930s. We have to consider also how far the existing condition of the people can be regarded as a guaranteed foundation for further advances and what dangers there are of things getting worse again instead of better. A worsening of Great Britain's economic position would not, of course, necessarily mean that we should go back to the old injustices and inhumanities that have been mitigated during and since the war. But it would clearly mean a fall, instead of a further advance, in living standards and an intensified struggle to retain larger shares in a smaller cake. If it involved a recurrence of serious unemployment, the economic power of the Trade Unions would be greatly undermined; and this would probably lead to an intensification of the political struggle as the workers attempted to make up for their economic weakness by more energetic use of their political power. For the theoretician it would be a matter of great interest to discover to what extent such an attempt could succeed; but politics and economics do not exist in order to provide material for social scientists or political speculators. They exist rather as structures for the furtherance of practical human ends—of good government and high production fairly shared—however differently 'goodness' and 'fairness' in these fields may be understood by different groups and interests.

Other things being equal, it is clearly a common interest of all classes that production shall be as great as possible within the limits set by the demand for leisure and for tolerable conditions of work. The total level of production is so important a factor in determining standards of living, not for one class but for all, that there is bound to be a general desire to keep it as high as possible, within these limits. Even those who, fearing glut or aiming at monopoly, wish to keep down the production of some particular kind of good or service wish the output of other things to increase and know that, the bigger the whole cake is, the bigger their share in it is likely to be. A cake, of any size, can no doubt be distributed better or worse; but this does not invalidate the fact that, from country to country, the size of the product per head of population is the principal factor affecting the standards of living of the common people.

The World is Still Very Poor. High production, then, is a matter of general interest, and will continue to be so until the world passes, if it ever does, into a condition of such plenty that no desires for goods and services remain unsatisfied—or at all events, none that are compatible with plenty for all. There is, however, clearly no country—not even the United States—in which such a state of affairs either exists or is likely to for as far ahead as it is at all profitable to look. Moreover, if we consider the world as a whole, sheer primary poverty is still the rule for the majority of mankind. The Soviet Union has demonstrated how fast a country, by intensified effort, can pass from primitive to highly industrialized methods; but it has also shown that such development is relatively slow in its effects on the general standards of living. Nor must it be left out of account that industrialization and the urbanization that goes with it create new needs as fast as they provide for meeting them—

or even faster, or that increased production involves much greater difficulties among crowded peasant populations, where land is scarce, than in vast underpopulated areas such as Russia was at the time of the Revolution.

Both nationally and on a worldwide scale higher production is a necessary condition of social, as well as of economic, progress. The more advanced countries need more for themselves, and are also under an obligation, not only morally but also in their own interest, to help forward the productive development of the rest of the world. In the case of Great Britain there is a special responsibility for furthering colonial development and for aiding India in facing its exceedingly difficult economic problems. But this obligation cannot be met unless the British economy can maintain a favourable balance of current payments and thus provide itself with a surplus for investing or giving to countries in greater need. Great Britain has a large task to face in modernizing its own productive equipment, and needs for this purpose to apply a high proportion of current output to home investment at the expense of higher immediate consumption; but over and above this it is called upon to provide funds for overseas use in the development of the less advanced areas.

International Factors in the Condition of the British Economy. This requirement raises special problems in view of Great Britain's high dependence on imports of both foodstuffs and industrial materials; for nearly all these imports have to be paid for out of the proceeds of exports of goods and services. In order to find customers, British industries must be able to sell at competitive prices: they must accordingly not merely increase the efficiency of production but do this as rapidly as the countries which are their chief competitors in world markets. Failure to achieve this rate of progress would involve loss of export markets on a scale that would soon not merely leave no surplus for investment abroad, but would render it impracticable to purchase the imports needed for maintaining full employment and for maintaining standards of living. Doubtless, the fall in exports could be stemmed temporarily by currency depreciation, which would reduce the price of British goods to overseas buyers; but this is a game at which more than one can play, and even if other countries did not reduce their currency values, it would mean a rise in the sterling prices of imports to the detriment of British consumers.

Comparative Incomes and Industrial Production. The pace at which British industries need to advance in efficiency is thus set mainly not by what may appear reasonable to British manufacturers or workers, but rather by the pace actually achieved in other advanced countries— notably the United States and Germany, which are Great Britain's principal competitors in the export of the classes of manufactured goods most important in world markets of to-day and to-morrow. As we saw (on p. 59) comparisons of productivity between countries are difficult to make with any approach to accuracy, and the usable statistics are few. The indexes of national production, however, furnish, despite their shortcomings, a rough indication of relative rates of advance; and in this respect Great Britain's record is no longer so satisfactory as it was a few years ago. We saw (on p. 68) that between 1938 and 1954 British industrial production rose by about 50 per cent, whereas that of the United States rose by more than 160 per cent and that of Canada by 140 per cent. The increase in Western Germany was 77 per cent and in Sweden 72 per cent; and even France showed an advance of 54 per cent. If we take 1950 instead of 1938 as the base year for comparison, the British position appears even less favourable. Here are the figures on this basis for a few of the leading countries.

TABLE 199

Index Numbers of Industrial Production in Certain Countries, 1950-4

	1950	1951	1952	1953	1954
United Kingdom	100	106·5	100	106	112
U.S.A.	100	106·5	110	119·5	111
W. Germany	100	120	128	139·5	156·5
France	100	112·5	118	114	125
Belgium	100	115·5	112	112	121½
Sweden	100	104·5	103	103	106½

On this basis, Great Britain, though ahead of Sweden, was badly behind Western Germany, France and Belgium and also, save in 1954, a year of mild recession in America, a long way behind the United States.

Comparative Price Movements. These, of course, are figures of total industrial production, and not of costs or prices, which are the significant factors in respect of external trade. In terms of unit prices of exports, figures are available only by regions and not for separate countries. Over the world as a whole, as far as statistics are to hand, export prices rose between 1950 and 1954 by about 11 per cent—made up of a rise of 22 per cent in 1951 and a series of drops in each of the following years. British export prices rose less rapidly, by 17 per cent, in 1951, but continued to rise, to 24 per cent over the 1950 level in 1952, and then dropped by stages to 18 per cent above that level in 1954. North American export prices rose less sharply, by 15 per cent in 1951 and by one point further in 1952, and then dropped by 1954 to 13 per cent above the level of 1950. For continental Western Europe there were rises of 22 per cent in 1951 and of four points more in 1952, followed by drops of 11 per cent above the 1950 level in 1954. Thus, in 1954, British export prices showed a greater increase over those of 1950 than the prices of the principal competing areas. It has been argued that in

1950, as an effect of recent devaluation, the British prices were unduly low; and they almost certainly were so in 1951, when the prices of primary materials were much too high. But by 1954 this effect of devaluation had certainly worn off, and there is certainly no room to-day for higher export prices without consequent loss of trade. With the rapid revival of Western Germany and the re-entry of Japan into the world market selling conditions have become much more keenly competitive than they were a few years ago. Export markets can be held and expanded only by keeping in step with rival exporters; and this means keeping costs down to a competitive level as other countries improve their productive efficiency.

The Limits to Wage-advances. This is an important factor in limiting the wage-advances which British export industries can afford to concede. The existence of high profits provides a strong inducement to Trade Unionists to believe that their employers can afford to increase wages; but the position is less simple than it appears. Even if employers can afford more, there are limits to what the British economy as a whole can afford to add to its wages bill. Higher wages, if they are not cancelled out by price-increases, mean higher consumption of imported as well as of home-produced goods, and thus put an additional strain on the balance of payments; and if prices are raised, in relation to those charged by other countries, some export sales are bound to be lost, and the balance of payments to be affected adversely in that way. To say this is not to say that there is no room for further wage-advances in the export trades: it is only to argue that the higher wages need to be earned by increasing production in step with other exporting countries.

The only condition, however, on which the British workers can be expected to accept policies of 'wage-restraint' in collective bargaining is that the distribution of incomes shall not be altered to their disadvantage by financial manipulation. Given this, the Trade Unions seem unlikely to press their claims to a point at which export trade would be endangered or the external value of the pound sterling seriously threatened. If there has been, in 1955, some tendency to press harder for wage-advances, the main reason for this has been a feeling among many workers that the sweeping away of 'controls' has allowed luxury spending and investment catering for it to advance too fast, and has thus set in motion inflationary forces that need to be checked in the general interest. The Government's attempt to hold these tendencies in check by purely monetary measures is regarded as bad, because it fails to discriminate between desirable and undesirable expansion and reacts particularly on the costs of house-building, in which interest rates are an important factor. High food prices are also resented; and the Government's refusal to give full effect to the views of the Monopolies Commission (see p. 261) is a further cause of complaint. The fact, however, remains that the British workers, if they demand a rising standard of life, will have to help in ensuring it by doing their best to increase their output at least as fast as their competitors in the world market.

The Coming of 'Automation'.   It may be that industry in all the advanced countries is on the threshold of a further leap forward, based on the peaceful application of atomic power and on the rapid development of the new methods of production that have been given the unhappy name of 'automation'. But it would be unwise to count these chickens before they have been hatched; for although nuclear energy will before long undoubtedly be making some contribution towards the solution of our difficult fuel problems no one can say how great this contribution will be, or what will be its effects on the costs of production. Nor can much be usefully said at present about 'automation' or its consequences on the demand for labour, skilled or unskilled. There have been already, for the most part in the United States, developments of automatic factory and machine control which have made it possible for one man to do the work of hundreds; and such methods are spreading fast in certain branches of industry, notably in chemical manufacture and in the production of electro-technical goods such as radio and television sets. The new electronic methods are also invading the field of office work, where the mechanical computer can displace the labour of large numbers of routine clerical workers and can also play a large part in the calculations needed for production planning. The limit to the application of these methods at present lies largely in the high cost of installing the new devices; for this makes them economic only where output is on a very large scale. It seems clear that they are destined to give the very large-scale producing unit an additional advantage over smaller rivals wherever there is a mass market to be provided for, and that in the long (but perhaps not very long) run they will involve wholesale scrapping of existing plant and vast new investment in capital goods designed to apply the new techniques.

These developments can clearly be of immense benefit to mankind, by making possible both greatly increased production and an immense reduction in the burden of work. They hold out the hope—but at present it is only the hope—of putting an end to poverty on a worldwide scale and at the same time of making possible a vast increase in leisure for all mankind. But, the more rapidly the great change comes, the more difficult problems it is likely to raise. It will be no benefit to mankind, but rather a curse, if millions of workers are displaced from employment and can find no new openings for work, if traditional skills are rendered obsolete in a moment, and no better provision is made for the victims than a profitless and meagre existence on inadequate social security payments. A sudden fall in the demand for labour could destroy at a blow the recently organized power of Trade Unions and could place dictatorial economic power in the hands of giant firms equipped with the new techniques. To combat such a situation the workers would have only their political power as voters; and this they might not learn to use effectively until terrible mischief had been done.

The workers, however, cannot wish to put themselves in opposition to a development which holds out the promise of greatly increased wealth obtained with much less human effort. Their only practicable course is not to resist the growth of automation but to insist on it being sensibly controlled in the interests of humanity and on its benefits being diffused, so as to reach above all the countries which are in the greatest need of increased production. If automatic methods are left to develop without such control, the main advances are certain to be made for some time to come chiefly in the wealthiest countries, and above all in the United States, where there exist both a vast home market and abundant supplies of capital for investment in new techniques. The poorer countries lack both the capital and the ready markets needed for taking advantage of the new Industrial Revolution that is on the way.

Technological Unemployment and its Effects.   Even the wealthiest countries will run into disaster if they increase their output by leaps and bounds and at the same time displace workers and deprive them of the means of buying what is being produced. Even the 'annual wage', on which the American Trade Unions are now beginning to insist, can give no more than temporary protection against the loss of a job; and no capitalist country will easily reconcile itself to maintaining unemployed persons at the same standards as they received when they were at work. In the past, it has usually been argued that, even if technological unemployment could cause grave hardship to particular groups of workers, fresh jobs would before long become available to absorb those who had been displaced; but such a contention can hardly hold good where great masses of workers are being eliminated and replaced by purely automatic devices. In such circumstances, quite revolutionary reductions in working hours may be needed for the avoidance of mass unemployment—unless indeed the automatized country is prepared to give away its products to poorer countries on an enormous scale.

Great Britain is certainly much worse placed than the United States for a very rapid development of automatic methods. Capital is scarce, even in relation to existing demands for it (see p. 99), and most industries would find great difficulty in providing the new investment needed for a rapid introduction of the new methods. If, however, the United States not only makes very rapid strides at home but also makes large foreign investments in such countries as Western Germany and Japan,

Great Britain will be compelled to mend its pace, by the fear of losing exports if it lags behind; and this will involve an additional diversion of resources to capital formation at the immediate sacrifice of higher consumption (or at the expense of armaments), though in the longer run the increase in productivity should suffice to cover both needs.

In the *News Chronicle* of September 8, 1955, Walter Reuther, then President of the United States Congress of Industrial Organizations, had an interesting article discussing the problems of 'automation' in American industry. He cited examples from the motor-car industry, the television and radio industries, and from large-scale office work showing the tremendous effects of electronic methods in displacing labour. In the electronics industry, he said, production has gone up in five years by 275 per cent, with only 40 per cent more workers employed. He was evidently disturbed about the possible repercussions of a rapid spread of these methods; but his conclusion was not that they should be opposed. On the contrary, he welcomed them and expressed confidence that they would be successfully dealt with so as to protect the workers from adverse effects. 'For the first time,' he concluded, 'instead of one country struggling to get its share at the expense of another, we have the tools to create abundance for all.'

This attitude is clearly sound; but we must not too easily take it for granted that these tools will be used for that purpose. Let us not forget to how small an extent even to-day the productive inventions and discoveries of the past two centuries have spread beyond a fairly narrow group of countries, even now that Russia has been added to the list. New methods of production and the knowledge how to use them do not spread of themselves. They usually require both heavy capital expenditure which backward countries cannot afford and a widespread education in technological and manual skills which they do not possess and can acquire only at considerable cost. This is the likelier to hold good for 'automation' because it can for the most part be successfully applied only at very high cost and on a very large scale and does not lend itself to relatively modest experiments. Doubtless, what has been done in Russia has opened men's eyes to the possibility of much swifter transformations than were formerly deemed possible; but few countries can be in a position to divert productive resources from consumption to investment on the massive scale that was rendered possible by the combined influence of political dictatorship and the presence of vast unused resources in relatively underpopulated regions, such as Russia.

If 'automation' is to narrow, instead of widening yet further, the gap in living standards between the advanced and the underdeveloped countries, there will have to be a really colossal export of capital from the one group to the other, by way of outright gifts as well as loans. There will also have to be a tremendous effort to train technologists, technicians, and skilled workers in the underdeveloped areas to take charge of the new equipment. The 'War on Want' will need to be waged at an expense comparable with that of great military wars if 'automation' is to be made a means of relieving mankind from bondage, and not of creating new discrepancies and antagonisms between the peoples.

The Need for New Capital Equipment. This book, however, is not about the world as a whole, but about Great Britain. Nor is it, save incidentally, about the future: its purpose is to describe, not to prophesy. We are accordingly concerned only with considering how far the improvements that have been achieved in Great Britain since the 1930s can be regarded as lasting and as providing the foundation for a continued advance. Broadly, the conclusion is that the British economy must expect to face in the near future serious economic difficulties, that large further improvements will be dependent on success in raising productivity fully as fast as it is raised in other advanced countries, and that this is likely to involve very great transformations in capital equipment, in business organization, and in the use and distribution of man-power—transformations which are certain to arouse strong resistance because they will upset many established ways of living and will call for high qualities of adaptability and initiative in every part of the economic structure. The British people are in no condition to settle down and take things easy after the upsets of the past two decades. Ever since 1945 Great Britain has barely got over one financial crisis before getting involved in the next; and even to-day we appear to be on the verge of another. At the bottom of them all is the precarious state of the international balance of payments, arising out of Britain's exceptionally high dependence on imports of materials as well as of foodstuffs, and therefore on exports to pay for them. This means, in effect, that the standards of consumption that can be afforded depend on the prosperity of the export trades and cannot be maintained or improved except by advances in productivity which allow more goods and services to be sold to overseas buyers. Our difficulty is, quite simply, that we are seeking to spend on consumption *plus* investments *plus* armaments more than we can afford to spend, so that inflationary tendencies are always making themselves felt and needing to be corrected.

The Dangers of Deflation. The traditional way of correcting such tendencies is by deflation—that is to say, by cutting down the supply of bank money and increasing rates of interest. This, however, means deliberately causing unemployment and using the occasion to cut wages as well as profit-margins. It is an essentially undiscriminating financial weapon which hits good and bad projects alike and inflicts widespread loss and suffering while 'equilibrium' is being restored. Nor does it necessarily produce, even in the long run, the desired effects. It is very much easier to throw men out of work by deflation than to get them back to work when prices have been brought down. To-day, no Chancellor of the Exchequer or Governor of the Bank of England dare deliberately induce serious unemployment with the object of compelling the Trade Unions to accept wage-reductions, or drive numerous firms into bankruptcy in order to speed up the elimination of high-cost producers. Pressure of public opinion has forced Governments, of whatever party, to accept the obligation of seeking to maintain full employment; and this renders it impracticable to use the weapons of financial stringency in the old ways. In effect, this weapon never did work except by achieving too much. In order to achieve a mild deflation it was necessary to engender a slump. This did not prevent its use as long as the powers that were could afford to be callous about the suffering they caused. But nowadays the unemployed have claims to be maintained, if not well, at least at a tolerable standard; and public opinion will not stand for letting them stew in their own juice. Nor will Trade Unionists submit to wage-cuts without putting up a political as well as an economic struggle. Consequently, less devastating methods of coping with inflationary conditions need to be found. Budgeting for a surplus, by imposing higher taxation, is one method; but it too encounters strong resistance from those on whom the taxes are to fall. 'Controls' of various kinds are another, in order to cut down the less desirable forms of spending without reducing those which should be maintained in the national interest; but 'controls' too are unpopular, especially with the middle classes and with business men, and Conservative Governments are particularly reluctant to make use of them. Therefore, on the whole, some amount of inflationary pressure is allowed to continue unchecked; and the result is crisis, whenever the external conditions change for the worse. Great Britain, in the world of to-day, can just manage to avoid crisis while the external conditions are favourable: whenever they go wrong, the precariousness of the country's external balance makes itself plain.

An Overstrained Economy.   The root difficulty is that the British economy is being overstrained. It is not that the wage-level is too high in any absolute sense, but that the combined demands of consumption, investment and armaments add up to more than can be met out of current resources. Investment cannot be cut without disastrous effects in the future; and accordingly, unless productivity can be increased at a greater rate, it is a question of cutting either consumption or expenditure on defence. Those who regard the continuance of rearmament at the prodigiously high level of recent years as a national necessity are bound to conclude that the remedy lies in cutting consumption. I do not accept this conclusion: I believe that the right course is to make drastic reductions in armament expenditure. But even if I did agree that it is necessary to reduce consumption, the question would remain

'Whose consumption is to be curtailed?' In my view, if such cuts are to be made at all, they should be at the expense of luxury and not of the standards of living of the main body of the people. Pensioners, recipients of social service benefits, and wage and low-salary earners generally, should be the last victims, and not among the first. Unearned incomes should be taxed more heavily, and so should all incomes in the higher middle ranges. Large expenses allowances should be drastically pared; and capital expenditure directed to catering for luxury should give way to more desirable forms of investment. There is no case for a return to 'rationing'; but without that there could be a resumption of 'controls' over such things as luxury building. The spread of private motoring expenditure could be checked both by higher taxes on powerful cars and by compelling the motor industry to sell more of its products overseas. There are many ways in which the relatively moderate deflation of consumers' expenditure that is needed could be brought about without wielding the sledge-hammer of general financial deflation.

Who is Spending Too Much?   It may be objected that a considerable proportion of to-day's luxury spending is done, not by the rich, but by the more highly-paid wage-earners whose regular day-to-day costs of living have not risen *pari passu* with their weekly earnings. This is no doubt true, as the extensive purchases of television sets and the higher spending on children's toys and clothing seem to indicate. But I fail to see why objection should be taken to such spending, which is one of the signs of the improved status of the wage-earners and presumably yields them more satisfaction than they would get by spending on other things.

The tendency to attribute over-consumption to unduly high wages is indeed a hangover from a social order that is happily passing away. One remembers the shocked tone of voice in which comfortably-off persons used to reprove the highly paid wage-earners for acquiring pianos during the first world war, and the similar noises that have accompanied every addition to the personal possessions of members of the 'lower classes'. The attitude that led to such comments still lingers on in many predominantly middle-class circles; but it has become a reactionary grumble without effective significance, and is a good deal less prevalent than it used to be. No doubt, where families or individuals experience a rather sudden change in spending power, it takes them some time to adapt themselves fully to their new conditions and to discover how to re-distribute their spending to the best advantage. This process of learning involves mistakes, and therefore waste; but it is a necessary element in any change in the position of groups or classes; and it is for those who experience it, and not for the 'superior' classes, to find out by trial or error what suits them best. If those whose real incomes increase tend to prefer more spending power to more leisure, that—until 'automation' has advanced much further than at present—is all to the good; for, whatever may happen in the future, for the time being Great Britain is short of man-power for producing as much as it needs.

Are Most of Us Doing a Fair Day's Work?   Those who say wages are too high are apt to say also that there is less readiness than there used to be to do a fair day's work. But where is the evidence for this belief? It is not disputed that production per man-hour has increased and is increasing over industry as a whole. It is, of course, impossible to say how much of the increase is due to harder work and how much to technical improvements in productive processes. No doubt, a good deal has been done to reduce by mechanization the amount of physically hard labour, which left the performer of it fit for nothing at the end of the working day. But many workers hold that there has been a counter-vailing increase in nervous strain, at any rate in some occupations. Personally, I feel little doubt that the overall burden of work has been in some degree lightened; but this does not mean that the pace of work has grown slack. The pace is indeed in many occupations effectively set nowadays by the machine, especially where mass-production methods have been applied. In such cases the worker has to work at a rate not of his choosing. Where this does not apply—for example, over most of the building industry—it is true that output fell off fairly sharply during the years just after the war. But it has been recovering fairly well in more recent years; and I can find no warrant for any general charge of 'slacking' on the job. In general, what is needed is not *harder* work, but better equipment and organization. There is still far too much out-of-date plant in use; and there are still far too many firms whose manage-ments are ill equipped to apply up-to-date methods.

Science in Industry.   There is indeed a widening gulf not only between individual managements but also between those industries whose tech-niques rest on increasingly complicated scientific foundations and those which are still mainly matters of expert practice of traditionally based methods. In the field of applied research it is often difficult for the scientists from their research stations and laboratories to make their ideas intelligible to managements which have no scientific staffs of their own. This applies especially where the scale of production is still relatively small, as in many branches of the textile and clothing trades. As against this the chemical and electro-technical industries of necessity employ an increasingly large force of scientists and tech-nicians; and the growth of electronics is beginning to spread advanced scientific techniques into new fields, such as large-scale office work. Even apart from what is called 'automation', industrial management is coming more and more to require the use of mathematical and scientific techniques—for example, in production planning. But managers brought up in the old ways cannot in most cases acquire such techniques, or afford to hire competent exponents of them if their output is modest in scale: nor are old factory buildings for the most part suitable for their practice. Hence the urgent need for more technically trained persons, at both higher and lower levels, and also for new factory buildings on sites suitable for the proper routing of successive processes and for the most economical use of power and recovery of waste products.

The Need for Re-planning. The deficiencies of many existing factories are due in part to the fact that they were not planned with a view to either the scale of output or the processes for which they are currently used, but have been expanded or adapted piecemeal as businesses have grown, often on sites inconveniently shaped or affording too little room. Apart from productive defects, such factories are often unable to provide proper space for canteens, industrial health services, and amenities regarded as requisite under modern conditions of employment. The need for such provision reinforces the direct economies of large-scale production in favouring the big against the small establishment. It is moreover often easier for a big than for a small establishment to change its location, though something has been done to make movement easier for the small firm by providing rentable buildings on Industrial Trading Estates. For the big factory the main problem is often that of procuring a suitable supply of labour. Modern ideas of Town and Country Planning involve attempting to diversify local employment openings so as to secure a right balance of demand for male and female and for skilled and less skilled workers. A firm which changes its location may be able to take with it a nucleus of skilled employees or of workers with long service; but for the greater part of its labour force it must usually rely on local residents or on attracting new workers to settle within easy reach—and in the latter case houses need to be built in sufficient numbers to provide the requisite accommodation. Since the Barlow Commission on the Distribution of the Industrial Population produced its report in 1940 growing attention has been given to this aspect of Town and Country Planning, especially during and immediately after the war; but industrial re-location is a long-term problem, complicated by the limited total capacity of the building industry and by the competition for its services for the building of factories, houses, schools, and many other kinds of construction. Even apart from the objections of employers to being told where to build or to refusal of permission to build where they please, planned re-location has been slowed down both by the limits of capital supply and by shortages of building capacity. Even when the housing shortage has been overtaken there should be no lack of work for the building industry for a long time to come in view of the need for extensive modernization and re-location of productive plants.

The Condition of Britain—Non-economic Factors. No attempt has been made in this book to evaluate the non-economic aspects of the change that has come over the British people since the 1930s, save in such fields as education and health. These matters have been left out of this study, not as unimportant, but because they are for the most part immeasurable in objective terms. It is easy enough to record the increase in the numbers of motor vehicles, radio and television sets, and other 'gadgets' produced for the home market (see pp. 66 and 86); but the figures do not tell us of themselves what have been the effects on the quality or pleasantness of living, either for the possessors of these amenities or for others whom they affect. Evidently, the growth of motor traffic is by no means an unmixed blessing. It has caused increasing road congestion, which is a nuisance not only to motorists but also to cyclists and pedestrians and to all who suffer from the excessive noise in overcrowded towns—to say nothing of the effects of vibration on buildings. The air too has been invaded by the nuisance of noise, especially since the advent of jet propulsion; many of us find ourselves disturbed by night as well as by day, in what were formerly quiet neighbourhoods. But who is to say how much the people, especially the younger people, mind the noise, or are even consciously aware of it? Again, radio and television are often praised because the whole family can share in the entertainment they provide. But who can tell us how many unwilling listeners and viewers are victims rather than beneficiaries, particularly in households which have no convenient other room to which they can escape? Indeed, who can say how far people have developed the capacity not to listen or not to view, or even not to hear or see at all while they carry on other avocations? 'Background' noises from a radio set to which no one is really listening have become a common occurrence: I do not know how many television sets show their pictures for how long to nobody at all who is consciously looking at them—or how many will when the novelty has worn off.

The Road Problem. The tone of these questions will probably be enough to inform my readers that I personally dislike both radio and television—and, I may add, the cinema as well. I also dislike noise as a perpetual background. That, however, is neither here nor there; for my tastes in these respects are clearly exceptional. If most people want these things and do not feel or are prepared to put up with the drawbacks they involve, clearly their demands must be met, and all the distressed minority can ask for is that, as far as practicable, the inconveniences shall be reduced. For example, could not cars be so designed as to make less racket in starting up at traffic points, or radio sets to turn themselves off after a time if nobody is listening? And cannot we afford, in face of the immense increase in motor traffic, to build better roads and provide more parking space? Can we not even drive some of the huger and more mountainous lorries off the roads by real co-ordination of rail and road traffic? Are not these the only practicable methods of reducing the monstrous total of road accidents?

The Effects of Better Distribution of Incomes. I am aware that the growing noisiness of the modern world is partly the outcome of a rising standard of living. As people get 'better off', they move about more and take more room. It used to be possible to pack away a large part of the population into a small space, from which it emerged but little to trouble its 'betters'. In an extreme form, this had its inconveniences and dangers—as when epidemics spread from slums and overcrowded working-class quarters into 'respectable' neighbourhoods. The public health movements of the nineteenth century owed not a little to these inconveniences. But nowadays the poorer classes cannot be so easily isolated, and even when they are, they take up much more room on modern housing estates and can get out of them much more often. Already, in the United States, a considerable proportion of manual workers can afford to keep a car, and do; and before long we must expect the same thing to happen here. Obviously it ought to happen; but it is likely to be an infernal nuisance when it does and to call for an immense public expenditure in road-building and maintenance and in the provision of public parking places and garages. Such expenditure will indeed become, if it has not already, a necessary part of the social services of the 'Welfare State'.

Security and Insecurity. If it is difficult to evaluate the effects on happiness and well-being of such things as the growth of motor traffic and of television and radio, it is still harder to estimate the effects of the social services on human attitudes and states of mind. In one sense there has been a great increase in the 'security' of life. Unemployment and sickness have become much less menacing than they were, and the receipt of income much more regular for the common run of the employed and self-employed. But in another sense 'security' has sensationally diminished with the advent of atomic power. We have been living for some years now in the knowledge that a new world war might come at any moment and that its effects might well be so devastating as to sweep our entire civilization away. But it is quite extraordinarily difficult to tell how this danger—now, happily, to some extent reduced —has affected people's minds and sense of security. Has it done more or less to create a feeling of insecurity than the 'Welfare State' has done to make people feel more secure? I think the answer is that most people do not reckon the one against the other, but keep the two in different compartments of their minds. The gains of the 'Welfare State' are largely measurable: we know roughly what we shall get if we fall sick and what provision will be made for us in hospital if we need it, and also what our incomes will be (though not what they will buy) when we grow old. But the consequences of atomic war are not calculable by the ordinary citizen; and because they are not, I think he shoves them away into the back of his mind and is much less disturbed by them than he would be by a much smaller but more calculable risk. That is why, though there is a deep and general desire for peace, there is no widespread peace movement. Most people prefer not to think about the danger of war, and do not take part in movements that would compel them to think about it. Probably they are happier so: it does not make for happiness to think about horrors that may wreck one's life and the lives of those one loves.

Discounting the Future: Personal Saving in Post-war Britain. Yet the sense of living on the edge of an abyss, even if largely repressed, can hardly be without some effect. It must make, in some degree, for a higher valuation of present as against future goods. It must do something towards strengthening the mood of *carpe diem.* But how much? Nobody, I think, knows the answer, even in his own case. Certainly no one knows how much, if at all, this factor of insecurity has been influencing habits of saving. There have been too many other influences at work for this one to be effectively isolated, even if the study of saving habits had been pursued much more actively than it has been in fact. We know indeed that up to 1951 savings out of personal incomes were making practically no net contribution to the accumulation of capital —indeed, less than none after allowing for depreciation of existing assets—but that from 1952 onwards such savings increased very sharply, from £113 million in 1951 to £628 million the following year, to £760 million in 1953, and to £773 million in 1954. We also know something about the movement of particular kinds of saving. Building Societies, for example, show the following figures since 1948.

TABLE 200

Building Societies. Changes in Funds since 1948 (£million)

	1948	1949	1950	1951	1952	1953	1954
Net Increase in Shares and Deposits	78	96	110	97	119	157	217
Repayments	161	161	164	169	160	167	196
Advances	264	276	270	268	266	300	373
Total Shares and Deposits	961	1057	1168	1265	1384	1540	1757
Total Balance Due on Mortgages	837	954	1060	1158	1263	1396	1574
Total Investments and other Assets	201	188	196	199	215	245	293

Other forms of saving about which there is information include contributions to private superannuation schemes and to life insurance. These are estimated at the following amounts in recent years.

TABLE 201

Life Insurance and Superannuation Contributions and Provisions, and Benefits Paid

(£*million*)

	1948	1949	1950	1951	1952	1953	1954
Employers' Contributions	188	215	244	274	308	332	352
Employees' Contributions and Individual Provisions	294	309	328	353	372	395	431
Pensions and Benefits Paid	307	334	359	381	402	425	452
Net Increase of Funds	211	230	262	301	342	381	427

We know also the figures of investment and disinvestment in National Savings, which, after allowing for increases in accrued interest, have shown the following changes (in £million) since 1948:

TABLE 202

National Savings

1948	1949	1950	1951	1952	1953	1954
+26	+62	−7	+1	−81	−45	+86

And we have estimates of the net changes in personal, as distinct from business, bank deposits, as follows:

TABLE 203

Personal Bank Deposits, 1948–54

+62	−26	−14	−26	+60	+82	+78

The Oxford Savings Surveys. Finally, much light has been thrown on saving habits among different sections of the population by the series of Savings Surveys, on a sample basis, conducted by the Oxford University Institute of Statistics in 1952, 1953 and 1954.[1] These Surveys confirm the official data in showing a very rapid rise of savings in 1952 and 1953. They also emphasize the great importance of contractual savings, mainly for life insurance, superannuation, and house purchase by instalments. On the average of the income units studied, total net savings come to £4 per annum in 1952 and 1953, and to £11 in 1954; whereas contractual saving taken by itself averaged £18, £17 and £21 in the three years in question, the balance being made up mainly

[1] Reports on these have been published in a number of issues of the *Bulletin* of the Institute, 1953–5.

of dissaving in national savings certificates and bonds and in other liquid assets. Out of every hundred income units in 1952, 13·3 neither saved nor dissaved on balance; nearly 54·5 made some net savings, and 29 dissaved, leaving a residue of 3·2 per cent unknown. By 1954 the 13·3 per cent neither saving nor dissaving had fallen to about 11·9 per cent, the 'savers' had become 57·7 per cent and the 'dissavers' 30·6 per cent, leaving an unknown residue of 2·4 per cent. The amounts saved or dissaved were in most cases small. In 1952 62 per cent of the savers saved less than £25, and only 9 per cent more than £100; and of the dissavers 41 per cent dissaved less than £25, and only 20 per cent more than £100. In 1954 the corresponding proportions were, for the savers, 54 per cent and over 13 per cent, and for the dissavers 42·5 per cent and 14·4 per cent. The incomes covered by the sample averaged £424 in 1952 and £477 in 1954 and included every range from under £100 to more than £2,000 a year. The actual distribution in 1954 was 4·5 per cent under £100, 57·5 between £100 and £500, 32·8 between £500 and £1,000, and 5·3 over £1,000. The proportions in 1952 were, naturally, in a period of rising money incomes, higher in the lower and lower in the higher ranges.

The Distribution of Ownership. An attempt was made in the Survey to measure the net money 'worth' of the income recipients who made up the samples in 1953 and 1954. Out of every hundred such persons 34·6 per cent in 1953 and 34·2 per cent in 1954 had no net 'worth' at all, or even a minus amount, their debts exceeding or equalling their assets. 17·2 per cent in 1953 and 14·2 per cent in 1954 were worth less than £50, and another 6·1 and 5·6 per cent less than £100. 14·2 per cent and 15·4 per cent were worth from £100 to £400, and 8·3 per cent and 10 per cent from £400 to £1,000. 17 per cent and 20·3 per cent were worth more than £1,000. This leaves an unascertained residue of 2·7 per cent in 1953, but of only 0·4 per cent in 1954. In 1953 about 50 per cent, and in 1954 59·6 per cent, of all the net 'worth' belonged to the few with more than £5,000, and 75·5 per cent in 1953 and 80·7 per cent in 1954 to those with more than £1,000—that is, to under 10 per cent and 10·6 per cent of the total number.

Sources of Personal Saving. The Savings Survey also breaks up the total of personal savings into groups based on the source of income. The figures which emerge from this analysis in respect of 1953 are shown in Table 204 (overleaf).

The self-employed group shows a high propensity to save partly because it has to provide more towards its own insurance and partly because its saving includes an element of investment in its own business or calling. The managerial and technical group shows both a high ratio of saving to numbers and a considerable propensity to dissave—that is to say, different numbers of the group behave in very different ways.

TABLE 204

Shares in Total Personal Savings by Source of Income

	Percentage of all Incomes Studied	Percentage share in net saving	Percentage share in net dissaving
Self-employed	4·4	26·9	7·0
Managerial and Technical	7·3	20·8	17·4
Clerical and Commercial	13·9	11·8	14·9
Skilled Manual	34·7	27·0	30·8
Unskilled Manual	17·0	8·5	9·4
Retired and Unoccupied	22·8	5·0	20·5

The 'black-coat' group of employees comes nearer to a balance between numbers and both saving and dissaving. The skilled manual workers both save and dissave rather less than in proportion to their numbers. Both the unskilled manual workers and the retired and unoccupied— the latter mostly elderly persons—save very much less than in proportion to their numbers; but whereas the unskilled do not dissave largely, the retired and unoccupied do, as many of them are using up savings to provide for their old age.

There is naturally a correlation between saving and size of income. Here are the figures in this respect for 1953.

TABLE 205

Saving and Dissaving in relation to Size of Income

	Percentage of Incomes Studied	Percentage share in net saving	Percentage share in net dissaving
Income under—			
£100	5·4	0·4	4·8
£100–£300	31·0	7·4	17·8
£300–£500	33·5	20·6	24·5
£500–£600	12·2	14·5	14·3
£600–£800	10·7	14·9	19·2
£800–£1,000	3·9	8·3	6·9
£1,000–£2,000	2·6	15·4	9·3
Over £2,000	0·9	18·5	3·1

Thus, almost 34 per cent of the saving, but only 12·4 per cent of the dissaving, is done out of the 3·5 per cent of incomes which exceed £1,000. Above the level of £500 the contributions to saving are more than proportionate to the numbers in each group; but the dissavings are more than proportionate to the numbers in all the income groups above £500. There is nothing surprising in these figures; but it is valuable to have them in mind. Nor is it surprising to find either that at all income levels the greater part of the net saving or dissaving is accounted for by a quite small proportion of the persons in each group, or that persons who are buying their houses by instalments show, in comparison with others, a high ratio of saving to income. It is more interesting, but still not surprising, to find that both incomes and savings tend on the average to be highest for the age-group 35–44.

Many further useful data can be procured from these Surveys by those who consult the articles based on them in the *Bulletin of the Oxford University Institute of Statistics*, which is also a valuable source for many other purposes. It is unfortunate that there are no surveys for earlier years to show how saving and dissaving habits have been changing in recent years. It is to be hoped that similar data will be regularly collected in future.

Impersonal Saving. All these figures of personal savings of course leave out the savings made not out of personal incomes but by means of the undistributed surpluses of companies or corporations or by public bodies through their budgetary surpluses. These forms of capital formation have been considered in earlier sections of this book (see pp. 104 and 106). Naturally these forms of saving react on the savings made out of personal incomes. Surpluses arising out of taxes are derived directly or indirectly from such incomes and reduce the spending power of the taxpayers; and undistributed profits reduce the amounts paid out in dividends and largely replace investment in companies out of personal savings. The more is saved in these ways, the less needs to be saved out of personal incomes in order to achieve any given level of total investment; and the tendency to rely less on personal savings for industrial development has been marked for a long time past, and has increased notably since 1945. In these circumstances personal saving tends to take on more and more a contractual character: its main uses, except in small-scale business, are the buying of houses by instalments and the provision for life insurances and for superannuation. This contractual character has a strong steadying influence on the amount of personal saving. A person whose income falls cannot easily vary his contractual obligations, unless he is forced radically to alter his way of life. He will try to keep up his payments by drawing on other resources, if he has any, or by economizing on other things.

Contractual saving thus acts as a stabilizing factor, especially in the middle ranges of incomes. The growth of private superannuation schemes, to which firms as well as employees contribute, has been greatest in the case of managerial and other staff workers; and house-purchase through Building Societies is also most prevalent among these groups and in the middle income ranges generally.

Co-operative Investment. Outside the contractual range personal savings are now of little account. Indeed, these other savings seem to be heavily outweighed by dissavings on the showing of the past few years. In view of the increase in contractual saving, this does not imply a decline in thrift, though such a decline has probably occurred among the groups less affected by savings of the contractual kind. It may be significant that the share capital of Co-operative Societies was substantially less in 1954 than in 1946—£233 million as against £247 million—despite a considerable rise in membership. Co-operative loan capital was indeed slightly higher at the later date—£51·75 million as against £50·8 million in 1946; but this rise is too small to be of real account. The decline in share capital took place between 1947 and 1951, since when there has been a slow recovery; but the bulk of Co-operative capital is held by a very small fraction of the membership, and it is clear that this highly distinctive form of working-class investment has received but scanty reinforcement from the rising wage-incomes of the working-class consumers. Even the better paid manual workers save little except under contract. Their contractual savings, however, have clearly increased.

Practicable Sources of Additional Capital. Under these conditions it is evident that any considerable increase in the proportion of total output devoted to capital accumulation will need to come either from undistributed profits or from budget surpluses, or of course from both—unless indeed it is to come from the inflation of bank deposits leading to higher prices uncompensated by larger money incomes to the workers. But, as we have seen, British industries cannot afford to price themselves out of world markets, as they would soon do if bank inflation were allowed to proceed unchecked. With shareholders increasingly resistant to dividend limitation and workers determined not to allow the standard of real wages to fall, budgetary policy is left as the only effective means of raising the rate of capital accumulation. Not even a Conservative Chancellor of the Exchequer can afford under present conditions to listen to the clamour of those who cry out against 'excessive' taxation—unless he is prepared to face the hostility of those who would be damaged by 'economies' at the expense of the social services.

But the scope for further direct taxation of really large personal incomes is already very limited. In 1954 the total of all personal incomes which exceeded £2,000 after payment of direct taxes was only £357 million, accruing to about 134,000 individuals; and out of this there were local rates and other charges to be met. If all these incomes were reduced to a flat £2,000 net and the proceeds applied to investment, there would be at most an addition of 5 per cent to the total of gross investment, which stood at £2,837 million in 1954. This sum is almost £450 million in excess of the total of retained personal incomes over £750. In order to get any really big contribution towards investment from higher direct taxation it would be necessary to bear more heavily on the middle incomes down to the £500 level—and this would adversely affect nearly eight million payers of direct tax. The alternative, of course, is to increase indirect taxes; but no really big sum could be raised in this way without regressive taxes on mass consumption.

Can We Hold Our Gains? It is not easy in a country which has recently won some improvement in its general standards of living, and is eager to win more, to direct an increasing proportion of the national product to capital accumulation unless total output is rising very fast. Certainly, during the past few years, British output has not been rising fast enough for this to be done without great difficulty. This brings us back to the point that the urgent need for the time being is to achieve higher all-round productivity and to guide a high proportion of the increase into investment until the productive structure has been thoroughly re-equipped. Here, of course, the great difficulty is that, in the main, the higher productivity can only follow on the investment and cannot precede it. Accordingly, Chancellors of the Exchequer have to walk the right-rope, with one eye on the foreign exchanges and the other swivelling between the demands of higher wages and salaries and the claims that are put out for higher profits and immunity from business controls. From this uncomfortable situation there is no present escape. But it is an unpleasant rather than a disastrous dilemma—at any rate up to now. For, difficult though the situation is, there is a surplus on the current balance of payments and the British people is not actually living beyond its means, even if it is saving less than prudence would require. Moreover, for the time being most people are living better than in the past, and the great gains that have been made in reducing sheer wretchedness represent a victory for human decency on which it would be criminal, as well as disastrous, to go back except under the direst compulsion.

SOURCES

GENERAL

Annual Abstract of Statistics. No. 92. Central Statistical Office. 1955. (New Series from 1946.)

Monthly Digest of Statistics (from 1946). Central Statistical Office.

Statistical Yearbook of the United Nations, 1955. U.N. 1956.

United Nations Monthly Bulletin of Statistics (from 1947). U.N.

National Income and Expenditure, 1955. (Annual from 1941, with comparisons from 1938.) Central Statistical Office. 1955.

National Income and Expenditure, 1948–55. Preliminary Estimates. Cmd. 9729. Central Statistical Office. 1956.

Economic Survey, 1956. (Annual from 1947.) Cmd. 9728. 1956.

Bulletin for Industry. Treasury. (Monthly from 1948.)

Statistics relating to the War Effort of the United Kingdom. Cmd. 6564. 1944.

Statistical Material presented during the Washington Negotiations. Cmd. 6707. 1945.

Statistics of National Product and Expenditure, 1938 and 1947–52. O.E.E.C. 1954.

Digest of Welsh Statistics, No. 2. 1955.

Digest of Scottish Statistics, No. 6. 1955.

Wales and Monmouthshire. Report of Government Action for the Year 1954–5. Cmd. 9592. 1955.

Industry and Employment in Scotland, 1954. Cmd. 9410. 1955.

Unofficial

Bulletin of the Oxford University Institute of Statistics. (Monthly to 1954: now quarterly.)

London and Cambridge Economic Bulletin. (Now quarterly supplement to *The Times Review of Industry*.)

AGRICULTURE, LAND, FORESTRY, FISHING

Agricultural Statistics, 1952–3. United Kingdom. Part I. 1955.

Agricultural Statistics, England and Wales, Part I, 1952–3. 1955. Part II. Prices of Agricultural Produce, 1948–50. 1955.

Agricultural Statistics, 1953. Scotland. 1955.

Agriculture in Scotland. Report for 1954. Cmd. 9411. 1955.

Yearbook of Food and Agricultural Statistics, 1954. Parts I and II. F.A.O. 1954–5.

The State of Food and Agriculture 1955. F.A.O. 1955.

Grain Crops, 1954. Commonwealth Economic Committee. 1954.

Farm Incomes in England and Wales, 1953–4. Farm Management Survey. 1955.

Cereals Deficiency Payment Scheme, 1955. 1955.

Ministry of Agriculture and Fisheries. Annual Review and Determination of Guarantees. 1955. Cmd. 9406. 1955.
Agricultural Land Commission. Accounts for 1953–4. H.C. 85. 1955.
Agricultural Land Commission. Report for 1954–5. H.C. 941. 1955.
Central Land Board. Report for 1954–5. H.C. 221. 1955.
National Land Fund. Accounts 1953–4. H.C. 227. 1954.
Chief Land Registrar. Report 1954–5. 1955
Crown Lands. Report of the Committee. Cmd. 9483. 1955.
National Parks Commission. Report 1953–4. H.C. 6. 1954.
Forestry Commission 34th Annual Report 1953–4. H.C. 18. 1955.
Herring Industry Board. Annual Report, 1954. Cmd. 9492. 1955.
White Fish Authority. Fourth Annual Report, 1954–5. H.C. 57. 1955.
Fisheries of Scotland. Report for 1954. Cmd. 9416. 1955.

ASSURANCE COMPANIES, FRIENDLY SOCIETIES, etc.

Assurance Companies. Returns for 1954. 2 volumes, 1955.
Assurance Companies. Summary of Statements of Assurance Business, 1954. 1955.
Chief Registrar of Friendly Societies. Report for 1953. Part I. General. 1955.
Chief Registrar of Friendly Societies. Report for 1953. Part II. Friendly Societies. 1955.
Chief Registrar of Friendly Societies. Report for 1954. Part III. Industrial and Provident Societies. 1955.
Chief Registrar of Friendly Societies. Report for 1954. Part V. Building Societies. 1955.
Industrial Assurance Commissioner. Report for 1953. 1954.

Unofficial
Lord Beveridge. *Voluntary Action*. 1948.

BALANCE OF PAYMENTS

United Kingdom Balance of Payments, 1946–55. (Half-yearly from 1948.) Cmd. 9585. 1955.
United Kingdom Balance of Payments, 1946–54. No. 2. Cmd. 9430. 1955.
Memorandum on the Sterling Assets of the British Colonies. Colonial Office. 1953.
Post-War Contribution of British Agriculture to the Saving of Foreign Exchange. 1947.
International Monetary Fund. Balance of Payments Yearbook, 1947–53. I.M.F. 1955.
American Aid and European Payments, 1953–4. H.C. 71. 1955.
Agreement for Inter-European Payments and Compensations for 1948–9. Cmd. 7456. 1948.
Agreement for Inter-European Payments and Compensations for 1949–50. Cmd. 7812. 1949.
Agreement for the Establishment of a European Payments Union, and Protocol. Cmd. 8064. 1950.

Agreement for the Establishment of a European Payments Union, 1950, as amended to June 1954. O.E.E.C. 1954.

European Payments Union. Annual Report, 1954–5. O.E.E.C. 1956.

European Payments Union. Directions for the Application of the Agreement to June 1954. O.E.E.C. 1954.

Organization for European Economic Co-operation. Private United States Investment in Europe and the Overseas Territories. 1954.

BROADCASTING, FILMS, TELEVISION

British Broadcasting Corporation. Annual Report and Accounts, 1954–5. Cmd. 9533. 1955.

British Broadcasting Corporation. Copy of an Agreement dated June 28, 1954, between the Postmaster-General and the B.B.C. Cmd. 9196. 1954.

National Film Finance Corporation. Annual Report, 1954–5. Cmd. 9464. 1955.

Cinematographic Films Council. Report, 1954–5. H.C. 14. 1955.

Independent Television Authority. Licence granted by H.M. Postmaster-General to the Independent Television Authority. Cmd. 9451. 1955.

BUSINESS STRUCTURE

Companies. *General Annual Report for* 1954. 1955.

CO-OPERATIVE MOVEMENT

Report of the Chief Registrar of Friendly Societies for 1953. *Part III.* Industrial and Provident Societies. 1954.

Unofficial

Co-operative Union. *Review of Co-operative Statistics*, 1955. (Annual.)

Co-operative Productive Federation. *The Co-operator's Year Book*, 1955. (Annual.)

Co-operative Wholesale Society. *The People's Year Book*, 1955. (Annual.)

J. Bailey. *The British Co-operative Movement*. 1955.

G. D. H. Cole. *The British Co-operative Movement in a Socialist Society*. 1951.

DEFENCE

Statement on Defence 1955. Cmd. 9391. 1955. And for 1956 Cmd. 9691. 1956.

Ministry of Defence Estimate for 1955–6. H.C. 57. 1955.

Programme of Nuclear Power. Cmd. 9389. 1955.

North Atlantic Treaty Organization. The First Five Years, 1949–54. By Lord Ismay. N.A.T.O. 1955.

DISTRIBUTION

Report of the Census of Distribution and other Services, 1950. Vol. II. Retail and Service Trades. General Tables, 1954. Vol. III. Wholesale Trades. 1955.

Censuses of Production and Distribution. Report of the Verdon-Smith Committee. Cmd. 9276. 1954.

EDUCATION

Education in 1954, being the Report of the Ministry of Education. Cmd. 9521. 1955.

Education in Scotland, 1954. Cmd. 9428. 1955.

Public Education in Scotland. Memorandum, 1952. Revised, 1955.

The Health of the School Child. Report of the Chief Medical Officer of the Ministry of Education for 1952 and 1953. 1954.

Ministry of Education Estimates, 1955–6. Memorandum. Cmd. 9415. 1955.

International Yearbook of Education, 1953. U.N.E.S.C.O. 1954.

Basic Facts and Figures. U.N.E.S.C.O. 1954.

Seven to Eleven. Ministry of Education Pamphlet No. 15. 1949.

The New Secondary Education. Ministry of Education Pamphlet No. 9. 1947.

Story of a School. Ministry of Education Pamphlet No. 14. 1949.

Early Leaving. Report of the Central Advisory Council for Education. 1954.

The Road to the Sixth Form. Ministry of Education Pamphlet No. 1919. 1951.

Maintenance Rates for Students at Universities. Ministry of Education Memo. 502. 1955.

Scales of Salaries for Teachers in Establishments for Further Education. Report of Burnham Committee. 1954.

Technical Education. Cmd. 9703. 1956.

Scientific Research in British Universities, 1953–4. D.S.I.R. 1954.

Organization and Finance of Adult Education in England and Wales (Ashby Committee Report). 1954.

University Grants Committee. University Development, 1935–47. 1948.

University Grants Committee. University Development, 1947–52. Cmd. 8875. 1953.

University Grants Committee. Returns from Universities and University Colleges, 1953–4. Cmd. 9477. 1955.

Reports of the Committee on Scales of Salaries for Teachers. 1954.

Reports of the Committee on Scales of Salaries for Teachers. Addendum, 1955.

Unofficial

G. A. N. Lowndes. *The British Educational System* (Hutchinson's University Library). 1955.

EUROPE

O.E.E.C. at Work for Europe, 1948–54. O.E.E.C. 1954.

O.E.E.C. From Recovery towards Economic Strength. O.E.E.C. 1955.

U.N. Economic Survey of Europe since the War. E.C.E. Geneva. 1953.

U.N. Growth and Stagnation in the European Economy. E.C.E. Geneva. 1954.

U.N. Economic Survey of Europe in 1955. E.C.E. Geneva. 1956.

U.N. Economic Commission for Europe. Annual Report, 1954–5. U.N. 1955.

HEALTH

Report of the Ministry of Health, 1954. Part I. National Health Service. Cmd. 9566. 1955.

Report of the Ministry of Health, 1954. Part II. On the State of the Public Health, being the Annual Report of the Chief Medical Officer. Cmd. 9627. 1955.

Department of Health for Scotland and Scottish Health Services Council Reports for 1954. Cmd. 9417. 1955.

Central Health Services Council:

Report for 1954. H.C. 142. 1955.

Report of the Committee on General Practice. 1954.

Report of the Joint Committee on Prescribing, 1953. 1954.

Report on Hospital Pharmaceutical Service. 1955.

Report on the Internal Administration of Hospitals. 1954.

National Health Service:

Report of a Committee into the Cost. Cmd. 9663. 1956.

Hospital Costing Returns, 1954–5. 1955.

Summarized Accounts of Hospitals, etc. 1953–4 (England and Wales). H.C. 135. 1955.

Summarized Accounts of Hospitals, etc. 1953–4 (Scotland). H.C. 136. 1955.

National Health Service, Scotland. Analysis of Running Costs of Hospitals, 1953–4. 1955.

Medical Research Council. Report for 1953–4. Cmd. 9506. 1955.

World Health Organization. The Work of W.H.O. 1954. W.H.O. 1955.

World Health Organization. Annual Epidemiological and Vital Statistics, 1952. Parts I and II. W.H.O. 1955.

HOUSING

Ministry of Housing and Local Government. Report for 1950–54. Cmd. 9559. 1955.

Housing Returns for England and Wales and for Scotland. (Monthly.)

Rents of Houses Owned by Local Authorities in Scotland, 1953. Cmd. 9235. 1954.

Slum Clearance Procedure. Ministry of Housing and Local Government Circular 75/54. 1954.

Town and Country Planning Act. First Review of Approved Development Plans. 1955.

New Town Acts. Accounts and Reports for 1954–5. H.C. 91. 1955.

Building Research Board. Report for 1954. D.S.I.R. 1955.

Royal Commission on the Distribution of the Industrial Population. Report. Cmd. 6153. 1940.

Town and Country Planning Acts, 1954. How to Claim Payments. 1955.

LOCAL GOVERNMENT

Local Government in Britain. Central Office of Information. 1955.

Local Government Financial Statistics, England and Wales, 1952–3. 1954.

Rates and Rateable Values in England and Wales, 1954–5. 1955.

Return of Rates in Scotland, 1953–4 and 1954–5. 1955.

Local Government Man-power Committee. Second Report, 1951. Cmd. 8421. 1951.

Unofficial

G. D. H. Cole. *Local and Regional Government.* 1947.

INSURANCE, PENSIONS AND ASSISTANCE

Ministry of Pensions and National Insurance. Report for 1954. Cmd. 9495. 1955.

Ministry of Pensions and National Insurance. Everybody's Guide to National Insurance. 1955.

Economic and Financial Problems of the Provision for Old Age. (Phillips Committee Report.) Cmd. 9333. 1954.

National Insurance Funds:

Accounts 1953–4. H.C. 107. 1955.

Increase of Benefit, etc. Regulations. Report of N.I. Advisory Committee. H.C. 102. 1955.

Maternity Benefit. H.C. 103. 1955.

Benefit, Review of Rates and Amounts. Memo and Report. Cmd. 9338. 1954.

Industrial Injuries Act. Fourth Interim Report by the Government Actuary. H.C. 192. 1954.

Report by the Government Actuary on the First Quinquennial Review. H.C. 22. 1955.

National Assistance Board. Report for 1954. Cmd. 9530. 1955.

Unofficial

National Council of Social Service. Public Social Services. 1951 (and later Supplements).

The Times. The Future of Pensions. By a Special Correspondent. March 1–3, 1955.

LABOUR

Annual Report of the Ministry of Labour and National Service for 1954. Cmd. 9522. 1955.

Annual Report of the Chief Inspector of Factories for 1954. Cmd. 9605. 1955.

Reasons Given for Retiring or Continuing at Work. M. of Pensions and National Insurance. 1954.

Staffs Employed in Government Departments. Jan. 1, 1955. Cmd. 9400. 1955.

Ministry of Labour Gazette. (Monthly.)

Economic Implications of Full Employment. Cmd. 9725. 1956.

Employment of Older Men and Women, Report on. Cmd. 9628. 1955.

MONEY AND BANKING

Bank of England Report for the Year ended February 28, 1955. Cmd. 9541. 1955.

Royal Mint. Annual Report for 1954. 1956.

Post Office Savings Bank Account for 1952. 1954.

Trustee Savings Banks Account for 1953–4. 1955.

International Financial Statistics. (Monthly.) I.M.F.

Commonwealth and the Sterling Area. 74th Statistical Abstract, 1950–3. 1955.

Unofficial

G. D. H. Cole. *Money, Trade and Investment.* 1954.

P.-W.C.B.—H H

MONOPOLIES

Monopolies and Restrictive Practices Commission. Annual Report for 1954. H.C. 78. 1955. For 1955. H.C. 201. 1956.

Monopolies and Restrictive Practices Commission. Report on the Supply of Buildings in the Greater London Area. H.C. 264. 1954.

Monopolies and Restrictive Practices Commission. Report on Collective Discrimination. Cmd. 9504. 1955. Report on Tyres. H.C. 133. 1955.

Report of the Committee on Resale Price Maintenance. Cmd. 7696. 1949.

Board of Trade. Statement on Resale Price Maintenance. Cmd. 8274. 1951.

NATIONALIZED INDUSTRIES

Report of the Minister of Fuel and Power for 1954–5. Electricity. H.C. 73. 1955.

Report of the Minister of Fuel and Power for 1954–5. H.C. 87. 1955.

Ministry of Fuel and Power. Statistical Digest, 1954. 1955.

Fuel Research Board. Report for 1953. D.S.I.R. 1954.

British Electricity Authority. Seventh Annual Report and Accounts. 1954–5. H.C. 72. 1955.

Gas Council. Sixth Report and Accounts, 1954–5. H.C. 86. 1955.

National Coal Board. Annual Report and Accounts for 1954. H.C. 1. 1955.

National Coal Board. Report of Advisory Committee on Organization (Fleck Committee). 1955.

Industrial and Domestic Coal Consumers' Councils. Reports, 1954–5. H.C. 36. 1955.

H.M. Inspectors of Mines and Quarries. Reports, 1953 and 1954. 1955.

H.M. Chief Inspector of Mines. Report for 1952. 1955.

Statistical Summary of the Mineral Industry, 1948–53. Colonial Office. 1955.

Iron and Steel Board. Report, 1953–4. H.C. 138. 1955.

Iron and Steel Board. Realization Account. Transactions to March 1954. H.C. 92. 1955.

Development of the Iron and Steel Industry, 1953–8. H.C. 49. 1955.

Agreement covering the relations between the United Kingdom and the European Coal and Steel Community, December 21, 1954. Cmd. 9346. 1954.

Cable and Wireless Ltd. Accounts for 1954–5 and Report. Cmd. 9546. 1955.

Post Office. Commercial Accounts and Balance Sheets for 1953–4. H.C. 299. 1954.

Raw Cotton Commission. Annual Report, 1953–4. H.C. 13. 1955.

Select Committee on Nationalized Industries. Report and Minutes of Evidence. H.C. 120. 1955.

Unofficial

H. A. Clegg and T. E. Chester. *The Future of Nationalization.* 195 .

PARLIAMENT, PARTIES AND ELECTIONS

Boundary Commission for England. First Periodical Report. Cmd. 9311. 1954.

Boundary Commission for Scotland. First Periodical Report. Cmd. 9312. 1954.

Boundary Commission for Wales. First Periodical Report. Cmd. 9313. 1954
Boundary Commission for N. Ireland. First Periodical Report. Cmd. 9314. 1954.
Parliamentary Constituencies. Statement showing Electorates proposed to be altered. Cmd. 9219. 1954.

Unofficial

J. Bonham. *The Middle Class Vote*. 1954.
R. T. Mackenzie. *British Political Parties*. 1955.
D. E. Butler. *The Electoral System in Britain, 1918-1951*. 1953.

POPULATION

Census, 1951. Great Britain. One Per Cent Sample Tables. 2 Volumes. 1952.
Census, 1951. England and Wales. County Reports. 1955.
Census, 1951. Scotland. County Reports.
General Registry Office. England and Wales. Estimates of the Population of England and Wales, June 1954. 1955.
General Registry Office. England and Wales:
Statistical Review, 1951. Text Volume, 1955.
Statistical Review, 1950. Text Medical. 1954.
Statistical Review, 1953. Tables, Part I. Medical, 1954.
Statistical Review, 1953. Tables, Part II. Civil. 1955.
General Registry Office. Scotland. Annual Report for 1954. 1955.
Royal Commission on Population:
Report. Cmd. 7695. 1949.
Papers. Vol. I. Family Limitation. 1949.
    „   Vol. II. Reports and Selected Papers of the Statistics Committee. 1950.
    „   Vol. III. Report of the Economics Committee. 1950.
    „   Vol. V. Memoranda Presented to the Commission. 1950.
Overseas Migration Board. First Annual Report. Cmd. 9261. 1954.

OCCUPATIONS

Census, 1951. Great Britain. One Per Cent Sample Tables, Part I. 1952.
Ministry of Labour Gazette. (Monthly.)

PRODUCTION

Census of Production, 1951. Trade Reports (in course of publication). 1955-6.

CONSUMPTION

Domestic Food Consumption and Expenditure, 1953. Fourth Report of the National Food Survey Committee. 1955.
Ready Reckoner of Food Values. Revised Edition. Ministry of Education. 1955.
Overseas Food Corporation. Report and Accounts 1953-4. H.C. 296. 1954.

PUBLIC FINANCE

Statement of Revenue and Expenditure. 1955–6. H.C. 114. 1955.

Civil Estimates, 1955–6. H.C. 63. 1955. 1956–7. H.C. 188. 1956.

Civil Estimates, 1955–6. Memorandum. H.C. 63M. 1955.

Estimates for Revenue Departments, 1955–6. H.C. 63 xi. 1955.

Public Income and Expenditure of the United Kingdom, 1954–5. H.C. 129. 1955.

Return of the National Debt, 1938–9 to 1953–4. Cmd. 9297. 1954.

Report of the Commissioners of Customs and Excise, 1954–5. Cmd. 9675. 1956.

Report of the Commissioners of Inland Revenue, 1954–5. Cmd. 9667. 1956.

Public Works Loan Board. Annual Report, 1954–5. 1955.

General Report of the Public Trustee for 1954–5. 1955.

Government Information Services. Estimated Expenditure, 1954–5. Cmd. 9192. 1954.

Marshall Aid Commemoration Commission. First Annual Report, 1953–4. Cmd. 9404. 1955.

Report of the Committee on Taxation of Trading Profits (Millard Tucker Committee). Cmd. 8189. 1955.

Trading Accounts and Balance Sheets, 1953–4. H.C. 298. 1955.

Royal Commission on the Taxation of Profits and Income. Final Report. Cmd. 9474. 1955.

SCIENCE AND RESEARCH

Advisory Council on Scientific Policy. Eighth Report, 1954–5. Cmd. 9537. 1955.

Department of Scientific and Industrial Research. Report for 1953–4. Cmd. 9386. 1955. For 1954–5. Cmd. 9690. 1956.

National Physical Laboratory. Report for 1954. 1955.

Report upon the Work of the Government Chemist Department, 1954–5. 1955.

Radio Research Board. Report for 1954. D.S.I.R. 1955.

Chemistry Research, 1954. D.S.I.R. 1955.

Road Research Board. Report for 1954. D.S.I.R. 1955.

National Research Development Corporation. Report and Accounts 1953–4. H.C. 27. 1955.

Scientific Research in British Universities, 1954–5. D.S.I.R. 1955.

U.K. Atomic Energy Authority. Report 1954–5. H.C. 95. 1955.

TRADE

Trade of the United Kingdom with Commonwealth Countries and Foreign Countries. Annual Statement, 1953. 4 volumes. 1955.

Accounts relating to the Trade and Navigation of the United Kingdom. (Monthly.) (3 years' figures in December issue.) December 1955. H.C. 41 xi. 1956.

Trade of the United Kingdom with Selected Countries, 1953, compared with 1951 and 1952. 1954.

Trade Facilities Acts. Accounts to March 1955. 1955.
International Trade Statistics Yearbook, 1954. U.N. 1956.
International Trade, 1953. G.A.T.T. 1954.
Commodity Trade Statistics, 1953. U.N. 1954.
General Agreement on Tariffs and Trade. Statement of Policy with Revised
    Text. Cmd. 9413. 1955.
General Agreement on Tariffs and Trade. Statement of H.M. Government on
    the Question of Japan's Accession. Cmd. 9449. 1955.
General Agreement on Tariffs and Trade. Basic Instruments and Selected
    Documents. Vol. I and Supplements. Revised. 1955.
General Agreement on Tariffs and Trade. Review, October 1954–March 1955.
    Cmd. 9414. 1955.

TRADE UNIONS AND INDUSTRIAL RELATIONS

Report of the Chief Registrar of Friendly Societies for 1954. Part IV. Trade
    Unions, 1955.
Ministry of Labour Gazette. (Monthly.)
Human Relations in Industry, 1953–4. D.S.I.R. 1954.

Unofficial

G. D. H. Cole. *An Introduction to Trade Unionism.* Revised edition, 1955.
V. L. Allen. *Power in Trade Unions.* 1954.
Reports of the Trades Union Congress. (Annual.)
J. H. Richardson. *An Introduction to the Study of Industrial Relations.* 1954.
A. Flanders and H. A. Clegg (editors). *The System of Industrial Relations in
    Great Britain.* 1954.

TRANSPORT

British Transport Commission. Seventh Annual Report and Accounts, 1954.
    Vol. I. Report. H.C. 20–1. 1955.
British Transport Commission. Seventh Annual Report and Accounts, 1954.
    Vol. II. Accounts. H.C. 20–2. 1955.
Central Transport Consultative Committee. Annual Report, 1954. H.C. 62.
    1955.
Railways Reorganization Scheme, 1954. Cmd. 9191. 1954.
Road Haulage Disposal Board. Third Report. H.C. 4. 1955.
Public Road Passenger Transport Statistics, 1954. 1956.
Road Fund Accounts, 1953–4. H.C. 35. 1955.
Road Fund Report. 1953–4. 1955.
Return of Mechanically Propelled Road Vehicles, 1954. 1954.
British Overseas Airways Corporation. Report and Accounts for 1953–4.
    H.C. 266. 1954.
British European Airways Corporation. Report and Accounts for 1953–4.
    H.C. 265. 1954.
Air Transport Advisory Council. Report for 1953–4. H.C. 267. 1954.

470   SOURCES

UNITED NATIONS, etc.

United Nations:
  Statistical Yearbook, 1955. U.N. 1956.
  World Economic Report, 1953–4. U.N. 1955.
  Annual Report of the Secretary-General, 1953–4. U.N. 1954.
  Yearbook, 1954. U.N. 1956.
  Yearbook of Human Rights, 1952. U.N. 1955.
  Demographic Yearbook, 1955. U.N. 1956.
  Catalogue of Economic and Social Projects. U.N. 1954.
  Ten Years of Publications, 1945–55. U.N. 1955.
  Economic Survey of Latin America, 1953. U.N. 1954.
  Economic Survey of Europe in 1954. U.N. 1955.
  Processes and Problems of Industrialization in Underdeveloped Countries.
    U.N. 1954.
  Children's Fund. Report and Accounts for 1953. U.N. 1954.
  U.N.E.S.C.O. Report of the Director-General and the Executive Board, 1953.
    U.N.E.S.C.O. 1954.
  Economic and Social Council. Report of the Tenth Session of the Com-
    mission on Human Rights. 1954.
  International Court of Justice. Yearbook, 1954–5. I.C.J. 1955.

WAGES AND SALARIES

Time Rates of Wages and Hours of Labour. April 1, 1955. Ministry of Labour
    1955. (Annual.)
Ministry of Labour Gazette. (Monthly.)
Equal Pay for Men and Women Civil Servants. Treasury Minute, February 2,
    1955. Cmd. 9380. 1955.

Unofficial

Barbara Wootton. *The Social Foundations of Wage Policy*. 1954.
Trades Union Congress. Monthly Summary of Minimum Remuneration
    fixed by Wages Councils.

APPENDIX

SUPPLEMENTARY STATISTICS FOR 1955 AND 1956

Note: The text of the present volume was finished before the end of 1955; and in most cases the statistics stop at 1954. For the convenience of readers I give (June 1956) some of the more important figures already available for 1955, and in a few cases for early 1956. Many of the 1955 figures are not yet available, and some that are are only provisional.

Page in text where earlier figures can be found.	Subject.	Date.	
4	Population (*de facto*) thousands	June 1955	E. and W. 44,441; Scot. 5,133; N. Ireland 1,394 U.K. 50,968 Males 24,523 Fem. 26,445
6	Live Births	1955	786,200
6	Deaths	1955	595,700
6	Excess of Births	1955	190,500
6	Marriages	1955	410,100
46	Man-power, thousands	Dec. 1955	Male 16,122 Fem. 7,896 Total 24,018
47	In Forces and Women's Services, thousands	Dec. 1955	779
53	Unemployed, thousands	Average, 1955	U.K. 264·5 G.B. 232·2
61	Production. Gross National Product at Market Prices	1955	£m.16,634
61	Production. Gross National Product at Factor Cost	1955	£m.16,489
61	Net Income from Abroad	1955	£m.145
63, 83, 96	Consumption. Consumers' Expenditure	1955	£m.12,677 (Food 4,136; Drink and Tobacco 1,757; Housing, Fuel and Light 1,639; Household Goods 994; Clothing 1,200; Private Motoring and Cycling

Page.	Subject.	Date.	
			570; Other Goods and Services 2,381)
65	Index of Industrial Production	1955 (1948 = 100)	Mining and Quarrying 108; Manufacturing 142; Chemicals 177; Metal, Engineering and Ship-building 150; (Vehicles only 172); Textiles and Clothing 116; Food, Drink and Tobacco 117; Paper and Printing 169; Building and Contracting 116; Gas, Electricity and Water 153
68	Industrial Production in Certain Countries	1955 (1948 = 100)	U.K. 135; U.S.A. 134; W. Germany 326; France 152; Belgium 132; Canada 136; Japan 305; Sweden 122; Yugoslavia 161
74	Industrial Productivity and Employment	1948–1955 (1948 = 100)	See Table 'A'

TABLE 'A'

	Industrial Production.	Industrial Employment.	Output per Man-Year.
1949	106	102	105
1950	114	103	110
1951	117	106	111
1952	114	105	109
1953	121	106	114
1954	130	108	120
1955	136	111	123

Page.	Subject.	Date.	
90	Food Consumption	1954	Annual Consumption in lb. per head 1954 (revised figures). Dairy Products 52·7; Meat 104·3; Poultry, Game and Fish 25·1; Eggs and Egg Products 29·1; Oils and Fats 48·7; Sugar and Syrups 111·4; Potatoes 221·9; Pulses and Nuts 12·2; Fruit 125·0; Vegetables 125·5; Grain Products 200·9; Tea 9·7
		1955	1955 (provisional

Page.	Subject.	Date.	
			figures). Dairy Products 52·6; Meat 110·0; Poultry, Game and Fish 24·8; Eggs, etc. 29·5; Oils and Fats 48·5; Sugar, etc. 114·9; Potatoes 222·7; Pulses and Nuts 12·3; Fruit 126·5; Vegetables 125·3; Grain Products 196·5; Tea 9·3
106	Gross Fixed Capital Formation	1955	(At 1948 prices) £m.2,019. Increase over 1954 at 1954 factor cost £m.185 = 7½ per cent.
107	Gross Fixed Capital Formation	1955	(At 1948 prices). Vehicles, Ships and Aircraft £m.293; Plant and Machinery £m.747; New Dwellings £m.480; Other New Buildings and Works £m.499
110	Gross Fixed Capital Formation	1955	By Industry Groups £m. Agriculture, Forestry and Fishing 72; Mining and Quarrying 71; Manufacturing 530; Building and Contracting 45; Gas, Electricity and Water 234; Transport and Communications 203; Distribution and other Services 209; New Dwellings 480; Social Services 72; Other Public Services 58; Fees and Stamp Duties 45
116	Depreciation Allowances	1955	£m.967
124	National Coal Board	1955	Deficit on year's working, £m.19·6
124	Transport Commission	1955	Deficit on year's working, £m.30·6
124	Combined British Airways	1955–6	Surplus on year's working, £m.1·0
132	Coal Supplies	1955	Production, m. tons: deep-mined 210·2; opencast 11·4; Imports 11·5;

Page.	Subject.	Date.	
			Exports 12·0; Foreign Bunkers 2·2
157	Steel Production in Leading Countries	1955	(m. *metric* tons): U.K. 20·2; U.S.A. 106·2; W. Germany 21·3; France and Saar 15·8; Belgium and Luxemburg 9·1; Italy 5·4; U.S.S.R. 45·9
158	Steel Supplies	1955	Production, crude steel (m. tons): 19·79; Imports 1·86; Exports 3·35; Total Supply 21·57; Home Use 18·22
163	Currency Circulation	1955	(£m.) Coin 163; B. of England Notes 1,795·1; Scottish and N. Irish Notes 109; Notes and Coin in Bank of England 37; in other Banks 373; in hands of Public 1,657. Total (per cent. of 1938) 375
		1956	Total Notes and Coin, April 1956 2,158
166	London Clearing Banks. Deposits and Advances	1955	Total Deposits £m.6,454 (current 4,113, deposit 2,340)
		(April) 1956	Total Deposits £m.6,112 (current 3,887; deposit 2,225)
		1955–6	Advances—1955 £m.2,019 1956 (April) 1,909
172	Exchange Rates	1955	£1 = U.S. dollars 2·79; Canadian dollars 2·75; French francs 978·1
176	External Trade	1955	(£m.) Total Imports 3,889·2; U.K. Exports 2,905·2; Re-exports 118·8; Visible Adverse Balance 865·2
		1955	Total Imports (1950 = 100) 127; U.K. Exports (1950 = 100) 112
196	U.K. Balance of Payments	1955	*Adverse* Balance of Current Payments £m.103, or, excluding Defence Aid, £m.147; Invisible Items £m.205. (Shipping

Page.	Subject.	Date.	
			£m.457—337; Interest, Profits and Dividends £m.317—258; Travel £m.111—123; Migrants' Funds £m.—15; Government Payments £m.60—241; Other Receipts £m.234)
199, 217	Terms of Trade	1955	(1954 = 100) 101
219	Retail Prices	1956	See Note on page 220
224	Personal Incomes, Sources	1955	(£m.) *From Employment* Total 11,050 (70·5 per cent). Wages and Salaries 10·040 (64·0 per cent). Forces' Pay 351 (2·2 per cent). Employers' Contributions 659 (N.I. 279, Other 380)=4·2 per cent (N.I. 1·8 per cent, Other 2·4 per cent) *From Self-Employment* Total 1,702 (10·8 per cent); Professions 281 (1·8 per cent); Farmers 381 (2·4 per cent); Other, 1,040 (6·6 per cent) *Rent, Interest and Dividends* 1,817 (11·6 per cent) *National Insurance Benefits and other Public Grants* 1,119 (7·1 per cent) *Total of Personal Incomes* 15,688
237	Average Weekly Earnings	Oct. 1955	All workers covered 187s. 2d. (Men 222s. 11d., Youths 94s. 2d., Women 115s. 5d., Girls 75s. 8d.)
241	Index of Wage-rates	Dec. 1955	(June 1947=100) All Workers 154 (Men 153, Women 158, Juveniles 166)
		April 1956	(June 1947=100) All Workers 163 (Men 162, Women 165, Juveniles 178)

Page.	Subject.	Date.	
247	Rent and Profits	1955	(£m.) Rent 785; Gross Profits, Companies 2,867; Public Corporations 297; Other Public Enterprises 110
251	Equity Shares, Prices and Yields	1955	Price (1938 = 100) 215; Yield per cent 6·17
		April 1956	Price (1938 = 100) 200; Yield per cent 6·83
253	Average Dividend Rates	1955	17·8 per cent
		1956 (1st quarter)	12·5 per cent
282	Retail Sales	1955	(1950 = 100) 140
289	Public Revenue	1955	(£m.) Taxes on Income, 2,297; on Capital, 184; on Expenditure, 2,144; Insurance Contributions, 593; Local Rates, 476; Total 5,674
302	Government Expenditure	1955	(£m.) 5,592 (including gross surplus of £m. 510)
304	Local Authorities' Current Expenditure	1955	(£m.) 1,091 (including government grants of £m. 470)
306	Defence Expenditure	1955	£m.1,505
306	Defence Estimates	1956–7	Gross £m.1,549. Less American Aid £m.50 = £m.1,499
311	Social Services		

Total Public Expenditure (including Local Authorities and Insurance Funds). £m.

	1954–5	1955–6 (Estimate)
N. Insurance	551·6	664·0
Old Age Pensions (non-contributory)	19·0	17·4
N. Assistance	129·2	120·2
War, etc., Pensions	85·4	87·8
Family Allowances	107·2	108·7
Rehabilitation	3·7	3·2
Nutrition Services	78·3	88·9
Education	445·1	488·4
Child Care	18·8	19·2
N. Health Service	499·6	541·6
Other Health Services	14·5	15·3
Housing	105·0	99·4
Total	2,057·4	2,254·1

Page.	Subject.	Date.	
	Of which:		
	Grants to Persons		971·0 1,090·8
	Administration		107·1 114·2
	Other Expenditure		979·3 1,049·1
311	Government Grants to	1954–5	£m.76·7
	Insurance Funds	1955–6	(est.) 100·1
338	Children under 15 (thousands)	June 1955	U.K. 11,700
355	Universities. G.B.	1953–4	Income £m. from Government Grants 21·9 (=70·5 per cent); from Local Authorities 1·1 (=3·6 per cent); from Endowments 1·3 (=4·3 per cent). Total Income 31·1
359	Housing, G.B.	1955	New Houses Completed (thousands) 317. (E. and W. 283, Scotland 34)
360	Housing, G.B.	1955	(Thousands) For Local Authorities 192; for Private Owners 113; Others 12
362	Road Vehicles. Licences Current	1955	(Thousands) Total 6,412 (Cars 3,526; Motor-cycles and Tricycles 1,256; Goods Vehicles 1,070; Public Conveyances 105; Others 456)
	Road Casualties	1955	Total 268,000; Deaths 5,526; Serious Injuries 62,106
372	New Towns	1955	Populations (thousands) Dec. 1955. Basildon 34·6; Bracknell 9·8; Crawley 29; Harlow 28; Hatfield 13·5; Hemel Hempstead 39·6; Stevenage 20; Welwyn 25·7; Corby 23; Cwmbran 18; E. Kilbride 14·5; Glenrothes 6·8; Newton Aycliffe 7·5; Peterlee 7·5; Total 277·5 New Schools completed or under construction 112

Page.	Subject.	Date.	
			Capital spent by Corporations to Dec. 1955 £m. 137·9
379	Birth and Death Rates	1955	U.K. Birth-rate 15·4; Death-rate 11·7; U.S.A. Birth-rate 24·6; Death-rate 9·3
401	Municipal Elections, E. and W.	1956	Labour: gains 294, losses 90 = +204 Conservatives: gains 74, losses 235 = −161 Liberals: gains 17, losses 12 = +5 Independents: gains 48, losses 95 = −47 Communists: gains 4, losses 0 = +4 Labour controls 52 out of 83 County Boroughs, 20 out of 28 Metropolitan Borough Councils
423	Industrial Disputes	1955	(Provisional) Number of Disputes beginning in year 2,404; Workers involved directly 599,000, indirectly 60,000; Working Days lost 3,754,000

INDEX